Foundations in Accountancy

FAB

ACCA

PAPER F1

ACCOUNTANT IN BUSINESS

INTERACTIVE TEXT

BPP Learning Media is an **ACCA Approved Content Provider** for the Foundations in Accountancy qualification. This means we work closely with ACCA to ensure this Interactive Text contains the information you need to pass your exam.

In this Interactive Text, which has been reviewed by the **ACCA examination team**, we:

- **Highlight** the **most important elements** in the syllabus and the **key skills** you need

- **Signpost** how each chapter links to the syllabus and the study guide

- **Provide** lots of **exam focus points** demonstrating what the examination team will want you to do

- **Emphasise key points** in regular **fast forward summaries**

- **Test your knowledge** in **quick quizzes**

- **Examine your understanding** in our **practice question bank**

- **Reference all the important topics** in our **full index**

BPP's **Practice & Revision Kit** also supports this paper.

FOR EXAMS FROM 1 SEPTEMBER 2017 TO 31 AUGUST 2018

BPP
LEARNING MEDIA

First edition March 2011
Sixth edition January 2017

ISBN 9781 5097 1133 8
Previous ISBN 9781 4727 4589 7
eISBN 9781 5097 1142 0

British Library Cataloguing-in-Publication Data
A catalogue record for this book is available from
the British Library

Published by

BPP Learning Media Ltd
BPP House, Aldine Place
142-144 Uxbridge Road
London W12 8AA

www.bpp.com/learningmedia

Printed in the United Kingdom by

Wheatons Exeter Ltd
Hennock Road
Marsh Barton
Exeter
EX2 8RP

Your learning materials, published by BPP
Learning Media Ltd, are printed on paper
obtained from traceable sustainable sources.

Contents

Helping you to pass

BPP Learning Media – ACCA Approved Content Provider

As an ACCA **Approved Content Provider**, BPP Learning Media gives you the **opportunity** to use study materials reviewed by the ACCA examination team. By incorporating the examination team's comments and suggestions regarding the depth and breadth of syllabus coverage, the BPP Learning Media Interactive Text provides excellent, **ACCA-approved** support for your studies.

The PER alert!

To become a Certified Accounting Technician or qualify as an ACCA member, you not only have to pass all your exams but also fulfil a **practical experience requirement** (PER). To help you to recognise areas of the syllabus that you might be able to apply in the workplace to achieve different performance objectives, we have introduced the '**PER alert**' feature. You will find this feature throughout the Interactive Text to remind you that what you are **learning in order to pass** your Foundations in Accountancy and ACCA exams is **equally useful to the fulfilment of the PER requirement**.

Your achievement of the PER should now be recorded in your online *My Experience* record.

Tackling studying

Studying can be a daunting prospect, particularly when you have lots of other commitments. The **different features** of the Interactive Text, the **purposes** of which are explained fully on the **Chapter features** page, will help you whilst studying and improve your chances of **exam success**.

Developing exam awareness

Our Interactive Texts are completely **focused** on helping you pass your exam.

Our advice on **Studying FAB/F1** outlines the **content** of the paper, the **recommended approach to studying** and any **brought forward knowledge** you are expected to have.

Exam focus points are included within the chapters to highlight when and how specific topics might be examined.

Testing what you can do

Testing yourself helps you develop the skills you need to pass the exam and also confirms that you can recall what you have learnt.

We include **Questions** – lots of them – both within chapters and in the **Practice Question Bank**, as well as **Quick Quizzes** at the end of each chapter to test your knowledge of the chapter content.

v

Chapter features

Each chapter contains a number of helpful features to guide you through each topic.

| Topic list | What you will be studying in this chapter and the relevant section numbers, together with the ACCA syllabus references. |

| Introduction | Puts the chapter content in the context of the syllabus as a whole. |

| Study Guide | Links the chapter content with ACCA guidance. |

| Fast Forward | Summarises the content of main chapter headings, allowing you to preview and review each section easily. |

| EXAMPLE | Demonstrates how to apply key knowledge and techniques. |

| Key Term | Definitions of important concepts that can often earn you easy marks in exams. |

| Exam Focus Point | When and how specific topics were examined, or how they may be examined in the future. |

| Formula | Formulae that are not given in the exam but which have to be learnt. |

| PER Alert | Gives you a useful indication of syllabus areas that closely relate to performance objectives in your Practical Experience Requirement (PER). |

| Question | Gives you essential practice of techniques covered in the chapter. |

| **Chapter Roundup** | A full list of the Fast Forwards included in the chapter, providing an easy source of review. |

| **Quick Quiz** | A quick test of your knowledge of the main topics in the chapter. |

| **Practice Question Bank** | Found at the back of the Interactive Text with more comprehensive chapter questions. Cross referenced for easy navigation. |

Studying FAB/F1

How to Use this Interactive Text

Aim of this Interactive Text

To provide the knowledge and practice to help you succeed in the examination for Paper FAB/F1 *Accountant in Business*.

To pass the examination you need a thorough understanding of all areas covered by the syllabus and teaching guide.

Recommended approach

(a) To pass you need to be able to answer questions on **everything** specified by the syllabus and teaching guide. Read the Interactive Text very carefully and do not skip any of it.

(b) Learning is an **active** process. Do **all** the questions as you work through the Interactive Text so you can be sure you really understand what you have read.

(c) After you have covered the material in the Interactive Text, work through the **Practice Question Bank**, checking your answers carefully against the **Practice Answer Bank**.

(d) Before you take the exam, check that you still remember the material using the following quick revision plan.

    (i) Read through the **chapter topic list** at the beginning of each chapter. Are there any gaps in your knowledge? If so, study the section again.

    (ii) Read and learn the **key terms**.

    (iii) Look at the **exam focus points**. These show the ways in which topics might be examined.

    (iv) Read the **chapter roundups**, which are a summary of the **fast forwards** in each chapter.

    (v) Do the **quick quizzes** again. If you know what you're doing, they shouldn't take long.

This approach is only a suggestion. You or your college may well adapt it to suit your needs. Remember this is a **practical** course.

(a) Try to relate the material to your experience in the workplace or any other work experience you may have had.

(b) Try to make as many links as you can to other papers at the Introductory and Intermediate levels.

For practice and revision use BPP Learning Media's Practice & Revision Kit and Passcards.

What FAB/F1 is about

The overall aim of the *Accountant in Business* syllabus is to introduce accountancy firmly in its context as a central business function. This encompasses:

- Business organisation, stakeholders and the business environment
- Business structure, functions and governance, including social responsibility
- Accounting and its relationship with other business functions
- Audit and internal control
- People management issues
- Effectiveness and communications
- Professional ethics in the business environment

Brought forward knowledge

There is no assumed brought forward knowledge for this paper.

Approach to examining the syllabus

Paper FAB/F1 is a two-hour paper. It can be taken as a written paper or a computer-based examination. The questions in the computer-based examination are objective test questions or multiple task questions – multiple choice, number entry, multiple response, multiple response matching, picklists and hotspots. (See page x for frequently asked questions about computer-based examinations.)

The written examination is structured as follows:

	Number of marks
16 one mark objective test questions	16
30 two mark objective test questions	60
6 four mark multiple task questions (One on each area of the syllabus)	24
	100

Syllabus and Study Guide

The complete FAB/FA syllabus and study guide can be found by visiting the exam resource finder on the ACCA website: www.accaglobal.com/uk/en/student/exam-support-resources.html

The Computer-Based Examination

Computer based examinations (CBEs) are available for the first seven Foundations in Accountancy papers (not papers FAU, FTX or FFM) and ACCA papers F1, F2, and F3, in addition to the conventional paper based examination.

Computer based examinations must be taken at an ACCA CBE Licensed Centre.

How does CBE work?

- Questions are displayed on a monitor.

- Candidates enter their answer directly onto the computer.

- Candidates have two hours to complete the examination.

- When the candidate has completed their examination, the final percentage score is calculated and displayed on screen.

- Candidates are provided with a Provisional Result Notification showing their results before leaving the examination room.

- The CBE Licensed Centre uploads the results to the ACCA (as proof of the candidate's performance) within 72 hours.

- Candidates can check their exam status on the ACCA website by logging into myACCA.

Benefits

- **Flexibility** as a CBE can be sat at any time.

- **Resits** can also be taken at any time and there is no restriction on the number of times a candidate can sit a CBE.

- **Instant feedback** is provided as the computer displays the results at the end of the CBE.

- Results are notified to ACCA within 72 hours.

CBE question types

- Multiple choice – choose one answer from four options

- Multiple response – select more than one response by clicking the appropriate tick boxes

- Multiple response matching – select a response to a number of related statements by choosing one option from a number of drop down menus

- Number entry – key in a numerical response to a question

- Multiple task questions – a series of short questions related to one scenario. Question formats could include number entry, drop-down lists, multiple choice, multiple response and hotspot

For more information on computer-based exams, visit the ACCA website.
www.accaglobal.com/en/student/Exams/Computer-based-exams.html

Tackling Multiple Choice Questions

MCQs are part of all Foundations in Accountancy exams.

The MCQs in your exam contain up to four possible answers. You have to **choose the option that best answers the question**. The incorrect options are called distractors. There is a skill in answering MCQs quickly and correctly. By practising MCQs you can develop this skill, giving you a better chance of passing the exam.

You may wish to follow the approach outlined below, or you may prefer to adapt it.

Step 1	Skim read all the MCQs and identify what appear to be the easier questions.
Step 2	Attempt each question – **starting with the easier questions** identified in Step 1. Read the question **thoroughly**. You may prefer to work out the answer before looking at the options, or you may prefer to look at the options at the beginning. Adopt the method that works best for you.
Step 3	Read the four options and see if one matches your own answer. Be careful with numerical questions, as the distracters are designed to match answers that incorporate common errors. Check that your calculation is correct. Have you followed the requirement exactly? Have you included every stage of the calculation?
Step 4	You may find that none of the options matches your answer. • Re-read the question to ensure that you understand it and are answering the requirement. • Eliminate any obviously wrong answers. • Consider which of the remaining answers is the most likely to be correct and select the option.
Step 5	If you are still unsure make a note and continue to the next question.
Step 6	Revisit unanswered questions. When you come back to a question after a break you often find you are able to answer it correctly straight away. If you are still unsure have a guess. You are not penalised for incorrect answers, so **never leave a question unanswered!**

After extensive practice and revision of MCQs, you may find that you recognise a question when you sit the exam. Be aware that the detail and/or requirement may be different. If the question seems familiar read the requirement and options carefully – do not assume that it is identical.

Tempting though it might be, don't try to predict where the correct answers might fall based on any kind of pattern you think you might perceive in this section. The distribution of the correct answers do not follow any predictable pattern in this exam!

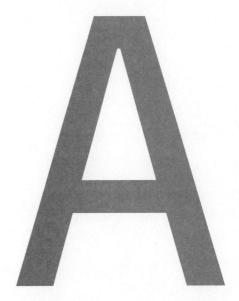

part

A

The business organisation, its stakeholders and the external environment

01

Business organisations and their stakeholders

Organisations develop out of the need to **co-ordinate** work **(Section 1)** but this can be achieved in different ways. In this chapter we will also look at the different types of organisation **(Section 2)**.

The objectives, policies, procedures and management/leadership style of an organisation will all be influenced in part by its stakeholders. Different stakeholder groups have different degrees of power and interest, and management must respond to each in a different way **(Section 3)**.

TOPIC LIST	SYLLABUS REFERENCE
1 Purpose of business organisations	A1 (a) – (d)
2 Types of business organisation	A1 (e)
3 Stakeholder goals and objectives	A2 (a) – (e)

Study Guide

		Intellectual level
A1	**The purpose and types of business organisation**	
(a)	Define 'business organisations' and explain why they are formed.	K
(b)	Describe common features of business organisations.	K
(c)	Outline how business organisations differ.	K
(d)	List the industrial and commercial sectors in which business organisations operate.	K
(e)	Identify the different types of business organisation and their main characteristics:	K
	(i) Commercial	
	(ii) Not-for-profit	
	(iii) Public sector	
	(iv) Non-governmental organisations	
	(v) Co-operatives	
A2	**Stakeholders in business organisations**	
(a)	Define stakeholders and explain the agency relationship in business and how it may vary in different types of business organisation.	K
(b)	Define internal, connected and external stakeholders and explain their impact on the organisation.	K
(c)	Identify the main stakeholder groups and the objectives of each group.	K
(d)	Explain how the different stakeholder groups interact and how their objectives may conflict with one another.	K
(e)	Compare the power and influence of various stakeholder groups and how their needs should be accounted for, such as under the Mendelow framework.	K

EXAM FOCUS POINT

This chapter lays the foundation for an understanding of what organisations are and how they are controlled. According to the Study Guide, it is not sufficient to simply understand these topics – you must also be able to **apply** your knowledge.

1 Purpose of business organisations

1.1 What all organisations have in common

An **organisation** is: 'a **social arrangement** which pursues collective **goals**, which **controls** its own performance and which has a **boundary** separating it from its environment'.

Here are some examples of organisations.

- A multinational car manufacturer (eg Ford)
- An accountancy firm (eg Ernst & Young)
- A charity (eg Oxfam)

- A local authority
- A trade union (eg Unison)
- An army

The common characteristics of organisations are as follows.

(a)   Organisations are preoccupied with **performance**, and meeting or improving their standards.

(b)   Organisations contain formal, documented **systems and procedures** which enable them to control what they do.

(c)   Different people do different things, or **specialise** in one activity.

(d)   They pursue a **variety of objectives** and goals.

(e)   Most organisations obtain **inputs** (eg materials), and **process** them into **outputs** (eg for others to buy).

1.2 Why do organisations exist?

Organisations can achieve results which individuals cannot achieve by themselves.

(a)   Organisations **overcome people's individual limitations**, whether physical or intellectual.

(b)   Organisations **enable people to specialise** in what they do best.

(c)   Organisations **save time**, because people can work together or do two aspects of a different task at the same time.

(d)   Organisations **accumulate** and share **knowledge**.

(e)   Organisations enable **synergy**: by bringing **together** two individuals their combined output will exceed their output if they continued working separately.

In brief, organisations enable people to be **more productive**.

1.3 How organisations differ

The common elements of organisations were described earlier, but organisations also differ in many ways. Here are some possible differences.

(a)   **Ownership**

Some organisations are owned by private owners or shareholders. These are private sector organisations. Public sector organisations are owned by the government.

(b)   **Control**

Some organisations are controlled by the owners themselves but many are controlled by people working on their behalf. Some are indirectly controlled by government-sponsored regulators.

(c)   **Activity**

What organisations actually do can vary enormously. They could be manufacturing organisations, for example, or they could be a healthcare service.

(d)   **Profit or non-profit orientation**

Some businesses exist to make a profit. Others, for example the army, are not profit orientated.

(e)   **Legal status**

Organisations may be limited companies or partnerships.

(f)   **Size**

The business may be a small family business or a multinational corporation.

(g)   **Sources of finance**

Businesses can raise finance by borrowing from banks or government funding or issuing shares.

(h)   **Technology**

Businesses have varying degrees of technology use. For example, computer firms will have high use of technology but a corner shop will have very low use.

1.4 What the organisation does

Organisations do many different types of work. Here are some examples.

Industry	Activity
Agriculture	Producing and processing food
Manufacturing	Acquiring raw materials and, by the application of labour and technology, turning them into a product (eg a car)
Extractive/raw materials	Extracting and refining raw materials (eg mining)
Energy	Converting one resource (eg coal) into another (eg electricity)
Retailing/distribution	Delivering goods to the end consumer
Intellectual production	Producing **intellectual property** (eg software, publishing, films, music)
Service industries	Including retailing, distribution, transport, banking, various business services (eg accountancy, advertising) and public services such as education, medicine

2 Types of business organisation

2.1 Profit vs not-for-profit orientation

An important difference in the list above is between profit orientated ('commercial') and not for profit orientated ('non-profit') organisations.

The basic difference in outlook is expressed in the diagram below. Note the distinction between **primary** and **secondary** goals. A primary goal is the most important: the other goals support it.

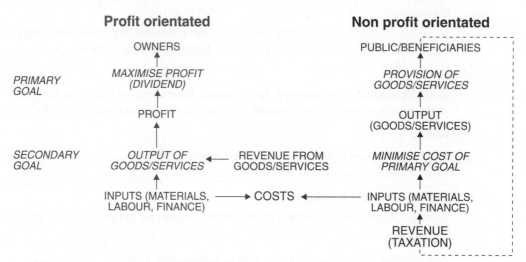

2.2 Private vs public sector

- **Private sector.** Organisations not owned or run by central or local government, or government agencies

- **Public sector.** Organisations owned or run by central or local government or government agencies

2.3 Private sector commercial business organisations

A **commercial** business organisation exists to make a profit. In other words, the costs of its activities should be less than the revenues it earns from providing goods or services. Profits are not incidental to its activities but the driving factor.

Business organisations come in all different shapes and sizes, and there is a choice of legal structure.

2.3.1 Legal status

Someone setting up a business can choose to go into business **alone**, take on one or more **partners** who also share the profits of the business, or set up a **limited company**.

2.3.2 Limited companies

A limited company has a separate legal personality from its owners (shareholders). The shareholders cannot normally be sued for the debts of the business unless they have given some personal guarantee. Their risk is generally restricted to the amount that they have invested in the company when buying the shares. This is called limited liability.

Whereas sole traderships and partnerships are normally small or medium-sized businesses, limited company status is used for businesses of any size.

The **ownership** and **control** of a limited company are **legally separate** even though they may be vested in the same individual or individuals.

(a)   **Shareholders are the owners** but have limited rights, as shareholders, over the day to day running of the company. They provide capital and receive a return. Shareholders could be large institutional investors (such as insurance companies and pension funds), private individuals, or employees.

(b)   **Directors are appointed by shareholders to run the company**. In the UK, the board of directors controls management and staff, and is accountable to the shareholders, but it has responsibilities towards both groups – owners and employees alike.

(i)   **Executive directors** participate in the daily operations of the organisation.

(ii)   **Non-executive directors** are invited to join in an advisory capacity, usually to bring their particular skills or experience to the discussions of the board to exercise some overall guidance.

(c)   **Operational management** usually consists of career managers who are recruited to operate the business, and are accountable to the board.

2.3.3 Types of limited company

In the UK, limited companies come in two types: **private limited companies** (eg X Limited) and **public limited companies** (eg X plc). They differ as follows.

(a)   **Number of shareholders.** Most private companies are owned by only a small number of shareholders. Public companies generally are owned by a wider proportion of the investing public.

(b)   **Transferability of shares.** Shares in public companies can be offered to the general public. In practice this means that they can be traded on a stock exchange. Shares in private companies, on the other hand, are rarely transferable without the consent of the shareholders.

(c)   **Directors as shareholders.** The directors of a private limited company are more likely to hold a substantial portion of the company's shares than the directors of a public company.

(d) Source of capital

    (i) A private company's share capital will normally be provided from three sources.

        (1) The founder or promoter

        (2) Business associates of the founder or employer

        (3) Venture capitalists

    (ii) A public company's share capital, in addition, can be raised from the public directly, or through institutional investors, using recognised markets.

Many companies start in a small way, often as family businesses which operate as private companies, then grow to the point where they become public companies and can invite investors to subscribe for shares. The new capital thus made available enables the firm to expand its activities and achieve the advantages of large scale operation.

2.3.4 Advantages and disadvantages of limited companies

Advantages

- **More money** is available for investment.
- **Risk is reduced** for investors thanks to limited liability.
- They have a **separate legal personality.** A company can own property, make contracts etc.
- **Ownership** is legally **separate** from **control**. Investors need not get involved in operations.
- **No restrictions on size** apply. Some companies have millions of shareholders.
- They offer **flexibility**. Capital and enterprise can be brought together.

Disadvantages

- Legal **compliance costs**. Because of limited liability, the financial statements of most limited companies have to be **audited**, and then published for shareholders.

- **Shareholders** have **little** practical **power**, other than to sell their shares to a new group of managers, although they can vote to sack the directors.

2.4 The public sector

The **public sector** comprises all organisations owned and run by the government and local government. Here are some examples.

- The armed forces
- Most schools and universities
- Government departments

Public sector organisations have a variety of objectives.

- The UK Pensions Service administers part of the social security system relating to pensions, benefits and retirement information.

- The Post Office makes a **profit** from mail services, although it does have a **social function** too.

2.4.1 Key characteristics of the public sector

(a) **Accountability**, ultimately, to Parliament

(b) **Funding**. The public sector can obtain funds in three main ways.

    (i) Raising taxes

    (ii) Making charges (eg for prescriptions)

    (iii) Borrowing

(c) **Demand for services**. There is a relationship between the price charged for something and the 'demand'. In the public sector demand for many services is practically limitless.

(d) **Limited resources**. Despite the potentially huge demand for public services, constraints on government expenditure mean that resources are limited and that demand cannot always be met.

2.4.2 Advantages

(a) **Fairness**. The public sector can ensure that everyone has access to health services.

(b) **Filling the gaps left by the private sector**. This can be done by providing **public goods**, such as street lighting.

(c) **Public interest**. Governments once believed the public interest was best served if the state ran certain services.

(d) **Economies of scale**. Costs can be spread if everything is centralised.

(e) **Cheaper finance**. Taxes or borrowing backed by government guarantees might be cheaper than borrowing at commercial rates.

(f) **Efficiency**. The public sector is sometimes more efficient than the private sector. The UK's National Health Service, despite its well-publicised problems, has lower administration costs and serves more of the population than the private sector does in the US.

2.4.3 Disadvantages

(a) **Accountability**. Inefficiency may be ignored as taxpayers bear losses.

(b) **Interference**. Politicians may not be familiar with the operation of a business and yet political pressures and indecision may influence adversely the decision-making process. Pressures to get elected may lead to the deferral of necessary but unpopular decisions.

(c) **Cost**. There can be conflict between economy of operation and adequacy of service. The public will demand as perfect a service as possible but will not wish to bear the cost involved.

2.5 Non-governmental organisations

A non-governmental organisation (NGO) is a legally constituted organisation of people acting together independently from any form of government.

Non-governmental organisations (NGOs) are bodies which are not directly linked with national government. The description 'NGO' generally applies to groups whose primary aim is not a commercial one, but within this the term is applied to a diverse range of activities, aimed at promoting social, political or environmental change. However, NGOs are not necessarily charities and, although they may have political aims, they are not political parties.

NGOs need to engage in fund raising and mobilisation of resources in order to ensure that they are operating effectively and efficiently (for example in terms of donations received, volunteer labour or materials). This process may require quite complex levels of organisation. The following are some organisational features of NGOs.

- Staffing by volunteers as well as full-time paid employees
- Finance from grants or contracts
- Skills in advertising and media relations
- Some kind of national 'headquarters'
- Planning and budgeting expertise

It can be seen, therefore, that NGOs may need to possess an efficient level of organisation structure, much in the same way as a traditional commercial undertaking.

EXAM FOCUS POINT

There are two articles on the ACCA website entitled "Not-for-profit organisations I" and "Not-for-profit organisations II" that are relevant to material in this section.

CASE STUDY

The United Nations (UN) has various NGOs, such as UNESCO (UN Educational, Scientific and Cultural Organisation) and UNICEF (UN Children's Fund).

2.6 Co-operative societies and mutual associations

Co-operatives are businesses owned by their workers or customers, who share the profits. Here are some of the features they have in common.

- Open membership
- Democratic control (one member, one vote)
- Distribution of the surplus in proportion to purchases
- Promotion of education

Although limited companies also have some measure of democratic control, this is on the basis of one share, one vote. So one shareholder could dominate a company if they hold a majority of shares. This would not happen in a co-operative.

CASE STUDY

A major example of a co-operative in the UK is the *Co-operative Retail Store* network. In addition there is the *Co-operative Wholesale Society* and the *Co-operative Bank*. Another example is the *John Lewis Partnership*.

Mutual associations are similar to co-operatives in that they are 'owned' by their members rather than outside investors.

(a) Some financial companies used to be mutual associations. However, building societies in the UK such as the Abbey National and the Halifax converted from being mutual associations to being banks. The Nationwide Building Society has held out against this, so far citing the lower interest rates it can offer to borrowers.

(b) **Credit unions** are examples of mutual associations. They are financial institutions owned and controlled by their members.

QUESTION

Legal form

Florence Nightingale runs a successful and growing small business as a sole trader. She wishes to expand the business and has her eyes on Scutari Ltd, a small private limited company in the same line. After the acquisition, she runs the two businesses as if they were one operation making no distinction between them. What is the legal form of the business she is running?

ANSWER

This is quite a tricky question. For example, if suppliers have contracts with Scutari Ltd, the contract is with the company, and Florence is not legally liable for the company's debts. If their contracts are with Florence, then they are dealing with her personally. Florence has to make a choice.

(a) She can run the entire business as a sole trader, in which case Scutari Ltd's assets must be transferred to her.

(b) She can run her entire business as a limited company, in which case she would contribute the assets of her business as capital to the company.

(c) She can ensure that the two business are legally distinct in their assets, liabilities, income and expenditure.

3 Stakeholder goals and objectives

Managers are not completely free to set objectives: they have different groups of stakeholders to consider. The managers act as **agents** for the stakeholders, whose influence varies from organisation to organisation.

The **agency relationship** in business therefore refers to the separation between an organisation's owners (the shareholders) as the 'principal', and those managing the organisation on their behalf (the company directors) as their 'agents'.

Those running the company should do so in a way that best serves the interests of shareholders (rather than pursuing their own interests). It is important that management interests are aligned with the organisation's goals, so that they act in a way that benefits shareholders and other stakeholders.

The concept of agency is particularly relevant for large organisations, where there is a large separation between company ownership and its management.

> **Stakeholders** are those individuals or groups that, potentially, have an interest in what the organisation does. These stakeholders can be within the organisation, connected to the organisation or external to the organisation.

There are three broad types of stakeholder in an organisation, as follows.

- **Internal** stakeholders (employees, management)
- **Connected** stakeholders (shareholders, customers, suppliers, financiers)
- **External** stakeholders (the community, government, pressure groups)

3.1 Internal stakeholders: employees and management

Because **employees and management** are so intimately connected with the company, their objectives are likely to have a strong influence on how it is run. They are interested in the following issues.

(a) The **organisation's continuation and growth**. Management and employees have a special interest in the organisation's continued existence.

(b) **Individual interests and goals**. Managers and employees have individual interests and goals which can be harnessed to the goals of the organisation.

Internal stakeholder	Interests to defend	Response risk
Managers and employees	<ul><li>Jobs/careers</li><li>Money</li><li>Promotion</li><li>Benefits</li><li>Satisfaction</li></ul>	<ul><li>Pursuit of 'systems goals' rather than shareholder interests</li><li>Industrial action</li><li>Negative power to impede implementation</li><li>Refusal to relocate</li><li>Resignation</li></ul>

3.2 Connected stakeholders

If management performance is measured and rewarded by reference to changes in **shareholder value** then shareholders will be happy, because managers are likely to encourage long-term share price growth.

Connected stakeholder	Interests to defend	Response risk
Shareholders (corporate strategy)	<ul><li>Increase in shareholder wealth, measured by profitability, P/E ratios, market capitalisation, dividends and yield</li><li>Risk</li></ul>	<ul><li>Sell shares (eg to predator) or boot out management</li></ul>

Bankers (cash flows)	• Security of loan • Adherence to loan agreements	• Denial of credit • Higher interest charges • Receivership
Suppliers (purchase strategy)	• Profitable sales • Payment for goods • Long-term relationship	• Refusal of credit • Court action • Wind down relationships
Customers (product market strategy)	• Goods as promised • Future benefits	• Buy elsewhere • Sue

3.3 External stakeholders

External stakeholder groups – the government, local authorities, pressure groups, the community at large, professional bodies – are likely to have quite diverse objectives.

External stakeholder	Interests to defend	Response risk
Government	• Jobs • Training • Tax	• Tax increases • Regulation • Legal action
Interest/pressure groups	• Pollution • Rights • Other	• Publicity • Direct action • Sabotage • Pressure on government
Professional bodies	• Members' ethics	• Imposition of ethical standards

3.4 Another approach

Stakeholders may also be analysed by reference to whether they have a **contractual relationship** with the organisation. Stakeholders who have such a relationship are called **primary stakeholders**, while those who do not are known as **secondary stakeholders**. The primary stakeholder category thus includes **internal** and **connected** stakeholders, while the secondary stakeholder category equates to **external** stakeholder status.

3.5 Stakeholder conflict

Since their interests may be widely different, **conflict between stakeholders** can be quite common. Managers must take the potential for such conflict into account when setting policy and be prepared to deal with it if it arises in a form that affects the organisation.

A relationship in which **conflict** between stakeholders is vividly characterised is that between **managers and shareholders**. The relationship can run into trouble when the managers' decisions focus on maintaining the corporation as a **vehicle for their managerial skills** while the shareholders wish to see radical changes so as to enhance their **dividend stream and increase the value of their shares**. The shareholders may feel that the business is a **managerial corporation** run for the benefit of managers and employees without regard for the objectives of the owners. The conflict in this case can be seriously detrimental to the company's stability.

(a) Shareholders may **force resignations and divestments of businesses**, while managers may seek to preserve their empire and provide growth at the same time by undertaking risky policies.

(b) In most cases, however, managers cannot but acknowledge that the shareholders have the **major stake** as owners of the company and its assets. Most companies therefore focus on making profits and increasing the market value of the company's shares, sometimes at the expense of the long-term benefit of the company. Hence long-term strategic plans may be 'hijacked' by the need to make a sizeable profit in one particular year; planning horizons are reduced and investment in long-term business prospects may be shelved.

Clearly, each stakeholder group considers itself in some way **a client of the organisation**, thus broadening the debate about organisation effectiveness.

3.6 Stakeholder mapping: power and interest

Mendelow (1991) suggests that stakeholders may be positioned on a matrix whose axes are power held and likelihood of showing an interest in the organisation's activities. These factors will help define the type of relationship the organisation should seek with its stakeholders.

Level of interest

	Low	High
High	C	D
Low	A	B

(Power on vertical axis, High to Low)

(a)   **Key players** are found in segment D: strategy must be **acceptable** to them, at least. An example would be a major customer. These stakeholders may even participate in decision-making.

(b)   Stakeholders in segment C must be treated with care. While often passive, they are capable of moving to segment D. They should therefore be **kept satisfied**. Large institutional shareholders might fall into segment C.

(c)   Stakeholders in segment B do not have great ability to influence strategy, but their views can be important in influencing more powerful stakeholders, perhaps by lobbying. They should therefore be **kept informed**. Community representatives and charities might fall into segment B.

(d)   Minimal effort is expended on segment A.

A single stakeholder map is unlikely to be appropriate for all circumstances. In particular, stakeholders may move from quadrant to quadrant when different potential future strategies are considered.

Stakeholder mapping is used to assess the **significance** of stakeholder groups. This in turn has implications for the organisation.

(a)   The framework of **corporate governance** should recognise stakeholders' levels of interest and power.

(b)   It may be appropriate to seek to **reposition** certain stakeholders and discourage others from repositioning themselves, depending on their attitudes.

(c)   Key **blockers** and **facilitators** of change must be identified.

Each of these groups has three basic choices.

•   **Loyalty**. They can do as they are told.

•   **Exit**. For example by selling their shares, or getting a new job.

•   **Voice**. They can stay and try to change the system. Those who choose **voice** are those who can, to varying degrees, influence the organisation. Influence implies a degree of power and willingness to exercise it.

Existing structures and systems can channel stakeholder influence.

(a)   They are the **location of power**, giving groups of people varying degrees of influence over strategic choices.

(b)   They are **conduits of information**, which shape strategic decisions.

(c) They **limit choices** or give some options priority over others. These may be physical or ethical constraints over what is possible.

(d) They **embody culture**.

(e) They **determine the successful implementation** of strategy.

(f) The **firm has different degrees of dependency** on various stakeholder groups. A company with a cash flow crisis will be more beholden to its bankers than one with regular cash surpluses.

So, different stakeholders will have their own views as to strategy. As some stakeholders have **negative power**, in other words power to impede or disrupt the decision, their likely response might be considered.

EXAM FOCUS POINT

There is an article on the ACCA website entitled "Communicating core values and mission" that is relevant to material in this section.

3.7 The strategic value of stakeholders

The firm can make strategic gains from managing stakeholder relationships. Over the years various theories and studies have revealed the following correlations.

(a) A correlation between **employee** and **customer loyalty** (eg reduced staff turnover in service firms generally results in more repeat business).

(b) **Continuity** and **stability** in relationships with employees, customers and suppliers is important in enabling organisations to respond to certain types of change, necessary for business as a sustained activity.

Responsibilities towards customers are mainly those of providing a product or service of a quality that customers expect, and of dealing honestly and fairly with customers.

Responsibilities towards suppliers are expressed mainly in terms of trading relationships.

(a) The organisation's size could give it considerable power as a buyer. One ethical guideline might be that the organisation should not use its power unscrupulously.

(b) Suppliers might rely on getting prompt payment in accordance with the terms of trade negotiated with its customers.

(c) All information obtained from suppliers and potential suppliers should be kept confidential.

3.8 Measuring stakeholder satisfaction

We have already considered ways in which stakeholders may be classified and given some instances of their probable interests. Measuring the success the organisation achieves in satisfying stakeholder interests is likely to be difficult, since many of their expectations relate to **qualitative** rather than **quantitative** matters. It is, for example, difficult to measure good corporate citizenship. On the other hand, some of the more important stakeholder groups do have fairly specific interests, the satisfaction of which should be fairly amenable to measurement. Here are some examples of possible measures.

Stakeholder group	Measure
Employees	Staff turnover; pay and benefits relative to market rate; job vacancies
Government	Pollution measures; promptness of filing annual returns; accident rate; energy efficiency
Distributors	Share of joint promotions paid for; rate of running out of inventory

PER performance objectives PO2 requires you to be able to demonstrate your skills in stakeholder relationship management. This could cover communications with internal and external colleagues, maintaining good business relationships, drafting reports, making presentations, using technology effectively and even addressing complaints. It all requires an understanding of stakeholder needs, as covered in this chapter.

CHAPTER ROUNDUP

↳ Organisations can achieve results which individuals cannot achieve by themselves.

↳ An important difference in the list above is between profit orientated ('commercial') and non profit orientated organisations.

↳ A non-governmental organisation (NGO) is a legally constituted organisation of people acting together independently from any form of government.

↳ Stakeholders are those individuals or groups that, potentially, have an interest in what the organisation does. These stakeholders can be within the organisation, connected to the organisation or external to the organisation.

QUICK QUIZ

1 Which of the following defines an organisation?

A A social arrangement which pursues collective goals, which controls its own performance and which has a boundary separating it from its environment

B A social arrangement which exists to make a profit, controls its own performance and which operates within certain boundaries

2 A private sector organisation is one owned or run by:

A Central government
B Local government
C Government agencies
D None of the above

3 Businesses owned by their workers or customers who share the profits are called

A Limited companies   C Co-operatives
B Private limited companies   D Partnerships

4 Which one of the following are examples of internal stakeholders?

A Shareholders   C Suppliers
B Employees   D Financiers

5 According to Mendelow's matrix, stakeholders in segment C (low interest, high power) should be kept informed. Is this true or false?

ANSWERS TO QUICK QUIZ

1   A.   This is the definition of an organisation. Not all organisations exist to make a profit.

2   D.   None of the above. A **public** sector organisation is owned or run by central or local government.

3   C.   Co-operatives are owned by their workers or customers.

4   B.   The others are all connected stakeholders.

5   False. Stakeholders in this segment should be kept satisfied.

Now try ...

Attempt the questions below from the **Practice Question Bank**

Q1 ~~Answers~~ Business org & their environment.

Q2 &

Q3 B

Q4 &

PART 1

CHAPTER

02

The aim of environmental analysis (Section 1) is to review the environment for **opportunities** and **threats**, and to secure environmental fit. An organisation has many interchanges with its environment. It draws inputs from it and outputs goods and services to it. The environment is a major source of uncertainty.

An organisation is affected by **general environmental trends**, usefully summarised in the **PEST** model (**Section 1**). The PEST model is drawn out into its component elements in **Sections 2 to 10**, which cover legal aspects (employment legislation, data protection and health and safety), social and cultural trends, the impact of technology on organisations and environmental factors. External competitive forces, as identified by Michael Porter, are covered in **Sections 11 and 13**.

The internal capabilities of the organisation are analysed in the value chain framework (**Section 12**). While the value chain has an internal rather than an external focus, it is included in this chapter as a method of improving a company's competitive position in the wider market.

The business environment

TOPIC LIST	SYLLABUS REFERENCE
1 Analysing the business environment	A3 (a),(b)
2 The political and legal environment	A3 (a),(b)
3 Employment protection	A3 (c)
4 Data protection and security	A3 (d)
5 Health and safety	A3 (e),(f)
6 Consumer protection	A3 (g)
7 Social and demographic trends	A6 (a),(c)
8 Cultural trends	A6 (b)
9 The impact of technology on organisations	A7 (a),(b)
10 Environmental factors	A8 (a) – (c)
11 Competitive forces	A9 (a)
12 Converting resources: the value chain	A9 (b), A9 (d)
13 Competitive advantage – Porter's five forces model	A9 (c)

Study Guide	**Intellectual level**

A3 Political and legal factors affecting business

(a) Explain how the political system and government policy affect the organisation. — K

(b) Describe the sources of legal authority, including supra-national bodies, national and regional governments. — K

(c) Explain how the law protects the employee and the implications of employment legislation for the manager and the organisation. — K

(d) Identify the principles of data protection and security. — K

(e) Explain how the law promotes and protects health and safety in the workplace. — K

(f) Recognise the responsibility of the individual and organisation for compliance with laws on data protection, security and health and safety. — K

(g) Outline principles of consumer protection, such as sale of goods and simple contract. — K

A6 Social and demographic factors

(a) Explain the medium- and long-term effects of social and demographic trends on business outcomes and the economy. — K

(b) Describe the impact of changes in social structure, values, attitudes and tastes on the organisation. — K

(c) Identify and explain the measures that governments may take in response to the medium and long-term impact of demographic change. — K

A7 Technological factors

(a) Explain the potential effects of technological change on the organisation structure and strategy:
   (i) Downsizing
   (ii) Delayering
   (iii) Outsourcing

(b) Describe the impact of information technology and information systems development on business processes. — K

A8 Environmental factors

(a) List ways in which the business can affect or be affected by its physical environment. — K

(b) Describe ways in which businesses can operate more efficiently and effectively to limit damage to the environment. — K

(c) Identify the benefits of economic sustainability to stakeholders. — K

A9 Competitive factors

(a) Identify a business's strengths, weaknesses, opportunities and threats (SWOT) in a market and the main sources of competitive advantage. — K

(b) Identify the main elements within Porter's value chain and explain the meaning of a value network. — K

(c) Explain the factors or forces that influence the level of competitiveness in an industry or sector using Porter's five forces model. — K

(d) Describe the activities of an organisation that affect its competitiveness: K

    (i)   Purchasing

    (ii) Production

    (iii) Marketing

    (iv) Service

EXAM FOCUS POINT

The topics covered in this large chapter have been heavily tested in the past, so this is a very important area. Note that exam questions will **not** be country specific.

1 Analysing the business environment

Whatever the overall strategic management method used, no organisation is likely to achieve its aims if it fails to take into account the **characteristics of the environment** in which it operates.

The environment is everything that surrounds an organisation, physically and socially.

Environmental analysis is one of the inputs to the strategy-making process. Johnson and Scholes suggest the following procedure:

Step 1	Assess the nature of the environment (eg is it changing?).

Step 2	Identify those influences which have affected the organisation in the past or which are likely to do so in future.

Step 3	Prepare a structural analysis identifying the 'key forces at work in the immediate or competitive environment'.

↓

These steps should identify important developments. Then the following questions should be asked.

↓

Step 4	What is the organisation's position in relation to other organisations?

Step 5	What threats and/or opportunities are posed by the environment?

An organisation's environment may be examined in a number of ways.

(a) **Global/local**. Some organisations operate worldwide. However, they still have to be sensitive to the local requirements of the countries or markets they operate in or export to. Some companies are much more exposed to global competition than others.

(b)   **General/task**: this is the method we will use.

   (i)   The **general (or macro) environment** covers all those factors influencing all organisations indirectly, for example: general economic trends, population growth, new technology. These factors are abbreviated to PEST (political-legal, economic, social-cultural, technological) factors.

   (ii) The **task (or micro) environment** includes those areas which have a direct impact on the organisation, such as its ability to acquire raw materials, its competitors and its customers. Porter (1980) analyses the task environment into **five competitive forces**, which are discussed in Section 13.

The distinction is not hard and fast, and is drawn for convenience only.

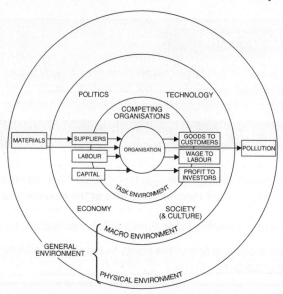

EXAM FOCUS POINT

PEST analysis is a useful tool to employ as an initial survey of conditions and options.

The environment is a source of **uncertainty**. In other words, decision-makers do not have sufficient information about environmental factors, and many things are out of their control. The overall degree of uncertainty may be assessed along two axes: simplicity/complexity and stability/dynamism.

(a)   **Simplicity/complexity**

   (i)   The **variety of influences** faced by an organisation. The more open an organisation is, the greater the variety of influences. The greater the number of markets the organisation operates in, the greater the number of influences to which it is subject.

   (ii) The amount of **knowledge necessary**. Some environments, to be handled successfully, require knowledge. All businesses need to have knowledge of the tax system, for example, but only pharmaceuticals businesses need to know about mandatory testing procedures for new drugs.

   (iii) The **interconnectedness** of environmental influences causes complexity. Importing and exporting companies are sensitive to exchange rates, which themselves are sensitive to interest rates. Interest rates then influence a company's borrowing costs. Scenario-building and modelling are ways of dealing with complexities to develop an understanding of environmental conditions.

(b) **Stability/dynamism**

    (i) An area of the environment is stable if it remains the same. (For example, investors get nervous about a change in government.) Firms which can predict demand face a stable environment.

    (ii) An unstable environment changes often. The environment of many fashion goods is unstable.

As a rule of thumb, use the following checklist for uncertainty.

- **Simple** (few environmental influences to worry about) **and stable:** low uncertainty
- **Complex and stable**: low to moderate uncertainty
- **Simple and unstable**: moderate to high uncertainty
- **Complex and unstable**: high uncertainty

1.1 The changing environment

Changes in the business environment have been driven by a number of developments. Here are some of the changes that have happened.

(a) **Globalisation** of business – increased competition and global customers as domestic markets become saturated, with companies able to compete easily anywhere in the world

(b) **Science and technology** developments, especially in communications (the internet) and transport (particularly air travel)

(c) Mergers, acquisitions and strategic **alliances**

(d) Changing **customer values** and behaviour

(e) Increased **scrutiny of business decisions** by government and the public

(f) Increased **liberalisation** of trade, and **deregulation** and co-operation between business and government easing access to foreign markets

(g) Changes in **business practices** – downsizing, outsourcing and re-engineering

(h) Changes in the **social and business relationships** between companies and their employees, customers and other stakeholders

As companies have become exposed to more international competition, at the same time as having greater access to international markets, their preferred choice of **organisational structure** has been affected. This has been evident, as discussed earlier, in the shift away from mechanistic and bureaucratic organisations towards flatter structures with more flexible operating arrangements. Network forms of organisation and 'virtual' organisations are another manifestation of this trend. The need for strategic **international alliances** has increased with the need to understand and access foreign markets. The development of **communications technology** (email, the internet) is the key factor that has made such relationships possible.

Some firms have been changing the structure of their workforces for the sake of greater flexibility in responding to competitor activity or customer needs. This so-called '**flexible firm**' comprises a **core** of full-time permanent staff who possess the key skills, and **peripheral** part-timers and temporary or contract workers. This workforce can be flexed in a number of ways to meet changes in the market.

2 The political and legal environment

> **Government policy** influences the economic environment, the framework of laws, industry structure and certain operational issues. Political instability is a cause of risk. Different approaches to the **political environment** apply in different countries. **International trade** is subject to a further layer of international law and regulation.

The **political environment** affects the firm in a number of ways.

- A basic legal framework generally exists.

- The Government can take a particular stance on an issue of direct relevance to a business or industry.

- The Government's overall conduct of its economic policy is relevant to business.

2.1 The political and legal environment

Laws come from common law, parliamentary legislation and government regulations derived from it, and obligations under treaties such as those establishing the European Union.

Legal factors affecting all companies

Factor	Example
General legal framework: contract, tort, agency	Basic ways of doing business, negligence proceedings
Criminal law	Theft, insider dealing, bribery, deception
Company law	Directors and their duties, reporting requirements, takeover proceedings, shareholders' rights, insolvency
Employment law	Trade Union recognition, Social Chapter provisions, minimum wage, unfair dismissal, redundancy, maternity, Equal Opportunities
Health and safety	Fire precautions, safety procedures
Data protection	Use of information about employees and customers
Marketing and sales	Laws to protect consumers (eg refunds and replacement, 'cooling off' period after credit agreements), what is or isn't allowed in advertising
Environment	Pollution control, waste disposal
Tax law	Corporation tax payment, collection of income tax (PAYE) and National Insurance contributions, sales tax (VAT)

Some legal and regulatory factors affect **particular industries**, if the public interest is served. For example, in the UK, electricity and gas, telecommunications, water and rail transport are subject to **regulators** who have influence over market access, competition and pricing policy (can restrict price increase). These UK bodies are called Offer, Ofgem, Ofcom, Ofwat and ORR respectively. Other countries will have similar regulators.

This is because:

- The industries are, effectively, monopolies
- Large sums of public money are involved (eg in subsidies to rail companies)

2.2 The impact of government

Porter notes several ways whereby the **Government** can directly affect the **economic structure** of an industry. They are explained below.

Capacity expansion	Government policy can encourage firms to increase or cut their capacity.
	(a) The UK tax system offers 'capital allowances' to encourage investment in equipment.
	(b) A variety of incentives, funded by the EU and national governments, exist for locating capacity in a particular area.
	(c) **Incentives** are used to encourage investment by overseas firms.
Demand	• The Government is a major customer.
	• Government can also influence demand by legislation, tax reliefs or subsidies.
Divestment and rationalisation	In some European countries, the state takes many decisions regarding the selling off or closure of businesses, especially in sensitive areas such as defence.
Emerging industries	Can be promoted by the Government or damaged by it.
Entry barriers	Government policy can discourage firms from entering an industry, by restricting investment or competition or by making it harder, by use of quotas and tariffs, for overseas firms to compete in the domestic market.
Competition	(a) The Government's **purchasing decisions** will have a strong influence on the strength of one firm relative to another in the market (eg armaments).
	(b) **Regulations and controls** in an industry will affect the growth and profits of the industry – eg minimum product quality standards.
	(c) As a supplier of **infrastructure** (eg roads), the Government is also in a position to influence competition in an industry.
	(d) Governments and supra-national institutions such as the EU might impose policies which keep an industry **fragmented**, and prevent the concentration of too much market share in the hands of one or two producers.

In some industries, governments regulate the adoption of **new products**. This is well illustrated by the pharmaceuticals industry, where new drugs or medicines must in many countries undergo stringent testing and obtain government approval before they can be marketed.

National and EU institutions also affect the operating activities of some organisations, for example:

- Anti-discrimination legislation
- Health and safety legislation
- Product safety and standardisation (especially EU standards)
- Workers' rights (eg unfair dismissal, maternity leave)
- Training and education policies (which can determine the 'standard' of recruits)

QUESTION

Government impact

How do you think government policy affects the pharmaceutical industry in your country?

ANSWER

Using the example of the UK.

(a)   The Government must authorise most new drugs (eg for safety before they can be sold).

(b)   The UK Government is a major purchaser of pharmaceuticals for the national health service, and so has significant buying power.

(c)   Health education policies affect consumer demand.

(d)   Funding of universities affects the science base for recruitment.

(e)   Employment practices, such as working hours, are influenced by EU employment directives.

2.3 Influencing government

Businesses are able to influence government policies in a number of ways.

(a)   They can employ **lobbyists** to put their case to individual ministers or civil servants.

(b)   They can give MPs **non-executive directorships**, in the hope that the MP will take an interest in all legislation that affects them.

(c)   They can try to **influence public opinion**, and hence the legislative agenda, by advertising.

Of particular importance is the need to influence the decision-making processes of the European Commission. EU regulations, for practical purposes, take priority over national law. They are arrived at after a great deal of negotiation, and for this reason alone, are difficult to change. It is therefore much better to influence the **drafting process** of new regulations than to try to get them changed once they have been implemented.

The EU will have an increasing role in the conduct of **European businesses** in:

* Product standards
* Environmental protection
* Monetary policy (a European Central Bank might set interest rates)
* Research and development
* Regional policy
* Labour costs (wages, pensions)

In addition, an EU-Africa Business Forum has been set up to improve investment and the business climate in Africa.

2.4 Political risk and political change

Changes in UK law are often predictable. A government will publish a **green paper** discussing a proposed change in the law, before issuing a **white paper** and passing a bill through Parliament. Plans should be formulated about what to do if the change takes place.

However, it is **political change** which complicates the planning activities of many firms. Many economic forecasts ignore the implications of a change in government policy.

(a)   At **national level**, political influence is significant and includes legislation on trading, pricing, dividends, tax and employment as well as health and safety (to list but a few).

(b)   Politics at **international level** also has a direct bearing on organisations. EU directives affect all countries in the EU.

The **political risk** in a decision is the risk that political factors will invalidate the strategy and perhaps severely damage the firm. Examples are wars, political chaos, corruption and nationalisation.

2.5 International trade

The political environment is of particular importance in **international trade**. Such trade is governed by an extra layer of legislation contained in treaties and agreements and is potentially subject to a **higher level of political risk**. This may be manifested in a variety of ways, such as taxation law, labour regulation and economic policy on such matters as ownership. At worst, there is a threat of expropriation or nationalisation. Failure to repress lawlessness and corruption are further complicating factors, as is open or covert refusal to consider international bidders for government contracts.

2.6 The European Union

The European Union operates a **single European market**, allowing for the **free movement** of labour, goods and services, and **free competition**.

The EU single market programme has involved areas as diverse as **harmonising technical standards**, opening up areas such as telecommunications to competition, consumer protection, mutual recognition of professional qualifications, and so on.

2.7 International trade liberalisation: the World Trade Organisation (WTO)

The **World Trade Organisation** was set up to promote free trade and resolve disputes between trading partners.

The theory of **comparative advantage** suggests that **free trade** is the best way to promote global economic growth and, by implication, domestic prosperity. In other words, people should be free to buy and sell goods and services anywhere in the world.

3 Employment protection

Much legislation has been aimed at the idea of 'employment protection'. As a result, all forms of **termination of employment** must be treated with great care.

3.1 Retirement

In the UK, many employees are taking **early retirement** perhaps as a result of corporate downsizing, but many people still search for work at an older age and there are pressure groups seeking to ban **ageism** in recruitment. Retirement ages for men and women are being **equalised**.

Organisations **encourage retirement** for a variety of reasons.

- Promotion opportunities are created for younger workers.
- Early retirement is an alternative to redundancy.
- The age structure of an organisation may become unbalanced.
- The cost of providing pensions rises with age.

3.2 Resignation

People resign for many reasons, personal and occupational. Employees who are particularly valuable should be encouraged to stay. Particular problems the employee has been experiencing (eg salary) may be solvable, though not always in the short term.

In any case, an **exit interview**, when the leaver explains the decision to go, is a valuable source of information.

The **period of notice** required for the employee to leave should be set out in the contract of employment, but some leeway may be negotiated on this.

3.3 Dismissal

There are three forms of termination that constitute dismissal under UK law (Employment Rights Act 1996, (TSO, 1996)).

(a)   The termination of an employee's contract **by the employer**

(b)   The ending of a fixed-term contract **without renewal** on the same terms: in effect, there is no such thing as a fixed-term contract of employment

(c)   Resignation by the **employee** where the **employer's conduct** breaches the contract of employment: this is **constructive dismissal**

The **statutory minimum** period of notice to be given is determined by the employee's length of continuous service with the employer. Longer periods may be written into the contract, at the employer's discretion, and by agreement. Either party may waive their right to notice, or accept payment in lieu of notice. An employee is entitled to a written statement of the **reasons** for dismissal.

3.4 Wrongful dismissal

Wrongful dismissal is dismissal that breaches the **contract of employment**. An example would be failure to give the contractual period of notice (assuming the circumstances did not justify summary dismissal). Wrongful dismissal relates to the method of dismissal.

3.5 Unfair dismissal

The legal concept of unfair dismissal gives protection to the employee against **arbitrary** dismissal; that is, dismissal without good reason. A dismissal need not be wrongful to be unfair. The basic principle is that any dismissal is potentially unfair. Under employment protection legislation, the employee has to **prove** that they have been dismissed. The onus is then on the **employer to prove** that the dismissal was **fair**. Examples of dismissals that would be unfair would be dismissing an employee who has legitimately 'whistleblown' on unethical practices or dismissal as a result of an employee joining a trade union.

3.6 Disciplinary procedures

The use of a disciplinary system can be evidence in certain situations that an employee has not been dismissed unfairly.

3.7 Redundancy

Redundancy is dismissal under two circumstances.

(a)   The employer has ceased to carry on the business at all or in the place where the employee was employed.

(b)   The requirements of the business for employees to carry out work of a particular kind have ceased or diminished or are expected to.

Compensation is a legal entitlement, and encourages employees to accept redundancy without damage to industrial relations.

The employee is **not entitled** to compensation in three circumstances.

(a)   The employer has made an offer of suitable alternative employment and the employee has **unreasonably** rejected it.

(b)   The employee is of pensionable age or over, or has less than two years' continuous employment.

(c)   The employee's conduct merits **dismissal without notice**.

There are certain legal minima for compensation offered, based on age and length of service.

3.7.1 Procedure for handling redundancies

From a purely humane point of view, it is obviously desirable to consult with employees or their representatives. Notice of impending redundancies is a legal duty for redundancies over a certain number.

The impact of a redundancy programme can be reduced in several ways.

- Retirement of staff over the normal retirement age
- Early retirement of staff approaching normal retirement age
- Restrictions on recruitment to reduce the workforce over time by natural wastage
- Dismissal of part-time or short-term contract staff
- Offering retraining and/or redeployment within the organisation
- Seeking voluntary redundancies

Where management have to choose between individuals doing the same work, they may dismiss the less competent or require people to re-apply for the job. The LIFO principle may be applied, so that newcomers are dismissed before long-serving employees.

Many large organisations provide benefits in excess of the statutory minimum with regard to consultation periods, terms, notice periods, counselling and aid with job search, training in job-search skills, and so on.

Many firms provide advice and **outplacement** counselling to help redundant employees find work elsewhere.

3.8 Equal opportunities

Some groups are discriminated against with little or no justification. This applies particularly in employment matters. There are laws and regulations to help prevent this and to redress the balance.

The subject of equal opportunities is covered, in detail, in Chapter 13.

4 Data protection and security

Privacy is the right of the individual not to suffer unauthorised disclosure of information.

Privacy is the right of the individual to control the use of information about them, including information on financial status, health and lifestyle (ie prevent unauthorised disclosure).

4.1 Why is privacy an important issue?

In recent years, there has been a growing fear that the ever-increasing amount of **information** about individuals held by organisations could be misused.

In particular, it was felt that an individual could easily be harmed by the existence of computerised data about them which was inaccurate or misleading and which could be **transferred to unauthorised third parties** at high speed and little cost.

In the UK the current legislation covering this area is the **Data Protection Act 1998**.

4.2 The Data Protection Act 1998

The (UK) **Data Protection Act 1998** protects individuals about whom data is held. Both manual and computerised information must comply with the Act.

The Data Protection Act 1998 (TSO, 1998) is an attempt to protect the **individual**. The terms of the Act cover data about individuals – **not data about corporate bodies**. (Remember that you will not be

examined on the details of the UK's Data Protection Act but the syllabus states that you must be able to identify the principles of data protection and security).

4.3 Definitions of terms used in the Act

In order to understand the Act it is necessary to know some of the technical terms used in it.

- **Personal data** is information about a living individual, including expressions of opinion about them. Data about organisations is not personal data.

- **Data users** are organisations or individuals who control personal data and the use of personal data.

- A **data subject** is an individual who is the subject of personal data.

4.4 The data protection principles

The **UK Data Protection Act** includes eight **Data Protection Principles** with which data users must comply.

DATA PROTECTION PRINCIPLES

Schedule 1 of the Act contains the data protection principles.

1 Personal data shall be processed fairly and lawfully in accordance with the Act.

2 Personal data shall be obtained only for one or more specified and lawful purposes, and shall not be further processed in any manner incompatible with that purpose or those purposes.

3 Personal data shall be adequate, relevant and not excessive in relation to the purpose or purposes for which they are processed.

4 Personal data shall be accurate and, where necessary, kept up to date.

5 Personal data processed for any purpose or purposes shall not be kept for longer than is necessary for that purpose or those purposes.

6 Personal data shall be processed in accordance with the rights of data subjects under this Act.

7 Appropriate technical and organisational measures shall be taken against unauthorised or unlawful processing of personal data and against accidental loss or destruction of, or damage to, personal data.

8 Personal data shall not be transferred to a country or territory outside the European Economic Area unless that country or territory ensures an adequate level of protection for the rights and freedoms of data subjects in relation to the processing of personal data.

The Act has two main aims:

(a) To protect **individual privacy**. Previous UK law only applied to **computer-based** information. The 1998 Act applies to **all personal data, in any form.**

(b) To **harmonise data protection legislation** so that, in the interests of improving the operation of the single European market, there can be a **free flow of personal data** between the member states of the EU.

4.4.1 The rights of data subjects

The Act establishes the following rights for data subjects.

(a) A data subject may seek **compensation** through the courts for damage and any associated distress caused by the **loss**, **destruction** or **unauthorised disclosure** of data about themselves or by **inaccurate data** about themselves.

(b) A data subject may apply to the courts for **inaccurate data** to be **put right** or even **wiped off** the data user's files altogether. Such applications may also be made to the Registrar.

(c) A data subject may obtain **access** to personal data of which they are the subject. (This is known as the 'subject access' provision.) In other words, a data subject can ask to see their personal data that the data user is holding.

(d) A data subject can **sue** a data user for any **damage or distress** caused to him by personal data about them which is **incorrect** or **misleading** as to matter of **fact** (rather than opinion).

QUESTION   Data protection

Your managing director has asked you to recommend measures that your company, which is based in the UK, could take to ensure compliance with data protection legislation. Suggest what measures should be taken.

ANSWER

Measures could include the following.

- Obtain consent from individuals to hold any sensitive personal data you need.
- Supply individuals with a copy of any personal data you hold about them if so requested.
- Consider if you may need to obtain consent to process personal data.
- Ensure you do not pass on personal data to unauthorised parties.

5 Health and safety

People should be able to be confident that they will not be exposed to excessive risk when they are at work. This means that risk and danger must be actively managed.

5.1 Importance of maintaining health and safety at work

- An employer has **legal obligations** under UK and EU law.
- Accidents and illness **cost the employer money**.
- The company's **image** in the marketplace and society may suffer.

The **major legislation in the UK** covers a number of Acts of Parliament. EU law will become more important in the future. The most important piece of legislation in this area in the UK is the Health and Safety at Work Act 1974 (HMSO, 1974). Remember that UK law will not feature in the exam but you do need to be aware of health and safety best practices.

5.2 Employers' duties

A senior manager must be specified as responsible for ensuring that problems are solved and rules observed.

(a) All **work practices** must be safe.

(b) The work **environment** must be safe and healthy.

(c) All plant and equipment must be maintained to the necessary standard.

(d) Information, instruction, training and supervision should **encourage safe working practices**. Employers must provide training and information to all staff.

(e) The safety policy should be clearly **communicated** to all staff.

(f) Employers must carry out **risk assessments**, generally in writing, of all work hazards. Assessment should be continuous. They must **assess the risks to anyone else affected by their work activities**.

(g)   They must **share hazard and risk information** with other employers, including those on adjoining premises, other site occupiers and all subcontractors coming onto the premises.

(h)   They must **introduce controls** to reduce risks.

(i)   They should **revise safety policies** in the light of the above, or initiate safety policies if none were in place previously.

(j)   They must **identify employees** who are especially at risk.

(k)   They must employ competent safety and health **advisers**.

The Safety Representative Regulations provide that a **safety representative** may be appointed by a recognised trade union, and for **safety committees** to be set up at the request of employee representatives. Safety representatives are entitled to paid time off work to carry out their duties.

5.3 Employee duties

(a)   Take reasonable care of themselves and others

(b)   Allow the employer to carry out their duties (including enforcing safety rules)

(c)   Not interfere intentionally or recklessly with any machinery or equipment

(d)   Inform the employer of any situation which may be a danger (this does not reduce the employer's responsibilities in any way)

(e)   Use all equipment properly

QUESTION

Work environment

What aspects of your own work environment (if any) do you think are:

* A hindrance to your work?   • A hazard to your health or safety?
* A source of dissatisfaction?

5.4 Accident and safety policies

Accidents are **expensive**.

(a)   Time is lost by the injured employee and other staff.

(b)   Costs caused by disruption to operations, for example repair costs and production 'downtime' following damage to equipment.

(c)   Compensation payments or fines resulting from legal action and increased insurance premiums.

(d)   Output from the injured employee on return to work is often reduced.

(e)   Recruiting and training a replacement for the injured worker will have its own cost.

An employee who is injured as a result of either the **employer's failure to take reasonable care** or a breach of **statutory duty** can **sue**.

(a)   An employee is not deemed to consent to the risk of injury because they are aware of the risk. It is the employer's duty to provide a safe working system.

(b)   Employees can become inattentive or careless in doing work which is monotonous or imposes stress. This factor too must be allowed for in the employer's safety precautions.

(c)   The employer should encourage and insist on proper use of safety equipment.

(d)   Many dangers can be caused by carelessness or other fault of an otherwise competent employee, possibly by their mere thoughtlessness.

Reducing the frequency and severity of accidents

(a) Develop safety consciousness among staff.

(b) Develop effective consultative **participation**.

(c) Give adequate **instruction** in safety rules and measures.

(d) **Materials handling should be minimised**.

(e) **Good maintenance** pays dividends.

(f) Implement in full the **code of practice** for the industry.

(g) **Safety inspections** should be carried out regularly.

Accident reporting systems

(a) Accidents should be reported on an **accident report form** and records kept. Accidents resulting in death, major injury (such as the loss of an eye or a finger) or more than three days off work for the victim must be notified to the Health and Safety Executive.

(b) **Statistical trends** should be monitored to reveal areas where recurring accidents suggest the need for special investigation, but only more serious incidents will have to be followed-up in depth.

(c) **Follow-up** should be clearly aimed at preventing recurrence – not placing blame.

(d) Risk audit or sampling should be carried out regularly to prevent accidents.

(e) There should be a procedure for reporting 'near-misses', anonymously if necessary, to encourage openness.

5.5 Health and safety policy

In order to enhance safety awareness, promote good practice and comply with legal obligations, many employers have a **health and safety policy** for their staff. Such a policy will have a number of features.

(a) Statement of **principles**

(b) Detail of **safety procedures**

(c) **Compliance with the law**

(d) **Detailed instructions** on how to use equipment

(e) **Training requirements**

Senior managers must set a good example.

(a) **Visibly reacting to breaches** of the policy (eg if the fire doors are blocked open, remove the blockage).

(b) **Ensuring that the policy is communicated** to staff (eg memoranda, newsletters).

(c) **Setting priorities for operations**.

(d) Involving staff in the health and safety process.

6 Consumer protection

We will now look at those aspects of law and regulation which apply to consumer protection, including **contract law and the sale of goods**. All countries have their own legislation dealing with these topics. These are the general principles.

6.1 What is a contract?

A contract is a legally binding agreement.

A contract is a legally binding agreement. In all areas of life we make contracts. If you buy or sell a house, a contract is made and 'exchanged'. When you start a job, you will probably have a contract of employment. When you go into a shop and buy something, you have entered into an agreement with the shopkeeper – you agree that the shopkeeper will give you the goods and you will give them the money.

Under contract law, the money that you give in exchange for the goods is referred to as the '**consideration**'. For a contract to take place, there must be **agreement** between the parties. This requires an **offer** made by one party, **acceptance** by the other party and, in England and Wales (but not Scotland), some **consideration** passing between them.

An important point about contracts is that they do not have to be written. They do not even have to be spoken. A customer picking up something in a supermarket and walking to the checkout is making an offer to the shop, and that offer is **implied** by their behaviour.

Any business buying and selling goods is continually making and discharging (completing) contracts. Probably none of the parties involved give much thought to the legal aspect of what they are doing **until something goes wrong**.

When one party to a contract fails to carry out his part of the agreement, the other party can take legal action against them for **breach of contract**. So if a business has a customer who is failing to pay, they can take them to court.

Where one party makes a misrepresentation to the other, the contract is considered **void.** For example, A sells goods to B, who sells them on to C. B then fails to pay A for the goods and disappears without trace. If A can demonstrate that they were genuinely mistaken as to the identity of B and would not have dealt with them had they known who B really was, then A can recover the goods which were subject to the original contract from C. This is because the law takes the view in such a situation that the original contract between A and B was no contract at all. Therefore C, who was an innocent third party acting in good faith, has to return the goods to A and either bear the loss or find and sue B.

6.2 Sale of goods and services

An important area of contract law is the law concerning the **sale of goods**. UK legislation also covers contracts where the **supply of services** is the major part of the contract. For example, contracts of repair, where the supply of goods may be incidental to the provision of a service.

Imagine that you are about to enter into a contract for the purchase of some goods. What might you be concerned about?

- You may want the goods delivered for a particular occasion or **date**.
- Are the goods stolen, ie does the seller have a **right to sell the goods**?
- You would expect the goods to be the same type and quality as the description or any sample.
- The goods should be of **reasonable quality** and **suitable for their purpose**.

The UK's Consumer Rights Act 2015 (TSO, 2015) legislation covers these matters and a number of other important issues. We will use UK legislation as an example in the following sections. Its provisions are regarded as **implied terms** of most contracts for the sale of goods.

6.2.1 Implied terms

A sale of goods is subject to the following provisions.

- Title, or the seller's right to sell the goods
- Description of the goods
- Quality of the goods
- Fitness of the goods for the purpose for which they are supplied

6.2.2 Time of performance

If goods arrive too late, they may be useless.

The terms of the contract will determine whether a particular timescale is a condition of performance. If it is, a breach of such terms entitles the injured party to treat the contract as discharged.

In commercial contracts for the supply of goods for business or industrial use, it will be assumed that **time is of the essence**, even where there is no express term to that effect.

6.2.3 Seller's title

You cannot sell something that is not yours to sell. It is an implied condition that the seller has a **right to sell the goods**, or will have, at the time of sale.

If the seller delivers goods without having the right to sell, the buyer does not get to own the goods, which is the essential basis of the contract. If the buyer subsequently has to return the goods to the real owner, they may recover the entire price from the seller.

6.2.4 Example: Seller's title

R bought a car from D, which D had unknowingly bought from a thief. When this was discovered, the car was returned to the true owner. R sued D for the return of the full purchase price (as damages). The court decided that, although R had used the car for several months, they had not had ownership of it, which is what they had paid for. D therefore had to repay the full amount.

6.2.5 Goods to correspond with contract description

If you have agreed to buy certain goods on the basis of the description (whether the buyer's or the seller's), you expect the goods to correspond to the description.

This is implied, under the Act, in any contract for sale of goods 'by description'. The description may be of ingredients, components, age, date of shipment, packing, quantity etc.

6.2.6 Example: Sale by description

A seller advertised a secondhand reaping machine, describing it as new the previous year. The buyer bought it without seeing it. When it arrived they found that it was much more than a year old and rejected it. The seller sued for the price. It was held that this was a sale by description, the goods had not corresponded to the description, and the buyer was therefore entitled to reject the goods.

6.2.7 Satisfactory quality

All goods supplied under a contract for the sale of goods **in the course of a business** must be of **'satisfactory quality'**. They should meet the standard that a reasonable person would regard as satisfactory, taking account of any description of the goods, the price and other relevant circumstances.

In deciding whether goods are of satisfactory quality, the following should be taken into account.

(a)   **Fitness for all the purposes for which goods of the kind in question are commonly supplied**. A hot water bottle that deteriorated when filled with hot water, for example, would not be of satisfactory quality. A bucket needs to hold a variety of substances, and be handled in a variety of ways, without leakage, damage, immediate deterioration, and so on.

(b)   **Appearance and finish**. Previous to 1994, goods with superficial damage, but which operated properly in the main, could be of merchantable quality. Satisfactory quality includes freedom from dents, marks, scratches, and so on – unless they have clearly been allowed for in the description and price.

(c)   **Freedom from minor defects**.

(d)   **Safety**.

(e)   **Durability**. They have to remain of satisfactory quality for a period which could be expected by a reasonable person.

QUESTION   Refund

Peter buys an electronic keyboard from his local catalogue store. He pays $199 for it. He returns to the store the next day complaining that, although the main keys work, none of the pre-set rhythm buttons seem to function. He demands an immediate refund. The sales assistant refuses to given him a refund or take back the goods, and instead gives him a card with the name and address of the manufacturer, suggesting that Peter contacts them to obtain a refund or a replacement.

(a)   Was the sales assistant legally justified in refusing to give a refund?   Yes/No
(b)   Give briefly a reason for your answer.

ANSWER

(a)   No

(b)   Contracts of sale are between the buyer and the seller, not between the buyer and the manufacturer.

6.2.8 Fitness of goods for a disclosed purpose

If you tell a seller (explicitly or by implication) that you intend to use goods for a particular purpose, you expect the goods supplied to be reasonably fit for that purpose.

This is an implied term, under the Act, unless it can be shown that the seller may not have known whether the goods were suitable for a purpose which was not familiar to them and the buyer may have been in a better position to tell.

Like 'satisfactory quality', this condition only applies to goods sold **in the course of a business**.

7 Social and demographic trends

7.1 Population and the labour market

> Population affects an organisation's supply of labour and hence its policies towards recruiting and managing human resources.

This section uses the example of the UK.

Growing populations offer a larger labour market.

- Increasing birth rates mean more young people.
- Falling death rates mean more elderly people – some of these will continue working.

The changing age structure of the labour force. Fewer young people might mean that young people will become more expensive. The number of 16 year olds entering the labour force peaked in the late 1970s, but has been falling ever since.

Women are increasing their participation in the labour force.

The increasing participation of women occurs for four reasons.

- More part-time jobs
- Rising male unemployment as many industries which employed men have declined
- The growth of the service sector
- An increase in the average age at which women have children

7.2 Implications for employers

How organisations can cope with these demographic and educational trends

(a) Establish the **labour market** the organisation is in (eg young people, part-time workers). In other words, 'Who do we want to recruit?'

(b) Discover the organisation's **catchment areas** (ie location of potential recruits).

(c) Discern the **supply side trends** in the catchment area labour force (eg how many school leavers are expected? What is the rate of growth/decline of the local population?).

(d) Examine **education trends** in the area.

(e) Assess the **demand from other employers** for the **skills** you need (eg if there is a large concentration of, say, electronics companies in the region, then they will be interested in hiring people with similar skills).

(f) Assess whether some of your demand can be satisfied by a supply from **other sources.**

Organisations will need proper resourcing strategies to make sure their demand for labour is properly met.

7.3 Family life cycle

An example of a use of demography by marketing people is **family life cycle** (FLC). This is a summary of demographic variables.

- It combines the effects of age, marital status, career status (income) and the presence or absence of children.

- It is able to identify the various stages through which households progress. It is clear that particular products and services can be marketed to people at specific stages of the life cycle.

7.4 Social structures and class

Social class: Society can be divided into broad groups, whose members share common features, such as **occupation, income level** and **education background**. These groups are known as social classes.

In sociological terms, a class is more than a group of people with various things in common, however. Classes fit into a social structure, in which some classes have advantage over others.

- Access to power
- Educational attainment
- Income
- Inherited wealth
- Status or esteem

It is possible to infer shared values, attitudes and behaviour within a social class as distinct from those of a higher or lower class: some research has been able to relate consumption behaviour to class standing. (This makes social class an attractive proposition for market segmentation.)

7.5 Socio-economic position, income and wealth

While there are some real differences between the groups, 'social class' for marketing or planning purposes should be used with caution. Sometimes people's lifestyles are a reflection of their economic condition in society, not the **reason for their position**.

7.6 Socio-economic status

QUESTION   Socio-economic status

'Comparing people's income is a simple matter. All you need to do is compare income after direct tax and social security contributions to see how well off people are.'
Do you agree with this statement?

ANSWER

Unfortunately the issue is not that simple. Firstly, there is indirect taxation (for example, sales tax). Households on different incomes are more or less exposed to this. Secondly, there is the issue of mortgage interest relief which is available in some countries. It is not available to people renting their accommodation. Thirdly, there are additional social benefits such as education. It is difficult to combine these factors.

7.7 Buying patterns

Buying behaviour is an important aspect of marketing. Many factors influence the buying decisions of individuals and households. Demography and the class structure are relevant in that they can be both **behavioural determinants** and **inhibitors**.

(a)   **Behavioural determinants encourage** people to buy a product or service. They include the individual's personality, culture, social class, and the importance of the purchase decision (eg a necessity such as food or water, or a luxury).

(b)   **Inhibitors** are factors that make the person **less likely** to purchase something (eg low income).

Socio-economic status can be related to buying patterns in a number of ways, both in the amount people have to spend and what they spend it on. It affects both the quantity of goods and services supplied and the proportion of their income that households spend on goods and services.

8 Cultural trends

Organisations are part of the wider social environment.

Examples of how cultural trends can change organisations are given in this section.

8.1 Health and diet issues

There have been significant changes in some countries in attitudes to diet and health.

Some people are slowly moving to a healthier diet. In addition, there has been an increase in vegetarianism, and 'green consumerism'. This includes a concern with 'organic food' now found in many supermarkets.

8.2 Impact of health and diet on businesses

Growing market. There is a growing market for sports-related goods (even though, as is the case with running shoes, sporting goods might be purchased as fashion accessories).

Employee health. Employers are concerned with the effect of ill-health on productivity. Some employers provide gyms and physical recreation facilities. Others offer counselling programmes to employees who may be struggling with stress or health problems.

New foods. The health food and supplement market has grown significantly over the past decade. Some foods and supplements claim health benefits including improved mental focus and concentration.

Convenience food. There is a market for **new sorts of convenience food**.

Organic foods. Organic foods (grown without artificial pesticides, hormones etc) are more popular. This could lead to a healthier workforce, or on the other hand may increase days lost to issues of food health (eg food poisoning).

8.3 Women in work

Over the past few decades, in most countries the number of women in the workforce has increased significantly. A related trend is an increase in part-time working and and flexible working. In the UK, more than five times as many women as men are part-timers.

There was once widespread discrimination against women.

- Overt discrimination is where one group is treated less favourably than another.

- Indirect discrimination makes it harder for somebody of a particular group to fulfil requirements.

Furthermore, the principle of **equal pay for equal work** and for **equal value** is enshrined in legislation. This is covered in more detail in Chapter 13.

8.4 Environmentalism

Issues relating to the effect of an organisation's activities on the physical environment have come to the fore in recent years. This will be dealt with in detail later in this chapter.

8.5 The business response

(a) **'Green products'**. Companies like The Body Shop have cleverly exploited ecological friendliness as a marketing tool. Supermarkets now stock cleaning products which are supposed to be kind to nature.

(b) **Changed practices**. Bad publicity has led to improvements. A consumer campaign to boycott tuna from companies whose methods of fishing endangered the lives of dolphins has led to changed fishing techniques.

(c)   **Limits**. There may be a limit to how much consumers are prepared to alter their lifestyles, or pay, for the sake of ecological correctness.

(d)   **Education and confusion**. Consumers may be imperfectly educated about environmental issues. For example, much recycled paper has simply replaced paper produced from trees from properly managed (ie sustainably developed) forests. There is widespread confusion as to green labelling.

(e)   **Environmental impact assessments**. Companies review not just the finished product but their production processes too.

As far as **pollution** goes, it is likely that government will take an increased interest in this area. Companies might have to face a variety of measures designed to deal with pollution.

9   The impact of technology on organisations

9.1 Organisation structure

> Information systems and information technology have played a significant role in the development of the modern business environment, including encouraging the **flattening** of **organisation hierarchies** and widening **spans of control**.

Information systems and information technology have played a significant role in the development of the modern business environment. For example, modern communications technology makes decentralised organisations possible, allowing decision-making to be passed down to 'empowered' workers or outsourced to external companies.

There is a trend towards smaller, more **agile companies**. **Flexibility** and speed are increasingly seen as the key to competitive advantage. Advances in IT have allowed complex operating processes to be accelerated and made feedback information available almost immediately.

9.1.1 Span of control

Span of control, or 'span of management', refers to the number of subordinates responsible to a superior. If a manager has five subordinates, the span of control is five.

Business automation and rationalisation, and improved management information systems, have often resulted in reduced staffing levels. In particular, layers of middle management have been removed in many organisations. This has been termed **'delayering'**. Managers or staff 'lower down' the hierarchy have been empowered to make decisions previously made by middle managers. Information technology has therefore had the effect of flattening organisation hierarchies and **widening spans of control**.

There is no universally 'correct' size for the span of control. The appropriate span of control will depend on:

(a)   The **ability of the manager**. A good organiser and communicator will be able to control a larger number. The manager's workload is also relevant.

(b)   The **ability of subordinates**. The more experienced, able, trustworthy and well-trained subordinates are, the easier it is to control larger numbers.

(c)   The **nature of the task**. It is easier for a supervisor to control a large number of people if they are all doing routine, repetitive or similar tasks.

(d)   The **geographical dispersal of subordinates**. A manager may be able to manage a larger group (wider span of control) more easily if subordinates are located together, for example in the same building as the manager.

(e)   The availability of **good quality information**. Relevant, timely information reduces uncertainty and may enable a manager to manage a larger group.

9.1.2 Tall and flat organisations

An **information system**, such as an intranet, can help provide organisation unity and coherency in flat, decentralised organisations.

The trend towards flatter structures is evidenced by talk of an 'e-lance economy', characterised by shifting **coalitions** of small firms collaborating on particular **projects**.

9.1.3 Organisation structure and information systems

The structure of an organisation and the way in which the organisation's information system is arranged are **related** issues.

Centralised systems means holding and processing data in a central place, such as a computer centre at head office. Data will be collected at 'remote' (ie geographically separate) offices and other locations and sent in to the central location.

Decentralised systems have the data/information processing carried out at several different locations, away from the 'centre' or 'head office'.

9.2 Other effects of IT on organisations

Other **effects of IT on organisations** include:

- Routine processing (bigger volumes, greater speed, greater accuracy)
- Digital information and record keeping
- New skills required and new ways of working
- Reliance on IT
- New methods of communication and of providing customer service
- Interoperability (encourages collaboration across organisation boundaries) and open systems
- The view of information as a valuable resource
- The view of information as a commodity which can be bought, sold or exchanged ('information market')

9.2.1 Routine processing

Information technology enables the processing of data to be performed in bigger volumes, at greater speed and with greater accuracy.

9.2.2 Digital information and recordkeeping

Information storage and transmission is now largely digital rather than paper-based. However, many people like 'hard copies' and print out information as required. Far from reducing the use of paper, computer systems seem to have encouraged greater use of paper.

The nature and quality of management information has also changed.

(a) Managers have access to more information – for example from an ESS. Information is also likely to be more timely, accurate, reliable and up to date.

(b) More detailed planning is possible through the use of models (eg spreadsheets).

(c) Information for control should be more readily available.

(d) Decision-making should improve as a consequence of better quality information.

9.2.3 Employment issues

The infiltration of IT into almost every area of business means that the vast majority of employees are now expected to utilise information technology. IT skills are required and new ways of working have emerged.

9.2.4 Technological change

A reliance on information technology commits an organisation to **continual change**. Systems are likely to be superseded after a few years.

9.2.5 Customer service

Information technology has enabled organisations to provide better customer service. Customer databases, EDI, extranets, websites and data mining can all be applied to improving service levels.

9.2.6 Information markets

The term **'information market'** reflects the growing view that information is a **commodity** which can be bought, sold or exchanged.

There has been a growing realisation that information is a resource and that it has many of the characteristics of any other resource. A key theme of this syllabus is the benefits which information, properly managed and used, can bring to an organisation.

9.2.7 Developments in communications

Communications technology is probably having a greater impact on organisational life than computers are at present. **Email** provides a quick and **efficient** means of communicating worldwide.

Mobile and WiFi technology allow **flexibility** in communication. Short Message Service (SMS) messages, often referred to as 'text messages', provide another option for short, concise, instant communication. Computer Telephony Integration (CTI) systems can **route** incoming calls (they can be frustrating, particularly for callers with non-standard enquiries). CTI also enables information about callers to be gathered and stored, allowing **personalised** communication.

Computer conferencing systems and organisation-wide **intranets** and bulletin boards encourage **communication** – both formal and **informal**.

Video-calls (for example Skype) and videoconferencing facilitate virtual face-to-face contact between people who are spread widely across the world. If a video-conference is deemed sufficient, **travel costs** can be reduced.

9.3 IT and the employee/employer relationship

The widespread use of information technology in the workplace has affected the relationship between **employers and employees**.

- Reduced need to follow the chain-of-command
- Information overload
- Nature of work
- Close business relationships regardless of geographical location
- More flexible working arrangements
- Greater monitoring and control

Delayering has gone hand in hand with a trend towards **downsizing** whereby large numbers of managers and staff have been made redundant.

9.4 Homeworking and supervision

Advances in communications technology have, for some tasks, reduced the need for the **actual presence of an individual in the office**. This is particularly true of tasks involving computers.

(a) The employee can, for example, do tasks involving data entry at home.

(b) The keyed-in data can be sent over a telecommunications link to head office.

(c) Some firms see benefits in employing the services of a pool of freelance workers, when there is a demand. This approach is being adopted in publishing and journalism.

This is sometimes known as homeworking (or, occasionally, telecommuting if it involves IT). The practice is not new in itself, but it is relatively new to the management of the office.

9.5 Outsourcing

Outsourcing is the contracting out of specified operations or services to an external vendor. There are various outsourcing options available, with different levels of control maintained 'in-house'. Outsourcing has **advantages** (eg use of highly skilled people) and **disadvantages** (eg lack of control).

Outsourcing is the contracting out of specified operations or services to an external vendor.

9.5.1 Types of outsourcing

There are four **broad classifications** of outsourcing, as described in the following table.

Classification	Comment
Ad hoc	The organisation has a short-term requirement for increased IS/IT skills. An example would be employing programmers on a short-term contract to help with the programming of bespoke software.
Project management	The development and installation of a particular IS/IT project is outsourced; for example, a new accounting system.
Partial	Some IT/IS services are outsourced. Examples include hardware maintenance, network management or ongoing website management.
Total	An external supplier provides the vast majority of an organisation's IS/IT services, eg third party owns or is responsible for IT equipment, software and staff.

9.5.2 The advantages and disadvantages of outsourcing

Advantages of outsourcing

The **advantages** of outsourcing are as follows.

(a)   Outsourcing can remove uncertainty about **cost**, as there is often a long-term contract where services are specified in advance for a **fixed price**. If computing services are inefficient, the costs will be borne by the FM company. This is also an incentive to the third party to provide a high quality service.

(b)   Long-term contracts (maybe up to ten years) encourage **planning** for the future.

(c)   Outsourcing can bring the benefits of **economies of scale**. For example, a FM company may conduct research into new technologies that benefits a number of their clients.

(d)   A specialist organisation is able to retain **skills and knowledge**. Many organisations would not have a sufficiently well-developed IT department to offer IT staff opportunities for career development. Talented staff would leave to pursue their careers elsewhere.

(e)   New skills and knowledge become available. A specialist company can **share** staff with **specific expertise** between several clients. This allows the outsourcing company to take advantage of new developments without the need to recruit new people or retrain existing staff, and without the cost.

(f)   **Flexibility** (contract permitting). Resources may be able to be scaled up or down depending on demand. For instance, during a major changeover from one system to another the number of IT staff needed may be twice as large as it will be once the new system is working satisfactorily. An outsourcing organisation is more able to arrange its work on a **project** basis, whereby some staff will expect to be moved periodically from one project to the next.

Disadvantages of outsourcing

Some possible **drawbacks** are outlined below.

(a)   It is arguable that information and its provision is an **inherent part of the business** and of management. Unlike office cleaning, or catering, an organisation's IT services may be too important to be contracted out. Information is at the heart of management.

(b)   A company may have highly **confidential information** and to let outsiders handle it could be seen as **risky** in commercial and/or legal terms.

(c)   If a third party is handling IS/IT services there is no onus on internal management to keep up with new developments or to suggest new ideas. Consequently, opportunities to gain **competitive advantage** may be missed. Any new technology or application devised by the third party is likely to be available to competitors.

(d)   An organisation may find itself **locked in** to an unsatisfactory contract. The decision may be very difficult to reverse. If the service provider supplies unsatisfactory levels of service, the effort and expense the organisation would incur to rebuild its own computing function or to move to another provider could be substantial.

(e)   The use of an outside organisation does not encourage awareness of the potential **costs** and benefits of IS/IT within the organisation. If managers cannot manage in-house IS/IT resources effectively, then it could be argued that they will not be able to manage an arrangement to outsource effectively either.

10 Environmental factors

There is increasing concern about businesses' relationship with the natural environment. Businesses may suffer **significant costs** and a **loss of reputation** if problems arise.

10.1 Significance of environmental effects

There is a general issue for society of whether environmental problems, such as climate change, actually exist. There are some who believe that environmental changes are just natural events in the lifecycle of the planet. If environmental problems do exist, the issue is how serious are they? There is an additional issue of whether business activities have contributed to environmental change. Clearly there are concerns which need to be closely examined.

10.2 Impact on environment of economic activities

Environmental footprint is the impact that a business's activities have on the environment, including its resource environment and pollution emissions.

At an individual firm or business level, environmental impact can be measured in terms of environmental costs in various areas. Much business activity takes place at some cost to the environment. Examples of impacts on the environment include:

- Depletion of natural resources
- Noise and aesthetic impacts
- Residual air and water emissions
- Long-term waste disposal (exacerbated by excessive product packaging)
- Uncompensated health effects
- Change in the local quality of life (through for example the impact of tourism)

CASE STUDY

Plastic shopping bags are widely recognised as a blight on the environment. Most supermarkets now charge customers for plastic bags, in an attempt to:

- Encourage customers to reduce their bag usage by changing from single use carrier bags to reusable bags

- Raise monies for environmental projects to counterbalance the adverse impact of the bags and other aspects of supermarket operations

10.3 Impact on organisation of environmental costs

In addition, an IFAC report listed a large number of costs that a business might suffer internally.

Direct or indirect environmental costs

- Waste management
- Remediation costs or expenses
- Compliance costs
- Permit fees
- Environmental training
- Environmentally driven research and development
- Environmentally related maintenance
- Legal costs and fines
- Environmental assurance bonds
- Environmental certification and labelling
- Natural resource inputs
- Record keeping and reporting

Contingent or intangible environmental costs

- Uncertain future remediation or compensation costs
- Risk posed by future regulatory changes
- Product quality
- Employee health and safety
- Environmental knowledge assets
- Sustainability of raw material inputs
- Risk of impaired assets
- Public/customer perception

Clearly failing to take sufficient account of environmental impact can have a significant impact on the business's accounts as well as the outside world.

EXAM FOCUS POINT

You may be asked about the main impacts on the environment that a particular organisation's activities are likely to have. You will need to use a little imagination, but hopefully the ideas we suggest in this chapter will help you come up with suggestions.

10.4 Social impacts of activities

Partly because of the publicity generated by reports, there is now significant focus on the environmental impact of businesses' activities. However, corporate social responsibility does not start and end with the environment. Organisations need to consider other aspects of corporate social responsibilities such has how people in developing countries are treated.

10.4.1 Stakeholder expectations

Pressures on organisations to widen the scope of their corporate public accountability come from **increasing expectations of stakeholders** and knowledge about the **consequences of ignoring such pressures**.

Stakeholders in this respect include communities (particularly where operations are based), customers (product safety issues), suppliers and supply chain participants and competitors. Issues such as plant closures, pollution, job creation, sourcing, etc can have powerful **social effects** for good or ill on these stakeholders.

10.4.2 Reputation risk

Increasingly a business must have the reputation of being a **responsible business** that enhances long-term shareholder value by addressing the needs of its **stakeholders** – employees, customers, suppliers, the community and the environment.

> ### EXAM FOCUS POINT
>
> There was an article on *Communicating core values and mission* in the 29 March 2012 edition of *Student Accountant.* You are recommended to read this article and others mentioned later in this text.

10.5 Corporate social responsibility and risk management

Corporate social responsibility (CSR) can be described as an organisation monitoring its activities to ensure its active compliance with the spirit of the law, ethical standards and international norms. The goal of CSR is to get the organisation to take responsibility for its actions and to encourage a positive impact on the environment, consumers and stakeholders generally.

CSR can provide value to an organisation through risk management by encouraging the organisation to 'do the right thing'. CSR can also help a business to think about sustainability; for example in its use of resources. Raw materials may be purchased from renewable sources, or the business may decide to switch to 'green' energy, such as wind or solar power.

In order to publicise its CSR policies, the organisation may include a customised report on CSR with its financial statements eg as part of the directors' report or as a separate statement.

11 Competitive forces

11.1 SWOT analysis

A method of environmental analysis which looks at an organisation's internal strengths and weaknesses as well as external opportunities and threats is known as SWOT analysis.

11.1.1 Internal appraisal: strengths and weaknesses

An internal appraisal will identify:

(a)   The areas of the organisation that have **strengths** that should be exploited by suitable strategies
(b)   The areas of the organisation that have **weaknesses** which need strategies to improve them

The strengths and weaknesses analysis is intended to shape the organisation's approach to the external world. For instance, the identification of shortcomings in products could lead to a programme of product development.

11.1.2 External appraisal: opportunities and threats

The external appraisal identifies **opportunities** that can be exploited by the organisation's strengths and also to anticipate environmental **threats** against which the company must protect itself.

Opportunities

(a)   What opportunities exist in the business environment?
(b)   What is their inherent profit-making potential?
(c)   Can the organisation exploit the worthwhile opportunities?
(d)   What is the comparative capability profile of competitors?
(e)   What is the company's comparative performance potential in this field of opportunity?

Threats

(a)   What threats might arise to the company or its business environment?
(b)   How will competitors be affected?
(c)   How will the company be affected?

11.2 Using a SWOT analysis

The SWOT analysis can be used in one of two ways.

(a)   The organisation can develop **resource-based strategies** which enable the organisation to extend the use of its strengths. This is common in retailing, for example, as supermarket chains extend their own brands from food to other areas.

(b)   The business can develop **positioning-based strategies**. In other words, identifying what opportunities are available and what the firm has to do exploit them.

12 Converting resources: the value chain

The **value chain** describes those activities of the organisation that add value to purchased inputs. Primary activities are involved in the production of goods and services. Support activities provide necessary assistance. **Linkages** are the relationships between activities. Managing the value chain, which includes relationships with outside suppliers, can be a source of strategic advantage.

The **value chain** model of corporate activities offers a bird's eye view of the firm and what it does. Competitive advantage arises out of the way in which firms organise and perform **activities** to add value.

12.1 Value activities

Value activities are the means by which a firm creates value in its products.

Activities incur costs and, in combination with other activities, provide a product or service which earns revenue.

12.2 Example

Let us explain this point by using the example of a **restaurant**. A restaurant's activities can be divided into buying food, cooking it, and serving it (to customers). There is no reason, in theory, why the customers should not do all these things themselves, at home. The customer, however, is not only prepared to **pay for someone else** to do all this but also **pays more than the cost of** the resources (food, wages, and so on). The ultimate value a firm creates is measured by the amount customers are willing to pay for its products or services above the cost of carrying out value activities. A firm is profitable if the realised value to customers exceeds the collective cost of performing the activities.

(a)   Customers **purchase value**, which they measure by comparing a firm's products and services with similar offerings by competitors.

(b)   The business **creates value** by carrying out its activities either more efficiently than other businesses, or by combining them in such a way as to provide a unique product or service.

QUESTION

Value activities

Outline different ways in which the restaurant can create value.

ANSWER

Here are some ideas. Each of these options is a way of organising the activities of buying, cooking and serving food in a way that customers will value.

(a)   It can become more efficient, by automating the production of food, as in a fast food chain.

(b)   The chef can develop commercial relationships with growers, so he or she can obtain the best quality fresh produce.

(c)   The chef can specialise in a particular type of cuisine (eg Nepalese, Korean).

(d)   The restaurant can be sumptuously decorated for those customers who value atmosphere and a sense of occasion, in addition to a restaurant's purely gastronomic pleasures.

(e)   The restaurant can serve a particular type of customer (eg celebrities).

12.3 The value chain

Porter's Value Chain (Porter, 1985) groups the various activities of an organisation into a **value chain**. Here is a diagram.

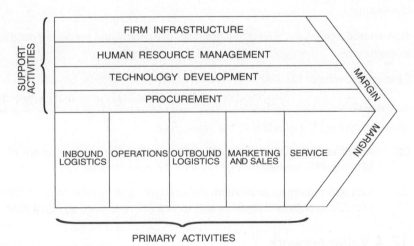

The **margin** is the excess the customer is prepared to **pay** over the **cost** to the firm of obtaining resource inputs and providing value activities. It represents the **value created** by the **value activities** themselves and by the **management of the linkages** between them.

EXAM FOCUS POINT

This diagram is worth committing to memory, as the terms may be referred to in an exam question.

Activity	Comment
Inbound logistics	Receiving, handling and storing inputs to the production system: warehousing, transport, inventory control, and so on
Operations (production)	Convert resource inputs into a final product. Resource inputs are not only materials. People are a resource, especially in service industries
Outbound logistics	Storing the product and its distribution to customers: packaging, testing, delivery, and so on
Marketing and sales	Informing customers about the product, persuading them to buy it, and enabling them to do so: advertising, promotion, and so on
Service	Installing products and \ or the act of performing the service for the client or customer. Includes all aspects of post-sales service delivery

Support activities provide purchased inputs, human resources, technology and infrastructural functions to support the primary activities.

Activity	Comment
Procurement (purchasing)	Acquire the resource inputs to the primary activities (eg purchase of materials, subcomponents equipment)
Technology development	Product design, improving processes and/or resource utilisation
Human resource management	Recruiting, training, developing and rewarding people
Firm infrastructure	Planning, finance, quality control: Porter believes they are crucially important to an organisation's strategic capability in all primary activities

Linkages connect the activities of the value chain.

(a) **Activities in the value chain affect one another**. For example, more costly product design or better quality production might reduce the need for after-sales service.

(b) **Linkages require co-ordination**. For example, Just In Time requires smooth functioning of operations, outbound logistics and service activities such as installation.

12.4 Value network

Activities and linkages that add value do not stop at the organisation's **boundaries**. For example, when a restaurant serves a meal, the quality of the ingredients – although they are chosen by the cook – is determined by the grower. The grower has added value, and the grower's success in growing produce of good quality is as important to the customer's ultimate satisfaction as the skills of the chef.

According to Johnson et al, (2005), an organisation's value chain is connected to the value chains of suppliers, distributors and customers in what may be referred to as a **value network**.

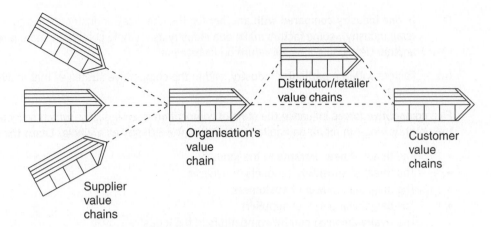

Organisation's value chain

Supplier value chains

Distributor/retailer value chains

Customer value chains

A value network generates value through exchanges between two or more organisations. Exchanges may include both tangible (for example goods) and intangible (for example knowledge such as collaborative design).

EXAM FOCUS POINT

Attempt the following question from a past exam. In the exam report it was mentioned that only 31% of students chose the correct answer.

QUESTION

Primary activity

BCD Co is a large trading company. Steve is the administration manager and is also responsible for legal and compliance functions. Sheila is responsible for after-sales service and has responsibility for ensuring that customers who have purchased goods from BCD Co are fully satisfied. Sunny deals with suppliers and negotiates on the price and quality of inventory. He is also responsible for identifying the most appropriate suppliers of plant and machinery for the factory. Sam is the information technology manager and is responsible for all information systems within the company.

According to Porter's value chain, which of the managers is involved in a primary activity as opposed to a support activity?

A   Steve   C   Sunny
B   Sheila   D   Sam

ANSWER

B   The exam report highlighted that the word 'administration' indicates that Steve is in a support role and that 'information technology' indicates that Sam is in a support role. Sunny's responsibilities describe procurement which is also a support role.

13   Competitive advantage – Porter's five forces model

The **competitive environment** is structured by five forces: **barriers to entry**; **substitute products**; the bargaining power of **customers**; the bargaining power of **suppliers**; **competitive rivalry**.

In discussing competition, Porter (Porter, 1980) distinguishes between factors which characterise the nature of competition.

(a) **In one industry compared with another** (eg the chemicals industry compared with the clothing retail industry), some factors make one industry as a whole potentially more profitable than another (ie yielding a bigger return on investment).

(b) Factors **within a particular industry** lead to the competitive strategies that individual firms might select.

Five **competitive forces** influence the state of competition in an industry, which collectively determine the profit (ie long-run return on capital) potential of the industry as a whole. **Learn them.**

- The threat of **new entrants** to the industry
- The threat of **substitute** products or services
- The bargaining power of **customers**
- The bargaining power of **suppliers**
- The **rivalry** amongst current competitors in the industry

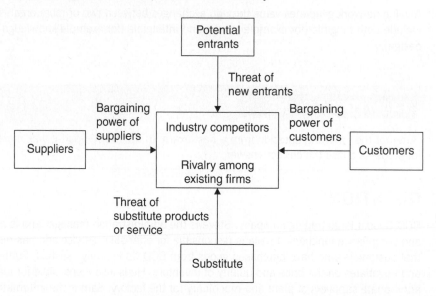

13.1 The threat of new entrants (and barriers to entry to keep them out)

A new entrant into an industry will bring extra capacity and more competition. The strength of this threat is likely to vary from industry to industry and depends on two things.

- The strength of the **barriers to entry**. Barriers to entry discourage new entrants.
- The likely **response of existing competitors** to the new entrant.

13.2 The threat from substitute products

A **substitute product** is a good or service produced by **another industry** which satisfies the same customer needs.

CASE STUDY

The Channel Tunnel

Passengers have several ways of getting from London to Paris, and the pricing policies of the various industries transporting them there reflects this.

(a) 'Le Shuttle' carries cars in the Channel Tunnel. Its main competitors come from the **ferry** companies, offering a substitute service. Therefore, you will find that Le Shuttle sets its prices with reference to ferry company prices, and vice versa.

(b) Eurostar is the rail service from London to Paris/Brussels. Its main competitors are not the ferry companies but the **airlines**.

13.3 The bargaining power of customers

Customers want better quality products and services at a lower price. Satisfying this want might force down the profitability of suppliers in the industry. Just how strong the position of customers will be depends on a number of factors including:

- How much the customer buys

- How critical the product is to the customer's own business

- Switching costs (ie the cost of switching supplier)

- Whether the products are standard items (hence easily copied) or specialised

- The customer's own profitability: a customer who makes low profits will be forced to insist on low prices from suppliers

- Customer's ability to bypass the supplier (or take over the supplier)

- The skills of the customer purchasing staff, or the price awareness of consumers

When product quality is important to the customer, the customer is less likely to be price-sensitive, and so the industry might be more profitable as a consequence.

13.4 The bargaining power of suppliers

Suppliers can exert pressure for higher prices. The ability of suppliers to get higher prices depends on several factors.

- Whether there are just **one or two dominant suppliers** to the industry, able to charge monopoly or oligopoly prices

- The threat of **new entrants** or substitute products to the **supplier's industry**

- Whether the suppliers have **other customers** outside the industry, and do not rely on the industry for the majority of their sales

- The **importance of the supplier's product** to the customer's business

- Whether the supplier has a **differentiated product** which buyers need to obtain

- Whether **switching costs** for customers would be high

13.5 The rivalry amongst current competitors in the industry

The **intensity of competitive rivalry** within an industry will affect the profitability of the industry as a whole. Competitive actions might take the form of price competition, advertising battles, sales promotion campaigns, introducing new products for the market, improving after-sales service or providing guarantees or warranties. Competition can stimulate demand, expanding the market, or it can leave demand unchanged, in which case individual competitors will make less money, unless they are able to cut costs.

PER performance objective PO3 requires you to demonstrate practical experience of strategy and innovation. This would mean that you need to be familiar with your employer's business, the sector in which it operates and the wider business environment, as covered in this chapter.

CHAPTER ROUNDUP

- Whatever the overall strategic management method used, no organisation is likely to achieve its aims if it fails to take into account the **characteristics of the environment** in which it operates.

- **Government policy** influences the economic environment, the framework of laws, industry structure and certain operational issues. Political instability is a cause of risk. Different approaches to the **political environment** apply in different countries. **International trade** is subject to a further layer of international law and regulation.

- Much legislation (and not enough economic knowledge) has been aimed at the idea of 'employment protection'. As a result, all forms of **termination of employment** must be treated with great care.

- **Privacy** is the right of the individual not to suffer unauthorised disclosure of information.

- The (UK) **Data Protection Act 1998** protects individuals about whom data is held. Both manual and computerised information must comply with the Act.

- The **UK Data Protection Act** includes eight **Data Protection Principles** with which data users must comply.

- People should be able to be confident that they will not be exposed to excessive risk when they are at work. This means that risk and danger must be actively managed.

- A contract is a legally binding agreement.

- Population affects an organisation's supply of labour and hence its policies towards recruiting and managing human resources.

- Organisations are part of the wider social environment

- Information systems and information technology have played a significant role in the development of the modern business environment, including encouraging the **flattening** of **organisation hierarchies** and widening **spans of control**.

- Other **effects of IT on organisations** include:

  - Routine processing (bigger volumes, greater speed, greater accuracy)

  - Digital information and record keeping

  - New skills required and new ways of working

  - Reliance on IT

  - New methods of communication and of providing customer service

  - Interoperability (encourages collaboration across organisation boundaries) and open systems

  - The view of information as a valuable resource

  - The view of information as a commodity which can be bought, sold or exchanged ('information market')

- There is increasing concern about businesses' relationship with the natural environment. Businesses may suffer **significant costs** and a **loss of reputation** if problems arise.

- A method of environmental analysis which looks at an organisation's internal **strengths** and **weaknesses** as well as external **opportunities** and **threats** is known as **SWOT** analysis

- The **value chain** describes those activities of the organisation that add value to purchased inputs. Primary activities are involved in the production of goods and services. Support activities provide necessary assistance. **Linkages** are the relationships between activities. Managing the value chain, which includes relationships with outside suppliers, can be a source of strategic advantage.

- The **competitive environment** is structured by five forces: **barriers to entry; substitute products**; the bargaining power of **customers**; the bargaining power of **suppliers; competitive rivalry**.

QUICK QUIZ

1   Environmental analysis is relevant when undertaking the strategy-making process. Is this true or false?

2   Give four types of legal factor affecting a company.

3   How can businesses influence government policy?

4   Which of the following types of dismissal relates to the method of dismissal?

    A   Unfair dismissal
    B   Wrongful dismissal
    C   Forced dismissal

5   An individual who is the subject of personal data is a data ....

6   How can senior managers promote health and safety awareness?

7   Information technology has encouraged which three of the following?

    A   Flattening of organisation hierarchies
    B   Widening spans of control
    C   Smaller volumes of routine processing
    D   More flexible working arrangements

8   Downsizing can reduce capacity. Is this true or false?

9   What are the five competitive forces?

10 Which one of the following is a primary activity in the value chain?

    A   Technology department
    B   Procurement
    C   Human resources management
    D   Marketing and sales

11 The purpose of value chain analysis is to understand customer price and quality preferences. True or false?

ANSWERS TO QUICK QUIZ

1   True.   The environment is everything that surrounds an organisation and so understanding it is one of the key inputs to the strategy-making process.

2   **Four from:**

General legal framework (eg contract)	Data protection
Criminal	Marketing and sales
Company	Environment
Employment	Taxation
Health and safety	

3   Employ lobbyists; hand out non-executive directorships; try to influence public opinion.

4   B   Wrongful dismissal relates to the method of dismissal. Unfair dismissal is dismissal without good reason.

5   An individual who is the subject of personal data is a data subject.

6
- Visibly reacting to policy breaches
- Ensuring that the policy is communicated
- Setting priorities
- Involving staff in the health and safety process

7   A, B, D. Information technology means that greater volumes of data can be processed more quickly and with greater accuracy.

8   True. It can make organisations leaner and more flexible, but also can reduce capacity.

9
- Threat of new entrants
- Threat of substitute products
- Bargaining power of customers
- Bargaining power of suppliers
- Rivalry amongst current competition

10   D   Marketing and sales

11   False. The main purpose is to understand how the company creates value from its various activities.

Now try ...

Attempt the questions below from the **Practice Question Bank**

Q5

Q6

Q7

Q8

Q9

Q10

Q11

Q12

The macroeconomic environment

In this chapter we present an overview of the goals of macroeconomic policy concentrating on fiscal policy and monetary policy.

Section 1 considers the circular flow of income in the economy and this leads us on to the explanation of supply and demand in **Section 2.**

In macroeconomics we are concerned with spending, investment, price levels, employment and output in the economy as a whole (**Section 3**).

Broadly speaking, macroeconomists divide into the two camps of the Keynesians and the monetarists. These two camps have had differing ideas about how national income can be made to grow, how full employment can be achieved and how booms and slumps of trade cycles can be smoothed out (**Section 4**).

There are also different views about the causes of inflation and the effectiveness of government measures to stimulate the economy (**Sections 5-7**).

We consider the Government's policies (**Section 8**) for managing the economy and the role of fiscal policy (**Section 9**) in affecting demand and examine the types of taxation and the role of taxation in creating incentives. This is followed by a discussion of the conduct of monetary policy (**Section 10**).

The balance of payments (**Section 11**) is a statistical 'accounting' record of a country's international trade transactions (the purchase and sale of goods and services) and capital transactions (the acquisition and disposal of assets and liabilities) with other countries during a period of time.

TOPIC LIST	SYLLABUS REFERENCE
1 The structure and objectives of the economy	A4 (a),(d)
2 Factors which affect the economy	A4 (e)
3 The determination of national income	A4 (b)
4 The business cycle	A4 (b)
5 Inflation and its consequences	A4 (c)(i)
6 Unemployment	A4 (c)(ii)
7 The objective of economic growth	A4 (c)(iii)
8 Government policies for managing the economy	A4 (a),(c)
9 Fiscal policy	A4 (e)
10 Monetary policy	A4 (e)
11 The balance of payments	A4 (c)(iv)

Study Guide	Intellectual level
A4 Macro-economic factors	
(a) Define macroeconomic policy and explain its objectives.	K
(b) Explain the main determinants of the level of business activity in the economy and how variations in the level of business activity affect individuals, households and businesses.	K
(c) Explain the impact of economic issues on the individual, the household and the business: (i) Inflation (ii) Unemployment (iii) Stagnation (iv) International payments disequilibrium	K
(d) Describe the main types of economic policy that may be implemented by government and supra-national bodies to maximise economic welfare.	K
(e) Recognise the impact of fiscal and monetary policy measures on the individual, the household and businesses.	K

EXAM FOCUS POINT

You might consider macroeconomic factors to be a peripheral area of this syllabus, but the detail in this chapter does lend itself to the type of questions which are set under this examination.

1 The structure and objectives of the economy

Macroeconomics is the study of the aggregated effects of the decisions of individual economic units (such as households or businesses). It looks at a complete national economy, or the international economic system as a whole.

Macroeconomic policy describes the policies and actions a government takes to control economic issues, including economic growth, inflation, employment and trade performance.

We look in detail at macroeconomic policy and objectives later in this chapter (in Section 8). We now turn our attention to the flow of income and expenditure in an economy.

1.1 Income and expenditure flows

There is a circular flow of income in an economy, which means that expenditure, output and income will all have the same total value.

Firms must pay households for the factors of production (this generally means that firms pay wages to members of households) and households must pay firms for goods and services. The income of firms is the sales revenue from the sales of goods and services.

This creates a circular flow of income and expenditure, as illustrated in Figure 1. This is a basic **closed economy**, without foreign trade. It assumes the economy has only two sectors (firms and households), with no government intervention and no imports or exports. In this model, we assume that households spend all that they earn (in economics this spending is known as consumption), and all the firms' goods and services are sold to the households.

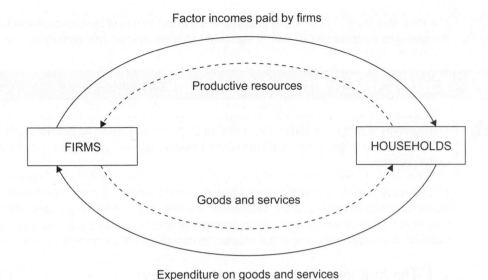

Figure 1 Circular flow of income

Households earn **income** because they have provided labour which enables firms to provide goods and services. The income earned is used as **expenditure** on these goods and services that are made.

(a)   The **total sales value** of goods produced should equal the **total expenditure** on goods, assuming that all goods that are produced are also sold.

(b)   The amount of **expenditure** should also equal the **total income** of households, because it is households that consume the goods and they must have income to afford to pay for them.

At this stage we are assuming there are no withdrawals from, or injections into, the circular flow of income.

1.2 Withdrawals and injections into the circular flow of income

Now we assume that there are withdrawals from the circular flow of income (savings, taxation, import expenditure) and injections into the circular flow (investment, government spending, export income).

Our simplified diagram of the circular flow of income in Figure 1 needs to be amended to allow for these two things.

Be aware that saving is different from investment. Saving simply means withdrawing money from circulation. Think of it as cash kept in a money box rather than being put into a bank to earn interest. Whereas investment covers expenditure on capital items, such as plant, machinery, roads and houses.

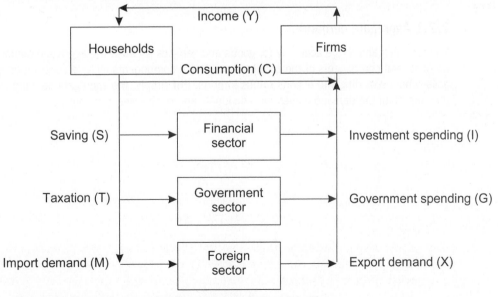

Figure 2 Circular flow of income showing withdrawals and injections

The important point to note is that changes in behaviour of one of the components of the circular flow (for example, investment) can lead to significant changes in economic performance as a whole.

2 Factors which affect the economy

The economy is rarely in a stable state because of the various changing factors which influence it. These include investment levels, the multiplier effect, inflation, savings, confidence, interest rates and exchange rates.

The economy is explained by the various factors that influence it, such as investment levels, the multiplier effect, inflation, savings, confidence, interest rates and exchange rates. These factors are subject to change which means that the economy is rarely in a stable state. Economists use the business cycle (explained later in the chapter) to describe the fluctuating level of activity in the economy.

2.1 The multiplier in the national economy

The **multiplier** involves the **process of circulation of income** in the national economy, whereby an injection of a certain size leads to a much larger increase in national income. **An initial increase in expenditure will have a snowball effect**, leading to further and further expenditures in the economy. Since total expenditure in the economy is one way of measuring national income, it follows that an initial increase in expenditure will cause an even larger increase in national income. The increase in national income will be a multiple of the initial increase in spending, with the size of the multiple depending on such factors as what proportion of any new investment is spent or what proportion is saved.

If you find this hard to visualise, think of an increase in government spending on the construction of roads. The government would spend money paying firms of road contractors, who in turn will purchase raw materials from suppliers, and subcontract other work. All these firms employ workers who will receive wages that they can spend on goods and services of other firms. The new roads in turn might stimulate new economic activity, for example amongst road hauliers, house builders and estate agents.

Depending on the size of the multiplier, an increase in investment would therefore have repercussions throughout the economy, increasing the size of the national income by a multiple of the size of the original increase in investment.

2.2 Aggregate supply and demand

Two of the main problems in the economy are inflation and unemployment. In order to understand how these problems arise, it is first necessary to understand aggregate demand, aggregate supply and how these combine to determine the level of national income and prices in the economy.

2.2.1 Aggregate demand

The total demand in the economy for goods and services is called the aggregate demand and it is made up of several components of the circular flow. These components include consumption, investment, government spending and exports minus imports. Put simply, the aggregate demand curve represents the sum of all the demand curves for individuals and businesses in a country.

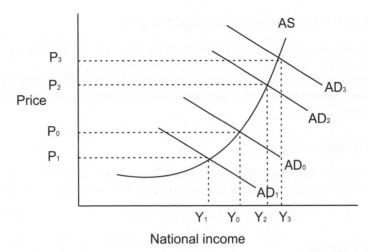

Figure 3 The aggregate supply and demand model

Figure 3 shows that the aggregate demand curve slopes from left to right (ie demand will rise as prices fall because people can afford more) but may shift as shown. A shift may be due to a factor such as an increase or decrease in consumer confidence. This is explained below.

2.2.2 Aggregate supply

The aggregate supply refers to the ability of the economy to produce goods and services. Aggregate supply is positively related to the price level. This is because a price rise will make more profitable sales and encourage organisations to increase their output. The aggregate supply curve slopes upwards from left to right and does not shift in the short term, as shown in Figure 3.

Where the aggregate demand curve intersects with the aggregate supply curve, the total demand for goods and services in the economy is equal to the total supply of goods and services in the economy. (This is known as the equilibrium level of national income.)

Note that the graph highlights the fact that a change in either the aggregate supply or demand will have an effect on the price level and the national income. Assuming that employment levels are related to national income levels, the model shows how unemployment and inflation (a change in price level) could arise.

2.2.3 A shift in aggregate demand

Say, for example, that the equilibrium level is currently where national income = Y_0 and price = P_0. Then suppose there is a drop in consumer confidence so consumers stop spending (ie demand falls). The new equilibrium would be where national income = Y_1 and where price = P_1. If, on the other hand, consumer confidence increased (for example due to more access to affordable credit), consumers would buy more (an increase in demand) and so the new equilibrium would be where national income = Y_2 and price = P_2.

3   The determination of national income

Equilibrium national income is determined using aggregate supply and aggregate demand analysis.

3.1 Aggregate demand and supply equilibrium

Aggregate demand (AD) is total planned or desired consumption demand in the economy for consumer goods and services and also for capital goods, no matter whether the buyers are households, firms or government.

3.2 Full-employment national income

If one aim of a country's economic policy is full employment, then the ideal equilibrium level of national income will be where AD and AS are in balance at the full employment level of national income, without any inflationary gap – in other words, where aggregate demand at current price levels is exactly sufficient to encourage firms to produce at an output capacity where the country's resources are fully employed.

3.3 Inflationary gaps

In a situation where resources are already fully employed, there may be an **inflationary gap** since increases in demand will cause price changes, but no variations in real output.

A shift in demand or supply will not only change the national income, it will also change price levels.

3.4 Example

If you are not sure about this point, a simple numerical example might help to explain it better. Suppose that in Ruritania there is full employment and all other economic resources are fully employed. The country produces 1,000 units of output with these resources. Total expenditure (that is, aggregate demand) in the economy is 100,000 Ruritanian dollars, or 100 dollars per unit. The country does not have any external trade, and so it cannot obtain extra goods by importing them. Because of pay rises and easier credit terms for consumers, total expenditure now rises to 120,000 Ruritanian dollars. The economy is fully employed, and cannot produce more than 1,000 units. If expenditure rises by 20%, to buy the same number of units, it follows that prices must rise by 20% too. In other words, when an economy is at full employment, any increase in aggregate demand will result in price inflation.

3.5 Deflationary gap

In a situation **where there is unemployment of resources** there is said to be a **deflationary gap**. Prices are fairly constant and real output changes as aggregate demand varies. A deflationary gap can be described as the extent to which the aggregate demand function will have to shift upward to produce the full employment level of national income.

3.6 Stagflation

In the 1970s there was a problem with **stagflation**: a combination of unacceptably high unemployment, unacceptably high inflation and low/negative economic growth. One of the causes was diagnosed as the major rises in the price of crude oil that took place. The cost of energy rose and this had the effect of rendering some production unprofitable.

National income fell, and both prices and unemployment rose. Any long-term major increase in costs (a **price shock**) is likely to have this effect.

3.7 Summary

An equilibrium national income will be reached where aggregate demand equals aggregate supply. There are two possible equilibria.

(a)   One is at a level of demand which exceeds the productive capabilities of the economy at full employment, and there is insufficient output capacity in the economy to meet demand at current prices. There is then an **inflationary gap**.

(b)   The other is at a level of employment which is below the full employment level of national income. The difference between actual national income and full employment national income is called a **deflationary gap**. To create full employment, the total national income (expenditure) must be increased by the amount of the deflationary gap.

4 The business cycle

> **Business cycles** or **trade cycles** are the continual sequence of rapid growth in national income, followed by a slowdown in growth and then a fall in national income (recession). After this recession comes growth again, and when this has reached a peak, the cycle turns into recession once more.

4.1 Phases in the business cycle

Four main phases of the business cycle can be distinguished.

- Recession
- Depression
- Recovery
- Boom

Recession tends to occur quickly, while recovery is typically a slower process.

4.2 Diagrammatic explanation

At point A in the diagram below, the economy is entering a recession. In the recession phase, consumer demand falls and many investment projects already undertaken begin to look unprofitable. Orders will be cut, inventory levels will be reduced and business failures will occur as firms find themselves unable to sell their goods. Production and employment will fall. The general price level will begin to fall. Business and consumer confidence are diminished and investment remains low, while the economic outlook appears to be poor. Eventually, in the absence of any stimulus to aggregate demand, a period of full **depression** sets in and the economy will reach point B.

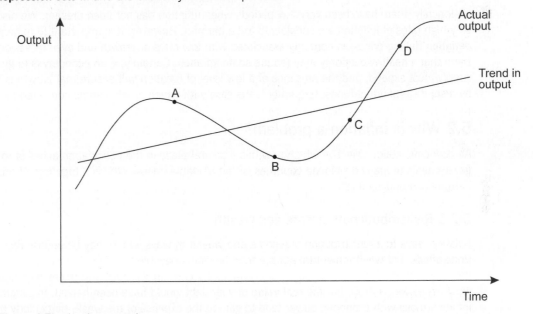

Figure 4 The business cycle

At point C the economy has reached the **recovery** phase of the cycle. Once begun, the phase of recovery is likely to quicken as confidence returns. Output, employment and income will all begin to rise. Rising production, sales and profit levels will lead to optimistic business expectations, and new investment will be more readily undertaken. The rising level of demand can be met through increased production by bringing existing capacity into use and by hiring unemployed labour. The average price level will remain constant or begin to rise slowly.

In the recovery phase, decisions to purchase new materials and machinery may lead to benefits in efficiency from new technology. This can enhance the relative rate of economic growth in the recovery phase once it is underway.

As recovery proceeds, the output level climbs above its trend path, reaching point D, in the **boom** phase of the cycle. During the boom, capacity and labour will become fully utilised. This may cause bottlenecks in some industries which are unable to meet increases in demand, for example because they have no spare capacity or they lack certain categories of skilled labour, or they face shortages of key material inputs. Further rises in demand will, therefore, tend to be met by increases in prices rather than by increases in production. In general, business will be profitable, with few firms facing losses. Expectations of the future may be very optimistic and the level of investment expenditure high.

It can be argued that wide fluctuations in levels of economic activity are damaging to the overall economic well-being of society. The inflation and speculation which accompanies boom periods may be inequitable in their impact on different sections of the population, while the bottom of the trade cycle may bring high unemployment. Governments generally seek to stabilise the economic system, trying to avoid the distortions of a widely fluctuating trade cycle.

5 Inflation and its consequences

High rates of **inflation** are harmful to an economy. Inflation redistributes income and wealth. Uncertainty about the value of money makes business planning more difficult. Constantly changing prices impose extra costs.

5.1 Inflation

Inflation is the name given to an increase in price levels generally. It is also manifest in the decline in the purchasing power of money.

Historically, there have been very few periods when inflation has not been present. We discuss below why high rates of inflation are considered to be harmful. However, it is important to remember that **deflation** (falling prices) is normally associated with low rates of growth and even recession. It would seem that a healthy economy may require some inflation. Certainly, if an economy is to grow, the money supply must expand, and the presence of a low level of inflation will ensure that growth is not hampered by a shortage of liquid funds. (Liquidity is the ease with which assets can be converted into cash.)

5.2 Why is inflation a problem?

An economic policy objective which now has a central place in the policy approaches of the governments of many developed countries is that of stable prices. Why is a **high** rate of price inflation harmful and undesirable?

5.2.1 Redistribution of income and wealth

Inflation leads to a redistribution of income and wealth in ways which may be undesirable. Redistribution of wealth might take place from accounts payable to accounts receivable. This is because debts lose 'real' value with inflation. For example, if you owed $1,000, and prices then doubled, you would still owe $1,000, but the **real value** of your debt would have been halved. In general, in times of inflation those with economic power tend to gain at the expense of the weak, particularly those on fixed incomes.

5.2.2 Balance of payments effects

If a country has a higher rate of inflation than its major trading partners, its exports will become relatively expensive and imports relatively cheap. As a result, the balance of trade will suffer, affecting employment in exporting industries and in industries producing import-substitutes. Eventually, the exchange rate will be affected.

5.2.3 Uncertainty of the value of money and prices

If the rate of inflation is imperfectly anticipated, no one has certain knowledge of the true rate of inflation. As a result, no one has certain knowledge of the value of money or of the real meaning of prices. If the rate of inflation becomes excessive, and there is 'hyperinflation', this problem becomes so exaggerated that money becomes worthless, so that people are unwilling to use it and are forced to resort to barter. In less extreme circumstances, the results are less dramatic, but the same problem exists. As prices convey less information, the process of resource allocation is less efficient and rational decision-making is almost impossible.

5.2.4 Resource costs of changing prices

A fourth reason to aim for stable prices is the resource cost of frequently changing prices. In times of high inflation, substantial labour time is spent on planning and implementing price changes. Customers may also have to spend more time making price comparisons if they seek to buy from the lowest cost source.

5.2.5 Economic growth and investment

It is sometimes claimed that inflation is harmful to a country's economic growth and level of investment.. Although some studies have indicated that the adverse influence of inflation on economic growth and investment appears to be small in the short term, it could affect a country's standard of living fairly significantly over the long term.

5.3 Consumer price indices

We have already referred to the way in which inflation erodes the real value of money. In order to measure changes in the real value of money as a single figure, we need to group all goods and services into a single price index.

A consumer price index is based on a chosen 'basket' of items which consumers purchase. A weighting is decided for each item according to the average spending on the item by consumers.

Consumer price indices may be used for several purposes, for example as an indicator of inflationary pressures in the economy, as a benchmark for wage negotiations and to determine annual increases in government benefits payments. Countries commonly have more than one consumer price index because one composite index may be considered too wide a grouping for different purposes.

5.3.1 The RPI and the CPI

One important measure of the general rate of inflation in the UK used over many years has been the **Retail Prices Index (RPI)**. The RPI measures the percentage changes month by month in the average level of prices of the commodities and services, including housing costs, purchased by the great majority of households in the UK. The items of expenditure within the RPI are intended to be a representative list of items, current prices for which are collected at regular intervals.

Since 2003, the Harmonised Index of Consumer Prices (HICP) has been used as the basis for the UK's inflation target. The UK HICP is called the **Consumer Prices Index (CPI)**. The CPI excludes most housing costs.

5.3.2 The underlying rate of inflation

The term **underlying rate of inflation** is usually used to refer to the RPI adjusted to exclude mortgage costs and sometimes other elements as well (such as the local council tax). The effects of interest rate changes on mortgage costs help to make the RPI fluctuate more widely than the underlying rate of inflation.

RPIX is the underlying rate of inflation measured as the increase in the RPI excluding mortgage interest payments. Another measure, called **RPIY**, goes further and excludes the effects of sales tax (VAT) changes as well.

5.4 Causes of inflation

The following can cause inflation:

- Demand pull factors
- Cost push factors
- Import cost factors
- Expectations
- Excessive growth in the money supply

5.4.1 Demand pull inflation

Demand pull inflation arises from an excess of aggregate demand over the productive capacity of the economy.

Demand pull inflation occurs when the economy is buoyant and there is a high aggregate demand, in excess of the economy's ability to supply.

(a)   Because aggregate demand exceeds supply, prices rise.

(b)   Since supply needs to be raised to meet the higher demand, there will be an increase in demand for factors of production, and so factor rewards (wages, interest rates, and so on) will also rise.

(c)   Since aggregate demand exceeds the output capability of the economy, it should follow that demand pull inflation can only exist when unemployment is low. A feature of inflation in the UK in the 1970s and early 1980s, however, was high inflation coupled with high unemployment.

Demand pull inflation: inflation resulting from a persistent excess of aggregate demand over aggregate supply. Supply reaches a limit on capacity at the full employment level.

5.4.2 Cost push inflation

Cost push inflation arises from increases in the costs of production.

Cost push inflation occurs where the costs of factors of production rise regardless of whether or not they are in short supply. This appears to be particularly the case with wages.

Cost push inflation: inflation resulting from an increase in the costs of production of goods and services, eg through escalating prices of imported raw materials or from wage increases.

5.4.3 Import cost factors

Import cost push inflation occurs when the cost of essential imports rise regardless of whether or not they are in short supply. This has occurred in the past with the oil price rises of the 1970s. Additionally, a fall in the value of a country's currency will have import cost push effects since a weakening currency increases the price of imports.

5.4.4 Expectations and inflation

A further problem is that once the rate of inflation has begun to increase, a serious danger of **expectational inflation** will occur. This means, regardless of whether the factors that have caused inflation are still persistent or not, there will arise a generally held view of what inflation is likely to be, and so to protect future income, wages and prices will be raised now by the expected amount of future inflation. This can lead to the vicious circle known as the **wage-price spiral**, in which inflation becomes a relatively permanent feature because of people's expectations that it will occur.

5.4.5 Money supply growth

Monetarists have argued that inflation is caused by **increases in the supply of money**. There is a considerable debate as to whether increases in the money supply are a **cause** of inflation or whether increases in the money supply are a **symptom** of inflation. Monetarists have argued that since inflation is caused by an increase in the money supply, inflation can be brought under control by reducing the rate of growth of the money supply.

6 Unemployment

6.1 The rate of unemployment

The **rate of unemployment** in an economy can be calculated as:

$$\frac{\text{Number of unemployed}}{\text{Total workforce}} \times 100\%$$

The number of unemployed at any time is measured by government statistics.

If the flow of workers through unemployment is constant then the size of the unemployed labour force will also be constant.

Flows into unemployment are:

(a)   Members of the working labour force **becoming** unemployed

- Redundancies
- Lay-offs
- Voluntarily quitting a job

(b)   People **out** of the labour force **joining** the unemployed

- School leavers without a job
- Others (for example, carers) rejoining the workforce but having no job yet

Flows out of unemployment are:

- Unemployed people finding jobs
- Laid-off workers being re-employed
- Unemployed people stopping the search for work

In the UK, the monthly unemployment statistics published by the Office for National Statistics (ONS) count only the jobless who receive benefits.

The ONS also produce figures based on a quarterly survey of the labour force known as the International Labour organisation measure (ILO measure) that provides seasonally adjusted monthly data. This figure is considered to be more useful because it is also an internationally comparable measure.

6.2 Consequences of unemployment

Unemployment results in the following problems.

(a)   **Loss of output**. If labour is unemployed, the economy is not producing as much output as it could. Thus, total national income is less than it could be.

(b)   **Loss of human capital.** If there is unemployment, the unemployed labour will gradually lose its skills, because skills can only be maintained by working.

(c)   **Increasing inequalities in the distribution of income**. Unemployed people earn less than employed people, and so when unemployment is increasing, the poor get poorer.

(d)   **Social costs**. Unemployment brings social problems of personal suffering and distress, and possibly also increases in crime, such as theft and vandalism.

(e)   **Increased burden of welfare payments**. This can have a major impact on government fiscal policy.

6.3 Causes of unemployment

Unemployment may be classified into several categories depending on the underlying causes.

Category	Comments
Real wage unemployment	This type of unemployment is caused when the supply of labour exceeds the demand for labour, but real wages do not fall for the labour market to clear. This type of unemployment is normally caused by strong trade unions which resist a fall in their wages. Another cause of this type of unemployment is the minimum wage rate, when it is set above the market clearing level.
Frictional	It is inevitable that some unemployment is caused not so much because there are not enough jobs to go round, but because of the **friction** in the labour market (difficulty in matching quickly workers with jobs), caused perhaps by a lack of knowledge about job opportunities. In general, it takes time to match prospective employees with employers, and individuals will be unemployed during the search period for a new job. Frictional unemployment is temporary, lasting for the period of transition from one job to the next.
Seasonal	This occurs in certain industries, for example building, tourism and farming, where the demand for labour fluctuates in seasonal patterns throughout the year.
Structural	This occurs where long-term changes occur in the conditions of an industry. A feature of structural unemployment is high regional unemployment in the location of the industry affected. The primary cause is a significant reduction in the level of demand.
Technological	This is a form of structural unemployment, which occurs when new technologies are introduced. (a) Old skills are no longer required. (b) There is likely to be a labour saving aspect, with machines doing the job that people used to do. With automation, employment levels in an industry can fall sharply, even when the industry's total output is increasing.
Cyclical or demand-deficient	It has been the experience of the past that domestic and foreign trade go through cycles of boom, decline, recession, recovery, then boom again, and so on. (a) During recovery and boom years, the demand for output and jobs is high, and unemployment is low. (b) During decline and recession years, the demand for output and jobs falls, and unemployment rises to a high level. Cyclical unemployment can be long term, and a government might try to reduce it by doing what it can to minimise a recession or to encourage faster economic growth.

Seasonal employment and frictional unemployment will be short term. Structural unemployment, technological unemployment and cyclical unemployment are all longer term, and more serious.

6.4 Government employment policies

Job creation and reducing unemployment should often mean the same thing, but it is possible to create more jobs without reducing unemployment.

(a)   This can happen when there is a greater number of people entering the jobs market than there are new jobs being created. For example, if 500,000 new jobs are created during the course of one year, but 750,000 extra school leavers are looking for jobs, there will be an increase in unemployment of 250,000.

(b)   It is also possible to reduce the official unemployment figures without creating jobs. For example, individuals who enrol for a government-financed training scheme are taken off the unemployment register, even though they do not have full-time jobs.

A government can try several options to create jobs or reduce unemployment.

(a)   **Spending more money directly on jobs** (for example hiring more civil servants)

(b)   **Encouraging growth** in the private sector of the economy; when aggregate demand is growing, firms will probably want to increase output to meet demand, and so will hire more labour

(c)   **Encouraging training in job skills**, as there might be a high level of unemployment amongst unskilled workers, and at the same time a shortage of skilled workers – a government can help to finance training schemes, in order to provide a 'pool' of workers who have the skills that firms need and will pay for

(d)   **Offering grant assistance to employers** in key regional areas

(e)   **Encouraging labour mobility** by offering individuals financial assistance with relocation expenses, and improving the flow of information on vacancies

Other policies may be directed at reducing real wages to market clearing levels.

(a)   Abolishing **closed shop** agreements, which restrict certain jobs to trade union members
(b)   Abolishing **minimum wage regulations**, where such regulations exist

QUESTION

Types of unemployment

Match the terms (a), (b) and (c) below with definitions A, B and C.

(a)   Structural unemployment   (c)   Frictional unemployment
(b)   Cyclical unemployment

A   Unemployment arising from a difficulty in matching unemployed workers with available jobs
B   Unemployment occurring in the downswing of an economy in between two booms
C   Unemployment arising from a long-term decline in a particular industry

ANSWER

The pairings are (a) C, (b) B and (c) A.

7   The objective of economic growth

7.1 Economic growth

Economic growth may be measured by increases in the **real** gross national product (GNP) per head of the population.

It is not unusual to find economic growth measured simply as increases in total GNP, regardless of inflation and changes in population size. Over periods in which the population changes relatively little, this approach will be satisfactory.

Economic growth may be **balanced**, when all sectors of the economy expand together, or **unbalanced**. Less developed countries in particular find it difficult to achieve economic growth, because many of the factors necessary for growth are absent in these countries.

Actual economic growth is the annual percentage increase in national output, which typically fluctuates in accordance with the trade cycle. **Potential economic growth** is the rate at which the economy would grow if all resources (eg people and machinery) were utilised.

7.2 Actual growth

Actual growth in the long run is determined by two factors.

- The growth in **potential output** (in other words the aggregate supply)
- The growth in **aggregate demand (AD)**

These factors should move in step with one another as we explained in Section 2.2 and Figure 3.

7.3 Potential growth

The causes of growth in **potential** output are the determinants of the capacity of the economy (the supply side) rather than actual spending (the demand side), and are as follows.

(a) There may be increases in the **amount of resources** available.

    (i)   **Land and raw materials**. Land is virtually in fixed supply, but new natural resources are continually being discovered.

    (ii)   **Labour** (the size of the working population). The output per head will be affected by the proportion of the population which is non-working.

    (iii)   **Capital** (eg machinery).

(b) Increases in the **productivity of resources** may result from technological progress or changed labour practices, for example.

7.4 Factors needed for sustained economic growth

Sustained economic growth depends heavily on an adequate level of new investment, which will be undertaken if there are **expectations** of future growth in demand. After investment has taken place on the basis of expectations, the level of income will increase, by the operation of the multiplier. But there is no reason why the actual level of income should end up increasing as much as the investing business people thought it would. It follows that investment, a factor in growth, is dependent on **business confidence** in the future, which is reflected in expectations of growth in consumption.

7.5 Natural resources

The rate of extraction of natural resources will impose a limit on the rate of growth. Production which uses up a country's natural resources, such as oil, coal and other minerals, depletes the stock of available resources; it is therefore, in a sense, **disinvestment**.

7.6 Technological progress

Technological progress is a very important source of faster economic growth.

- The same amounts of the factors of production can produce a higher output.
- New products will be developed, thus adding to output growth.

There can be technical progress in the labour force. If workers are better educated and better trained they will be able to produce more. For example, if there is a fault in the production process, a skilled worker will be able to deal with it quickly, whereas an unskilled worker might have to call for a superior instead.

Technological progress can be divided into three types.

(a) **Capital saving**: technical advances that use less capital and the same amount of labour per unit of output

(b) **Neutral**: technical advances that require labour and capital in the same proportions as before, using less of each per unit of output

(c) **Labour-saving**: technical advances that uses less labour and the same amount of capital per unit of output

If technological progress is of type (c) and the new technology seems to be labour-saving, then unemployment will rise unless there is either a simultaneous **expansion of demand** or a **reduction in hours** worked by each person. In the latter case there is no productivity increase associated with the technological progress.

Technological progress may therefore stimulate growth but at the same time conflict with the goal of full employment. A further consequence of this could be that those people in work would benefit from economic growth in the form of higher wages, but those people put out of work by the new technology would be left with a lower income. There is thus a danger that the rich will get richer and the poor will get poorer in spite of economic growth, and this would be regarded by many people as an undesirable development.

7.7 External trade influences on economic growth

An improvement in the **terms of trade** (the quantity of imports that can be bought in exchange for a given quantity of exports) means that more imports can be bought or alternatively a given volume of exports will earn higher profits. This will boost investment and hence growth. The rate of growth of the rest of the world is important for an economy that has a large foreign trade sector. If trading partners have slow growth, the amount of exports a country can sell to them will grow only slowly, and this limits the country's own opportunities for investment and growth.

7.8 Advantages and disadvantages of economic growth

Economic growth should lead to a higher income per head which can in turn lead to higher levels of consumption and a better standard of living.

A country with economic growth is more easily able to provide welfare services without creating intolerable tax burdens on the community.

There are possible disadvantages to growth, however.

(a)   Growth implies faster use of **natural resources**. Without growth, these resources would last longer.

(b)   Much economic activity tends to create **pollution**, such as acid rain and nuclear waste. It leads to emissions which threaten to produce disruptive climatic changes through an increase in the 'greenhouse effect'. It results in more roads, new and larger towns, and less unspoilt countryside.

(c)   There is a danger that some sections of the population, unable to adapt to the demands for new skills and more training, will not find jobs in the developing economy. This **structural unemployment** might create a large section of the community which gains no benefit from the increase in national income.

(d)   In order to achieve growth, firms need to **invest more** and this requires financing. This finance can only come from **higher savings** which in turn require the population to consume less. In the short run, therefore, higher growth requires a cut in consumption.

8 Government policies for managing the economy

Macroeconomic policy objectives relate to economic growth, inflation, unemployment and the balance of payments.

All modern governments are expected to manage their national economies to some extent. Electorates generally suppose that government action can support or hinder the growth of prosperity and look to them for serviceable macroeconomic policies.

There are four main objectives of economic policy, though debate continues about their relative priority.

(a)   **To achieve economic growth**, and growth in national income per head of the population. Growth implies an increase in national income in real terms. Increases caused by price inflation are not real increases at all.

(b)   **To control price inflation** (to achieve stable prices). This has become a central objective of UK economic policy in recent years.

(c)   **To achieve full employment**. Full employment does not mean that everyone who wants a job has one all the time, but it does mean that unemployment levels are low, and involuntary unemployment is short term.

(d)   **To achieve a balance between exports and imports** (on the country's balance of payments accounts) over a period of years. The wealth of a country relative to others, a country's creditworthiness as a borrower, and the goodwill between countries in international relations might all depend on the achievement of an external balance over time.

The problem with trying to satisfy these objectives is that when any are satisfied, they invariably cause a problem with the others. For example, creating full employment may lead to increased inflation rates. As explained later in the chapter, governments use 'fiscal' or 'monetary' policies to manage these objectives.

8.1 Government spending

Governments spend money. Expenditure must be allocated between departments and functions such as health, social services, education, transport, defence, grants to industry, and so on.

- Wages and salaries to employees
- Materials, supplies and services
- Capital equipment
- Interest on borrowings and repayments of capital
- Benefits and pensions to those entitled to such

8.2 Significance of government tax and spending decisions to companies

(a)   Expenditure decisions by government affect **suppliers to the Government**, such as producers of defence equipment, medicines and medical equipment, and school text books.

(b)   There is a **'knock-on' effect** throughout the economy of government spending; that is, companies might supply companies which in turn supply the Government.

(c)   Taxation affects **consumers' purchasing power**.

(d)   **Taxes** on company profits and tax allowances affect the after-tax return on investment that companies achieve.

(e)   **Investment** by the public sector will tend to be directed towards activities in which the public sector is involved or on fulfilling social needs. Hence industries in these fields will benefit.

(f)   Public sector investment might have a longer **time scale** (eg health) or have less quantifiable economic benefits (eg education) than the private sector is able to cope with.

8.3 Economic planning

At one time, many people believed the Government should plan economic activity in detail. This is now out of favour, perhaps as a result of the failure of communism in the eastern bloc. In this model, government is a **director** of economic activity.

Economic planning on a lesser scale, with the Government as an **enabler** of private sector activity and as corrector of market imperfections, is now seen by many as more appropriate.

(a)   Government's most important economic role is the legal system relating to business. Law relating to property, contracts in corporation, competition, employment, and so on provides a framework which enables businesses to be done with confidence.

(b)   Government also has a responsibility for macroeconomic management. Such management, like the legal framework, should provide stable conditions in which business can operate with confidence.

(c)   Governments can raise **trade barriers** to protect domestic industry, although the trend has been to lower such barriers.

(d)   Governments can **subsidise exports, or promote them** in other ways (eg by trade missions, export credit insurance and so forth).

(e)   Governments can also encourage **inward investment** by foreign countries..

(f)   **Regional policy** is an example of small scale economic planning.

    (i)   Tax incentives or grants for investing in certain areas

    (ii)   Relaxing or enforcing town and county planning restrictions

    (iii)   Developing **new towns** to reduce population pressure in major conurbations, although this policy is perhaps a thing of the past

    (iv)   Promotion of infrastructure developments (eg roads, rail, airports)

The Government also attempts to influence businesses by persuasion and encouraging certain actions.

8.4 State influences over organisations

Government influences are outlined in the diagram below.

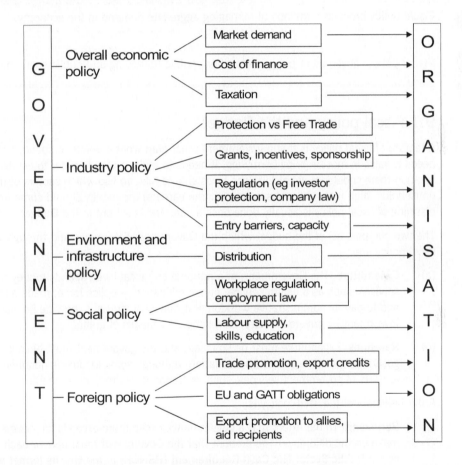

8.5 Government influence over commercial decisions

Decision	Comment
Output capacity	Grants or tax incentives to invest
Competition	Forbid or allow takeovers/mergers Outlaw anti-competitive practices Opening markets to new entrants (eg gas)
Monopolies	Break them up; regulate them
Sales demand	Government policy affects demand

8.6 Government influence over operational decisions

Decision	Comment
Health and safety	Legislation, regulations
Employment	Equal opportunities legislation
Consumers	Product safety standards
Tax	Sales tax procedures, income tax, accounting control

As well as State influences, there are other influences which affect groups of nations rather than a single nation, for example the EU. These are known as supra-national bodies. We looked at these in Chapter 2.

9 Fiscal policy

Fiscal policy provides a method of managing **aggregate demand** in the economy.

Fiscal policy: government policy on taxation, public borrowing and public spending.

9.1 Fiscal policy and the Budget

A feature of fiscal policy is that a government must **plan** what it wants to spend, and so how much it needs to raise in income or by borrowing. It needs to make a plan in order to establish how much taxation there should be, what form the taxes should take and so which sectors of the economy (firms or households, high income earners or low income earners) the money should come from. This formal planning of fiscal policy is usually done once a year and is set out in **the Budget**.

The two components of the budget which the Government determines and through which it exercises its fiscal policy are:

(a) **Expenditure.** The Government, at a national and local level, spends money to provide goods and services, such as a health service, public education, a police force, roads and public buildings, and to pay its administrative workforce. It may also, perhaps, provide finance to encourage investment by private industry, for example by means of grants.

(b) **Revenues.** Expenditure must be financed, and the government must have income. Most government income comes from **taxation**, although some income is obtained from **direct charges** to users of government services, such as National Health Service charges.

A third element of the fiscal policy is:

(c) **Borrowing.** To the extent that a government's expenditure exceeds its income it must borrow to make up the difference. The amount that the Government must borrow each year is now known as the **Public Sector Net Cash Requirement (PSNCR)** in the UK. Its former name was **Public Sector Borrowing Requirement (PSBR)**. Where the Government borrows from has an impact on the effectiveness of fiscal policy.

9.2 Budget surplus and budget deficit

If a government decides to use fiscal policy to influence demand in the economy, it can choose either expenditure changes or tax changes as its policy instrument.

Suppose, for example, that the Government wants to stimulate demand in the economy.

If the Government kept its own spending at the same level, but **reduced levels of taxation**, it would **stimulate demand** in the economy because firms and households would have more of their own money after tax for consumption or saving/investing.

(a) **It can increase demand directly by spending more itself** – eg on the health service or education, and by employing more people itself.

  (i) This extra spending could be financed by higher taxes, but this would reduce spending by the private sector of the economy because the private sector's after-tax income would be lower.

  (ii) The extra government spending could also be financed by extra government borrowing. Just as individuals can borrow money for spending, so too can a government.

(b) **It can increase demand indirectly by reducing taxation** and so allowing firms and individuals more after-tax income to spend (or save).

  (i) Cuts in taxation can be matched by cuts in government spending, in which case total demand in the economy will not be stimulated significantly, if at all.

  (ii) Alternatively, tax cuts can be financed by more government borrowing.

Just as aggregate demand in the economy can be boosted by either more government spending or by tax cuts, financed in either case by a higher PSNCR, so too can demand in the economy be reduced by cutting government spending or by raising taxes, and using the savings or higher income to cut government borrowing.

Expenditure changes and tax changes are not mutually exclusive options, of course. A government has several options.

(a) Increase expenditure and reduce taxes, with these changes financed by a higher PSNCR
(b) Reduce expenditure and increase taxes, with these changes reducing the size of the PSNCR
(c) Increase expenditure and partly or wholly finance this extra spending with higher taxes
(d) Reduce expenditure and use these savings to reduce taxes

When a government's income exceeds its expenditure, and there is a negative PSNCR or **Public Sector Debt Repayment (PSDR)**, we say that the Government is running a **budget surplus**. This may be a deliberate policy (known as contractionary policy) to reduce the size of the money supply by taking money out of the economy. When a government's expenditure exceeds its income, so that it must borrow to make up the difference, there is a PSNCR and we say that the Government is running a **budget deficit**. When the government is injecting money into the economy, this is known as expansionary policy.

9.3 Functions of taxation

Taxation has several functions. Some of these include the following.

(a) **To raise revenues for the Government** as well as for local authorities and similar public bodies (eg the European Union).

(b) **To cause certain products to be priced to take into account their social costs**. (For example, smoking entails certain social costs, such as hospital care.)

(c) **To redistribute income and wealth**.

(d) **To protect industries from foreign competition.** If the Government levies a duty on all imported goods, much of the duty will be passed on to the consumer in the form of higher prices, making imported goods more expensive.

9.4 Direct and indirect taxes

A government must decide how it intends to raise tax revenues, from **direct or indirect taxes**, and in what proportions tax revenues will be raised from each source.

A **direct tax** is paid direct by a person to the Revenue authority. Examples of direct taxes in the UK are income tax, corporation tax, capital gains tax and inheritance tax. A direct tax can be levied on income and profits, or on wealth. Direct taxes tend to be progressive or proportional taxes. They are also usually unavoidable, which means that they must be paid by everyone.

An **indirect tax** is collected by the Revenue authority from an intermediary (a supplier) who then attempts to pass on the tax to consumers in the price of goods they sell. Indirect taxes are of two types.

- A specific tax is charged as a **fixed sum** per unit sold.

- An ad valorem tax is charged as a **fixed percentage** of the price of the good.

9.5 Tax and income levels

Note the following distinctions.

(a) A **regressive tax** takes a higher **proportion** of a poor person's salary than of a rich person's. Television licences and road tax are examples of regressive taxes since they are the same for all people.

(b) A **proportional tax** takes the **same proportion** of income in tax from all levels of income.

(c) A **progressive tax** takes a **higher proportion** of income in tax as income rises. Income tax as a whole is progressive, since the first part of an individual's income is tax free due to personal allowances and the rate of tax increases in steps in the UK from 20p in £1 to 45p in £1 as taxable income rises.

Direct taxes tend to be **progressive** or **proportional**. Income tax is usually progressive, with high rates of tax charged on higher bands of taxable income. **Indirect taxes** can be **regressive**, when the taxes are placed on essential commodities or commodities consumed by poorer people in greater quantities.

10 Monetary policy

Monetary policy uses money supply, interest rates or credit controls to influence aggregate demand.

Monetary policy: government policy on the money supply, the monetary system, interest rates, exchange rates and the availability of credit.

Monetary and fiscal policies attempt to attain the macroeconomic policy objectives by influencing aggregate demand.

QUESTION

Effects of policy

How are businesses affected by fiscal and monetary policy?

ANSWER

Businesses are affected by a government's tax policy (eg corporation tax rates) and monetary policy (high interest rates increase the cost of investment, and depress consumer demand).

10.1 Objectives of monetary policy

Monetary policy can be used as a means towards achieving ultimate economic objectives for inflation, the balance of trade, full employment and real economic growth. To achieve these **ultimate objectives**, the authorities will set **intermediate objectives** for monetary policy.

In the UK, the ultimate objective of monetary policy in recent years has been principally to reduce the rate of inflation to a sustainable low level. The intermediate objectives of monetary policy have related to the level of interest rates, growth in the money supply, the exchange rate for sterling, the expansion of credit and the growth of national income.

BPP
LEARNING MEDIA

10.2 The money supply as a target of monetary policy

To monetarist economists, the **money supply** is an obvious intermediate target of economic policy. This is because they claim that an increase in the money supply will raise prices and incomes and this in turn will raise the demand for money to spend. The current trend is to call this **quantitative easing**, a policy whereby a government prints more money in order to stimulate the economy.

When such a policy is first introduced, the short-term effect would be unpredictable for three reasons.

(a) The effect on interest rates might be erratic.

(b) There might be a time lag before anything can be done. For example, it takes time to cut government spending and hence to use reduction in government borrowing as an instrument of monetary policy.

(c) There might be a time lag before control of the money supply alters expectations about inflation and wage demands.

Growth in the money supply, if it is a monetary policy target, should therefore be a **medium-term target**.

10.3 Interest rates as a target for monetary policy

The authorities might decide that **interest rates** – the price of money – should be a target of monetary policy. This would be appropriate if it is considered that there is a direct relationship between interest rates and the level of expenditure in the economy, or between interest rates and the rate of inflation.

A rise in interest rates will raise the price of borrowing in the internal economy for both companies and individuals. If companies see the rise as relatively permanent, rates of return on investments will become less attractive and **investment plans may be curtailed**. Corporate profits will fall as a result of higher interest payments. Companies will reduce inventory levels as the cost of having money tied up in inventory rises. Individuals should be expected to reduce or postpone consumption in order to reduce borrowings, and should become less willing to borrow for house purchase.

Although it is generally accepted that there is likely to be a connection between interest rates and investment (by companies) and consumer expenditure, **the connection is not a stable and predictable one**, and interest rate changes are only likely to affect the level of expenditure after a **considerable time lag**.

Other effects of raising interest rates

(a) High interest rates will keep the value of sterling higher than it would otherwise be. This will keep the cost of exports high, and so discourage the purchase of exports. This may be necessary to protect the balance of payments and to prevent 'import-cost-push' inflation. UK manufacturers have complained bitterly about this effect and BMW cited it as one of the reasons for disposing of Rover.

(b) High interest rates will attract foreign investors into sterling investments, and so provide capital inflows which help to finance the large UK balance of payments deficit.

An important reason for pursuing an interest rate policy is that the authorities are able to influence interest rates much more effectively and rapidly than they can influence other policy targets, such as the money supply or the volume of credit.

10.4 The exchange rate as a target of monetary policy

Why the exchange rate is a target

(a) If the exchange rate falls, exports become cheaper to overseas buyers and so more competitive in export markets. Imports will become more expensive and so less competitive against goods produced by manufacturers at home. A fall in the exchange rate might therefore be good for a domestic economy, by giving a **stimulus to exports** and **reducing demand for imports**.

(b) An increase in the exchange rate will have the opposite effect, with dearer exports and cheaper imports. If the exchange rate rises and imports become cheaper, there should be a reduction in the rate of domestic inflation. A fall in the exchange rate, on the other hand, tends to increase the cost of imports and adds to the rate of domestic inflation.

When a country's economy is heavily dependent on overseas trade, as the UK economy is, it might be appropriate for government policy to establish a target exchange value for the domestic currency. However, the exchange rate is dependent on both the domestic rate of inflation and the level of interest rates. Targets for the exchange rate cannot be achieved unless the rate of inflation at home is first brought under control.

10.5 Targets and indicators

An economic indicator provides information about economic conditions and might be used as a way of judging the performance of government.

(a) A **leading indicator** is one which gives an advance indication of what will happen to the economy in the future. It can therefore be used to predict future conditions. For example, a fall in the value of sterling by, say, 2% might be used to predict what will happen to the balance of payments and to the rate of inflation.

(b) A **coincident indicator** is one which gives an indication of changes in economic conditions **at the same time** that these changes are occurring. For example, if the narrow money supply rises by 5%, this might 'confirm' that the rate of increase in GDP over the same period of time has been about the same, 5% in 'money' terms.

(c) A **lagging indicator**, you will have guessed, is one which 'lags behind' the economic cycle. Unemployment, to take an example, often continues to rise until after a recession has ended and only starts to fall again after recovery has begun.

There are a number of monetary indicators.

(a) The size of the money stock

(b) Interest rates such as the banks' base rate of interest, the Treasury bill rate and the yield on long-dated government securities

(c) The exchange rate against another currency, for example the US dollar, or the trade-weighted exchange rate index

(d) The size of the Government's borrowing

(e) Government borrowing as a percentage of Gross Domestic Product

10.6 Monetary policy and fiscal policy

Monetary policy can be made to act as a subsidiary support to fiscal policy and demand management. Since budgets are once-a-year events, a government must use non-fiscal measures in between budgets to make adjustments to its control of the economy.

(a) A policy of **low interest rates** or the absence of any form of credit control might stimulate bank lending, which in turn would increase expenditure (demand) in the economy.

(b) **High interest rates** might act as a deterrent to borrowing and so reduce spending in the economy.

(c) Strict **credit controls** (for example restrictions on bank lending) might be introduced to reduce lending and so reduce demand in the economy.

Alternatively, monetary policy might be given prominence over fiscal policy as the most effective approach by a government to achieving its main economic policy objectives. This might not, however, be possible: from 1990 to 1992, for example, monetary policy in the UK was heavily constrained by the need to set interest rates at levels which maintained sterling's position in the European exchange rate mechanism (ERM). From 1997, the Government has given the Bank of England the role of setting interest rates, although it is still the Government which sets an inflation target. If the UK joined a single European currency, interest rates would largely be determined at the European level.

10.7 Monetary policy, inflation control and economic growth

Monetarists argue that monetary control will put the brake on inflation, but how does this help the economy? We might argue like this.

(a)   High inflation increases **economic uncertainty**. Bringing inflation under control will restore business confidence and help international trade by stabilising the exchange rate.

(b)   A resurgence of business confidence through lower interest rates (due to less uncertainty and lower inflation) will **stimulate investment** and real output.

(c)   A **controlled growth in the money supply** will provide higher incomes for individuals to purchase the higher output.

11   The balance of payments

The **balance of payments accounts** consist of a current account with visibles and invisibles sections and transactions in capital (external assets and liabilities including official financing).

11.1 The nature of the balance of payments

EXAM FOCUS POINT

Confusion of the balance of payments with the Government budget is common. Make sure that the distinction is clear in **your** mind.

Under the current method of presentation of the UK balance of payments statistics, **current account** transactions are subdivided into four parts.

- Trade in goods
- Trade in services
- Income
- Transfers

Before 1996, the term **visibles** was used in official statistics for trade in goods and the term **invisibles** was used for the rest. These terms have now been dropped in order to give more emphasis to the balances for trade in goods and services, although you may still find them mentioned.

Income is divided into two parts.

(a)   Income from employment of UK residents by overseas firms

(b)   Income from capital investment overseas

Transfers are also divided into two parts.

(a)   Public sector payments to and receipts from overseas bodies, such as the EU. Typically these are interest payments

(b)   Non-government sector payments to and receipts from bodies, such as the EU

The **capital account** balance is made up of public sector flows of **capital** into and out of the country, such as government loans to other countries.

The balance on the **financial account** is made up of flows of capital to and from the non-government sector, such as direct investment in overseas facilities; portfolio investment (in shares, bonds, and so on); and speculative flows of currency. Movements on government foreign currency reserves are also included under this heading.

When journalists or economists speak of the balance of payments they are usually referring to the deficit or surplus on the **current account**, or possibly to the surplus or deficit on trade in goods only (this is also known as the **balance of trade**).

EXAM FOCUS POINT

Do not equate a trade surplus or deficit with a 'profit' or 'loss' for the country. A country is not like a company and the trade balance has nothing to do with profits and losses.

11.2 Equilibrium in the balance of payments

A balance of payments is in equilibrium if, over a period of years, the exchange rate remains stable and autonomous credits and debits are equal in value (the annual trade in goods and services is in overall balance). However, equilibrium will not exist if these things require the government to introduce measures which create unemployment or higher prices, sacrifice economic growth or impose trade barriers (eg import tariffs and import quotas).

11.3 Surplus or deficit in the current account

A surplus or deficit on the balance of payments usually means a **surplus or deficit on the current account**.

A problem arises for a country's balance of payments when the country has a deficit on current account year after year, although there can be problems too for a country which enjoys a continual current account **surplus**.

The problems of a **deficit** on the current account are probably the more obvious. When a country is continually in deficit, it is importing more goods and services that it is exporting. This leads to two possible consequences.

(a)   It may borrow more and more from abroad, to build up external liabilities which match the deficit on the current account, for example encouraging foreign investors to lend more by purchasing the government's gilt-edged securities.

(b)   It may sell more and more of its assets. This has been happening recently in the US, for example, where a large deficit on the US current account has resulted in large purchases of shares in US companies by foreign firms.

Even so, the demand to buy the country's currency in the foreign exchange markets will be weaker than the supply of the country's currency for sale. As a consequence, there will be pressure on the exchange rate to depreciate in value.

If a country has a **surplus** on the current account year after year, it might invest the surplus abroad or add it to official reserves. The balance of payments position would be strong. There is the problem, however, that if one country which is a major trading nation (such as Japan) has a continuous surplus on its balance of payments current account, other countries must be in continual deficit. These other countries can run down their official reserves, perhaps to nothing, and borrow as much as they can to meet the payments overseas, but eventually they will run out of money entirely and be unable even to pay their debts. Political pressure might therefore build up within the importing countries to impose tariffs or import quotas.

11.4 How can a government rectify a current account deficit?

The government of a country with a balance of payments deficit will usually be expected to take measures to reduce or eliminate the deficit. A current account deficit may be rectified by one or more of the following measures.

(a)   A depreciation of the currency (called **devaluation** when deliberately instigated by the government, for example by changing the value of the currency within a controlled exchange rate system)

(b)   Direct measures to restrict imports, such as tariffs or import quotas or exchange control regulations

(c)   Domestic deflation to reduce aggregate demand in the domestic economy

The first two are **expenditure switching** policies, which transfer resources and expenditure away from imports and towards domestic products, while the last is an **expenditure reducing** policy.

CHAPTER ROUNDUP

- ↳ **Macroeconomics** is the study of the aggregated effects of the decisions of individual economic units (such as households or businesses). It looks at a complete national economy, or the international economic system as a whole

- ↳ There is a circular flow of income in an economy, which means that expenditure, output and income will all have the same total value.

- ↳ The economy is rarely in a stable state because of the various changing factors which influence it. These include investment levels, the multiplier effect, inflation, savings, confidence, interest rates and exchange rates.

- ↳ **Equilibrium national income** is determined using aggregate supply and aggregate demand analysis.

- ↳ **Business cycles** or **trade cycles** are the continual sequence of rapid growth in national income, followed by a slowdown in growth and then a fall in national income. After this recession comes growth again, and when this has reached a peak, the cycle turns into recession once more.

- ↳ High rates of **inflation** are harmful to an economy. Inflation redistributes income and wealth. Uncertainty about the value of money makes business planning more difficult. Constantly changing prices impose extra costs.

- ↳ **Demand pull inflation** arises from an excess of aggregate demand over the productive capacity of the economy.

- ↳ **Cost push inflation** arises from increases in the costs of production.

- ↳ The number of unemployed at any time is measured by government statistics.

- ↳ **Economic growth** may be measured by increases in the **real** gross national product (GNP) per head of the population.

- ↳ **Macroeconomic policy objectives** relate to economic growth, inflation, unemployment and the balance of payments.

- ↳ **Fiscal policy** provides a method of managing **aggregate demand** in the economy.

- ↳ If a government decides to use fiscal policy to influence demand in the economy, it can choose either expenditure changes or tax changes as its policy instrument.

- ↳ A government must decide how it intends to raise tax revenues, from **direct or indirect taxes**, and in what proportions tax revenues will be raised from each source.

- ↳ **Direct taxes** have the quality of being **progressive** or **proportional**. Income tax is usually progressive, with high rates of tax charged on higher bands of taxable income. **Indirect taxes** can be **regressive**, when the taxes are placed on essential commodities or commodities consumed by poorer people in greater quantities.

- ↳ **Monetary policy** uses money supply, interest rates or credit controls to influence aggregate demand.

- ↳ The **balance of payments accounts** consist of a current account with visibles and invisibles sections and transactions in capital (external assets and liabilities, including official financing).

- ↳ A surplus or deficit on the balance of payments usually means a **surplus or deficit on the current account**.

QUICK QUIZ

1   Government policy on taxation, public borrowing and public spending is:

A   Monetary policy   B   Fiscal policy

2   A government can increase demand by using fiscal policy.

True ☐   False ☐

3   A tax which takes a higher proportion of a poor person's salary than of a rich person's is:

A   Proportional tax   C   Progressive tax
B   Regressive tax   D   Indirect tax

4   High rates of personal income tax are thought to have a disincentive effect. This refers to the likelihood that the high rates of tax will:

A   Encourage illegal tax evasion by individuals
B   Lead to a reduction in the supply of labour
C   Lead to a reduction in savings by individuals
D   Discourage company investment

5   The government of a certain country decides to introduce a poll tax, which will involve a flat rate levy of $200 on every adult member of the population. This new tax could be described as:

A   Regressive   C   Progressive
B   Proportional   D   *Ad valorem*

6   Which of the following will **not** be the immediate purpose of a tax measure by the Government?

A   To discourage an activity regarded as socially undesirable
B   To influence interest rates
C   To protect a domestic industry from foreign competition
D   To price certain products so as to take into account their social cost

7   Which of the following government aims might be achieved by means of fiscal policy? 1. A redistribution of income between firms and households. 2. A reduction in aggregate monetary demand. 3. A change in the pattern of consumer demand.

A   Objectives 1 and 2 only   C   Objectives 2 and 3 only
B   Objectives 1 and 3 only   D   Objectives 1, 2 and 3

8   Other things remaining the same, an increase in the money supply will tend to reduce:

A   Interest rates   C   The volume of bank overdrafts
B   Liquidity preference   D   Prices and incomes

9   Injections into the economy are:

A   Consumption and Investment
B   Investment and Government Expenditure
C   Investment, Government Expenditure and Export Demand
D   Consumption, Investment, Government Expenditure and Export Demand

10   A deflationary gap occurs when:

A   Aggregate demand is insufficient to buy up all the goods and services the company is capable of producing.

B   Aggregate demand is more than sufficient to buy up all the goods and services produced by an economy.

C   A government attempts to spend its way out of recession.

D   A government is cutting its level of expenditure.

ANSWERS TO QUICK QUIZ

1	B	Monetary policy is policy on the money supply, monetary system, interest rates, exchange rates and the availability of credit.
2	True.	A government can increase demand by spending more itself or by reducing taxation so that firms and households have more after-tax income to spend.
3	B	This is the definition of regressive tax.
4	B	The disincentive effect refers specifically to the disincentive of individuals to work.
5	A	A flat-rate poll tax, with no concession for the lower paid, would take a higher proportion of the income of lower-income earners than of higher-income earners. This is a regressive tax system.
6	B	The main purpose of taxation will be to raise revenue for the government. Other aims might be to redistribute wealth or affect demand in the economy. Changes in rate of tax do not have a direct influence on interest rates, which can be influenced by a government's **monetary** policies.
7	D	Objective 1 could be achieved by raising (or lowering) taxes on firms and lowering (or raising) taxes on households. Objective 2 could be achieved by raising taxation in order to reduce consumers' disposable income and so to reduce aggregate expenditure in the economy: these consequences should lead to a fall in the demand for money. Objective 3 can be achieved either by taxing income or by means of selective indirect taxes on certain goods.
8	A	Lower interest rates should be a consequence of an increase in the money supply, with a movement along the liquidity preference curve rather than a shift in the liquidity preference curve.
9	C	
10	A	

Now try ...

Attempt the questions below from the **Practice Question Bank**

Q13

Q14

Q15

Q16

04

We start by looking at the definition of the micro environment (**Section 1**) and the differences between the micro and macro environments (**Section 2**).

Next we shall examine the concept of a market which, in economics, goes beyond the idea of a single geographical place where people meet to buy and sell goods (**Section 3**).

We will then look in more depth at the microeconomic level of the individual firm, individual markets and consumers (or households). This means looking at what influences the amount of a product which is demanded or supplied and analysing how price and output are determined through the interaction of **demand** and **supply** (**Sections 4 to 8**).

Microeconomic factors

Study Guide

Intellectual level

A5 Microeconomic factors

(a) Define the concept of demand and supply for goods and services.   K

(b) Explain elasticity of demand and the impact of substitute and complementary goods.   K

(c) Explain the economic behaviour of costs in the short and long term.   K

(d) Define perfect competition, oligopoly, monopolistic competition and monopoly.   K

EXAM FOCUS POINT

There is an article on the ACCA website entitled "Introduction to microeconomics" that is relevant to material in this chapter.

1   The micro environment

The **micro environment** refers to the immediate operational environment, including suppliers, competitors, customers, stakeholders and intermediaries.

The micro environment includes all factors which impact directly on a firm and its activities in relation to a particular market in which it operates, and also any internal aspects of the organisation which influence the development of a marketing strategy.

The **micro environment** includes the groups and organisations that have a two-way operation relationship with the business, and which the business can **control** and **influence** to some degree.

1.1 Supply and demand

An organisation's micro environment consists of itself and its current and potential **customers, suppliers** and **intermediaries**. The competition also has a key influence on the micro environment.

The organisation is an open system, with boundaries to its immediate environment. The organisation must establish relationships across these boundaries to obtain supplies and credit. It also must have linkages to the marketplace, either directly to end customers or indirectly through intermediaries.

Competitors also form part of the micro environment and senior management must understand the relationships that exist between competitors in the micro environment of the organisation. This was covered in more detail in Chapter 1 where we took a closer look at the **stakeholders** of an organisation.

We might need to remind ourselves of some of the underlying relationships between an organisation and the other organisations in its environment.

The **market economy** based on **capitalism** contrasts with the centrally planned economy in which the State controls production, as in Soviet Russia up to the 1980s, for example. A feature of market economies is that many firms compete with each other to create a customer. This is a spur to innovation and marketing activities which are the distinguishing characteristics of business organisation.

The micro environment

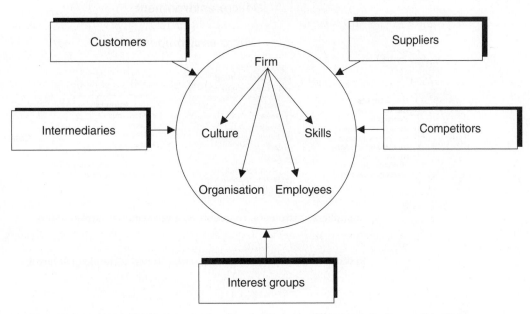

Elements of the micro environment

The micro environment comprises not just those firms that an organisation **actually** does business with. It also includes those firms and individuals that an organisation could **potentially** do business with.

Therefore it includes not just current customers, but potential customers who may currently be served by another organisation. Thus, an important element in understanding the micro environment is **competition** between organisations in order to:

- Win customers
- Obtain supplies
- Get access to the best intermediaries

The micro environment is of general importance to the marketing process for several reasons. In general, the micro environment is the **immediate or operational environment**; it drives the tactical responses of management on a daily basis. The marketer can utilise the marketing mix to influence and affect the stakeholders of a business.

Remember that the micro environment contains both **actual** and **potential** customers – management can use the marketing mix to **convert** potential customers into actual customers; however, to do this requires an understanding of the needs and wants of those potential customers.

2 Internal and external micro and macro environments

 For the **organisation as a system**, we need to consider the various forces which have an impact internally and externally.

The diagram which follows highlights the organisation (which is a social system) taking inputs and transforming them into outputs for consumption. The process is cyclical in nature, those consuming the end output providing feedback which is used to adapt the inputs selected and the transformation process in the future. The purpose of this feedback is to better meet the needs of these consumers (customers, end-users etc). This process also happens within the context of the micro and macro environments, which have factors and forces that will have an impact on all elements within this process.

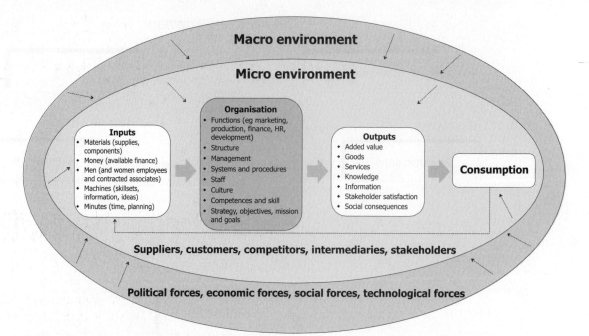

There are four main elements to the system: the inputs, the transformational process which occurs within the organisation, the output and then the final consumption of these outputs. The inputs can be remembered using a common abbreviation, the 5Ms.

The **5Ms** refer to inputs that an organisation requires in order to function. They are:

1   Materials
2   Money
3   Men (ie human resource)
4   Machines
5   Management

Each of the 5Ms needs to be carefully employed, as each is a valuable resource in enabling the organisation to meet its goals.

The competence and skill employed within the organisation should be used in a way to enable the transformation of these inputs into something valuable or important to the customer. Mullins (2005) noted that organisations even within the same sector may have radically different goals, procedures, methods of operating, styles of management, systems, structure and behaviour of staff. Despite these differences, Mullins identified four factors that all organisations require in order to function:

- **People** – behind every action, document written, presentation, decision made are **human interactions**

- **Objectives** – which form the **basis** of an organisation and determine the nature of the outputs and the series of activities to achieve them

- **Structure** – is needed by which to **channel and co-ordinate** efforts and interactions

- **Management** – is required to **direct and control** efforts in order to pursue objectives

EXAM FOCUS POINT

You are not expected to discuss different forms and methods of **management**. However, it is useful for you to appreciate that effective strategic management is at the core of the organisation's ability to transform inputs and to be able to offer a competitive offering of value to customers.

The output and consumption elements of our diagram outline that the process is ongoing and that once something is created by the organisation (the product or service) it is passed on. Marketing as a discipline reminds us that, in order for this process to continue, the organisation needs to ensure that the output will meet the needs of specified customers and this must relate to the **customer value proposition**.

The **customer value proposition** consists of the sum total of benefits which a vendor promises that a customer will receive in return for the customer's associated payment (or other value-transfer).

In simple words: value proposition = what the customer gets for what the customer pays.

Accordingly, a customer can evaluate a company's value proposition on two broad dimensions with multiple subsets:

1   Relative performance: what the customer gets from the vendor relative to a competitor's offering

2   Price: which consists of the payment the customer makes to acquire the product or service; plus the access cost

The vendor-company's marketing and sales efforts offer a customer value proposition; the vendor-company's delivery and customer-service processes then fulfil that value proposition.

When faced with their next purchase decision, whose product or service is a customer most likely to buy? Will it be yours or will it be that of a key competitor? This is the most important question most business managers will have to answer. Most of the time, customers will make that decision based on the benefits that are most valuable to them, and the price they must pay to receive those benefits. In other words, most purchase decisions are based upon perceived value – the trade-off between the quality of the most desirable benefits and the price paid for those benefits.

CASE STUDY

Imagine the following scenario for a hypothetical organisation called Premier Motors which produces high-performance sports cars.

If, for example, Premier Motors has used the very best input resources available to them and has the ultimate management and organisational workings to produce the most exceptional cars ever designed, you might think that this would be highly lucrative. If, however, they were based in Mongolia, which has one of the lowest levels of car ownership, they would not have a significant local customer base. Equally, they would find that to transport the product to other parts of the world would be very expensive. For some exceptionally wealthy consumers the opportunity to purchase the best car in the world regardless of cost would mean that there is a market for the cars; however, the potential size of this market is highly limited and not necessarily cost effective in the long term.

We now need to add in the additional environmental elements to our example. In the micro environment, the lack of many customers is clearly a disadvantage. Also, within the high-performance sports car market Premier Motors may well have a number of competitors who may not produce such exceptional cars but are more affordable and therefore have a larger market. At the macro level, in times of economic prosperity there may be a larger global number of 'high worth' individuals, while in turbulent economic times there may be a reduced propensity to purchase such ostentatious cars not only for financial reasons but also possibly due to a change in social and cultural expectations.

Although this is a completely fictitious and extreme example, it at least demonstrates how the whole process is embedded in a complex picture to be assessed and anticipated by the marketer.

3   The concept of a market

In a free market, the **price mechanism** signals demand and supply conditions to producers and consumers. It therefore determines the activities of both producers and consumers, influencing the levels of demand for and the supply of goods.

3.1 What is a market?

A market involves **the buyers and sellers of a good who influence its price**. Markets can be worldwide, as in the case of oil, wheat, cotton and copper for example. Others are more localised, such as the housing market or the market for secondhand cars.

A market can be defined as a situation in which potential buyers and potential sellers (**suppliers**) of a good or service come together for the purpose of exchange.

Suppliers and potential suppliers are referred to in economics as **firms**. The potential purchasers of consumer goods are known as **households**.

However, some markets have buyers who are other firms or government authorities. For example, a manufacturing firm buys raw materials and components to go into the products that it makes. Service industries and government departments must similarly buy in supplies in order to do their own work. The demand for goods by firms and government authorities is a **derived demand**, in that it depends on the demand from households for the goods and services that they produce and provide.

Markets for different goods or commodities are often interrelated. All commodities compete for households' income so that if more is spent in one market, there will be less to spend in other markets. Further, if markets for similar goods are separated geographically, there will be some price differential at which it will be worthwhile for the consumer to buy in the lower price market and pay shipping costs, rather than buy in a geographically nearer market.

3.2 Price theory and the market

Price theory is concerned with how market prices for goods are arrived at, through the interaction of demand and supply.

A good or service has a **price** if it is **useful** as well as **scarce**. Its usefulness is shown by the fact that consumers demand it. In a world populated entirely by vegetarians, meat would not command a price, no matter how few cows or sheep there were because no one would want to eat meat.

3.3 Utility

Utility is the word used to describe the pleasure or satisfaction or benefit derived by a person from the consumption of goods. **Total utility** is the total satisfaction that people derive from spending their income and consuming goods.

Marginal utility is the **satisfaction gained** from consuming one **additional** unit of a good or the **satisfaction forgone** by consuming one unit **less**. If someone eats six apples and then eats a seventh, total utility refers to the satisfaction they derive from all seven apples together, while marginal utility refers to the additional satisfaction from eating the seventh apple, having already eaten six.

3.4 Assumptions about consumer rationality

Economists assume that consumers act rationally. This means, in turn, that:

(a)   Generally the consumer prefers more goods to less.

(b)   Generally the consumer is willing to substitute one good for another, provided its price is right.

(c)   Choices are transitive. This means that if, at a given time, a commodity A is preferred to B and B is preferred to C then we can conclude that commodity A is preferred to commodity C.

Acting rationally means that the consumer attempts to **maximise the total utility** attainable with a **limited income**. When the consumer decides to buy another unit of a good they are deciding that its marginal utility exceeds the marginal utility that would be yielded by any **alternative** use of the price they pay.

If a person has maximised their total utility, it follows that they have allocated their expenditure in such a way that the utility gained from spending the last penny spent on each good will be equal.

We are now going to look at demand and supply in turn, before considering how they (demand and supply) interact through the price mechanism.

4 The demand schedule

The position of the **demand curve** is determined by the demand conditions, which include consumers' tastes and preferences, and consumers' incomes.

4.1 The concept of demand

Demand for a good or service is the quantity of that good or service that potential purchasers would be willing and able to buy, or attempt to buy, at any possible price.

Demand might be satisfied, and so actual quantities bought would equal demand. On the other hand, some demand might be unsatisfied, with the number of would-be purchasers trying to buy a good being too great for the supply of that good. In which case, demand is said to exceed supply.

The phrase 'willing and able to buy' in the key term above is important. Demand does not mean the quantity that potential purchasers wish they could buy. For example, a million households might wish that they owned a luxury yacht, but there might only be actual attempts to buy 100 luxury yachts at a given price. **Economic demand needs to be effective**. That is, it must be supported by available money (ie willing and able to buy), rather than just being a general desire for goods or services.

4.2 The demand schedule and the demand curve

The relationship between demand and price can be shown graphically as a **demand curve**. The demand curve of a single consumer or household is derived by estimating how much of the good the consumer or household would demand at various hypothetical market prices. Suppose that the following **demand schedule** shows demand for biscuits by one household over a period of one month.

Price per kg $	Quantity demanded kg
1	9.75
2	8
3	6.25
4	4.5
5	2.75
6	1

Notice that we show demand falling as price increases. This is what normally happens with most goods. This is because purchasers have a limited amount of money to spend and must choose between goods that compete for their attention. When the price of one good rises, it is likely that other goods will seem relatively more attractive and so demand will switch away from the more expensive good to the cheaper alternative. So the shape of the demand curve is determined by the consumer acting **rationally**; with demand tending to be higher at a low price, and lower at a high price for most goods and services.

We can show this schedule graphically, with **price on the y axis** and **quantity demanded on the x axis.** If we assume that there is complete divisibility, so that price and quantity can both change in infinitely small steps, we can draw a demand curve by joining the points represented in the schedule by a continuous line (Figure 1). This is the household's demand curve for biscuits in the particular market we are looking at.

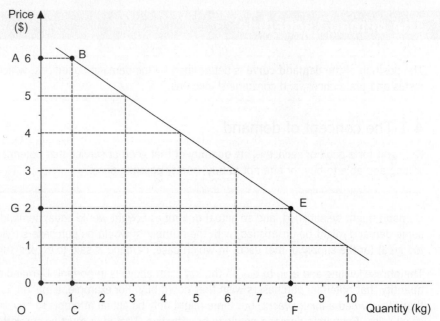

Figure 1 Graph of a demand schedule

The area of each rectangle in Figure 1 represents consumers' total money outlay at the price in question. For example, at a price of $6, demand would be 1 kilogram and total spending would be $6, represented by rectangle ABCO. Similarly, at a price of $2, demand would be 8 kilograms and the total spending of $16 is represented by rectangle GEFO.

EXAM FOCUS POINT

Sketching demand and/or supply curves may be a useful way of analysing an exam question.

In Figure 1, the demand curve happens to be a straight line. Straight line demand curves are often used as an illustration in economics because it is convenient to draw them this way. In reality, a demand curve is more likely to be a curved line convex to the origin. As you will be able to appreciate, such a demand curve means that there are progressively larger increases in quantity demanded as price falls (Figure 2). This happens because of the fall in marginal utility experienced as consumption of a good increases.

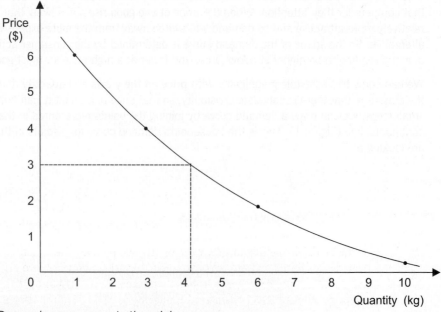

Figure 2 Demand curve convex to the origin

QUESTION

Refer to Figure 2. The price of the commodity is currently $3 per kilo, and demand is approximately 4 kilograms at that price. What would be the (approximate) demand for the commodity if the price fell to $2 per kilo? And what would be the demand if the price rose to $4 per kilo?

ANSWER

Demand rises to (approximately) 6 kilos at the reduced price of $2 per kilo. If the price rises to $4 per kilo, demand falls to (approximately) 3 kilos.

Note that changes in demand caused by changes in price are represented by movements **along the demand curve**, from one point to another. These changes in quantity demanded in response to a change in price are called **expansions** or **contractions** in demand. The price has changed, and the quantity demanded changes (prompting a movement along the curve), but **the demand curve itself remains the same**.

4.3 The market demand curve

In the example above, we have been looking at the demand schedule of a single household. A **market demand curve** is a similar curve, but it expresses the expected total quantity of the good that would be demanded by **all consumers together**, at any given price.

Market demand is the total quantity of a product that **all** purchasers would want to buy at each price level. A market demand schedule and a market demand curve are therefore simply the sum of all the individual demand schedules and demand curves put together. Market demand curves would be similar to those in Figures 1 and 2 – sloping downwards from left to right – but with quantities demanded (total market demand) being higher at each price level.

A **demand curve generally slopes down from left to right**.

(a)   As we saw earlier, the curve is downward sloping because progressively larger quantities are demanded as price falls.

(b)   A fall in the good's price means that it becomes cheaper both in relation to the household's income and also in relation to other (substitute) products. Therefore the overall size of the market for the good increases. The converse argument applies to an increase in prices; the size of the market will shrink as the good becomes more expensive.

Several factors influence the total market demand for a good. One of these factors is obviously its price, but there are other factors too, and to help you to appreciate some of these other factors, you need to recognise that households buy not just one good with their money but a whole range of goods and services.

Factors determining demand for a good

*   The **price** of the good
*   The size of **households' income** (income effect)
*   The price of other **substitute goods** (substitution effect)
*   **Tastes** and fashion
*   **Expectations** of future price changes
*   The **distribution of income** among households

The **income effect** reflects the impact of a price change on consumers' income. If the price of a good falls, all other things being equal, consumers become better off, as their real income has increased. Therefore they can afford to buy more of the good, following its fall in price.

The income effect can also be reinforced by the **substitution effect**. The substitution effect occurs when consumers buy more of one good and less of another good because of relative price changes between the two goods. For example, if two types of bread are considered substitutes, the price of bread 1 falls relative to the price of bread 2, then consumers will buy more of 1 than 2: they substitute bread 1 for bread 2.

A demand curve shows how the quantity demanded will change in response to a change in price **provided that all other conditions affecting demand are unchanged** – that is, provided that there is no change in the prices of other goods, tastes, expectations or the distribution of household income. (This assumption that 'all other things remain equal' is referred to as *ceteris paribus*.)

Make sure you remember this point about a movement along the demand curve reflecting a change in price when other factors are unchanged. We will return to it later to examine what happens to the demand curve when the other conditions affecting demand are changed.

4.4 Substitutes and complements

- Substitute goods are goods that are alternatives to each other, so that an **increase** in the demand for one is likely to cause a **decrease** in the demand for another. Switching demand from one good to another 'rival' good is **substitution**.

- Complements are goods that tend to be bought and used together, so that an **increase** in the demand for one is likely to cause an **increase** in the demand for the other.

A change in the price of one good will not necessarily change the demand for another good. For example, we would not expect an increase in the price of televisions to affect the demand for bread. However, there are goods for which the market demand is interconnected. These interrelated goods are referred to as either **substitutes** or **complements**.

Examples of substitute goods and services

- Rival brands of the same commodity, like Coca-Cola and Pepsi-Cola
- Tea and coffee
- Some different forms of entertainment

Substitution takes place when the price of one good rises relative to a substitute good.

By contrast, complements are connected in the sense that demand for one is likely to lead to demand for the other.

Examples of complements

- Cups and saucers
- Bread and butter
- Motor cars and the components and raw materials that go into their manufacture

QUESTION

Substitutes and complements

What might be the effect of an increase in the ownership of domestic deep freezers on the demand for perishable food products?

ANSWER

(a) Domestic deep freezers and perishable products are complements because people buy deep freezers to store perishable products.

(b) Perishable products are supplied either as fresh produce (for example, fresh meat and fresh vegetables) or as frozen produce, which can be kept for a short time in a refrigerator but for longer in a freezer. The demand for frozen produce will rise, while the demand for fresh produce will fall.

(c) Wider ownership of deep freezers is likely to increase bulk buying of perishable products. Suppliers can save some packaging costs, and can therefore offer lower prices for bulk purchases.

4.5 The price elasticity of demand

Elasticity, in general, refers to the relationship between two variables. Price elasticity of demand explains the relationship between **change in quantity demanded** and **changes in price**.

If prices went **up** by 10%, would the quantity demanded **fall** by the same percentage?

Price elasticity of demand (PED) is a measure of the extent of change in the market demand for a good in response to a change in its price. The demand for a good is said to be **inelastic** when changes in price have a relatively *small* effect on the quantity of the good demanded. The demand for a good is said to be **elastic** when changes in price have a relatively *large* effect on the quantity of a good demanded. 'Relatively small' and 'relatively large' here equate to 'less than 1' and 'greater than 1' respectively.

The coefficient of PED is measured as:

$$\frac{\text{Percentage change in quantity demanded}}{\text{Percentage change in price}}$$

Since demand usually increases when the price falls, and decreases when the price rises, elasticity has a negative value. **However, it is usual to ignore the minus sign**, and just describe the absolute value of the coefficient. Inelastic demand has a coefficient of less than 1, while elastic demand is greater than 1.

This can be expressed as:

$$\frac{\frac{\Delta Q}{Q} \times 100}{\frac{\Delta P}{P} \times 100}$$

where Δ is the symbol for 'change in'
Q is the quantity demanded of the good
P is the price of the good

If we are measuring the responsiveness of demand to a large change in price, we can measure elasticity between two points on the demand curve, and the resulting measure is called the **arc elasticity of demand**. We calculate the arc elasticity of demand from the percentage change in quantity relative to **average** quantity for the relevant range of output and from the percentage price change relative to the **average** of the corresponding price range.

If we wish to measure the responsiveness of demand at one particular point in the demand curve, we can calculate a **point elasticity of demand**, without averaging price and quantity over a range. In doing so, it is convenient to assume that the demand curve is a straight line unless told otherwise.

4.6 Example: arc elasticity of demand

The price of a good is $1.20 per unit and annual demand is 800,000 units. Market research indicates that an increase in price of 10 cents per unit will result in a fall in annual demand of 70,000 units.

What is the price elasticity of demand measuring the responsiveness of demand over this range of price increase?

Solution

Annual demand at $1.20 per unit is 800,000 units.
Annual demand at $1.30 per unit is 730,000 units.
Average quantity over the range is 765,000 units.

Average price is $1.25.

% change in demand $\dfrac{70,000}{765,000} \times 100\% = 9.15\%$

% change in price $\dfrac{10c}{125c} \times 100\% = 8\%$

Price elasticity of demand $= \dfrac{-9.15}{8} = -1.14$

Ignoring the minus sign, the arc elasticity is 1.14.

The demand for this good, over the range of annual demand 730,000 to 800,000 units, is **elastic** because the price elasticity of demand is greater than 1. Now try the following exercise yourself.

QUESTION   Arc price elasticity of demand

If the price per unit of X rises from $1.40 to $1.60, it is expected that monthly demand will fall from 220,000 units to 200,000 units.

What is the arc price elasticity of demand over these ranges of price and output?

ANSWER

Monthly demand at $1.40 per unit = 220,000 units
Monthly demand at $1.60 per unit = 200,000 units
Average quantity = 210,000 units
Average price = $1.50

% change in demand $\dfrac{20,000}{210,000} \times 100\% = 9.52\%$

% change in price $\dfrac{20}{150} \times 100\% = 13.33\%$

Arc price elasticity of demand $= \dfrac{-9.52}{13.33} = -0.71\%$

Ignoring the minus sign, the arc elasticity is 0.71.

Demand is **inelastic** over the demand range considered, because the price elasticity of demand (ignoring the minus sign) is less than 1.

4.7 Example: point elasticity of demand

The price of a good is $1.20 per unit and annual demand is 800,000. Market research indicates that an increase in price of 10 cents per unit will result in a fall in annual demand for the good of 70,000 units.

Required

Calculate the elasticity of demand at the current price of $1.20.

Solution

We are asked to calculate the elasticity at a particular price. We assume that the demand curve is a straight line.

At a price of $1.20, annual demand is 800,000 units. For a price rise:

% change in demand $\qquad \dfrac{70,000}{800,000} \times 100\% = 8.75\%$ (fall)

% change in price $\qquad \dfrac{10c}{120c} \times 100\% = 8.33\%$ (rise)

Price elasticity of demand at price $1.20 = $\qquad \dfrac{-8.75}{8.33} = -1.05$

Ignoring the minus sign, the price elasticity at this point is 1.05. Demand is **elastic** at this point, because the elasticity is greater than 1.

QUESTION
Point price elasticity of demand

If the price per unit of x rises from $1.40 to $1.60, it is expected that monthly demand will fall from 220,000 units to 200,000 units.

What is the point price elasticity of demand when the price is $1.40?

ANSWER

We assume that the demand curve is a straight line.

At a price of $1.40, demand is 220,000 units.

For a price rise of 20 cents to $1.60:

% change in demand $\qquad \dfrac{20,000}{220,000} \times 100\% = 9.09\%$ (fall)

% change in price $\qquad \dfrac{20c}{140c} \times 100\% = 14.29\%$ (rise)

Price elasticity of demand = $\qquad \dfrac{9.09}{-14.29} = -0.64$

or 0.64 ignoring the minus sign.

Demand is **inelastic** at this point, because it is less than 1.

QUESTION
Range of elasticity

A shop sells 100 shirts each month at a price of $20. When the price is increased to $24, the total sales revenue rises by 14%. Within which range does the price elasticity of demand lie?

A Under 0.15
B Greater than 0.15 and less than 0.5
C Greater than 0.5 and less than 1.0
D Greater than 1.0

ANSWER

B   Total revenue of $20 = 100 × $20 = $2,000
     Total revenue at $24 = $2,000 × 1.14 = $2,280
     Number sold at $24 = $2,280 ÷ 24 = 95

Price elasticity of demand

Point method Arc method

$$\frac{\frac{5}{100} \times 100}{\frac{4}{20} \times 100} = \frac{5\%}{20\%} = 0.25 \qquad \frac{\frac{5}{97\frac{1}{2}} \times 100}{\frac{4}{22} \times 100} = \frac{5.13\%}{18.2\%} = 0.28$$

4.8 Income elasticity of demand

> **Income elasticity of demand** measures the responsiveness of demand to changes in household income.
> **Cross elasticity of demand** is determined by the availability of substitute (competitors') products.

It is possible to construct other measures of elasticity than price elasticity, and an important one which you need to know about is **income elasticity of demand**. The income elasticity of demand for a good indicates the responsiveness of demand to changes in **household incomes**.

When household income rises people will not only increase their demand for existing goods but also start to demand new goods which they could not previously afford.

$$\text{Income elasticity of demand} = \frac{\% \text{ change in quantity demanded}}{\% \text{ change in income}}$$

(a)   Demand for a good is **income elastic** if income elasticity is greater than 1; in other words, if quantity demanded rises by a larger percentage than the rise in income. For example, if the demand for compact discs will rise by 10% if household income rises by 7%, we would say that the demand for compact discs is income elastic.

(b)   Demand for a good is **income inelastic** if income elasticity is between 0 and 1, and the quantity demanded rises less than the proportionate increase in income. For example, if the demand for books rises by 6% if household income rises by 10%, we would say that the demand for books is income inelastic.

The change in quantity demanded takes the form of a **shift in the position of the demand curve**, not a movement along it, since it is **not** stimulated by a change in price.

Goods whose income elasticity of demand is positive are said to be **normal goods**, meaning that demand for them will rise when household income rises. If income elasticity is **negative**, the commodity is called an **inferior good** since demand for it falls as income rises.

Inferiority in this sense is an observable fact about the consumer's demand preferences, rather than a statement about the quality of the good itself.

Inter-city bus travel is an example of an inferior good. Bus travel is cheaper than air or rail travel, but takes longer. When consumers have limited income, they are prepared to forgo the increased time taken to travel in return for the cheaper cost. However, as their income increases, they will choose the more rapid modes of transport over the slower, albeit cheaper, bus travel. Therefore demand for bus travel will fall as income rises.

Income elasticity of demand can be summarised as follows.

Elasticity	Value	Type of good	Example
Negative	–ve	Inferior	Inter-city bus travel
Inelastic	0 – 1	Necessity	Basic food stuffs
Elastic	> 1	Luxury	Yachts, sports cars

For most commodities, an increase in income will increase demand. The exact effect on demand will depend on the type of product. For example, the demand for some products like bread will not increase much as= income rises. Therefore, bread has a low income elasticity of demand. In contrast, the demand for luxuries increases rapidly as income rises and luxury goods therefore have a high income elasticity of demand.

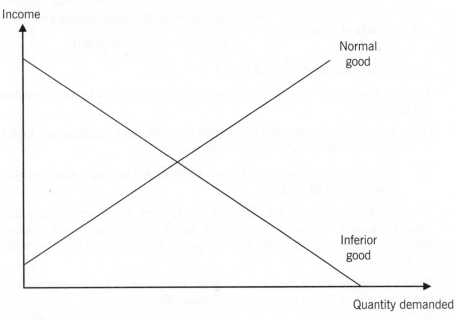

Figure 3 Demand curves for normal and inferior goods

QUESTION

Elasticity of demand and supply

What will be the effect on price, quantity demanded and quantity supplied of luxury sports cars, given a significant reduction in income tax?

ANSWER

The demand curve for sports cars will shift to the right. Price, quantity demanded and quantity supplied will all go up.

The effect of a cut in income tax is to leave households with more to spend. Sports cars are a luxury good, so their income elasticity of demand is likely to be quite high. The percentage increase in demand for the cars is therefore likely to be greater than the percentage increase in after-tax household income.

We can illustrate the change diagrammatically:

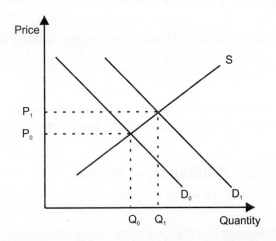

The shift in the demand curve (from D_0 to D_1) means that the equilibrium quantity demanded and supplied shifts from Q_0 to Q_1 and the equilibrium price increases from P_0 to P_1.

4.9 Cross elasticity of demand

Cross elasticity of demand is the responsiveness of quantity demanded for one good following a change in price of another good.

$$\text{Cross elasticity of demand} = \frac{\% \text{ change in quantity demanded of good A} *}{\% \text{ change in the price of good B}}$$

*(assuming no change in the price of A)

The cross elasticity of demand depends upon the degree to which goods are **substitutes or complements**.

(a)   If the two goods are **substitutes, cross elasticity will be positive** and a fall in the price of one will reduce the amount demanded of the other.

(b)   If the goods are **complements, cross elasticity will be negative** and a fall in the price of one will raise demand for the other.

For example, assume bread and butter are complements. If the price of bread increases, demand for bread and then, in turn, butter will decrease. So, as a fraction, we have a negative value (quantity of butter demanded) over a positive value (increase in price) meaning the cross elasticity of demand is negative.

Cross elasticity involves a comparison between two products. The concept is a useful one in the context of considering substitutes and complementary products.

The value of the cross-elasticity of demand shows the strength of the relationship between the two goods. Indices tending towards 1 or −1 indicate a strong relationship; statistics tending towards zero indicate a weak relationship.

Cross-elasticity	Value	Example
Perfect complements	−1	
Complements	−ve	Bread and butter
Unrelated products	0	Bread and cars
Substitutes	+ve	White bread and brown bread
Perfect substitutes	+1	

EXAM FOCUS POINT

Make sure you know how to calculate the different types of elasticity, and how to distinguish between complements and substitutes.

Remember that cross elasticity of demand (like other measures of elasticity) measures the **percentage** change in the quantity demanded for one good, in response to the **percentage** change in the price of another.

4.10 Market demand and the distribution of income

Market demand for a good is influenced by the way in which the national income is shared among households.

In a country with many rich and many poor households and few middle income ones, we might expect a relatively large demand for luxury cars and yachts and also for bread and potatoes. In a country with many middle-income households, we might expect high demand for medium-sized cars and TV sets, and other middle income goods.

QUESTION

What do you think might be the demand for swimming pools amongst a population of five households enjoying total annual income of $1m, if the distribution of income is either as under assumption 1 or as under assumption 2?

	Annual income	
	Assumption 1	Assumption 2
	$	$
Household 1	950,000	200,000
Household 2	12,500	200,000
Household 3	12,500	200,000
Household 4	12,500	200,000
Household 5	12,500	200,000

ANSWER

Under assumption 1, the demand for swimming pools will be confined to household 1. Even if this household owns three or four properties, the demand for swimming pools is likely to be less than under assumption 2, where potentially all five households might want one.

4.11 Shifts of the demand curve

So far, we have been looking at the way a change in price affects the quantity demanded, depicted as a movement **along** the demand curve. However, when there is a **change in the conditions of demand**, the quantity demanded will change even if price remains constant. In this case, there will be a different price/quantity demand schedule and so **a different demand curve**. We refer to such a change as a **shift of the demand curve**.

Figure 4 depicts a rise in demand at each price level, with the demand curve shifting to the right, from D_0 to D_1. For example, at price P_1, demand for the good would rise from X to Y. This shift could be caused by any of the following **conditions of demand**.

- A rise in **household income** (including a reduction in direct taxes)
- A rise in the price of **substitutes**
- A fall in the price of **complements**
- A change in **tastes** towards this product
- An **expected rise** in the price of the product
- An **increase** in population

Figure 4 shows an outward shift in the demand curve, but conversely a fall in demand at each price level would be represented by a shift in the opposite direction: to the **left** of the demand curve. Such a shift may be caused by the opposite of the conditions of demand shown above.

4.12 Demand, fashion and expectations

A change in fashion or tastes will also alter the demand for a product. For example, if it becomes fashionable for middle-class households in the UK to drink wine with their meals, expenditure on wine will increase. There may be passing 'crazes', such as roller blades or skateboards. And tastes can be affected by advertisers and suppliers trying to 'create' demand for their products. However, the effect of a product becoming fashionable will be that demand for it rises without its price having to be reduced.

If consumers believe that prices will rise, or that shortages will occur, they may attempt to stock up on the product before these changes occur. Again, this could lead to increases in demand, despite the price of the good remaining unchanged.

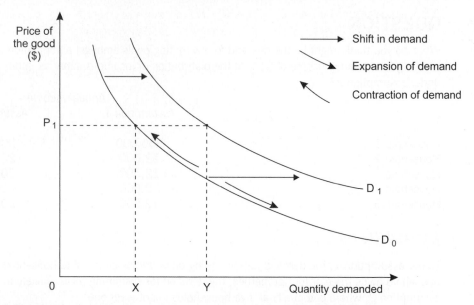

Figure 4 Changes in quantity demanded and outward shift of the demand curve

EXAM FOCUS POINT

The difference between a change in demand and a shift of the demand curve is of fundamental importance. Remember:

(a) Movements along a demand curve (contractions or expansions) for a good are caused solely by changes in its price.

(b) Variations in the conditions of demand create shifts in the demand curve.

QUESTION

Substitutes and complements

In County X, a recent fall in the price of DVDs has seen demand for DVDs increase significantly. However, cinema operators have reported a decline in customer numbers, which they believe is due to people preferring to buy DVDs to watch rather than going to the cinema.

What effect is the fall in the price of DVDs likely to have on the demand curves for:

(a) DVD players?
(b) Cinema tickets?

ANSWER

(a) There is likely to have been an outward shift in the demand curve for DVD players. DVD players are complements to the DVDs themselves because people will need to buy the DVD players in order to watch their DVDs. So, the increased demand for DVDs will lead to an increase in demand for DVD players even though their price may be unchanged. This results in an **outward shift** in their demand curve (an expansion of demand).

(b) There is likely to be an inward shift in the demand curve for cinema tickets (a contraction of demand). Even though the price of cinema tickets has not changed, people are demanding less of them because they are choosing to watch DVDs instead. Cinema tickets are a substitute product to DVDs, and a fall in the price of a substitute leads to an inward shift of the demand curve for a product.

5 The supply schedule

The **supply curve** shows the quantity of a good which would be supplied by producers at a given price.

5.1 The concept of supply

Supply refers to the quantity of a good that existing suppliers or would-be suppliers would want to produce for the market at a given price.

As with demand, supply relates to a period of time – for example, we might refer to an annual rate of supply or to a monthly rate.

The quantity of a good supplied to a market varies up or down for two reasons.

(a)   Existing suppliers may increase or reduce their output quantities.

(b)   Firms may stop production altogether and leave the market, or new firms may enter the market and start to produce the good.

If the quantity that firms want to produce at a given price exceeds the quantity that households (consumers) would demand, there will be an **excess of supply**, with firms competing to win what sales demand there is. Oversupply and competition would then be expected to result in price competitiveness and **a fall in prices**.

As with demand, a distinction needs to be made.

(a)   An individual firm's supply schedule is the quantity of the good that the individual firm would want to supply to the market at any given price.

(b)   Market supply is the total quantity of the good that all firms in the market would want to supply at a given price.

5.2 The supply curve

A **supply schedule** and **supply curve** can be created both for an individual supplier and for all firms which produce the good.

A supply curve is constructed in a similar manner to a demand curve (from a schedule of quantities supplied at different prices) but shows the quantity suppliers are willing to produce at different price levels. It is an **upward sloping curve from left to right**, because greater quantities will be supplied at higher prices.

We usually assume that suppliers aim to maximise their profits, and the upward slope of the supply curve reflects this desire to make profit (ie they are prepared to supply more of something, the higher the price that is being paid for it).

5.3 Short run supply curve

Following the assumption that suppliers are profit maximisers, they will produce at the point where marginal costs equals marginal revenue. For now, it is only necessary to note that producing at the level of output where marginal revenue equals marginal cost is the profit-maximising position for a firm.

Therefore, the amount a firm will supply will be affected by the costs of production (marginal and average costs).

We will look at supply in both the short run and the long run.

Short run supply curve

A firm's short run average cost curve is U shaped, with marginal cost (MC) rising and falling more steeply than average cost (AC).

If we assume there is a single, constant selling price for all firms, then a firm's average revenue (AR) and marginal revenue (MR) will be identical. We can show this as Price = Average Revenue = Marginal Revenue.

We know that the firm will supply where MC = MR in order to maximise profit. Consequently, the firm's chosen levels of output (forming its supply curve) are as shown in Figure 5 below.

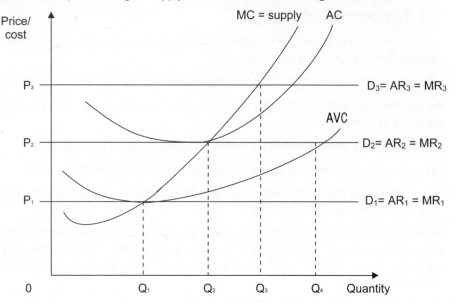

Figure 5 Short run supply curve

We can see that at price P_1 the firm supplies Q_1 output, because MC = MR_1. When price rises to P_2, the output increases to Q_2 and so on, provided that the firm has the capacity to increase its sales output. In these conditions, the firm's **marginal cost curve becomes its supply curve**.

However, remember there is a minimum price level below which a firm will not supply. In the short run, a firm will only continue to supply if the selling price covers all its **variable costs**.

At P_2 and Q_4, the supplier's AR will be less than its AC but greater than its average variable cost (AVC). Because AC > AR the firm makes a loss, but some of its fixed costs are still paid for, because AR > AVC.

If the firm had stopped producing altogether, it would still incur its fixed costs even though there will be no sales income to pay for any of these fixed costs. So it would have been financially worse off than it was by producing at a level where AR > AVC, even though it made a loss at this point.

Therefore, in the short run, the firm's **supply curve** is represented by the part of its **marginal cost curve** shown **above** the **average variable cost curve (AVC)**.

EXAM FOCUS POINT

It is important that you remember that a firm will continue to produce in the short run if price is greater than average variable costs, even if price is less than average total costs.

Cost-plus pricing

The idea of the marginal cost curve representing the supply curve is the traditional theory of a firm's short run supply curve. However, more recent theories of the firm incorporate a cost-plus pricing approach.

Under a cost-plus pricing approach, a firm adds a profit margin to its average cost at any level of output in order to establish its selling price. This alternative theory produces a horizontal supply curve.

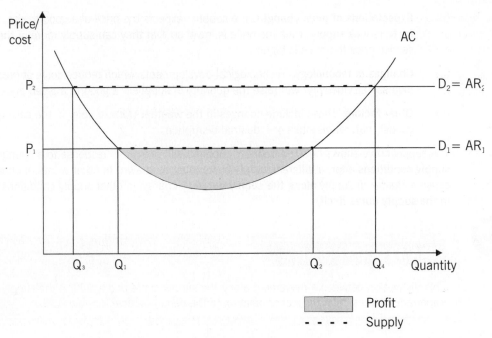

Figure 6 Short run supply curves based on cost-plus pricing

A rational (profit maximising, or loss minimising) firm will only supply where AR > AC. So the minimum and maximum levels of output occur at Q_1 and Q_2 respectively, at price P_1; that is, where AR crosses the AC curve (AC = AR).

Changes in the market price will lead to changes in output. (Note, we are still assuming a single, constant selling price for all firms in the industry.) A higher price (P_2) will lead to a new supply curve, between Q_3 and Q_4.

5.4 Long run supply curve

In traditional theory, the **marginal cost curve remains the supply curve** in the long run. However, it may no longer be upward sloping.

The supply curve was upward sloping in the short run because of the impact of diminishing returns on the marginal cost curve. However, this is only a short run phenomenon, because the constraint of one factor of production being fixed is only a short run condition.

In the long run, the supply curve could still be upward sloping (if the firm suffers from diseconomies of scale) but it could equally be downward sloping to the right if the firm benefits from economies of scale. The curve could even be horizontal if the firm's marginal cost remained constant at all levels of output.

The full cost-plus pricing theory also retains a horizontal supply curve in the long run. The level of the curve relative to the short run will depend on whether the firm experiences any economies or diseconomies of scale. However, the maximum and minimum output levels will still be where AC = AR.

5.5 Factors influencing the supply quantity

The quantity supplied of a good depends, as you might expect, on prices and costs. More specifically, it depends on the following factors.

(a)　The **costs of making the good**. These include raw materials costs, which ultimately depend on the prices of factors of production (wages, interest rates, land rents and profit expectations).

(b)　The **prices of other goods**. When a supplier can switch readily from supplying one good to another, the goods concerned are called **substitutes in supply**. An increase in the price of one such good would make the supply of another good whose price does not rise less attractive to suppliers. When a production process has two or more distinct and separate outputs, the goods produced are known as **goods in joint supply** or **complements in production**. Goods in joint supply include, for example, meat and hides. If the price of beef rises, more will be supplied and there will be an accompanying increase in the supply of cow hide.

(c)   **Expectations of price changes**. If a supplier expects the price of a good to rise, they are likely to try to reduce supply while the price is lower so that they can supply more of their product or service once the price is higher.

(d)   **Changes in technology**. Technological developments which reduce costs of production (and increase productivity) will raise the quantity of supply of a good at a given price.

(e)   **Other factors**. These include changes in the weather (for example, in the case of agricultural goods), natural disasters or industrial disruption.

The supply curve shows how the quantity supplied will change in response to a change in price. If **supply conditions** alter, a different supply curve must be drawn. In other words, a change in price will cause a change in supply **along the supply curve**. A change in other supply conditions will cause a **shift in the supply curve itself**.

> ### EXAM FOCUS POINT
>
> This distinction between a movement along the supply curve and a shift in the supply curve is just as important as the similar distinction relating to the demand curve.

5.6 Shifts of the market supply curve

The **market supply curve** is the aggregate of all the supply curves of individual firms in the market. A shift of the market supply curve occurs when supply conditions (other than the price of the good itself) change. Figure 7 shows a shift in the supply curve from S_0 to S_1. A **rightward** (or **downward**) shift of the curve shows an expansion of supply and may be caused by the factors below.

(a)   A fall in the cost of factors of production, for example a reduction in the cost of raw material inputs

(b)   A fall in the price of other goods; the production of other goods becomes relatively less attractive as their price falls and firms are therefore likely to shift resources away from the goods whose price is falling and into the production of higher priced goods that offer increased profits. We therefore expect that (*ceteris paribus*) the supply of one good will rise as the prices of other goods fall (and vice versa).

(c)   Technological progress, which reduces unit costs and also increases production capabilities

(d)   Improvements in productivity or more efficient use of existing factors of production, which again will reduce unit cost

A shift of the supply curve is the result of changes in costs, either in absolute terms or relative to the costs of other goods. If the price of the good is P_1, suppliers would be willing to increase supply from Q_0 to Q_1 under the new supply conditions (Figure 7).

Conversely, we might see a **leftward** (or **upward**) shift in the supply curve if the cost of supply increases. This would mean that at the existing price, a firm's output will decrease and less will be supplied.

This is also illustrated on Figure 7: at price P_1, the quantity supplied now falls from Q_0 to Q_2, as the supply curve shifts from S_0 to S_2.

In order for the supplier to restore output levels to the original Q_0, price would have to increase to P_2.

An upward (leftward) shift ($S_0 \rightarrow S_2$) in supply could be caused by:

(a)   An increase in the cost of factors of production

(b)   A rise in the price of other goods which would make them relatively more attractive to the producer

(c)   An increase in indirect taxes, or a reduction in a subsidy, which would make supply at existing prices less profitable

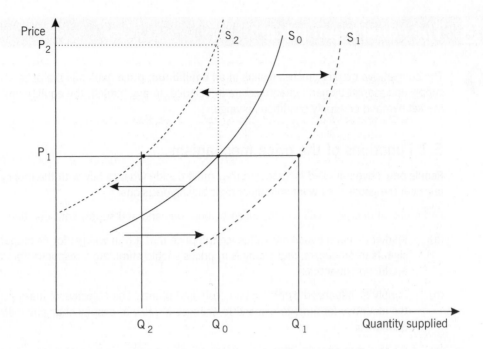

Figure 7 Shifts in the supply curve

We need to distinguish between short run and long run responses of both supply and demand. **In the short run** both supply and demand are **relatively unresponsive** to changes in price compared with the **long run**.

(a)   **In the case of supply**, changes in the quantity of a good supplied often require the laying off or hiring of new workers, or the installation of new machinery. All of these changes, brought about by management decisions, take some time to implement.

(b)   **In the case of demand**, it takes time for consumers to adjust their buying patterns, although demand will often respond more rapidly than supply to changes in price or other demand conditions.

In some markets, responses to changes in price are relatively rapid. In others, response times are much longer. In stock markets for example, the supply and demand for company shares respond very rapidly to price changes, whereas in the markets for fuel oils or agrichemicals response times are much longer.

QUESTION

Quantity supplied

What effect will higher grain prices have on the supply curve of a cereal manufacturer who makes cereals from grain?

ANSWER

The higher price of grain will cause the supply curve to shift leftwards (or upwards). The increase in grain prices increase the cereal manufacturer's production costs, making supply at existing prices less profitable.

6 The equilibrium price

The competitive market process results in an **equilibrium price**, which is the price at which market supply and market demand quantities are in balance. In any market, the equilibrium price will change if market demand or supply conditions change.

6.1 Functions of the price mechanism

People only have a limited income and they must decide what to buy with the money they have. The prices of the goods they want will affect their buying decisions.

Firms' output decisions will be influenced by both demand and supply considerations.

(a) Market demand conditions influence the price that a firm will get for its output. Prices act as **signals** to producers, and changes in prices should stimulate a response from a firm to change its production quantities.

(b) Supply is influenced by production costs and profits. The objective of maximising profits provides the **incentive** for firms to respond to changes in price or cost by changing their production quantities.

(c) When a firm operates efficiently, responding to changes in market prices and controlling its costs, it is **rewarded** with profit.

Decisions by firms about what industry to operate in and what markets to produce for will be influenced by the prices obtainable. Although some firms have been established in one industry for many years, others are continually opening up, closing down or switching to new industries and new markets. Over time, firms in an industry might also increase or reduce the volume of goods they sell.

Sometimes, however, price will not represent the economic cost of a good or service. For example, price may be higher than costs due to **taxes** imposed by government. The sales price of cigarettes and alcohol is much higher than the cost of producing them, due to the imposition of taxes and duty.

By contrast, a **subsidy** may bring about an artificially low price.

However, in the main, we will be looking at price as an indicator of the exchange value of goods and services, as determined by the market forces of supply and demand.

6.2 The price mechanism and the equilibrium price

The **price mechanism** brings demand and supply into equilibrium, and the **equilibrium price** for a good is the price at which the volume demanded by consumers and the volume that firms would be willing to supply is the same. This is also known as the **market clearing price**, since at this price there will be neither surplus nor shortage in the market.

The way demand and supply interact to come to the equilibrium price can be illustrated by drawing the market demand curve and the market supply curve on the same graph (Figure 8).

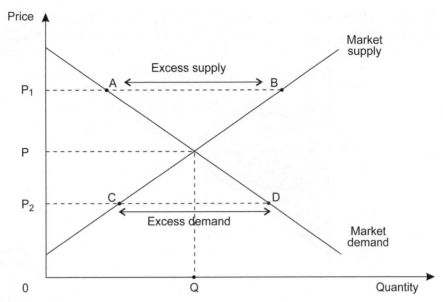

Figure 8 Market equilibrium

Figure 8 shows the planned (or *ex ante*) demand and planned supply at a set of prices.

At price P_1 in Figure 8, suppliers want to produce a greater quantity than the market demands, meaning that there is excess supply, equal to the distance AB. Suppliers would react as the stock of unsold goods accumulates.

(a)   They would cut down the current level of production in order to sell unwanted inventories.

(b)   They would also reduce prices in order to encourage sales.

The opposite will happen at price P_2 where there is an excess of demand over supply shown by the distance CD. Supply and price would increase. Faced with an excess of demand, manufacturers would be able to raise their prices. This would make supplying the good more profitable and supply would increase.

At price P the amount that sellers are willing and able to supply is equal to the amount that customers are willing and able to buy. Consumers will be willing to spend a total of (P × Q) on buying Q units of the product, and suppliers will be willing to supply Q units to earn revenue of (P × Q). P is the **equilibrium price**.

The forces of supply and demand push a market to its equilibrium price and quantity. Note carefully the following key points.

(a)   If there is no change in conditions of supply or demand, the **equilibrium price will prevail** in the market and will remain stable.

(b)   If price is not at the equilibrium, the market is in **disequilibrium** and supply and demand will push prices towards the equilibrium price.

(c)   In any market there will only be one equilibrium position where the market is cleared.

(d)   Shifts in the supply curve or demand curve will change the equilibrium price (and the quantity traded).

6.3 Consumer surplus and producer surplus

The **marginal utility** derived by different consumers from consumption of a unit quantity of a good will vary and so, therefore, will the price they would offer to buy that good. Because of this, consumers may be able to buy the good at a prevailing market price **lower than the price they were prepared to pay**. You will be familiar with this idea from your own experience, where you would have been prepared to pay a certain amount for a holiday or a specific item of clothing, for example, but you have been able to buy them at a lower price than you had anticipated. This situation (where the market price is lower than the price the consumer was prepared to pay) is called a **consumer surplus**, and it can be represented as shown in Figure 9.

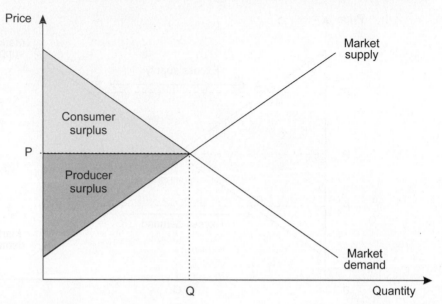

Figure 9 Consumer surplus and producer surplus

In the same way that consumers may be able to buy a good for less than they would be prepared to pay, so producers may be able to sell a good at a higher price than they would have accepted.

In this case, there is a producer surplus. Figure 9 illustrates this. The area of producer surplus on the graph represents the suppliers in the market who would be prepared to sell quantities of the good at less than the market price.

7 Demand and supply analysis

The effects of **demand and supply conditions** on markets can be analysed by studying the behaviour of both demand and supply curves.

7.1 Case example

In this section we look at a case example involving the analysis of demand and supply conditions. We will examine the likely effects on the price and quantity sold of secondhand cars in the event of:

(a)   A large increase in petrol prices
(b)   A big increase in the price of new cars
(c)   A massive investment in public transport

7.2 Analysis

Petrol and cars are **complementary** products; hence, any change in the market for petrol (part (a) of this case example) would be expected to affect the market for secondhand cars. The demand for petrol, however, is likely to be relatively unresponsive to a change in price, so a change in price will only have a small impact on the quantity demanded. Consequently, a major change in its price will be necessary to affect the demand for any complementary product. Figure 10 assumes that there is a large increase in the price of fuel (petrol) as stated above.

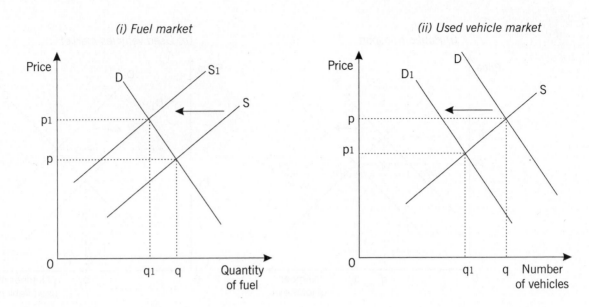

Figure 10

In this instance, we have assumed that the rise in the price of fuel results from a change in the conditions of supply. This is the basis of the new supply curve S_1 shifting to the left of the existing one (Figure 10 (i)). A rise in the price of fuel is a rise in the cost of owning and running a car. There will thus be a fall in the demand for secondhand cars and a fall in the price and quantity sold (Figure 10 (ii)).

Part (b) of this case example involves new vehicles and used vehicles as **substitute** products.

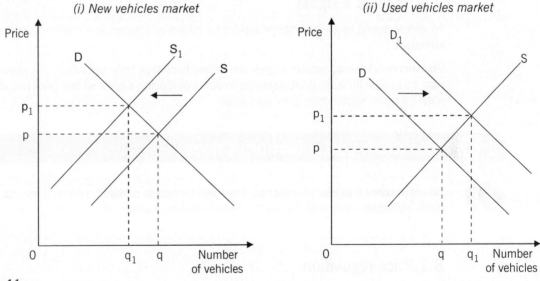

Figure 11

It is assumed that the increase in the price of new cars is the result of a major increase in supply costs. The rise in price causes a switch of demand into secondhand vehicles, so pushing up their price and leading to an increase in the number sold (Figure 11(ii)).

The increased price of new vehicles could alternatively result from an increase in the demand for them.

Case example, part (c) involves another 'product' which is in competition with secondhand cars. If there is a reduction in the price of public transport services following the outward shift in supply, this could be the result (Figure 12).

(i) Public transport

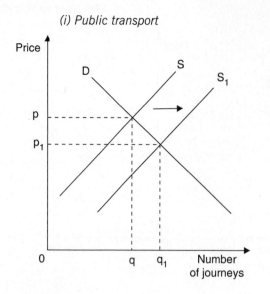

(ii) Used vehicles market

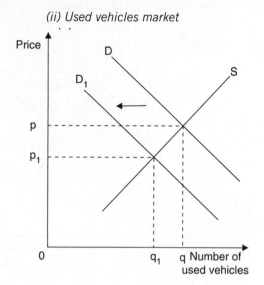

Figure 12

In part (c) of our case example, the fall in public transport prices leads to an expansion in demand for public transport (Figure 12(i)) while the demand for secondhand cars falls (with a new demand line D_1 in Figure 12(ii)) together with a fall in price. However, the relationship between public transport and the market for secondhand cars is likely to be a highly complex and indeterminate one. Thus, people might make greater use of public transport while the ownership of cars (including secondhand cars) could continue to increase.

7.3 Price as a signal

As well as acting as an information system for buyers and sellers in a market, price can also act as a **stimulant**.

Price information may prompt buyers and sellers to change their behaviour. For example, a price rise may encourage firms to divert resources towards producing a good whose price has risen, in order to obtain a better reward from their resources.

8 Maximum and minimum prices

Where **maximum prices** are imposed, there will be **excess demand**: rationing may be necessary, and black marketeers may seek to operate. Where **minimum prices** are imposed, producers will make **excess supply**.

8.1 Price regulation

The regulation of prices provides an illustration of how demand and supply analysis can be applied. Governments might try to control prices in two ways.

(a) They might set a **maximum price** (or **price ceiling**) for a good, perhaps as part of an anti-inflationary economic policy.

(b) They might set a **minimum price** (or **price floor**) for a good. The EU Common Agricultural Policy (CAP) is an example of a price floor, aimed to ensure that farmers receive at least the minimum prices for their produce.

8.2 Maximum prices

The Government may try to prevent prices of goods rising by establishing a price ceiling **below** the equilibrium price. (Note: the price ceiling has to be below the equilibrium price. If the price ceiling is higher than the equilibrium price, setting a price ceiling will have no effect at all on the operation of market forces. Make sure that you understand why this is so.)

If the maximum price M is lower than what the equilibrium price would be, there will be an excess of demand over supply (Figure 13). The low price attracts customers, but deters suppliers. Because the price ceiling M is below the equilibrium price P, producers will reduce the quantity of goods supplied to the marketplace from Q to A. However, the quantity demanded will increase from Q to B because of the fall in price. The excess quantity demanded is AB.

Because the market is now in disequilibrium, the limited supply has to be allocated by a means other than price.

To prevent an unfair allocation of the units of the good that are available, the Government might have to introduce **rationing** (as with petrol coupons) or a **waiting list** (as for local authority housing). Rationing and **black marketeers** tend to go together. In Figure 13 consumers demand quantity B but can only get A. However, for quantity A they are prepared to pay price Z, which is well above the official price M. The black marketeers step in to exploit the gap. The commodity may be sold on ration at the official price M, but black marketeers may sell illicit production at price Z.

Note also that maximum prices can lead to a misallocation of resources. Producers will reduce output of the products subject to price controls because they are now relatively less profitable than those products not subject to price controls.

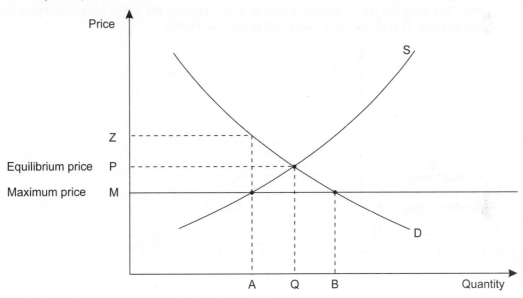

Figure 13 Maximum price below equilibrium price

QUESTION

Equilibrium

Supply of and demand for good Q are initially in equilibrium as shown in the diagram below.

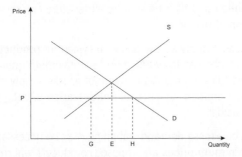

The Government introduces a maximum price P. What effect will this have on the quantity of good Q purchased?

A   It will rise from G to E   C   It will fall from H to G
B   It will rise from E to H   D   It will fall from E to G

ANSWER

D   The initial equilibrium quantity is E (where supply and demand curves intersect). Quantity demanded at the controlled price P will be H. However, only quantity G will be supplied and purchases will therefore be limited to this amount. Therefore, the quantity purchased will fall from E to G due to the shortage of supply available.

8.3 Minimum prices

Minimum price legislation aims to ensure that suppliers earn at least the minimum price (or floor price) for each unit of output they sell.

If the minimum price is set below the market equilibrium there is no effect. But if it is set above the market price, it will cause an excess supply (see surplus 'AB' in Figure 14). This has been a recurring problem in Europe, where minimum prices guaranteed by agricultural subsidies have resulted in the 'butter mountains' and 'wine lakes' of past years.

In Figure 14, the minimum price Z is set above the equilibrium price P. The quantity demanded falls from Q to A but the quantity supplied increases to B because the higher price encourages suppliers to supply more. There is excess supply equal to the quantity AB.

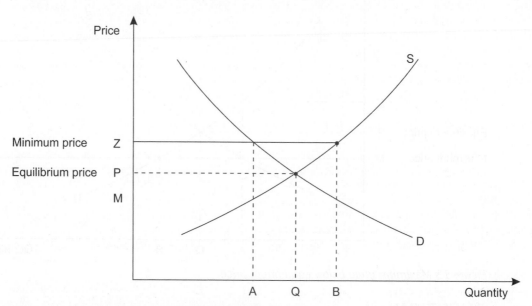

Figure 14 Minimum price above equilibrium price

The problem with floor prices is that more of the good will be produced than can be sold at the minimum price, and so surplus quantities will build up, which have to be either stored or destroyed. Either way, the floor prices lead to a misallocation of resources.

To try to prevent oversupply and 'dumping' of excess supply at low prices, a system of **production quotas** might be introduced whereby each supplier is only allowed to produce up to a maximum quantity and no more. For some types of produce, the EU tried to overcome the problem of excess supply by imposing quotas on farmers. From 1992, the EU Common Agricultural Policy started to oblige farmers to take land out of production: this is called 'set-aside'.

Where **maximum prices** are imposed, there will be **excess demand**: rationing may be necessary, and black marketeers may seek to operate. Where **minimum prices** are imposed, producers will make **excess supply**.

QUESTION

What are the economic impacts of the Common Agricultural Policy (CAP) and other floor price schemes?

ANSWER

CAP guarantees a minimum price above the market equilibrium price. Therefore it encourages an excess of supply over demand, creating surplus production of agricultural goods.

However, it provides price and income stability for the farmers producing the goods.

8.4 Minimum wages

A minimum wage is an application of floor pricing in the labour market.

The UK now has minimum wage legislation. The purpose of a minimum wage is to ensure that low-paid workers earn enough to have an acceptable standard of living. If a minimum wage is enforced by legislation (a **statutory minimum wage**), or negotiated nationally for an industry by a trade union, the minimum wage will probably be above the current wage level for the jobs concerned. This would have two consequences.

- To raise wage levels for workers employed to a level above the 'equilibrium' wage rate
- To reduce the demand for labour and so cause job losses

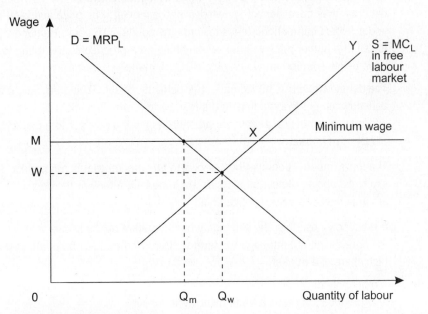

Figure 15 Minimum wage

Without a minimum wage, Q_w workers would be employed at wage rate W (Figure 15).

QUESTION

By reference to Figure 15, work out what happens when a minimum wage M, higher than the existing rate W, is imposed.

ANSWER

The supply curve for labour is now the line MXY.

Demand for labour from employers will fall to Q_m, but Q_m workers will at least earn a higher wage.

However, *ceteris paribus*, the imposition of the minimum wage would create unemployment at $Q_w - Q_m$.

In practice, there may be a temptation for firms to ignore the floor price, for example by establishing informal arrangements with workers whereby they work for less than the minimum wage. However, while this would provide employment for the workers, it raises ethical issues about their treatment.

9 Competition and restrictive practices

9.1 Types of competition

The way in which firms are structured in an industry and the way they compete with each other are often described using the – terms perfect competition, imperfect competition, monopoly, oligopoly or monopolistic competition.

The explanation in the table that follows is based on an article that appeared in *Student Accountant*.

Type of market / competition	Comment
Perfect competition	A perfectly competitive market has many firms producing the same (ie homogeneous) goods or services. The market is easy to enter and exit.
	Under perfect competition producers and consumers have all the information they require – they have 'perfect knowledge' of the market. The price and level of output under perfect competition tends towards the equilibrium point. Producers attempting to sell at a higher price will not sell anything, and producers attempting to sell as a price below equilibrium would obtain 100% market share.
	The demand 'curve' is horizontal – it is 'perfectly elastic'. There are few, if any, truly perfectly competitive markets in the real world. Some financial markets in which information is freely available are probably as close as we get to a perfectly competitive market.
Imperfect competition	The term 'imperfect competition' apples to any market that is not perfect. As we explained above, almost all markets are imperfect, although the degree to which they are imperfect can vary significantly.
Monopoly	A monopoly describes the situation where a market has only one producer. That is the pure definition, although the term is often used to describe a firm that has a very high share of a market.
	A monopoly may come about because the producer has a statutory right to be the only producer, perhaps a 'state owned enterprise'.
	If left uncontrolled, a monopoly can set its own price in the marketplace, which can result in what economists refer to as 'super-normal profits'. For this reason, monopolies are usually subject to control by government or a government agency.
Oligopoly	An oligopoly arises when a market has a few dominant producers. Each of the few producers has a high level of influence – and a high level of knowledge of their competitor strategies. If an oligopoly has only two firms, it is referred to as a duopoly.
	Oligopolistic markets are often characterised by complex product differentiation, significant barriers to entry and a high level of influence on prices.
	An example of an oligopoly is the retail petrol and diesel market – several large companies including Exxon Mobil, Shell and BP control the majority of the market (although fuel outlets linked to supermarkets are gaining market share). An example of a duopoly would be the two major cola producers, The Coca-Cola Company and Pepsi Co.

Type of market / competition	Comment
Monopolistic competition	Monopolistic competition arises when the market comprises many producers who tend to use product differentiation to distinguish themselves from others.
	Although their products may be very similar, because producers differentiate their products they are able to create a short-term 'monopoly', as customers see their product as unique. Therefore, for monopolistic competition to exist, consumers must perceive differences in the products offered by different firms.
	Monopolistic competition tends to have fewer barriers to entry or exit than oligopolistic competition.

9.2 Restrictive practices

As well as 'imperfections' in the market, the market may also be subject to restrictive or anti-competitive activities; some examples follow.

- Dumping – selling product at a loss
- Exclusive dealing – being bound by contract to only buy from or sell to one business
- Price fixing – two or more businesses agree to sell at the same price
- Refusal to deal – businesses refusing to use a certain vendor
- Limit pricing – effectively a monopoly which is intended to discourage entry into the market
- Retail price maintenance – reseller cannot set independent price
- Government subsidies – deemed to be unfair to competitors

ᒼ The **micro environment** refers to the immediate operational environment, including suppliers, competitors, customers, stakeholders and intermediaries.

ᒼ For the **organisation as a system**, we need to consider the various forces which have an impact internally and externally.

ᒼ In a free market, the **price mechanism** signals demand and supply conditions to producers and consumers. It therefore determines the activities of both producers and consumers, influencing the levels of demand for and the supply of goods.

ᒼ The position of the **demand curve** is determined by the demand conditions, which include consumers' tastes and preferences, and consumers' incomes.

ᒼ Elasticity, in general, refers to the relationship between two variables. Price elasticity of demand explains the relationship between **change in quantity demanded** and **changes in price**.

ᒼ **Income elasticity of demand** measures the responsiveness of demand to changes in household income. **Cross elasticity of demand** is determined by the availability of substitute (competitors') products.

ᒼ The **supply curve** shows the quantity of a good which would be supplied by producers at a given price.

ᒼ The competitive market process results in an **equilibrium price**, which is the price at which market supply and market demand quantities are in balance. In any market, the equilibrium price will change if market demand or supply conditions change.

ᒼ The **price mechanism** brings demand and supply into equilibrium, and the **equilibrium price** for a good is the price at which the volume demanded by consumers and the volume that firms would be willing to supply is the same. This is also known as the **market clearing price**, since at this price there will be neither surplus nor shortage in the market.

ᒼ The effects of **demand and supply** conditions on markets can be analysed by studying the behaviour of both demand and supply curves.

ᒼ Where **maximum prices** are imposed, there will be **excess demand**: rationing may be necessary, and black marketeers may seek to operate. Where **minimum prices** are imposed, producers will make **excess supply**.

ᒼ The way in which firms are structured in an industry and the way they compete with each other are often described using terms perfect competition, imperfect competition, monopoly, oligopoly or monopolistic competition.

QUICK QUIZ

1   What factors influence demand for a good?

2   What are (a) substitutes and (b) complements?

3   What factors affect the supply quantity?

4   What is meant by equilibrium price?

5   A demand curve is drawn on all **except** which of the following assumptions?

    A   Incomes do not change.
    B   Prices of substitutes are fixed.
    C   Price of the good is constant.
    D   There are no changes in tastes and preferences.

6   The diagram shown relates to the demand for and supply of Scotch whiskey. The market is initially in equilibrium at point X. The government imposes a specific tax on Scotch while, at the same time, the price of Irish Whiskey (a substitute for Scotch Whisky) rises. Which point, A, B, C or D, represents the new market equilibrium?

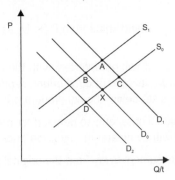

7   A price ceiling set above the equilibrium market price will result in:

    A   Market failure
    B   Excess supply over demand
    C   Market equilibrium
    D   Excess demand over supply

8   Which one of the following would normally cause a rightward shift in the demand curve for a product?

    A   A fall in the price of a substitute product
    B   A reduction in direct taxation on incomes
    C   A reduction in price of the product
    D   An increase in the price of a complementary product

9   What is an inferior good?

    A   A good of such poor quality that demand for it is very weak
    B   A good of lesser quality than a substitute good, so that the price of the substitute is higher
    C   A good for which the cross elasticity of demand with a substitute product is greater than 1
    D   A good for which demand will fall as household income rises

10 In traditional theory, which of the following best describes a firm's short run supply curve:

    A   Its marginal cost curve where price is less than average variable costs
    B   Its marginal cost curve where price is greater than average variable costs
    C   Its average cost curve where price is less than marginal cost
    D   Its average cost curve where price is greater than marginal cost

ANSWERS TO QUICK QUIZ

1   The price of the good
     The price of other goods
     Household income
     Taste and fashion

2   Substitutes are goods that are alternatives to each other (for example, Coke and Pepsi)

     Complements are goods which are bought and used together (for example, cars and petrol)

3   The price obtainable for the good
     The prices obtainable for other goods, particularly goods in joint supply
     The costs of making the good
     Disruptions such as bad weather and strikes

4   The price at which the volume of demand and the volume of supply are equal; there is neither surplus nor shortage.

5   C   Demand curves express the quantity demanded at each given market price. Non-price determinants such as income must be held constant when looking at the effect of price movements in isolation.

6   A   Supply shifts from S_0 to S_1, reflecting the per-unit tax. Demand shifts from D_0 to D_1 as the price of a substitute (Irish whiskey) rises.

7   C   If the price ceiling is above the equilibrium market price, it will not interfere with the working of the price mechanism. The market will not be forced from its current equilibrium. A price ceiling only affects the workings of the price mechanism if it is set **below** the equilibrium price.

8   B   A reduction in income tax will increase 'real' household income, and so demand for normal products will shift to the right, ie quantity demanded will be greater at any given price.

          A fall in the price of a substitute good would entice consumers away from the original good. This would cause a leftward shift in the demand curve.

          A change in the price of the good itself does not cause a shift in the curve but a movement along it.

          Complementary products tend to be bought and used together, so an increase in the price of one will lead to a reduction in demand for the other, reflected in a leftward shift in the demand curve.

9   D   Inferior goods are defined in terms of the relationship between quantity demanded and income. The issue of substitutes is not relevant.

10   B   The marginal cost curve represents the firm's supply curve, but a firm will only continue to supply in the short run provided that the selling price covers its variable costs and therefore allows it to make a contribution to covering fixed costs.

Now try ...

Attempt the questions below from the **Practice Question Bank**

Q17

Q18

Q19

Q20

Q21

Q22

part

B

Business organisation structure, functions and governance

Business organisation, structure and strategy

Section 1 examines the importance of **informal networks** in shaping organisational culture.

There are various influences on organisational structure (**Section 2**). Most firms have some sort of **organisation hierarchy** reflecting the levels of strategy making (**Section 3**). We can see the **strategic apex** (eg Board of Directors) at the top, through ranks of **middle managers** to the **operating core** where the work is done.

Businesses may need to group employees into departments on some basis, which may involve choices as to the degree of centralisation needed (**Section 4**).

Study Guide	Intellectual level
B1 The formal and informal business organisation	
(a) Explain the informal organisation and its relationship with the formal organisation.	K
(b) Describe the impact of the informal organisation on the business.	K
B2 Business organisation structure and design	
(a) Describe Mintzberg's components of the organisation and explain the different ways in which organisations may be structured: (i) Entrepreneurial (ii) Functional (iii) Matrix (iv) Divisional: (geographical, by product, or by customer type) (v) Boundaryless: (virtual, hollow or modular)	K
(b) Explain basic organisational structure concepts: (I) Separation of ownership and management (II) Separation of direction and management (iii) Span of control and scalar chain (iv) Tall and flat organisations (v) Outsourcing and offshoring (vi) Shared services approach	K
(c) Explain the characteristics of the strategic, tactical and operational levels in the organisation in the context of the Anthony hierarchy.	K
(d) Explain centralisation and decentralisation and list their advantages and disadvantages.	K

EXAM FOCUS POINT

This chapter lays the foundation for an understanding of what organisations are, what they do and how they do it. Remember that the exam may require you to **apply** this knowledge.

1 The informal organisation

1.1 What is the 'informal organisation'?

An **informal organisation** always exists alongside the formal one. This consists of social relationships, informal communication networks, behavioural norms and power/influence structures, all of which may 'by-pass' formal organisational arrangements. This may be detrimental or beneficial to the organisation, depending how it is managed.

An **informal organisation** exists side by side with the formal one, whose key structural characteristics and features were examined in detail in Chapter 1. When people work together, they establish social relationships and customary ways of doing things. Unlike the formal organisation, the **informal organisation** is loosely structured, flexible and spontaneous. It embraces such mechanisms as:

(a) Social relationships and groupings (eg cliques) within – or across – formal structures

(b) The 'grapevine', 'bush telegraph', or informal communication which by-passes the formal reporting channels and routes

(c)   Behavioural norms and ways of doing things, both social and work-related, which may circumvent formal procedures and systems (for good or ill). New members must 'learn the ropes' and get used to 'the way we do things here'

(d)   Power/influence structures, irrespective of organisational authority: informal leaders are those who are trusted and looked to for advice

1.2 Benefits (or the role of) the informal organisation

Benefits of the informal organisation for managers include the following.

(a)   **Employee commitment**. The meeting of employees' social needs may contribute to morale and job satisfaction, with benefits in reduced absenteeism and labour turnover.

(b)   **Knowledge sharing**. The availability of information through informal networks can give employees a wider perspective on their role in the task and the organisation, potentially stimulating 'big picture' problem-solving, cross-boundary co-operation and innovation.

(c)   **Speed**. Informal networks and methods may sometimes be more efficient in achieving organisational goals, where the formal organisation has rigid procedures or lengthy communication channels, enabling decisions to be taken and implemented more rapidly.

(d)   **Responsiveness**. The directness, information-richness and flexibility of the informal organisation may be particularly helpful in conditions of rapid environmental change, facilitating both the mechanisms and culture of anti-bureaucratic responsiveness.

(e)   **Co-operation**. The formation and strengthening of interpersonal networks can facilitate team working and co-ordination across organisational boundaries. It may reduce organisational politics – or utilise this positively by mobilising effective decision-making coalitions and bypassing communication blocks.

1.3 Managerial problems of informal organisation

Each of the positive attributes of informal organisation could as easily be detrimental if the power of the informal organisation is directed towards goals unrelated to, or at odds with, those of the formal organisation.

(a)   Social groupings may act collectively against organisational interests, strengthened by collective power and information networks. Even if they are aligned with organisational goals, group/network maintenance may take a lot of time and energy away from tasks.

(b)   The grapevine is notoriously inaccurate and can carry morale-damaging rumours.

(c)   The informal organisation can become too important in fulfilling employees' needs: individuals can suffer acutely when excluded from cliques and networks.

(d)   Informal work practices may 'cut corners', violating safety or quality assurance measures.

Managers can **minimise problems** by:

(a)   Meeting employees' **needs** as far as possible via the **formal** organisation: providing information, encouragement, social interaction, and so on

(b)   Harnessing the **dynamics** of the informal organisation – for example by using informal leaders to secure employee commitment to goals or changes

(c)   Involving **managers** themselves in the informal structure, so that they support information sharing, the breaking down of unhelpful rules, and so on

EXAM FOCUS POINT

Culture impacts on other topics, such as motivation, leadership and teams. It is also an important and fashionable topic in its own right – including the influence of national cultures, with increasingly globalised management.

1.4 Group norms

A work group establishes **norms** or acceptable levels and methods of behaviour, to which all members of the group are expected to conform. This group attitude will have a negative effect on an organisation if it sets unreasonably low production norms. Groups often apply unfair treatment or discrimination against others who break their rules.

Norms are partly the product of role and role expectations of how people in certain positions behave, as conceived by people in related positions.

The general nature of group pressure is to require the individual to share in the group's own identity, and individuals may react to group norms and customs in a variety of ways.

- **Compliance** – toeing the line without real commitment
- **Internalisation** – full acceptance and identification
- **Counter-conformity** – rejecting the group and/or its norms

There are some circumstances which put strong pressure on the individual.

- The issue is not clear-cut.
- The individual lacks support for their own attitude or behaviour.
- The individual is exposed to other members of the group for a length of time.

Norms may be reinforced in various ways by the group.

(a) **Identification**: the use of badges, symbols, perhaps special modes of speech, in-jokes, and so on – the marks of belonging, prestige and acceptance. There may even be initiation rites which mark the boundaries of membership.

(b) **Sanctions** of various kinds. Deviant behaviour may be dealt with by ostracising or ignoring the member concerned, by ridicule or reprimand, even by physical hostility. The threat of expulsion is the final sanction.

The group's power to induce conformity depends on the degree to which the individual values his membership of the group and the rewards it may offer, or wishes to avoid the negative sanctions at its disposal.

1.4.1 The Hawthorne Studies

The work of the **human relations school** of management theory sheds light on the importance of groups within an organisation. Interesting findings emerged from studies conducted at the Hawthorne plant of the Western Electric Company by Professor Elton Mayo of the Harvard Business School (Mayo, 1933). One conclusion was that informal groups exercise a powerful influence in the workplace: supervisors and managers need to take account of social needs if they wish to secure commitment to organisational goals. The studies also showed that people tend to perform better when they believe they are being treated well and are valued.

2 Organisational structure

2.1 Components of the organisation (Mintzberg)

Mintzberg believes that **all** organisations can be analysed into five components, according to how they relate to the work of the organisation, and how they prefer to co-ordinate.

Mintzberg's five components (Mintzberg, 1979)

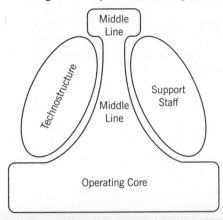

Component	Job	Preferred means of co-ordination
Strategic apex	Ensures the organisation follows its mission Manages the organisation's relationship with the environment	Direct supervision (especially in small businesses)
Operating core	People directly involved in the process of obtaining inputs, and converting them into outputs	Mutual adjustment; standardisation of skills
Middle line	Converts the desires of the strategic apex into the work done by the operating core	Standardisation of outputs (results)
Technostructure	• Analysers determine the best way of doing a job • Planners determine outputs (eg goods must achieve a specified level of quality) • Personnel analysts standardise skills (eg training programmes)	Standardisation of work processes or outputs
Support staff	Ancillary services such as public relations, legal counsel, the cafeteria. Support staff do not plan or standardise production. They function independently of the operating core.	Mutual adjustment

2.2 Categories of organisation (Mintzberg, 1979)

Based on the organisational model above, Mintzberg described five categories of organisation structure.

2.2.1 Simple structure

The simple structure is centralised and often autocratic, with power concentrated at the strategic apex. Typically, control is exerted by the chief executive or a small executive team. This structure can be very flexible and informal, but it is also very vulnerable, with so much power and control concentrated in the hands of a few people.

2.2.2 Machine bureaucracy

This structure relies heavily on a good technostructure. Strategic planners and financial controllers are influential, with multiple layers of management, formal (often rigid) procedures and standardised production processes. Motivation can be difficult, and organisations of this type tend to be inflexible.

2.2.3 Professional bureaucracy

The professional bureaucracy is based on clear lines of authority and standard practices. The practices are often built on standards set by law, regulations or independent external bodies, such as professional associations (eg law, accountancy). The operating core is the major coordinating influence and people are usually well motivated.

2.2.4 Divisionalised

In a divisionalised structure, a small central core provides guidelines for business units that enjoy a high degree of autonomy. The middle line forms a strong coordinating influence, as it translates the demands of the central core into the objectives of the operating core.

2.2.5 Adhocracy

The adhocracy is task or project-based, and needs to respond quickly to changing demands such as rapidly evolving markets, or technological innovation. Defined processes are less important as a result. Research and development is usually the primary driver of adhocracies.

So, in most organisations, tasks and people are grouped together in some way: on the basis of specialisation, say, or shared technology or customer base. This is known as **departmentation**. Different patterns of departmentation are possible, and the pattern selected will depend on the individual circumstances of the organisation.

> ### EXAM FOCUS POINT
>
> There is an article on the ACCA website entitled "Mintzberg's theory on organisations" that is relevant to material in this section.

2.3 Functional departmentation

> Organisations can be **departmentalised** on a **functional** basis (with separate departments for production, marketing, finance, etc), a **geographical** basis (by region or country), a **product** basis (eg worldwide divisions for product X, Y, etc), a **brand** basis, or a **matrix** basis (eg someone selling product X in country A would report to both a product X manager and a country A manager). Organisation structures often feature a variety of these types, as **hybrid** structures.

Functional organisation involves grouping together people who do similar tasks. Primary functions in a manufacturing company might be production, sales, finance and general administration. Sub-departments of marketing might be market research, advertising, PR, and so on.

Advantages include:

(a)   **Expertise is pooled** thanks to the division of work into specialist areas.

(b)   It **avoids duplication** (eg one management accounts department rather than several) and enables economies of scale.

(c)   It **facilitates** the recruitment, management and development of functional specialists.

(d)   It suits **centralised** businesses.

Disadvantages include:

(a)   It focuses on internal **processes** and **inputs**, rather than the **customer** and **outputs**, which are what ultimately drive a business. Inward-looking businesses are less able to adapt to changing demands.

(b)   **Communication problems** may arise between different functions, which each have their own jargon.

(c)   **Poor co-ordination**, especially if rooted in a tall organisation structure. Decisions by one function/department involving another might have to be referred upwards, and dealt with at a higher level, thereby increasing the burdens on senior management.

(d)   Functional structures create **vertical barriers** to information and work flow.

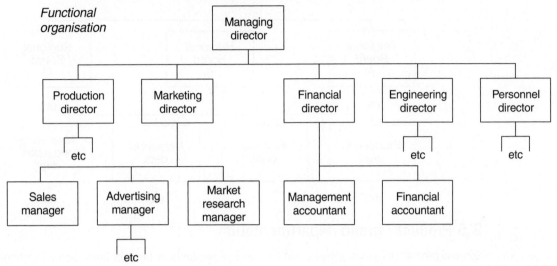

Adapted from: (Johnson et al, 2005: p.399)

2.4 Geographic departmentation

Where the organisation is structured according to geographic area, some authority is retained at Head Office but day-to-day operations are handled on a **territorial** basis (eg Southern region, Western region). Many sales departments are organised territorially.

There are **advantages** to geographic departmentation.

(a)   There is **local decision-making** at the point of contact between the organisation (eg a salesperson) and its customers, suppliers or other stakeholders.

(b)   It may be **cheaper** to establish area factories/offices than to service markets from one location (eg costs of transportation and travelling may be reduced).

But there are **disadvantages** too.

(a)   **Duplication** and possible loss of economies of scale might arise. For example, a national organisation divided into ten regions might have a customer liaison department in each regional office. If the organisation did all customer liaison work from head office (centralised) it might need fewer managerial staff.

(b)   **Inconsistency** in methods or standards may develop across different areas.

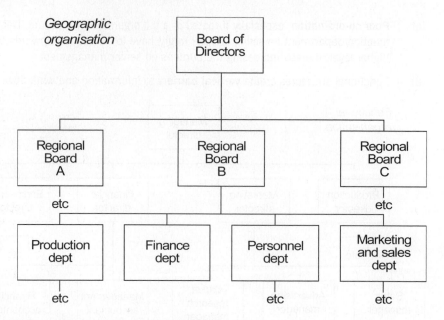

2.5 Product / brand departmentation

Some organisations group activities on the basis of **products** or product lines. Some functional departmentation remains (eg manufacturing, distribution, marketing and sales) but a divisional manager is given responsibility for the product or product line, with authority over personnel of different functions.

Advantages include:

(a)   **Accountability**. Individual managers can be held accountable for the profitability of individual products.

(b)   **Specialisation**. For example, some salespeople will be trained to sell a specific product in which they may develop technical expertise and thereby offer a better sales service to customers.

(c)   **Co-ordination**. The different functional activities and efforts required to make and sell each product can be co-ordinated and integrated by the divisional/product manager.

Disadvantages include:

(a)   It **increases the overhead costs** and managerial complexity of the organisation.
(b)   Different product divisions may **fail to share resources** and customers.

A **brand** is the name (eg 'Persil') or design which identifies the products or services of a manufacturer or provider and distinguishes them from those of competitors. (Large organisations may produce a number of different brands of the same basic product, such as washing powder or toothpaste.) Branding brings the product to the attention of buyers and creates brand **recognition**, **differentiation** and **loyalty**: often customers do not realise that two 'rival' brands are in fact produced by the same manufacturer.

(a)   Because each brand is packaged, promoted and sold in a distinctive way, the need for specialisation may make brand departmentation effective. As with product departmentation, some functional departmentation remains but brand managers have responsibility for the brand's marketing and this can affect every function.

(b)   Brand departmentation has similar advantages/disadvantages to product departmentation.

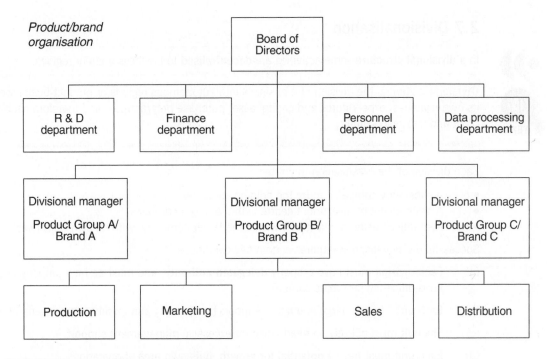

Product/brand organisation

2.6 Customer departmentation

An organisation may organise its activities on the basis of types of customer, or market segment.

(a) Departmentation by customer is commonly associated with **sales departments** and selling effort, but it might also be used by a jobbing or contracting firm where a team of managers may be given the responsibility of liaising with major customers (eg discussing specifications and completion dates, quality of work, progress chasing etc).

(b) Many businesses distinguish between **business customers** and **consumers**.

QUESTION

Types of organisation

Looking at the 'Product/Brand Organisation' chart following Section 2.4 above, what types of organisation can you identify, and why are these appropriate for their purposes? What **added** type of organisation might this firm use, and in what circumstances?

ANSWER

- At the head office level, there is **functional** organisation. This enables standardisation of policy and activity in key 'staff' or support functions shared by the various divisions.

- At divisional level, there is **product/brand** organisation. This allows the distinctive culture and attributes of each product/brand to be addressed in production processes and marketing approach.

- For each product/brand, there is **functional** organisation, enabling specialist expertise to be directed at the different activities required to produce, market and distribute a product.

- This firm may further organise its marketing department by **customer**, if its customer base includes key (high-value, long-term) customer accounts with diverse service needs, for example.

- It may further organise its sales and distribution departments by **geographical area**, if the customer base is internationally or regionally dispersed: local market conditions and values, and logistical requirements of distribution, can then be taken more specifically into account.

2.7 Divisionalisation

In a **divisional structure** some activities are **decentralised** to business units or regions.

Divisionalisation is the division of a business into autonomous regions or product businesses, each with its own revenues, expenditures and capital asset purchase programmes, and therefore each with its own profit and loss responsibility.

Each division of the organisation might be:

- A subsidiary company under the holding company
- A profit centre or investment centre within a single company
- A strategic business unit (SBU) within the larger company, with its own objectives

Successful divisionalisation requires certain key conditions.

(a) Each division must have **properly delegated authority**, and must be held properly accountable to head office (eg for profits earned).

(b) Each unit must be **large enough** to support the quantity and quality of management it needs.

(c) The unit must not rely on head office for excessive **management support**.

(d) Each unit must have a **potential for growth** in its own area of operations.

(e) There should be **scope and challenge** in the job for the management of each unit.

(f) If units deal with each other, it should be as an **'arm's length' transaction**.

The advantages and disadvantages of divisionalisation may be summarised as follows.

Advantages	Disadvantages
Focuses the attention of management below 'top level' on business performance	In some businesses, it is impossible to identify completely independent products or markets for which separate divisions can be set up.
Reduces the likelihood of unprofitable products and activities being continued	Divisionalisation is only possible at a fairly senior management level, because there is a limit to how much discretion can be used in the division of work. For example, every product needs a manufacturing function and a selling function.
Encourages a greater attention to efficiency, lower costs and higher profits	There may be more resource problems. Many divisions get their resources from head office in competition with other divisions.
Gives more authority to junior managers, and so grooms them for more senior positions in the future (planned managerial succession)	
Reduces the number of levels of management, meaning that the top executives in each division should be able to report directly to the chief executive of the holding company	

2.8 Hybrid structures

Organisation structures are rarely composed of only one type of organisation. 'Hybrid' structures may involve a mix of functional departmentation, ensuring specialised attention to key functions, with elements of (for example):

(a) Product organisation, to suit the requirements of brand marketing or production technologies

(b) Customer organisation, particularly in marketing departments, to service key accounts

(c)   Territorial organisation, particularly of sales and distribution departments, to service local
        requirements for marketing or distribution in dispersed regions or countries

2.9 The simple structure (or entrepreneurial structure)

> The strategic apex exerts a pull to centralise, leading to the **simple structure**.

The **strategic apex** wishes to retain control over decision-making, and so exercises a **pull to centralise**
(Mintzberg, 1979). Mintzberg believes that this leads to a **simple structure**.

Simple structure

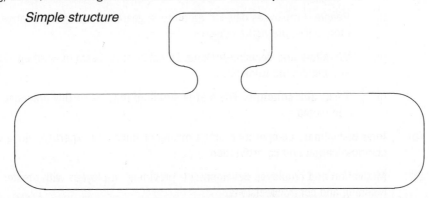

(a)   **The simple structure is characteristic of small, young organisations**. The strategic apex is a
        small group, or possibly one person, which exercises direct control over the people making up the
        operating core. There is little, if any, role for technical or support staff.

(b)   In small firms, a single entrepreneur or management team will dominate (as in the power
        culture). If it grows, the organisation might need more managerial skills than the apex can
        provide. Strategies might be made on the basis of the manager's hunches.

(c)   Centralisation is advantageous, as it reflects management's full knowledge of the operating core
        and its processes. However, senior managers might intervene too much.

(d)   It is risky, as it depends on the expertise of one person. Such an organisation might be prone to
        succession crises. This problem is often encountered in family businesses.

(e)   This structure can handle an environment that is relatively simple but fast moving, where
        standardisation cannot be used to co-ordinate activities.

(f)   **Co-ordination is achieved by direct supervision**, with few formal devices. It is thus flexible.

(g)   This structure has its own particular characteristics: wide span of control; no middle line and
        hence minimal hierarchy; and no technostructure, implying little formalisation or standardisation
        of behaviour.

2.10 Matrix and project organisation

Where hybrid organisation 'mixes' organisation types, **matrix** organisation actually **crosses** functional and
product/customer/project organisation.

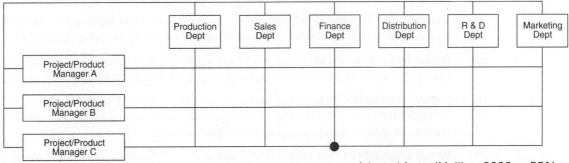

Adapted from: (Mullins, 2002: p.551)

The employees represented by the dot in the above diagram, for example, are responsible to:

- The finance manager for their work in accounting and finance for their functional department; and

- The project manager C for their work on the project team: budgeting, management reporting and payroll relevant to the project, say.

Advantages of matrix organisation include:

(a) Greater **flexibility** of:

    (i) **People**. Employees develop an attitude geared to accepting change, and departmental monopolies are broken down.

    (ii) **Workflow and decision-making**. Direct contact between staff encourages problem solving and big-picture thinking.

    (iii) **Tasks and structure**. The matrix structure may be readily amended, once projects are completed.

(b) **Inter-disciplinary co-operation** and a mixing of skills and expertise, along with **improved communication** and **co-ordination**

(c) **Motivation and employee development**: providing employees with greater participation in planning and control decisions

(d) **Market awareness**: the organisation tends to become more customer/quality focused

(e) **Horizontal workflow**: bureaucratic obstacles are removed, and department specialisms become less powerful

There are **disadvantages**, however.

(a) **Dual authority** threatens a **conflict** between functional managers and product/project/area managers.

(b) An individual with two or more bosses may suffer stress from **conflicting demands** or **ambiguous roles**.

(c) **Cost**: product management posts are added, meetings have to be held, and so on.

(d) **Slower decision-making** due to the added complexity.

2.11 The new organisation

Some recent trends have emerged from the focus on **flexibility** as a key organisational value.

(a) **Flat structures**. The flattening of hierarchies does away with levels of organisation which lengthened lines of communication and decision-making. Flat structures are more responsive because there is a more direct relationship between the organisation's strategic centre and the operational units serving the customer.

(b) **'Horizontal structures'**. There is increased recognition that functional versatility (through multi-functional project teams and multi-skilling, for example) is the key to flexibility.

(c) **'Chunked' and 'unglued' structures**. So far, this has meant team working and decentralisation, or empowerment, creating smaller and more flexible units within the overall structure.

(d) **Output-focused structures**. The key to all the above trends is the focus on results, and on the customer, instead of internal processes and functions for their own sake.

(e) **'Jobless' structures**. The employee becomes not a job-holder but a seller of skills. This is a concrete expression of the concept of **employability**, which says that a person needs to have a portfolio of skills which are valuable on the open market.

(f) **Virtual organisations**. The organisation may consist of individuals, teams, companies or stakeholders. Members are geographically dispersed and the organisation usually only exists electronically on the internet, without any physical premises. This creates cost savings from not having the costs associated with physical locations, such as rent. For example, Amazon operates

as a virtual retailer without incurring the cost of retail premises. These organisations are entirely reliant on their technology and any problems could affect the operation of the organisation.

(g) In a **hollow organisation** people and activities are split between core and non-core competencies. All non-core processes and activities are outsourced. For example, the sports shoe and clothing manufacturer Nike outsources production to sub-contracters – but the activity seen as core and key, product design, is retained in-house. Such organisations can then focus on their core activities, but this structure depends on being able to find reliable subcontractors.

(h) In **modular organisations** different elements or components of the product or service the organisation produces are outsourced to different suppliers. The retained people within the organisation assemble or combine these elements to produce the final product or service. This structure enables the organisation to be more flexible and to respond to market needs more quickly, but also depends on reliable suppliers. For example, a motor vehicle dealership may recognise that its sales, repair and customer service modules are performing well, but that its finance and accounting services are inefficient. The dealership may, as a result, outsource that module.

(i) **Boundaryless organisations** remove both the internal barriers that separate the hierarchy levels, different functions and different departments, and also remove the barriers between the organisation and its suppliers, customers and competitors. To help eliminate boundaries, managers may use virtual, hollow or modular structures. This helps to eliminate bureaucracy and helps to reduce costs.

EXAM FOCUS POINT

The examining team has commented that newer organisational models (such as hollow, modular and virtual) presented difficulties for some recent candidates. You can expect them to be tested again.

2.12 Span of control

Span of control or **'span of management'** refers to the number of subordinates responsible to a superior.

The span of control refers to the number of subordinates immediately reporting to a superior official.

In other words, if a manager has five subordinates, the span of control is five.

A number of factors influence the span of control.

(a) A manager's **capabilities** limit the span of control: there are physical and mental limitations to any single manager's ability to control people and activities.

(b) The **nature of the manager's workload**

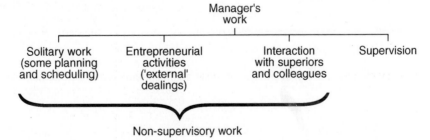

The more non-supervisory work in a manager's workload:

(i) The narrower the span of control
(ii) The greater the delegation of authority to subordinates

(c) The **geographical dispersion** of subordinates: dispersed teams require more effort to supervise.

2.13 Tall and flat organisations

Recent trends have been towards **delayering** organisations of levels of management. In other words, **tall organisations** (with many management levels, and narrow spans of control) are turning into **flat organisations** (with fewer management levels, and wider spans of control) as a result of technological changes and the granting of more decision-making power to front-line employees.

The span of control concept has implications for the length of the **scalar chain**

- The **scalar chain** is the chain of command from the most senior to the most junior.

- A **tall organisation** is one which, in relation to its size, has a large number of levels of management hierarchy. This implies a **narrow** span of control.

- A **flat organisation** is one which, in relation to its size, has a small number of hierarchical levels. This implies a **wide** span of control.

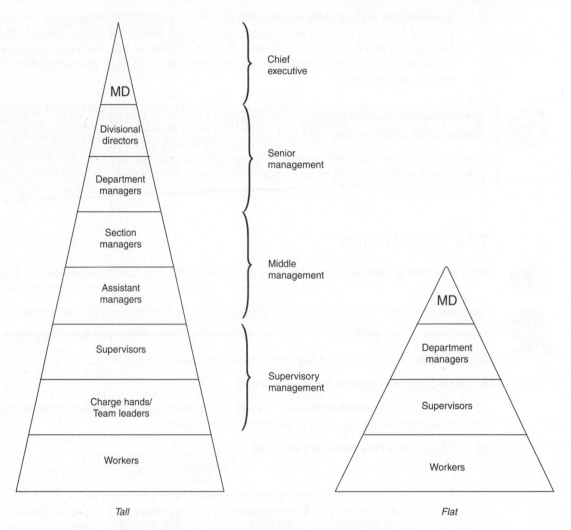

Tall

Flat

The advantages and disadvantages of these organisational forms can be summarised as follows.

Tall organisation

For	Against
Narrow control spans	Inhibits delegation
Small groups enable team members to participate in decisions	Rigid supervision can be imposed, blocking initiative
A large number of steps on the promotional ladders – assists management training and career planning	The same work passes through too many hands Increases administration and overhead costs Slow decision making and responses, as the strategic apex is further away

Flat organisation

For	Against
More opportunity for delegation	Requires that jobs **can** be delegated. Managers may only get a superficial idea of what goes on. If they are overworked they are more likely to be involved in crisis management
Relatively cheap	Sacrifices control
In theory, speeds up communication between strategic apex and operating core	Middle managers are often necessary to convert the grand vision of the strategic apex into operational terms

2.14 Delayering

Delayering is the reduction of the number of management levels from bottom to top.

Many organisations are delayering. Middle-line jobs are vanishing. Organisations are increasing the average span of control, reducing management levels and becoming flatter.

(a) **Information technology**. This reduces the need for middle managers to process information.

(b) **Empowerment**. Many organisations, especially service businesses, are keen to delegate authority down the line to the lowest possible level. Front-line workers in the operating core are allowed to take decisions, in order to increase responsiveness to customer demands.

(c) **Economy**. Delayering reduces managerial/supervisory costs.

(d) **Fashion**. Delayering is fashionable: if senior managers believe that tall structures are inherently inflexible, they might cut the numbers of management levels.

This topic was also covered in Chapter 2, when discussing the impact of technology on the organisation.

2.15 Outsourcing and offshoring

Outsourcing, as explained in Chapter 2, is the contracting out of specified operations or services to an external vendor. Outsourcing impacts organisation structure by removing the outsourced activity from the organisation.

A related concept to outsourcing is offshoring. Whereas outsourcing involves an organisation sending work to an external organisation, offshoring involves sending work overseas. Work sent overseas may still be done within the organisation; for example, if a UK bank sets up its own call centre in India, that is offshoring but is not outsourcing. If, on the other hand, a UK business contracts with an external call centre based in India to deal with customer service telephone enquiries, that is both outsourcing and offshoring.

Offshoring is often used by organisations who want to make use of cheaper labour in overseas markets. The disadvantages of offshoring come from possible cultural and language barriers and a loss of customer focus if the offshoring company no longer has day-to-day contact with its customers.

2.16 Shared services approach

Under a shared services approach, a single service centre is established to provide a support function across an organisation. Previously, the service may have been provided in a more fragmented way.

The shared services business unit, created within the company, is accountable for delivering the service to agreed service levels. Although the service provider is part of the organisation, the relationship it has with other parts of the organisation is similar to that of an external service provider. The shared services unit has the mindset of a business and views the rest of the organisation as their customers.

The shared services approach aims to enable better use of resources across the organisation, resulting in lower costs but with the protection of agreed service levels.

IT and HR are two functions often seen as suitable for the shared services approach, but the approach could be applied to a wide range of activities.

The disadvantages to the shared services approach are that services are likely to be less tailored and more generic and also that there is less job diversity within the organisation.

3 Levels of strategy in the organisation

There are many levels of strategy in an organisation.

- **Corporate**: the general direction of the whole organisation
- **Business**: how the organisation or its SBUs tackle particular markets
- **Operational/functional**: specific strategies for different departments of the business

Any level of the organisation can have objectives and devise strategies to achieve them. The strategic management process is multi-layered.

It is generally agreed that there are three levels of strategy: corporate, business and functional/operational. The distinction between corporate and business strategy arises because of the development of the divisionalised business organisation, which typically has a corporate centre and a number of strategic business units (SBUs).

3.1 Corporate strategies

Corporate strategy is concerned with what types of business the organisation is in.

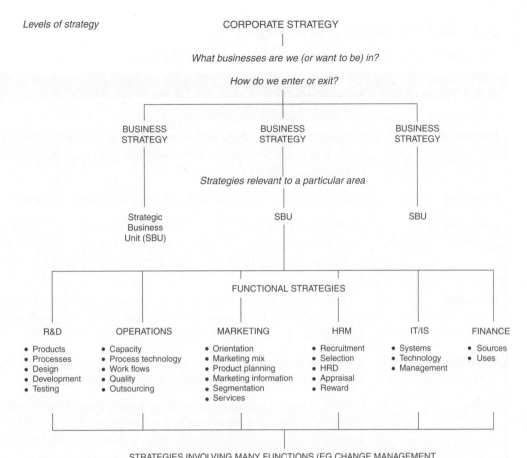

Defining aspects of corporate strategy

Characteristic	Comment
Scope of activities	Strategy and strategic management impact on the whole organisation: all parts of the business operation should support and further the strategic plan.
Environment	The organisation counters threats and exploits opportunities in the environment (customers, clients, competitors).
Resources	Strategy involves choices about allocating or obtaining corporate resources now and in future.
Values	The value systems of people with power in the organisation influence its strategy.
Timescale	Corporate strategy has a long-term impact.
Complexity	Corporate strategy involves uncertainty about the future, integrating the operations of the organisation and change.

3.2 Business strategy

Business strategy: how an organisation approaches a particular product market area

Business strategy can involve decisions such as whether to segment the market and specialise in particularly profitable areas, or to compete by offering a wider range of products.

As we noted earlier, some large, diversified firms have separate **strategic business units** (SBUs) dealing with particular areas. Business strategy for such large organisations is strategy at the SBU level.

3.3 Functional/operational strategies

Functional/operational strategies deal with specialised areas of activity.

Functional area	Comment
R&D	New products and techniques
Purchasing	Ensuring that the firm acquires the raw materials and other supplies that it needs at the best price possible, and with assurances over quality and delivery in accordance with production schedules
Production	Factory location, manufacturing techniques, outsourcing, and so on
Direct service provision	The provision of services to customers (as opposed to the production of goods) encompassing a range of activities, depending on the business concerned – eg consultancy, accounting, payroll services, tax advice, facilities management etc
Marketing	Devising products and services, pricing, promoting and distributing them, in order to satisfy customer needs at a profit. Marketing and corporate strategies are interrelated
Administration	General support to other business functions in their day to day activities – call handling, reception duties, maintenance of records etc
Finance	Ensuring that the firm has enough financial resources to fund its other strategies by identifying sources of finance and using them effectively. The full role of the finance and accounting function is covered in detail in Chapter 8
Human resources management	Secure personnel of the right skills in the right quantity at the right time, and to ensure that they have the right skills and values to promote the firm's overall goals
Information systems	A firm's information systems are becoming increasingly important, as an item of expenditure, as administrative support and as a tool for competitive strength. Not all information technology applications are strategic, and the strategic value of IT will vary from case to case

3.4 The Anthony hierarchy

Managerial activity can be described in the following hierarchy (Anthony, 1965).

(a) **Strategic management** (carried out by senior management) is concerned with direction setting, policy making and crisis handling. The time frame of decisions made at strategic management level would typically have implications for three to five years.

(b) **Tactical management** (carried out by middle management) is concerned with establishing means to the corporate ends, mobilising resources and innovating (finding new ways to achieve business goals). Decisions made at this level would have medium-term implications.

(c) **Operational management** (carried out by supervisors and operatives) is concerned with routine activities to carry out tactical plans. Decisions at this level would deal with short-term matters.

EXAM FOCUS POINT

One of the basic organisational structure concepts is that of the separation between direction setting for the business, and day-to-day management processes. This distinction is specified in the Study Guide.

4 Centralisation and decentralisation

4.1 What is centralisation?

A **centralised** organisation is one in which authority is concentrated in one place.

We can look at centralisation in two ways.

(a) **Geography**. Some functions may be centralised rather than 'scattered' in different offices, departments or locations.

So, for example, secretarial support, IT support and information storage (filing) may be centralised in specialist departments (whose services are shared by other functions) rather than carried out by staff/equipment duplicated in each departmental office.

(b) **Authority**. Centralisation also refers to the extent to which people have to refer decisions upwards to their superiors. Decentralisation therefore implies increased delegation, empowerment and autonomy at lower levels of the organisation.

4.2 Advantages and disadvantages of centralisation

Centralisation offers greater control and co-ordination; **decentralisation** offers greater flexibility.

The table below summarises some of the arguments in favour of centralisation and decentralisation.

Pro centralisation	Pro decentralisation/delegation
Decisions are made at one point and so are easier to co-ordinate.	Avoids overburdening top managers, in terms of workload and stress
Senior managers can take a wider view of problems and consequences.	Improves motivation of more junior managers who are given responsibility
Senior management can balance the interests of different functions – eg by deciding on the resources to allocate to each.	Greater awareness of local problems by decision makers (geographically dispersed organisations are often decentralised on a regional/area basis for this reason)
Quality of decisions is (theoretically) higher due to senior managers' skills and experience.	Greater speed of decision-making, and response to changing events, since no need to refer decisions upwards. This is particularly important in rapidly changing markets.
It is possibly cheaper, by reducing number of managers needed and so lower costs of overheads.	Helps develop the skills of junior managers: supports managerial succession
Crisis decisions are taken more quickly at the centre, without need to refer back.	Separate spheres of responsibility can be identified: controls, performance measurement and accountability are better.
Policies, procedures and documentation can be standardised organisation-wide.	Communication technology allows decisions to be made locally, with information and input from head office if required.

CHAPTER ROUNDUP

↪ An **informal organisation** always exists alongside the formal one. This consists of social relationships, informal communication networks, behavioural norms and power/influence structures, all of which may 'by-pass' formal organisational arrangements. This may be detrimental or beneficial to the organisation, depending how it is managed.

↪ Mintzberg believes that **all** organisations can be analysed into five components, according to how they relate to the work of the organisation, and how they prefer to co-ordinate.

↪ Organisations can be **departmentalised** on a **functional** basis (with separate departments for production, marketing, finance, etc), a **geographical** basis (by region or country), a **product** basis (eg worldwide divisions for product X, Y, etc), a **brand** basis, or a **matrix** basis (eg someone selling product X in country A would report to both a product X manager and a country A manager). Organisation structures often feature a variety of these types, as **hybrid** structures.

↪ In a **divisional structure** some activities are **decentralised** to business units or regions.

↪ The strategic apex exerts a pull to centralise, leading to the **simple structure**.

↪ **Span of control** or '**span of management**' refers to the number of subordinates responsible to a superior.

↪ Recent trends have been towards **delayering** organisations of levels of management. In other words, **tall organisations** (with many management levels, and narrow spans of control) are turning into **flat organisations** (with fewer management levels, and wider spans of control) as a result of technological changes and the granting of more decision-making power to front-line employees.

↪ There are many levels of strategy in an organisation.

   – **Corporate**: the general direction of the whole organisation
   – **Business**: how the organisation or its SBUs tackle particular markets
   – **Operational/functional**: specific strategies for different departments of the business

↪ A **centralised** organisation is one in which authority is concentrated in one place.

QUICK QUIZ

1 List the potential benefits of the informal organisation.

2 What, in Mintzberg's view, are the five component parts of an organisation?

3 Grouping people together who do similar tasks is called

   A   Task departmentation   C   Product departmentation
   B   Geographic departmentation   D   Functional departmentation

4 Fill in the blanks.

Divisionalisation is the division of a business into .... regions or products each with its own .... and .... responsibility.

5 The span of control refers to the chain of command from the most senior to the most junior.

Is this true or false?

6 *Delete as appropriate

A tall organisation has a large number of levels of management. This implies a narrow*/wide* span of control.

7 Delayering would:

   A   Make an organisation taller   B   Make an organisation flatter

BPP
LEARNING MEDIA

ANSWERS TO QUICK QUIZ

1   Meeting of employee needs offering morale and job satisfaction; knowledge sharing; speed of operation; responsiveness to change; support for team working and co-ordination

2   Strategic apex; technostructure; support staff; middle line; operating core.

3   D.   This is the definition of functional departmentation.

4   autonomous; profit; loss

5   False.   This refers to the scalar chain. The span of control refers to the number of subordinates responsible to a superior.

6   A tall organisation has a large number of levels of management. This implies a **narrow** span of control.

7   B.   Delayering is the reduction of the number of management levels from bottom to top so this would make an organisation flatter.

Now try ...

Attempt the questions below from the **Practice Question Bank**

Q23

Q24

Q25

Q26

Q27

Organisational culture and committees

Firms which employ many people need to group people into departments (**Section 1**).

Organisation culture is, broadly, the distinctive way an organisation does things: its particular 'style'. We explore how this reveals itself in **Sections 2 and 3** of this chapter.

Like **structure**, the concept of **culture** gives us a way of talking about how organisations 'work'. The contributions of Schein, Handy and Hofstede are specifically mentioned in the Study Guide. Particular structures suit particular cultures – as we see in **Section 4**: Handy's is a useful model, which should be learned in detail. The impact of national culture on organisational culture outlined by Hofstede is useful when discussing management in multi-national and cross-cultural contexts. With increasing globalisation and workforce diversity, this is useful awareness.

The chapter concludes with a discussion of the work of committees (**Section 5**). Committees are one of the main mechanisms for organisational consultation and communication.

At this point in your studies, you may find it helpful to reread Chapter 2, Section 9 on the impact of technology on organisations.

B2 Business organisation structure and design

(e) Describe the roles and functions of the main departments in a business organisation:　K
  (i)   Research and development
  (ii) Purchasing
  (iii) Production
  (iv) Direct service provision
  (v)   Marketing
  (vi) Administration
  (vii) Finance

(f) Explain the role of marketing in an organisation:　K
  (i)   The definition of marketing
  (ii) The marketing mix
  (iii) The relationship of the marketing plan to the strategic plan

B3 Organisational culture in business

(a) Define organisational culture.　K

(b) Describe the factors that shape the culture of the organisation.　K

(c) Explain the contribution made by writers on culture:　K
  (i)   Schein – determinants of organisational culture
  (ii) Handy – four cultural stereotypes
  (iii) Hofstede – international perspectives on culture

B4 Committees in business organisations

(a) Explain the purposes of committees.　K

(b) Describe the types of committee used by business organisations.　K

(c) List the advantages and disadvantages of committees.　K

(d) Explain the roles of the Chair and Secretary of a committee.　K

C1 The relationship between accounting and other business functions

(a) Explain the relationship between accounting and other key functions within the business, such as procurement, production and marketing.　K

(b) Explain financial considerations in production and production planning.　K

(c) Identify the financial issues associated with marketing.　S

(d) Identify the financial costs and benefits of effective service provision.　S

C2 Accounting and finance functions within business

(a) Explain the contribution of the accounting function to the formulation, implementation, and control of the organisation's policies, procedures and performance.　K

(b) Identify and describe the main financial accounting functions in business:　K
  (i)   Recording financial information
  (ii) Codifying and processing financial information
  (iii) Preparing financial statements

(c) Identify and describe the main management accounting and performance management functions in business: K

    (i)   Recording and analysing costs and revenues

    (ii)   Providing management accounting information for decision-making

    (iii)   Planning and preparing budgets and exercising budgetary control

(d) Identify and describe the main finance and treasury functions: K

    (i)   Calculating and mitigating business tax liabilities

    (ii)   Evaluating and obtaining finance

    (iii)   Managing working capital

    (iv)   Treasury and risk management

EXAM FOCUS POINT

Cultural influences provide a good source of potential exam questions.

1 Organisational departments and functions

1.1 Research and development

Research may be **pure**, **applied** or **development**. It may be intended to improve **products** or **processes**. R&D should support the organisation's strategy and be closely co-ordinated with marketing.

- **Pure research** is original research to obtain new scientific or technical knowledge or understanding. There is no obvious commercial or practical end in view.

- **Applied research** is also original research work like pure research, but it has a specific practical aim or application (eg research on improvements in the effectiveness of medicines etc).

- **Development** is the use of existing scientific and technical knowledge to produce new (or substantially improved) products or systems, prior to starting commercial production operations.

Many organisations employ **specialist staff** to conduct research and development (R&D). They may be organised in a separate functional department of their own. In an organisation run on a product division basis, R&D staff may be employed by each division.

1.1.1 Product and process research

There are two categories of R&D.

- **Product research** is based on creating new products and developing existing ones; in other words, the organisation's 'offer' to the market.

- **Process research** is based on improving the way in which those products or services are made or delivered, or the efficiency with which they are made or delivered.

Product research – new product development

The new product development process must be carefully controlled; new products are a major source of competitive advantage but can cost a great deal of money to bring to market. A screening process is necessary to ensure that resources are concentrated on projects with a high probability of success.

Process research

Process research involves attention to how the goods/services are produced. Process research has these aspects.

(a) **Processes**. These are crucial in service industries (eg fast food), as part of the services sold.

(b) **Productivity**. Efficient processes save money and time.

(c) **Planning**. If you know how long certain stages in a project are likely to take, you can plan the most efficient sequence.

(d) **Quality management**. Performed effectively, this leads to enhanced quality.

R&D should be closely co-ordinated with marketing

(a) Customer needs, as identified by marketers, should be a vital input to new product developments.

(b) The R&D department might identify possible changes to product specifications so that a variety of marketing mixes can be tried out and screened.

1.2 Purchasing

Purchasing makes a major contribution to cost and quality management in any business and in retail is a vital element of strategy. The purchasing mix is:

- Quantity
- Price
- Quality
- Delivery

Purchasing is 'the acquisition of material resources and business services for use by the organisation'.

1.2.1 Importance of purchasing

Cost. Raw materials and subcomponents purchases are a major cost for many firms.

Quality. The quality of input resources affects the quality of outputs and the efficiency of the production function.

Strategy. In retailing, buying goods for resale is one of the most important activities of the business.

Position of purchasing within the organisation

Where purchasing is of strategic importance, the most senior purchasing executive may be on the **board of directors** or, at least, report to the managing director.

Where raw materials are an important cost, the purchasing officer may work in the **production function**.

In any event, the purchasing officer must **liaise with the finance department**, especially with regard to payment of payables.

The purchasing manager's responsibilities include:

(a) **Inputs for production**. Acquiring raw materials, components, sub-assemblies, consumable stores and capital equipment for the production function.

(b) **Inputs for administration**. Purchasing supplies and equipment for all areas of the business (eg microcomputers, motor cars, telephone systems, office furniture, paper and other stationery items).

(c)   **Cost control.** Ensuring that the organisation obtains value for money over the long term consistent with quality.

(d)   **Liaison with the R&D department.** to find suppliers for materials which are to the specifications required by the designers.

(e)   **Supplier management.** Locating suppliers and dealing with them (eg discussing prices, discounts, delivery lead times, specifications; chasing late deliveries; sanctioning payments).

(f)   **Evaluating purchasing alternatives**. Obtaining information on availability, quality, prices, distribution and suppliers for the evaluation of purchasing alternatives.

(g)   **Ensuring co-ordination between purchasing and inventory control**. Ensuring appropriate levels of inventory.

1.2.2 The purchasing mix

The purchasing manager has to obtain the best purchasing mix.

- Quantity
- Quality
- Price
- Delivery

(a)   **Quantity.** The size and timing of purchase orders will be dictated by the balance between two things.

    (i)   Delays in production caused by insufficient inventory

    (ii)   Costs of holding inventory: tied up capital, storage space, deterioration, insurance, risk of pilferage

    A system of inventory control will set **optimum reorder levels** (the inventory level at which supplies must be replenished so as to arrive in time to meet demand) to ensure **economic order quantities** (EOQ) are obtained for individual inventory items.

(b)   **Quality.** The production department will need to be consulted about the quality of goods required for the manufacturing process, and the marketing department about the quality of goods acceptable to customers. Purchased components might be an important constituent of product quality.

(c)   **Price.** Favourable short-term trends in prices may influence the buying decision, but purchasing should have an eye to the best **value** over a period of time – considering quality, delivery, urgency of order, inventory-holding requirements, and so on.

(d)   **Delivery.** The **lead time** between placing and delivery of an order can be crucial to efficient inventory control and production planning. The reliability of suppliers' delivery arrangements must also be assessed.

1.2.3 Purchasing and profits

The professionalism of the purchasing function affects profit in three ways. Effective purchasing does three things.

- It obtains the **best value for money**, giving the company more flexibility in its pricing strategy.

- It assists in meeting **quality targets**, with an impact on a firm's long-term marketing strategy if quality is an issue.

- It minimises the amount of purchased material held as inventory, so minimising inventory-holding costs.

1.3 Production

> **The production function** plans, organises, directs and controls the necessary activities to provide products and services, creating outputs which have added value over the value of inputs.

Activity	Example
Obtain **inputs** to the production 'system', such as plant facilities, materials and labour	Inputs: timber, screws, nails, adhesives, varnish, stain, templates, cutting tools, carpenters
Adding of value. The activities below occupy most of the production manager's attention. • Scheduling jobs on machines • Assigning labour to jobs • Controlling the quality of production and/or service delivery • Improving methods of work • Managing materials and equipment, to avoid waste	Operations: sawing, sanding, assembly, finishing
Create **outputs**, ie finished products and services	Outputs: tables, chairs, cabinets, and so on

1.3.1 Production management decisions

Longer-term decisions

These are related to setting up the production organisation.

- Selection of equipment and processes
- Job design and methods
- Factory location and layout
- Ensuring the right number and skills of employees

Short-term decisions

These are concerned with the running and control of the organisation.

- Production and control
- Quality management
- Maintenance
- Labour control and supervision
- Inventory control

1.3.2 Relationships with other functions

Longer-term decisions, particularly relating to design and the innovation of improved products, cannot be taken by the production department alone; its activities must be **integrated with other functions** in the firm.

- **Product design** is co-ordinated with **R&D**. Production should advise R&D as to the consequences of particular designs for the manufacturing process.

- **Job design** will involve consultation with **human resources** specialists.

- The quantities needed to be produced will be notified by the **sales department**.

- The **human resources department** will be involved in managing the workforce.

- The **finance department** might indicate the resources available for new equipment.

1.4 Service operations

> **Services** are intangible, cannot be stored, are inherently variable in quality and nature and their purchase results in no transfer of property. The people and processes involved in providing them are therefore of paramount importance.

Many products have a service element. Service businesses include health care, restaurants, tourism, financial services, education and all the professions.

1.4.1 The nature of services

Intangibility. Unlike goods, there are no substantial material or physical aspects to a service. A service cannot be packaged in a bag and carried home, such as a live musical performance.

Inseparability. Many services are **created** at the same time as they are **consumed**, for example dental treatment. Associated with this is **perishability**. Services cannot be stored. The services of a dentist are purchased for a **period of time**. The service they offer cannot be used later.

Variability. It may be hard to attain precise standardisation of the service offered. The quality of the service may depend heavily on **who** (or what) delivers the service, and exactly **when** it takes place.

Ownership. Services differ from consumer goods: they do **not normally result in the transfer of property**. The purchase of a service only confers on the customer access to, or a right to use, a facility, not ownership.

1.4.2 Implications of service provision

Poor service quality on one occasion (eg lack of punctuality of trains, staff rudeness, a bank's incompetence) is likely to lead to **widespread distrust** of everything the organisation does.

Services often have added **complexity.** For example, if the service is intangible offering a complicated future benefit then attracting customers means promoting an attractive image and ensuring that the service lives up to its reputation, consistently.

Pricing of services is often complicated, especially if large numbers of people are involved in providing the service.

Human resources management is a key ingredient in the services marketing mix, as so many services are produced and consumed in a specific social context.

Dimensions of service operations

Determinants	Comments
Tangibles	The physical evidence, such as the quality of fixtures and fittings of the company's service area, must be consistent with the desired image.
Reliability	Getting it right first time is very important, not only to ensure repeat business but, in financial services, as a matter of ethics, if the customer is buying a future benefit.
Responsiveness	The staff's willingness to deal with the customer's queries must be apparent.
Communication	Staff should talk to customers in non-technical language which they can understand.
Credibility	The organisation should be perceived as honest, trustworthy and acting in the best interests of customers.
Security	This is specially relevant to medical and financial services organisations. The customer needs to feel that the conversations with bank service staff are private and confidential. This factor should influence the design of the service area.

Determinants	Comments
Competence	All the service staff need to appear competent in understanding the product range and interpreting the needs of the customers. In part this can be achieved through training programmes.
Courtesy	Customers (even rude ones) should perceive service staff as polite, respectful and friendly. This basic requirement is often difficult to achieve in practice, although training programmes can help.
Understanding customers' needs	The use of computer-based customer databases can be very impressive in this context. The service personnel can then call up the customer's records and use these data in the service process, thus personalising the process. Service staff need to meet customer needs rather than try to sell products. This is a subtle but important difference.
Access	Minimising queues, having a fair queuing system and speedy but accurate service are all factors which can avoid customers' irritation building up. A pleasant, relaxing environment is a useful design factor in this context.

1.5 Marketing

The **marketing function** manages an organisation's relationships with its customers.

Marketing is 'the management process which identifies, anticipates and satisfies customer needs profitably'.

(Chartered Institute of Marketing, 2015)

1.5.1 Models of marketing

Marketing activities in organisations can be grouped broadly into four roles.

(a) **Sales support**. The emphasis in this role is essentially reactive: marketing supports the direct sales force. It may include such activities as telesales or telemarketing, responding to inquiries, co-ordinating diaries, customer database management, organising exhibitions or other sales promotions, and administering agents. These activities usually come under a sales and marketing director or manager.

(b) **Marketing communications**. The emphasis in this role is more proactive: marketing promotes the organisation and its product or service at a tactical level. It typically includes activities such as providing brochures and catalogues to support the sales force.

(c) **Operational marketing**. The emphasis in this role is for marketing to support the organisation with a co-ordinated range of marketing activities including marketing research; brand management; product development and management; corporate and marketing communications; and customer relationship management. Given this breadth of activities, planning is also a function usually performed in this role but at an operational or functional level.

(d) **Strategic marketing**. The emphasis in this role is for marketing to contribute to the creation of competitive strategy. As such, it is practised in customer-focused and larger organisations. In a large or diversified organisation, it may also be responsible for the co-ordination of marketing departments or activities in separate business units.

Operational marketing activities

- Research and analysis
- Contributing to strategy and marketing planning
- Managing brands
- Implementing marketing programmes
- Measuring effectiveness
- Managing marketing teams

The operational marketing role, where it exists, will be performed by a marketing function in a business.

1.5.2 Marketing strategy and corporate strategy

So, what is the relationship between marketing and strategic management? The two are closely linked since there can be no corporate plan which does not involve products/services and customers.

Corporate strategic plans aim to guide the overall development of an organisation. Marketing planning is subordinate to corporate planning but makes a significant contribution to it and is concerned with many of the same issues. The marketing department is probably the most important source of information for the development of corporate strategy. The corporate audit of product/market strengths and weaknesses, and much of its external environmental analysis is directly informed by the **marketing audit**.

Specific marketing strategies will be determined within the overall corporate strategy. To be effective, these plans will be interdependent with those for other functions of the organisation.

(a)   The **strategic** component of marketing planning focuses on the direction which an organisation will take in relation to a specific market, or set of markets, in order to achieve a specified set of objectives.

(b)   Marketing planning also requires an **operational** component that defines tasks and activities to be undertaken in order to achieve the desired strategy. The **marketing plan** is concerned uniquely with **products** and **markets**.

Marketing management aims to ensure the company is pursuing effective policies to promote its products, markets and distribution channels. This involves exercising strategic control of marketing, and the means to apply strategic control is known as the **marketing audit**. Not only is the marketing audit an important aspect of **marketing control** but it can also be used to provide much information and analysis for the **corporate planning process**.

EXAM FOCUS POINT

There is an article on the ACCA website entitled "The role of marketing" that is relevant to material in this section.

1.5.3 Marketing orientation

Different organisations have different orientations towards the customer.

Orientation	Description
Production orientation	'Customers will buy whatever we produce – our job is to make as many as we can'. (Demand exceeds available supply.)
Product orientation, a variant of production orientation	'Add more features to the product – demand will pick up'. Such firms do not research what customers actually want.
Sales orientation	Customers are naturally sales resistant so the product must be sold actively and aggressively and customers must be persuaded to buy them.
Marketing orientation	The key task of the organisation is to determine the needs, wants and values of a target market and to adapt the organisation to delivering the desired satisfactions more effectively and efficiently than its competitors.

Market orientation   *Sales/production orientation*

```
Determine customer needs          Determine whether product
                                        can be made
        │                                    │
        ▼                                    ▼
   Invest resources                    Invest resources
        │                                    │
        ▼                                    ▼
  Make product/service                  Make product
        │                                    │
        ▼                                    ▼
Market the product/service        Sell the product (profit via
(Profit via customer satisfaction)     increased turnover)
        │
        ▼
   Market feedback
```

1.5.4 Satisfying customer needs: the marketing mix

Before you continue, recall the Chartered Institute of Marketing's definition at the beginning of this section. The last word is **profitably**. After all, customers would be absolutely delighted if you were to satisfy **all** their needs for exotic holidays, caviar, champagne, private jets and so forth, for nothing. The marketing orientation is a way of doing business that seeks to provide satisfaction of customer wants at a **profit**.

The marketing mix is the set of controllable variables and their levels that an organisation uses to influence the target market. According to McCathy (1964), these variables are product, price, place and promotion and are known as the 4Ps.

There is thus a balance to be achieved between organisational capacity and customer requirements. This balance is expressed in the **marketing mix**, which is the framework in which the customer and the business deal with each other.

Product

The **product** element of the marketing mix is what is being sold, whether this be widgets, power stations, haircuts, holidays or financial advice. (A product could be a **service**.) Product issues include:

- Design (size, shape)
- Features
- Quality and reliability
- Packaging

- Safety
- Ecological friendliness
- What it does
- Image

The **implication of the marketing orientation** is that the **product or service** is not a 'thing' with 'features' but, from the customer's point of view, is a **package of benefits**, **which meets a need or provides a solution** to a problem.

Core and augmented product

(a)   The **core product** is a product's essential features. The core product of a credit card is the ability to borrow up to a certain limit and pay off in varied instalments.

(b)   **Augmentations** are additional benefits. Most credit cards offer travel insurance, for instance.

Marketing managers make the following distinction.

(a)   Product **class**. This is a broad category of product, such as cars, washing machines and so forth. This corresponds to the core or generic product identified above.

(b)   Product **form**. This category refers to the different types of product within a product class. The product class 'cars' may have several forms, including five-door hatchbacks, four-wheel drive vehicles, hearses and so forth.

(c)   **Brand or make.** This refers to the particular brand or make of the product form. For example, the Nissan Micra, Vauxhall Corsa and Rover 100 are, broadly speaking, examples of the same product form.

When considering the marketing mix, the **product life cycle** is relevant. A product may be expected to go through the life cycle stages of introduction, growth, maturity, decline and senility. A **different marketing approach is appropriate to each stage**, and different levels of sales and profit can be expected. Note that the product life cycle is a **model** of what **might** happen, **not a law** prescribing what **will** happen. In other words, not all products go through these stages or even have a life cycle.

Marketing personnel do not decide how the product appears. Production and design staff must also be consulted.

Place: distribution

Place covers two main issues.

(a)   **Outlets.** Where products are sold, for example in supermarkets and shops.

  (i)   For most consumer goods, this involves one or more **intermediaries**, such as wholesalers, and then retailers.

  (ii) **Direct distribution** occurs when a firm runs its own shops or, via **mail order,** uses the postal service to bypass intermediaries.

(b)   **Logistics**

  Even where intermediaries are used, a manufacturer still has to distribute products to wholesalers and retailers. Logistics involves managing how resources are obtained, moved and stored.

Promotion: marketing communications

Promotion in the marketing mix includes all marketing communications, by which the public knows about the product or service.

Promotion is traditionally the main responsibility of marketing personnel, and is their most visible role. Promotion is intended to stimulate the potential customer through four behavioural stages.

- **Awareness** of the product
- **Interest** in the product
- **Desire** to buy
- **Action:** an actual purchase   (AIDA)

Some types of promotion

- **Advertising**: newspapers, TV, cinema, internet websites
- **Sales promotion**: money-off coupons, 'two for the price of one' offers
- **Direct selling**: by sales personnel
- **Public relations**: crisis management, obtaining favourable press coverage

Price

Products have to be sold at a price which meets the organisation's profit objectives. Pricing is a very practical matter and important part of marketing work.

(a)   The **price element of the mix** itself covers the basic price, discounts, credit terms and interest free credit.

(b)   **Price is influenced by demand** and the product's stage in its life cycle.

  (i)   **Penetration** pricing: a low price is charged to persuade as many people as possible to buy the product in its early stages.

  (ii) **Skimming**: prices are set to cream off the highest level of profits even though this restricts the number of people able to afford the product.

(c) **Price is also part of the image** of the product: rightly or wrongly, a high-priced product is often assumed to be of better quality than a cheaply priced product. A high price also conveys an image of exclusivity.

(d) Price is a weapon against **competitors**.

Service marketing

In addition, for **services** (eg hospital care, air travel) there are three more Ps.

(a) The **people** who deliver the service (eg smiling or surly staff).
(b) The **processes** by which the service is delivered (eg queuing systems at Disney World).
(c) The **physical evidence** of the service (such as a glossy brochure).

This **extended marketing mix** can also be applied to the supply of goods.

QUESTION

Marketing concept

'An accounts department is not making goods and selling them and so does not need the marketing concept.' Is this a fair comment?

ANSWER

No.

(a) The accounts department supplies information to various other parts of the organisation. Providing information is its service, and the other parts of the organisation are, effectively, its customers.

(b) An accounts department deals with customers all the time, especially credit customers: after all, it sends out the bills and collects the money. As its activities are directly involved with customers, it must take the marketing philosophy on board, too.

1.5.5 The ideal marketing mix

The ideal marketing mix is one which holds a **proper balance** between each of these elements.

(a) One marketing activity in the mix will not be fully effective unless proper attention is given to all the other activities. For example, if a company launches a costly promotion campaign which emphasises the superior quality of a product, the outlay on advertising, packaging and personal selling will be wasted if the quality does not live up to customer expectations.

(b) A company might also place too much emphasis on one aspect of the marketing mix, and much of the effort and expenditure might not be justified for the additional returns it obtains. It might, for example, place too much importance on price reductions to earn higher profits, when in fact a smaller price reduction and greater spending on sales promotion or product design might have a more profitable effect.

1.5.6 Market segmentation

Market segmentation occurs when the market can be broken up into different segments whose customers have common needs and preferences for products and/or services. Segmentation could be on bases such as geography, age, gender or income level. Separate identification of segments means that customers may be charged a different amount.

Mass marketing occurs when a business decides to ignore market segments and go to the market as a whole with one standard offering.

Targeted marketing happens when a business targets one particular market segment, eg geographic (a country or area), age or gender, similar lifestyles, degree of loyalty.

In **differentiated marketing**, a business decides to target several segments with different marketing mix strategies, whereas **undifferentiated marketing** is the same as mass marketing.

1.6 Administration

In many organisations administrative functions are carried out at head office as much as possible. When this is the case, the administration function is said to be **centralised**. A **centralised** administration department involves as many administrative tasks as possible being carried out at a single central location.

1.6.1 Advantages of a centralised administration office

(a)   It provides **consistency**, for example the same account codes are likely to be used no matter which part of the organisation submits an invoice. Everyone uses the same data and information.

(b)   It gives better **security/control** over operations and it is easier to enforce standards.

(c)   **Head office** is in a better position to know what is going on.

(d)   There may be **economies of scale** available, for example in purchasing computer equipment and supplies.

(e)   Administration staff are in a **single location** and more expert staff are likely to be employed. Career paths may be more clearly defined.

1.6.2 Disadvantages of a centralised administration office

(a)   Local offices might **have to wait** for tasks to be carried out.

(b)   There is a **reliance on head office** as local offices are less self-sufficient.

(c)   A system fault or hold-up at head office will **impact across the organisation**.

1.7 The finance function

In many companies, the finance function is one of the most important expert roles in the organisation.

Note that Chapter 8 also looks at the role of the finance function in the context of the **specific role** of accounting in the organisation.

Role

- **Raising money**, ensuring it is available for those who need it
- **Recording and controlling** what happens to money, eg payroll and credit control
- Providing **information to managers** to help them make decisions
- **Reporting** to stakeholders, such as shareholders and tax authorities

1.7.1 The importance of finance and finance management

A distinction can be made between 'financial management' and 'management of finance'.

(a)   **Financial management**

   (i)   Investment decisions

   (ii)   Financing decisions (how to pay for investments)

   (iii)   Dividend decisions (how much to give to shareholders)

   (iv)   Operating decisions that affect profits (such as decisions on cost reductions or price increases).

(b)   **Management of finance** is the responsibility for the handling of cash, invoices and other financial documents and for recording the affairs of the business in the books of account.

1.7.2 Raising money: sources of finance

A company might raise new funds from the following sources, using the expertise in its treasury department if it has one.

(a)   **The capital markets**, such as the Stock Exchange or the Alternative Investment Market, are markets for trading **long-term** financial instruments such as equities and debentures. Companies will go to them for three services.

(i)   New share issues, for example by companies acquiring a stock market listing for the first time

(ii)   Rights issues (ie when existing companies issue shares to investors for money)

(iii)   Issues of loan capital

(b)   **Money markets**, on the other hand, are markets for trading **short-term** financial instruments, bills of exchange and certificates of deposits.

(c)   **Retained earnings**, when profits earned in a year may be kept in the company as opposed to being distributed to shareholders.

(d)   **Bank borrowings** (on a short- or long-term basis). Interest payments cannot be reduced to reflect changed circumstances.

(e)   **Government sources** (grants, tax reliefs)

(f)   **Venture capital**

(g)   The **international money and capital markets** (eurocommercial paper, eurobonds and eurocurrency borrowing)

QUESTION

Finance function

What sources of finance are available to a public sector organisation?

ANSWER

- Taxation of incomes and company profits, excise, sales tax (VAT) receipts (central government)
- Sale of gilts (government securities) to investors
- Borrowing from external sources (eg issuing eurobonds)
- Council tax
- User fees (eg charge for using a leisure facility)
- Retail prices (eg train fares)
- Other special charges (eg the 'nuclear levy' on electricity bills)
- Charging overseas users (eg universities for overseas students)
- Funds from central government
- Issuing of municipal bonds (on the money markets)
- Long-term loan finance (eg for local authorities)

Management at this level involves:

(a)   Decisions as to the **right mix of share and loan capital**

(b)   Decisions as to **when that capital should be raised** (eg to fund a major acquisition)

(c)   **Keeping these important shareholders and lenders informed** about the company and its prospects

Much of the **internal** financial management of a company is conducted with the shareholders' return in mind. For example, a company embarking on an investment project will assess its worth by the return or value expected.

1.7.3 Financial accounting

(a)   **Recording financial transactions.** Financial accounting covers the classification and recording of transactions in monetary terms in accordance with established concepts, principles, accounting standards and legal requirements. It presents as accurate a view as possible of the effect of those transactions over a period of time and at the end of the time. In the UK the Companies Act **requires** directors of companies to maintain adequate records to show transactions, assets and liabilities and from which accounts can be prepared to show profit or loss for the accounting reference period and a statement of financial position (balance sheet), detailing assets and liabilities and capital at the end of that reference period.

(b)   **Reporting to shareholders.** In addition, the information must be reported to the **shareholders** in accordance with the detailed disclosure requirements of the Companies Act. All this information will be subject to statutory **audit**. Other organisations, such as building societies and charities, are subject to similar legislation.

1.7.4 Treasury management

Treasury management **plans and controls** the **sources and uses of funds** by the organisation. This is achieved by a range of techniques.

(a)   **Cash budgeting**, daily, weekly, monthly, quarterly and annually

(b)   Arranging **a bank overdraft facility**; borrowing funds in the money markets and capital markets

(c)   **Repaying** sums borrowed when the loans mature

(d)   Comparing actual **cash flows** against budget

(e)   Possibly, the **cashier's duties** of making payments to suppliers, paying wages and banking receipts

(f)   Managing **foreign currency dealings**, to limit the firm's exposure to the risk of losses arising from changes in exchange rates

1.7.5 Working capital and other matters

A company's management of its working capital is vital for business success. Working capital consists of cash, accounts receivable, accounts payable and inventory.

Receivables. Receivables can be managed by effective **credit control**. Poor credit control has its own penalties.

(a)   **Irrecoverable debts**. Sales revenue is not received for goods sold. If the purchaser does not pay for goods received, and no effort is made to recover the debt, the goods have, in effect, been given away.

(b)   A company which cannot collect its debts in time might have to use bank **overdraft finance** to pay its bills. If the bank is concerned about the security of its loan, this might mean the company is vulnerable to increases in interest rates, and the bank's credit decisions.

Payables. Many companies delay paying suppliers as long as possible. In effect, they are using suppliers as a sort of credit finance. Payments to suppliers are an outflow of funds. However, in the long term it may be more important to establish reliable commercial relationships with them than squeeze every pound out of them in the short term. Large companies are now required to disclose their policies on paying suppliers in their annual financial statements.

Inventory. Inventory levels are a focus of some of the production systems discussed earlier. Inventory holding costs must always be managed.

The finance department is often responsible for **payroll**. HR and production provide details of wage rates, time sheets and so forth.

1.7.6 Management accounting information

The finance function plays a critical role in providing information to management to assist in **planning, decision-making and control.** This is called management accounting.

(a)   **Planning**

    (i)   The finance function draws up **budgets** which direct and allocate resources.

    (ii)   The finance function also produces **forecasts** of anticipated future results.

(b)   **Decision-making.** The finance function is often involved in assessing and modelling the expenditure and cash flow implications of proposed decisions.

(c)   **Control**

(i)   **Budgets are also used to monitor performance**. The finance function regularly provides information comparing budgeted revenues and costs for a period, with **actual results** and comparisons from previous months.

(ii) **Management accountants** are involved in assessing the contribution which products, services, processes and other operations make to overall profitability.

(iii) **Costing based on predetermined standards** provides the information which enables managers to identify weaknesses and look for remedies all in a timely manner.

The success of management accountants in meeting their job objectives will depend on two things.

- The quality of the information they provide
- Whether the information they provide to other managers is used properly

1.7.7 Co-ordination with other departments

Instead of being seen as helpers and advisers to other managers, management accountants are sometimes regarded as an adversary who tries to **find fault**. However, close co-ordination with other departments is essential.

(a)   The **payables ledger section** relies on the purchasing department to send copies of purchase orders and confirm the validity of invoices received from suppliers, and also to inform the payables ledger staff about any despatches concerning goods received, or purchases returns. The section also relies on the cashier to inform it of all payments of invoices.

(b)   The **receivables ledger section** relies on **sales staff** to send copies of sales order or confirmations of goods delivered to customers, and on the cashier to pass on information about payments received.

(c)   The receivables ledger section must also co-operate with **debt collection staff**, by helping to prepare monthly statements and lists of aged receivables. **Credit control** work and the work of the debt collection staff are also closely interdependent, relying on the free exchange of information between them.

(d)   The **financial accounting** staff responsible for the preparation of the annual accounts might rely on the management accounting staff for data about inventory records, so as to place a value on closing inventory in the accounts.

As **information providers** to other managers in other departments in the organisation, accountants cannot be fully effective unless they work in co-operation with these other managers.

1.7.8 The finance department and strategic planning

The role of finance is threefold.

(a)   Finance is a **resource**, which can be deployed so that objectives are met.

(b)   A firm's objectives are often **expressed in financial or semi-financial terms**.

(c)   **Financial controls** are often used to plan and control the implementation of strategies. Financial indicators are often used for detailed performance assessment.

As a planning medium and tool for monitoring, financial management makes a variety of strategic contributions.

(a)   **Ensuring that resources of finance are available**. Issues of raising equity or loan capital are important here. The amount of resources that the strategy will consume needs to be assessed, and the likely cost of those resources established. Cash flow forecasting will also be necessary.

(b)   **Integrating the strategy into budgets** for revenues, operating costs and capital expenditure over a period. The budgeting process serves as a planning tool and a means of financial control and monitoring.

(c)   **Establishing the necessary performance measures**, in line with other departments for monitoring strategic objectives.

(d)   **Establishing priorities** if, for example, altered conditions make some aspects of the strategy hard to fulfil.

(e)   **Assisting in the modelling process**. Financial models are simplified representations of the business. It is easier to experiment with models, to see the effect of changes in variables, than with the business itself.

1.8 Human resources

Human resource management (HRM) is the process of evaluating an organisation's human resource needs, finding people to fill those needs, and getting the best work from each employee by providing the right incentives and job environment – with the overall aim of helping achieve organisational goals.

1.8.1 Scope of human resource management

Human resource management (HRM) is concerned with the most effective use of human resources. It deals with organisation, staffing levels, motivation, employee relations and employee services.

Human resource management (HRM) is concerned with a strategic approach to people at work and their relationships as they arise in the working environment.

The objectives of HRM

It is possible to identify **four main objectives of HRM**.

(a)   To develop an effective human component for the organisation which will respond effectively to change.

(b)   To obtain and develop the human resources required by the organisation and to use and motivate them effectively.

(c)   To create and maintain a co-operative climate of relationships within the organisation.

(d)   To meet the organisation's social and legal responsibilities relating to the human resource.

1.8.2 Why is HRM important?

Effective human resource management and employee development are strategically necessary for the following reasons.

(a)   To **increase productivity**. Developing employee skills might make employees more productive, hence the recent emphasis on public debate on the value of training.

(b)   To **enhance group learning**. Employees work more and more in multi-skilled teams. Each employee has to be competent at several tasks. Some employees have to be trained to work together (ie in team working skills).

(c)   To **reduce staff turnover**. Reducing staff turnover, apart from cutting recruitment costs, can also increase the effectiveness of operations. In service businesses, such as hotels or retail outlets, reductions in staff turnover can be linked with repeat visits by customers. As it is cheaper to keep existing customers than to find new ones, this can have a significant effect on profitability.

(d)   To **encourage initiative**. Organisations can gain significant advantage from encouraging and exploiting the present and potential abilities of the people within them.

1.8.3 The human resource cycle

A relatively simple model that provides a framework for explaining the nature and significance of HRM is the human resource cycle (Fombrun et al 1984).

Human resource cycle

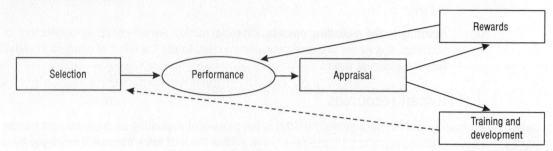

Selection is important to ensure the organisation obtains people with the qualities and skills required.

Appraisal enables targets to be set that contribute to the achievement of the overall strategic objectives of the organisation. It also identifies skills and performance gaps, and provides information relevant to reward levels.

Training and development ensure skills remain up to date, relevant, and comparable with (or better than) the best in the industry.

The **reward system** should motivate and ensure valued staff are retained.

Performance depends on each of the four components and how they are co-ordinated.

These topics are all covered in Part D of the Interactive Text.

1.8.4 The HR plan

HRM planning should be based on the **organisation's strategic planning processes**, in relation to analysis of the labour market, forecasting of the external supply and internal demand for labour, job analysis and plan implementation.

Human resource planning concerns the acquisition, utilisation, improvement and return of an enterprise's human resources. Human resource planning deals with:

* Recruitment
* Retention (company loyalty, to retain skills and reduce staff turnover)
* Downsizing (reducing staff numbers)
* Training and retraining to enhance the skills base

The process of human resources planning

1. STRATEGIC ANALYSIS

* Of the environment
* Of the organisation's manpower strengths and weaknesses, opportunities and threats
* Of the organisation's use of employees
* Of the organisation's objectives

2. FORECASTING

* Of internal demand and supply
* Of external supply

1.8.5 Control over the HR plan

Once the HR plan has been established, regular **control reports** should be produced.

(a)   **Actual** numbers recruited, leaving and promoted should be compared with **planned** numbers. Action may be required to correct any imbalance – depending on the cause.

(b)   Actual pay, conditions of employment and training should be compared with assumptions in the HR plan. Do divergences explain any excessive staff turnover?

(c)   Periodically, the HR plan itself should be reviewed and brought up to date.

2   What is culture?

2.1 Spheres of culture

Culture is 'the collective programming of the mind which distinguishes the members of one category of people from another' *(Hofstede)*. It may be identified as ways of behaving, and ways of understanding, that are shared by a group of people.

Edgar Schein (Schein, 1985) defines organisational culture as 'the set of shared, taken-for-granted implicit assumptions that a group holds and that determines how it perceives, thinks about and reacts to its environment'. He also suggests that the culture of an organisation is grounded in the founder's basic beliefs, values and assumptions, and embedded in the organisation over time – what Schein calls 'the residue of success'.

Culture may therefore be identified as ways of behaving, and ways of understanding, that are shared by a group of people. Referring to it as: 'The way we do things round here', Schein (Schein, 1985) says that organisational culture matters because cultural elements determine strategy, goals and modes of operating.

Culture can be discussed on many different levels. The 'category' or 'group' of people whose shared behaviours and meanings may constitute a culture include:

- A nation, region or ethnic group
- Women versus men ('gender culture')
- A social class (eg 'working class culture')
- A profession or occupation
- A type of business (eg 'advertising culture')
- An organisation (**'organisational culture'**)

If you are a male (or female) accountant in an organisation operating in a given business sector in a particular region of your country of residence (which may not be your country of origin), you may be influenced by all these different spheres of culture!

2.2 Elements of culture

Elements of culture include:

- Observable behaviour
- Underlying values and beliefs which give meaning to the observable elements
- Hidden assumptions, which unconsciously shape values and beliefs

It is suggested that there are different levels at which culture can be understood (Schein, 1985). For Schein, culture is the most difficult organisational attribute to change, outlasting products, founders and leaders as the organisation grows. His model describes three **determinants of culture**.

(a)   **The first level**. The **observable**, expressed or 'explicit' elements of culture

   (i)   **Behaviour**: norms of personal and interpersonal behaviour; customs and rules about behaviour that is acceptable or unacceptable.

   (ii)   **Artefacts**: concrete expressions such as architecture and interior design (eg of office premises), dress codes and symbols.

   (iii)   **Attitudes**: patterns of collective behaviour such as greeting styles, business formalities, social courtesies and ceremonies.

(b)   **The second level**. Beneath these observable phenomena lie **values and beliefs** and the professed culture, which give the behaviour and attitudes their special meaning and significance. For example, the design of office space may imply status and honour, or reflect the importance of privacy within a culture: it 'means' more than the observable features. Values and beliefs may be overtly expressed in slogans or the mission statement.

(c)   **The third level**. Beneath values and beliefs lie **assumptions**: foundational ideas ('unspoken rules') that are no longer consciously recognised or questioned by the culture, but which 'program' its ways of thinking and behaving.

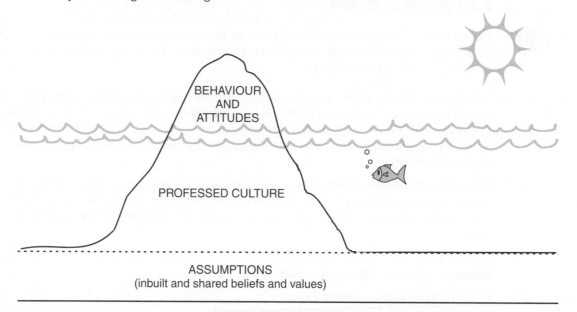

ASSUMPTIONS
(inbuilt and shared beliefs and values)

3 Organisation culture

3.1 Manifestations of culture in organisations

Organisation culture is **'the way we do things round here'** (Schein, 1985).

Examples of organisation culture include the following.

Item	Example
Beliefs and values, which are often unquestioned	'The customer is always right'.
Behaviour	In the City of London, standard business dress is still generally taken for granted and even 'dress down Fridays' have their rules.
Artefacts	Microsoft encourages communication between employees by setting aside spaces for the purpose.
Rituals	In some firms, salespeople compete with each other, and there is a reward, given at a ceremony, for the salesperson who does best in any period.
Symbols	Corporate logos are an example of symbols, but they are directed outwards. Within the organisation, symbols can represent power: dress, make and model of car, office size and equipment and access to facilities can all be important symbols.

Manifestations of culture in an organisation may thus include:

- How formal the organisation structure is
- Communication: are senior managers approachable?
- Office layout
- The type of people employed
- Symbols, legends, corporate myths
- Management style
- Freedom for subordinates to show initiative
- Attitudes to quality
- Attitudes to risk
- Attitudes to the customer
- Attitudes to technology

QUESTION

Manifestations of culture

What do you think would differentiate the culture of:

- A regiment in the Army?   •   An advertising agency?

ANSWER

Here are some hints. The Army is very disciplined. Decisions are made by officers; behaviour between ranks is sometimes very formal. The organisation values loyalty, courage and discipline and teamwork. Symbols and artefacts include uniforms, medals, regimental badges, and so on. Rituals include corporate expressions such as parades and ceremonies.

An advertising agency, with a different mission, is more fluid. Individual flair and creativity, within the commercial needs of the firm, is expected. Artefacts may include the style of creative offices, awards or prizes, and the agency logo. Rituals may include various award ceremonies, team meetings and social gatherings.

3.2 What shapes organisation culture?

Influences on organisational culture include:

(a) The organisation's **founder**. A strong set of values and assumptions is set up by the organisation's founder, and even after they have retired, these values have their own momentum. Or, to put it another way, an organisation might find it hard to shake off its original culture.

(b) The organisation's **history**

  (i) Culture reflects the era when the organisation was founded.

  (ii) The effect of history can be determined by stories, rituals and symbolic behaviour. They legitimise behaviour and promote priorities.

(c) **Leadership and management style**. An organisation with a strong culture recruits and develops managers who naturally conform to it and who perpetuate the culture.

(d) The **organisation's environment**. As we have seen, nations, regions, occupations and business types have their own distinctive cultures, and these will affect the organisation's style.

> **Cultural values** can be used to guide organisational processes without the need for tight control. They can also be used to motivate employees, by emphasising the heroic dimension of the task. Culture can also be used to drive change, although – since values are difficult to change – it can also be a powerful force for preserving the *status quo*.

4 Culture and structure

> **Handy** (2007) classifies four types of culture, to which he gives the names of Greek deities.
>
> - **Power** culture (Zeus) is shaped by one individual.
> - **Role** culture (Apollo) is a bureaucratic culture shaped by rationality, rules and procedures.
> - **Task** culture (Athena) is shaped by a focus on outputs and results.
> - **Existential** or person culture (Dionysus) is shaped by the interests of individuals.

The four types are differentiated by their structures, processes and management methods. The differences are so significant as to create **distinctive cultures**, to each of which Handy gives the name of a Greek God.

Zeus **Power culture** The organisation is controlled by a key central figure, owner or founder. Power is direct, personal, informal. Suits small organisations where people get on well.	Apollo **Role culture** Classical, rational organisation: bureaucracy. Stable, slow-changing, formalised, impersonal. Authority based on position and function.
Athena **Task culture** Management is directed at outputs: problems solved, projects completed. Team based, horizontally structured, flexible, valuing expertise – to get the job done.	Dionysus **Person culture** The purpose of the organisation is to serve the interests of the individuals who make it up: management is directed at facilitating, administering.

4.1 Power culture

Zeus is the god representing the **power culture** or **club culture**. Zeus is a dynamic entrepreneur who rules with snap decisions. Power and influence stem from a central source, perhaps the owner-directors or the founder of the business. The degree of formalisation is limited, and there are few rules and procedures. Such a firm is likely to be organised on a functional basis.

(a)   The organisation is capable of adapting quickly to meet change.

(b)   Personal influence decreases as the size of an organisation gets bigger. The power culture is therefore best suited to smaller entrepreneurial organisations, where the leaders have direct communication with all employees.

(c)   Personnel have to get on well with each other for this culture to work. These organisations are clubs of 'like-minded people introduced by the like-minded people, working on empathetic initiative with personal contact rather than formal liaison.'

4.2 Role culture

Apollo is the god of the **role culture** or **bureaucracy**. There is a presumption of logic and rationality.

(a)   These organisations have a formal structure, and operate by well-established rules and procedures.

(b)   Individuals are required to perform their job to the full, but not to overstep the boundaries of their authority. Individuals who work for such organisations tend to learn an expertise without experiencing risk; many do their job adequately, but are not over-ambitious.

(c)   The bureaucratic style, as we have seen, can be very efficient in a stable environment, when the organisation is large and when the work is predictable.

4.3 Task culture

Athena is the goddess of the **task culture**. Management is seen as completing a succession of projects or solving problems.

(a)   The task culture is reflected in project teams and task forces. In such organisations, there is no dominant or clear leader. The principal concern in a task culture is to get the job done. Therefore the individuals who are important are the experts with the ability to accomplish a particular aspect of the task.

(b)   Performance is judged by results.

(c)   Task cultures are expensive, as experts demand a market price.

(d)   Task cultures also depend on variety, and to tap creativity requires a tolerance of perhaps costly mistakes.

4.4 Person culture

Dionysus is the god of the **existential** or **person culture**. In the three other cultures, the individual is subordinate to the organisation or task. An existential culture is found in an organisation whose purpose is to serve the interests of the individuals within it. These organisations are rare, although an example might be a partnership of a few individuals who do all the work of the organisation themselves (with perhaps a little secretarial or clerical assistance): for example, barristers (in the UK) working through chambers.

Management positions in these organisations are often lower in status than the professionals and are labelled secretaries, administrators, bursars, registrars or clerks.

The organisation depends on the talent of the individuals; management is derived from the consent of the managed, rather than the delegated authority of the owners.

> **EXAM FOCUS POINT**
>
> Do not neglect the key link between **culture** and **structure**!

4.5 A contingency approach

When thinking about these four types of culture, remember that they do not necessarily equate to specific organisation types, though some styles of organisation culture may accompany particular organisation structures. Also, it is quite possible for different cultures to prevail in different parts of the same organisation, especially large ones with many departments and sites. In other words, as the contingency approach says: 'it all depends'.

Handy also matched appropriate cultural models to Robert **Anthony's** classification of managerial activity, which we discussed in Chapter 5.

(a)   **Strategic management** (carried out by senior management) is concerned with direction setting, policy making and crisis handling. It therefore suits a **power culture**.

(b)   **Tactical management** (carried out by middle management) is concerned with establishing means to the corporate ends, mobilising resources and innovating (finding new ways of achieving goals). It therefore suits a **task culture**.

(c)   **Operational management** (carried out by supervisors and operatives) is concerned with routine activities to carry out tactical plans. It therefore suits a **role culture**.

QUESTION

Review the following statements. Ascribe each of them to one of Handy's four corporate cultures.

People are controlled and influenced by:

(a) The personal exercise of rewards, punishments or charisma

(b) Impersonal exercise of economic and political power to enforce procedures and standards of performance

(c) Communication and discussion of task requirements leading to appropriate action motivated by personal commitment to goal achievement

(d) Intrinsic interest and enjoyment in the activities to be done and/or concern and caring for the needs of the other people involved

ANSWER

(a) Zeus/power culture

(b) Apollo/role culture

(c) Athena/task culture

(d) Dionysus/person culture

4.6 The impact of national culture

National culture influences organisation culture in various ways. One model of these effects is the 'Hofstede model' which describes four dimensions on which cultures differ.

- Power distance
- Individualism/collectivism
- Uncertainty avoidance
- Masculinity/femininity

Different countries have different ways of doing business, and different cultural values and assumptions which influence business and management styles.

4.7 The Hofstede model

Hofstede (2011) carried out cross-cultural research at 66 national offices of IBM and formulated one of the most influential models of work-related cultural differences.

The Hofstede model describes four main dimensions of difference between national cultures, which impact on all aspects of management and organisational behaviour: motivation, team working, leadership style, conflict management and HR policies.

(a) **Power distance**: the extent to which unequal distribution of power is accepted

    (i) **High** PD cultures (as in Latin, near Eastern and less developed Asian countries) accept greater centralisation, a top-down chain of command and closer supervision. Subordinates have little expectation of influencing decisions.

    (ii) **Low** PD cultures (as in Germanic, Anglo and Nordic countries) expect less centralisation and flatter organisational structures. Subordinates expect involvement and participation in decision-making. (Japan is a medium PD culture.)

(b) **Uncertainty avoidance**: the extent to which security, order and control are preferred to ambiguity, uncertainty and change

    (i) **High** UA cultures (as in Latin, near Eastern and Germanic countries and Japan) respect control, certainty and ritual. They value task structure, written rules and regulations, specialists and experts, and standardisation. There is a strong need for consensus: deviance and dissent are not tolerated. The work ethic is strong.

    (ii) **Low** UA cultures (as in Anglo and Nordic countries) respect flexibility and creativity. They have less task structure and written rules, more generalists and greater variability. There is more tolerance of risk, dissent, conflict and deviation from norms.

(c) **Individualism**: the extent to which people prefer to live and work in individualist (focusing on the 'I' identity) or collectivist (focusing on the 'we' identity) ways

    (i) **High** individualism cultures (as in Anglo, more developed Latin and Nordic countries) emphasise autonomy and individual choice and responsibility. They prize individual initiative. The organisation is impersonal and tends to defend business interests: task achievement is more important than relationships. Management is seen in an individual context.

    (ii) **Low** individualism (or collectivist) cultures (as in less developed Latin, near Eastern and less developed Asian countries) emphasise interdependence, reciprocal obligation and social acceptability. The organisation is seen as a 'family' and tends to defend employees' interests: relationships are more important than task achievement. Management is seen in a team context. (Japan and Germany are 'medium' cultures on this dimension.)

(d) **Masculinity**: the extent to which social gender roles are distinct (Note that this is different from the usual sense in which the terms 'masculine' and 'feminine' are used.)

    (i) **High** masculinity cultures (as in Japan and Germanic and Anglo countries) clearly differentiate gender roles. Masculine values of assertiveness, competition, decisiveness and material success are dominant. Feminine values of modesty, tenderness, consensus, focus on relationships and quality of working life are less highly regarded, and confined to women.

    (ii) **Low** masculinity (or Feminine) cultures (as in Nordic countries) minimise gender roles. Feminine values are dominant – and both men and women are allowed to behave accordingly.

QUESTION

National culture and management style

According to the Hofstede model, what issues might arise in the following cases?

(a) The newly appointed Spanish (more developed Latin) R&D manager of a UK (Anglo) firm asks to see the Rules and Procedures Manual for the department.

(b) A US-trained (Anglo) manager attempts to implement a system of Management by Objectives (MbO) in Thailand (less developed Asian).

(c) A Dutch (Nordic) HR manager of a US (Anglo) subsidiary in the Netherlands is instructed to implement downsizing measures.

ANSWER

(a) A high-UA manager, expecting to find detailed and generally adhered-to rules for everything, may be horrified by the adhocracy of a low-UA organisation: if they attempt to impose a high-UA culture, there may be resistance from employees and management.

(b) A high-individuality manager may implement MbO on the basis of individual performance targets, results and rewards: this may fail to motivate collectivist workers, for whom group processes and performance is more important.

(c) A low-masculinity manager may try to shelter the workforce from the effects of downsizing, taking time for consultation, retraining, voluntary measures, and so on: this may seem unacceptably 'soft' to a high-masculinity parent firm.

EXAM FOCUS POINT

The following question appeared in a past exam and the exam report said that only 27% of students got it right.

QUESTION

Hofstede

Research has indicated that workers in country A display characteristics such as toughness and the desire for material wealth and possessions, while workers in country B value personal relationships, belonging and the quality of life.

According to Hofstede's theory, these distinctions relate to which of the following cultural dimensions?

A   Masculinity/femininity   C   Individualism-collectivism
B   Power distance   D   Uncertainty avoidance

ANSWER

A   The exam report highlighted that this question was one of ten questions on the paper that referred to management theories or needed knowledge of management theories. Make sure that you learn your theories!

5 Committees

Within an organisation, committees can consist entirely of executives or may be instruments for joint consultation between employers and employees. They are a key part of organisational communication processes, which are covered in Chapter 18.

5.1 Purposes of committees

(a)   **Creating new ideas**. Group creativity may be achieved by a brainstorming committee or think tank.

(b)   **Communication**. They can be an excellent means of **communication**. For example, they can be used to exchange ideas and get feedback before a decision is taken or to inform managers about policies, plans, actual results, and so on.

(c)   **Democratic**. They are democratic, because they allow for greater **participation** in the decision-making process. **Problem solving** can be facilitated by consultations between interested parties.

(d)   **Combining abilities**. Committees enable the differing skills of its various members to be brought together to deal with a problem. In theory, the quality of committee decisions should be of a high standard.

(e)   **Co-ordination**. Committees should enable the maximum co-ordination of all parties involved in a decision to be achieved, for example in co-ordinating the budgets of each department and compiling a master budget.

(f)   **Representation**. Committees enable all relevant interests to be involved in the decision-making process and they bring together the specialised knowledge of working people into a working combination.

(g)   **Recommendations**. Making **recommendations** for others to follow is a key output from committee processes.

5.1.1 The committee Chair

There are a number of recognised qualities of a good Chair (though common sense may dictate many others, varying with circumstances).

(a)   The Chair will have to give **immediate rulings** on points of dispute or doubt, so they should have:

   (i)   A sound knowledge of the relevant issues
   (ii)   An ability to make up his/her mind
   (iii)   Skill in communicating clearly, but tactfully and in a courteous manner

(b)   The Chair should be and be seen to be **impartial**. There will be times when criticism is expressed which they personally may find unfair, or when there is a strong clash of opinion between other committee members. In either situation, whatever their personal views, the Chair should treat opponents with equal fairness.

(c)   The Chair should have the **discretion** to know when to insist on **strict observance** of correct procedure, and when a certain amount of **relaxation** will ease the tension.

(d)   The Chair should be **punctual** and regular in attendance at meetings. If they cannot give the duties the appropriate amount of time and attention, they should consider resigning.

5.1.2 The committee secretary

(a)   Duties **before** committee meeting:

(i)   Fixing the date and time of the meeting
(ii)   Choosing and preparing the location of the meeting
(iii)   Preparing and issuing various documents

(b)   Duties **at** the meeting: assisting the Chair, making notes

(c)   Duties **after** the meeting: preparing minutes, acting on and communicating decisions

5.2 Types of committee

Committees can be classified according to the **power** they exercise.

(a)   **Executive committees** have the power to govern or administer. The board of directors of a limited company is itself a 'committee' appointed by the shareholders, to the extent that it governs or administers.

(b)   **Standing committees** are formed for a particular purpose on a **permanent basis**. Their role is to deal with routine business delegated to them at weekly or monthly meetings.

(c)   **Ad hoc committees** are formed to complete a particular task (eg fact-finding and reporting on a particular problem before being wound up).

(d)   **Sub-committees** may be appointed by committees to relieve the parent committee of some of its routine work.

(e)   **Joint committees** may be formed to co-ordinate the activities of two or more committees; for example, representatives from employers and employees may meet in a Joint Consultative Committee. This kind of committee can either be permanent or appointed for a special purpose.

(f)   **Management committees** in many businesses contain executives at a number of levels, not all the decisions in a firm need to be taken by the Board.

5.3 Advantages of committees

(a)   **Consolidation of power and authority**. The pooled authority of a committee may enable a decision to be made for which an individual's authority would not be sufficient. Examples of a **plural executive** include a Board of Directors or the Cabinet of the Government.

(b)   **Delegation**. A committee can further delegate responsibility, for example to a subcommittee.

(c)   **Blurring responsibility**. When a committee makes a decision, no individual will be held responsible for the consequences of the decision.

(d)   **Delay**. A committee is used to gain time (eg a manager may set up a committee to investigate a problem when they want to delay their decision, or a company may refer a labour relations problem to a committee to defer a crisis with a trade union).

5.4 Disadvantages of committees

(a)   They are **apt to be too large for constructive action**, since the time taken by a committee to resolve a problem tends to be in direct proportion to its size.

(b) Committees are **time consuming and expensive**. In addition to the cost of highly paid executives' time, secretarial costs will be incurred.

(c) **Delays may occur if matters of a routine nature are entrusted to committees**; committees must not be given responsibilities which they would carry out inefficiently.

(d) **Operations may be jeopardised by the frequent attendance of executives at meetings**, and by distracting them from their real duties.

(e) **Incorrect or ineffective decisions** may be made, if members are unfamiliar with the issues. Occasionally, there may be a **total failure to reach any decision at all.**

(f) The fact that there is no individual responsibility for decisions might invite **compromise** instead of clear-cut decisions. Moreover, members may avoid responsibility for poor results arising from decisions taken by the committee. Weak management can hide behind committee decisions.

5.5 Using committees successfully

(a) Well-defined areas of authority, timescales of operations and purpose should be specified in writing.

(b) The **Chair** should have the qualities of leadership to co-ordinate and motivate the other committee members.

(c) The committee should not be so large as to be unmanageable.

(d) The members of the committee should have the necessary skills and experience to do the committee's work; where the committee is expected to liaise with functional departments, the members must also have sufficient status and influence with those departments.

(e) Minutes of the meetings should be taken and circulated by the **Secretary**, with any action points arising out of the meetings notified to the members responsible for doing the work.

(f) In order to conduct business and make decisions there is usually a minimum number of members required to be in attendance at the meeting. This minimum number of members is known as a quorum and it is usually over 50% of members.

(g) Above all, an efficient committee must provide benefits that justify its cost.

(h) Finally, if at all possible, the committee should be allowed plenty of time to reach decisions, enabling members to form sub-groups.

EXAM FOCUS POINT

There is an article on the ACCA website entitled "Corporate governance: the board of directors and standing committees" that is relevant to material in this section.

PER performance objective PO3 requires you to demonstrate contribution to strategy and innovation. Knowledge of organisational culture, and working effectively with internal committees on business issues and challenges, may help in this context.

CHAPTER ROUNDUP

- Research may be **pure**, **applied** or **development**. It may be intended to improve **products** or **processes**.

- R&D should support the organisation's strategy and be closely co-ordinated with marketing.

- **Purchasing** makes a major contribution to cost and quality management in any business and in retail is a vital element of strategy. The purchasing mix is:

  - Quantity
  - Price
  - Quality
  - Delivery

- **The production function** plans, organises, directs and controls the necessary activities to provide products and services, creating outputs which have added value over the value of inputs.

- **Services** are intangible, cannot be stored, are inherently variable in quality and nature and their purchase results in no transfer of property. The people and processes involved in providing them are therefore of paramount importance.

- The **marketing function** manages an organisation's relationships with its customers.

- **Human resource management** (HRM) is concerned with the most effective use of human resources. It deals with organisation, staffing levels, motivation, employee relations and employee services.

- **HRM planning** should be based on the **organisation's strategic planning processes**, with relation to analysis of the labour market, forecasting of the external supply and internal demand for labour, job analysis and plan implementation.

- **Culture** is 'the collective programming of the mind which distinguishes the members of one category of people from another' (Hofstede). It may be identified as ways of behaving, and ways of understanding, that are shared by a group of people.

- **Elements of culture** include:

  - Observable behaviour
  - Underlying values and beliefs which give meaning to the observable elements
  - Hidden assumptions, which unconsciously shape values and beliefs

- Organisation culture is **'the way we do things round here'**.

- **Cultural values** can be used to guide organisational processes without the need for tight control. They can also be used to motivate employees, by emphasising the heroic dimension of the task. Culture can also be used to drive change, although – since values are difficult to change – it can also be a powerful force for preserving the status quo.

- **Harrison** classified four types of culture, to which **Handy** gave the names of Greek deities.

  - **Power** culture (Zeus) is shaped by one individual.
  - **Role** culture (Apollo) is a bureaucratic culture shaped by rationality, rules and procedures.
  - **Task** culture (Athena) is shaped by a focus on outputs and results.
  - **Existential** or person culture (Dionysus) is shaped by the interests of individuals.

- **National culture** influences organisation culture in various ways. One model of these effects is the 'Hofstede model' which describes four dimensions on which cultures differ.

  - Power distance
  - Uncertainty avoidance
  - Individualism/collectivism
  - Masculinity/femininity

- Within an organisation, committees can consist entirely of executives or may be instruments for joint consultation between employers and employees. They are a key part of organisational communication processes, which are covered in Chapter 18.

QUICK QUIZ

1   What is the main intention behind R&D?

2   What are the elements of the purchasing mix?

    A   Place, product, price, promotion   C   Product, quality, price, delivery
    B   Quantity, quality, price, delivery   D   Place, product, price, delivery

3   Choose the correct word to fill in the blank: planning, production, promotion

    The .... function plans, organises and controls the necessary activities to provide products and services.

4   Marketing is the management process which identifies, anticipates and satisfies customer needs, regardless of expense.

    Is this true or false?

5   Which two of the following are roles of the finance function?

    ☐   To provide information to managers for decision-making

    ☐   To ensure compliance with social and legal responsibilities

    ☐   To record and control what happens to money

6   What are the four main objectives of HRM?

7   Selection is important to ensure that the organisation obtains people with the qualities and skills required.

    Is this true or false?

8   What are the elements of culture?

9   'Bureaucracy' is another name for a:

    A   Power culture   C   Task culture
    B   Role culture   D   Existential culture

10   A project team is most likely to be a role culture. True or false?

11   According to Hofstede, the extent to which security, order and control are preferred to ambiguity and change is called

    A   Masculinity   C   Power distance
    B   Individualism   D   Uncertainty avoidance

12   What is the name of a committee with the power to govern or administer?

    A   Joint committee   C   Executive committee
    B   Ad hoc committee   D   Standing committee

1   To improve products or processes and so support the organisation's strategy.

2   B. Note that A is the marketing mix.

3   Production

4   False. Marketing must be done profitably.

5   ☑ To provide information to managers for decision-making

     ☑ To record and control what happens to money

6   • To develop an effective human component for the company
     • To obtain, develop and motivate staff
     • To create positive relationships
     • To ensure compliance with social and legal responsibilities

7   True

8   Observable phenomena (behaviour, artefacts, rituals), values and beliefs, assumptions

9   B   Role culture

10   False. It is most likely to be a task culture.

11   D   Uncertainty avoidance

12   C   Executive committee. Committees can be classified according to the **power** that they exercise.

Now try ...

Attempt the questions below from the **Practice Question Bank**

Q28

Q29

Q30

Q31

07

There have been a number of reports worldwide on corporate governance, but understanding the underlying principles of corporate governance are more important than getting to grips with the detailed provisions laid down in each report. **Sections 1 and 2** of this chapter cover the main areas of corporate governance.

Section 3 and 4 go on to discuss the role of the board and how it communicates with shareholders.

Corporate social responsibility is covered in **Sections 5 and 6** of the chapter. While some argue that business has a social responsibility for the cost of its activities, this is controversial. However, there does now seem to be widespread acceptance that commercial organisations should devote some of their resources to the promotion of wider social aims that are not necessarily mandated by either law or the rules of ethics.

Corporate governance and social responsibility

Study Guide | Intellectual level

B5 Governance and social responsibility in business

(a) Explain the agency concept in relation to corporate governance. | K

(b) Define corporate governance and social responsibility and explain their importance in contemporary organisations. | K

(c) Explain the responsibility of organisations to maintain appropriate standards of corporate governance and corporate social responsibility. | K

(d) Briefly explain the main recommendations of best practice in effective corporate governance: | K

   (i) Executive and non-executive directors

   (ii) Remuneration committees

   (iii) Audit committees

   (iv) Public oversight

(e) Explain how organisations take account of their social responsibility objectives through analysis of the needs of internal, connected and external stakeholders. | K

(f) Identify the social and environmental responsibilities of business organisations to internal, connected and external stakeholders. | K

EXAM FOCUS POINT

There is an article on the ACCA website entitled "Corporate governance: the board of directors and standing committees" that is relevant to material in this chapter.

---

1 Principles of corporate governance

Most corporate governance reports are based around the principles of **integrity**, **accountability**, **independence** and **good management** but there is disagreement on how much these principles need to be supplemented by detailed rules.

1.1 What is corporate governance?

Corporate governance is the system by which organisations are directed and controlled by senior officers.

Most countries adopt a principles-based approach to corporate governance, meaning that 'best practice' guidelines are set out for companies to follow. The Organisation for Economic Co-operation and Development published its 'Principles of Corporate Governance' in 2004. In summary:

- *Rights of shareholders*: The corporate governance framework should protect shareholders and their rights

- *Equitable treatment of shareholders*: All shareholders should be treated fairly and on equal terms.

- *Stakeholders*: The corporate governance framework should recognise the legal rights of stakeholders and facilitate cooperation with them

- *Disclosure and transparency*: Companies should make relevant, timely disclosures on matters affecting financial performance, management and ownership of the business.

- *Board of directors*: The board of directors should set the direction of the company and monitor management, underpinning the board's accountability to the company and its members

Although mostly discussed in relation to large quoted companies, governance is an issue for all corporate bodies; commercial and not for profit.

There are a number of elements in corporate governance.

(a) The management and **reduction of risk** is fundamental in all definitions of good governance.

(b) **Overall performance enhanced** by **good supervision** and **management** within **set best practice guidelines** underpins most definitions.

(c) Good governance provides a **framework** for an organisation to pursue its strategy in an **ethical and effective** way from the perspective of all stakeholder groups affected, and offers safeguards against misuse of resources, physical or intellectual.

(d) Good governance is not just about externally established codes; it also requires a willingness to **apply the spirit** as well as the letter of the law.

(e) **Accountability** is generally a major theme in all governance frameworks. There is a free flow of information in the form of accounts and other reports. However, issues of commercial confidentiality can get in the way of too much 'openness'.

Extensive abuses have led to a variety of measures intended to improve the quality of corporate governance.

(a) The development of **accounting standards** has been driven in part by the need to prevent abuses in financial reporting.

(b) The various professional bodies all have their own **codes of professional conduct**.

(c) A series of major financial scandals has led to government intervention in the UK in the form of **commissions on standards of behaviour**, each producing its code of conduct.

1.2 Definitions

1.2.1 Integrity

Integrity in business means dealing honestly with employees, customers and all business contacts.

1.2.2 Accountability

Accountability means the business being answerable for its actions.

1.2.3 Independence

Independence in this context means that there must be independent people within the organisation checking that the business is complying with its code of governance.

1.2.4 Good management

Good management in business means setting best practice guidelines.

1.3 Perspectives on governance

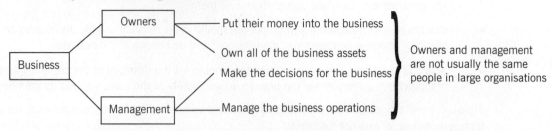

In a small business the shareholders (ie owners) are likely to be the directors and so the owners and the managers are the same and there are no issues.

In larger businesses the shareholders (ie owners) will not necessarily be involved in the day-to-day running and management of the business. The owners and the managers will not be the same and so there may be a conflict of interest.

1.3.1 The agency concept

When applied to corporate governance, the agency concept refers to the organisation owners (the shareholders) as the 'principal' and those managing the company (the company directors) as their 'agents'.

The corporate governance framework should therefore aim to ensure that those running the company do so in a way that best serves the interests of shareholders (rather than pursuing their own interests). Ensuring that the way in which managers and directors are rewarded encourages them to act in a way that benefits shareholders is also important (see agency theory below).

Debates about the place of governance are founded on three differing views associated with the **ownership** and **management** of organisations.

The agency concept is particularly relevant for large organisations, where there is a greater degree of separation between ownership and management. This is particularly the case for public listed companies.

1.3.2 Stewardship theory

Some approaches to good governance view the management of an organisation as the **stewards** of its assets, charged with their employment and deployment in ways consistent with the overall strategy of the organisation. With this approach, power is seen to be vested in the stewards; that is, the executive managers.

Other interest groups take little or no part in the running of the company and receive relevant information via established reporting mechanisms (audited accounts, annual reports, etc). Technically, shareholders or members/owners have the right to dismiss their stewards if they are dissatisfied by their stewardship, via a vote at an annual general meeting.

1.3.3 Agency theory

Under **agency theory**, it is recognised that management are likely to pursue their own interests. It is important therefore that management interests (including their remuneration) are aligned with the organisation's goals. Only when these goals are aligned and consistent will managers act in a way that benefits shareholders and other stakeholders.

1.3.4 Stakeholder theory

The stakeholder approach takes a much more **'organic' view** of the organisation, imbuing it with a 'life' of its own, in keeping with the notion of a separate legal personage. Stakeholder theory is effectively a development of the notion of stewardship, stating that management has a **duty of care, not just to the owners** of the company in terms of maximising shareholder value, but also to the **wider community** of interest, or stakeholders.

1.4 Governance principles

As mentioned above, most corporate governance codes are based on a **set of principles** founded upon ideas of what corporate governance is meant to achieve. This list is based on a number of reports.

(a)   To **minimise risk**, especially financial, legal and reputational risks, by requiring compliance with accepted good practice in the jurisdiction in question and ensuring appropriate systems of financial control are in place, in particular systems for monitoring risk, financial control and compliance with the law

(b)   To **ensure adherence** to and **satisfaction** of the **strategic objectives** of the organisation, thus aiding effective management

(c)   To **fulfil responsibilities to all stakeholders** and to **minimise potential conflicts of interest** between the owners, managers and wider stakeholder community, however defined and to treat each category **fairly**

(d)   To **establish clear accountability** at senior levels within an organisation

(e)   To **maintain the independence** of those who scrutinise the behaviour of the organisation and its senior executive managers. Independence is particularly important for **non-executive directors,** and **internal and external auditors**

(f)   To **provide accurate and timely reporting of trustworthy/independent financial and operational data** to both the management and owners/members of the organisation to give them a true and balanced picture of what is happening in the organisation

(g)   To **encourage more proactive involvement** of owners/members in the effective management of the organisation through recognising their responsibilities of oversight and input to decision-making processes via voting or other mechanisms.

(h)   To promote integrity; that is, straightforward dealing and completeness.

1.5 Principles vs rules

A continuing debate on corporate governance is over whether the guidance should predominantly be in the form of principles, or whether there is a need for detailed laws or regulations.

The UK came out very firmly in favour of a principles-based approach in the FRC's UK Corporate Governance Code (2016). The FRC preferred relaxing the regulatory burden on companies and was against treating the corporate governance codes as sets of prescriptive rules. The Code contains **guidelines** which will normally be appropriate but the differing circumstances of companies meant that sometimes there are valid reasons for exceptions.

Some critics believe that the principles set out in the Code are so broad that they are of very little use as a guide to best corporate governance practice.

In the US, the emphasis is on a rules-based approach and this is typified by the Sarbanes-Oxley Act 2002 (see Section 2.4.1 of this chapter).

2 Developments in corporate governance

Good corporate governance involves **risk management** and **internal control, accountability** to stakeholders and other shareholders and conducting business in an **ethical and effective way.**

2.1 The driving forces of governance development

Corporate governance issues came to prominence in the UK and Europe in the late 1980s. The main, but not the only, drivers associated with the increasing demand for the development of governance were as follows.

(a)   **Increasing internationalisation and globalisation** meant that investors, and institutional investors in particular, began to invest outside their home countries.

(b)   The **differential treatment of domestic and foreign investors**, both in terms of reporting and associated rights/dividends, caused many investors to call for parity of treatment.

(c)   Issues concerning **financial reporting** were raised by many investors and were the focus of much debate and litigation. Shareholder confidence in many instances was eroded and, while focus solely on accounting and reporting issues is inadequate, the regulation of practices such as off-balance sheet financing has led to greater transparency and a reduction in risks faced by investors.

(d)   The characteristics of individual countries may have a **significant influence** in the way corporate governance has developed. The King report emphasises the importance of qualities that are fundamental to the South African culture such as collectiveness, consensus, helpfulness, fairness, consultation and religious faith in the development of best practice. (Note that you will not be examined on individual reports.)

(e)   An increasing number of **high profile corporate scandals** and collapses prompted the development of governance codes in the early 1990s. However, scandals since then have raised questions about further measures that may be necessary.

2.2 Features of poor corporate governance

The scandals over the last 25 years have highlighted the need for guidance in order to tackle the various risks and problems that can arise in organisations' systems of governance.

2.2.1 Domination by a single individual

A feature of many corporate governance scandals has been boards dominated by a single senior executive, with other board members merely acting as a rubber stamp. Sometimes the single individual may bypass the board to action their own interests.

Even if an organisation is not dominated by a single individual, there may be other weaknesses. The organisation may be run by a small group centred round the chief executive and chief financial officer, and appointments may be made by personal recommendation rather than a formal, objective process.

2.2.2 Lack of involvement of board

Boards that meet irregularly or fail to consider systematically the organisation's activities and risks are clearly weak. Sometimes the failure to carry out proper oversight is due to a **lack of information** being provided.

2.2.3 Lack of adequate control function

One possible weakness is a **lack of an internal audit function**, or an ineffective internal audit function. Another is a **lack of adequate technical knowledge** in key roles, for example in the audit committee or in senior compliance positions. A rapid turnover of staff involved in accounting or control may suggest inadequate resourcing, and will make control more difficult because of lack of continuity.

2.2.4 Lack of supervision

Employees who are not properly supervised can create large losses for the organisation through their own incompetence, negligence or fraudulent activity. The behaviour of Nick Leeson, the employee who caused the collapse of Barings bank, was not challenged because he appeared to be successful, whereas he was using unauthorised accounts to cover up his large trading losses. Leeson was able to do this because he was in charge of dealing and settlement, a systems weakness or **lack of segregation of key roles** that featured in other financial frauds.

2.2.5 Lack of independent scrutiny

External auditors may not carry out the necessary questioning of senior management because of fears of losing the audit, and internal audit do not ask awkward questions because the chief financial officer determines their employment prospects. Often corporate collapses are followed by criticisms of external auditors where poorly planned and focused audit work failed to identify illegal use of client monies.

2.2.6 Lack of contact with shareholders

Often board members may have grown up with the company but lose touch with the interests and views of shareholders. One possible symptom of this is the payment of remuneration packages that do not appear to be warranted by results.

2.2.7 Emphasis on short-term profitability

Emphasis on success or getting results can lead to the concealment of problems or errors, or manipulation of accounts to achieve desired results.

2.2.8 Misleading accounts and information

Misleading figures are often symptomatic of other problems (or are designed to conceal other problems) but clearly poor quality accounting information is a major problem if markets are trying to make a fair assessment of the company's value. Giving out misleading information was a major issue in the UK's Equitable Life scandal where the company gave contradictory information to savers, independent advisers, media and regulators.

QUESTION

Governance

Techpoint plc is a medium-sized public company that produces a range of components used in the manufacture of computers.

The board of directors consists of chairman Max Mallory, chief executive Richard Mallory and finance director Linda Mallory, all of whom are siblings. There are five other unrelated executive directors. All directors receive bonuses based on sales. The company's sales are made by individual salesmen and women, each of whom have the authority to enter the company into contracts unlimited in value without the need to refer to a superior or consult with other departments. It is this flexibility that has enabled the company to be very profitable in past years. However, a number of bad contracts in the current year have meant that the finance director has reclassed them as 'costs' to maintain healthy sales and to protect the directors' bonuses.

What are the corporate governance issues at Techpoint plc?

ANSWER

The main corporate governance issues are:

(a) **Domination by a small group**

   All the key directors are related which gives them power over the other executives.

(b) **Short-term view**

   Directors' bonuses are based on short-term sales and have resulted in the manipulation of accounts to achieve them.

(c) **Lack of supervision**

   The sales force can tie the company into large loss-making contracts without any checks. There is no authorisation or communication with other departments which means the company may take on contracts that it cannot fulfil. The company has been hit hard with bad contracts in the current year.

2.3 Risks of poor corporate governance

Clearly the ultimate risk is of the organisation **making such large losses** that **bankruptcy** becomes inevitable. The organisation may also be closed down as a result of **serious regulatory breaches**, for example misapplying investors' monies.

2.4 Reports on corporate governance

A number of reports have been produced in various countries aiming to address the risk and problems posed by poor corporate governance.

2.4.1 US

In the US, corporate scandals have led to the Sarbanes-Oxley Act 2002. The Act established the Public Company Accounting Oversight Board (PCAOB). Its aim is to protect investors and other stakeholders by ensuring that the auditor of a company's financial statements has adhered to strict guidelines. While this applies chiefly to US auditing firms, the principle of **public oversight** is applicable to other countries in that regulation of the auditing profession (whether through registration and inspection, or self-regulation) is seen as very important, both in improving audit quality and emphasising the importance of compliance with standards in a company's control environment.

EXAM FOCUS POINT

The responsibilities of a Public Oversight Board appeared under the old syllabus.

The following question appeared in a past exam, and the exam report said that only 47% of students answered it correctly.

QUESTION

Codes of practice

In most countries, what is the usual purpose of codes of practice on corporate governance?

A   To establish legally binding requirements to which all companies must adhere
B   To set down detailed rules to regulate the ways in which companies must operate
C   To provide guidance on the standards of best practice that companies should adopt
D   To provide a comprehensive framework for management and administration

ANSWER

C   A principles-based approach (rather than a rules-based approach) is normally used in codes of practice, so the words 'legally binding' and 'detailed rules' should have told you that options A and B were incorrect. Corporate governance standards are set at the highest level in an organisation, so option D is incorrect, as it refers to lower levels of management and administration.

3 Role of the board

The board should be responsible for taking major **policy** and **strategic** decisions.

Directors should have a **mix of skills** and their **performance** should be assessed regularly.

Appointments should be conducted by formal procedures administered by a **nomination committee**.

3.1 Scope of role

Note that some countries have one-tier boards (the **unitary system**) and others have two-tier boards. In the unitary system the board of directors is legally charged with the responsibility to govern the company, serving together on one board comprising both executive and non-executive directors. In the two-tier system there is an executive management board of directors and this is monitored by a supervisory board of directors. Paper F1 we will concentrate on a one-tier board system.

The King report provides a good summary of the role of the board.

*   to define the purpose of the company
*   to define the values by which the company will perform its daily duties

- to identify the stakeholders relevant to the company
- to develop a strategy combining these factors
- to ensure implementation of this strategy

If the board is to act effectively, its role must be defined carefully. The Cadbury report suggests that the board should have a **formal schedule of matters** specifically reserved to it for decision. Some would be decisions such as **mergers and takeovers** that are **fundamental** to the business and hence should not be taken just by executive managers. Other decisions would include **acquisitions and disposals of assets of the company** or its subsidiaries that are material to the company and **investments, capital projects, bank borrowing** facilities, **loans** and their repayment, and foreign currency transactions, all above a certain size (to be determined by the board).

Other tasks the board should perform include:

- Monitoring the chief executive officer

- Overseeing strategy

- Monitoring risks and control systems

- Monitoring the human capital aspects of the company in regard to succession, morale, training, remuneration, etc

- Ensuring that there is effective communication of its strategic plans, both internally and externally

3.2 Role of chairman

The chairman is the leader of the board of directors. It is the chairman's responsibility to ensure that the board operates efficiently and effectively, promoting regular attendance at meetings, and full involvement by all members. The chairman decides the scope of each meeting and is responsible for ensuring that all matters are discussed fully.

3.3 Role of chief executive

The chief executive officer (CEO) is the leader of the executive team and is responsible for the day-to-day management of the organisation. As well as attending board meetings, the CEO will usually chair the management committee or executive committee. While most companies have monthly board meetings, it is common for management/executive committee meetings to be held more often.

3.4 Role of company secretary

The company secretary is effectively the chief administrative officer and is appointed by the company's directors. He or she is legally responsible for acting on the company's behalf to undertake specific requirements, which are written into the Companies Act.

The duties of a company secretary include preparing and filing the following documents with Companies House each year.

- Confirmation statements – giving details of share capital and directorships held

- Financial statements – outlining the company's assets and liabilities

- Director's reports which, depending on the company's turnover, may also require a full business review and details of the individual responsible for approving accounts

- Depending on company turnover, the company secretary may also need to file an auditor's report

Other duties which fall under the remit of the company secretary include:

- Maintaining statutory books and records ie a register of directors and shareholders and any charges held on the company assets

- Safeguarding legal documents including share certificates, certificates of incorporation and other official documentation

- Organising board meetings of shareholders and taking formal minutes

In addition to these duties, the company secretary is required to establish and maintain a registered office for official communications.

3.5 Attributes of directors

In order to carry out effective scrutiny, directors need to have **relevant expertise** in industry, company, functional area and governance. The board as a whole needs to contain a **mix of expertise** and show a **balance** between **executive management** and **independent non-executive directors**. The King report stresses the importance also of having a good **demographic balance.**

New and existing directors should also have **appropriate training** to develop the knowledge and skills required.

3.5.1 Nomination committee

In order to ensure that balance of the board is maintained, the UK Corporate Governance Code (FRC, 2016) states that the board should set up a **nomination committee** to oversee the process for board appointments and make recommendations to the board. The nomination committee needs to consider the balance between executives and independent non-executives, the skills possessed by the board, the need for continuity and the desirable **size** of the board. Recent corporate governance guidance has laid more emphasis on the need to attract board members from a **diverse range** of backgrounds.

3.6 Possession of necessary information

In many corporate scandals the board was not given full information. The UK Corporate Governance Code (FRC, 2016) stresses that directors should have access to **appropriate information** of **sufficient quality** to make sound judgements.

3.7 Performance of board

Appraisal of the board's performance is an important control over it. The UK Corporate Governance Code (FRC, 2016) recommends that **performance of the board** should be **assessed** once a year. **Separate appraisal** of the chairman and chief executive should also be carried out, with links to the remuneration process.

3.8 Increased accountability and responsibility

Corporate governance rules have created standards of '**best practice**' that all companies, not just listed ones, are encouraged to follow.

These standards have raised public expectations of directors' conduct, and widened the range of stakeholders taking an interest in a company's governance.

Directors now **face increased risk** of:

- **Legal action**, as they are now more accountable for their actions and responsible to a wider range of stakeholders
- **Dismissal**, as service contracts are shorter in length and directors must stand for re-election by the shareholders regularly

Directors have had to alter their behaviour to counter these increased risks. They are devoting more time to meeting the requirements of '**best practice**', and to investor/stakeholder relations.

However, this would result in directors' attention being diverted away from making the company profitable, potentially damaging the long-term success of the business.

3.9 Division of responsibilities

For best performance, it is important for a company to have a division of responsibilities at the head of an organisation. The simplest way to do this is to require the roles of **Chair** and **chief executive** to be held by two different people.

This division has not been made legally mandatory in the UK but the UK Corporate Governance Code (FRC, 2016) states that the roles of chairman and chief executive should not be exercised by the same individual. The division of responsibilities between the chairman and chief executive should be clearly established, set out in writing and agreed by the board.

Division of responsibilities at the head of an organisation is most simply achieved by separating the roles of Chair and chief executive.

Independent non-executive directors have a key role in governance. Their number and status should mean that their views carry significant weight.

3.10 Non-executive directors

Non-executive directors have no executive (managerial) responsibilities.

Non-executive directors are not employees of the company but they do take part in decision-making at board meetings. They do not take part in the day-to-day running of the company.

Non-executive directors should provide a **balancing influence**, and play a key role in **reducing conflicts of interest** between management (including executive directors) and shareholders. They should provide reassurance to shareholders, particularly institutional shareholders, that management is acting in the interests of the organisation.

3.10.1 Role of non-executive directors

The role of non-executive directors includes:

(a) **Strategy**: non-executive directors should contribute to, and challenge the direction of, strategy.

(b) **Performance**: non-executive directors should scrutinise the performance of management in meeting goals and objectives, and monitor the reporting of performance.

(c) **Risk**: non-executive directors should satisfy themselves that financial information is accurate and that financial controls and systems of risk management are robust.

(d) **Directors and managers**: non-executive directors are responsible for determining appropriate levels of remuneration for executives, and are key figures in the appointment and removal of senior managers and in succession planning.

3.10.2 Benefits of effective non-executive directors

Non-executive directors can bring a number of benefits to a board of directors.

(a) They may have external experience and knowledge which executive directors do not possess.

(b) Non-executive directors can provide a wider perspective than executive directors who may be more involved in detailed operations.

(c) Good non-executive directors are often a comfort factor for third parties such as investors or suppliers.

(d) The most important advantage perhaps lies in the dual nature of the non-executive director's role. Non-executive directors are full board members who are expected to have the level of knowledge that full board membership implies. At the same time they are meant to provide the so-called strong, independent element on the board. This should imply that they have the knowledge and detachment to be able to assess fairly the remuneration of executive directors when serving on the remuneration committee, and to be able to discuss knowledgeably with auditors the affairs of the company on the audit committee.

3.10.3 Problems with non-executive directors

Nevertheless, there are a number of difficulties connected with the role of non-executive director.

(a) In many organisations, non-executive directors may **lack independence**. (For example, potential non-executive directors are more likely to agree to serve if they admire the company's Chair or its way of operating.)

(b) There may be a **prejudice in certain companies** against widening the recruitment of non-executive directors to include people proposed other than by the board or to include stakeholder representatives.

(c) Non-executive directors may have **difficulty imposing** their views upon the board. It may be easy to dismiss the views of non-executive directors as irrelevant to the company's needs.

(d) Perhaps the biggest problem which non-executive directors face is the **limited time** they can devote to the role. If they are to contribute valuably, they are likely to have other, time-consuming commitments.

3.10.4 Independence of non-executive directors

Various safeguards can be put in place to ensure that non-executive directors remain independent. Those suggested by the corporate governance reports include:

(a) Non-executive directors should have **no business**, **financial** or other **connection** with the company, apart from fees and shareholdings. Recent reports such as the UK's Higgs report have widened the scope of business connections to include anyone who has been an employee or had a material business relationship over the last few years, or served on the board for more than ten years.

(b) They should **not take part in share option schemes** and their service should not be pensionable, to maintain their independent status.

(c) **Appointments** should be for a **specified term** and reappointment should not be automatic. The board as a whole should decide on their nomination and selection.

(d) Procedures should exist whereby non-executive directors may take **independent advice**, at the company's expense if necessary.

EXAM FOCUS POINT

In the context of non-executive directors, watch out for threats to, or questions over, their independence.

3.11 Remuneration, nomination, audit and risk committees

Directors' remuneration should be set by a **remuneration committee** consisting of independent non-executive directors.

Remuneration should be dependent on **organisation** and **individual performance**.

Accounts should disclose **remuneration policy** and (in detail) the **packages of individual directors**.

3.11.1 Need for guidance

Directors' being paid excessive salaries and bonuses has been seen as one of the major corporate abuses for a large number of years. It is thus inevitable that the corporate governance provisions have targeted it.

The following are principles of what a good remuneration policy should involve.

- Directors' remuneration should be set by **independent members** of the board.

- Any form of bonus should be related to **measurable performance** or enhanced shareholder value.

- There should be **full transparency of directors' remuneration** including pension rights in the annual accounts.

3.11.2 Standing committees

The term 'standing committee' refers to any committee that is a permanent feature within the organisation. In the context of corporate governance, it refers to committees made up of members of the board with specified duties. There are four committees usually appointed by public companies:

- Remuneration committee
- Audit committee
- Nominations committee
- Risk committee

EXAM FOCUS POINT

The Syllabus and Study Guide for Paper F1/FAB require students to study only two committees. These are the remuneration committee and the audit committee

3.11.2 Remuneration committee

The remuneration committee plays the key role in establishing remuneration arrangements. In order to be effective, the committee needs to **determine** both the organisation's **general policy** on the **remuneration of executive directors** and **specific remuneration packages** for each director.

Measures to ensure that the committee is **independent** include not just requiring that the committee is staffed by non-executive directors, but also placing limits on the members' connection with the organisation. Measures to ensure independence include stating that the committee should have no personal interests other than as shareholders, no conflicts of interest and no day-to-day involvement in running the business.

3.11.3 Audit committee

Audit committees of **independent non-executive directors** should liaise with **external audit, supervise internal audit**, and **review** the **annual accounts** and **internal controls**.

The main duties of the audit committee are as follows.

Duty	Committee's task
Review of financial statements and systems	They should review both the quarterly (if published) and annual accounts.
Liaison with external auditors	They appoint and remove external auditors and should help external auditors resolve any problems they may encounter.
Review of internal audit	They should look at the objectivity, technical knowledge and professional standards of the internal auditors. They should also review the scope, resources and results of the audit.
Review of internal control	They should play a significant role in reviewing the adequacy of internal controls.
Investigations	They will be involved in implementing and reviewing the results of one-off investigations.
Review of risk management	They must ensure that there is a formal policy in place and review the arrangements for risk management. (This may be carried out by a separate risk committee instead, see below.)

4 Reporting on corporate governance

Annual reports must **convey** a **fair and balanced view** of the organisation. They should state whether the organisation has complied with governance regulations and codes, and give specific disclosures about the board, internal control reviews, going concern status and relations with stakeholders.

4.1 Reporting requirements

Listed companies are required to make the following general disclosures.

(a) A **narrative statement** of how they have **applied the principles** set out in the UK Corporate Governance Code, providing explanations which enable their shareholders to assess how the principles have been applied

(b) A **statement** as to whether or not they **complied** throughout the accounting period with the **provisions** set out in the UK Corporate Governance Code. Listed companies that did not comply throughout the accounting period with all the provisions must specify the provisions with which they did not comply, and give reasons for non-compliance.

The corporate governance reports also suggest that the directors should **explain** their **responsibility for preparing accounts**. They should **report that the business is a going concern**, with supporting assumptions and qualifications as necessary.

In addition, further statements may be required depending on the jurisdiction, such as:

(a) Information about the **board of directors**: the composition of the board in the year, information about the independence of the non-executives, frequency of and attendance at board meetings, and how the board's performance has been evaluated.

(b) Brief report on the **remuneration, audit and nomination committees** covering terms of reference, composition and frequency of meetings

(c) Information about **relations with auditors** including reasons for change and steps taken to ensure auditor objectivity and independence when non-audit services have been provided

(d) A statement that the directors have reviewed the **effectiveness** of **internal controls**, including risk management

(e) A statement on relations and **dialogue with shareholders**

(f) A statement that the company is a **going concern**

(g) **Sustainability reporting,** including the nature and extent of social, transformation, ethical, safety, health and environmental management policies and practices

(h) An **operating and financial review**.

Furthermore, the information that organisations provide cannot just be backward looking. Companies will need to weigh the need to keep commercially sensitive information private with the expectations that investors will receive full and frank disclosures.

5 Corporate social responsibility

There is a fundamental split of views about the nature of corporate responsibility.

- The **strong stakeholder view** that a range of goals should be pursued
- The view that the business organisation is a purely **economic force**, subject to law

Expectations about the exercise of **social responsibility** by organisations are subject to the same split of views as corporate ethical responsibility. One definition of corporate social responsibility is that set of actions which the organisation is not obliged to take, taken for the well-being of stakeholders and the public.

5.1 Corporate social responsibility

Businesses, particularly large ones, are subject to increasing expectations that they will exercise **social responsibility**. This is an ill-defined concept, but appears to focus on the provision of specific benefits to society in general, such as charitable donations, the creation or preservation of employment, and spending on environmental improvement or maintenance. A great deal of the pressure is created by the activity of minority action groups and is aimed at businesses because they are perceived to possess extensive resources. The momentum of such arguments is now so great that the notion of social responsibility has become almost inextricably confused with the matter of ethics. It is important to remember the distinction. Social responsibility and ethical behaviour are not the same thing.

In this context, you should remember that a business managed with the sole objective of maximising shareholder wealth can be run in just as ethical a fashion as one in which far wider stakeholder responsibility is assumed. On the other hand, there is no doubt that many large businesses have behaved irresponsibly in the past and some continue to do so.

5.1.1 Strategies for social responsibility

Proactive strategy	A strategy which a business follows where it is prepared to take full responsibility for its actions. A company which discovers a fault in a product and recalls the product without being forced to, before any injury or damage is caused, acts in a proactive way.
Reactive strategy	This involves allowing a situation to continue unresolved until the public, government or consumer groups find out about it.
Defence strategy	This involves minimising or attempting to avoid additional obligations arising from a particular problem.
Accommodation strategy	This approach involves taking responsibility for actions, probably when one of the following happens. - Encouragement from special interest groups - Perception that a failure to act will result in government intervention

5.2 Against corporate social responsibility

Milton Friedman (1970) argued against corporate social responsibility along the following lines.

(a) Businesses do not have responsibilities; only people have responsibilities. Managers in charge of corporations are responsible to the owners of the business, by whom they are employed.

(b) These employers may have charity as their aim, but 'generally [their aim] will be to make as much money as possible while conforming to the basic rules of the society, both those embodied in law and those embodied in ethical custom.'

(c) If the statement that a manager has social responsibilities is to have any meaning, 'it must mean that he is to act in some way that is not in the interest of his employers.'

(d)   If managers do this they are, generally speaking, spending the owners' money for purposes other than those they have authorised.

5.3 The stakeholder view

How much organisations consider the interests of other stakeholders will depend on their **legal responsibilities** and their view of stakeholders as partners.

The **stakeholder view** is that many groups have a stake in what the organisation does. This is particularly important in the business context, where shareholders own the business but employees, customers and government also have particularly strong claims to having their interests considered. This is fundamentally an argument derived from **natural law theory** and is based on the notion of individual and collective **rights**.

6 Ethics, law, governance and social responsibility

6.1 A brief recap

This chapter has developed the concept of corporate governance and business social responsibility. Since the management and owners of companies are not necessarily the same people, it is important for management to be encouraged to act in the best interests of the owners and other stakeholders.

6.2 Interaction of ethics, law, governance and social responsibility

By pulling together all we have already studied, we find:

- Ethics are values and principles that society **expects** companies and individuals to follow.
- Laws are rules that a company and individuals **must** follow.

Corporate governance requirements and social responsibility may be viewed as additional rules and guidance for companies and individuals. They bridge the gap between what the law requires and what society expects. This is because the law does not always encourage them to behave in an ethical or socially responsible manner.

6.2.1 Levels of regulation

One way of examining how the subjects are related is to look at how regulated they are.

The relationship between law, governance, social responsibility and ethics			
Law	Corporate governance	Social responsibility	Ethics
Rules individuals and companies **must follow**. The **minimum level of behaviour** society allows.	**Publicly listed companies only** are regulated. Others are **encouraged** to follow 'best practice'.	**No regulation.** Individuals and companies have a free choice. **Some social pressure** to act in a socially responsible manner.	**Values and principles.** Individuals and companies are **expected to follow**. Adopting an ethical position is down to free choice.
More regulation, less freedom of choice		Less regulation, more freedom of choice	

From the table above, we can see that the law is highly regulated, corporate governance is less regulated and, social responsibility and ethics have no regulation, as adoption is down to free choice.

6.2.2 Effect on corporate behaviour

Perhaps more importantly, we should examine the effect each has on corporate behaviour.

An important point to remember is that companies do not make decisions by themselves. Human individuals (usually the directors) make the significant policy choices.

The following diagram demonstrates the interaction of law, ethics and social responsibility on the company.

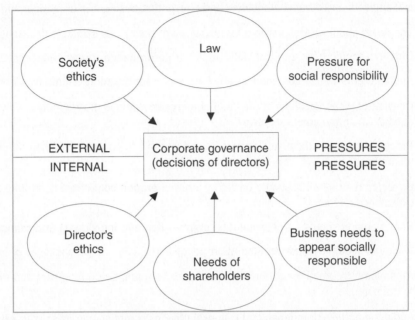

We can see that many factors will influence the behaviour of a company. The main external influence is the law, as it sets the minimum level of behaviour expected. Society's ethical views and needs for social responsibility will have an influence, as companies will respect them as far as necessary to remain profitable.

Directors are greatly influenced by the need to deliver the results that shareholders require, for example increasing the company's share price or dividend. To achieve this may require breaking their own personal ethical beliefs.

Remember, businesses do not necessarily have to act ethically. In most cases they are run for the benefit of the owners (the shareholders) rather than for the benefit of society as a whole.

PER performance objective PO4 requires you to contribute to the effective governance, risk management and control of an organisation. The material covered in this chapter (and expanded upon later in your studies in Paper P1), will help in this context.

CHAPTER ROUNDUP

↳ Most corporate governance reports are based around the principles of **integrity**, **accountability**, **independence** and **good management** but there is disagreement on how much these principles need to be supplemented by detailed rules.

↳ Good corporate governance involves **risk management** and **internal control, accountability** to stakeholders and other shareholders and conducting business in an **ethical and effective way.**

↳ The board should be responsible for taking major **policy** and **strategic** decisions.

Directors should have a **mix of skills** and their **performance** should be assessed regularly.

Appointments should be conducted by formal procedures administered by a **nomination committee.**

↳ **Division of responsibilities** at the head of an organisation is most simply achieved by separating the roles of Chair and chief executive.

Independent non-executive directors have a key role in governance. Their number and status should mean that their views carry significant weight.

↳ Directors' remuneration should be set by a **remuneration committee** consisting of independent non-executive directors.

Remuneration should be dependent on **organisation** and **individual performance.**

Accounts should disclose **remuneration policy** and (in detail) the **packages of individual directors.**

↳ A nomination committee should be in place for selecting board members and making recommendations to the board.

↳ Audit committees of **independent non-executive directors** should liaise with **external audit, supervise internal audit**, and **review** the **annual accounts** and **internal controls.**

↳ Annual reports must **convey** a **fair and balanced view** of the organisation. They should state whether the organisation has complied with governance regulations and codes, and give specific disclosures about the board, internal control reviews, going concern status and relations with stakeholders.

↳ There is a fundamental split of views about the nature of corporate responsibility.

- The **strong stakeholder view** that a range of goals should be pursued
- The view that the business organisation is a purely **economic force**, subject to law

Expectations about the exercise of **social responsibility** by organisations are subject to the same split of views as corporate ethical responsibility. One definition of corporate social responsibility is that set of actions which the organisation is not obliged to take, taken for the well-being of stakeholders and the public.

1 Choose the correct word from the following to fill the gap: cost/internal control/risk.

The management and reduction of .... is fundamental in all definitions of good governance.

2 Features of good corporate governance include the following.

	True	False
Splitting the roles of Chair and chief executive	☐	☐
Appointing a majority of executive directors on the board	☐	☐

3 Audit committees are generally staffed by executive directors.

True ☐   False ☐

4 Which of the following is a nomination committee responsible for?

A   Review of financial statements   C   Recommending potential board members
B   Review of internal control

5 Which two of the following are symptoms of poor corporate governance?

A   Lack of board involvement
B   Bonuses for directors
C   The finance director also performing the role of company secretary
D   Inadequate supervision

6 What is 'the stakeholder view'?

7 A strategy for social responsibility which involves allowing a situation to continue unresolved until the public finds out about it is a:

A   Proactive strategy   C   Defence strategy
B   Reactive strategy   D   Accommodation strategy

ANSWERS TO QUICK QUIZ

1   The management and reduction of risk is fundamental in all definitions of good governance.

2

	True	False
Splitting the roles of chair and chief executive	✓	
Appointing a majority of executive directors on the board		✓

Governance principles suggest that there should be a balance between executive and non-executive directors.

3   False. They should be staffed by non-executive directors (excluding the chair).

4   C   The audit committee would be responsible for A and B.

5   A   Lack of board involvement   D   Inadequate supervision

6   This view is that many groups have a stake in what the organisation does.

7   B   Reactive strategy

Now try ...

Attempt the questions below from the **Practice Question Bank**

Q32

Q33

Q34

Q35

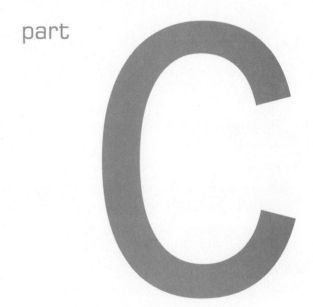

part

C

Accounting and reporting systems, controls and compliance

08

It is important to understand why accounts are prepared. **Sections 1 and 2** of this chapter introduce some basic ideas about accounts and give an indication of their purpose. You also need to consider what makes accounting information useful, and the qualities which such information should have.

We outline the standard setting process in **Section 3**.

In **Section 4**, we will look at the types of accounting information produced.

Sections 5 and 6 examine the main transactions and financial systems undertaken by a business, before going on to consider manual and computerised financial systems in **Section 7**.

Questions may ask you to discuss the advantages and disadvantages of databases and spreadsheets (**Section 8**).

The role of accounting

TOPIC LIST	SYLLABUS REFERENCE
1 The purpose of accounting information	C2 (a),(b)
2 Nature, principles and scope of accounting	C2 (a),(b)
3 The regulatory system	C2 (a), C3 (a)-(c)
4 Internal and external financial information	C4 (a),(b)
5 Control over business transactions	C5 (a)
6 The main business financial systems	C5 (b)-(f)
7 Manual and computerised accounting systems	C5 (g),(h)
8 Databases and spreadsheets	C5 (g)

Study Guide	Intellectual level

C2 Accounting and finance functions within business

(a) Explain the contribution of the accounting function to the formulation, implementation, and control of the organisation's policies, procedures, and performance. — K

(b) Identify and describe the main financial accounting functions in business: — K

   (i) Recording financial information

   (ii) Codifying and processing financial information

   (iii) Preparing financial statements

C3 Principles of law and regulation governing accounting and audit

(a) Explain basic legal requirements in relation to retaining and submitting proper records and preparing and auditing financial reports. — K

(b) Explain the broad consequences of failing to comply with the legal requirements for maintaining and filing accounting records. — K

(c) Explain how the international accountancy profession regulates itself through the establishment of reporting standards and their monitoring. — K

C4 The sources and purpose of internal and external financial information, provided by business

(a) Explain the various business purposes for which the following financial information is required. — K

   (i) The statement of profit or loss

   (ii) The statement of financial position

   (iii) The statement of cash flows

   (iv) Sustainability and integrated reports

(b) Describe the main purposes of the following types of management accounting reports. — K

   (i) Cost schedules

   (ii) Budgets

   (iii) Variance reports

C5 Financial systems, procedures and related IT applications

(a) Identify an organisation's system requirements in relation to the objectives and policies of the organisation. — S

(b) Describe the main financial systems used within an organisation. — S

   (i) Purchases and sales invoicing

   (ii) Payroll

   (iii) Credit control

   (iv) Cash and working capital management

(c) Explain why it is important to adhere to policies and procedures for handling clients' money. — K

(d) Identify weaknesses, potential for error and inefficiencies in accounting systems. — S

(e) Recommend improvements to accounting systems to prevent error and fraud and to improve overall efficiency. — S

(f) Explain why appropriate controls are necessary in relation to business and IT systems and procedures. — S

(g) Understand business uses of computers and IT software applications. — S

   (i) Spreadsheet applications

   (ii) Database systems

   (iii) Accounting packages

Study Guide

	Intellectual level
(h) Describe and compare the relative benefits and limitations of manual and automated financial systems that may be used in an organisation.	K

EXAM FOCUS POINT

The specifics of accounting systems are highly likely to be examined. The business needs of the users of accounting information are also a 'hot topic'.

1 The purpose of accounting information

Accounting is a way of recording, analysing and summarising transactions of a business.

1.1 What is accounting?

*   The transactions are recorded in 'books of prime entry'.
*   The transactions are then analysed and posted to the ledgers.
*   Finally the transactions are summarised in the financial statements.

The accounting function is part of the broader business system, and does not operate in isolation. It handles the financial operations of the organisation, but also provides information and advice to other departments.

Accounts are produced to aid management in planning, control and decision-making and to comply with statutory regulations. **The accounting system must be adequate to fulfil these functions**. An organisation's accounting systems are affected by the nature of its business transactions and the sort of business it is.

Factor	Example
Size	A small business like a greengrocer will have a simple accounting system, where the main accounting record will probably be the till roll. A large retail business, such as a chain of supermarkets, will have elaborate accounting systems covering a large number of product ranges and sites.
Type of organisation	A service business might need to record the time employees take on particular jobs. Accounting on a job or client basis might also be a feature of service businesses. A public sector organisation, such as a government department, may be more concerned with the monitoring of expenditure against performance targets than recording revenue. A manufacturing company will account both for unit sales and revenue, but needs to keep track of costs for decision-making purposes and so forth.
Organisation structure	In a business managed by area, accounts will be prepared on an area basis. In a functional organisation, the accounts staff are in a separate department.

Be aware that accounting work has to comply with a wide range of regulations to avoid penalties, including law such as the Companies Act. As a result, it tends to be rather formalised and procedural in order to make sure that nothing is overlooked. Organisations often lay down their accounting rules and procedures in writing, and this may form part of an organisation manual or procedures manual.

1.2 The need for accounts

Renaissance scholar Luca Pacioli wrote the first printed explanation of double-entry bookkeeping in 1494. Double-entry bookkeeping involves entering every transaction as a **debit** in one account and a corresponding **credit** in another account, and ensuring that they 'balance'. Pacioli's description of the method was widely influential.

The first English book on the subject was written in 1543. The practice of double entry bookkeeping has barely changed since then and is standard across the world, based upon the concept that every transaction has a dual effect that balances to zero. The original role of the accounting function was to record financial information and this is still its main focus.

Why do businesses need to produce accounts? If a business is being run efficiently, why should it have to go through all the bother of accounting procedures in order to produce financial information?

A business should produce information about its activities because there are various groups of people who want or need to know that information. This sounds rather vague: to make it clearer, we should look more closely at the classes of people who might need information about a business. We need also to think about what information in particular is of interest to the members of each class.

Large businesses are usually of interest to a greater variety of people than small businesses, so we will consider the case of a large public company whose shares can be purchased and sold on the Stock Exchange.

1.3 Users of financial statements and accounting information

The people who might be interested in financial information about a large public company may be classified as follows.

(a) **Managers of the company**. These are people appointed by the company's owners to supervise the day-to-day activities of the company. They need information about the company's financial situation as it is currently and as it is expected to be in the future. This is to enable them to manage the business efficiently and to take effective control and planning decisions.

(b) **Shareholders of the company**, ie the company's owners. These will want to assess how effectively management is performing its stewardship function. They will want to know how profitably management is running the company's operations and how much profit they can afford to withdraw from the business for their own use.

(c) **Trade contacts**, including suppliers who provide goods to the company on credit and customers who purchase the goods or services provided by the company. **Suppliers** will want to know about the company's ability to pay its debts; **customers** need to know that the company is a secure source of supply and is in no danger of having to close down.

(d) **Providers of finance to the company**. These might include a bank which permits the company to operate an overdraft, or provides longer-term finance by granting a loan. The bank will want to ensure that the company is able to keep up with interest payments, and eventually to repay the amounts advanced.

(e) **Her Majesty's Revenue and Customs**, who will want to know about business profits in order to assess the tax payable by the company.

(f) **Employees of the company**. These should have a right to information about the company's financial situation, because their future careers and the size of their wages and salaries depend on it.

(g) **Financial analysts and advisers**, who need information for their clients or audience. For example, stockbrokers will need information to advise investors in stocks and shares; credit agencies will want information to advise potential suppliers of goods to the company; and journalists need information for their reading public.

(h) **Governments and their agencies.** Governments and their agencies are interested in the allocation of resources and therefore in the activities of enterprises. They also require information in order to provide a basis for national statistics.

(i)   **The public**. Enterprises affect members of the public in a variety of ways. For example, enterprises may make a substantial contribution to a local economy by providing employment and using local suppliers. Another important factor is the effect of an enterprise on the environment, for example as regards pollution.

Accounting information is organised into financial statements to satisfy the **information needs** of these different groups. Not all will be equally satisfied.

Managers of a business need the most information, to help them take their planning and control decisions; and they obviously have 'special' access to information about the business, because they can get people to give them the types of statements they want. When managers want a large amount of information about the costs and profitability of individual products, or different parts of their business, they can arrange to obtain it through a system of cost and management accounting.

QUESTION

Information

It is easy to see how 'internal' people get hold of accounting information. A manager, for example, can just go along to the accounts department and ask the staff there to prepare whatever accounting statements they need. But external users of accounts cannot do this. How, in practice, can a business contact or a financial analyst access accounting information about a company?

ANSWER

Limited companies (though not other forms of business such as a sole trader) are required to make certain accounting information public. They do so by filing the required information with the Registrar of Companies at Companies House. The information filed at Companies House is available, at a fee, to any member of the public. Other sources include financial comment in the press and company brochures.

In addition to management information, financial statements are prepared and perhaps published for the benefit of other user groups.

(a)   The **law** provides for the provision of some information. The Companies Acts require every company to publish accounting information for its shareholders; and companies must also file a copy of their accounts with the Registrar of Companies, so that any member of the public who so wishes can go and look at them.

(b)   The **HM Revenue and Customs** authorities will receive the information they need to make tax assessments.

(c)   A **bank** might demand a forecast of a company's expected future cash flows as a pre-condition of granting an overdraft.

(d)   The **professional accountancy bodies** have been jointly responsible for issuing **accounting standards** and some standards require companies to publish certain additional information. Accountants, as members of these professional bodies, are placed under a strong obligation to ensure that company accounts conform to the requirements of the standards.

(e)   Some companies provide, voluntarily, specially prepared financial information for issue to their employees. These statements are known as **employee reports**.

EXAM FOCUS POINT

You may be asked about what information would be needed by managers, employees or shareholders.

1.3.1 Non-commercial undertakings

It is not only businesses that need to prepare accounts. **Charities and clubs**, for example, prepare financial statements every year. Accounts also need to be prepared for **government** (public sector organisations).

1.4 Qualities of good information

You should be able to identify the qualities of good information. Below are some features that accounting information should have if it is to be useful.

(a) **Relevance**. The information provided should satisfy the needs of information users. In the case of company accounts, clearly a wide range of information will be needed to satisfy a wide range of users.

(b) **Comprehensibility**. Information may be difficult to understand because it is scant or incomplete; but too much detail is also a defect which can cause difficulties of understanding.

(c) **Reliability**. Information will be more reliable if it is independently verified. The law requires that the accounts published by limited companies should be verified by auditors, who must be independent of the company and must hold an approved qualification.

(d) **Completeness**. A company's accounts should present a rounded picture of its economic activities.

(e) **Objectivity**. Information should be as objective (free from bias) as possible. In the context of preparing accounts, management may be inclined to paint a rosy picture of a company's profitability to make their own performance look impressive.

(f) **Timeliness**. The value of information decreases if it cannot be used to impact events. Increasingly, organisations need 'real-time' information to enable informed decision-making.

(g) **Comparability**. Information should be produced on a consistent basis so that valid comparisons can be made with information from previous periods and with information produced by other sources (for example the accounts of similar companies operating in the same line of business).

1.5 The structure of the accounting function

In UK companies, the head of the accounting management structure is usually the **finance director**. The finance director has a seat on the **board of directors** and is responsible for routine accounting matters and also for broad financial policy.

In many larger companies the finance director has one or more deputies below him.

(a) Some responsibilities of the **Financial Controller**

- Routine accounting
- Providing accounting reports for other departments
- Cashiers' duties and cash control

(b) Management accounting is such an important function that a **Management Accountant** is often appointed with status equal to the financial controller and separate responsibilities.

- Cost accounting
- Budgets and budgetary control
- Financial management of projects

(c) A very large organisation might have a **Treasurer** in charge of treasury work.

- Raising funds by borrowing
- Investing surplus funds on the money market or other investment markets
- Cash flow control

Sections in the accounts department

(a) The **financial accounts** section is divided up into sections, with a supervisor responsible for each section (eg for credit control, payroll, purchase ledger, sales ledger).

(b) Similarly, **management accounting** work is divided up, with a number of cost accountants as supervisors of sections responsible for keeping cost records of different items (eg materials, labour and overheads; or production, research and development, and marketing).

(c)   Some companies that spend large amounts on **capital projects** might have a section assigned exclusively to capital project appraisal (payback appraisal, DCF appraisal, sensitivity analysis, the capital budget).

An accounts function is depicted in the following diagram. People are grouped together by the type of work they do. In an area structure, accounts staff might be dispersed throughout the different regions of an organisation. Management accounting work is often decentralised to departments because it provides vital information for management control purposes.

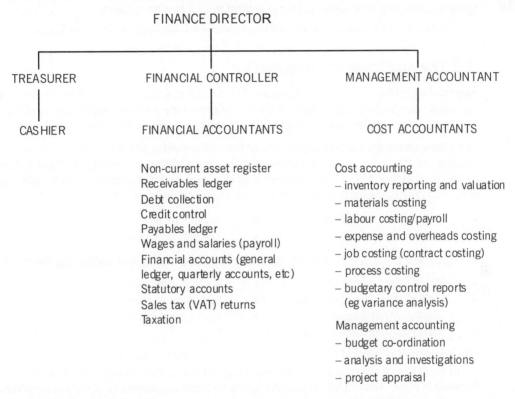

FINANCE DIRECTOR

TREASURER   FINANCIAL CONTROLLER   MANAGEMENT ACCOUNTANT

CASHIER   FINANCIAL ACCOUNTANTS   COST ACCOUNTANTS

Non-current asset register
Receivables ledger
Debt collection
Credit control
Payables ledger
Wages and salaries (payroll)
Financial accounts (general ledger, quarterly accounts, etc)
Statutory accounts
Sales tax (VAT) returns
Taxation

Cost accounting
– inventory reporting and valuation
– materials costing
– labour costing/payroll
– expense and overheads costing
– job costing (contract costing)
– process costing
– budgetary control reports (eg variance analysis)

Management accounting
– budget co-ordination
– analysis and investigations
– project appraisal

Note that some of these functions may be brought together under a single job description, particularly in smaller businesses. For example, there may be one person who does the job of a financial accountant and a cost accountant.

Many organisations have an **internal audit department**. This functions as an internal financial control. One of its responsibilities is to control the risks of fraud and error. For this reason it should be separate from the finance department and the chief internal auditor should report to the audit committee of the board of directors, bypassing the Financial Director. Internal audit is covered in Chapter 9.

2 Nature, principles and scope of accounting

You may have a wide understanding of what accounting is about. Your job may be in one area or type of accounting, but you must understand the breadth of work which an accountant undertakes.

2.1 Financial accounting and management accounting

KEY TERM

Financial accounting is mainly a method of reporting the results and financial position of a business.

It is not primarily concerned with providing information towards the more efficient conduct of the business. Although financial accounts are of interest to management, their principal function is to satisfy the information needs of persons not involved in the day-to-day running of the business.

This is particularly clear in the context of the published accounts of limited companies. **Accounting Standards** (and company law) prescribe that a company should **produce accounts to be presented to**

the shareholders. There are usually detailed regulations on what the accounts must contain and this enables shareholders to assess how well the directors (or management board) have run the company. Also there are certain outsiders who need information about a company: suppliers, customers, employees, tax authorities, the general public. Their information needs are satisfied, wholly or in part, by the company's published financial statements.

Management (or cost) accounting is a management information system which analyses data to provide information as a basis for managerial action. The concern of a management accountant is to present accounting information in the form most helpful to management.

2.2 The application of information

Financial reporting is not an optional extra. The published accounts are an important source of communication with outsiders. Reported levels of profit determine the return that investors can receive. They also indirectly affect the company's cost of capital by affecting the share price.

The **management accountant** is even nearer the policy-making and management process. This is because the management accountant is not primarily interested in reporting to interested parties external to the organisation. After all, the requirements of external users of accounts may be different to those involved in managing and running the business in several respects.

- Aggregation of information
- Classification of data
- Level of detail
- The period covered

Internally, accountants therefore provide information for **planning and controlling** the business.

- Competitors' performance
- Cost/profit centre performance
- Desirability of investments
- Past cost information
- Product profitability
- Sensitivity analysis
- Alternative options

The accountant provides information essential for the current management and decision-making of the business. If line decisions are assessed in accounting terms, even in part, then the accountant will be involved in them. Accountants assess the future financial consequences of certain decisions.

2.2.1 Control and stewardship

The accountant's staff authority is generally expressed in procedures and rules. For example, staff have formal expenditure limits. In many respects, money and funds are a business's lifeblood, and monitoring their flow is a necessary precaution. If the flow of funds dries up, a business can fail very easily. **Proper financial control ensures that the business is adequately financed to meet its obligations**.

EXAM FOCUS POINT

It is important that you understand this distinction between management accounting and financial accounting. You should bear in mind the different reasons for preparing management and financial accounts, and the different people to whom they are addressed.

2.3 Financial management

Financial management is a separate discipline from both management accounting and financial accounting, although in a small organisation the three roles may be carried out by the same person.

The financial manager is responsible for raising finance and controlling financial resources, including the following decisions.

- Should the firm borrow from a bank or raise funds by issuing shares?
- How much should be paid as a dividend?
- Should the firm spend money on new machinery?
- How much credit should be given to customers?
- How much discount should be given to customers who pay early?

2.4 Auditing

The annual accounts of a limited company above a certain size (in terms of revenue) must generally be **audited** by a person independent of the company. The members of the company usually appoint a firm of registered auditors to investigate the financial statements and report as to whether or not they show a true and fair view. When the auditors have completed their work they must prepare a **report** explaining the work that they have done and the **opinion** they have formed.

In simple cases they will be able to report that they have carried out their work in accordance with the Auditing Standards and that, in their opinion, the accounts show a true and fair view and are properly prepared in accordance with company legislation. This is described as an **unqualified** (or 'clean') audit report.

Sometimes the auditors may disagree with management on a point in the accounts. If they are unable to persuade the management to change the accounts, and if the item at issue is large or otherwise important, it is the auditors' duty to prepare a **qualified report**, setting out the matter(s) on which they disagree with the management.

The financial statements to which the auditors refer in their report comprise the following.

- The profit or loss account (sometimes referred to as the income statement)
- The statement of financial position (formerly called the balance sheet)
- The statement of cash flows (formerly called the cash flow statement)
- Supporting notes

The auditors' report is included as part of the company's published accounts. It is addressed to the members of the company (not to the management).

2.4.1 Internal audit

Internal auditors are employees of the company whose duties are fixed by management and who report on the effectiveness of internal control systems.

2.5 Other departments and sections

Accounting management provides a good example of the **need for close co-ordination** between managers and sections, and this need is particularly acute in financial accounts work because of the **internal controls dividing up responsibilities**.

Department	Accounts section	Relationship
Purchases dept (PD)	Payables ledger (PL) Cashier (C)	PD advises PL of purchase orders PD indicates valid invoices C informs PD and PL of payment
Human resources dept	Payroll	Personnel gives details of wage rates, starters and leavers to payroll
Sales dept (SD) **Credit control (CC)**	Receivables ledger (RL)	SD advises RL of sales order RL might give CC information about overdue debts RL might give details about debtors ageing and other reports
Operations, inventory controllers	Cost accounting staff	Operations might give details of movements of inventory, so that the accounts staff can value inventory and provide costing reports
Senior management	Financial accounting and cost accounting staff	The accounts department as a whole produces management information for decision-making and control

Importance of the relationship

The accounts department is crucial to the organisation.

- If it provides the wrong information, managers will make bad decisions.
- If it confuses the data, important transactions might slip through the net, and fraud may result.
- There is a legal duty to ensure that accounting records are in good order.

3 The regulatory system

> You should be able to outline the factors which have shaped the development of financial accounting.

3.1 Introduction

You may be aware that there have been considerable upheavals in financial reporting, mainly in response to criticism. The purpose of this section is to give a **general picture** of some of the factors which have shaped financial accounting. We will concentrate on the accounts of limited companies because this is the type of organisation whose accounts are most closely regulated by statute or otherwise.

The following factors can be identified.

- Company law
- Accounting concepts and individual judgement
- Accounting standards
- The European Union
- Other international influences
- Generally accepted accounting practice (GAAP)

3.2 Company law

Limited companies are required by law (the UK Companies Act 2006 or CA 2006 for example) to prepare and publish accounts annually. The form and content of the UK accounts are regulated primarily by CA 2006, but must also comply with accounting standards.

The Companies Act 2006 (TSO, 2006) requires companies to keep proper accounting records in order to be able to prepare financial statements. These statements are then required to be audited and an auditor's report appended (see Section 2.4 above), before being filed at Companies House. These financial statements are then available for inspection by members of the public. A company can be fined for failing to keep proper accounting records or for failing to file financial statements within the statutory period after the year end.

3.3 Accounting concepts and individual judgement

Financial statements are prepared on the basis of a number of fundamental accounting concepts (or accounting principles as they are called in the UK Companies Act 2006). Many figures in financial statements are derived from the application of judgement in putting those concepts into practice.

It is clear that different people exercising their judgement on the same facts can arrive at very different conclusions. Other examples of areas where the judgement of different people may differ are as follows.

- Valuation of buildings in times of rising property prices

- Research and development. Is it right to treat this only as an expense? In a sense it is an investment to generate future revenue.

- Accounting for inflation

- Brands such as 'Jaffa Cakes' or 'Walkman'. Are they assets in the same way that a forklift truck is an asset?

Working from the same data, different groups of people would produce very different financial statements. If the exercise of judgement is completely unfettered any comparability between the accounts of different organisations will disappear. This will be all the more significant in cases where deliberate manipulation occurs in order to present accounts in the most favourable light.

3.4 UK accounting standards

In an attempt to deal with some of the subjectivity, and to achieve comparability between different organisations, **accounting standards** were developed.

3.4.1 The old UK regime

Between 1970 and 1990 the standards (Statements of Standard Accounting Practice or SSAPs) were devised by the **Accounting Standards Committee**. However, it was felt that these standards were too much concerned with detailed rules in which companies found it all too easy to find loopholes.

The Accounting Standards Committee was replaced in 1990 by the **Financial Reporting Council**. Its subsidiary, the **Accounting Standards Board** (ASB), issued standards 'concerned with principles rather than fine details'. Its standards were called Financial Reporting Standards (FRSs). However, it adopted all existing SSAPs and some of these are still relevant, although most have been replaced by FRSs. It was supported in its aim by the Urgent Issues Task Force and the Review Panel.

3.4.2 The current UK regime

In 2012, a number of reforms took place that made the FRC a unified regulatory body. As part of this reform, the Accounting Council and the UITF was disbanded and responsibility for setting accounting standards came under the FRC Board.

3.4.3 Accounting standards and the law

The Companies Act 2006 (TSO, 2006) requires companies to include a note to the accounts stating that the accounts have been prepared in accordance with **applicable accounting standards** or, alternatively, giving details of material departures from those standards, with reasons. The Review Panel and the Secretary of State for Trade and Industry have the power to apply to the court for revision of the accounts where non-compliance is not justified.

These provisions mean that accounting standards now have the force of law, whereas previously they had no legal standing in statute.

3.5 The European Union

Since the United Kingdom became a member of the European Union (EU) it has been obliged to comply with legal requirements decided on by the EU. It does this by enacting UK laws to implement EU directives. For example, all companies listed on an EU Stock Exchange are required to use International Financial Reporting Standards (IFRSs) when preparing their consolidated financial statements.

EXAM FOCUS POINT

Although your syllabus does not require you to be an expert on EU procedure, you should be aware that the form and content of company accounts can be influenced by international developments.

3.6 International Accounting Standards Board

One important influence on financial accounting is the **International Accounting Standards Board** (IASB). The forerunner of the IASB was set up in 1973 to work for the improvement and harmonisation of financial reporting. Its members are the professional accounting bodies. The structure of the IASB was reorganised in May 2000.

The objectives of the IASB are:

(a) To **develop**, in the public interest, a single set of high quality, understandable and enforceable **global accounting standards** that require high quality, transparent and comparable information in financial statements and other financial reporting to help participants in the world's capital markets and other users make economic decisions

(b) To promote the use and **rigorous application** of those standards.

(c) To bring about **convergence of national accounting standards** and International Accounting Standards to high quality solutions

3.6.1 The use and application of International Financial Reporting Standards (IFRSs)

IFRSs have helped both to improve and to harmonise financial reporting around the world. The standards are used:

- As national requirements, often after a national process
- As the basis for all or some national requirements
- As an international benchmark for those countries which develop their own requirements
- By regulatory authorities for domestic and foreign companies
- By companies themselves

3.7 Generally Accepted Accounting Practice (GAAP)

This term signifies all the rules, from whatever source, which govern accounting.

GAAP is a set of rules governing accounting. The rules may derive from:

- Company law (mainly CA 2006)
- Accounting standards
- International accounting standards and statutory requirements in other countries (particularly the US)
- Stock Exchange requirements

3.8 True and fair view

True and fair view is not defined in company law or accounting standards. For practical purposes, it can be taken to mean accurate and not misleading.

Company law requires that:

- The statement of financial position must give a **true and fair view of the state of affairs** of the company as at the end of the financial year.

- The profit or loss account (income statement) must give a **true and fair view of the profit or loss** of the company for the financial year.

3.8.1 True and fair 'override'

The Companies Act 2006 (TSO, 2006) states that the directors may depart from any of its provisions if these are inconsistent with the requirement to give a true and fair view. This is commonly referred to as the 'true and fair override'. It has been treated as an important loophole in the law and has been the cause of much argument and dissatisfaction within the accounting profession.

QUESTION

Forces

List the forces that have shaped financial accounting, stating the effect of each.

ANSWER

(a)   **Company law** requires companies to prepare accounts and regulates their form and content.
(b)   **Accounting concepts** are applied by individuals using their **subjective judgement**.
(c)   **Accounting standards** help to eliminate subjectivity.
(d)   The **European Union** issues directives on accounting matters which we must apply.
(e)   **International Financial Reporting Standards** aim to harmonise accounting around the world.
(f)   **GAAP** is a collection of rules from various sources, governing accounting.

4   Internal and external financial information

The two most important external financial statements are the statement of financial position and the profit or loss account. Reports produced for internal purposes include budgets and costing schedules.

4.1 External reports

Businesses prepare financial statements for **external stakeholders**, such as shareholders, banks, suppliers and the Government.

The main reports produced for external purposes are the financial statements, which give the historic position of the business. The main statements are as follows.

- The profit or loss account (also known as the income statement, or statement of profit or loss)
- The statement of financial position (also known as a balance sheet)
- The statement of cash flows

4.2 The profit or loss account

The **profit or loss account** is a record of income generated and expenditure incurred over a given period.

The profit or loss account of a limited liability company will be made up for the period of a year, commencing from the date of the previous year's accounts. It shows whether the business has more income than expenditure (a profit) or vice versa (a loss) during a period.

Management accountants might need quarterly or monthly income statements for internal purposes.

Organisations which are not run for profit (charities etc) produce a similar statement called an **income and expenditure account** which shows the surplus of income over expenditure (or a deficit where expenditure exceeds income).

4.3 The statement of financial position

The **statement of financial position** is a list of all the assets owned by a business and all the liabilities owed by a business at a particular date.

Assets are the business's resources, eg buildings to operate from, plant and machinery to manufacture goods, inventory to sell and cars for its employees. These are all resources which it uses in its operations. Also, it may have bank balances, cash and amounts of money owed to it. These provide the funds it needs to carry out its operations and are also assets. It may owe money to the bank or to suppliers: these are liabilities.

4.4 The statement of cash flows

The **statement of cash flows** shows sources of cash generated during a period and how these funds have been spent.

The statement of cash flows takes the information presented in the profit or loss account and statement of financial position and analyses it into cash flows from different types of activity (such as operating (trading profit or loss) and investing (eg buying or selling non-current assets)).

4.5 Sustainability and integrated reports

Pressure from shareholders, customers, regulators and the media has led to companies recognising the need to collect and report non-financial data.

Integrated reporting refers to the integration (combining) of financial and non-financial information into a single document. However, there are considerable differences of opinion over the type of non-financial information that should be included, and how it should relate to financial data.

One area on which most agree information should be reported is sustainability. Sustainability is concerned with protecting the environment from damage – to be sustainable, an activity should be able to continue forever.

4.6 Internal reports

Businesses will wish to prepare internal reports to help them run the day-to-day operations of the business.

Examples of internal reports include the following.

- Cost schedules
- Budgets
- Variance reports

4.7 Cost schedules

Cost schedules are needed at regular intervals to enable managers to keep a check on what the business is spending. Cost schedules may be produced, for example, for the following areas.

- Wages and salaries
- Departmental costs
- Cost of sales
- Selling expenses
- Administration costs

4.8 Budgets

Most businesses will prepare a budget. This may be a budget for the year ahead, showing projected sales, the costs involved in generating those sales, overheads and projected profits. Budgets may be produced for the business as a whole and for individual departments. The finance department will also produce a cash flow budget (or cash flow forecast) identifying the amounts of cash likely to come into and out of the business each week or month. This will enable the department to identify potential problems and arrange overdraft facilities or loans with the bank well in advance.

4.9 Variance reports

Once the budget has been agreed, the actual costs must be measured. The cost schedules should be compared to the budget and any differences accounted for. These differences are called variances and the variance report details the differences between actual and budgeted costs, and explains any material variances. Action can then be taken as needed.

5 Control over business transactions

5.1 Office organisation

There are a number of areas or functions to be administered and managed within a business. For example, the 'head office' of a business may cover the following areas:

- Purchasing
- Sales and marketing
- Human resources
- General administration
- Finance

5.1.1 Purchasing

Whether a business manufactures products or sells bought-in products, there will be a large purchasing function, either purchasing raw materials for manufacture or purchasing finished goods for resale. The function of the purchasing department will be to ensure that the business purchases from suppliers providing the best overall deal in terms of price, service, delivery time and quality. The purchasing department will also be responsible for ensuring that only necessary purchases are made by the business.

5.1.2 Human resources

Any business that employs a significant number of people is likely to have a human resources function. This area of the office will be responsible for the hiring and firing of staff, for training of staff and for the general welfare of the employees.

5.1.3 Finance

The finance function is also very wide ranging. On a day-to-day level the accounts department will deal with the sending invoices to customers, receiving invoices from suppliers, payment of suppliers, receiving money from customers and making other payments, such as purchases of non-current assets and payment of employees. The higher levels of management in the accounting function may also be responsible for management of the cash balances and for the overall financing of the organisation.

5.1.4 Sales and marketing

The selling and marketing function will deal with all aspects of taking sales orders, advertising, and any sales personnel.

5.1.5 General administration

General administration functions are very wide ranging but might include secretarial support, dealing with telephone queries and arranging matters such as rent of properties.

QUESTION

Departmental functions

Which of the following is not a function of the purchasing department?

A   Ensuring that only required goods are purchased
B   Ensuring that suppliers used give the best price
C   Paying suppliers' invoices
D   Negotiating discounts with suppliers

ANSWER

The answer is C. Paying suppliers' invoices.

5.2 Policies

In any organisation there is a need for order, co-ordination and control to ensure efficiency. To achieve this, management often implement rules and procedures. For example there will be authorisation policies for the purchase of non-current assets, procedures for choosing new suppliers, procedures for accepting new customers, etc.

Policies and procedures may be grouped in the form of a **policy manual**, perhaps stored on the organisation's computer network for easy reference. Although a policy manual is to be recommended as a form of control over the activities of employees, care must be taken that strict adherence to the rules does not create inflexibility.

5.3 Business transactions

It was mentioned earlier that businesses come in all shapes and forms. However, there will be a number of types of transaction which will be common to most businesses.

- Making sales
- Making purchases
- Paying expenses
- Paying employees
- Purchasing non-current assets

This diagram shows, in a simplified form, the flow of funds, documentation and information.

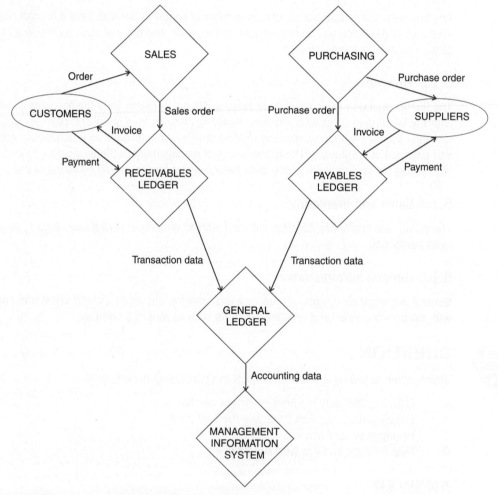

Effective systems and procedures should ensure that:

- Relationships with customers are effectively managed
- Relationships with suppliers are effectively managed
- Office functions interrelate properly and are not duplicated

Within the overall system, which we can consider to be how each department relates to the other departments and to outside bodies, there will be sub-systems. For instance, the purchase ledger function will have its own system, which will be designed to ensure that only authorised payments are made, that no invoice ever gets paid twice and that expenses are coded to the correct accounts.

Weaknesses in office procedures may be signalled by:

- Arguments over job functions
- Missing paperwork
- Disputes with customers/suppliers
- Goods not delivered

5.3.1 Sales

In a retail organisation sales are of course made on the shop floor. However, in a **manufacturing organisation**, there will normally be a **sales and marketing function** whose responsibility is to **market** the organisation's **products** and take orders from customers. Often the day-to-day responsibility for taking orders will be with the salesmen and women. This may be done over the telephone or via personal visits to customers or potential customers.

If a sale is being made to an **existing customer**, provided that customer has not exceeded their credit balance then the procedure will be for the **salesperson** to **take details** of the order and pass those details to the stores department **for despatch** and to the **accounts department for invoicing** of the customer.

However, if the sale is to a **new customer**, then a more **senior** level of management will have to be involved if the sale is to be on credit. The **credit status** of the new customer must be **determined** and a decision made as to whether sales on credit should be made to this customer.

Once the **goods** have been **despatched** to the customer, **responsibility** then **passes** to the **accounting function** to invoice the customer for the goods and to ensure that payment is received.

5.3.2 Purchases

The making of **purchases** will initially be **started** by either the **purchasing department or** the **stores department**. The need for the purchase of more goods will be recognised by, for example, the stores manager when he realises that an item of inventory is running low. He will then **complete** a **purchase requisition** which must be **authorised** and then the **purchasing function** will determine the most **appropriate supplier** on the basis of price, delivery and quality. An order will be placed by the purchasing function and the goods will normally be received by the stores department.

After this, **responsibility** then goes to the **accounting department** which will await the arrival of the invoice for the goods from the suppliers, check that the invoice is accurate and for goods that have in fact been received and then in due course pay the amount due to the supplier.

5.3.3 Overheads

Organisations will incur a variety of expenses such as rent and rates, insurance, telephone bills, energy bills, advertising expenses, etc. In some cases these will be incurred by a specific department of the business, such as the marketing department investing in an advertising campaign, or alternatively the receipt of the telephone bill will be part of the **general administration of the business**.

When bills for **expenses** are received they will be passed to the **accounting function** which will check that the expense has been incurred or is reasonable and then will process the expense for payment.

5.3.4 Payroll

Every week and/or every month the employees of the business must be paid. For this process to take place there are a lot of calculations to be made and a lot of paperwork to be filled out. In **larger organisations** there will be a **payroll department** which will deal with this; otherwise, it will be the **responsibility** of the payroll clerk in the **accounting function**.

The payroll function will determine the gross pay for each employee, based on a variety of different remuneration schemes, and then will calculate the statutory and other deductions that must be made before calculating the net pay due to the employee. Finally the payroll function must then organise the method of payment to the employees.

5.3.5 Capital expenditure

From time to time an organisation will need to purchase non-current assets. These are **assets** that are to be **used** in the business for the **medium to long term** rather than being purchased for resale. This will include items such as machinery, cars, computer equipment, office furniture, etc.

In order for the purchase of non-current assets to be put in motion the manager of the department which requires the asset must firstly fill out a **purchase requisition**. As most non-current assets are relatively expensive this will probably have to be **authorised** by more **senior management**. Once the requisition has been authorised the purchasing function will then find the most appropriate supplier for the assets.

Once a purchase order has been placed the details will then be passed to the **accounting function** which will then process and pay the invoice when it is received.

QUESTION

Purchasing function

Which of the following personnel in an organisation would not be involved in the purchase of materials?

A   Credit controller   C   Accountant
B   Stores manager   D   Purchasing manager

ANSWER

A. The credit controller chases unpaid debts.

5.4 Control over transactions

As you may have noticed in the last section, any transaction that a business is involved in will tend to involve a number of different people within the organisation. You will have also noticed the requirement for transactions to be authorised.

The management of a reasonably large business cannot have the time to personally be involved in every transaction of the business. However, in order to keep control of the sources of income of the business and the expenditure that the business incurs, it is important that transactions are authorised by a responsible member of the management team.

In particular, this means that management must have control over the following areas.

(a)   **Sales on credit made to new customers**. If a sale is made on credit the goods are sent out with a promise from the customer to pay in the future, therefore the management of the business must be as certain as they can be that this new customer can, and will, pay for the goods. This means that the credit controller must be happy that the new customer has a good credit rating and is fairly certain to pay for the goods.

(b)   **Purchases of goods or non-current assets and payments for expenses**. This is money going out of the business therefore it is essential that these are necessary and valid expenditures so a responsible official must authorise them.

(c)   **Payroll**. One of the largest payments made by most organisations is that of the wages bill for their employees. It is essential that only bona fide employees are paid for the actual hours that they have worked therefore authorisation of the payroll is a very important part of any business.

5.5 Financial control procedures

Financial control procedures exist specifically to ensure that:

- Financial transactions are properly carried out.
- The assets of the business are safeguarded.
- Accurate and timely management information is produced.

These are some examples of financial control procedures:

- Cheques over a certain amount to need two signatories
- Authorisation limits for purchase orders
- Authorisation for petty cash and expenses claims
- Effective credit control procedures
- Computer security procedures and access levels

Weaknesses in financial control procedures may be signalled by:

- Cash or cheques going missing
- Excessive bad or doubtful debts
- Customers not paying within credit terms
- Suppliers not being paid on time
- Unauthorised purchases being made
- Failure to produce accounts or other reports at the specified time

6 The main business financial systems

6.1 Controlling the payroll system

Key controls over payroll cover:

- Documentation and authorisation of staff changes
- Calculation of wages and salaries
- Payment of wages and salaries
- Authorisation of deductions

The purpose of a payroll system is to compute the gross wages and salaries of employees and produce payslips, cheques and/or listings sent to banks instructing them to make payments. A computerised payroll system will be expected to carry out these tasks in accordance with how much employees should receive, how they should receive it and when it should be paid. The system should also be able to calculate tax deductions, national insurance deductions, savings, loan repayments, etc as well as printing various other outputs connected with employees' pay.

6.1.1 Data held on a payroll file

Payroll files will consist of an individual record for each employee.

(a) **Standing** data on each employee will include:

    (i)   Personal details (eg name, employee number, job grade, address)
    (ii)   Rate of pay
    (iii) Details of deductions (including tax code)
    (iv) Holidays

(b) **Variable** (transaction) data will include:

    (i)   Gross pay to date
    (ii)   Tax to date
    (iii) Pension contributions etc

6.1.2 Inputs to a payroll system

The main inputs into a **wages system** (ie into a weekly paid payroll) are as follows.

(a) Clock cards or timesheets (sometimes both are used). Details of overtime worked will normally be shown on these documents. Sometimes payroll might be directly linked to an electronic time recording system.

(b) Amount of bonus, or appropriate details if the bonus is calculated by the computer.

Salary systems (ie a monthly paid payroll) are similar to those for wages but it is usual for the monthly salary to be generated by the computer from details held on the master file and therefore (with the exception of overtime, bonuses, etc) there is no need for any transaction input. So the inputs for a salary system are just overtime, bonuses, etc (because the basic salary is already on the master file).

6.1.3 Processing in a payroll system

The primary action involved in processing a payroll is calculating an employee's gross pay, calculating and implementing the various deductions in order to find net pay, and then making payment by the appropriate method.

In the case of wages, this means taking the input data on hours worked and pay details, and calculating the weekly wage due to the employee. The same calculation is carried out every week.

In the case of salaries, payroll processing might just mean picking an option to pay all the monthly paid employees the same amount as they received the previous month. This could happen in theory, but in practice there are usually some amendments to make to the monthly pay details, and these are implemented during payroll processing.

6.1.4 Outputs from a payroll system

Typical outputs in a payroll system are:

(a)   Payslips

(b)   Payroll (this is often a copy of the payslips)

(c)   Payroll analysis, including analysis of deductions (tax, national insurance, etc) and details for costing purposes

(d)   Various forms required for income tax purposes

(e)   Coin analysis, cheques, credit transfer forms

(f)   In some cases, a floppy disk with payment details for despatch to the bank and payment through the BACS system

Segregation of duties within the payroll department is particularly important. Well-planned fraud, such as the payment of 'ghost' employees, then requires collusion involving two or more people, and is consequently less likely to take place.

The most important aims of the control system relating to wages and salaries are:

Feature	Aims
Setting of wages and salaries	• **Employees** are **only paid** for **work** that they have **done**. • **Gross pay** has been **calculated correctly** and **authorised**.
Recording of wages and salaries	• **Gross** and **net pay** and **deductions** are **accurately recorded** on the payroll. • **Wages** and **salaries paid** are **recorded correctly** in the **bank** and **cash records**. • Wages and salaries are **correctly recorded** in the **general ledger**.
Payment of wages and salaries	• The **correct employees** are **paid**.
Deductions	• Statutory and non-statutory **deductions** have been **calculated correctly** and are **authorised**. • The **correct amounts** are **paid** to the **taxation authorities**.

BPP LEARNING MEDIA

6.1.5 Controls

While in practice separate arrangements are generally made for dealing with wages and salaries, the considerations involved are broadly similar and for convenience the two aspects are here treated together.

Responsibility for the preparation of pay sheets should be delegated to a suitable person, and adequate staff appointed to assist them. The extent to which the staff responsible for preparing wages and salaries may perform other duties should be clearly defined. In this connection full advantage should be taken where possible of the **division of duties**, and checks available where automatic wage-accounting systems are in use.

Setting of wages and salaries

- **Staffing** and **segregation of duties**
- **Maintenance of personnel records** and regular checking of wages and salaries to details in personnel records
- **Authorisation** required for:
    - Engagement and discharge of employees
    - Changes in pay rates
    - Overtime
    - Non-statutory deductions (for example pension contributions)
    - Advances of pay
- **Recording** of **changes** in **personnel** and **pay rates**
- **Recording** of hours worked by **timesheets, clocking in and out** arrangements
- **Review of hours worked**
- **Recording** of **advances** of **pay**
- **Holiday pay** arrangements
- **Answering queries**
- **Review** of **wages against budget**

Recording of wages and salaries

- **Bases** for **compilation** of payroll
- **Preparation, checking** and **approval** of payroll
- Dealing with **non-routine matters**

Payment of cash wages

- **Segregation of duties**
    - Cash sheet preparation
    - Filling of pay packets
    - Distribution of wages
- **Authorisation** of **wage cheque**
- **Custody** of cash
    - Encashment of cheque
    - Security of pay packets
    - Security of transit arrangements
    - Security and prompt banking of unclaimed wages
- **Verification of identity**
- **Recording** of distribution

Payment of salaries

- **Preparation** and **signing** of cheques and bank transfer lists
- **Comparison** of **cheques** and **bank transfer list** with payroll
- **Maintenance** and **reconciliation** of wages and salaries bank account

Deductions from pay

- **Maintenance** of **separate employees' records**, with which pay lists may be compared as necessary

- **Reconciliation** of **total pay** and **deductions** between one pay day and the next

- **Surprise cash counts**

- **Comparison** of actual pay totals with **budget estimates** or standard costs and the investigation of variances

- **Agreement** of **gross earnings** and **total tax deducted** with income tax returns to the HM Revenue and Customs

Appropriate arrangements should be made for dealing with statutory and other authorised deductions from pay, such as national insurance, income tax, pension fund contributions and savings held in trust. A primary consideration is the establishment of adequate controls over the **records**, and **authorisation** of deductions.

6.2 The purchases and sales cycles

The purchases and sales systems will be the most important components of most company accounting systems.

6.2.1 Purchase and sales systems

Purchasing is an important area to control, especially where items of high value are concerned. There are likely to be specific authorisation procedures for the purchase of non-current assets.

6.2.2 Payables ledger system

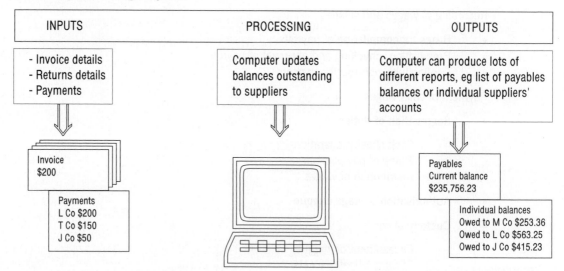

Businesses have to ensure that only **properly authorised purchases** which are necessary for the business are made. All stages of the purchase process – ordering, receiving goods and being charged for them – should be documented and matched. In this way it can be ensured that the business gets what it ordered and only pays for what it orders and receives. The payables ledger makes it possible for the business to keep track of what it owes each supplier.

The most important aims of the control system relating to payables and purchases are:

Feature	Aims
Ordering	• All **orders for**, and expenditure on, **goods and services** are properly **authorised**, and are for **goods and services** that are actually **received** and are **for the company**. • **Orders** are only **made** to **authorised suppliers**. • **Orders** are **made** at **competitive prices**.
Receipt and invoices	• **Goods and services** received are **used** for the **organisation's purposes** and not private purposes. • **Goods and services** are **only accepted** if they have been **ordered**, and the **order** has been authorised. • All **goods and services received** are accurately **recorded**. • **Liabilities** are **recognised** for all **goods and services** that have been **received**. • All **credits** to which business is due are **claimed**. • **Receipt** of goods and services is **necessary** to **establish** a **liability**.
Accounting	• All expenditure is authorised and is for goods that are actually received. • All expenditure that is made is recorded correctly in the general and payables ledger. • All credit notes that are received are recorded in the general and payables ledger. • All entries in the payables ledger are made to the correct payables ledger accounts. • Cut-off is applied correctly to the payables ledger.

6.2.3 Controls

The purchasing system tests will be based around:

- Buying (authorisation)
- Goods inwards (custody)
- Accounting (recording)

ORDERING

- Use certain suppliers only
- Obtain authorisation
- Use prenumbered forms

GOODS RECEIVED

- Compare goods received note with purchase order
- Check condition of goods received
- Check supplier invoice correct
- Record goods returned

ACCOUNTING/RECORDING

- Segregate duties of accounting and checking
- Record purchases/returns promptly
- Compare supplier statements to payables ledger
- Check payment properly authorised

6.3 Controlling the sales cycle

Like the purchase cycle, the sales system tests will be based around:

- Selling (authorisation)
- Goods outwards (custody)
- Accounting (recording)

For sales, businesses want to give credit only to customers who will pay their debts. The processes of handling sales, matched orders, despatching goods and invoicing all need to be **documented** and **matched**, so that customers receive what they ordered and are correctly billed. The **receivables ledger** makes it possible to keep track of what is owed by each customer.

6.3.1 Receivables ledger system

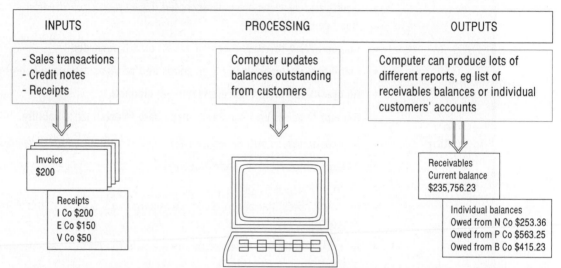

There are a number of controls which need to be in place over sales and receivables. Bear in mind that, quite apart from safeguarding actual transactions, there must be no possibility of turnover figures being falsified. A number of people may have bonuses and commissions based on them!

The most important aims of the control system relating to receivables and sales are these:

Feature	Aims
Ordering and granting of credit	• **Goods** and **services** are **only supplied** to **customers** with **good credit ratings**. • **Customers** are encouraged to **pay promptly**. • **Orders** are **recorded correctly**. • **Orders** are **fulfilled**.
Despatch and invoicing	• All **despatches** of goods are **recorded**. • All **goods and services** sold are **correctly invoiced**. • All **invoices** raised **relate to goods and services** that have been **supplied** by the business. • **Credit notes** are only given for **valid reasons**.
Recording, accounting and credit control	• All sales that have been **invoiced** are **recorded** in the general and receivables ledgers. • All **credit notes** that have been **issued** are **recorded** in the general and receivables ledgers. • All **entries** in the receivables ledger are **made** to the **correct** receivables ledger **accounts**. • **Cut-off** is applied correctly to the receivables ledger. • Potentially **doubtful debts** are **identified**.

6.3.2 Controls

The tests of controls of the **sales system** will be based around:

- Selling (authorisation)
- Accounting (recording)
- Goods outwards (custody)

 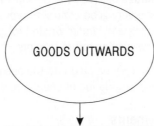 

SELLING	GOODS OUTWARDS	ACCOUNTING/RECORDING
- Segregate duties of credit control, invoicing and despatch - Obtain authorisation for credit terms for customers - Use prenumbered forms	- Authorisation of despatch of goods - Check condition of goods returned - Check signature of delivery notes - Match sales invoices with despatch and delivery notes and sales orders	- Segregate duties of accounting and checking - Record sales sequentially - Match cash receipts to invoices - Prepare regular receivables statements - Retain customer remittance advice - Review and follow up overdue accounts

6.4 Controlling cash

Cash and petty cash must be regularly reconciled.

Although we still talk in terms of cash, very few business transactions involve its use. Even at the retail level, many purchases are now being made by debit and credit card.

When we consider sales and purchases made on credit between businesses, transfer of funds will probably be by:

- Company cheque
- Internet transfer, or in some cases
- Bank transfer
- Standing order/direct debit

The only use of cash in non-retail businesses will probably be for petty cash. So what controls need to be in place?

6.4.1 Control over receipts

In any business controls over cash **receipts** are fundamental if the company is to keep a healthy cash position. **Control over cash receipts** will concentrate on three main areas.

- Receipts must be **banked promptly**.
- The **record of receipts must be complete**.
- The loss of receipts through **theft or accident** must be prevented.

The difference between these three controls can be demonstrated with an example.

6.4.2 Example: control over cash receipts

Suppose that your company sells goods for $10,000 during the month of April to XYZ & Co. You receive a payment of $10,000 by cheque along with a remittance advice which shows exactly which invoices the cheque covers.

(a)   You examine the cheque to ensure it is valid and completed correctly and you pay it in to the company account within 24 hours as company policy dictates (**banked promptly**).

(b)   A colleague records the cheque details and compares the amount of the cheque to the remittance advice (**checking for completeness**). Usually the payment would also be checked against the total amount owed by the customer as part of the completeness check.

(c)   The **segregation of duties** between the person who banks the money and the person who records it is considered to be a very good control to prevent **theft and accidental loss**. This prevents the fraud known as 'teeming and lading' where receipts for customers are misappropriated and this is then covered up by misposting future receipts.

(d)   Now that cheques can only be paid into the account in whose name they are made out, the opportunities for misappropriation of cheque receipts are much less.

6.4.3 Controls over payments

Controls over payments by a business must be **strict**. This should apply to all payments, from the smallest to the largest. The need for controls should be fairly obvious: if any business allowed some of its employees to pay out its money without needing to obtain permission, the scope for cheating and dishonesty would be very wide.

There are three main steps in applying controls over payments.

Step 1	Obtaining **documentary evidence** of the reason why the payment is being made and the amount of the payment. In the case of payments to suppliers, the documentary evidence will be a supplier's invoice (or statement).

Step 2	**Authorisation** of the payment, which means giving formal 'official' approval to make the payment.

Step 3	**Restricting the authority to actually make the payment** to certain specified individuals.

The difference between Steps 1, 2 and 3 can be illustrated with an example.

6.4.4 Example: controlling a payment

Suppose that a company buys goods costing $5,000.

Step 1	It will receive an invoice from the supplier. This is the **documentary evidence** of the reason for and amount of the payment.

Step 2	The invoice will be approved by the purchasing director. This approval is the **authorisation of the payment**.

Step 3	At some time later, the payment will be made to the supplier, probably by cheque. For a payment of $5,000, perhaps only the finance director or managing director will be permitted to sign the cheque, and so the **authority to make the payment** would be limited to these two people.

6.4.5 Authorisation

Every payment must be approved by an **authorised person**. This person will often be a manager or supervisor in the department that initiated the expense, but every organisation has its own system. The following control limits must be set.

*   **Which individuals** can authorise particular expenses
*   The **maximum amount** of expenditure that an individual can authorise

The controls described above are designed to **prevent** fraud and error in the cash cycle. The most important controls designed to **detect** fraud and error which may already have taken place are **reconciliations**.

Petty cash should be reconciled whenever there is a need to replenish the float. The vouchers plus the remaining cash should equal the original float. If this balances, the only other check needed is to make sure that the vouchers are all valid and authorised.

A **bank reconciliation** should be done at least once a month. Many businesses, even those with sophisticated computer systems, still keep a manual cash book. If not, a printout of the bank record from the computer can be used. This is reconciled to the bank statement. There will always be differences, but they should come into the following categories.

* Timing differences due to unpresented cheques
* Timing differences due to uncredited lodgements
* Standing orders and direct debits not entered in the cash book
* Bank charges not entered in the cash book
* Funds received by transfer and not recorded in the cash book

6.5 Reviewing controls

Controls should be regularly checked and any problems reported to management.

It is not sufficient to set up controls and assume that they work. The control system needs to be regularly tested and reviewed by means of an internal audit (see next chapter). This will highlight any problems in practice and the internal auditors can make recommendations to the management for improvements to the control system. This will help to prevent error and fraud and to improve efficiency.

7   Manual and computerised accounting systems

Most accounting systems are computerised and anyone training to be an accountant should be able to work with computerised systems. The most important point to remember is that the **principles** of computerised accounting are the same as those of **manual accounting**.

Most references to computerised accounting talk about accounting **packages**. This is a rather general term, but most of us can probably name the accounting package that we use at work. An accounting package consists of several accounting **modules**, eg receivables ledger, general ledger.

We are going to look specifically at 'applications software'; that is, packages of computer programs that carry out specific tasks.

(a)   Some applications are devoted specifically to an accounting task, for example a payroll package, a non-current asset register or a inventory control package.

(b)   Other applications have many uses in business, including their use for accounting purposes. Examples of this are databases and spreadsheets, which are covered in Section 8.

7.1 Accounting packages

Accounting functions retain the same names in computerised systems as in more traditional written records. Computerised accounting still uses the familiar ideas of day books, ledger accounts, double entry, trial balance and financial statements. The principles of working with computerised sales, purchase and nominal ledgers are exactly what would be expected in the manual methods they replace.

The only difference is that these various books of account have become invisible. Ledgers are now computer files which are held in a computer-sensible form, ready to be called on.

7.2 Manual systems vs computerised systems

In many situations manual systems are inferior to computerised systems in terms of productivity, speed, accessibility, quality of output, incidence of errors, 'bulk' and when making corrections.

Disadvantages of manual systems include the following.

Disadvantage	Comment
Productivity	**Productivity** is usually lower, particularly in routine or operational situations such as transaction processing.
Slower	Processing is **slower** where large volumes of data need to be dealt with.
Risk of errors	The **risk of errors** is greater, especially in repetitive work like payroll calculations.
Less accessible	Information on manual systems is generally **less accessible**. Access to information is often restricted to one user at a time.
Alterations	It is difficult to make **corrections**. If a manual document contains errors or needs updating it is often necessary to recreate the **whole** document from scratch.
Quality of output	**Quality of output** is less consistent and often not well designed. At worst, handwritten records may be illegible and so completely useless.
Bulk	Paper-based systems are generally very **bulky** both to handle and to store

However, don't assume that computerised systems are best in every situation. For example, a post-it note stuck on a colleague's desk with a brief message may in some cases be quicker than typing up an email message.

7.3 Coding

Computers require vital information to be expressed in the form of codes. For example, general ledger accounts might be coded individually by means of a two-digit code.

00   Ordinary share capital
01   Share premium
05   Statement of profit or loss and other comprehensive income
15   Purchases
22   Receivables control account
41   Payables control account
42   Interest
43   Dividends

In the same way, individual accounts must be given a unique code number in the receivables ledger and payables ledger.

7.3.1 Example: coding

When an invoice is received from a supplier (example code 1234) for $3,000 for the purchase of raw materials, the transaction might be coded for input to the computer as:

	General ledger			Inventory	
Supplier Code	Debit	Credit	Value	Code	Quantity
1234	15	41	$3,000	56742	150

Code 15 in our example represents purchases, and code 41 the payables control account from the list in Paragraph 6.3. This single input could be used to update the payables ledger, the general ledger and the inventory ledger. The inventory code may enable further analysis to be carried out, perhaps allocating the cost to a particular department or product. Thus the needs of both financial accounting and cost accounting can be fulfilled at once.

7.4 Modules and accounting packages

A **module** is a program which deals with one particular part of a business accounting system.

An accounting package will consist of several modules. A simple accounting package might consist of only one module (in which case it is called a standalone module), but more often it will consist of several modules. The name given to a set of several modules is a **suite**. An accounting package, therefore, might have separate modules for:

- Invoicing
- Inventory
- Receivables ledger
- Payables ledger
- General ledger
- Payroll
- Cash book
- Job costing
- Non-current asset register
- Report generator

7.5 Integrated software

Control is enhanced by an **integrated accounting system**.

Each module may be integrated with the others, so that data entered in one module will be passed automatically or by simple operator request through into any other module where the data is of some relevance. For example, if there is an input into the invoicing module authorising the despatch of an invoice to a customer, there might be **automatic links**:

(a) To the receivables ledger, to update the file by posting the invoice to the customer's account

(b) To the inventory module, to update the inventory file by:

    (i)   Reducing the quantity and value of inventory in hand
    (ii)   Recording the inventory movement

(c) To the general ledger, to update the file by posting the sale to the sales account

(d) To the job costing module, to record the sales value of the job on the job cost file

(e) To the report generator, to update the sales analysis and sales totals which are on file and awaiting inclusion in management reports

A diagram of an **integrated accounting system** is given below.

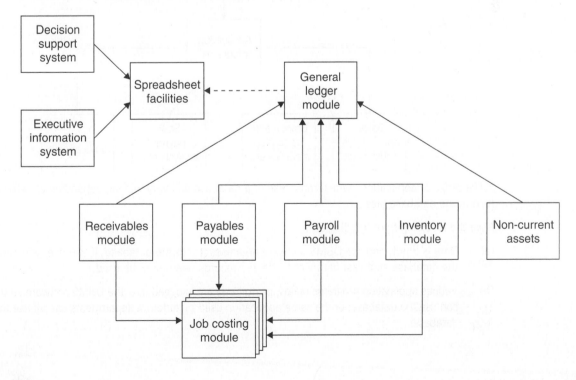

7.5.1 Advantages

(a) It becomes possible to make just one entry in one of the ledgers which automatically updates the others.

(b) Users can specify reports, and the software will automatically extract the required data from all the relevant files.

(c) Both of the above simplify the workload of the user, and the irritating need to constantly load and unload disks is eliminated.

7.5.2 Disadvantages

(a) Usually, it requires more computer memory than separate (standalone) systems – which means there is less space in which to store actual data.

(b) Because one program is expected to do everything, the user may find that an integrated package has fewer facilities than a set of specialised modules.

8 Databases and spreadsheets

> A **database** may be described as a 'pool' of data, which can be used by any number of applications. Its use is not restricted to the accounts department.

The database approach can also be summarised diagrammatically.

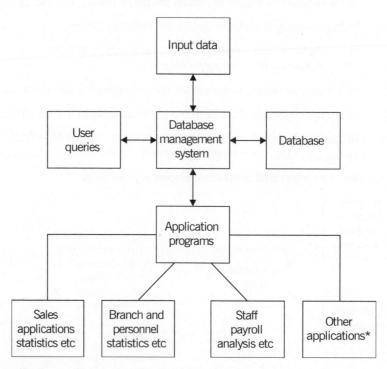

* The range of applications which make use of a database will vary widely, depending on what data is held in the database files.

Note the following from the diagram.

(a) Data is input, and the DBMS software organises it into the database. If you like, you can think of the database as a vast library of fields and records, waiting to be used.

(b) Various application programs (sales, payroll etc) are 'plugged into' the DBMS software so that they can use the database, or the same application used by different departments can all use the database.

(c)   As there is only one pool of data, there is no need for different departments to keep many different files with duplicated information.

8.1 Objectives of a database

The main virtues of a database are as follows.

(a)   There is **common data** for all users to share.

(b)   The extra effort of keeping **duplicate files** in different departments is avoided.

(c)   Conflicts between departments who use **inconsistent data are avoided**.

A database should have four major objectives.

(a)   It should be **shared**. Different users should be able to access the **same data** in the database for their own processing applications (and at the **same time** in some systems) thus removing the need for duplicating data on different files.

(b)   The **integrity** of the database must be preserved. This means that one user should not be allowed to alter the data on file so as to spoil the database records for other users. However, users must be able to update the data on file, and so make valid alterations to the data.

(c)   The database system should provide for the needs of different users, who each have their own processing requirements and data access methods. In other words, the database should provide for the **operational requirements of all its users**.

(d)   The database should be capable of **evolving**, both in the short term (it must be kept updated) and in the longer term (it must be able to meet the future data processing needs of users, not just their current needs).

8.2 Example: Non-current assets and databases

An organisation, especially a large one, may possess a large quantity of non-current assets. Before computerisation these would have been kept in a manual non-current asset register. A database enables this non-current asset register to be stored in an electronic form. A database file for non-current assets might contain most or all of the following categories of information.

(a)   Code number to give the asset a unique identification in the database

(b)   Type of asset (for example motor car, leasehold premises), for published accounts purposes

(c)   More detailed description of the asset (for example serial number, car registration number, make)

(d)   Physical location of the asset (for example address)

(e)   Organisational location of the asset (for example accounts department)

(f)   Person responsible for the asset (for example, in the case of a company-owned car, the person who uses it)

(g)   Original cost of the asset

(h)   Date of purchase

(i)   Depreciation rate and method applied to the asset

(j)   Accumulated depreciation to date

(k)   Net book value of the asset

(l)   Estimated residual value

(m)   Date when the physical existence of the asset was last verified

(n)   Supplier

Obviously, the details kept about the asset would depend on the type of asset it is.

Any kind of computerised non-current asset record will improve efficiency in accounting for non-current assets because of the ease and speed with which any necessary calculations can be made. Most obvious

is the calculation of the depreciation provision which can be an extremely onerous task if it is done monthly and there are frequent acquisitions and disposals and many different depreciation rates in use.

The particular advantage of using a database for the non-current asset function is its flexibility in generating reports for different purposes. Aside from basic cost and net book value information a database with fields such as those listed above in the record of each asset could compile reports analysing assets according to location, say, or by manufacturer. This information could be used to help compare the performance of different divisions, perhaps, or to assess the useful life of assets supplied by different manufacturers. There may be as many more possibilities as there are permutations of the individual pieces of data.

8.3 Spreadsheets

Spreadsheets, too, are often used both in financial accounting and cost accounting.

A spreadsheet is essentially an electronic piece of paper divided into rows and columns with a built-in pencil, eraser and calculator. It provides an easy way of performing numerical calculations.

The intersection of each column and row of a spreadsheet is referred to as a cell. A cell can contain text, numbers or formulae. Use of a formula means that the cell which contains the formula will display the results of a calculation based on data in other cells. If the numbers in those other cells change, the result displayed in the formula cell will also change accordingly. With this facility, a spreadsheet is used to create financial models.

Below is a spreadsheet processing budgeted sales figures for three geographical areas for the first quarter of the year.

	A	B	C	D	E
1	**BUDGETED SALES FIGURES**				
2		Jan	Feb	Mar	Total
3		£'000	£'000	£'000	£'000
4	North	2,431	3,001	2,189	7,621
5	South	6,532	5,826	6,124	18,482
6	West	895	432	596	1,923
7	Total	9,858	9,259	8,909	28,026

8.4 The use of spreadsheets

Spreadsheets have many uses, both for accounting and for other purposes. It is perfectly possible, for example, to create proforma statements of financial position and statements of comprehensive income on a spreadsheet, or set up the notes for financial accounts, like the non-current assets note.

CHAPTER ROUNDUP

↳ Accounting is a way of recording, analysing and summarising transactions of a business.

↳ You may have a wide understanding of what accounting is about. Your job may be in one area or type of accounting, but you must understand the breadth of work which an accountant undertakes.

↳ You should be able to outline the factors which have shaped the development of financial accounting.

↳ The two most important external financial statements are the statement of financial position and the profit or loss account. Reports produced for internal purposes include budgets and costing schedules.

↳ Businesses prepare financial statements for **external stakeholders**, such as shareholders, banks, suppliers and the Government.

↳ The **profit or loss account** is a record of income generated and expenditure incurred over a given period.

↳ The **statement of financial position** is a list of all the assets owned by a business and all the liabilities owed by a business at a particular date.

↳ The **statement of cash flows** shows sources of cash generated during a period and how these funds have been spent.

↳ Businesses will wish to prepare internal reports to help them run the day-to-day operations of the business.

↳ Key controls over payroll cover:

  – Documentation and authorisation of staff charges
  – Calculation of wages and salaries
  – Payment of wages and salaries
  – Authorisation of deductions

↳ The purchases and sales systems will be the most important components of most company accounting systems.

↳ The purchasing system tests will be based around:

  – Buying (authorisation)
  – Goods inwards (custody)
  – Accounting (recording)

↳ Like the purchase cycle, the sales system tests will be based around:

  – Selling (authorisation)
  – Goods outwards (custody)
  – Accounting (recording)

↳ The tests of controls of the **sales system** will be based around:

  – Selling (authorisation)
  – Goods outwards (custody)
  – Accounting (recording)

↳ Cash and petty cash must be regularly reconciled.

↳ Controls should be regularly checked and any problems reported to management.

↳ In **many situations manual systems are inferior to computerised systems** in terms of productivity, speed, accessibility, quality of output, incidence of errors, 'bulk' and when making corrections.

↳ Control is enhanced by an **integrated accounting system**.

↳ A **database** may be described as a 'pool' of data, which can be used by any number of applications. Its use is not restricted to the accounts department.

↳ **Spreadsheets**, too, are often used both in financial accounting and cost accounting.

QUICK QUIZ

1 Transactions are initially recorded in which of the following?

   A   Books of first entry   C   Books of prime entry
   B   Books of ledger entry   D   Books of financial entry

2 The person responsible for cost accounting is most likely to be the company treasurer. Is this true or false?

3 Internal auditors are employed by

   A   The company that they audit   C   Either A or B
   B   An independent auditing/accounting firm

4 Which of the following factors have not influenced financial accounting?

   A   National legislation   C   Accounting standards
   B   Economic factors   D   GAAP

5 What does GAAP stand for?

   A   Group audit and accountancy policy   C   Generally accepted audit policy
   B   Generally accepted accounting practice   D   Guidelines for accepted accounting principles

6 What do the key controls over payroll cover?

7 What are the three main steps in controlling payments?

8 A series of cells arranged in columns and rows which can contain calculations, numbers or text is called a:

   A   Word document   C   Calculation sheet
   B   Spreadsheet   D   Cell document

ANSWERS TO QUICK QUIZ

1   C   Books of prime entry.

2   False. Cost accounting is usually done by the management accountant.

3   A   Internal auditors are employees of the company that they audit.

4   B   Economic factors do not influence the development of financial accounting.

5   B   Generally accepted accounting practice.

6   Controls cover documentation and authorisation of staff changes, calculation and payment of wages and salaries, and authorisation of deductions.

7   The three steps are: obtaining documentary evidence of the amount and reason for payment, obtaining authorisation and restricting the authority to actually make the payment to certain specified individuals.

8   B   Spreadsheet.

Now try ...

Attempt the questions below from the **Practice Question Bank**

Q36

Q37

Q38

Q39

Q40

Q41

Q42

Control, security and audit

In this chapter we move to the main elements of internal control systems that organisations operate (**Section 1**). Controls must be linked to organisational objectives and the main risks that organisations face (**Section 2**). In addition, internal control systems do not just consist of the controls themselves but also the control environment within which controls operate.

Internal audit is a key part of the control system of larger companies (**Section 3**) and the external audit function exists to review controls and report on the financial statements (**Section 4**).

Organisations are becoming increasingly **reliant on computerised information systems**. It is vital therefore to ensure these systems are secure – to protect the information held on them, to ensure operations run smoothly, to prevent theft and to ensure compliance with legislation (**Sections 5 and 6**).

Security and legal issues are likely to crop up regularly in the examination.

Study Guide	Intellectual level
C2 Accounting and finance functions within business	
(e) Identify and describe the main audit and assurance roles in business.	K
(i) Internal audit	
(ii) External audit	
(f) Explain the main functions of the internal auditor and the external auditor and how they differ.	K
C6 Internal controls, authorisation, security and compliance within business	
(a) Explain internal control and internal check.	K
(b) Explain the importance of internal financial controls in an organisation.	K
(c) Describe the responsibilities of management for internal financial control.	K
(d) Describe the features of effective internal financial control procedures in an organisation, including authorisation.	K
(e) Identify and describe the types of information technology and information systems used by the business organisation for internal control.	S
(f) Identify and describe features for protecting the security of IT systems and software within business.	S
(g) Describe general and application systems controls in business.	K

EXAM FOCUS POINT

The syllabus regards internal control as a specific and very important business function, supported by effective and secure management information.

1 Internal control systems

Internal controls should help organisations counter risks, maintain the quality of reporting and comply with laws and regulations. They provide reasonable assurance that the organisations will fulfil their objectives.

1.1 Direction of control systems

In order for internal controls to function properly, they have to be well directed. Managers and staff will be more able (and willing) to implement controls successfully if it can be demonstrated to them what the objectives of the control systems are, while objectives provide a yardstick for the board when they come to monitor and assess how controls have been operating.

1.2 Purposes of internal control systems

An internal control system should:

(a) Facilitate the business' **effective** and **efficient operation** by enabling it to respond appropriately to significant **business, operational, financial, compliance** and other risks to achieving its objectives, including the **safeguarding of assets** from inappropriate use or from loss and fraud and ensuring that **liabilities** are **identified** and **managed**

(b)   Help ensure the **quality** of **internal** and **external reporting**, requiring the **maintenance** of **proper records and processes** that generate a flow of **timely, relevant and reliable information** from within the organisation and from external sources

(c)   Help ensure **compliance with applicable laws and regulations**, and also with internal policies with respect to the conduct of business'

A sound system of internal control reduces but does not eliminate the possibilities of **poorly judged decisions, human error, deliberate circumvention of controls, management override of controls** and **unforeseeable circumstances**. Systems will provide reasonable (not absolute) assurance that the company will not be hindered in achieving its business objectives and in the orderly and legitimate conduct of its business, but won't provide certain protection against all possible problems.

1.3 Need for control framework

Internal control frameworks include the **control environment** within which **internal controls** operate. Other important elements are the **risk assessment and response processes**, the **sharing of information** and **monitoring** the environment and operation of the control system.

Organisations need to consider the overall framework of controls since controls are unlikely to be very effective if they are developed sporadically around the organisation, and their effectiveness will be very difficult to measure by internal audit and ultimately by senior management.

1.4 Control environment and control procedures

The **internal control system** comprises the **control environment** and **control procedures**. It includes all the policies and procedures (internal controls) adopted by the directors and management of an entity to assist in achieving their objective of ensuring, as far as practicable, the orderly and efficient conduct of its business, including adherence to internal policies, the safeguarding of assets, the prevention and detection of fraud and error, the accuracy and completeness of the accounting records, and the timely preparation of reliable financial information. Internal controls may be incorporated within computerised accounting systems. However, the internal control system extends beyond those matters which relate directly to the accounting system.

Perhaps the simplest framework for internal control draws a distinction between

- **Control environment** – the overall context of control, in particular the attitude of directors and managers towards control

- **Control procedures** – the detailed controls in place

The Turnbull report on Internal Control also highlights the importance of

- **Information** and **communication processes**
- **Processes** for **monitoring** the **continuing effectiveness** of the system of internal control

However, any internal control system can only provide the directors with **reasonable assurance** that their objectives are reached. This is because of **inherent limitations**, such as **human error** or **fraud**, collusion between employees and controls being overridden by managers.

2   Internal control environment and procedures

The **control environment** is influenced by **management's attitude** towards control, the **organisational structure** and the **values** and **abilities** of employees.

2.1 Nature of control environment

The **control environment** is the overall attitude, awareness and actions of directors and management regarding internal controls and their importance in the entity. The control environment encompasses the management style, and corporate culture and values shared by all employees. It provides the background against which the various other controls are operated.

The following are elements of a strong control environment.

- **Clear strategies** for dealing with the significant risks that have been identified

- The company's **culture, code of conduct, human resource policies** and **performance reward systems** supporting the business objectives and risk management and internal control systems

- Senior management demonstrating through its actions and policies commitment to **competence, integrity** and **fostering a climate of trust** within the company

- **Clear definition** of **authority, responsibility** and **accountability** so that decisions are made and actions are taken by the appropriate people

- **Communication** to employees of what is expected of them and scope of their freedom to act

- People in the company having the **knowledge, skills** and **tools** to support the achievements of the organisation's objectives and to manage effectively its risks

However, a strong control environment does not, by itself, ensure the effectiveness of the overall internal control system although it will have a major influence on it.

The control environment will have a major impact on the establishment of business objectives, the structuring of business activities and dealing with risks.

Controls can be classified in various ways including **administrative** and **accounting; prevent, detect** and **correct; discretionary** and **non-discretionary; voluntary** and **mandated; manual** and **automated.**

The mnemonic **SPAMSOAP** can be used to remember the main types of control.

2.2 Classification of control procedures

You may find internal controls classified in different ways; these are considered below. Classification of controls can be important because different classifications of control are tested in different ways.

Classification	Detail
Administration	These are concerned with achieving the objectives of the organisation and with implementing policies. These controls relate to channels of communication and reporting responsibilities.
Accounting	These controls aim to provide accurate accounting records and to achieve accountability. They apply to recording transactions and establishing responsibilities for records, transactions and assets.
Prevent	These are controls designed to prevent errors from happening in the first place. For example, checking invoices from suppliers against goods received notes before paying the invoices.
Detect	These are designed to detect errors once they have happened. Examples include bank reconciliations and physical checks of inventory against inventory records.
Correct	These are designed to minimise or negate the effect of errors. An example would be a back-up of computer input at the end of the day.

QUESTION

Prevent controls

How can prevent controls be used to measure performance and efficiency?

ANSWER

In the above examples the system outputs could include information about, say, the time lag between delivery of goods and invoicing:

(a) As a measure of the **efficiency of the invoicing section**

(b) As an **indicator of the speed and effectiveness** of **communications** between the despatch department and the invoicing department

(c) As **relevant background information** in assessing the effectiveness of cash management

You should be able to think of plenty of other examples. Credit notes reflect customer dissatisfaction, for example: how quickly are they issued?

2.2.1 Other classifications

Classification	Detail
Discretionary	These are controls which are subject to human discretion. For example, checking a signature on a purchase order
Non-discretionary	These are controls which are provided automatically by the system and cannot be overridden. For example, entering a pin number at a cash dispensing machine
Voluntary	These controls are chosen by the organisation to support the management of the business.
Mandated	These controls are required by law and imposed by external authorities.
Manual	These controls demonstrate a one-to-one relationship between the processing functions and controls, and the human functions.
Automated	These controls are programmed procedures designed to prevent, detect and correct errors all the way through processing.
General	These controls are used to reduce the risks associated with the computer environment. General controls are controls which relate to the environment in which the application is operated. For example, change management controls are designed to ensure that changes meet the organisation's requirements and have been authorised.
Application	These controls are used to reduce the risks associated with the computer environment. Application controls are controls that prevent, detect and correct errors. For example, completeness checks to ensure that all records have been processed from initiation to completion.
Financial	These controls focus on the key transaction areas, with the emphasis being on the safeguarding of assets and the maintenance of proper accounting records and reliable financial information.

2.3 Types of financial control procedure

The following is a useful summary of the types of financial control procedure, it is often remembered as a mnemonic, 'SPAMSOAP'.

(a) **Segregation of duties.** For example, the chairman/Chief Executive roles should be split.

(b)   **Physical**. These are measures to secure the custody of assets, eg only authorised personnel are allowed to move funds on to the money market.

(c)   **Authorisation and approval**. All transactions should require authorisation or approval by an appropriate responsible person; limits for the authorisations should be specified, eg a remuneration committee is staffed by non-executive directors (NEDs) to decide directors' pay.

(d)   **Management**. Management should provide control through analysis and review of accounts, eg variance analysis, provision of internal audit services.

(e)   **Supervision**. Supervision of the recording and operations of day-to-day transactions ensures that all individuals are aware that their work will be checked, reducing the risk of falsification or errors, eg budgets, managers' review, exception or variance reports.

(f)   **Organisation**. By identifying reporting lines, levels of authority and responsibility, this ensures everyone is aware of their control (and other) responsibilities, especially in ensuring adherence to management policies, eg avoid staff reporting to more than one manager. Procedures manuals will be helpful here.

(g)   **Arithmetical and accounting**. The correct and accurate recording and processing of transactions eg reconciliations and trial balances should be checked.

(h)   **Personnel**. Attention should be given to selection, training and qualifications of personnel, as well as personal qualities; the quality of any system is dependent on the competence and integrity of those who carry out control operations, eg use only qualified staff as internal auditors.

2.4 Internal checks

Internal controls should not be confused with **internal checks**, which have a more restricted definition.

Internal checks are defined as the checks on the day-to-day transactions whereby the work of one person is proved independently or is complementary to the work of another, the object being the prevention or early detection of errors and fraud. It includes matters such as the delegation and allocation of authority and the division of work, the method of recording transactions and the use of independently ascertained totals, against which a large number of individual items can be proved.

Internal checks are an important feature of the day-to-day control of financial transactions and the accounting system. **Arithmetical** internal checks include pre-lists, post-lists and control totals.

- A pre-list is a list that is drawn up before any processing takes place.

- A post-list is a list that is drawn up during or after processing.

- A control total is a total of any sort used for control purposes by comparing it with another total that ought to be the same.

A pre-list total is a control total so that, for example, when cash is received by post and a pre-list prepared and the receipts are recorded individually in the cash book, and a total of amounts entered in the cash book is obtained by adding up the individual entries, the control total obtained from the cash book can be compared with, and should agree with, the pre-list control total. Control totals, as you should already be aware, are frequently used in computer processing.

2.5 Aims of internal checks

Segregate tasks, so that the responsibility for particular actions, or for defaults or omissions, can be traced to an individual person.

Create and preserve the records that act as confirmation of physical facts and accounting entries.

Break down routine procedures into separate steps or stages, so as to facilitate an even flow of work and avoid bottlenecks.

Reduce the possibility of fraud and error. The aim should be to **prevent** fraud and error rather than to be able to **detect** it after it has happened. Efficient internal checks make extensive fraud virtually impossible, except by means of collusion between two or more people.

Internal checks, importantly, imply a **division of work**, so that the work of one person is either **proved independently** or else is complementary to the work of another person.

2.6 Characteristics of a good internal control system

(a) **A clearly defined organisation structure**

   (i) **Different operations must be separated** into appropriate divisions and subdivisions.

   (ii) Officers must **be appointed to assume responsibility** for each division.

   (iii) **Clear lines of responsibility** must exist between each division and subdivision and the board.

   (iv) There must be overall **co-ordination of the company's activities** (through corporate planning).

(b) **Adequate internal checks**

   (i) **Separation of duties** for **authorising** a transaction, **custody** of the assets obtained by means of the transaction and **recording** the transaction.

   (ii) **'Proof measures'** such as control totals, pre-lists and bank reconciliations should be used.

(c) **Acknowledgement** of work done: persons who carry out a particular job should acknowledge their work by means of signatures, initials, rubber stamps, and so on

(d) Protective devices for **physical security**

(e) **Formal documents should acknowledge the transfer of responsibility for goods.** When goods are received, a goods-received note should be used to acknowledge receipt by the storekeeper.

(f) **Pre-review:** the authorisation of a transaction (for example a cash payment, or the purchase of an asset) should not be given by the person responsible without first checking that all the proper procedures have been carried out

(g) A clearly defined **system for authorising transactions** within specified spending limits

(h) **Post-review:** completed transactions should be reviewed after they have happened; for example, monthly statements of account from suppliers should be checked against the purchase ledger accounts of those suppliers.

(i) There should be **authorisation, custody** and **re-ordering** procedures.

   (i) Funds and property of the company should be kept under **proper custody**. Access to assets (either direct or by documentation) should be **limited to authorised personnel**.

   (ii) Expenditure should only be incurred after authorisation and all expenditures are properly accounted for.

   (iii) All revenue must be properly accounted for and received in due course.

(j) **Personnel** should have the capabilities and qualifications necessary to carry out their responsibilities properly.

(k) An **internal audit** department should be able to verify that the control system is working and to review the system to ensure that it is still appropriate for current circumstances.

2.7 Limitations on the effectiveness of internal controls

Not only must a control system include sufficient controls, but these **controls must also be applied properly and honestly**.

(a) Internal controls depending on **segregation of duties can be avoided by the collusion** of two or more people responsible for those duties.

(b) **Authorisation controls can be abused** by the person empowered to authorise the activities.

(c) **Management can often override the controls they have set up themselves.**

3 Internal audit and internal control

3.1 Internal audit

Internal audit has been defined as:

An independent appraisal activity established within an organisation as a service to it. It is a control which functions by examining and evaluating the adequacy and effectiveness of other controls. The investigative techniques developed are applied to the analysis of the effectiveness of all parts of an entity's operations and management.

The work of internal audit is distinct from the external audit which is carried out for the benefit of shareholders only and examines published accounts. **Internal audit is part of the internal control system**.

3.2 The need for internal audit

The role of internal audit will **vary** according to the **organisation's objectives** but is likely to include review **of internal control systems, risk management, legal compliance** and **value for money**.

The UK Corporate Governance Code (2016) states that companies without an internal audit function should **annually review** the need to have one and if none is present, to report on the reasons why one is absent..

The need for internal audit will depend on:

*   The **scale, diversity** and **complexity** of the company's activities
*   The number of employees
*   Cost-benefit considerations
*   **Changes** in the organisational structures, reporting processes or underlying information systems
*   **Changes** in **key risks**
*   **Problems** with **internal control systems**
*   An **increased number** of **unexplained** or **unacceptable** events

Although there may be alternative means of carrying out the routine work of internal audit, those carrying out the work may be involved in operations and hence lack **objectivity**.

3.3 Objectives of internal audit

The role of the internal auditor has expanded in recent years as internal auditors seek to monitor all aspects (not just accounting) of the business, and add value to their organisation. The work of the internal auditor is still prescribed by management, but it may cover the following broad areas.

(a) **Review of the accounting and internal control systems**. The establishment of adequate accounting and internal control systems is a responsibility of management and the directors. Internal audit is often assigned specific responsibility for the following tasks.

*   Reviewing the design of the systems
*   Monitoring the operation of the systems by risk assessment and detailed testing
*   Recommending cost-effective improvements

Review will cover both financial and non-financial controls.

(b) **Examination of financial and operating information**. This may include review of the means used to identify, measure, classify and report such information and specific enquiry into individual items including detailed testing of transactions, balances and procedures.

(c) **Review of the economy, efficiency and effectiveness** of operations

(d)   **Review of compliance** with laws, regulations and other external requirements and with internal policies and directives and other requirements including appropriate authorisation of transactions

(e)   **Review of the safeguarding of assets**

(f)   **Review of the implementation of corporate objectives**. This includes review of the effectiveness of planning, the relevance of standards and policies, the company's corporate governance procedures and the operation of specific procedures, such as communication of information.

(g)   **Identification of significant business** and financial **risks, monitoring** the **organisation's overall risk management policy** to ensure it operates effectively, and **monitoring** the **risk management strategies** to ensure they continue to operate effectively

(h)   **Special investigations** into particular areas, for example suspected fraud

3.4 Internal audit and risk management

Internal audit will play a significant part in the organisation's risk management processes, being required to assess and advise on how risks are countered. Internal audit's work will be influenced by the organisation's **appetite** for bearing risks, but internal audit will assess:

- The **adequacy of the risk management and response processes** for identifying, assessing, managing and reporting on risk

- The risk management and control **culture**

- The **internal controls** in operation to **limit risks**

- The **operation and effectiveness** of the **risk management processes**

The areas auditors will concentrate on will depend on the **scope** and **priority** of the assignment and the **risks identified**. Where the risk management framework is insufficient, auditors will have to rely on their own **risk assessment** and will focus on **recommending an appropriate framework**. Where a framework for risk management and control is embedded in operations, auditors will aim to use **management assessment of risks** and concentrate on **auditing the risk management processes**.

3.5 The features of internal audit

From these definitions the two main features of internal audit emerge.

(a)   **Independence**. Although an internal audit department is part of an organisation, it should be independent of the line management whose sphere of authority it may audit.

(b)   **Appraisal**. Internal audit is concerned with the appraisal of work done by other people in the organisation, and internal auditors should not carry out any of that work themselves. The appraisal of operations provides a service to management.

3.6 Types of audit

Internal audit is a management control, as it is a tool used to ensure that other internal controls are working satisfactorily. An internal audit department may be asked by management to look into any aspect of the organisation.

Five different types of audit can be distinguished. (The first three types are considered further in the following paragraphs.)

- Operational audit
- Systems audit
- Transactions audit
- Social audit
- Management investigations

Operational audits can be concerned with **any sphere** of a company's activities. Their prime objective is the monitoring of management's performance at every level, to ensure optimal functioning according to predetermined criteria. They concentrate on the outputs of the system, and the efficiency of the organisation. They are also known as **'management'**, **'efficiency'** or **'value for money'** audits.

A **systems audit** is based on a testing and evaluation of the **internal controls** within an organisation so that those controls may be relied on to ensure that resources are being managed effectively and information provided accurately. Two types of tests are used.

(a)   **Compliance tests** seek evidence that the internal controls are being applied as prescribed.

(b)   **Substantive tests** substantiate the entries in the figures in accounts. They are used to discover **errors and omissions**.

The auditor will be interested in a variety of processing errors when performing compliance tests.

- At the wrong time
- Incompleteness
- Omission
- Error
- Fraud

The key importance of the two types of test is that, **if the compliance tests reveal that internal controls are working satisfactorily, then the amount of substantive testing can be reduced**, and the internal auditor can concentrate the audit effort on those areas where controls do not exist or are not working satisfactorily.

3.7 Example

Suppose a department within a company processes travel claims which are eventually paid and recorded on the general ledger.

(a)   When conducting **compliance tests**, the internal auditor is **looking at the controls** in the travel claim section to see if they are working properly. This is not the same as looking at the travel claims themselves. For example, one of the internal controls might be that a clerk checks the addition on the travel claim and initials a box to say that they have done so. If they fail to perform this arithmetic check, then there has been a control failure – regardless of whether the travel claim had, in fact, been added up correctly or incorrectly.

(b)   When conducting **substantive tests**, the internal auditor is examining figures which they have extracted directly from the company's financial records. For this sort of test, the auditor is concerned only with establishing whether or not the figure in the ledger is correct. They are not concerned as to how it got there.

A transactions or probity audit aims to detect fraud and uses only substantive tests.

3.8 Accountability

The internal auditor is accountable to the highest executive level in the organisation, preferably to the audit committee of the Board of Directors. There are three main reasons for this requirement.

- The auditor needs access to all parts of the organisation.

- The auditor should be free to comment on the performance of management.

- The auditor's report may need to be actioned at the highest level to ensure its effective implementation.

EXAM FOCUS POINT

You may be examined on the accountability of the internal auditor.

3.9 Independence

Given an acceptable line of responsibility and clear terms of authority, it is vital that the internal auditor **is and is seen to be independent**. Independence for the internal auditor is established by three things.

- The responsibility structure
- The auditor's mandatory authority
- The auditor's own approach

Internal audit requires a highly professional approach which is objective, detached and honest. Independence is a fundamental concept of auditing and this applies just as much to the internal auditor as to the external auditor. The internal auditor should not install new procedures or systems; neither should they engage in any activity which they would normally appraise, as this might compromise their independence.

QUESTION

Internal control systems

The Midas Mail Order Company operates a central warehouse from which all merchandise is distributed by post or carrier to the company's 10,000 customers. An outline description of the sales and cash collection system is set out below.

Sales and cash collection system

Stage	Department/ staff responsible	Documentation
1 Customer orders merchandise (orders by phone or through the postal system)	Sales dept Sales assistants	Multiple copy order form (with date, quantities, price marked on them) Copies 1-3 sent to warehouse. Copy 4 sent to accounts dept. Copy 5 retained in sales dept
2 Merchandise requested from inventory rooms by despatch clerks	Storekeepers	Copies 1-3 handed to storekeepers. Forms marked as merchandise taken from inventory. (Note. If merchandise is not in inventories held, the storekeepers retain copies 1-3 until inventory room is refilled). Copies 1-2 handed to despatch clerks. Copy 3 retained by storekeepers.
3 Merchandise despatched	Despatch bay Despatch clerks	Copy 2 marked when goods despatched and sent to accounts department
4 Customers invoiced	Accounts dept: receivables ledger clerks	2-copy invoice prepared from invoiced details on copy 2 of order form received from despatch bay Copy 1 of invoice sent to customer. Copy 2 retained by accounts dept and posted to receivables ledger
5 Cash received (as cheques, bank giro credit, or cash)	Accounts dept: cashier	2-copy cash receipt list Copy 1 of cash receipt list retained by cashier Copy 2 passed to receivables ledger clerk

(a) State four objectives of an internal control system.

(b) For the Midas Mail Order Company list four major controls which you would expect to find in the operation of the accounting system described above, and explain the objective of each of these controls.

(c) For each of the four controls identified above, describe briefly two tests which you would expect an internal auditor to carry out to determine whether the control was operating satisfactorily.

ANSWER

(a) **Four objectives of an internal control system**

(i) To enable management to carry on the business of the enterprise in an orderly and efficient manner

(ii) To satisfy management that their policies are being adhered to

(iii) To ensure that the assets of the company are safeguarded

(iv) To ensure, as far as possible, that the enterprise maintains complete and accurate records

(b) **Four major controls**

(i) **Control over customers' creditworthiness**. Before any order is accepted for further processing, established procedures should be followed in order to check the creditworthiness of that customer. For new customers procedures should exist for obtaining appropriate references before any credit is extended. For all existing customers there should be established credit limits and before an order is processed the sales assistants should check to see that the value of the current order will not cause the customer's balance to rise above their agreed credit limit.

The objective of such procedures is to try to avoid the company supplying goods to customers who are unlikely to be able to pay for them. In this way the losses suffered by the company as a result of bad debts should be minimal.

(ii) **Control over the recording of sales and receivables**. The most significant document in the system is the multiple order form. These forms should be sequentially pre-numbered and controls should exist over the supplies of unused forms and also to ensure that all order forms completed can be traced through the various stages of processing and agreed to the other documents raised and the various entries made in the accounting records.

The main objective here will be to check the completeness of the company's recording procedures in relation to the income which it has earned and the assets which it holds in the form of receivables.

(iii) **Control over the issue of inventory and the despatch of goods**. Control procedures here should be such that goods are not issued from stores until a valid order form has been received and the fact of that issue is recorded both on the order form (copies 1-3) and in the inventory records maintained by the storekeepers.

The objectives here are to see that no goods are released from inventory without appropriate authority and that a record of inventory movements is maintained.

(iv) **Control over the invoicing of customers**. The main control requirement here will be to use sequentially pre-numbered invoices with checks being carried out to control the completeness of the sequence. Checks should also be conducted to ensure that all invoices are matched with the appropriate order form (copy 2) to confirm that invoices have been raised in respect of all completed orders.

The major concern here will be to ensure that no goods are despatched to customers without an invoice subsequently being raised.

(v) **(The question merely required four controls to be considered, but for the sake of completeness, each of the five main stages in processing as indicated by the question are considered here.)**

Control over monies received. There should be controls to ensure that there is an adequate segregation of duties between those members of staff responsible for the updating of the sales records in respect of monies received and those dealing with the receipt, recording and banking of monies. There should also be a regular independent review of aged debtor balances together with an overall reconciliation of the receivables control account with the total of outstanding debts on individual customer accounts.

The objectives here are to ensure that proper controls exist with regard to the complete and accurate recording of monies received, safe custody of the asset cash and the effectiveness of credit control procedures.

(c) Appropriate tests in relation to each of the controls identified in (b) above would be as follows.

(i) **Controls over customers' creditworthiness**

(1) For a sample of new accounts opened during the period check to see that suitable references were obtained before the company supplied any goods on credit terms and that the credit limit set was properly authorised and of a reasonable amount.

(2) For a sample of customers' orders check to see that, at the time they were accepted, their invoice value would not have been such as to cause the balance on those customers' account to go above their agreed credit limit.

(ii) **Controls over the recording of sales and receivables**

    (1) On a sample basis check the completeness of the sequence of order forms and also that unused inventory of order forms are securely stored.

    (2) For a sample of order forms raised during the period ensure that they can be traced through the system such that there is either evidence that the order was cancelled or that a valid invoice was subsequently raised.

(iii) **Control over the issue of inventory and the despatch of goods**

    (1) For a sample of entries in the inventory records check to ensure that a valid order form exists for all issues recorded as having been made.

    (2) Attend the inventory rooms to observe the procedures and check that goods are not issued unless a valid order form has been received and that the appropriate entries are made in the inventory records and on the order form at the time of issue.

(iv) **Control over the invoicing of customers**

    (1) On a sample basis check the completeness of the sequence of invoices raised and also that the unused inventory of invoice forms are securely stored.

    (2) For a sample of invoices raised during the period ensure that they have been properly matched with the appropriate order form (copy 2).

4 External audit

Internal auditors are **employees** of the organisation whose work is designed to **add value** and who report to the **audit committee. External auditors** are from **accountancy firms** and their role is to **report on the financial statements to shareholders**.

Both **internal and external auditors** review controls, and **external auditors** may **place reliance** on **internal auditors' work** providing they assess its worth.

External audit is a periodic examination of the books of account and records of an entity carried out by an independent third party (the auditor) to ensure that they have been properly maintained, are accurate and comply with established concepts, principles, accounting standards and legal requirements and give a true and fair view of the financial state of the entity.

It cannot be overemphasised that the **primary purpose** of an external audit is to review the books and records in order to give a **professional opinion** on whether the financial statements represent a **true and fair view** of the organisation.

4.1 Differences between internal and external audit

The following table highlights the differences between internal and external audit.

	Internal audit	External audit
Reason	Internal audit is an activity designed to **add value** and improve an **organisation's operations**.	External audit is an exercise to enable auditors to **express an opinion on the financial statements**.
Reporting to	Internal audit reports to the **board of directors**, or others charged with governance, such as the audit committee.	The external auditors report to the **shareholders**, or members, of a company on the stewardship of the directors.

	Internal audit	External audit
Relating to	Internal audit's work relates to the **operations of the organisation**.	External audit's work relates to the **financial statements**. They are concerned with the financial records that underlie these.
Relationship with the company	Internal auditors are very often **employees of the organisation**, although sometimes the internal audit function is outsourced.	External auditors are **independent of the company and its management**. They are appointed by the shareholders.

The table shows that, although some of the procedures that internal audit undertake are very similar to those undertaken by the external auditors, the whole **basis** and **reasoning** of their work is fundamentally **different**.

The **difference** in **objectives** is particularly important. Every definition of internal audit suggests that it has a **much wider scope** than external audit, which has the objective of considering whether the accounts give a true and fair view of the organisation's financial position.

EXAM FOCUS POINT

You must be aware of the primary purpose of an external audit. The examining team has commented that candidates do not always understand the distinction between the role and duties of internal auditors and those of external auditors, or the attributes of both.

4.2 Relationship between external and internal audit

Co-ordination between the external and internal auditors of an organisation will minimise duplication of work and encourage a wide coverage of audit issues and areas. Co-ordination should have the following features.

- Periodic meetings to plan the overall audit to ensure adequate coverage
- Periodic meetings to discuss matters of mutual interest
- Mutual access to audit programmes and working papers
- Exchange of audit reports and management letters
- Common development of audit techniques, methods and terminology

4.3 Assessment by external auditors

Where the external auditors wish to rely on the work of the internal auditors, then the external auditors must assess the internal audit function, as with any part of the system of internal control. The following important criteria will be considered by the external auditors.

(a)   **Organisational status**

Internal audit's specific status in the organisation and the effect this has on its ability to be objective. Ideally, the internal audit function should have a direct line of communication to the entity's main board or audit committee, and be free of any other operating responsibility. External auditors should consider any constraints or restrictions placed on internal audit.

(b)   **Scope of function**

The nature and extent of the assignments which internal audit performs. External auditors should also consider whether management and the directors act on internal audit recommendations and how this is evidenced.

(c) **Technical competence**

Whether internal audit work is performed by persons having adequate technical training and proficiency as internal auditors. External auditors may, for example, review the policies for hiring and training the internal audit staff and their experience and professional qualifications and also how work is assigned, delegated and reviewed.

(d) **Due professional care**

Whether internal audit work is properly planned, supervised, reviewed and documented. The existence of adequate audit manuals, work programmes and working papers may be considered, as well as consultation procedures.

QUESTION
External and internal audit

The growing recognition by management of the benefits of good internal control and the complexities of an adequate system of internal control have led to the development of internal auditing as a form of control over all other internal controls. The emergence of internal auditors as specialists in internal control is the result of an evolutionary process similar in many ways to the evolution of independent auditing.

Required

Explain why the internal and independent auditors' review of internal control procedures differ in purpose.

ANSWER

The internal auditors **review and test the system of internal control** and report to management in order to **improve the information** received by managers and to help in their task of running the company. The internal auditors will recommend changes to the system to make sure that management receive objective information that is efficiently produced. The internal auditors will also have a duty to search for and discover fraud.

The external auditors **review the system of internal control** in order to **determine the extent of the substantive work** required on the year-end accounts. The external **auditors report** to the **shareholders** rather than the managers or directors. It is usual, however, for the external auditors to issue a letter of weakness to the managers, laying out any areas of weakness and recommendations for improvement in the system of internal control. The external auditors report on the **truth and fairness** of the financial statements, not directly on the system of internal control. The auditors do not have a specific duty to detect fraud, although they should plan the audit procedures so as to have reasonable assurance that they will detect any material misstatement in the accounts on which they give an opinion.

---

5 IT systems security and safety

Security is the protection of data from accidental or deliberate threats and the protection of an information system from such threats.

5.1 The responsibilities of ownership

If you own **something that you value** – you **look after it. Information** is valuable and it deserves similar care.

Security, in information management terms, means the **protection of data** from accidental or deliberate threats which might cause unauthorised modification, disclosure or destruction of data, and the **protection of the information system** from the degradation or non-availability of services.

Security refers to **technical** issues related to the computer system, psychological and **behavioural** factors in the organisation and its employees, and protection against the unpredictable occurrences of the **natural world**.

Security can be subdivided into a number of aspects.

(a) **Prevention**. It is in practice impossible to prevent all threats cost effectively.

(b) **Detection**. Detection techniques are often combined with prevention techniques: a log can be maintained of unauthorised attempts to gain access to a computer system.

(c) **Deterrence**. As an example, computer misuse by personnel can be made grounds for disciplinary action.

(d) **Recovery procedures**. If the threat occurs, its consequences can be contained (for example checkpoint programs).

(e) **Correction procedures**. These ensure the vulnerability is dealt with (for example, by instituting stricter controls).

(f) **Threat avoidance**. This might mean changing the design of the system.

5.2 Physical threats

Physical threats to security may be natural or man made. They include fire, flooding, weather, lightning, terrorist activity and accidental damage.

The **physical environment** quite obviously has a major effect on information system security, and so planning it properly is an important precondition of an adequate security plan.

5.2.1 Fire

Fire is the **most serious hazard** to computer systems. Destruction of data can be even more costly than the destruction of hardware.

A fire safety plan is an essential feature of security procedures in order to prevent fire, detect fire and put out the fire.

5.2.2 Water

Water is a serious hazard. Flooding and water damage are often encountered following firefighting activities elsewhere in a building.

This problem can be countered by the use of waterproof ceilings and floors together with the provision of adequate drainage.

5.2.3 Weather

Wind, rain and storms can all cause substantial **damage to buildings**. In certain areas the risks are greater, for example the risk of typhoons in parts of the Far East. Many organisations make heavy use of prefabricated and portable offices, which are particularly vulnerable.

5.2.4 Lightning

Lightning and electrical storms can play havoc with power supplies, causing power failures coupled with power surges as services are restored.

Power failure can be protected against by the use of a **separate generator** or rechargeable battery. It may be sufficient to maintain power only long enough to close down the computer system in an orderly manner.

5.2.5 Terrorist activity

Political terrorism is the main risk, but there are also threats from individuals with **grudges**.

In some cases there is very little that an organisation can do: its buildings may just happen to be in the wrong place and bear the brunt of an attack aimed at another organisation or intended to cause general disruption. **Physical access** to buildings should be controlled (see the next section).

BPP
LEARNING MEDIA

5.2.6 Accidental damage

People are a physical threat to computer installations: there can be few of us who have not at some time spilt a cup of coffee over a desk covered with papers, or tripped and fallen doing some damage to ourselves or to an item of office equipment.

Combating accidental damage is a matter of having a good office layout and eliminating hazards, such as trailing cables.

QUESTION

Fire and flooding

You are the financial controller of your organisation. The company is in the process of installing a mainframe computer and, because your department will be the primary user, you have been co-opted onto the project team with responsibility for systems installation. You have a meeting at which the office services manager will be present, and you realise that no one has yet mentioned the risks of fire or flooding in the discussions about site selection. Make a note of the issues which you would like to raise under these headings.

ANSWER

(a) **Fire**. Fire security measures can usefully be categorised as preventative, detective and corrective. Preventative measures include siting of the computer in a building constructed of suitable materials and the use of a site which is not affected by the storage of inflammable materials (eg stationery, chemicals). Detective measures involve the use of smoke detectors. Corrective measures may include installation of a sprinkler system (water based or possibly gas based to avoid electrical problems), training of fire officers and good siting of exit signs and fire extinguishers.

(b) **Flooding**. Water damage may result from flooding or from fire recovery procedures. If possible, large installations should not be situated in basements.

5.3 Physical access controls

Physical access controls are designed to prevent **intruders** getting near to computer equipment and/or storage media.

Physical access controls including the following.

(a) **Personnel**, including receptionists and, outside working hours, security guards, can help control human access.

(b) **Door locks** can be used where frequency of use is low. (This is not practicable if the door is in frequent use.)

(c) Locks can be combined with:

(i) A **keypad system**, requiring a code to be entered
(ii) A **card entry system**, requiring a card to be 'swiped'

(d) Intruder **alarms** can also be used.

The best form of access control would be one which **recognised** individuals immediately, without the need for personnel or cards. However, machines that can identify a person's fingerprints or scan the pattern of a retina are relatively more **expensive**, so their use is less widespread.

It may not be cost effective or practical to use the same access controls in all areas. The **security requirements of different departments** should be estimated, and appropriate measures taken. Some areas will be very restricted, whereas others will be relatively open.

Important aspects of physical access of control are **door locks** and **card entry systems**. Computer theft is becoming more prevalent as equipment becomes smaller and more portable.

QUESTION

You are the chief accountant at your company. Your department, located in an open-plan office, has five networked desktop PCs, two laser printers and a dot matrix printer.

You have just read an article suggesting that the best form of security is to lock hardware away in fireproof cabinets, but you feel that this is impracticable. Make a note of any alternative security measures which you could adopt to protect the hardware.

ANSWER

(a) 'Postcode' all pieces of hardware. Invisible ink postcoding is popular, but visible marking is a better deterrent. Heated soldering irons are ideal for imprinting postcodes onto objects with a plastic casing.

(b) Mark the equipment in other ways. Some organisations spray their hardware with permanent paint, perhaps in a particular colour (bright red is popular) or using stencilled shapes.

(c) Hardware can be bolted to desks. If bolts are passed through the desk and through the bottom of the hardware casing, the equipment can be rendered immobile.

(d) Ensure that the organisation's standard security procedures (magnetic passes, keypad access to offices, signing in of visitors, etc) are followed.

6 Building controls into an information system

It is possible to **build controls into** a **computerised** information system. A **balance** must be struck between the degree of control and the requirement for a user-friendly system.

Controls can be classified as:

- Security controls   •   Contingency controls
- Integrity controls

6.1 Security controls

Security is needed to mitigate the risks to data which include:

- Human error

    – Entering incorrect transactions
    – Failing to correct errors
    – Processing the wrong files

- Technical error such as malfunctioning hardware or software

- Natural disasters such as fire, flooding, explosion, impact, lightning

- Deliberate actions such as fraud

- Commercial espionage

- Malicious damage

- Industrial action

- Malware programs that seek information or cause systems to crash

Examples of the last point include **phishing, pharming and Trojans. Phishing** may occur, for example, when an email is received that appears to come from a bank asking that you log on to a website to register your details. If you do log on, your details are stolen and may be used to clear out your bank account. Pharming is an attack on an organisation's website in order to redirect people to another, bogus website. The intention is to collect data in order to commit fraud (similar to phishing). A **Trojan** is a software program that masquerades as a desirable application, eg a virus checker. When downloaded, the Trojan introduces viruses that can completely wipe out a computer's systems.

6.2 Integrity controls

- **Data integrity** in the context of security is preserved when data is the same as in source documents and has not been accidentally or intentionally altered, destroyed or disclosed.

- **Systems integrity** refers to system operation conforming to the design specification despite attempts (deliberate or accidental) to make it behave incorrectly.

Data will maintain its **integrity** if it is **complete** and **not corrupted**. This means that:

(a) The original **input** of the data must be controlled in such a way as to ensure that the results are complete and correct.

(b) Any **processing and storage** of data must maintain the completeness and correctness of the data captured.

(c) Reports or other **output** should be set up so that they, too, are complete and correct.

6.2.1 Input controls

Input controls should ensure the **accuracy, completeness and validity** of input.

(a) **Data verification** involves ensuring data entered matches source documents.

(b) **Data validation** involves ensuring that data entered is not incomplete or unreasonable. Various checks can be used, depending on the data type.

    (i) **Check digits**. A digit calculated by the program and added to the code being checked to validate it, eg modulus 11 method

    (ii) **Control totals**. For example, a batch total totalling the entries in the batch

    (iii) **Hash totals**. A system-generated total used to check processing has been performed as intended

    (iv) **Range checks**. Used to check the value entered against a sensible range, eg statement of financial position account number must be between 5,000 and 9,999

    (v) **Limit checks**. Similar to a range check, but usually based on a upper limit, eg must be less than 999,999.99

Data may be **valid** (for example in the **correct format**) but still **not match source documents**.

6.2.2 Processing controls

Processing controls should ensure the **accuracy and completeness of processing**. Programs should be subject to development controls and to rigorous testing. Periodic running of test data is also recommended.

6.2.3 Output controls

Output controls should ensure the accuracy, completeness and security of output. The following measures are possible.

- Investigation and follow-up of error reports and exception reports
- Batch controls to ensure all items processed and returned
- Controls over distribution/copying of output
- Labelling of disks/tapes

6.2.4 Back-up controls

A **back-up** and **archive** strategy should include:

- Regular back up of data (at least daily)
- Archive plans
- A **disaster recovery** plan including off-site storage

Back-up controls aim to maintain system and data integrity. We have classified back-up controls as an integrity control rather than a contingency control (see later in this section) because back ups should be part of the day-to-day procedures of all computerised systems.

Back up means to make a copy in anticipation of future failure or corruption. A back-up copy of a file is a duplicate copy kept separately from the main system and only used if the original fails.

The **purpose of backing up data** is to ensure that the most recent usable copy of the data can be recovered and restored in the event of loss or corruption on the primary storage media.

In a well-planned data back-up scheme, a copy of backed-up data is delivered (preferably daily) to a secure **off-site** storage facility.

A tape **rotation scheme** can provide a restorable history from one day to several years, depending on the needs of the business.

A well-planned **back-up and archive strategy** should include:

(a) A plan and schedule for the **regular back up of critical data**
(b) **Archive plans**
(c) A **disaster recovery plan** that includes off-site storage

Regular tests should be undertaken to **verify that data backed up can be successfully restored**.

The **intervals** at which back ups are performed must be decided. Most organisations back up their data daily, but back ups may need to be performed more frequently, depending on the nature of the data and of the organisation.

Even with a well planned back-up strategy some re-inputting may be required. For example, if after three hours' work on a Wednesday a file becomes corrupt, the Tuesday version can be restored – but Wednesday's work will need to be re-input.

6.2.5 Archiving

A related concept is that of **archiving**. Archiving data is the process of moving data from primary storage, such as a hard disk, to tape or other portable media for long-term storage.

Archiving provides a legally acceptable **business history**, while freeing up **hard-disk space**. If archived data is needed, it can be restored from the archived tape to a hard disk. Archived data can be used to recover from site-wide disasters, such as fires or floods, where data on primary storage devices is destroyed. Archiving also helps avoid the slowdown in processing which may occur if large volumes of data build up on the main operational storage.

How long data should be retained will be influenced by:

- Legal obligations   •   Other business needs

Data stored for a long time should be tested periodically to ensure it is **still restorable** – it may be subject to **damage** from environmental conditions or mishandling.

6.2.6 Passwords and logical access systems

A **password** is a set of characters which may be allocated to a person, a terminal or a facility which is required to be keyed into the system before further access is permitted.

Unauthorised persons may circumvent physical access controls. A **logical access system** can prevent access to data and program files through measures such as the following.

- Identification of the user
- Checks on user authority
- Authentication of user identity

Virtually all computer installations use passwords. Failed access attempts may be logged. Passwords are not foolproof.

- Standard system passwords (such as 1234) given when old passwords are reset or provided to new employees must be changed.

- Passwords must never be divulged to others and must never be written down.

- Passwords must be changed regularly – and changed immediately if it is suspected that the password is known by others.

- Obvious passwords must not be used.

Passwords are also used by administrators to control access rights for the reading, modifying and deleting functions.

6.2.7 Administrative controls

Personnel selection is important. Some employees are always in a position of trust.

- Computer security officer
- Database administrator
- Senior systems analyst

Measures to control personnel include the following.

- Careful recruitment
- Systems logs
- Job rotation and enforced vacations
- Review and supervision

For other staff, **segregation of duties** remains a core security requirement. This involves division of responsibilities into separate roles.

- Data capture and data entry
- Systems analysis and programming
- Computer operations

6.2.8 Audit trail

An **audit trail** shows who has accessed a system and the operations performed.

The original concept of an audit trail is to enable a manager or auditor to follow transactions stage by stage through a system to ensure that they have been processed correctly. The intention is to:

- **Identify errors**
- **Detect fraud**

Modern integrated computer systems have cut out much of the time-consuming stage-by-stage working of older systems, but there should still be some **means of identifying individual records** and the **input and output documents** associated with the processing of any individual transaction.

An audit trail is a record showing who has accessed a computer system and what operations they have performed. Audit trails are useful both for maintaining security and for recovering lost transactions. Accounting systems include an audit trail component that is able to be output as a report.

In addition, there are separate audit trail software products that enable network administrators to monitor use of network resources.

An audit trail should be provided so that every transaction on a file contains a **unique reference** (eg a sales system transaction record should hold a reference to the customer order, delivery note and invoice).

Typical contents of an accounting software package audit trail include the following items.

(a) A system-generated **transaction number**
(b) A meaningful reference number eg invoice number
(c) Transaction type eg reversing journal, credit note, cashbook entry, etc
(d) Who input the transaction (user ID)
(e) Full **transaction details** eg net and gross amount, customer ID
(f) The **PC or terminal** used to enter the transaction
(g) The **date** and **time** of the entry
(h) Any additional reference or **narration** entered by the user

6.2.9 Systems integrity with a PC

Possible controls relevant to a standalone PC are as follows.

(a) Installation of a **password** routine which is activated whenever the computer is booted up, and activated after periods of inactivity.

(b) The use of additional passwords on 'sensitive' files eg employee salaries spreadsheet.

(c) Any data stored on floppy disk, DVD or CD should be locked away.

(d) **Physical access controls**, for example door locks activated by swipe cards or PIN numbers, to prevent access into the room(s) where the computers are kept.

6.2.10 Systems integrity with a LAN

The main additional risk (when compared with a standalone PC) is the risk of a fault **spreading across the system**. This is particularly true of **viruses**. A virus introduced onto one machine could replicate itself throughout the network. All files coming in to the organisation should be scanned using **anti-virus software** and all machines should have anti-virus software running constantly.

A further risk, depending on the type of network configuration, is that an extra PC could be 'plugged in' to the network to gain access to it. The **network management software** should detect and prevent breaches of this type.

6.2.11 Systems integrity with a WAN

Additional issues over and above those already described are related to the extensive communications links utilised by Wide Area Networks. Dedicated land lines for data transfer and encryption software may be required.

If **commercially sensitive data** is being transferred it would be necessary to specify high quality communications equipment and to use sophisticated network software to prevent and detect any security breaches.

6.3 Contingency controls

A contingency is an unscheduled interruption of computing services that requires measures outside the day-to-day routine operating procedures.

The preparation of a contingency plan (also known as a disaster recovery plan) is one of the stages in the development of an organisation-wide security policy. A contingency plan is necessary in case of a major **disaster**, or if some of the **security measures** discussed elsewhere **fail**.

A **disaster** occurs where the system for some reason breaks down, leading to potential **losses** of equipment, data or funds. The system **must recover as soon as possible** so that further losses are not incurred, and current losses can be rectified.

QUESTION

Causes of system breakdown

What actions or events might lead to a system breakdown?

ANSWER

System breakdowns can occur in a variety of circumstances, for example:

(a)   Fire destroying data files and equipment

(b)   Flooding

(c)   A computer virus completely destroying a data or program file

(d)   A technical fault in the equipment

(e)   Accidental destruction of telecommunications links (eg builders severing a cable)

(f)   Terrorist attack

(g)   System failure caused by software bugs which were not discovered at the design stage

(h)   Internal sabotage (eg logic bombs built into the software)

6.3.1 Disaster recovery plan

Any disaster recovery plan must provide for:

(a)   **Standby procedures** so that some operations can be performed while normal services are disrupted

(b)   **Recovery procedures** once the cause of the breakdown has been discovered or corrected

(c)   **Personnel management** policies to ensure that (a) and (b) above are implemented properly

6.3.2 Contents of a disaster recovery plan

A **disaster recovery plan** must cover all activities, from the initial response to a 'disaster' through to damage limitation and full recovery. Responsibilities must be clearly spelt out for all tasks.

PER performance objective PO4 requires you to contribute to the effective governance of an organisation and raise awareness of risk. The material covered in this chapter, and built on later in your studies in Paper P1, will help you achieve this.

↳ **Internal controls** should help organisations counter risks, maintain the quality of reporting and comply with laws and regulations. They provide reasonable assurance that the organisations will fulfil their objectives.

↳ Internal control frameworks include the **control environment** within which **internal controls** operate. Other important elements are the **risk assessment and response processes**, the **sharing of information** and **monitoring** the environment and operation of the control system.

↳ The **control environment** is influenced by **management's attitude** towards control, the **organisational structure** and the **values** and **abilities** of employees.

↳ Controls can be classified in various ways including **administrative** and **accounting**; **prevent**, **detect** and **correct**; **discretionary** and **non-discretionary**; **voluntary** and **mandated**; **manual** and **automated**.

The mnemonic **SPAMSOAP** can be used to remember the main types of control.

↳ The role of internal audit will **vary** according to the **organisation's objectives** but is likely to include review **of internal control systems, risk management, legal compliance** and **value for money**.

↳ **Internal auditors** are **employees** of the organisation whose work is designed to **add value** and who report to the **audit committee. External auditors** are from **accountancy firms** and their role is to **report on the financial statements to shareholders**.

↳ Both **internal and external auditors** review controls, and **external auditors** may **place reliance** on **internal auditors' work** providing they assess its worth.

↳ **Security** is the protection of data from accidental or deliberate threats and the protection of an information system from such threats.

↳ **Security**, in information management terms, means the **protection of data** from accidental or deliberate threats which might cause unauthorised modification, disclosure or destruction of data, and the **protection of the information system** from the degradation or non-availability of services.

↳ **Physical threats** to security may be natural or man made. They include fire, flooding, weather, lightning, terrorist activity and accidental damage.

↳ **Physical access controls** are designed to prevent **intruders** getting near to computer equipment and/or storage media.

↳ It is possible to **build controls into** a **computerised** information system. A **balance** must be struck between the degree of control and the requirement for a user-friendly system.

↳ A **back-up** and **archive** strategy should include:

- Regular back up of data (at least daily)
- Archive plans
- A **disaster recovery** plan including off-site storage

↳ An **audit trail** shows who has accessed a system and the operations performed.

↳ A **disaster recovery plan** must cover all activities, from the initial response to a 'disaster' through to damage limitation and full recovery. Responsibilities must be clearly spelt out for all tasks.

QUICK QUIZ

1   The internal control system comprises which two of the following.

A   Control accounting
B   Control environment
C   Control procedures
D   Control audit

2   Match the control and control type.

(a)   Checking of delivery notes against invoices
(b)   Back up of computer input
(c)   Bank reconciliation

(i)   Prevent
(ii)   Detect
(iii) Correct

3   A .... control is required by law and imposed by external authorities.

4   An operational audit is also known as: (tick all that apply).

A system audit   ☐   An efficiency audit   ☐

A management audit   ☐   A value for money audit   ☐

5   Internal auditors are not required to consider fraud.
True   ☐   False   ☐

6   A record showing who has accessed a computer system is called:

A   A fraud trail
B   An audit trail
C   A computer trail
D   A password trail

ANSWERS TO QUICK QUIZ

1   B, C   The internal control system comprises the control environment and control procedures

2   (a)   (i)   (c)   (ii)

     (b)   (iii)

3   A **mandated** control is required by law and imposed by external authorities.

4   A system audit   ☐   An efficiency audit   ☑

     A management audit   ☑   A value for money audit   ☑

5   False. Internal auditors should be alert to fraud as part of risk management.

6   B   An audit trail shows who has accessed a system and the operations performed.

Now try ...

Attempt the questions below from the **Practice Question Bank**

Q43

Q44

Q45

Q46

Q47

Q48

BPP
LEARNING MEDIA

This chapter considers the various types of fraud that an organisation may be prone to (**Section 1**) and which may have to be investigated by internal audit (**Chapter 9**). It is important that you are able to identify signs of fraud in different circumstances (**Section 2**).

You also need to have a good knowledge of both how fraud is prevented and detected. Although there may be significant costs involved in implementing a good system of fraud prevention, the consequences of successful fraud may be very serious, both for the reputation of the organisation and the position of its directors. **Sections 3, 4** and **5** explore these issues.

Money laundering can be a serious problem. **Section 6** shows how systems can be set up to help detect and prevent this.

Identifying and preventing fraud

Study Guide

<table>
<tr><td></td><td></td><td>Intellectual level</td></tr>
</table>

C7 Fraud and fraudulent behaviour and their prevention in business including money laundering

(a)	Explain the circumstances under which fraud is likely to arise.	K
(b)	Identify different types of fraud in the organisation.	K
(c)	Explain the implications of fraud for the organisation.	K
(d)	Explain the role and duties of individual managers in the fraud detection and prevention process.	K
(e)	Define the term money laundering.	K
(f)	Give examples of recognized offences under typical money laundering regulation.	K
(g)	Identify methods for detecting and preventing money laundering.	K
(h)	Explain how suspicions of money laundering should be reported to the appropriate authorities.	K

The practical aspects of fraud (where it might actually occur, how it can be detected) are the most likely topics to be examined.

---

1 What is fraud?

EXAM FOCUS POINT

In a corporate context fraud can fall into one of two main categories: **removal of funds or assets** from a business or the intentional **misrepresentation of the financial position of a business**.

Fraud may be generally defined as 'deprivation by deceit'. In a court case, fraud was defined as 'a false representation of fact made with the knowledge of its falsity, or without belief in its truth, or recklessly careless, whether it be true or false'.

In a corporate context, fraud can fall into one of two main categories.

Category	Comment
Removal of funds or assets from a business	The most obvious example of this is outright theft, either of cash or of other assets. However, this form of fraud also encompasses more subtle measures, such as overstatement of claims. (Paragraph 1.1)
Intentional misrepresentation of the financial position of the business	This includes the omission or misrecording of the company's accounting records. (Paragraph 1.2)

BPP
LEARNING MEDIA

EXAM FOCUS POINT

This is not an exhaustive list of examples. Every business is unique and offers different opportunities for fraud to be committed. You need to be able to think about a situation and identify for yourself areas and ways in which frauds could be occurring.

1.1 Removal of funds or assets from a business

Common frauds include payroll frauds, conspiracy with other parties and stealing assets. More subtle measures include teeming and lading and manipulation of bank reconciliations and cashbooks to conceal theft.

1.1.1 Theft of cash

Employees with access to cash may be tempted to steal it. A prime example is theft from petty cash. Small amounts taken at intervals may easily go unnoticed.

1.1.2 Theft of inventory

Similarly, employees may pilfer items of inventory. The most trivial example of this is employees taking office stationery, although larger items may also be taken. These examples are of unsophisticated types of fraud, which generally go undetected because of their immateriality. On the whole, such fraud will tend to be too insignificant to have any serious impact on results or long-term performance.

1.1.3 Payroll fraud

Employees within or outside the payroll department can perpetrate payroll fraud.

(a)   Employees external to the department can falsify their timesheets, for example by claiming overtime for hours which they did not really work.

(b)   Members of the payroll department may have the opportunity deliberately to miscalculate selected payslips, either by applying an inflated rate of pay or by altering the hours to which the rate is applied.

(c)   Alternatively, a fictitious member of staff can be added to the payroll list. The fraudster sets up a bank account in the bogus name and collects the extra cash themselves. This is most feasible in a large organisation with high numbers of personnel, where management is not personally acquainted with every employee.

1.1.4 Teeming and lading

This is one of the best known methods of fraud in the sales ledger area. Basically, **teeming and lading** is the theft of cash or cheque receipts. Setting subsequent receipts, not necessarily from the same customer, against the outstanding debt conceals the theft.

1.1.5 Fictitious customers

This is a more elaborate method of stealing inventory. Bogus orders are set up, and goods are despatched on credit. The 'customer' then fails to pay for the goods and the cost is eventually written off as a bad debt. For this type of fraud to work, the employee must have responsibility for taking goods orders as well as the authority to approve a new customer for credit.

1.1.6 Collusion with customers

Employees may collude with customers to defraud the business by manipulating prices or the quality or quantity of goods despatched.

(a)   For example, a sales manager or director could **reduce the price** charged to a customer in return for a cut of the saving. Alternatively, the employee could write off a debt or issue a credit note in return for a financial reward.

(b)   Another act of collusion might be for the employee to **suppress invoices** or underrecord quantities of despatched goods on delivery notes. Again, the customer would probably provide the employee with a financial incentive for doing this.

1.1.7 Bogus supply of goods or services

This typically involves senior staff who falsely invoice the firm for goods or services that were never supplied. One example would be the supply of consultancy services. To enhance authenticity, in many cases the individual involved will set up a personal company that invoices the business for its services. This type of fraud can be quite difficult to prove.

1.1.8 Paying for goods not received

Staff may collude with suppliers, who issue invoices for larger quantities of goods than were actually delivered. The additional payments made by the company are split between the two parties.

1.1.9 Meeting budgets/target performance measures

Management teams will readily agree that setting budgets and goals is an essential part of planning and an important ingredient for success. However, such targets can disguise frauds. In some cases, knowing that results are unlikely to be questioned once targets have been met, employees and/or management siphon off and pocket any profits in excess of the target.

1.1.10 Manipulation of bank reconciliations and cash books

Often the simplest techniques can hide the biggest frauds. We saw earlier how simple a technique teeming and lading is for concealing a theft. Similarly, other simple measures such as incorrect descriptions of items and use of compensating debits and credits to make a reconciliation work frequently ensure that fraudulent activities go undetected.

1.1.11 Misuse of pension funds or other assets

This type of fraud has received a high profile in the past. Ailing companies may raid the pension fund and steal assets to use as collateral in obtaining loan finance. Alternatively, company assets may be transferred to the fund at significant overvaluations.

1.1.12 Disposal of assets to employees

It may be possible for an employee to arrange to buy a company asset (eg a car) for personal use. In this situation, there may be scope to manipulate the book value of the asset so that the employee pays below market value for it. This could be achieved by overdepreciating the relevant asset.

1.2 Intentional misrepresentation of the financial position of the business

Here we consider examples in which the intention is to overstate profits. Note, however, that by reversing the logic we can also use them as examples of methods by which staff may deliberately understate profits. You should perform this exercise yourself.

1.2.1 Overvaluation of inventory

Inventory is a particularly attractive area for management wishing to inflate net assets artificially. There is a whole range of ways in which inventory may be incorrectly valued for accounts purposes.

(a)   Inventory records may be manipulated, particularly by deliberate miscounting at inventory counts.

(b)   Deliveries to customers may be omitted from the books.

(c)   Returns to suppliers may not be recorded.

(d)   Obsolete inventory may not be written off but rather held at cost on the statement of financial position.

1.2.2 Irrecoverable debt policy may not be enforced

Aged receivables who are obviously not going to pay should be written off. However, by not enforcing this policy, management can avoid the negative effects it would have on profits and net assets.

1.2.3 Fictitious sales

These can be channelled through the accounts in a number of ways.

QUESTION   Sales fraud

See if you can come up with three ways of generating fictitious sales transactions or sales values.

ANSWER

The following are just three obvious suggestions.

(a)   Generation of false invoices
(b)   Overcharging customers for goods or services
(c)   Selling goods to friends (with a promise of buying them back at a later date)

1.2.4 Manipulation of year-end events

Cut off dates provide management with opportunities for window dressing the financial statements. Sales made just before year end can be deliberately overinvoiced and credit notes issued with an apology at the start of the new year. This will enhance turnover and profit during the year just ended. Delaying the recording of pre-year-end purchases of goods not yet delivered can achieve the same objective.

1.2.5 Understating expenses

Clearly, failure to record all expenses accurately will inflate the reported profit figure.

1.2.6 Manipulation of depreciation figures

As an expense that does not have any cash flow effect, depreciation figures may be easily tampered with. Applying incorrect rates or inconsistent policies in order to understate depreciation will result in a higher profit and a higher net book value, giving a more favourable impression of financial health.

2 Potential for fraud

The UK has witnessed a number of high-profile frauds, most notably the BCCI, Maxwell and Barings Bank cases. The real incidence of fraud is difficult to gauge, particularly because companies are often loath to publicise such experiences. However, all businesses – without exception – face the **risk of fraud**: the directors' responsibility is to manage that risk.

2.1 Prerequisites for fraud

There are three broad **prerequisites** or 'preconditions' that must exist in order to make fraud a possibility: dishonesty, motivation and opportunity.

These are useful to know, because if one or more of them can be eliminated, the risk of fraud is reduced!

2.1.1 Dishonesty

Honesty is a subjective quality, which is interpreted variously according to different ethical, cultural and legal norms. However, we may define dishonesty as an individual's predisposition or tendency to act in ways which contravene accepted ethical, social, organisational and legal norms for fair and honest dealing. This tendency may arise from:

(a)   Personality factors: a high need for achievement, status or security; a competitive desire to gain advantage over others; low respect for authority.

(b)   Cultural factors: national or familial values, which may be more 'flexible' or anti-authority than the law and practice prevailing in the organisation. (Cultural values about the ethics of business 'bribes' (or 'gifts'), for example, vary widely. 'Lying' is also a very fluid concept: some cultures value 'saving face' (or agreeing) over giving strictly truthful responses.)

2.1.2 Motivation

In addition to a general predisposition or willingness to act dishonestly, should the opportunity arise, the individual needs a specific motivation to do so. We will be discussing the concept of motivation in Chapter 15 but, broadly, it involves a **calculation** of whether a given action is worthwhile. Individuals weigh up:

(a)   The **potential rewards** of an action: the satisfaction of some need, or the fulfilment of some goal; **in relation to**

(b)   The **potential sanctions** or negative consequences of an action, or the deprivations required to carry it through.

The individual's goal or motive for fraudulent behaviour may be:

(a)   Financial needs or wants, or envy of others (in the case of theft or fraud for monetary gain)
(b)   A desire to exercise negative power over those in authority
(c)   A desire to avoid punishment (in the case of cover ups, say)

2.1.3 Opportunity

Even if a person is willing to act dishonestly, and has a motive for doing so, they must still find an opportunity or opening to do so; a 'loophole' in the law or control system that:

- Allows fraudulent activity to go undetected, or
- Makes the risk of detection acceptable, given the rewards available.

An individual will have a high incentive to commit fraud if they are predisposed to **dishonesty** and the **rewards** for the particular fraud are high and there is an **opportunity** to commit fraudulent action with **little chance of detection** or with insignificant sanctions if caught.

QUESTION   Fraud strategies

Just considering the three prerequisites of fraud, what immediate control strategies can you suggest for preventing fraud?

ANSWER

(a)   Don't employ people with predispositions to **dishonesty**, if possible: undertake legitimate and appropriate background and CV checks when carrying out recruitment and selection. (The more opportunity for fraud there is in the job, the more carefully dishonesty should be screened.)

(b)   Reduce **motivations** for fraud. This is highly subjective, but the organisation should give attention to such matters as ensuring equity in pay and rewards; monitoring employees for signs of financial difficulty and its possible causes (eg gambling addiction) and offering counselling and support where required; providing generally good and equitable working terms and conditions; and establishing clear rules and strong sanctions for fraudulent behaviour.

(c)   Reduce **opportunities** for fraud. This is the function of a range of internal checks and controls, discussed in Section 4 of this chapter: separating duties so no one person has sole control over a system; requiring authorisations for expense/timesheets, cheques, and so on; using data security measures such as passwords; security checks; identification on office equipment to deter theft; and so on.

2.2 Assessing the risk of fraud

Signs of high fraud risk include indications of **lack of integrity**, **excessive pressures**, **poor control systems**, **unusual transactions** and **lack of audit evidence**.

The starting point for any management team wanting to set up internal controls to prevent and detect fraud must be an assessment of the extent to which the firm is exposed to the risk of fraud. The best approach is to consider separately the extent to which **external** and **internal** factors may present a risk of fraud.

2.2.1 External factors

Step 1	First, consider the marketplace as a whole. The general environment in which the business operates may exhibit factors that increase the risk of fraud. For instance, the trend to delayer may reduce the degree of supervision exercised in many organisations, perhaps without putting anything in its place.

Step 2	Next, narrow the focus a little and consider whether the industry in which the firm operates is particularly exposed to certain types of fraud. For example, the building industry may be particularly prone to the risk of theft of raw materials, the travel industry may face risks due to the extensive use of agents and intermediaries and the retail industry must be vigilant to the abuse of credit cards.

QUESTION   Risk factors

Think of some examples of such general external factors that might influence the degree of risk that a company is exposed to.

ANSWER

You might have thought of some of the following.

- Technological developments
- New legislation or regulations
- Economic or political changes
- Increased competition
- Changing customer needs

2.2.2 Internal factors

Having considered the big picture, the next step is to apply the same logic at company level. Focus on the general and specific risks in the firm itself.

Be alert to circumstances that might increase the risk profile of a company.

- Changed operating environment
- New personnel
- New or upgraded management information systems
- New overseas operations
- Rapid growth
- New technology
- New products
- Corporate restructuring

A number of factors tend to crop up time and time again as issues that might indicate potential fraud. Attention should be drawn to them if any of these factors come to light when assessing external and internal risks.

2.2.3 Business risks

> A number of factors tend to crop up frequently as **indicators** of potential fraud situations; these can be categorised under business and personnel risks.

An alert management team will always be aware of the industry or business environment in which the organisation operates.

(a) **Profit levels/margins deviating significantly from the industry norm**

As a rule of thumb, if things seem too good to be true, then they generally are. If any of the following happen, alarm bells should start ringing.

(i) The company suddenly starts to exhibit profits far above those achieved by other firms in the same industry.

(ii) Turnover rises rapidly but costs do not rise in line.

(iii) Demand for a particular product increases significantly.

(iv) Investors seem to find the firm unusually attractive.

Such patterns can indicate problems, such as the manipulation of accounting records, collusion with existing customers or the creation of fictitious customers.

Similarly, results showing that the organisation is underperforming relative to competitors may be an indication of theft, collusion with suppliers or deliberate errors in the accounting records.

(b) **Market opinion**

If the market has a low opinion of the firm, this might indicate something about the company's products, its people or its way of doing business.

(c) **Complex structures**

(i) Organisations with complex group structures, including numerous domestic and overseas subsidiaries and branches, may be more susceptible to fraud.

(ii) The sheer size of the group can offer plenty of opportunities to 'lose' transactions or to hide things in intercompany accounts.

(iii) Furthermore, vast staff numbers contribute to a certain degree of employee anonymity, making it easier to conceal fraudulent activities.

2.2.4 Personnel risks

Fraud is not usually an easy thing to hide. A person's behaviour often gives clues to the fact that they are engaging in fraud.

(a) **Secretive behaviour**
A High Court judge once described secrecy as 'the badge of fraud'. If an individual starts behaving in a more secretive way than is generally considered normal, then there may be cause for concern.

(b) **Expensive lifestyles**
A well-known indicator of fraud is a lifestyle beyond an individual's earnings. A recent case involved an Inspector of Taxes who started driving expensive sports cars, taking lavish holidays and so forth. It was later discovered that he was being paid by a wealthy businessman in return for assisting him to evade tax.

(c) **Long hours or untaken holidays**
Workaholics and staff who do not take their full holiday entitlement may be trying to prevent a temporary replacement from uncovering a fraud.

(d) **Autocratic management style**
In some organisations a sole manager or director has exclusive control over a significant part of the business. This can provide ample scope for fraud, particularly when the situation is compounded by little, if any, independent review of those activities by anyone else at a senior level.

BPP
LEARNING MEDIA

(e) **Lack of segregation of duties**

Employees occasionally have more than one area of responsibility, particularly in small businesses where staff numbers are low. This can make it easy for the employee to conduct and conceal fraudulent actions. For example, if the employee who prepares the payslips were also the person who authorises the payments, payroll fraud would be relatively simple to put into practice.

(f) **Low staff morale**

One motive for fraud is resentment towards the firm. Staff may start defrauding the firm because they feel that they are not rewarded sufficiently for their work or because they were passed over for a promotion that they believed they deserved. Alternatively, low staff morale may lead to the breakdown of internal controls, yielding opportunities for fraud.

2.3 Potential for computer fraud

Organisations are becoming increasingly dependent on computers for operational systems as well as accounting and management information. With this dependency comes an increased **exposure** to fraud. The computer is frequently the vehicle through which fraudulent activities are carried out.

Problems particularly associated with computers

(a) **Computer hackers.** The possibility of unknown persons trying to hack into the systems increases the potential for fraud against which the firm must protect itself.

(b) **Lack of training within the management team.** Many people have an inherent lack of understanding of how computer systems work. Senior management can often be the least computer literate. They may also be the most reluctant to receive training, preferring to delegate tasks to assistants. Without management realising it, junior staff can secure access to vast amounts of financial information and find ways to alter it.

(c) **Identifying the risks.** Most firms do not have the resources to keep up to date with the pace of development in computer technology. This makes it ever more difficult to check that all major loopholes in controls are closed, even if management are computer literate.

(d) **Need for ease of access and flexible systems.** In most cases, a firm uses computers in order to simplify and speed up operations. To meet these objectives, there is frequently a need for ease of access and flexible systems. However, implementing strict controls can sometimes suppress these features.

3   Implications of fraud for the organisation

While it is clear that fraud is bad for business, the precise ways in which the firm is affected depends on the type of fraud being carried on.

3.1 Removal of funds or assets from a business

Immediate financial implications

Profits are lower than they should be. The business has less cash or fewer assets, and therefore the net asset position is weakened. Returns to shareholders are likely to fall as a result.

Long-term effects on company performance

The reduction in working capital makes it more difficult for the company to operate effectively. In the most serious cases, fraud can ultimately result in the collapse of an otherwise successful business, such as Barings.

3.2 Intentional misrepresentation of the financial position of the business

Financial statements do not give a true and fair view of the financial situation of the business. Results may be either artificially enhanced or, less frequently, underreported.

It is also possible that managers in charge of a particular **division** can artificially enhance their division's results, thereby deceiving senior management.

QUESTION

Try to think of reasons why someone might want to:

(a)   Artificially enhance the results   (b)   Underreport the results

ANSWER

(a)   Reasons for overstating profits and/or net assets

    (i)   To ensure achievement on paper, may have to meet targets in order to secure a promotion, bonuses or remuneration may be linked to performance

    (ii)   Trying to conceal another form of fraud, such as theft

    (iii)   Need a healthy statement of financial position to convince bank to give loan finance

    (iv)   Ailing company may be trying to entice equity investors

(b)   Reasons for understating profits and/or net assets

    (i)   To facilitate a private purchase of an asset from the business at less than market value

    (ii)   To defraud HM Revenue & Customs by reducing taxable profits or gains

    (iii)   Trying to force the share price down so that shares can be bought below market value by friends or relatives

3.2.1 If results are overstated

A company may **distribute too much** of its profits to shareholders.

Retained profits will be lower than believed, leading to potential shortfalls in working capital. This makes the day-to-day activities more difficult to perform effectively.

Incorrect decisions will be made, based on inaccurate knowledge of available resources.

The effects of fraudulent activities can also affect **stakeholders** if the financial statements on which they rely are misrepresentations of the truth.

(a)   **Investors** making decisions based on inaccurate information will find actual returns deviating from expectations.

(b)   **Suppliers** will extend credit without knowing the financial position of the company.

3.2.2 If results are understated

Returns to investors may be reduced unnecessarily.

If the company is quoted on the stock exchange, the share price might fall and market strength may be eroded.

Access to loan finance may be restricted if assets are understated.

The **negative publicity** can damage the business by affecting the public's perceptions.

Legal consequences. Finally, fraudsters open themselves up to the possibility of arrest. Depending on the scale and seriousness of the offence some may even find themselves facing a prison sentence.

4 Systems for detecting and preventing fraud

4.1 Prioritising prevention

> In order to prevent fraud, managers must be aware of the **risks** and **signs** of fraud.

Prevention of fraud must be an **integral** part of **corporate strategy**. Managing the risk of fraud is a key part of managing business risks in general and, if the company's risk management procedures are poor, management of fraud risk is also likely to be unsuccessful.

Certain recent developments, notably downsizing, have however meant that certain controls that are designed to prevent fraud, for example segregation of duties, may not be possible. Hence it is equally important the control system is designed so as to **detect and investigate** fraud.

4.2 Reasons for fraud

Management must have an understanding of how and why frauds might arise. Examples include:

(a)   The risk of fraud may be increased by factors that are specific to the **industry**. Lower profit margins due to increased competition may be a temptation to manipulate results.

(b)   Factors specific to the **business** may also increase the risk of fraud.

   (i)   **Personnel** factors such as extensive authority given to dominant managers

   (ii)   **Organisation** factors such as unclear structure of responsibility or lack of supervision of remote locations

   (iii)   **Strategy** factors such as a lack of a business strategy or great emphasis being placed on reward by results

(c)   **Changes in circumstances** may also increase the risk of fraud. Often a control system may become inadequate as a result of changes in the business, particularly changes in technology or the internal organisation.

(d)   Certain areas, for example cash sales, are **normally high risk**.

4.3 Reasons for poor controls

Management also need to understand factors that may prevent controls from operating properly.

- Controls will not function well if there is a **lack of emphasis** on compliance or a **lack of understanding** of why the controls are required, how they should operate and who should be operating them.

- **Staff problems** such as understaffing and poor quality or poorly motivated staff can impede the operation of controls.

- **Changes in senior personnel** can lead to a lack of supervision during the transition period.

- **Emphasis on the autonomy of operational management** may lead to controls being bypassed.

4.4 General prevention policies

> Prevention policies include emphasis on **ethics** and **personnel and training procedures**. Controls within particular business areas such as **segregation of duties** and **documentation requirements** are also significant.

Management can implement certain general controls that are designed to prevent fraud.

(a)   **Emphasising ethics** can decrease the chances of fraud. Several businesses have formal codes of ethics which employees are required to sign covering areas such as gifts from customers. Management can also ensure that they set 'a good example'.

(b)   **Personnel controls** are a very important means of preventing fraud. Thorough **interviewing** and **recruitment procedures** including obtaining references can be an effective screening for dishonest employees. **Appraisal** and grievance systems can prevent staff demotivation.

(c)   **Training and raising awareness** can be important. There are many examples of frauds taking place where people who were unwittingly close were shocked that they had no idea what was happening. **Fraud awareness education** should therefore be an integral part of the training programme, particularly for managers and staff in **high risk areas** such as procurement, and staff with key roles in fraud prevention and detection, for example human resources.

4.5 Prevention of fraud in specific business areas

Controls will also be needed in specific areas of the business where a high risk of fraud has been identified.

(a)   **Segregation of duties** is a key control in fraud prevention. Ultimately operational pressures may mean that segregation is incomplete. Management should nevertheless identify certain functions that must be kept separate, for example separating the cheque signing function from the authorisation of payments.

(b)   **Appropriate documentation** should be required for all transactions.

(c)   **Limitation controls**, such as only allowing staff to choose suppliers from an approved list and limiting access to the computer network by means of passwords, can reduce the opportunities for fraud.

(d)   Certain actions should be **prohibited** such as leaving a computer terminal without logging off.

(e)   **Internal audit** work should **concentrate** on these areas.

4.6 Detection and prevention

A primary aim of any system of internal controls should be to **prevent fraud**. However, the very nature of fraud means that people will find ways to get around existing systems. It is equally important, therefore, to have controls in place to **detect fraud** if and when it happens.

4.7 Internal controls

Controls must be developed in a structured manner, taking the whole spectrum of risk into account and focusing on the key risks identified in each area of the business.

Let us think about appropriate controls that could be introduced to combat fraud.

4.8 Physical controls

Basic as it seems, physical security is an important tool in preventing fraud. Keeping tangible assets under lock and key makes it difficult for staff to access them and can go a long way towards discouraging theft.

4.9 Segregation of duties

Staff who have responsibility for a range of tasks have more scope for committing and concealing fraud. Therefore the obvious way to control the risk is to segregate duties.

If an employee's duties do not extend beyond one domain, it will be more difficult for an employee to conceal a fraud. It is more likely that it will be picked up at the next stage in the process.

So, for example, the employee responsible for recording sales orders should not be the same person responsible for maintaining inventory records. This will make it more difficult to falsify sales or inventory records, as a discrepancy between sales figures and inventory balances would show up.

Segregating responsibility for packaging goods for delivery from either of the recording tasks would also help to minimise the risk of theft and increase the likelihood of detection.

4.10 Authorisation policies

Requiring written authorisation by a senior member of staff is a good preventative tool. It increases accountability and also makes it harder to conceal a fraudulent transaction.

4.11 Customer signatures

Requiring customers to inspect and sign for receipt of goods or services ensures that they cannot claim that the delivery did not match their order.

It also provides confirmation that the delivery staff actually did their job and that what was delivered corresponded to what was recorded.

4.12 Using words rather than numbers

Insist that all quantities be written out in full. It is much more difficult to change text than to alter a figure.

4.13 Documentation

Separate documents should be used to record sales order, despatch, delivery and invoice details. A simple matching exercise will then pick up any discrepancies between them and lead to detection of any alterations.

4.14 Sequential numbering

Numbering order forms, delivery dockets or invoices makes it extremely simple to spot if something is missing.

4.15 Dates

Writing the date on forms and invoices assists in cut-off testing. For example, if a delivery docket is dated pre-year end but the sale is recorded post-year end it is possible that results are being manipulated.

4.16 Standard procedures

Standard procedures should be defined clearly for normal business operations and should be known to all staff. For example:

- Independent checks should be made on the existence of new customers.
- Credit should not be given to a new customer until his/her credit history has been investigated.
- All payments should be authorised by a senior member of staff.
- Wages/payslips must be collected in person.

Any deviations from these norms should become quite visible.

4.17 Holidays

As we have said, fraud is difficult to conceal. Enforcing holiday policy by insisting that all staff take their full holiday entitlement is therefore a crucial internal control. A two-week absence is frequently sufficient time for a fraud to come to light.

4.18 Recruitment policies

Personnel policies play a vital part in developing the corporate culture and deterring fraud. Something as obvious as checking the information and references provided by applicants may reduce the risk of appointing dishonest staff.

4.19 Computer security

This will be discussed in detail in Chapter 18. However, many of the above controls (access controls, segregation of duties, authorisations, and so on) will apply.

4.20 Manager and staff responsibilities

Managers and staff should be aware of their **responsibilities** to help in detecting fraud. Fraud detection is also helped by having **information readily available** and allowing **whistleblowing**.

If fraud is to be detected, it is important that everyone involved in detection should be aware of their responsibilities.

(a) **Operational managers** should be **alert for signs** of petty fraud, as well as checking the work staff have done and also being aware of what staff are doing.

(b) **Finance staff** should be alert for **unusual items** or **trends** in accounting data, as well as incomplete financial information.

(c) **Personnel staff** should be alert for **signs of discontent** or **low morale**, and also should (if possible) be aware of close personal relationships between staff who work together.

(d) **Internal audit staff** have responsibility for ensuring **systems** and controls are thoroughly **reviewed**. One-off exercises such as surprise visits may be undertaken alongside annual audit work.

(e) **External audit staff** are required to **assess** the **risk** that fraud may have a **material impact** on a company's accounts when planning their audit work. They are required to **report** all instances of fraud found to management, unless they suspect management of being involved in the fraud. The external auditors should also report to management any material weaknesses in the accounting and internal control systems.

(f) **Non-executive directors** should **act** on **signs** of **dishonesty** by senior executive management. The **audit committee** should **review the organisation's performance** in fraud prevention and report any suspicious matters to the board.

4.20.1 Fraud officer

Many large organisations have appointed a fraud officer, who is responsible for **initiating** and **overseeing fraud investigations**, **implementing the fraud response plan**, and for **any follow-up actions**. The fraud officer should be able to **talk to staff confidentially** and be able to **provide advice** without consulting senior management.

4.21 Availability of information

It is of course important that information should be available to enable management to identify signs of actual fraud, or of an environment where fraud may occur.

(a) **Cost and management accounting systems** should **provide** promptly **information** with sufficient detail to enable management to identify parts of the business whose performance is out of line with expectations. Actual results should be compared with budgeted results and explanations sought for significant variances.

(b) **Personnel procedures** such as **staff meetings**, **appraisals** and **exit interviews** may indicate low morale or staff who are under undue pressure.

(c) **Lines of reporting** should be **clear**. Staff should know to whom they should report any suspicions of fraud.

4.22 Whistleblowing

The likelihood of fraud detection may have been increased by recent legislation in a number of countries that provides **employment protection rights** to 'whistleblowers', employees who reveal fraud or malpractice in a workplace. The legislation covers disclosure of certain 'relevant failures', including committal of a criminal offence, failure to comply with legislation, endangering health and safety or damaging the environment.

Some employers are introducing a formal concerns procedure, which sets out how potential whistleblowers should communicate their concerns.

4.23 Investigation of fraud

Organisations should establish a **fraud response plan**, setting out how the **method** and **extent** of the fraud and **possible suspects** should be investigated.

If the worst does happen there should be a **fraud response plan**, a strategy for **investigating** and **dealing with the consequences** of frauds that have occurred.

Certain actions might have to be taken as soon as the fraud comes to light. These may include **ensuring the security of the records** that will be used to investigate what has happened, and also the **securing of assets** that may be vulnerable to theft. Procedures may have to include suspending staff, changing passwords and so on.

Investigation procedures should be designed with the following aims in mind:

(a) **Establishing** the **extent** of the loss, ascertain on whom it fell and assess how it may be recovered

(b) **Establishing how** the fraud **occurred**

(c) Considering **who else** may have been **implicated** in the fraud

(d) Assessing whether the **fraud** was not detected because **existing controls** were not operating properly, or whether existing controls would have been unlikely to prevent or identify the fraud

Key decisions in fraud investigation will include who will be **carrying out the investigation** and also whether the investigation will be **undercover**. Guidance produced by the accountancy firm KPMG has highlighted the importance of quickly obtaining a picture of the **activities** of the suspected fraudster by reviewing their personal paperwork (diaries, files, expense claims, etc) and also contacting the people who worked with them.

Ultimately the detection and prevention of fraud requires not only a **clear strategy** but also a **willingness to enforce controls**.

4.24 Evolving control systems

The environment in which organisations exist and operate changes constantly. The risks organisations face also change over time. Some risks will decrease with time, other risks will increase, new risks will arise.

For the systems intended to control and minimise the impact of risks to be effective they also must change and adapt. The control systems must evolve to deal with the risks present in the changing environment. Control systems must therefore be reviewed constantly and, if necessary, changed or adapted in order to cope with new risks.

This is particularly true where legislation changes, such as the relatively recent changes in the UK to money laundering and bribery legislation. Control systems must enable the organisation and the individuals that work within the organisation to meet their legal obligations under new legislation.

5 Responsibility for detecting and preventing fraud

It is the responsibility of the directors to take such steps as are reasonably open to them to **prevent and detect** fraud.

5.1 The responsibility of directors

In a **limited company**, or plc, it is the responsibility of the directors to prevent and detect fraud. They should:

(a)   Ensure that the **activities** of the entity are conducted honestly and that its **assets** are safeguarded

(b)   Establish arrangements to **deter** fraudulent or other dishonest conduct and to **detect** any that occurs

(c)   Ensure that, to the best of their knowledge and belief, **financial information**, whether used internally or for financial reporting, is reliable

5.2 The role of the auditor

The responsibility of the external auditor is only to express an opinion on whether the financial statements give a true and fair view of the company's financial situation and results.

The auditor should design audit procedures so as to have a **reasonable expectation** of detecting misstatements arising from fraud or error. It should be emphasised that, in the case of a sophisticated fraud, which has been designed to escape detection by the auditors, a **reasonable expectation** is all that they can have.

If the auditors become aware during the audit that fraud or error may exist, they should document their findings and report them to management.

In the case of fraud, the auditors should then consider whether the matter should be reported to an appropriate authority in the public interest. If they decide that this is the case, they request that **the directors** make the report. If the directors do not do so, or if the fraud casts doubt on the integrity of the directors, the auditors should make the report themselves.

If the auditors take the view that the financial statements are affected by fraud or error, they should qualify their report accordingly.

It is the responsibility of the **directors** to take reasonable steps to detect and prevent fraud and error.

EXAM FOCUS POINT

The examining team has commented that recent candidates have struggled to identify the appropriate action that should be taken by external auditors when evidence of fraud is uncovered.

6 Money laundering

The growth of globalisation has created more opportunities for money laundering which governments and international bodies are trying to combat with legislation.

One of the side effects of globalisation and the free movement of capital has been the growth in **money laundering**.

Money laundering constitutes any financial transactions whose purpose is to conceal the origins of the proceeds of criminal activity.

Money laundering is used by organised crime and terrorist organisations but it is also used in order to avoid the payment of taxes or to distort accounting information. Money laundering involves therefore a number of agents and entities from criminals and terrorists to companies and corrupt officials or states as well as tax havens.

6.1 Risks associated with a company's products and services

Some businesses are at higher risk than others of money laundering. For example, businesses dealing in luxury items of high value can be at risk of the products being resold through the black market or returned to the retailer in exchange for a legitimate cheque from them.

The increasing complexity of financial crime and its increase has prompted national governments and the European Union to legislate and regulate the conduct of transactions.

6.2 The effects of regulation

The following information relates specifically to European companies but similar regulations exist in other countries.

Affected companies must assess the risk of money laundering in their business and take necessary action to alleviate this risk.

6.2.1 Assessing risk – the risk-based approach

The risk-based approach consists of a number of steps.

- Identifying the money laundering risks that are relevant to the business

- Carrying out a detailed risk assessment on such areas as customer behaviour and delivery channels

- Designing and implementing controls to manage and reduce any identified risks

- Monitor the effectiveness of these controls and make improvements where necessary

- Maintain records of actions taken and reasons for these actions

The time and cost of carrying out such assessments will depend on the size and complexity of the business but will require considerable effort to ensure compliance with regulations.

6.2.2 Assessing the customer base

Businesses with certain types of customers are more at risk of money laundering activities and will therefore be required to take more stringent action to protect themselves. Types of customers that pose a risk include the following.

- New customers carrying out large, one-off transactions

- Customers who have been introduced by a third party who may not have assessed their risk potential thoroughly

- Customers who aren't local

- Customers whose businesses handle large amounts of cash

Other customers who might pose a risk include those who are unwilling to provide identification and who enter into transactions that do not make commercial sense. Before companies commence business dealings with a customer, they should conduct suitable customer due diligence.

6.2.3 Customer due diligence

This is an official term for taking steps to check that customers are who they say they are. In practice, the best and easiest way to do this is to ask for official documents or details from these, for example company registration details. For individuals a passport or driving licence, together with utility bills and bank statements, would suffice.

If customers are acting on behalf of a third party, it is important to identify who the third party is.

6.2.4 Applying customer due diligence

Businesses should apply customer due diligence whenever they feel it necessary but as a minimum in any of the following circumstances.

(a)   When establishing a business relationship. This is likely to be a relationship that will be ongoing therefore it is important to establish identify and credibility at the start. The organisation may have a responsibility to establish such information as the source and origin of funds that the customer will be using, copies of recent and current financial statements and details of the customer's business or employment.

(b)   When carrying out an 'occasional transaction' worth 15,000 euros or more – that is, transactions that are not carried out within an ongoing business relationship. The organisation should also look out for 'linked' transactions which are individual transactions of 15,000 euros or more that have been broken down into smaller, separate transactions to avoid due diligence checks.

(c)   When doubts exist about identification information obtained previously

(d)   When the customer's circumstances change – for example, a change in the ownership of the customer's business or a significant change in the type of business activity of the customer

6.2.5 Ongoing monitoring

It is important that an effective system of internal controls is in place to protect the business from being used for money laundering. Staff should be suitably trained in the implementation of these internal controls and be alert to any potential issues. A specific member of staff should be nominated as the person to whom any suspicious activities should be reported, known as the Money Laundering Reporting Officer.

Full documentation of anti-money laundering policies and procedures should be kept and updated as appropriate. Staff should be kept fully informed of any changes.

6.2.6 Maintaining full and up-to-date records

Businesses are generally required to keep full and up-to-date records for financial reporting and auditing purposes but these can also be used to demonstrate compliance with money laundering regulations. Such records will include receipts, invoices and customer correspondence. European money laundering regulations require that such information be kept for each customer for five years beginning on either the date a transaction is completed or the date a business relationship ends.

6.3 Categories of criminal offence

In the UK, there are various offences relating to **money laundering**, including tipping off a money launderer (or suspected money launderer) and failing to report reasonable suspicions.

There are **three categories of criminal offences** under the Criminal Justice Act 1993 (HMSO, 1993).

- **Laundering**: acquisition, possession or use of the proceeds of criminal conduct, or assisting another to retain the proceeds of criminal conduct and concealing, disguising, converting, transferring or removing criminal property. This relates to the nature, source, location, disposition, movement or ownership of the property. Money laundering includes possession of the proceeds of one's own crime and facilitating any handling or possession of criminal property, which may take any form, including in money or money's worth, securities, tangible property and intangible property.

- **Failure to report** by an individual: failure to disclose knowledge or suspicion of money laundering (suspicion is more than mere speculation, but falls short of proof or knowledge)

- **Tipping off**: disclosing information to any person if disclosure may prejudice an investigation into, drug trafficking, drug money laundering, terrorist-related activities, or laundering the proceeds of criminal conduct

For the purposes of laundering, '**criminal property**' is property which the alleged offender knows (or suspects) constitutes or represents being related to any criminal conduct. This is any conduct that constitutes or would constitute an offence in the UK.

In relation to **laundering**, a person may have a **defence** if they make a disclosure to the authorities:

- As soon as possible after the transaction
- Before the transaction takes place

Alternatively, they may have a defence if they can show there was a **reasonable excuse** for not making a disclosure.

In relation to **failure to report**, the person who suspects money laundering must disclose this to a nominated Money Laundering Reporting Officer (MLRO) within their organisation if it has one, or directly to the Serious Organised Crime Agency (SOCA) in the form of a Suspicious Activity Report (SAR). SOCA has responsibility in the UK for collecting and disseminating information related to all forms of serious organised crime, including money laundering and related activities. The nominated MLRO in an organisation acts as a filter and notifies SOCA too.

In relation to **tipping off**, this covers the situation when a person making a disclosure to the MLRO or SOCA also tells the person at the centre of their suspicions about the disclosure. There is a **defence** to the effect that the person did not know that tipping off would prejudice an investigation.

6.4 Penalties

The law sets out the following penalties in relation to money laundering.

(a)   14 years' imprisonment and/or a fine for knowingly assisting in the **laundering** of criminal funds

(b)   5 years' imprisonment and/or a fine for failure to report knowledge or the suspicion of money laundering and for 'tipping off' a suspected launderer; the suspected launderer must not be alerted

QUESTION

Money laundering

Why should a professional adviser not give a warning to a client whom they suspect of money laundering?

ANSWER

Tipping off a suspected money launderer is an offence. Alerting the suspect would be likely to hamper any subsequent investigation by the authorities.

6.5 Money laundering process

The money laundering process usually involves three phases.

- **Placement** – this is the initial disposal of the proceeds of the illegal activity into apparently legitimate business activity or property eg 'smurfing' whereby small amounts are banked with a number of institutions in order to avoid suspicion and anti-money laundering reporting requirements.

- **Layering** – this involves the transfer of monies from business to business or place to place to conceal the original source eg under- or overvaluing invoices to disguise the movement of money.

- **Integration** – having been layered, the money has the appearance of legitimate funds, eg an individual may use cash to gamble at a casino and receive a cheque for any winnings. This cheque can then be banked as proceeds from gambling, regardless of the original source of the money.

For accountants, the most worrying aspect of the law on money laundering relates to the offence of '**failing to disclose**'. It is relatively straightforward to identify actual 'knowledge' of money laundering, and therefore of the need to disclose it, but the term 'suspicion' of money laundering is not defined. The nearest there is to a definition is that suspicion is more than mere speculation but falls short of proof or knowledge. It is a question of judgement.

6.6 The role of the Financial Conduct Authority

In addition to UK legislation, there are other rules which apply to **investment firms** (that is, firms which sell financial services or shares).

The **FCA SYSC sourcebook** (FRC 2016) provides the following rules:

(a) **Control systems** in place to monitor possible money laundering activities

(b) A **Money Laundering Reporting Officer (MLRO)** who is responsible for the oversight of the anti-money laundering activities.

(c) **Internal reporting procedures**; staff must be able to identify suspicious transactions, understand reporting procedures, and be able to notify the MLRO of any person who they suspect of engaging in money laundering

(d) **Adequate records** such as:

   (i) A copy of the evidence of identity obtained

   (ii) A record of where a copy of the identity evidence can be obtained

   (iii) Procedures for internal and external reporting

   (iv) Evidence of an applicant's identity, which must be retained for five years from the end of the firm's relationship with the client

   (v) Money laundering training given to all staff who handle transactions (or who manage others who are responsible for handling transactions) that may involve money laundering

Although investment firms may be particularly at risk of being involved with clients who are seeking to launder money, **methods used** for laundering such dirty money **can be extremely complex**. They may involve **trusts, companies** (both offshore and onshore) and could involve the use of relatively complex bank instruments.

Therefore **all companies**, their **managers** and their **advisers need to be aware** of the issue of money laundering and not fall foul of the regulations.

There is a **legal requirement** for organisations to take the following actions.

- To set up procedures and establish accountabilities for senior individuals to take action to prevent money laundering

- To educate staff and employees about the potential problems of money laundering

- To obtain satisfactory evidence of identity where a transaction is for more than €15,000

- To report suspicious circumstances (according to the established procedures)

- Not to alert persons who are or might be investigated for money laundering

- To keep records of all transactions for five years

EXAM FOCUS POINT

You must be clear as to how this guidance seeks to prevent or minimise money laundering.

6.7 The costs of compliance

All of the activities listed above do not come cheaply, especially if policies and procedures are being established for the first time. In addition, regulations in the UK state that all accountants in public practice must be supervised and monitored in their compliance and registered with a supervisory body.

ACCA is one of the supervisory bodies and is responsible for monitoring its own members. Such supervision comes at a cost, however, and monitored firms are expected to pay a fee for this service.

6.8 Financial Action Task Force (FATF)

The Financial Action Task Force (FATF) is an inter-governmental body which develops and promotes policies, at national and international levels, to combat money laundering and terrorist financing. FATF currently has over 30 member states, including the UK, many EU states, Turkey, India, China, Japan, New Zealand, the US, Brazil and Argentina.

FATF members are committed to implementing FATF standards and having their anti-money laundering (AML)/counter-terrorist financing (CTF) systems mutually assessed. A country needs to do the following in order to implement FATF's recommendations effectively.

- Successfully investigate and prosecute money laundering and terrorist financing

- Deprive criminals of their criminal proceeds and the resources needed to finance their illicit activities

- Require financial institutions and other businesses and professions to implement effective measures to detect and prevent money laundering and terrorist financing

- Ensure that financial institutions and other businesses and professions comply with AML/CTF requirements

- Enhance the transparency of legal persons and arrangements

- Implement mechanisms to facilitate co-operation and co-ordination of AML/CTF efforts at the international and domestic level

6.9 International Monetary Fund (IMF)

The IMF is increasingly involved in addressing the risks of money laundering.

It promotes itself as a natural forum for sharing information, developing common approaches to issues and promoting desirable policies and standards in order to fight money laundering and the financing of terrorism.

PER performance objective PO4 requires you to contribute to the effective governance of an organisation and raise awareness of risk. The material covered in this chapter, and built on later in your studies in Paper P1, will help you achieve this.

CHAPTER ROUNDUP

⤷ The practical aspects of fraud (where it might actually occur, how it can be detected) are the most likely topics to be examined.

⤷ **Common frauds** include payroll frauds, conspiracy with other parties and stealing assets. More subtle measures including teeming and lading and manipulation of bank reconciliations and cashbooks to conceal theft.

⤷ There are three broad **prerequisites** or 'preconditions' that must exist in order to make fraud a possibility: dishonesty, motivation and opportunity.

⤷ Signs of high fraud risk include indications of **lack of integrity**, **excessive pressures**, **poor control systems**, **unusual transactions** and **lack of audit evidence**.

⤷ A number of factors tend to crop up frequently as **indicators** of potential fraud situations; these can be categorised under business and personnel risks.

⤷ In order to prevent fraud, managers must be aware of the **risks** and **signs** of fraud.

⤷ Prevention policies include emphasis on **ethics** and **personnel and training procedures**. Controls within particular business areas, such as **segregation of duties** and **documentation requirements**, are also significant.

⤷ Controls must be developed in a structured manner, taking account of the whole spectrum of risk and focusing on the key risks identified in each area of the business.

⤷ Managers and staff should be aware of their **responsibilities** to help in detecting fraud. Fraud detection is also helped by having **information readily available** and allowing **whistleblowing**.

⤷ Organisations should establish a **fraud response plan**, setting out how the **method** and **extent** of the fraud and **possible suspects** should be investigated.

⤷ It is the responsibility of the directors to take such steps as are reasonably open to them to **prevent and detect** fraud.

⤷ The growth of globalisation has created more opportunities for money laundering which governments and international bodies are trying to combat with legislation.

⤷ In the UK, there are various offences relating to money laundering, including tipping off a money launderer (or suspected money launderer) and failing to report reasonable suspicions.

QUICK QUIZ

1   Applying incorrect rates to understate depreciation will result in a higher profit, giving a more favourable impression of financial health. Is this true or false?

2   *True*   *False*

Computers increase the risk of fraud   ☐   ☐

Motivation is a prerequisite for fraud   ☐   ☐

3   Who has the primary responsibility for preventing and detecting fraud?

    A   The external auditors
    B   The internal auditors
    C   The directors
    D   The shareholders

4   List five examples of internal controls (not computer related).

5   What are the main factors that might prevent controls operating properly?

6   What are the main personnel controls that can be used to limit the risk of fraud?

ANSWERS TO QUICK QUIZ

1   True.   Depreciation does not have any actual cash flow which means it is easy to tamper with.

2   True, true. Computers tend to increase exposure to fraud because they are frequently the vehicles through which fraudulent activities are carried out.

3   C   The directors are responsible for taking steps to prevent and detect fraud.

4   Examples include physical controls, segregation of duties, authorisation policies, using words rather than numbers and enforcing holiday policy.

5   • Lack of emphasis on compliance
    • Lack of understanding of why controls are required
    • Staff problems
    • Changes in senior personnel
    • Excessive emphasis on the authority of line management

6   • Rigorous recruitment procedures including interviews and references
    • Appraisals
    • Procedures to deal with grievances

Now try ...

Attempt the questions below from the **Practice Question Bank**

Q49

Q50

Q51

Q52

Q53

Q54

Q55

part

D

Leading and managing individuals and teams

In this chapter, we attempt to get an overview of the manager's task (**Section 1**). What is management? How should people be managed? What do managers actually do to manage resources, activities and projects?

Section 2 traces the **development of management theory** from its focus on efficiency and control (classical and scientific management), through a recognition of the importance of people factors (human relations and neo-human relations), to a more complex understanding that a variety of factors influence the managerial role.

In **Section 3**, we note the difference between a manager and a **supervisor**: the interface between managerial and non-managerial levels of the organisation.

The theories discussed in this chapter are noted specifically in the syllabus Study Guide, and some are particularly useful as a framework for understanding management in general. The major challenge of this topic is learning the detail of the various theories.

In today's organisations, managers are also called on to be 'leaders'. We explore leadership as a separate function (and skill-set) of management in **Sections 4 and 5**.

Leading and managing people

Study Guide | Intellectual level

D1 Leadership, management and supervision

(a) Define leadership, management and supervision and explain the distinction between these terms.   K

(b) Explain the nature of management.   K

    (i) Scientific/classical theories of management Fayol, Taylor

    (ii) The human relations school – Mayo

    (iii) The functions of a manager – Mintzberg, Drucker

(c) Explain the areas of managerial authority and responsibility.   K

(d) Explain the situational, functional and contingency approaches to leadership with reference to the theories of Adair, Fiedler, Bennis, Kotter and Heifetz.   K

(e) Describe leadership styles and contexts using the models of Ashridge, and Blake and Mouton.   K

EXAM FOCUS POINT

There is an article on the ACCA website entitled "Theories of leadership style" that is relevant to material in this chapter.

1 The purpose and process of management

Management is responsible for using the organisation's resources to meet its goals. It is accountable to the owners: shareholders in a business, or government in the public sector.

1.1 Managing organisations

KEY TERM

Management may be defined, most simply, as 'getting things done through other people' (Stewart).

An organisation has been defined as 'a social arrangement for the controlled performance of collective goals.' This definition suggests the need for management.

(a) **Objectives** have to be set for the organisation.

(b) Somebody has to **monitor progress and results** to ensure that objectives are met.

(c) Somebody has to communicate and sustain **corporate values**, ethics and operating principles.

(d) Somebody has to look after the interests of the **organisation's owners** and other **stakeholders**.

QUESTION

Management structure

John, Paul, George and Ringo set up in business together as repairers of musical instruments. Each has contributed $5,000 as capital for the business. They are a bit uncertain as to how they should run the business and, when they discuss this in the pub, they decide that attention needs to be paid to planning what they do, reviewing what they do and controlling what they do.

Suggest two ways in which John, Paul, George and Ringo can manage the business assuming no other personnel are recruited.

ANSWER

The purpose of this exercise has been to get you to separate the issues of management functions from organisational structure and hierarchy. John, Paul, George and Ringo have a number of choices. Here are some extreme examples.

(a)   All the management activities are the job of one person.

In this case, Paul, for example, could plan, direct and control the work and the other three would do the work.

(b)   Division of management tasks between individuals could be carried out (repairing drums **and** ensuring plans are adhered to would be Ringo's job, and so on).

(c)   Management by committee. All of them could sit down and work out the plan together etc. In a small business with equal partners this is likely to be most effective.

Different organisations have different structures for carrying out management functions. For example, some organisations have separate strategic planning departments. Others do not.

In a **private sector business**, managers act, ultimately, on behalf of shareholders. In practical terms, shareholders rarely interfere, as long as the business delivers profits year on year.

In a **public sector organisation**, management acts on behalf of the Government. Politicians in a democracy are in turn accountable to the electorate. More of the objectives of a public sector organisation might be set by the 'owners' – ie the Government – rather than by the management. The Government might also tell senior management to carry out certain policies or plans, thereby restricting management's discretion.

1.2 Authority, accountability and responsibility

It is the role of the manager to **take responsibility** and **organise people** to get things done. This involves the use of **authority** and **power** and implies a hierarchy in which power is delegated downwards while **accountability** is rendered upwards.

Authority is the decision-making discretion given to a manager, while responsibility is the obligation to perform duties. Sufficient authority should be granted to permit the efficient discharge of the appointed responsibility. Delegation is essential wherever there is a hierarchy of management. Power is the **ability** to do something whereas authority is the **right** to do something; expert power is possessed by those acknowledged as experts.

It is easy to confuse **authority**, **accountability** and **responsibility** since they are all to do with the **allocation of power within an organisation**.

1.3 Authority

Organisational authority: the scope and amount of discretion given to a person to make decisions, by virtue of the position they hold in the organisation.

The authority and power structure of an organisation defines two things.

*   The part which each member of the organisation is expected to perform
*   The relationship between the members

A person's (or office's) authority can come from a variety of sources, including from above (supervisors) or below (if the position is elected). Managerial authority thus has three aspects.

*   Making decisions within the scope of one's own managerial authority
*   Assigning tasks to subordinates
*   Expecting and requiring satisfactory performance of these tasks by subordinates

1.4 Responsibility and accountability

Responsibility is the liability of a person to discharge duties. Responsibility is the obligation to do something; in an organisation, it is the duty of an official to carry out assigned tasks.

With responsibility, we must associate **accountability**. Managers are accountable **to** their superiors **for** their actions and are obliged to report to their superiors how well they have exercised the authority delegated to them.

1.5 Delegation

Delegation of authority occurs in an organisation where a superior gives a subordinate the discretion to make decisions within a certain sphere of influence. This can only occur if the superior initially possesses the authority to delegate; a subordinate cannot be given organisational authority to make decisions unless it would otherwise be the superior's right to make those decisions. Delegation of authority is the process by which a superior gives a subordinate the authority to carry out an aspect of the superior's job. Without delegation, a formal organisation could not exist.

When a superior delegates authority to a subordinate, the subordinate is accountable to the superior. However, the superior **remains fully accountable** to **their** superiors; responsibility and accountability cannot be abdicated by delegation.

As well as being essential for running an organisation, delegation brings a number of other benefits.

(a) **Training**. Subordinates gain experience of problems and responsibility, which helps to prepare them for promotion and contributes to the avoidance of crises of management succession.

(b) **Motivation**. Herzberg found that responsibility was an important factor in job satisfaction and motivation.

(c) **Assessment**. Subordinates' performance in relation to delegated responsibility can be used as a measure of their need for further training and experience and their readiness for promotion.

(d) **Decisions**. Delegation brings decisions closer to the situations that require them, potentially improving them by having them made by those with most knowledge of the problems and factors involved.

1.6 Authority and power

If an organisation is to function as a co-operative system of individuals, some people must have authority or power over others. Authority and power flow **downwards** through the formal organisation.

(a) **Authority** is the right to do something; in an organisation it is the right of a manager to require a subordinate to do something in order to achieve the goals of the organisation.

(b) **Power** is distinct from authority, but is often associated with it. **While authority is the right to do something, power is the ability to do it**.

Weber put the kind of authority we see in organisations into a wider context, proposing that there were three ways in which people could acquire legitimate power (or authority).

(a) **Charismatic authority** arises from the personality of the leader and their ability to inspire devotion through, for example, sanctity, heroism or example.

(b) **Traditional authority** rests on established belief in the importance of immemorial tradition and the status it confers.

(c) **Rational-legal** authority raises from the working of accepted normative rules, such as are found in organisations and democratic governments.

1.7 Power and influence

Influence is the process by which one person in an organisation, A, modifies the behaviour or attitudes of another person, B. An individual may have the ability to make others act in a certain way, without having the organisational authority to do so: informal leaders are frequently in this position.

The following types of power can be found in organisations.

Power	Detail
Physical power	This is the power of superior force.
Resource power	This is the control over resources which are valued by the individual or group.
Coercive power	This is power based on fear of punishment.
Reward power	This is related to resource power. Senior managers may have the power to grant pay increases to subordinates.
Position power or legitimate power	This is the power which is associated with a particular job in an organisation. It is more or less the same as authority.
Expert power	This is power which is based on expertise, although it only works if others acknowledge that expertise.
Referent power	This power lies in the personal qualities of the individual.
Negative power	This is the use of disruptive attitudes and behaviour to stop things from happening.

QUESTION

Power

What kind of power is used by a manager who promises a pay increase if productivity rises?

A	Position power	C	Reward power
B	Resource power	D	Referent power

ANSWER

C   Reward power: reward power is an aspect of resource power so, while Option B is not incorrect, it is not as good an answer as Option C.

1.8 Power centres

The **degree** of power people exercise, and the **types** of power they are able to exploit, differ depending in part on their position in the organisation hierarchy. The effects of personal power vary: the chief executive's use of personal power will be more far reaching in the organisation as a whole than that of a junior manager.

1.8.1 Senior management

Senior managers have coercive and reward powers, and most importantly take decisions relating to personnel.

1.8.2 Middle managers

Middle managers have a number of power sources. They have some reward power over their own subordinates. They may have expert power and negative power to delay or subvert decisions taken by senior managers. They need legitimate power, hence the need for formal job descriptions, authorisation limits, and so on.

1.8.3 Interest groups

There are also formal interest groups; that is, groups which are perceived to represent the interests of their members. Such groups tend to wield greater power in conflict situations than their members as individuals. Examples include trade unions and occupational and professional groups.

1.8.4 Departmental power

The power exercised by individual departments will vary.

Some departments in the technostructure exercise power by the use of **functional authority**, for instance, by specifying procedures. Other departments are important as they deal with **key strategic contingencies**.

1.9 The manager's role in organising work

Managers have **key roles** in work planning, resource allocation and project management.

1.9.1 Work planning

Work planning is the establishment of work methods and practices to ensure that predetermined objectives are efficiently met at all levels.

(a)   **Task sequencing** or **prioritisation** ie considering tasks in order of importance for achieving objectives and meeting deadlines

(b)   **Scheduling** or **timetabling tasks**, and allocating them to different individuals within appropriate time scales

(c)   Establishing **checks and controls** to ensure that:

   (i)   Priority deadlines are being met and work is not 'falling behind'
   (ii)   Routine tasks are achieving their objectives

(d)   **Contingency plans:** arrangements for what should be done if changes or problems occur, eg computer system failure or industrial action

(e)   **Co-ordinating** the efforts of individuals: integrating plans and schedules so that data and work flows smoothly from one stage of an operation to another

Some jobs (eg assembly line work) are entirely routine, and can be performed one step at a time, but for most people some kind of ongoing planning and adjustment will be required.

1.9.2 Assessing where resources are most usefully allocated

In broad terms, managers and supervisors have access to the following resources, which can be allocated or deployed to further the unit's objectives.

(a)   **Human resources**: staff time and skills
(b)   **Material resources**, including raw materials, equipment, machine time and office space
(c)   **Financial resources**, within budget guidelines
(d)   **Information**

The first three of these are sometimes called 'the 4Ms': Manpower, Machine capacity, Materials and Money.

A manager or supervisor may be responsible for allocating resources between:

(a)   Different ways to achieve the same objective (eg to increase total profits, sell more – or cut costs)
(b)   Competing areas, where total resources are limited

A piece of work will be **high priority** in the following cases.

•   If it has to be completed by a certain time (ie a deadline)
•   If other tasks depend on it
•   If other people depend on it
•   If it has an important potential consequence or impact

Routine priorities or regular peak times (eg tax returns) can be planned ahead of time, and other tasks planned around them.

Non-routine priorities occur when unexpected demands are made. Thus planning of work should cover routine scheduled peaks and contingency plans for unscheduled peaks and emergencies.

1.9.3 Projects

A **project** is 'an undertaking that has a beginning and an end and is carried out to meet established goals within cost, schedule and quality objectives'. (Haynes, 1997).

The main difference between project planning and other types of planning is that a project is not generally a repetitive activity. Projects generally:

- Have specific start and end points
- Have well-defined objectives, cost and time schedules
- Cut across organisational and functional boundaries

The relocation of offices, the introduction of a new information system or the launch of a new product may be undertaken as a project. Other examples include building/capital projects, such as factory construction or bridge building.

1.9.4 Project management

The job of **project management** is to foresee as many contingencies as possible and to plan, organise, co-ordinate and control activities.

Management task	Comment
Outline project planning	• Developing project targets such as overall costs or timescale (eg project should take 20 weeks) • Dividing the project into activities (eg analysis, programming, testing) and placing these activities into the right sequence, often a complicated task if overlapping • Developing the procedures and structures, managing the project (eg plan weekly team meetings, performance reviews)
Detailed planning	Identifying the tasks and resource requirements; network analysis for scheduling
Teambuilding	The project manager has to meld the various people into an effective team
Communication	The project manager must let key project stakeholders know what is going on, and ensure that members of the project team are properly briefed
Co-ordinating project activities	Between the project team and clients/users, and other external parties (eg suppliers of hardware and software)
Monitoring and control	The project manager should determine causes of any departure from the plan, and take corrective measures
Problem resolution	Unforeseen problems may arise, and it falls on the project manager to sort them out, or to delegate the responsibility for doing so to a subordinate

2 Writers on management

The classical writers on management and organisation were largely concerned with **efficiency**.

2.1 Henri Fayol: five functions of management

Fayol was an administrator and proposed universal principles of organisation.

Fayol was a French industrialist who put forward and popularised the concept of the '**universality of management principles**': in other words, the idea that all organisations could be structured and managed according to certain rational principles. Fayol himself recognised that applying such principles in practice was not simple: 'Seldom do we have to apply the same principles twice in identical conditions; allowance must be made for different and changing circumstances.'

Fayol (1967) classified five **functions of management** which apply to any organisation.

Function	Comment
Planning	Determining **objectives**, and strategies, policies, programmes and procedures for achieving those objectives, for the organisation and its sub-units
Organising	Establishing a **structure of tasks** which need to be performed to achieve the goals of the organisation; grouping these tasks into jobs for individuals or teams; allocating jobs to sections and departments; **delegating** authority to carry out the jobs; and providing **systems of information** and communication, for the co-ordination of activities
Commanding	Giving **instructions** to subordinates to carry out tasks, for which the manager has authority (to make decisions) and responsibility (for performance)
Co-ordinating	**Harmonising** the goals and activities of individuals and groups within the organisation. Management must reconcile differences in approach, effort, interest and timing in favour of overall (or 'super-ordinate') shared goals.
Controlling	**Measuring** and **correcting** the activities of individuals and groups, to ensure that their performance is in accordance with plans. Deviations from plans are identified and corrected

You may be struck by two key 'omissions' from Fayol's classification, from a more modern viewpoint.

(a) '**Motivating**' is not mentioned. It is assumed that subordinates will carry out tasks when 'commanded' or instructed to do so, regardless of whether or how far they may 'want' to.

(b) '**Communicating**' is not mentioned, although it is implied by the process of commanding (giving instructions), co-ordinating (sharing information) and controlling (giving feedback).

Fayol's classification reflects the classical view that saw the act of management as the controlling of resources and processes. The idea that management is an **interpersonal** process, involving communication and the ability to influence and motivate, is a more recent concept.

EXAM FOCUS POINT

Although Fayol's 'managerial functions' may seem like a minor topic – and rather old-fashioned – it is a foundational model. The five functions are a helpful framework or starting point for discussing the nature of management and supervision – even if you prefer more modern alternatives such as Mintzberg's more fluid managerial roles or more interpersonally-based interpretations (including 'leadership', discussed later in this chapter).

BPP
LEARNING MEDIA

2.2 F W Taylor: scientific management

Taylor was an engineer and sought the most efficient methods.

Frederick W Taylor pioneered the **scientific management** movement in the US. He was among the first to argue that management should be based on 'well-recognised, clearly defined and fixed principles, instead of depending on more or less hazy ideas.' Taylor was a very skilled engineer and took an engineering efficiency approach to management.

The principles of scientific management (Taylor, 1911) include the following.

(a)   The development of a true **science of work**. 'All knowledge which had hitherto been kept in the heads of workmen should be gathered and recorded by management. Every single subject, large and small, becomes the question for scientific investigation, for reduction to law.'

(b)   The **scientific selection** and **progressive development** of workers. Workers should be carefully trained and given jobs to which they are best suited.

(c)   The application of techniques to **plan**, **measure and control work** for maximum productivity

(d)   The constant and intimate **co-operation between management and workers**: 'the relations between employers and men form without question the most important part of this art'

In practice, scientific management techniques included the following key elements.

(a)   **Work study techniques** were used to analyse tasks and establish the most efficient methods to use. No variation was permitted in the way work was done, since the aim was to use the 'one best way'.

(b)   **Planning and doing were separated**. It was assumed that the persons who were intellectually equipped to do a particular type of work were probably unlikely to be able to plan it to the best advantage: this was the manager's job.

(c)   Jobs were **micro-designed**: divided into single, simple task components which formed a whole specialised 'job' for an individual, rather than permitting an individual to perform whole or part-task processes. (Task 'meaning' and 'significance', now considered essential to job satisfaction, had not yet emerged as important values.)

(d)   Workers were **paid incentives** on the basis of acceptance of the new methods and output norms; the new methods greatly increased productivity and profits. Pay was assumed to be the only important motivating force.

Scientific management as practised by Taylor and contemporaries such as Gilbreth and Gantt was very much about **manual work**. However, elements of scientific management are still practised today, whenever there is a concern for productivity and efficiency.

CASE STUDY

Persistent Taylorism?

It has been argued that elements of Taylorism – maximising managerial control through the micro-design of jobs, automation and close supervision – can be seen in the management of junior staff in businesses such as:

•   Large fast-food franchises (such as McDonald's).

•   Call centres, where calls are scripted, timed and monitored – and (in some reported cases) staff must ask permission to leave the 'floor' to go to the toilet

2.3 Elton Mayo: human relations

Mayo and his colleagues investigated individual and group behaviour at work, as a factor in productivity.

In the 1920s, research began to show that managers needed to consider the complexity of **human behaviour**. It was recognised that an exclusive focus on technical competence (under scientific management) had resulted in social incompetence: managers were not taught how to manage people. At the same time, it emerged that being a 'small cog in the machine' was experienced as alienating and demoralising by workers – whatever the financial incentives offered. A more complex picture of human motivation began to emerge.

Elton Mayo was Professor of Industrial Research at the Harvard Business School. He was involved in a series of large-scale studies at the Western Electric Company's Hawthorne works in Chicago between 1924 and 1932. These studies were originally firmly set in the context of scientific management in that they began with an experiment into the effect of lighting on work output. However, it rapidly became apparent that **worker attitudes** and **group relationships** were of greater importance in determining the levels of production achieved than the lighting itself.

An important element in the Hawthorne studies (Mayo, 1933) was the investigation of the dynamics of work groups. The group was very effective in enforcing its behavioural norms in such matters as 'freezing out' unpopular supervisors and restricting output. It was concluded that people are motivated at work by a variety of psychological needs, including social or 'belonging' needs. This became the basis of the **human relations school** of management theory.

2.3.1 Neo-human relations

Later writers focused on a wider variety of workers' 'higher-order' needs, including the need for challenge, responsibility and personal development in the job. This became known as the **neo-human relations school**, which proposed important theories of motivation and job satisfaction.

The human relations approaches contributed an important awareness of the influence of the human factor at work (and particularly in the work group) on organisational performance. Most of its theorists attempted to offer guidelines to enable practising managers to satisfy and motivate employees and so (theoretically) to obtain the benefits of improved productivity.

However, the approach tends to emphasise the importance of work to the workers without really addressing the economic issues: there is still no proven link between job satisfaction and motivation, or either of these and productivity or the achievement of organisational goals, as we will see in Chapter 15.

2.4 Modern writers on management

Subsequent writers have taken a more **flexible** view of what managers do.

In the second half of the 20th century, writing on management became more diverse.

(a)   The early emphasis on the organisation of work has been continued in the field of **supervisory studies** and the development of specific management techniques, such as **project management**. The search for efficiency continues in the field of **work study** and **industrial engineering**.

(b)   Human relations theory has been enhanced by developments in the study of motivation, group and individual behaviour, leadership and other aspects of **industrial psychology**.

(c)   There has been much new writing on the nature of the **manager's task**: what it is to be a manager and what managers do, in increasingly complex and chaotic business environments.

2.5 Peter Drucker: the management process

Drucker emphasised the economic objective of managers in businesses.

Drucker argued that the manager of a business has one basic function – **economic performance**. In this respect, the business manager is different from the manager of any other type of organisation. Management can only justify its existence and its authority by the economic results it produces, even though as a consequence of its actions, significant non-economic results occur as well.

2.5.1 Management tasks

Drucker (1993) described the jobs of management within this basic function of economic performance as follows.

(a) **Managing a business.** The purposes of the business are to create a customer and innovation.

(b) **Managing managers.** The requirements here are:

- Management by objectives (or performance management)
- Proper structure of managers' jobs
- Creating the right spirit (culture) in the organisation
- Making a provision for the managers of tomorrow (managerial succession)
- Arriving at sound principles of organisation structure

(c) **Managing workers and work**

A manager's performance in all areas of management, including management of the business, can be enhanced by a study of the principles of management, the acquisition of 'organised knowledge' (eg management techniques) and systematic self-assessment.

2.5.2 Management processes

Drucker (1989) also grouped the work of the manager into five categories.

(a) **Setting objectives for the organisation.** Managers decide what the objectives of the organisation should be and quantify the targets of achievement for each objective. They must then communicate these targets to other people in the organisation.

(b) **Organising the work.** The work to be done in the organisation must be divided into manageable activities and manageable jobs. The jobs must be integrated into a formal organisation structure, and people must be selected to do the jobs.

(c) **Motivating** employees and communicating information to them to enable them to do their work.

(d) **The job of measurement.** Management must:

(i) Establish **objectives** or yardsticks of performance for all personnel

(ii) Analyse **actual performance**, appraise it against the objectives or yardsticks which have been set, and analyse the comparison

(iii) **Communicate** the findings and explain their significance both to subordinate employees and to superiors

(e) **Developing people.** The manager 'brings out what is in them or he stifles them. He strengthens their integrity or he corrupts them'.

Every manager performs all five functions listed above, no matter how good or bad a manager they are. However, a bad manager performs these functions badly, whereas a good manager performs them well. Unlike Fayol, Drucker emphasised the importance of **communication** in the functions of management.

2.6 Mintzberg: the manager's role

Mintzberg described managerial roles, arguing that management is a disjointed, non-systematic activity.

Henry Mintzberg (1989) did a study of a relatively small sample of US corporations to see how senior managers actually spend their time. He suggests that in their daily working lives managers fulfil three **types** of managerial role.

Role category	Role	Comment
Interpersonal Based on manager's formal authority or position	**Figurehead** (or ceremonial)	A large part of a Chief Executive's time is spent representing the company at dinners, conferences, and so on.
	Leader	Hiring, firing and training staff, motivating employees, and reconciling individual goals with the objectives of the organisation.
	Liaison	Making contacts outside the vertical chain of command. Some managers spend up to half their meeting time with their peers rather than with their subordinates.
Informational Based on managers' access to: • Upward and downward channels • Many external contacts	**Monitor**	The manager monitors the environment, and receives information from subordinates, superiors and peers in other departments. Much of this information is of an informal nature, derived from the manager's network of contacts.
	Spokesperson	The manager provides information on behalf of the unit and/or organisation to interested parties.
	Disseminator	The manager disseminates relevant information to subordinates.
Decisional Based on the manager's formal authority and access to information, which allow him to take decisions relating to the work of the department as a whole.	**Entrepreneur**	A manager initiates projects to improve the department or to help it react to a changed environment.
	Disturbance handler	A manager has to respond to unexpected pressures, taking decisions when there is deviation from the plan.
	Resource allocator	A manager takes decisions relating to the mobilisation and distribution of limited resources to achieve objectives.
	Negotiator	Both inside and outside the organisation, negotiation takes up a great deal of management time.

Mintzberg's research challenged the classical view of the manager as separate to, or above, the routine demands of day-to-day work.

(a)   Managers are not always able to be reflective, systematic planners.

(b)   Managerial work is disjointed and discontinuous.

(c)   Managers do have routine duties to perform, especially of a ceremonial nature (receiving important guests) or related to authority (signing cheques as a signatory) – contrary to the myth that all routine work is done by juniors.

(d)   Managers prefer verbal and informal information to the formal output of management information systems. Verbal information is 'hotter' and probably easier to grasp.

(e)   Management cannot be reduced to a science or a profession. According to Mintzberg, managerial processes cannot be analysed scientifically or codified into an examinable body of theory.

Mintzberg states that general management is, in practice, a matter of **judgement and intuition**, gained from **experience** in **particular situations** rather than from abstract principles. 'Fragmentation and verbal communication' characterise the manager's work.

QUESTION   Managerial roles

Who suggested that a primary managerial role is 'developing people'?

A   Handy   C   Herzberg
B   Taylor   D   Drucker

ANSWER

The correct answer is D. Drucker.

3   Management and supervision

There are different levels of management in most organisations. A finance department in an organisation might be headed by the finance director (A) supported by a chief financial accountant (B) and chief management accountant (C). Lower down in the hierarchy assistant accountants might report to (B) and (C).

Supervision is the interface between the operational core (non-managerial workers) and management.

3.1 The supervisor's role

The supervisor is the lowest level of management, at the **interface** between managerial and non-managerial staff.

The key features of supervision are as follows.

(a)   A supervisor is usually a **front-line manager**, dealing with the levels of the organisation where the bread-and-butter work is done. They will deal with matters such as staffing and health and safety at the day-to-day operational level, where a manager might deal with them at a policy-making level.

(b)   A supervisor does not spend all their time on the managerial aspects of their job. Much of the time will be spent doing **technical/operational work**.

(c)   A supervisor is a **gatekeeper** or filter for communication between managerial and non-managerial staff, both **upward** (conveying reports and suggestions) and **downward** (conveying policies, instructions and feedback).

(d)   The supervisor monitors and controls work by means of **day-to-day, frequent and detailed information:** higher levels of management plan and control using longer-term, less frequent and less detailed information, which must be 'edited' or selected and reported by the supervisor.

Above the supervisor there may be several levels of management. Authority, responsibility and the timescale for decision-making all increase as the scalar chain is ascended. However, all managerial work may be considered to have some elements of similarity: it may be argued that supervisors carry out Fayol's five functions of management at a lower level.

QUESTION

Supervising work

Bert Close has decided to delegate the task of identifying the reasons for machine 'down' time (when machines are not working) over the past three months to Brenda Cartwright. This will involve her in talking to operators, foremen and supervisors and also liaising with other departments to establish the effects of this down time. What will Bert need to do to delegate this task effectively? List at least four items he will need to cover with Brenda.

ANSWER

- Identify task objectives
- Explain limits within which Brenda will work
- Deadlines

- Formats of reporting results
- Progress monitoring

---

4 What is leadership?

4.1 Management and leadership

There are many different definitions of **leadership**. Key themes (which are also used to distinguish leadership from management) include: interpersonal influence; securing willing commitment to shared goals; creating direction and energy; and an orientation to change.

The terms 'management' and 'leadership' are often used interchangeably. In some cases, management skills and theories have simply been relabelled to reflect the more fashionable term. However, there have been many attempts to distinguish meaningfully between them. It has been suggested that leadership and management involve two distinct sets of action. Management is about coping with **complexity**: its functions are to do with logic, structure, analysis and control, and are aimed at producing order, consistency and predictability. Leadership, by contrast, is about coping with **change**: its activities include creating a sense of direction, communicating strategy, and energising, inspiring and motivating others to translate the vision into action.

Management can be exercised over resources, activities, projects and other essential non-personal things. Leadership can only be exercised over **people**.

4.2 Key leadership skills

Key leadership skills may be identified in a range of interpersonal and business areas.

There are a range of business and managerial skills important to a good leader, including:

(a) **Entrepreneurship**: the ability to spot business opportunities and mobilise resources to capitalise on them

(b) **Interpersonal skills**, such as networking, rapport building, influencing, negotiating, conflict resolution, listening, counselling, coaching and communicating assertively

(c) **Decision-making and problem-solving** skills, including seeing the big picture

(d) **Time management and personal organisation**

(e) **Self-development** skills: the ability to learn continuously from experience, to grow in self-awareness and to exploit learning opportunities

4.3 Theories of leadership

There are three basic **schools of leadership theory**: trait ('qualities') theories, style theories and contingency (including situational and functional) theories.

There are three basic 'schools' of leadership theory.

School	Comment
Trait theories	Based on analysing the personality characteristics or preferences of successful leaders
Style theories	Based on the view that leadership is an interpersonal process whereby different leader behaviours influence people in different ways. More or less effective patterns of behaviour (or 'styles') can therefore be adopted
Contingency theories	Based on the belief that there is no 'one best way' of leading, but that effective leaders adapt their behaviour to the specific and changing variables in the leadership context: the nature of the task, the personalities of team members, the organisation culture, and so on

We will look at each of these in turn.

5 Leadership skills and styles

5.1 Trait or 'qualities' theories

Early theories suggested that there are certain personal **qualities** common to 'great men' or successful leaders. In other words, **'leaders are born, not made'**.

Various studies have attempted to determine exactly **which** qualities are essential in a leader. One American study cites the following.

- Judgement
- Drive
- Fairness
- Energy

- Initiative
- Human relations skill
- Ambition
- Emotional stability

- Integrity
- Decisiveness
- Dedication
- Co-operation

- Foresight
- Dependability
- Objectivity

Trait theory has been more or less discredited.

(a) The premise that certain traits (or qualities) are absolutely necessary for effective leadership has never been substantiated.

(b) The lists of traits proposed for leaders have been vast, varied and contradictory.

(c) Trait theories ignore the complexities of the leadership situation, and not everybody with leadership 'traits' turns out to be a good leader.

5.2 Style theories of leadership

Leadership styles are clusters of leadership behaviour that are used in different ways in different situations. While there are many different classifications of style, they mainly relate to the extent to which the leader is focused primarily on task/performance (directive behaviour) or relationships/people (supportive behaviour). Key style models include:

- The **Ashridge Model**: tells, sells, consults, joins
- **Blake and Mouton**'s **Managerial Grid**: concern for task, concern for people

There are various classifications of leadership style. Although the labels and definitions of styles vary, style models are often talking (broadly) about the same thing – a continuum of behaviours from:

(a)   Wholly task-focused, directive leadership behaviours (representing high leader control) at one extreme, and

(b)   Wholly people-focused, supportive/relational leadership behaviours (representing high subordinate discretion) at the other

EXAM FOCUS POINT

Leadership can be linked with theories of motivation and management style.

5.2.1 The Ashridge Management College model

The Research Unit at Ashridge Management College distinguished four different management styles (Goold and Campbell, 1988). (These are outlined, with their strengths and weaknesses, in the following table.) The researchers labelled their styles:

- Tells
- Sells
- Consults
- Joins

(a)   **Tells (autocratic)**
The 'tells' style is where the **leader makes all of the decisions** and issues instructions which must be obeyed without question. Quick decisions can be made when speed is required but it does not encourage initiative and commitment from subordinates.

(b)   **Sells (persuasive)**
This style is where the leader still makes all of the decisions but believes that **subordinates have to be motivated to accept them** and carry them out properly. Employees are made aware of the reasons for decisions but they may not accept the decisions.

(c)   **Consults**
This style is where the **leader confers with subordinates** and takes their views into account but retains the final say. This encourages motivation and employees can contribute their knowledge but it may take much longer to reach decisions.

(d)   **Joins (democratic)**
This style is where the leader and followers make the decision on the **basis of consensus**. This can provide high motivation and commitment from employees but decision-making might become a very long process.

The Ashridge studies found that:

(a)   In an ideal world, subordinates preferred the 'consults' style of leadership.

(b)   People led by a 'consults' manager had the most favourable attitude to their work.

(c)   Most subordinates feel they are being led by a 'tells' or 'sells' manager.

(d)   In practice, **consistency** was far more important to subordinates than any particular style. The least favourable attitudes were found among subordinates who were unable to perceive any consistent style of leadership in their superiors.

QUESTION

Styles of leadership

Suggest an appropriate style of leadership for each of the following situations. Think about your reasons for choosing each style in terms of the results you are trying to achieve, the need to secure commitment from others, and potential difficulties with both.

(a) Due to external factors, the budget for your department has been reduced and 25% of your staff must be made redundant. Records of each employee's performance are available.

(b) There is a recurring administrative problem which is minor, but irritating to everyone in your department. Several solutions have been tried in the past, but without success. You think you have a remedy which will work, but unknown problems may arise, depending on the decisions made.

ANSWER

(a) You may have to 'tell' here: nobody is going to like the idea and, since each person will have their own interests at heart, you are unlikely to reach consensus. You could attempt to 'sell', if you can see a positive side to the change in particular cases: opportunities for retraining, say.

(b) You could 'consult' here: explain your remedy to staff and see whether they can suggest potential problems. They may be in a position to offer solutions – and, since the problem affects them too, they should be committed to solving it.

5.2.2 Blake and Mouton's Managerial Grid

Robert Blake and Jane Mouton (1964) carried out research (The Ohio State Leadership Studies) into managerial behaviour and observed two basic dimensions of leadership: **concern for production** (or task performance) and **concern for people**.

Along each of these two dimensions, managers could be located at any point on a continuum from very low to very high concern. Blake and Mouton observed that the two concerns did not seem to correlate, positively or negatively: a high concern in one dimension, for example, did not seem to imply a high or low concern in the other dimension. Individual managers could therefore reflect various permutations of task/people concern.

Blake and Mouton modelled these permutations as a grid. One axis represented concern for people, and the other concern for production. Blake and Mouton allotted nine points to each axis, from 1 (low) to 9 (high).

A questionnaire was designed to enable users to analyse and plot the positions of individual respondents on the grid. This was to be used as a means of analysing individuals' **managerial styles** and areas of weakness or 'unbalance', for the purposes of management development.

The managerial grid

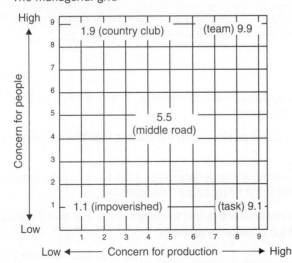

The extreme cases shown on the grid are:

(a) 1.1 **impoverished:** the manager is lazy, showing little interest in either staff or work.

(b) 1.9 **country club:** the manager is attentive to staff needs and has developed satisfying relationships. However, there is little attention paid to achieving results.

(c) 9.1 **task management:** almost total concentration on achieving results. People's needs are virtually ignored.

(d) 5.5 **middle of the road** or the **dampened pendulum:** adequate performance through balancing (or switching between) the necessity to get out work with team morale.

(e) 9.9 **team:** high work accomplishment through 'leading' committed people who identify themselves with the organisational aims.

The managerial grid was intended as an appraisal and management development tool. It recognises that a balance is required between concern for task and concern for people, and that a high degree of both is possible (and highly effective) at the same time.

5.2.3 Evaluating the managerial grid

The grid thus offers a number of useful insights for the identification of management **training and development** needs. It shows in an easily assimilated form where the behaviour and assumptions of a manager may exhibit a lack of balance between the dimensions and/or a low degree of concern in either dimension or both. It may also be used in team member selection, so that a 1.9 team leader is balanced by a 9.1 co-leader, for example.

However, the grid is a simplified model, and as such has practical limitations.

(a) It assumes that 9.9 is the desirable model for effective leadership. In some managerial contexts, this may not be so. Concern for people, for example, would not be necessary in a context of comprehensive automation: compliance is all that would be required.

(b) It is open to oversimplification. Scores can appear polarised, with judgements attached about individual managers' suitability or performance. The grid is intended as a simplified 'snapshot' of a manager's preferred style, not a comprehensive description of their performance.

(c) Organisational context and culture, technology and other 'givens' (Handy) influence the manager's style of leadership, not just the two dimensions described by the grid.

(d) Any managerial theory is only useful in so far as it is useable in practice by managers: if the grid is used only to inform managers that they 'must acquire greater concern for people', it may result in stress, uncertainty and inconsistent behaviour.

EXAM FOCUS POINT

The positions on Blake and Mouton's grid are a likely source of examination questions.

QUESTION

The managerial grid

Here are some statements about a manager's approach to meetings. Which position on Blake and Mouton's grid do you think each might represent?

(a) I attend because it is expected. I either go along with the majority position or avoid expressing my views.

(b) I try to come up with good ideas and push for a decision as soon as I can get a majority behind me. I don't mind stepping on people if it helps a sound decision.

(c) I like to be able to support what my boss wants and to recognise the merits of individual effort. When conflict rises, I do a good job of restoring harmony.

ANSWER

(a) 1.1: low task, low people   (c)   1.9: high people, low task
(b) 9.1: high task, low people

5.2.4 Limitations of style approaches

Perhaps the most important criticism of the style approach is that it does not consider all the variables that contribute to the practice of effective leadership.

(a) The manager's personality (or 'acting' ability) may simply not be **flexible** enough to utilise different styles effectively.

(b) The demands of the task, technology, organisation culture and other managers **constrain** the leader in the range of styles effectively open to them. (If their own boss practices an authoritarian style, and the team are incompetent and require close supervision, no amount of theorising on the desirability of participative management will make it possible ...)

(c) **Consistency** is important to subordinates. If a manager adapts their style to changing situations, they may simply perceive him to be fickle, or may suffer insecurity and stress.

In practice, it is often noted that there is no simple solution that an individual manager can use to decide which style to adopt to be most effective.

It is the consideration of this wide set of variables that has led to the development of the contingency approach to leadership.

5.3 Contingency approaches to leadership

In essence, contingency theory sees effective leadership as being dependent on a number of variable or contingent factors. There is no one right way to lead that will fit all situations. The ability of a manager to be a leader, and to influence their subordinate work group, depends on the particular situation and will vary from case to case.

Leaders need to adapt their style to the needs of the team and situation. This is the basis of **contingency approaches** such as:

- **Fiedler**'s 'psychologically close' and 'psychologically distant' styles
- **John Adair**'s 'action-centred' leadership model – based on 'situations' or 'functions'

5.3.1 F E Fiedler

Perhaps the leading advocate of contingency theory is Fiedler (1967). He carried out extensive research on the nature of leadership and found that people become leaders partly because of their own attributes and partly because of their situation. He studied the relationship between style of leadership and the effectiveness of the work group and identified two types of leader.

(a) **Psychologically distant managers** (PDMs) maintain distance from their subordinates.

(i) They formalise the roles and relationships between themselves and their superiors and subordinates.

(ii) They choose to be withdrawn and reserved in their interpersonal relationships within the organisation (despite having good interpersonal skills).

(iii) They prefer formal consultation methods rather than seeking the opinions of their staff informally.

PDMs judge subordinates on the basis of performance, and are primarily task oriented: Fiedler found that leaders of the most effective work groups tend to be PDMs.

Fiedler also argued that the leadership style adopted is relatively stable, and a feature of a leader's personality that could therefore be predicted.

(b)   **Psychologically close managers** (PCMs) are closer to their subordinates.

    (i)   They do not seek to formalise roles and relationships with superiors and subordinates.

    (ii)   They are more concerned about maintaining good human relationships at work than ensuring that tasks are carried out efficiently.

    (iii)   They prefer informal contacts to regular formal staff meetings.

Fiedler suggested that the effectiveness of a work group depended on the **situation**, made up of three key variables.

- The relationship **between the leader and the group** (trust, respect, and so on)
- The extent to which the **task** is defined and structured
- The **power** of the leader in relation to the group (authority, and power to reward and punish)

A situation is **favourable** to the leader when:

- The leader is liked and trusted by the group
- The tasks of the group are clearly defined and unambiguous
- The position power of the leader (ie to reward and punish with organisation backing) is high

Fiedler suggested that:

(a)   A structured (or psychologically distant) style works best when the situation is either very favourable, or very unfavourable to the leader.

(b)   A supportive (or psychologically close) style works best when the situation is moderately favourable to the leader.

(c)   'Group performance will be contingent upon the appropriate **matching of leadership styles** and the **degree of favourableness** of the group situation for the leader.' (Fiedler)

This is summed up in the diagram below.

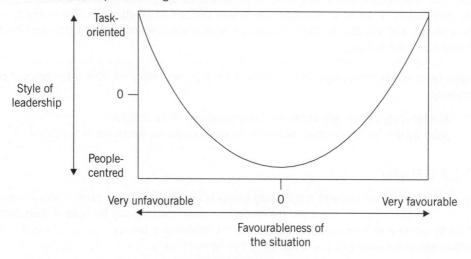

5.3.2 John Adair: action-centred leadership

The 'action-centred' or 'functional' leadership model (Adair, 1973) is part of the contingency school of thought, because it sees the leadership process in a context made up of three interrelated variables: **task needs**, the individual needs of group members and the **needs of the group** as a whole. These needs must be examined in the light of the whole situation, which dictates the relative priority that must be given to each of the three sets of needs. Effective leadership is a process of identifying and acting on that priority, exercising a relevant cluster of roles to meet the various needs.

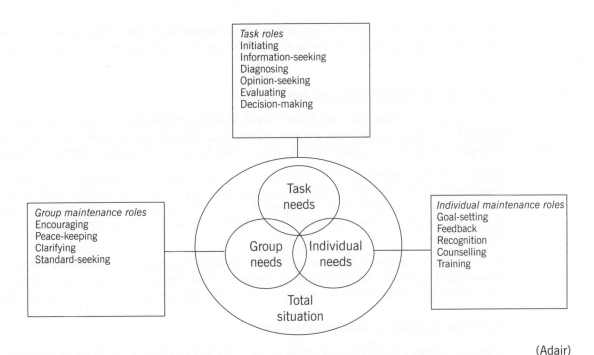

(Adair)

Adair argued that the common perception of leadership as 'decision-making' was inadequate to describe the range of action required by this complex situation. He developed a scheme of leadership training based on precept and practice in each of eight leadership 'activities' which are applied to task, team and individual: hence, the '**action-centred leadership**' model.

- Defining the task
- Planning
- Briefing
- Controlling

- Evaluating
- Motivating
- Organising
- Setting an example

5.3.3 Bennis: the distinction between management and leadership

Warren Bennis puts forward some specific differences between the role of the manager and the role of the leader.

(a)   **The manager** administers and maintains, by focusing on systems and controls and the short term.

(b)   **The leader** innovates, focuses on people and inspires trust, and holds a long-term view.

As a further distinction, Bennis distinguishes between the manager as someone who '**does things right**' and the leader who '**does the right thing**'.

Bennis studied leadership by examining leaders of every description in the hope of finding some common characteristics and concluded that there is no one right way to lead, but it does set out common competencies displayed by leaders. Bennis (1985) calls them:

(a)   The **management of attention**: a compelling cause or vision, to give focus
(b)   The **management of meaning**: the ability to communicate
(c)   The **management of trust**: being consistent and honest
(d)   The **management of self**: being aware of personal weaknesses and strengths

Other tasks of the leader that Bennis sees as important are:

(a)   Constantly reminding people why their work is important
(b)   Creating an atmosphere of trust
(c)   Encouraging curiosity and risk taking in the organisation culture
(d)   Fostering an atmosphere of 'hope' which can be particularly helpful when things go wrong

Bennis believes that leadership in the modern age is a **shared task**, with power spread around rather than centralised. It could be that the most important role of modern leaders is deciding who will be in their teams.

5.3.4 Heifetz: dispersed leadership

This approach recognises the importance of social relations, the need for a leader to be accepted and the fact that nobody will be an ideal leader in every circumstance. Also referred to as 'informal' or 'emergent', it proposes that individuals at all organisational levels can exert a 'leadership influence'.

Heifetz (1994) distinguishes between the exercise of 'leadership' and the exercise of 'authority'. This separates leadership from the formal organisational hierarchy and traditional positions of 'power'. The leader can only be identified by examining relationships with the 'followers' in the group – they could quite easily be someone who 'emerges', rather than someone who has been predefined as the leader from the outset.

This approach is more sociological and political in its basis than traditional management thinking, drawing as it does upon the prevailing organisational culture and context. A leader's individual qualities are less important than the leadership process, and the relationships created and sustained within it.

5.3.5 An appraisal of contingency theory

Contingency theory usefully makes people aware of the factors affecting the choice of leadership style. However, Schein has pointed out that:

(a)   Key variables such as task structure, power and relationships are difficult to measure in practice.

(b)   Contingency theories do not always take into account the need for the leader to have technical competence relevant to the task.

Perhaps the major difficulty for any leader seeking to apply contingency theory, however, is actually to modify their behaviour as the situation changes.

PER performance objective PO5 requires you to contribute to the effective leadership and management of an organisation – managing yourself, others and resources effectively. The material covered in this chapter will help you achieve this.

EXAM FOCUS POINT

The syllabus Study Guide specifically mentions the work of:

*   Adair
*   Bennis
*   Fiedler
*   Heifetz
*   Kotter

Keep in mind that most of the quoted theories are North American in origin, and do not necessarily take account of cultural differences in other countries.

↳ **Management** is responsible for using the organisation's resources to meet its goals. It is accountable to the owners: shareholders in a business, or government in the public sector.

↳ It is the role of the manager to **take responsibility** and **organise people** to get things done. This involves the use of **authority** and **power** and implies a hierarchy in which power is delegated downwards while **accountability** is rendered upwards.

Authority is the decision-making discretion given to a manager, while responsibility is the obligation to perform duties. Sufficient authority should be granted to permit the efficient discharge of the appointed responsibility. Delegation is essential wherever there is a hierarchy of management. Power is the **ability** to do something whereas authority is the **right** to do something; expert power is possessed by those acknowledged as experts.

↳ Managers have **key roles** in work planning, resource allocation and project management.

↳ The classical writers on management and organisation were largely concerned with **efficiency**.

↳ **Fayol** was an administrator and proposed universal principles of organisation.

↳ **Taylor** was an engineer and sought the most efficient methods.

↳ **Mayo** and his colleagues investigated individual and group behaviour at work as a factor in productivity.

↳ **Subsequent writers** have taken a more **flexible** view of what managers do.

↳ **Drucker** emphasised the economic objective of managers in businesses.

↳ **Mintzberg** described managerial roles, arguing that management is a disjointed, non-systematic activity.

↳ **Supervision** is the interface between the operational core (non-managerial workers) and management.

↳ There are many different definitions of **leadership**. Key themes (which are also used to distinguish leadership from management) include: interpersonal influence; securing willing commitment to shared goals; creating direction and energy; and an orientation to change.

↳ **Key leadership skills** may be identified in a range of interpersonal and business areas.

↳ There are three basic **schools of leadership theory**: trait ('qualities') theories, style theories and contingency (including situational and functional) theories.

↳ Early theories suggested that there are certain personal qualities common to 'great men' or successful leaders. In other words, **'leaders are born, not made'**.

↳ **Leadership styles** are clusters of leadership behaviour that are used in different ways in different situations. While there are many different classifications of style, they mainly relate to the extent to which the leader is focused primarily on task/performance (directive behaviour) or relationships/people (supportive behaviour). Key style models include:

– The **Ashridge Model**: tells, sells, consults, joins
– **Blake and Mouton**'s **Managerial Grid**: concern for task, concern for people

↳ Leaders need to adapt their style to the needs of the team and situation. This is the basis of **contingency approaches** such as:

– **Fiedler**'s 'psychologically close' and 'psychologically distant' styles
– **John Adair**'s 'action-centred' leadership model – based on 'situations' or 'functions'

1   Which of the following is **not** one of Fayol's five functions of management?

A   Commanding   C   Communicating
B   Controlling   D   Co-ordinating

2   Who argued that management should be based on 'well-recognised, clearly defined and fixed principles, instead of depending on more or less hazy ideas'?

A   Fayol   C   Adair
B   Taylor   D   Fielder

3   The Hawthorne studies found that individual attitudes and group relationships help determine the level of output. True or false?

4   The overriding responsibility of the management of a business, according to Drucker, is employee development. True or false?

5   What managerial roles did Mintzberg describe and what categories did he group them into?

6   Is the statement below true or false?

'Frederick Taylor, despite his engineering background, was primarily concerned with the satisfaction workers obtained from their jobs.'

7   Which of the following is not one of the interpersonal roles of managers identified by Henry Mintzberg?

A   Handling disturbances
B   Reconciling individual needs with the requirements of the organisation
C   Training staff
D   Liaising outside the scalar chain

8   Complete the statement below using one of the words in the list given in brackets.

'.................................... authority cuts across departmental boundaries and enables managers to take decisions that affect staff in departments other than their own.'

(managerial, line, staff, functional, financial, formal)

9   A 'manager' might also be identified as a transformational leader. True or false?

10 If a manager confers with subordinates, takes their views and feelings into account, but retains the right to make a final decision, this is a:

A   Tells style   C   Consults style
B   Sells style   D   Joins style

11 What is the most effective style suggested by Blake and Mouton's Managerial Grid? Why is it so effective in theory, and why might it not be effective in practice?

12 John Adair formulated the:

A   Best fit model of leadership   C   Follower-readiness model of leadership
B   Action-centred model of leadership   D   Trait theory of leadership

ANSWERS TO QUICK QUIZ

1   C   Communicating

2   B   Taylor pioneered the scientific management movement in the USA.

3   True. It was concluded that people are motivated at work by a variety of psychological needs, including social or 'belonging' needs.

4   False. The overriding responsibility is economic performance.

5 | Category | Roles |
    |---|---|
    | Interpersonal: | Figurehead; leader; liaison |
    | Informational: | Monitor; spokesperson; disseminator |
    | Decisional: | Entrepreneur; disturbance handler; resource allocator; negotiator |

6   False. Taylor was entirely concerned with engineering efficiency and believed that the increases in pay that ensued from the adoption of his method should be sufficiently motivating for any good worker.

7   A   This is a decisional role. The 'disturbances' referred to are unpredictable situations that require managerial input to resolve.

8   Functional

9   False. Management is identified with 'transactional' leadership.

10 C   Make sure you can define the other styles as well.

11 9.9. It is effective if there is sufficient time and resources to attend fully to people's needs, if the manager is good at dealing with people and if the people respond. It is ineffective when a task has to be completed in a certain way or by a certain deadline, whether or not people like it

12 B   (You should be able to identify A as the work of Handy, and C as the work of Hersey and Blanchard.)

Now try ...

Attempt the questions below from the **Practice Question Bank**

Q56

Q57

Q58

Q59

Q60

Q61

Q62

Recruitment and selection (**Section 1**) are two core activities in the field of Human Resource Management (HRM). Together, they are broadly aimed at ensuring that the organisation has the human resources (labour and skills) it needs, when it needs them, in order to fulfil its objectives.

In this chapter, we look at the process of **recruitment** (**Sections 2 and 3**), which is about **obtaining candidates** and advertising the vacancy in the labour market (**Section 4**).

We then go on to cover the process of **selection**, which is about deciding which of the applicants is the **right candidate**. Once candidates have applied, there needs to be a systematic process to separate out those who are most suitable for the job (**Section 5**).

In **Sections 6 to 9**, we examine a range of selection tools. **Interviews** are the most popular – but not necessarily the most effective in their ability to predict future job performance! Organisations are increasingly using 'back-up' methods such as tests and group assessments.

In **Section 10**, we complete the planning and control cycle by suggesting how a manager might **evaluate** the effectiveness of the recruitment and selection process – and what might be done to improve it where necessary.

Bear in mind what these procedures are designed to **do**: identify the best person for the job **and** ensure fair treatment for all potential applicants.

Recruitment and selection

Study Guide	Intellectual level

D2 Recruitment and selection of employees

(a)	Explain the importance of effective recruitment and selection to the organisation.	K
(b)	Describe the recruitment and selection process and explain the stages in this process.	K
(c)	Describe the roles of those involved in the recruitment and selection processes.	K
(d)	Describe the methods through which organisations seek to meet their recruitment needs.	K
(e)	Explain the advantages and disadvantages of different recruitment and selection methods.	K

EXAM FOCUS POINT

A question requirement on recruitment may be combined with a requirement relating to selection. Some aspects of recruitment and/or selection will inevitably come up in the exam. Bear in mind that there are a number of procedures and techniques involved in selection. This part of the syllabus is a rich source of questions.

1 Recruitment and selection

The process of recruitment should be part of the organisation's human resource plan. People are a major organisational resource and must be managed as such.

1.1 Overview of recruitment and selection

Effective recruitment practices ensure that a firm has enough **people with the right skills**.

The **overall aim of the recruitment and selection process** in an organisation is to obtain the quantity and quality of employees required to fulfil the objectives of the organisation.

This process can be broken down into three main stages.

(a) **Defining requirements**, including the preparation of job descriptions, job specifications and person specifications (or personnel specifications).

(b) **Attracting applicants**, including the evaluation and use of various methods for reaching appropriate sources of labour (both within and outside the organisation).

(c) **Selecting** the appropriate candidates for the job, or the appropriate job for the candidate.

- Recruitment is the part of the process concerned with finding applicants: it is a positive action by management, going into the labour market (internal and external), communicating opportunities and information, and generating interest.

- Selection is the part of the employee resourcing process which involves choosing between applicants for jobs: it is largely a 'negative' process, eliminating unsuitable applicants.

In times of low unemployment, employers have to compete to **attract** desirable categories of labour. In times of high unemployment, and therefore plentiful supply the problem is not in attracting candidates, but in deciding the best way to **select** them. In times of low demand for labour, however, socially responsible employers may have the additional policy of using **existing staff** (internal recruitment) rather than recruiting from outside, in order to downsize staff levels through natural wastage and redeployment.

1.2 The importance of recruitment and selection

The founding belief of the human resources management (HRM) approach is that employees represent a scarce and crucial resource which must be obtained, retained, developed and mobilised for organisational success.

(a)   Recruitment (and training) issues are central to the business strategy.

(b)   Organisations need to deploy skills in order to succeed. Although the labour market might seem a 'buyer's market', in practice there are:

(i)   Skill shortages in key sectors (eg computing services) and local areas

(ii)   Mismatches between available skill supply and the demands of particular markets and organisations

Even in conditions of high overall employment, particular skill shortages still exist and may indeed be more acute because of recessionary pressures on education and training. Engineers and software designers, among other specialist and highly trained groups, are the target of fierce competition among employers, forcing a revaluation of recruitment and retention policies.

2   Responsibility for recruitment and selection

The recruitment process involves **personnel specialists** and **line managers**, sometimes with the help of recruitment **consultants**.

The people involved in recruitment and selection vary from organisation to organisation.

2.1 Senior managers

Senior managers/directors may be involved in recruiting people – from within or outside the organisation – for **senior positions**, or in authorising key appointments. For most other positions, they will not be directly involved. However, they are responsible for **human resources (HR) planning**: identifying the overall skill needs of the organisation, and the types of people it wishes to employ (perhaps as part of the corporate mission statement).

2.2 The human resources department

Some firms employ specialists to manage their recruitment and other human resources (HR) activities, often under the authority of the **human resources manager**.

The role of the HR function in recruitment and selection may include:

*   Assessing needs for human resources (HR planning)
*   Maintaining records of people employed
*   Keeping in touch with trends in the labour market
*   Advertising for new employees
*   Ensuring the organisation complies with equal opportunities and other legislation
*   Designing application forms
*   Liaising with recruitment consultants
*   Preliminary interviews and selection testing

2.3 Line managers

In many cases the recruit's prospective boss will be involved in the recruitment.

(a)   In a small business they might have sole responsibility for recruitment.

(b)   In larger organisations, line managers may be responsible for:

- Asking for more human resources: notifying vacancies or issuing a job requisition
- Advising on skill requirements and attributes required
- Selection interviewing (perhaps collaborating with HR specialists)
- Having a final say in the selection decision

The current trend is towards devolving recruitment and selection (among other Human Resource Management activities) increasingly to line management.

2.4 Recruitment consultants

Specialist recruitment consultants or agencies may be contracted to perform some recruitment tasks on the organisation's behalf, including:

(a)   Analysing, or being informed of, the requirements

(b)   Helping to draw up, or offering advice on, job descriptions, person specifications and other recruitment and selection aids

(c)   Designing job advertisements (or using other, informal methods and contacts, eg by 'head hunting')

(d)   Screening applications, so that those most obviously unsuitable are weeded out immediately

(e)   Helping with shortlisting for interview

(f)   Advising on, or conducting, first-round interviews

(g)   Offering a list of suitable candidates with notes and recommendations

2.4.1 Factors in the outsourcing decision

The decision of whether or not to use consultants will depend on a number of factors.

(a)   **Cost**

(b)   The level of expertise, specialist **knowledge and contacts** which the consultant can bring to the process

(c)   The level of recruitment expertise available **within the organisation**

(d)   Whether there is a need for **impartiality** which can only be filled by an outsider trained in objective assessment; if fresh blood is desired in the organisation, it may be a mistake to have insiders selecting clones of the common organisational type

(e)   Whether the use of an outside agent will be **supported** or resented/rejected by in-house staff

(f)   Whether the organisation **culture** supports in-house staff in making HR decisions (consultants are not tied by status or rank and can discuss problems freely at all levels)

(g)   **Time**; consultants will need to learn about the vacancy, the organisation and its requirements

(h)   **Supply of labour**; if there is a large and reasonably accessible pool of labour from which to fill a post, consultants will be less valuable, and if the vacancy is a standard one, and there are ready channels for reaching labour (such as professional journals), the use of specialists may not be cost effective

3   The recruitment process

Recruitment is a systematic process of (a) identifying and defining skill needs and (b) attracting suitably skilled candidates.

BPP
LEARNING MEDIA

3.1 A systematic approach

The recruitment process is part of a wider whole.

(a) Detailed **human resource planning** defines what resources the organisation needs to meet its objectives, and what sources of labour (internal and external) are available. The organisation's skill requirements may be met through recruitment – but there may also be plans for reducing staff numbers, redeployment, training and development, promotion, retention (to reduce loss of skills through staff turnover), and so on.

(b) **Job analysis** produces two outputs.

    (i) A **job description**: a statement of the component tasks, duties, objectives and standards involved in a job

    (ii) A **person specification**: a reworking of the job description in terms of the kind of person needed to perform the job

(c) Recruitment as such **begins with the identification of vacancies**, from the requirements of the human resource plan or by a **job requisition** from a department that has a vacancy.

(d) Preparation and publication of **recruitment advertising** will have three aims.

    (i) Attract the attention and interest of potentially suitable candidates.

    (ii) Give a favourable (but accurate) impression of the job and the organisation.

    (iii) Equip those interested to make an appropriate application (how and to whom to apply, desired skills, qualifications, and so on).

(e) Recruitment merges into **selection** when processing applications and assessing candidates.

(f) **Notifying applicants** of the results of the selection process is the final stage of the combined recruitment and selection process.

3.2 Job analysis, competences and job design

3.2.1 Job analysis

Job analysis determines the requirement for a job. The job's tasks are set out in a job description. A **job specification** describes the skills or competences required for the job. A **person specification** describes the sort of person suitable for the job.

The management of the organisation needs to analyse the sort of work needed to be done in order to recruit effectively. The type of information needed is outlined below.

Type of information	Comments
Purpose of the job	This might seem obvious. As an accountant, you will be expected to analyse, prepare or provide financial information; but this has to be set in the context of the organisation as a whole.
Content of the job	The tasks you are expected to do. If the purpose of the job is to ensure, for example, that people get paid on time, the tasks involve include many activities related to payroll.
Accountabilities	These are the results for which you are responsible. In practice they might be phrased in the same way as a description of a task.
Performance criteria	These are the criteria which measure how good you are at the job. These are largely task related.
Responsibility	This denotes the importance of the job. For example, a person running a department and taking decisions involving large amounts of money is more responsible that someone who only does what they are told.

Type of information	Comments
Organisational factors	Who does the jobholder report to directly (line manager)?
Developmental factors	Likely promotion paths, if any, and career prospects. Some jobs are 'dead-end' if they lead nowhere.
Environmental factors	These include working conditions, security and safety issues and equipment.

3.2.2 Competences

A current approach to job design is the development and outlining of **competences**.

A person's competence is ' capacity that leads to behaviour that meets the job demands within the parameters of the organisational environment and that, in turn, brings about desired results'.

Some take this further and suggest that a competence embodies the ability to **transfer** skills and knowledge to new situations within the occupational area.

Different sorts of competences

(a)   **Behavioural/personal** competences are underlying personal characteristics and behaviour required for successful performance; for example, 'ability to relate well to others'. Most jobs require people to be good communicators.

(b)   **Work-based/occupational competences** are 'expectations of workplace performance and the outputs and standards people in specific roles are expected to obtain'. This approach is used in NVQ systems. They cover what people have to do to achieve the results of the job. For example, a competence for a Chartered Certified Accountant might be to 'produce financial and other statements and report to management'.

(c)   **Generic competences** can apply to all people in an occupation.

Some competences for managers are shown in the following table.

Competence area	Competence
Intellectual	• Strategic perspective • Analytical judgement • Planning and organising
Interpersonal	• Managing staff • Interpersonal sensitivity • Persuasiveness • Oral communication • Assertiveness and decisiveness
Adaptability	• Flexibility • Coping with change
Results	• Initiative • Motivation to achievement • Business sense

These competences can be elaborated by identifying **positive** and **negative** indicators.

3.2.3 Job design

Parameters of job design (Mintzberg, 1979).

(a)   **Job specialisation**

   (i)   **How many different tasks** are contained in the jobs and how broad and narrow are these tasks? **The task may be determined by operations management.** Until recently, there has

been a trend towards narrow specialisation, reinforced perhaps by demarcations laid down by trade unions. On the production line, a worker did the same task all the time. Modern techniques, however, require workers to be **multi-skilled**.

(ii) **To what extent does the worker have control over the work?** At one extreme ('scientific management') the worker has little control over the work. At the other extreme (eg an electrician) the worker controls the task.

(b) **Regulation of behaviour.** Co-ordination requires that organisations formalise behaviour so as to predict and control it.

(c) **Training** in **skills** and indoctrination in **organisational values**.

Belbin (1997) described a way of **tailoring job design** to delayered, team-based structures and flexible working systems.

(a) Flattened delayered hierarchies lead to greater flexibility but also to uncertainty and sometimes to a **loss of control**.

(b) Old hierarchies tended to be **clearer** in establishing responsibilities.

3.2.4 Job description

A **job description** sets out the purpose of the job, where it fits in the organisation structure, the context of the job, the accountabilities of the job and the main tasks the holder carries out.

Purposes of job descriptions

Purpose	Comment
Organisational	Defines the job's place in the organisational structure
Recruitment	Provides information for identifying the sort of person needed (person specification)
Legal	Provides the basis for a contract of employment
Performance	Performance objectives can be set around the job description

Contents of a job description

(a) **Job title** (eg Assistant Financial Controller). This indicates the function/department in which the job is performed, and the level of job within that function.

(b) **Reporting to** (eg the Assistant Financial Controller reports to the Financial Controller); in other words, the person's immediate boss (no other relationships are suggested here)

(c) **Subordinates** directly reporting to the job holder

(d) **Overall purpose** of the job, distinguishing it from other jobs

(e) **Principal accountabilities or main tasks**

(i) Group the main activities into a number of broad areas.

(ii) Define each activity as a statement of accountability: what the job holder is expected to achieve (eg **tests** new system to ensure they meet agreed systems specifications).

(f) The current fashion for multi-skilling means that **flexibility** is expected.

3.2.5 Role definitions

Whereas a **job** is a group of tasks, a role is more than this. A **role** is a part played by people in meeting their objectives by working competently and flexibly within the context of the organisation's objectives, structures and processes. A **role definition** is wider than a job description. It is less concerned with the details of the job content, but how people interpret the job.

3.2.6 Person specification

Possible areas the specification may cover include:

- Personal skills
- Qualifications
- Innate ability

- Motivation
- Personality

3.2.7 Rodger's Seven-point plan

Rodger (1952) devised a framework for the selection process that includes seven points.

Point	Examples
Physical make-up	Strength, appearance, health
Attainments	Qualifications, career achievements
General intelligence	Average, above average
Special aptitudes	Manual dexterity, mental sharpness
Interests	Mechanical, people-related
Disposition	Calm, independent
Circumstances	Location, car owner

The following diagram shows recruitment activities in more detail.

The Recruitment Process

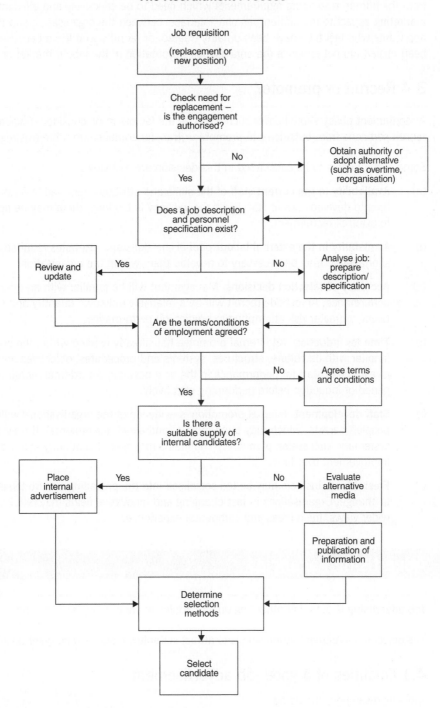

3.3 Recruitment policy

Detailed procedures for recruitment should only be devised and implemented in the context of a fair, consistent and coherent **policy**, or code of conduct.

A typical recruitment policy might deal with:

- Internal advertisement of vacancies, where possible
- Efficient and courteous processing of applications
- Fair and accurate provision of information to potential recruits
- Selection of candidates on the basis of suitability, without discrimination

Detailed procedures should be devised in order to make recruitment activity **systematic** and **consistent** throughout the organisation (especially where it is decentralised in the hands of line managers). Apart from the human resourcing requirements which need to be effectively and efficiently met, there is a **marketing** aspect to recruitment, as one 'interface' between the organisation and the outside world: applicants who feel they have been unfairly treated, or recruits who leave because they feel they have been misled, do not enhance the organisation's reputation in the labour market or the world at large.

3.4 Recruit or promote?

A recruitment policy should cover such areas as the factors to be considered when deciding whether to **recruit** someone from **outside** or to **promote** or **transfer** someone from the existing workforce instead.

Some of the factors to be considered in this decision are as follows.

(a) **Availability in the current staff** of the skills and attributes required to fill the vacancy. If the lead time to develop current staff to 'fit' the vacancy is too long, there may be no immediate alternative to external recruitment.

(b) **Availability in the external labour pool** of the skills and attributes required. Where there are skill shortages, it may be necessary to develop them within the organisation.

(c) **Accuracy of selection decisions**. Management will be familiar with an internal promotee and their performance. An outside recruit will be a relatively unknown quantity and the organisation will be taking a greater risk attempting to predict job performance.

(d) **Time for induction**. An internal promotee has already worked within the organisation and will be familiar with its culture, structures, systems and procedures, objectives and other personnel. This gives a head start for performance in the new position. An external recruit may have to undergo a period of induction before performing effectively.

(e) **Staff development**. Internal promotion is evidence of the organisation's willingness to develop people's careers, which may build morale (and avoid resentments). It may also be part of a systematic **succession plan** which maintains managerial continuity and individual performance improvement over time.

(f) **Fresh blood**. Insiders may be too socialised into the prevailing culture to see faults or be willing to change. Organisations in fast-changing and innovative fields may require new people with wider views, fresh ideas and competitor experience.

4   Advertising vacancies

Job advertising is aimed at attracting quality applicants and aiding self-selection.

The object of recruitment advertising is to attract suitable candidates and deter unsuitable candidates.

4.1 Qualities of a good job advertisement

Job advertisements should be:

(a) **Concise**, but comprehensive enough to be an accurate description of the job, its rewards and requirements

(b) **Attractive** to the maximum number of the right people

(c) **Positive and honest** about the organisation; disappointed expectations will be a prime source of dissatisfaction when an applicant actually comes into contact with the organisation

(d) **Relevant and appropriate to the job and the applicant**; skills, qualifications and special aptitudes required should be prominently set out, along with special features of the job that might attract – or indeed deter – applicants, such as shiftwork or extensive travel

4.2 Contents of a job advertisement

Typical contents of an advertisement targeted at external job seekers would include information about:

(a)   The **organisation**: its main business and location, at least

(b)   The **job**: title, main duties and responsibilities and special features

(c)   **Conditions**: special factors affecting the job

(d)   **Qualifications and experience** (required, and preferred); other attributes, aptitudes and/or knowledge required

(e)   **Rewards**: salary, benefits, opportunities for training, career development, and so on

(f)   **Application process**: how to apply, to whom, and by what date

It should encourage a degree of **self-selection**, so that the target population begins to narrow itself down. The information contained in the advertisement should deter unsuitable applicants as well as encourage potentially suitable ones.

4.3 Advertising media

> A number of print, electronic and interpersonal **media** are used for job **advertising**.

Media for recruitment advertising include the following.

(a)   **In-house magazine, noticeboards**, email or intranet. An organisation might invite applications from employees who would like a transfer or a promotion to the particular vacancy advertised, from within the internal labour pool.

(b)   **Professional and specialist newspapers or magazines**, such as *Accountancy Age, Marketing Week* or *Computing.*

(c)   **National newspapers**: often used for senior management jobs or vacancies for skilled workers, where potential applicants will not necessarily be found through local advertising.

(d)   **Local newspapers:** suitable for jobs where applicants are sought from the local area.

(e)   **Local radio, television and cinema**. These are becoming increasingly popular, especially for large-scale campaigns for large numbers of vacancies.

(f)   **Job centres**. Vacancies for unskilled work (rather than skilled work or management jobs) are advertised through local job centres, although in theory any type of job can be advertised here.

(g)   **School and university careers offices**. Ideally, the manager responsible for recruitment in an area should try to maintain a close liaison with careers officers. Some large organisations organise special meetings or **careers fairs** in universities and colleges, as a kind of showcase for the organisation and the careers it offers.

(h)   The **internet**. Many businesses advertise vacancies on their websites, or register vacancies with online databases. The advantages of '**e-recruitment**' include:

(i)   Large audience, reached at low cost

(ii)   Interactivity with links to information, downloadable application forms, email contacts, and so on

(iii)   Pre-selection of people with internet skills

4.4 Choosing

> The choice of advertising medium depends on such criteria as **reach, targeting** and **cost**.

There is a variety of advertising media available to recruiters. Factors influencing the choice of medium include the following.

(a) **The type of organisation**. A factory is likely to advertise a vacancy for an unskilled worker in a different way to a company advertising for a member of the Chartered Institute of Personnel and Development for an HRM position.

(b) **The type of job**. Managerial jobs may merit national advertisement, whereas semi-skilled jobs may only warrant local coverage, depending on the supply of suitable candidates in the local area. Specific skills may be most appropriately reached through trade, technical or professional journals, such as those for accountants or computer programmers.

(c) **The cost of advertising**. It is more expensive to advertise in a national newspaper than on local radio, and more expensive to advertise on local radio than in a local newspaper, etc.

(d) **The readership and circulation** (type and number of readers/listeners) of the medium, and its suitability for the number and type of people the organisation wants to reach.

(e) **The frequency** with which the organisation wants to advertise the job vacancy, and the duration of the recruitment process.

EXAM FOCUS POINT

A question might ask about a job advertisement that is discriminatory. This ties the material in this section with that in the following chapter on diversity and equal opportunities.

5 A systematic approach to selection

The process of **selection** begins when the recruiter receives details of candidates interested in the job. A systematic approach includes shortlisting, interviewing (and other selection methods), decision-making and follow-up.

A systematic approach to selection may be outlined as follows.

Step 1	Deal with responses to job advertisements. This might involve sending **application forms** to candidates.
Step 2	Assess each application against **key criteria** in the job advertisement and specification. Critical factors may include qualifications and experience.
Step 3	**Sort applications** into 'possible', 'unsuitable' and 'marginal'. 'Possibles' will then be more closely scrutinised, and a shortlist for interview drawn up. Ideally, this should be done by both the personnel specialist and the prospective manager of the successful candidate.
Step 4	Invite candidates **for interview**.
Step 5	Reinforce interviews with **selection testing**, if suitable.
Step 6	**Review** uninterviewed 'possibles', and 'marginals', and put potential future candidates on hold, or in reserve.
Step 7	Send **standard letters** to unsuccessful applicants, and inform them simply that they have not been successful. Reserves will be sent a holding letter: 'We will keep your details on file, and should any suitable vacancy arise in future ...'.
Step 8	Make a **provisional offer** to the successful candidate.

BPP
LEARNING MEDIA

6 | Selection methods in outline

All **selection methods** are **limited** in their ability to predict future job performance!

6.1 A range of methods

We will briefly list the main selection methods here. The more important are discussed in the following sections.

Methods	Examples
Interviewing	• Individual (one-to-one) • Interview panels • Selection boards
Selection tests	• Intelligence • Aptitude • Personality • Proficiency • Medical
Reference checking	• Job references • Character references
Work sampling	• Portfolios • Trial periods or exercises
Group selection methods	• Assessment centres

6.2 Which method is best?

Smith and Abrahamsen developed a scale that plots selection methods according to how accurately they predict a candidate's future performance in the job. This is known as a **predictive validity** scale. The scale ranges from 1 (meaning that a method is right every time) to 0 (meaning that a method is no better than chance).

Method	% use by firms	Predictive validity
Interviews	92	0.17
References	74	0.13
Work sampling	18	0.57
Assessment centres	14	0.40
Personality tests	13	0.40
Cognitive tests	11	0.54
Biodata (biography analysis)	4	0.40
Graphology (handwriting analysis)	3	0.00

The results surprisingly show a pattern of employers relying most heavily on the **least** accurate selection methods. Interviews in particular (for reasons which we will discuss below) seem not much better than tossing a coin.

7 | Interviews

Most firms use selection **interviews**, on a one-to-one or panel basis. Interviews have the advantage of flexibility, but have limitations as predictors of job performance.

Most firms use the interview as the main basis for selection decisions.

7.1 Purposes of selection interviews

Purposes of the selection interview include:

(a) Finding the **best person** for the job, by giving the organisation a chance to assess applicants (and particularly their interpersonal and communication skills) directly

(b) Making sure that applicants **understand** what the job involves, what career prospects there are, and other aspects of the employment relationship on offer

(c) Giving the best possible **impression** of the organisation as a prospective employer

(d) Offering **fair treatment** to all applicants, whether they get the job or not: in the UK, this is covered by anti-discrimination legislation, but it is also part of the organisation's 'employer brand' and reputation in the labour market

7.2 Preparation of the interview

Candidates should be given clear instructions about the date, time and location of the interview.

The layout of the interview room should be designed to create the desired impression of the organisation, and to create the atmosphere for the interview. In most cases, it will be designed to put the candidate at ease and facilitate communication (eg removing unnecessary formal barriers such as a desk between interviewers and interviewee) but it may also be used to create pressures on the candidate, to test their response to stress.

The agenda and questions should be at least partly prepared in advance, based on **documentation** such as:

(a) The job description (which sets out the requirements of the job)
(b) The person specification (which describes the ideal candidate)
(c) The application form and/or the applicant's CV (which outline the candidate's claim to suitability)

7.3 Conduct of the interview

Questions should be paced and put carefully. The interviewer should not be trying to confuse the candidate, plunging immediately into demanding questions or picking on isolated points; neither, however, should the interviewee be allowed to digress or gloss over important points. The interviewer must retain control over the information-gathering process.

Various questioning techniques may be used; they are listed in the table below.

Type of question	Comment
Open questions	('Who ...? What ...? Where ...? When ...? Why ....?) These force candidates to put together their own responses in complete sentences. This encourages them to talk, keeps the interview flowing, and is most revealing ('Why do you want to be an accountant?')
Probing questions	These aim to discover the deeper significance of the candidate's answers, especially if they are initially dubious, uninformative, too short, or too vague. ('But what was it about accountancy that **particularly** appealed to you?')
Closed questions	Invite only 'yes' or 'no' answers: ('Did you ...?, 'Have you ...?'). This may be useful where there are points to be pinned down ('Did you pass your exam?') but there are several disadvantages to such questions. (a) They elicit an answer **only** to the question asked. (b) Candidates cannot express their personality, or interact with the interviewer on a deeper level. (c) They make it easier for candidates to conceal things ('You never **asked** me...'). (d) They make the interviewer work very hard.

Problem solving questions	Present the candidate with a situation and ask them to explain how they would deal with it. ('How would you motivate your staff to do a task that they did not want to do?') Such questions are used to establish whether the candidate will be able to deal with the sort of problems that are likely to arise in the job.
Leading questions	Encourage the candidate to give a certain reply. ('We are looking for somebody who likes detailed figure work. How much do you enjoy dealing with numbers?' or 'Don't you agree that …?' or 'Surely …?'). The danger with this type of question is that the candidate will give the answer that they think the interviewer wants to hear.

QUESTION

Question types

Identify the type of question used in the following examples, and discuss the opportunities and constraints they offer the interviewee who must answer them.

(a)   'So, you're interested in a Business Studies degree, are you, Jo?

(b)   'Surely you're interested in Business Studies, Jo?'

(c)   'How about a really useful qualification like a Business Studies degree, Jo? Would you consider that?'

(d)   'Why are you interested in a Business Studies degree, Jo?

(e)   'Why particularly Business Studies, Jo?'

ANSWER

(a)   Closed. (The only answer is 'yes' or 'no', unless Jo expands on it, at her own initiative.)

(b)   Leading. (Even if Jo was not interested, she should get the message that 'yes' would be what the interviewer wanted, or expected, to hear.)

(c)   Leading closed multiple! ('Really useful' leads Jo to think that the 'correct' answer will be 'yes': there is not much opportunity for any other answer, without expanding on it unasked.)

(d)   Open. (Jo has to explain, in her own words.)

(e)   Probing. (If Jo's answer has been unconvincing, short or vague, this forces a specific answer.)

Evaluating the response to questions requires another set of interpersonal skills.

(a)   The interviewer must **listen carefully** to the responses and evaluate them so as to judge what the candidate is:

   (i)   Wanting to say
   (ii)   Trying not to say
   (iii)   Saying, but does not mean, or is lying about
   (iv)   Having difficulty saying

(b)   In addition, the interviewer will have to be aware when they are hearing:

   (i)   Something they need to know

   (ii)   Something they **do not** need to know

   (iii)   Only what they **expect** to hear

   (iv)   Inadequately – when their own attitudes, perhaps prejudices, are getting in the way of an objective response to the candidate

Candidates should also be given the opportunity to ask questions. The choice of questions might well have some influence on how the interviewers assess a candidate's interest in and understanding of the job. Moreover, there is information that the candidate will need to know about the organisation, the job, and indeed the interview process.

7.4 Types of interview

7.4.1 Individual interviews

Individual, one-to-one or face-to-face interviews are the most common selection method.

Advantages include:

(a)   Direct face-to-face communication, with opportunities for the interviewer to use both verbal and non-verbal cues to assess the candidate

(b)   Rapport between the candidate and the interviewer: each has to give attention solely to the other, and there is potentially a relaxed atmosphere, if the interviewer is willing to establish an informal style

(c)   Flexibility in the direction and follow-up of questions

Disadvantages include:.

(a)   The candidate may be able to disguise lack of knowledge in a specialist area of which the interviewer knows little.

(b)   The interviewer's perception may be selective or distorted, and this lack of objectivity may go unnoticed and unchecked.

(c)   The greater opportunity for personal rapport with the candidate may cause a weakening of the interviewer's objective judgement.

7.4.2 Panel interviews

Panel interviews are designed to overcome such disadvantages. A panel may consist of two or three people who together interview a single candidate: most commonly, an HR specialist and the departmental manager who will have responsibility for the successful candidate. This saves the firm time and enables better assessment.

7.4.3 Selection boards

Large formal panels, or **selection boards**, may also be convened where there are a number of individuals or groups with an interest in the selection.

Advantages include the following.

(a)   A number of people see candidates, and share information about them at a single meeting.

(b)   Similarly, they can compare their assessments on the spot, without a subsequent effort at liaison and communication.

Drawbacks include the following.

(a)   Questions tend to be more varied, and more random, since there is no single guiding force behind the interview strategy. The candidate may have trouble switching from one topic to another so quickly, especially if questions are not led up to, and not clearly put – as may happen if they are unplanned.

(b)   If there is a dominating member of the board, the interview may have greater continuity – but that individual may also influence the judgement of other members.

(c)   Some candidates may not perform well in a formal, artificial situation, such as the board interview, and may find such a situation extremely stressful.

(d)   Research shows that board members rarely agree with each other in their judgements about candidates.

7.5 Advantages of interviews

Interviews in general are by far the most popular selection method used by organisations. They offer some significant advantages.

(a) They are highly interactive, allowing flexible question and answers. This allows candidates opportunities to ask questions, and allows questions and responses to be adapted to the direction and style of the interview.

(b) They offer opportunities to use non-verbal communication, which might confirm or undermine spoken answers (eg a candidate looking hesitant or embarrassed when making competence claims). This is particularly helpful to interviewers when challenging or probing in relation to inconsistencies or gaps in a candidate's application or answers.

(c) They offer opportunities to assess a candidate's personal appearance (relevant in areas such as grooming), interpersonal and communication skills.

(d) They offer initial opportunities to evaluate rapport between the candidate and their potential colleagues/bosses.

7.6 The limitations of interviews

Interviews are criticised, however, because **they fail to provide accurate predictions** of how a person will perform in the job, partly because of the nature of interviews, partly because of errors of judgement by interviewers.

Problem	Comment
Scope	An interview is too **brief** to 'get to know' candidates in the kind of depth required to make an accurate prediction of work performance.
Artificiality	An interview is an **artificial situation**: candidates may be on their best behaviour or, conversely, so nervous that they do not do themselves justice. Neither situation reflects what the person is really like.
The halo effect	A tendency for people to make an **initial general judgement** about a person based on a single obvious attribute, such as being neatly dressed or well spoken. This single attribute will colour later perceptions, and make an interviewer mark the person up or down on every other factor in their assessment.
Contagious bias	The interviewer changes the behaviour of the applicant by **suggestion**. The applicant might be led by the wording of questions, or non-verbal cues from the interviewer, to change what they are doing or saying in response.
Stereotyping	Stereotyping groups together people who are assumed to share certain characteristics (women, say, or vegetarians), then attributes certain traits to the group as a whole. It then assumes that each individual member of the supposed group will possess that trait.
Incorrect assessment	Qualitative factors such as motivation, honesty or integrity are very difficult to define and assess objectively.
Logical error	For example, an interviewer might decide that a young candidate who has held two or three jobs in the past for only a short time will be unlikely to last long in any job. (This isn't necessarily the case.)

Problem	Comment
Inexperienced interviewers	Inexperienced or unskilled interviewers may undermine the process through:
	• Inability to evaluate information about a candidate properly
	• Failure to compare a candidate against the job description or person specification
	• Failure to take control of the direction and length of the interview
	• Using inappropriate question types to elicit data or put candidates at ease
	• A reluctance to probe into facts or challenge statements where necessary

EXAM FOCUS POINT

Interviews are relevant to many areas of personnel management. Many of the issues described above may also be relevant to appraisal interviews.

The limitations of interviews as a selection method is a particularly contentious issue which would lend itself to an exam question.

8 Selection testing

Selection tests can be used before or after interviews. Intelligence tests measure the candidate's general intellectual ability, and personality tests identify character traits and behavioural preferences. Other tests are more specific to the job (eg proficiency tests).

8.1 Types of selection test

In some job selection procedures, an interview is supplemented by some form of **selection test**. In order to be effective, tests must be:

(a) **Sensitive** enough to discriminate between different candidates

(b) **Standardised** on a representative sample of the population, so that a person's results can be interpreted meaningfully

(c) **Reliable**, in that the test should measure the same thing whenever and to whomever it is applied

(d) **Valid**, measuring what they are supposed to measure

There are two basic types of test.

(a) **Proficiency and attainment** tests measure an individual's demonstrated competence in particular job-related tasks.

(b) **Psychometric** tests measure such psychological factors as aptitude, intelligence and personality.

8.1.1 Proficiency, attainment or competence tests

Proficiency tests are designed to measure an individual's current ability to perform particular tasks or operations relevant to the job: for example, giving a secretarial candidate a typing test. **Attainment** (or competence) tests are a similar measurement of the standard an individual has reached at a particular skill. There is a wide range of proficiency-testing material available, including 'in-tray' exercises (simulating work tasks). **Work sampling** requires the candidate to demonstrate work outputs: selectors may observe the candidate working, or the candidate may bring a portfolio of past work.

8.1.2 Intelligence tests

Tests of general intellectual ability typically test memory, ability to think quickly and logically, and problem-solving skills. Most people have experience of IQ tests and the like, and few would dispute their validity as a good measure of general intellectual capacity. However, there is no agreed definition of intelligence, and tests have now been devised to measure other forms of intelligence, notably emotional intelligence factors (such as self-awareness, interpersonal ability and self-control).

8.1.3 Aptitude tests

Aptitude tests are designed to measure and predict an individual's potential for performing a job or learning new skills. Aptitudes include:

- **Reasoning**: verbal, numerical and abstract
- **Spatio-visual ability**: practical intelligence, non-verbal ability and creative ability
- **Perceptual speed and accuracy**: clerical ability
- **Physical abilities**: mechanical, manual, musical and athletic

8.1.4 Personality tests

Personality tests may measure a variety of characteristics, such as an applicant's skill in dealing with other people, ambition and motivation, or emotional stability. Examples include the 16PF, the Myers-Briggs Type Indicator™ and the Minnesota Multiphasic Personality Inventory (MMPI).

The validity of such tests has been much debated, but it seems that some have been shown by research to be valid predictors of job performance, so long as they are used properly.

8.2 Limitations of testing

Despite current enthusiasm for selection testing, it has its limitations.

(a)   There is not always a direct relationship between ability in the test and **ability in the job**: the job situation is very different from artificial test conditions.

(b)   The **interpretation of test results** is a skilled task, for which training and experience is essential. It is also highly subjective (particularly in the case of personality tests), which belies the apparent scientific nature of the approach.

(c)   Additional difficulties are experienced with **particular kinds of test**. For example:

(i)   An aptitude test measuring arithmetical ability would need to be constantly revised or its content might become known to later applicants.

(ii)   Personality tests can often give misleading results because applicants seem able to guess which answers will be looked at most favourably.

(iii)   It is difficult to design intelligence tests which give a fair chance to people from different cultures and social groups and which test the kind of intelligence that the organisation wants from its employees: the ability to score highly in IQ tests does not necessarily correlate with desirable traits, such as mature judgement or creativity, but merely mental ability.

(iv)   Most tests are subject to coaching and practice effects.

(d)   It is difficult to exclude **bias** from tests. Many tests (including personality tests) are tackled less successfully by women than by men, or by some candidates born overseas than by indigenous applicants, because of the particular aspect chosen for testing.

9 Other selection methods

9.1 Group selection methods (assessment centres)

> **Group selection methods** might be used by an organisation as the final stage of a selection process, as a more 'natural' and in-depth appraisal of candidates.

Group assessments (sometimes called **assessment centres**) tend to be used for posts requiring leadership, communication or teamworking skills: advertising agencies often use the method for selecting account executives, for example.

9.1.1 Methods used in group selection

Assessment centres are attended by a group of candidates and consist of a series of tests, interviews and group situations. In a typical assessment centre, following an introductory session to ensure candidates feel at ease, candidates face tests, interviews and group scenarios designed to establish their suitability for the role(s) on offer.

A variety of tools and techniques are used in group selection, including:

(a) **Group role-play exercises**, in which candidates can explore (and hopefully display) interpersonal skills and/or work through simulated managerial tasks.

(b) **Case studies**, where candidates' analytical and problem-solving abilities are tested in working through described situations/problems, as well as their interpersonal skills in taking part in (or leading) group discussion of the case study.

9.1.2 Advantages of group selection

These group sessions might be useful for the following reasons.

(a) They give the organisation's selectors a longer opportunity to study the candidates.

(b) They reveal more than application forms, interviews and tests alone about the ability of candidates to persuade others, negotiate with others, explain ideas to others, investigate problems efficiently, and so on. These are typically management skills.

(c) They reveal more about how the candidate's personality and skills will affect the work team and their own performance in the job.

9.2 Reference checking

> **References** provide further information about the prospective employee.

This may be of varying value, as the subjectivity and reliability of all but the most factual information provided by chosen reference sources must be questioned. A reference should contain two types of information.

(a) Straightforward **factual information**. This confirms the nature of the applicant's previous job(s), period of employment, pay and circumstances of leaving.

(b) **Opinions** about the applicant's personality and other attributes. These should obviously be treated with some caution. Allowances should be made for prejudice (favourable or unfavourable), charity (withholding detrimental remarks), and possibly fear of being actionable for libel (although references are privileged, as long as they are factually correct and devoid of malice).

At least two **employer** references are desirable, providing necessary factual information, and comparison of personal views. **Personal** references tell the prospective employer little more than that the applicant has a friend or two.

9.2.1 Written references

Written references save time, especially if a standardised letter or form has been pre-prepared. A simple letter inviting the previous employer to reply with the basic information and judgements required may suffice. A standard form may be more acceptable, and might pose a set of simple questions about:

- Job title
- Main duties and responsibilities
- Period of employment
- Pay/salary
- Attendance record

If a judgement of character and suitability is desired, it might be most tellingly formulated as the question: 'Would you re-employ this individual? (If not, why not?)'

9.2.2 Telephone references

Telephone references may be timesaving if standard reference letters or forms are not available. They may also elicit a more honest opinion than a carefully prepared written statement. For this reason, a telephone call may also be made to check or confirm a poor or grudging reference which the recruiter suspects may be prejudiced.

It should be noted that with the giving and taking up of references there are **legal issues** to consider. Those who issue references need to be aware of the potential for claims of negligence from the prospective employer relying on the reference, or even defamation from the employee about whom the reference is being written. In addition, confidentiality must never be breached. Former employees have sued for slander and subsequent employers have brought an action where a person was recommended for an unsuitable post and their incompetence caused damage. Because of the legal implications, employers nowadays write a reference that is purely factual, confirming the dates, salary and role of the person in question. An alternative new method of assessment for new recruits comes in the form of a detailed questionnaire, which has been designed to ask skill-based, quality questions that should provide accurate answers.

10 Evaluating recruitment and selection practices

The **effectiveness and cost effectiveness** of recruitment and selection should be systematically **evaluated**, using a variety of measures.

10.1 How effective are recruitment and selection?

To get a clear idea of how efficient their recruitment and selection practices are, firms can ask themselves these questions.

- Can we identify human resources requirements from the business plans?
- How fast do we respond to demands from line managers for human resources?
- Do we give/receive good advice on labour market trends?
- Do we select the right advertising media to reach the market?
- How effective (and cost effective) is our recruitment advertising?
- How do our recruits actually perform – do we end up employing the right people?
- Do we retain our new recruits?

Recruitment and selection practices can be reviewed in various ways.

Review	Comment
Performance indicators	Each stage of the process can be assessed by performance indicators; for example, the time it takes to process an application. Data can be collected to check any deviation from standard.
Cost effectiveness	For example, number of relevant responses per recruitment ad, or cost of various advertising media per application elicited (or person employed).

Monitoring the workforce	High staff turnover, absenteeism and other problems (particularly among new recruits) may reflect poor recruitment and selection. Lack of workforce diversity may highlight discriminatory practices.
Attitude surveys	The firm can ask its recruits what they thought of the process.
Actual individual job performance	A person's actual performance can be compared with what was expected when they were recruited.

10.2 Improving recruitment and selection procedures

A systematic model has been proposed in this chapter. If it is considered that recruitment and selection procedures need to be improved, attention may be given to such matters as:

(a)   Improvement of **policies and guidelines** for selectors: eg in equal opportunities and recruitment/promotion decisions

(b)   Establishment of **systematic procedures** for all stages of the process

(c)   Improved **education and training** of selectors: eg in interviewing skills and testing techniques

(d)   **Auditing of job advertising** content and media, in order to improve the attractiveness and realism of the organisation's offerings and the cost effectiveness of advertising

(e)   Widening the organisation's **repertoire of selection techniques**, to aim for the highest possible accuracy in predicting job performance and confirming candidate claims

(f)   The possible use of external recruitment and selection **agencies and consultants**

PER performance objective PO5 covers leadership and management. This could include recruitment and selection and other activities related to human resource management. For example, a professional accountant may be involved in the training of accounts department staff.

CHAPTER ROUNDUP

↳ Effective recruitment practices ensure that a firm has enough **people with the right skills**.

↳ The recruitment process involves **personnel specialists** and **line managers**, sometimes with the help of recruitment **consultants**.

↳ **Recruitment** is a systematic process of (a) identifying and defining skill needs and (b) attracting suitably skilled candidates.

↳ **Job analysis** determines the requirement for a job. The job's tasks are set out in a job description. A **job specification** describes the skills or competences required for the job. A **person specification** describes the sort of person suitable for the job.

↳ Detailed procedures for recruitment should only be devised and implemented in the context of a fair, consistent and coherent **policy**, or code of conduct.

↳ A recruitment policy should cover such areas as the factors to be considered when deciding whether to **recruit** someone from **outside** or to **promote** or **transfer** someone from the existing workforce instead.

↳ **Job advertising** is aimed at attracting quality applicants and aiding self-selection.

↳ A number of print, electronic and interpersonal **media** are used for job **advertising**.

↳ The choice of advertising medium depends on criteria such as **reach, targeting** and **cost**.

↳ The process of **selection** begins when the recruiter receives details of candidates interested in the job. A systematic approach includes shortlisting, interviewing (and other selection methods), decision-making and follow-up.

↳ All **selection methods** are **limited** in their ability to predict future job performance!

↳ Most firms use selection **interviews**, on a one-to-one or panel basis. Interviews have the advantage of flexibility, but have limitations as predictors of job performance.

↳ **Selection tests** can be used before or after interviews. Intelligence tests measure the candidate's general intellectual ability, and personality tests identify character traits and behavioural preferences. Other tests are more specific to the job (eg proficiency tests).

↳ **Group selection methods** might be used by an organisation as the final stage of a selection process, as a more 'natural' and in-depth appraisal of candidates.

↳ **References** provide further information about the prospective employee.

↳ The effectiveness and cost effectiveness of **recruitment and selection** should be systematically **evaluated**, using a variety of measures.

QUICK QUIZ

1   Put these stages of the recruitment and selection process into the correct order.

(a)   Select candidates
(b)   Attract potential employees
(c)   Identify/define requirements

2   List the factors determining whether a firm should use recruitment consultants.

3   What type of competence area would planning and organising be classed under?

A   Intellectual competence   B   Interpersonal competence
C   Adaptability competence   D   Results competence

4   The question 'Did you complete your accountancy qualification?' is:

A   An open question   C   A leading question
B   A closed question   D   A probing question

5   Interviews fail to predict performance accurately. True or false?

6   'Personality and cognitive tests are more reliable predictors of job performance than interviews.' True or false?

7   Firms can improve their recruitment and selection practices by doing which two of the following?

A   Clearly identifying what they want from the candidate
B   Not relying on interviews alone
C   Ensuring that new recruits are young

ANSWERS TO QUICK QUIZ

1   1 (c), 2 (b), 3 (a) Identify/define requirements, attract potential employees, select candidates.

2   Cost; expertise; impartiality; organisation structure and politics; time; supply of labour.

3   A   Planning and organising are classed as intellectual competences.

4   B   (You might try to rephrase this question as the other types, for extra practice.)

5   True.   This is due to brevity and artificiality of the interview situation combined with the bias and inexperience of interviewers.

6   True.

7   A and B. Ensuring that new recruits are young would be age discrimination and would prevent experienced, potentially more suitable applicants from applying.

Now try ...

Attempt the questions below from the **Practice Question Bank**

Q63

Q64

Q65

Q66

Diversity and equal opportunities

This chapter addresses a key issue in recruitment and selection (following on from Chapter 12), but it also has wider implications for HR policy and practice.

Employers are slowly starting to realise that equal opportunity policies have social and business benefits (as discussed in **Section 1**) and are seeking not just to comply with the legal framework **(Section 2)** but also to develop positive action initiatives **(Section 3)**.

It is also being recognised that the workforce is increasingly **diverse** – and not just in the rather 'obvious' ways referred to by equal opportunities. Managing diversity is discussed in **Section 4**.

This chapter refers to the UK framework. Non-UK students may choose to use this material or may prefer to make use of their knowledge of similar matters in their own countries. Arguably, the UK legal framework raises important issues and sets certain minimum standards which should be regarded as good practice in any employment market.

D2 Recruitment and selection of employees

(f) Explain the purposes and benefits of diversity and equal opportunities policies within the human resources plan.

K

(g) Explain the practical steps that an organisation may take to ensure the effectiveness of its diversity and equal opportunities policy.

K

EXAM FOCUS POINT

There is an article on the ACCA website entitled "Equal opportunities" that is relevant to material in this chapter.

1 Discrimination at work

1.1 Equal opportunities

Equal opportunities is an approach to the management of people at work based on equal access to benefits and fair treatment.

Equal opportunities is an approach to the management of people at work based on equal access and fair treatment, irrespective of gender, race, ethnicity, age, disability, sexual orientation or religious belief.

Equal opportunities employers will seek to redress inequalities (eg of access to jobs, training, promotion, pay or benefits) which are based around differences, where they have no relevance to work performance.

Certain aspects of equal opportunities (such as discrimination on the basis of sex, race or disability) are enshrined in law; others (such as, up to now, discrimination on the basis of age) rely on models of good practice.

1.1.1 Why is equal opportunities an issue?

Despite the fact that women have contributed directly to the national product since medieval times, the acceptance of women in paid employment, on equal terms to men, has been a slow process. Many assumptions about women's attitudes to work, and capabilities for various types of work, have only recently been re-examined. Meanwhile, earnings surveys report that, across all occupations, women are still earning less than males in the same occupational group.

The choice of jobs for the disabled is often restricted, resulting in higher and longer unemployment rates than those of the general population. Jobs are concentrated in plant/machine operative jobs, which tend to be low paid.

Despite demographic and educational changes (and associated skill shortages among the younger population) a certain amount of discrimination is still directed at mature-age workers.

1.1.2 Why is equal opportunity an issue for employers?

Sound **business arguments** can be made for having an equal opportunities policy.

Reasons argued for adopting non- or anti-discrimination measures include the following.

(a)   Common decency and fairness, in line with business ethics.

(b)   Good HR practice, to attract and retain the best people for the job, regardless of race or gender.

(c)   Compliance with relevant legislation and Codes of Practice, which are used by employment tribunals.

(d)   Widening the recruitment pool in times of skill shortages.

(e)   Other potential benefits to the business through its image as a good employer, and through the loyalty of customers who benefit from (or support) equality principles.

2   Equal opportunity

Discrimination of certain types is illegal in the UK on grounds of:

- Sex and marital status
- Colour, race, nationality and ethnic or national origin
- Disability
- Sexual orientation and religious beliefs
- Age

There are three types of discrimination.

- **Direct discrimination** occurs when one interested group is treated less favourably than another (except for exempted cases). It is unlikely that a prospective employer will practise direct discrimination without being aware of it.

- **Indirect discrimination** occurs when a policy or practice is fair in form, but discriminatory in operation. For example, requiring all applicants to be clean shaven would put members of some religious groups at a disadvantage. Another example would be a policy preventing staff working part time (those with children or family responsibilities could be disadvantaged).

- **Victimisation** occurs when a person is penalised for giving information or taking action in pursuit of a claim of discrimination.

In addition, **harassment** is the use of threatening, intimidatory, offensive or abusive language or behaviour.

QUESTION   Indirect discrimination

Suggest four examples of practices that would constitute indirect discrimination on the grounds of sex.

ANSWER

(a)   Advertising a vacancy in a primarily male environment, where women would be less likely to see it.

(b)   Offering less favourable terms to part-time workers (given that most of them are women).

(c)   Specifying age limits which would tend to exclude women who had taken time out of work for child-rearing.

(d)   Asking in selection interviews about plans to have a family (since this might be to the detriment of a woman, but not a man).

2.1 Applying the law

In the UK, the obligation of non-discrimination applies to all aspects of employment, including advertisements, recruitment and selection programmes, access to training, promotion, disciplinary procedures, redundancy and dismissal. The main source of legislation in this area is the Equality Act 2010 (TSO, 2010).

There are certain exceptions ('genuine occupational qualifications') in which discrimination of a sort may be permitted. For example, a firm may prefer a man over a woman if there are reasons of physiology (not strength), privacy/decency (closely defined) or legal restrictions, eg work outside the UK, where 'laws or customs are such that the duties could not, or could not effectively, be performed by a woman'.

The legislation does not permit **positive discrimination**: actions which give preference to a protected person, regardless of genuine suitability and qualification for the job.

EXAM FOCUS POINT

Bear in mind that the above provisions apply in the UK. Other countries, for reasons of social policy, may have different legislative measures in place. The principles of UK law may represent good practice anywhere.

Training may be given to particular groups exclusively, if the group has in the preceding year been substantially underrepresented. It is also permissible to encourage such groups to apply for jobs where such exclusive training is offered, and to apply for jobs in which they are underrepresented.

2.2 Disability discrimination

A country's disability discrimination law may, for example, make it unlawful for an employer to discriminate against a disabled person/employee in the following respects.

(a)   In deciding who to interview or who to employ, or in the terms of an employment offer

(b)   In the terms of employment and the opportunities for promotion, transfer, training or other benefits

(c)   By dismissal or any other disadvantage

The employer may also be forced to make reasonable adjustments to working arrangements or to the physical features of premises where these constitute a disadvantage to disabled people.

2.3 Sexual orientation and religious beliefs

A country's equality regulation may, for example, outlaw discrimination and harassment on grounds of sexual orientation and religious belief. Employers may be held responsible for conduct deemed offensive or harassing (including inappropriate jokes) in regard to either issue.

2.4 Age discrimination

A country's age discrimination regulations may suggest that employers should:

(a)   Recruit on the basis of skills and abilities; refrain from using age limits or phrases that imply restrictions (such as 'newly qualified' or 'recent graduate') in job advertisements; refrain from asking for medical references only from older applicants

(b)   Select on merit and use, where possible, a mixed-age panel of interviewers, trained to avoid decisions based on prejudices and stereotypes

(c)   Promote on the basis of ability, having openly advertised opportunities

(d)   Train and develop all employees and regularly review training to avoid age being a barrier

(e)   Base redundancy decisions on job-related criteria and ensure that retirement schemes are applied fairly

3 The practical implications

The practical implications of the legislation for employers are set out in **Codes of Practice**. These do not have the force of law, but may be taken into account by employment tribunals.

3.1 Formulating an effective equal opportunities policy

Many organisations now establish their own **policy statements** or **codes of practice on equal opportunities**: apart from anything else, a statement of the organisation's position may provide some protection in the event of complaints.

Some organisations make minimal efforts to avoid discrimination, paying lip-service to the idea only to the extent of claiming 'We are an Equal Opportunities Employer' on advertising literature. To turn such a claim into reality, the following are needed.

(a) **Support** from the top of the organisation for the formulation of a practical policy.

(b) A **working party** drawn from – for example – management, unions, minority groups, the HR function and staff representatives. This group's brief will be to produce a draft Policy and Code of Practice, which will be approved at senior level.

(c) **Action plans and resources** (including staff) to implement and monitor the policy, publicise it to staff, arrange training, and so on.

(d) **Monitoring** the numbers of women and ethnic minority staff can easily be done

- On entering (and applying to enter) the organisation
- On leaving the organisation
- On applying for transfers, promotions or training schemes

(It is less easy to determine the ethnic origins of the workforce through such methods as questionnaires: there is bound to be suspicion about the question's motives, and it may be offensive to some workers.)

(e) **Positive action**, namely the process of taking active steps to encourage people from disadvantaged groups to apply for jobs and training, and to compete for vacancies. (Note that this is not positive discrimination.) Examples might be using ethnic languages in job advertisements, or implementing training for women in management skills. In addition, there may be awareness training, counselling and disciplinary measures to manage sexual, racial and religious harassment.

3.2 Recruitment and selection

Recruitment and selection are areas of particular sensitivity to claims of discrimination – as well as genuine (though often unintended) inequality.

There is always a risk that disappointed job applicants, for example, will attribute their lack of success to discrimination, especially if the recruiting organisation's workforce is conspicuously lacking in representatives of the same ethnic minority, sex or group. The following guidelines should be borne in mind.

(a) **Advertising**

    (i)   Any wording that suggests preference for a particular group should be avoided (except for genuine occupational qualifications).

    (ii)   Employers must not indicate or imply any 'intention to discriminate'.

    (iii)   Recruitment literature should state that the organisation is an Equal Opportunities employer (where this can be justified).

    (iv)   The placing of advertisements only where the readership is predominantly of one race or sex is construed as indirect discrimination. This includes word-of-mouth recruiting from the existing workforce, if it is not broadly representative.

(b) **Recruitment agencies.** Instructions to an agency should not suggest any preference.

(c) **Application forms.** These should include no questions which are not work related (such as domestic details) and which only one group is asked to complete.

(d) **Interviews**

    (i)   Any non work related question must be asked of all subjects, if at all, and even then, some types of question may be construed as discriminatory. (You cannot, for example, ask only women about plans to have a family or care of dependants, or ask – in the most offensive case – about the Pill or PMT.)

    (ii)   It may be advisable to have a witness at interviews, or at least to take detailed notes, in the event that a claim of discrimination is made.

(e) **Selection tests.** These must be wholly relevant, and should not favour any particular group. Even personality tests have been shown to favour white male applicants.

(f) **Records**. Reasons for rejection, and interview notes, should be carefully recorded, so that in the event of investigation the details will be available.

3.3 Other initiatives

In addition to responding to legislative provisions, some employers have begun to address the **underlying problems** of discrimination.

Measures such as the following may be used as positive action initiatives.

(a) Putting equal opportunities **higher on the agenda** by appointing Equal Opportunities Managers (and even Directors) who report directly to the HR Director

(b) **Flexible hours** or part-time work, term-time or annual-hours contracts (to allow for school holidays) to help women to combine careers with family responsibilities; terms and conditions, however, must not be less favourable

(c) **Career-break or return-to-work** schemes for women

(d) **Fast-tracking school leavers**, as well as graduates, and posting managerial vacancies internally, giving more opportunities for movement up the ladder for groups (typically women and minorities) currently at lower levels of the organisation

(e) **Training for women-returners** or women in management to help women manage their career potential; assertiveness training may also be offered as part of such an initiative

(f) **Awareness training** for managers, to encourage them to think about equal opportunity policy

(g) **Counselling and disciplinary policies** to raise awareness and eradicate sexual, racial and religious harassment

(h) **Positive action** to encourage job and training applications from minority groups

4 Diversity

> The concept of **'managing diversity'** is based on the belief that the dimensions of individual difference on which organisations currently focus are crude and performance-irrelevant classifications of the most obvious differences between people.

Diversity in employment, as a concept, goes further than equal opportunities.

The ways in which people meaningfully differ in the workplace include not only race and ethnicity, age and gender, but personality, preferred working style, individual needs and goals, and so on.

4.1 Managing diversity

A 'managing diversity' orientation implies the need to be proactive in managing the needs of a diverse workforce in such areas (beyond the requirements of equal opportunity and discrimination regulations) as:

(a) Tolerance of individual differences
(b) Communicating effectively with (and motivating) ethnically diverse workforces
(c) Managing workers with increasingly diverse family structures and responsibilities
(d) Managing the adjustments to be made by an increasingly aged workforce
(e) Managing increasingly diverse career aspirations/patterns, flexible working, etc
(f) Dealing with differences in literacy, numeracy and qualifications in an international workforce
(g) Managing co-operative working in ethnically diverse teams

4.2 Diversity policy

Ingham (2003) suggests the following key steps in implementing a **diversity policy** taking into account all the equal opportunity requirements.

Step 1	**Analyse your business environment**
	(a) Internally – does the diversity of the organisation reflect the population in its labour market?
	(b) Externally – does the diversity of the workforce mirror that of the customer base?

Step 2	**Define diversity and its business benefits**
	(a) Legal, moral and social benefits
	(b) Business benefits: better understanding of market segments; positive employer brand; attraction and retention of talent
	(c) Employee benefits: more representative workforce; value and respect for people; opportunity to contribute fully; enhanced creativity

Step 3	**Introduce diversity policy into corporate strategy**
	Weave diversity into corporate values and mission

Step 4	**Embed diversity into core HR processes and system**
	Review and refocus recruitment and selection, induction, reward and recognition, career management and training and development

Step 5	Ensure leaders implement policy
	(a) Leaders and top management need to provide long-term commitment and resources
	(b) Use diversity as a key factor in coaching, awareness training and development of managers

Step 6	Involve staff at all levels
	• Educate the workforce through awareness training
	• Create a 'diversity handbook'
	• Set up diversity working parties and councils
	• Establish mentoring schemes

Step 7	Communicate, communicate, communicate
	• Communicate diversity policy and initiatives clearly
	• Internally: updates, briefings, training, intranet pages
	• Externally: to boost employer brand and recruitment

Step 8	Understand your company's needs
	(a) Match resources to the size of the organisation and the scale of change required
	(b) Consider using diversity consultants or best practice representatives to provide advice, support and training

Step 9	Evaluate
	• Benchmark progress at regular intervals
	• Internally: diversity score cards, employee climate surveys
	• Externally: focus groups, customer/supplier surveys

EXAM FOCUS POINT

The examining team has stated that, while the details of Ingham's framework will not be examined, it is useful in aiding an understanding of how diversity may be implemented.

CHAPTER ROUNDUP

↳ **Equal opportunities** is an approach to the management of people at work based on equal access to benefits and fair treatment.

↳ Sound **business arguments** can be made for having an equal opportunities policy.

↳ **Discrimination** of certain types is illegal in the UK on grounds of:

  – Sex and marital status
  – Colour, race, nationality and ethnic or national origin
  – Disability
  – Sexual orientation and religious beliefs
  – Age

↳ Many organisations now establish their own **policy statements** or **codes of practice on equal opportunities**: apart from anything else, a statement of the organisation's position may provide some protection in the event of complaints.

↳ **Recruitment and selection** are areas of particular sensitivity to claims of discrimination – as well as genuine (though often unintended) inequality.

↳ In addition to responding to legislative provisions, some employers have begun to address **the underlying problems** of discrimination.

↳ The concept of **'managing diversity'** is based on the belief that the dimensions of individual difference on which organisations currently focus are crude and performance-irrelevant classifications of the most obvious differences between people.

1   Matt Black and Di Gloss run a small DIY shop. They're recruiting an assistant. Matt puts up an ad on the noticeboard of his Men's Club. It says: 'Person required to assist in DIY shop. Full-time. Aged under 28. Contact ...' Two candidates turn up for interview the following day: a man and a woman (who's heard about the job by word of mouth, through Di). Matt interviews them both, asking work-related questions. He also asks the woman whether she has children and how much time she expects to spend dealing with family matters.

With reference to legislation to prevent sexual discrimination, Matt may have laid himself open to allegations of:

A   One count of discrimination   C   Four counts of discrimination
B   Two counts of discrimination   D   No discrimination at all

2   When a person is penalised for giving information or taking action in pursuit of a claim of discrimination, this is known as:

A   Direct discrimination   C   Victimisation
B   Indirect discrimination   D   Harassment

3   At which stages of the recruitment and selection process should the equal opportunities policy be implemented?

1   Advertising vacancies
2   Interviewing candidates
3   Selecting candidates
4   Offering candidates the job

A   1, 2 and 3 only
B   2, 3, and 4 only
C   1, 3 and 4 only
D   1, 2, 3 and 4

4   The process of taking active steps to encourage people from disadvantaged groups to apply for jobs and training is:

A   Positive action
B   Positive discrimination
C   Positive opportunity

5   Diversity in the workplace includes differences such as personality and preferred working style. True or false?

ANSWERS TO QUICK QUIZ

1   C   Advertising in a place where the readership is predominately male. Aged under 28.

Asking the women about (1) children and (2) time spent on family matters.

2   C   This is victimisation.

3   D   Equal opportunities should be applied at all stages.

4   A   Examples of positive action include using ethnic languages in job advertisements or implementing training for women in management skills.

5   True.   Diversity in employment, as a concept, goes further than equal opportunities.

Now try ...

Attempt the questions below from the **Practice Question Bank**

Q67

Q68

Q69

Individuals, groups and teams

It is a useful reminder that managers do not just manage activities, processes and resources: they manage **people**. Organisations are made up of individuals and groups, with their own goals, needs and ways of seeing things.

In **Section 1**, we look at some useful concepts for understanding the behaviour of **individuals** at work, and how it can be managed.

In **Sections 2 to 7**, we look at how people behave in informal groups and in the more structured environment of **teams**. In particular, we consider how to create and maintain effective teams at work.

One of the key points to grasp is that an **effective team** is one which not only achieves its task objectives, but satisfies the needs of its members as well. As you will see in this chapter, **teamwork** involves both **task** functions (getting the job done) and **maintenance** functions (keeping the team together).

Teamwork is one of the hottest concepts in modern management. Fortunately, there are some useful models which can be learned: perhaps the major challenge of this topic is to get their details straight in your mind.

D3 Individual and group behaviour in business organisations

(a) Describe the main characteristics of individual and group behaviour. — K

(b) Outline the contributions of individuals and teams to organisational success. — K

(c) Identify individual and team approaches to work. — K

D4 Team formation, development and management

(a) Explain the differences between a group and a team. — K

(b) Explain the purposes of a team. — K

(c) Explain the role of the manager in building the team and developing individuals within the team. — K
    (i) Belbin's team roles theory
    (ii) Tuckman's theory of team development

(d) List the characteristics of effective and ineffective teams. — K

(e) Describe tools and techniques that can be used to build the team and improve team effectiveness. — K

EXAM FOCUS POINT

Relationships within a team and the management of teams have often figured in the examination, including named models such as Tuckman and Belbin. The examining team has commented that candidates performed poorly on questions relating to Tuckman's team development theory.

1 Individuals

1.1 Personality

Personality is the total pattern of an individual's thoughts, feelings and behaviour. It is shaped by a variety of factors, both inherited and environmental.

In order to identify, describe and explain the differences between people, psychologists use the concept of **personality**.

Personality is the total pattern of characteristic ways of thinking, feeling and behaving that constitute the individual's distinctive method of relating to the environment.

1.1.1 Describing personality

Attempts to describe the 'components' of personality, or the ways people differ, focus on two broad concepts: traits and types.

(a) Personality **traits** are relatively stable, enduring qualities of an individual's personality which cause a tendency to behave in particular ways. For example, we might say that someone is 'impulsive'.

(b) Personality **types** are distinct clusters of personality characteristics, which reflect the psychological preferences of the individual. If we say that someone is an 'extrovert', for example, we may be suggesting that they are sociable, expressive, impulsive, practical and active.

The well-known **Myers Briggs Type Inventory**™ (Myers and Briggs Foundation, 2014) is based on detailed analysis of personality types. The aim of the inventory (and the value of personality theories to managers) is:

(a) To provide a shared language with which people can discuss and explore individual uniqueness (their own natural style) and ways of developing to their full potential

(b) To help people to understand areas of difference which might otherwise be the source of misunderstanding and miscommunication

(c) To encourage people to appreciate diversity by highlighting the value and complementary contributions of all personality types

Note that the Myers Briggs Type Inventory is not directly examinable; it is referred to as it helps explain the concept of personality types.

QUESTION Personality

How is your personality 'cut out' to be an accountant? This is not a technical question: it merely invites you to think about your personality traits – and stereotypes about the 'type of person' who chooses to be an accountant or makes a good accountant. (This will be useful when we look at recruitment and selection in Chapter 15.)

1.1.2 Managing personality

An individual's personality should be compatible with their work requirements in three ways.

Compatibility	Comments
With the **task**	Different personality types suit different types of work. A person who appears unsociable and inhibited will find sales work, involving a lot of social interactions, intensely stressful – and will probably not be very good at it.
With the **systems** and **management culture** of the organisation	Some people hate to be controlled, for example, but others want to be controlled and dependent in a work situation, because they find responsibility threatening.
With other **personalities** in the team	Personality clashes are a prime source of conflict at work. An achievement-oriented personality, for example, may become frustrated and annoyed by laid-back sociable types working (or not working) around them.

Where incompatibilities occur, the manager or supervisor has three options.

(a) **Restore compatibility**. This may be achieved by reassigning an individual to tasks more suited to their personality type, for example.

(b) **Achieve a compromise**. Individuals should be encouraged to understand the nature of their differences and modify their behaviour if necessary.

(c) **Remove the incompatible personality**. In the last resort, obstinately difficult or disruptive people may simply have to be weeded out of the team.

1.2 Perception

Perception is the process by which the brain selects and organises information in order to make sense of it. People behave according to what they perceive – not according to what really is.

Different people see things differently. Each individual behaves in a way that reflects their own interpretation of the world. The same single 'reality' may be perceived differently by different people.

Perception is the psychological process by which stimuli or incoming sensory data are selected and organised into patterns which are meaningful to the individual.

1.2.1 Processes of perception

The process of **perceptual selection** deals with how we gather and filter out incoming data. Perception may be determined by any or all of the following.

(a) **The context**. People see what they want to see: whatever is necessary or relevant in the situation in which they find themselves. You might notice articles on management in the newspapers while studying this module which normally you would not notice, for example.

(b) **The nature of the stimuli**. Our attention tends to be drawn to large, bright, loud, contrasting, unfamiliar, moving and repeated (not repetitive) stimuli. Advertisers know it.

(c) **Internal factors**. Our attention is drawn to stimuli that match our personality, needs, interests, expectations, and so on. If you are hungry, for example, you will pick the smell of food out of a mix of aromas.

(d) **Fear or trauma**. People are able to avoid seeing things that they **don't** want to see: things that are threatening to their security or self-image, or things that are too painful for them.

A complementary process of **perceptual organisation** deals with the interpretation of the data which has been gathered and filtered.

1.3 Attitudes

People develop **attitudes** about things based on what they think, what they feel and what they want to do about it. Attitudes are formed by perception, experience and personality which in turn are shaped by wider social influences.

Attitudes are our general standpoint on things: the positions we have adopted in regard to particular issues, things and people, as we perceive them.

An **attitude** is 'a mental state ... exerting a directive or dynamic influence upon the individual's response to all objects and situations with which it is related.'

Attitudes are thought to contain three basic components.

- Knowledge, beliefs or disbeliefs, perceptions
- Feelings and desires (positive or negative)
- Volition, will or the intention to perform an action

Behaviour in a work context will be influenced by:

(a) **Attitudes to work:** the individual's standpoint on working, work conditions, colleagues, the task, the organisation and management

(b) **Attitudes at work:** all sorts of attitudes which individuals may have about other people, politics, education or religion (among other things), and which they bring with them into the workplace – to act on, agree, disagree or discuss

Positive, negative or neutral attitudes to other workers, or groups of workers, to the various systems and operations of the organisation, to learning – or particular training initiatives – to communication or to the task itself will obviously influence performance at work.

QUESTION

Attitude

Suggest four elements which would make up a positive attitude to work. (An example might be the belief that you get a fair day's pay for a fair day's work.)

ANSWER

Elements of a positive attitude to work may include a willingness to:

(a)   Commit oneself to the objectives of the organisation, or adopt personal objectives that are compatible with those of the organisation

(b)   Accept the right of the organisation to set standards of acceptable behaviour for its members

(c)   Contribute to the development and improvement of work practices and performance

(d)   Take advantage of opportunities for personal development at work

1.4 Intelligence

Intelligence is a wider and more complex concept than the traditional view of 'IQ'. It includes useful attributes, such as:

(a)   **Analytic intelligence**: traditionally measured by IQ tests, including mental agility, logical reasoning and verbal fluency

(b)   **Spatial intelligence**: the ability to see patterns and connections, most obvious in the creative artist or scientist

(c)   **Practical intelligence**: practical aptitude, handiness

(d)   **Intrapersonal intelligence**: self-awareness, self-expression, self-control, handling stress

(e)   **Interpersonal intelligence**: empathy, understanding of the emotional needs of others, influence, conflict resolution, assertiveness, co-operation

Intra- and interpersonal intelligence have recently attracted attention through the work of Daniel **Goleman** (and others) as **emotional intelligence** (EQ). EQ is considered particularly important in managing people effectively, since it enables a person to manage the emotional components of situations, behaviour and communication.

1.5 Role theory

Role theory suggests that people behave in any situation according to other people's expectations of how they should behave in that situation.

A role may be seen as a part you play: people sometimes refer to wearing 'different hats' in different situations or groups of people.

(a)   A **role set** is a group of people who respond to you in a given role. Staff in the accounts department will relate to the account manager in his role as professional and superior – rather than as a father or husband (within the role set of the family) or friend (in the role set of non-work peers), and so on. Individuals need to be aware of which role set they are operating in, in order to behave appropriately for the role.

(b)   **Role ambiguity** may occur if you do not know what role you are operating in at a given time. If a manager tries to be 'friends' with staff, this may create ambiguity and people will not know where they stand.

(c)   **Role incompatibility** or **role conflict** occurs when you are expected to operate in two roles at once: for example, if you have to discipline a member of staff (in your role as superior) with whom you have become informally friendly (in your role as sociable person).

(d)   **Role signs** indicate what role you are in at a given moment, so that others relate to you in that role without ambiguity or confusion. Role signs at work have traditionally included such things as style of dress (signalling professionalism) and styles of address (signalling respect and relative status).

(e)   **Role models** are the individuals you aspire to be like: people you look up to and model your own behaviour on.

2 Groups

As an employee your relationship with the organisation is as an individual: the employment contract is with you as an individual, and you are recruited as an individual. In your working life, though, you will generally find yourself working as part of a **group** or **team**. If you are a supervisor or a manager, you may direct a team.

2.1 What is a group?

> A **group** is a collection of individuals who perceive themselves as a group. It thus has a sense of **identity**.

A group is any collection of people who perceive themselves to be a group.

Groups have certain attributes that a random crowd does not possess.

(a) **A sense of identity**. There are acknowledged boundaries to the group which define who is in and who is out, who is us and who is them.

(b) **Loyalty to the group**, and acceptance within the group. This generally expresses itself as conformity or the acceptance of the norms of behaviour and attitudes that bind the group together and exclude others from it.

(c) **Purpose and leadership**. Most groups have an express purpose, whatever field they are in: most will, spontaneously or formally, choose individuals or sub-groups to lead them towards the fulfilment of those goals.

2.2 Why form groups?

Any organisation is composed of many groups, with attributes of their own. People in organisations will be **drawn together into groups** by a variety of forces.

- A preference for small groups, where closer relationships can develop
- The need to belong and to make a contribution that will be noticed and appreciated
- Familiarity: a shared office or canteen
- Common rank, specialisms, objectives and interests
- The attractiveness of a particular group activity (joining an interesting club, say)
- Resources offered to groups (for example sports facilities)
- Power greater than the individuals could muster alone (trade union, pressure group)
- Formal directives

2.3 Formal and informal groups

Informal groups will invariably be present in any organisation. Informal groups include workplace cliques, and networks of people who regularly get together to exchange information, groups of 'mates' who socialise outside work, and so on. They have a constantly fluctuating membership and structure.

Formal groups will be intentionally organised by the organisation, for a task for which they are held responsible – they are task oriented, and become **teams**. Although many people enjoy working in teams, their popularity in the workplace arises because of their effectiveness in fulfilling the organisation's work.

QUESTION

Small groups

What groups are you a member of in your study or work environment(s)? How big are these groups? How does the size of your class, study group, work team – or whatever:

(a) Affect your ability to come up with questions or ideas?

(b) Give you help and support to do something you couldn't do alone?

ANSWER

Your primary groups are probably your tutor group or class. If at work, it would be the section in which you work. If the groups are large, you may feel reluctant to put forward ideas or ask questions, but even within a large group you should feel there is support and that help is at hand if you need it.

EXAM FOCUS POINT

Aspects to look out for in exam questions include the distinction between teams and groups; factors in team success; Belbin's team roles and Tuckman's team development model. Revise teambuilding carefully: it is another key issue.

2.4 Individual and group contribution

People **contribute differently in groups** (due to group dynamics and synergy) than they do individually. This may have a positive or negative effect.

People contribute different skills and attributes to the organisation as individuals than they do as group members because:

(a) Human behaviour is different in groups than in solo or interpersonal situations: **group dynamics** have an effect on performance.

(b) Groups offer **synergy**: $2 + 2 = 5$. The pooling and stimulation of ideas and energies in a group can allow greater contribution than individuals working on their own. ('None of us is as smart as all of us', Blanchard.)

(c) Group dynamics and synergy may also be **negative**: distracting the individual, stifling individual responsibility and flair, and so on. Individuals may contribute more and better in some situations.

Individuals contribute:	**Groups contribute:**
• A set of skills	• A mix of skills
• Objectives set by manager	• Some teams can set their own objectives under the corporate framework
• A point of view	• A number of different points of view, enabling a swift overview of different ways of looking at a problem
• Creative ideas related to the individual's expertise	• Creative ideas arising from new combinations of expertise
• 'I can't be in two places at once'	• Flexibility as team members can be deployed in different ways
• Limited opportunity for self-criticism	• Opportunity for exercising control

3 | Teams

A **team** is more than a group. It has joint **objectives** and **accountability** and may be set up by the organisation under the supervision or coaching of a team leader, although **self-managed teams** are growing in popularity.

> ### EXAM FOCUS POINT
>
> There is an article on the ACCA website entitled "The importance of teams" that is relevant to material in this section.

A **team** is a group of people with complementary skills who have a **common purpose** and objectives for which they hold themselves accountable.

3.1 Strengths of teamworking

Teamworking may be used for: **organising** work; **controlling** activities; **generating** ideas; **decision-making**; pooling **knowledge**.

Teams are particularly well adapted to the following purposes.

Type of role	Comments
Work organisation	Teams combine the skills of different individuals.
	Teams are a co-ordinating mechanism: they avoid complex communication between different business functions.
Control	Fear of letting down the team can be a powerful motivator: team loyalty can be used to control the performance and behaviour of individuals.
Idea generation	Teams can generate ideas, eg through brainstorming and information sharing.
Decision-making	Decisions are evaluated from more than one viewpoint, with pooled information. Teams make fewer, but better evaluated, decisions than individuals.

3.2 Limitations of teamworking

Problems with teams include **conflict** on the one hand, and **group think** (excessive cohesion) on the other.

Teams and teamworking are very much in fashion, but there are potential **drawbacks**.

(a)   Teamworking is not suitable for all jobs – although some managers do not like to admit this.

(b)   Teamwork should be introduced because it leads to better performance, not because people feel better or more secure.

(c)   Team processes (especially seeking consensus) can delay decision-making. The team may also produce the compromise decision, not the right decision.

(d)   Social relationships might be maintained at the expense of other aspects of performance.

(e)   Group norms may restrict individual personality and flair.

(f)   'Group think' (Janis, 1982): team consensus and cohesion may prevent consideration of alternatives or constructive criticism, leading the team to make risky, ill-considered decisions.

(g)   Personality clashes and political behaviour within a team can get in the way of effective performance.

3.3 Organising teamwork

Multi-disciplinary teams contain people from different departments, pooling the skills of specialists.

Multi-skilled teams contain people who themselves have more than one skill.

A team may be called together temporarily, to achieve specific task objectives (**project team**), or may be more or less permanent, with responsibilities for a particular product, product group or stage of the production process (a **product or process team**).

There are two basic approaches to the organisation of teamwork: multi-skilled teams and multi-disciplinary teams.

3.3.1 Multi-disciplinary teams

Multi-disciplinary teams bring together individuals with different skills and specialisms, so that their skills, experience and knowledge can be pooled or exchanged.

Multi-disciplinary teams can:

(a)   Increase workers' awareness of their overall objectives and targets

(b)   Aid co-ordination between different areas of the business

(c)   Help to generate solutions to problems and suggestions for improvements, since a multi-disciplinary team has access to more pieces of the jigsaw

3.3.2 Multi-skilled teams

A multi-skilled team brings together a number of individuals who can perform any of the group's tasks. These tasks can then be shared out in a more flexible way between group members according to who is available and best placed to do a given job at the time it is required. Multi-skilling is the cornerstone of team empowerment, since it cuts across the barriers of job descriptions and demarcations to enable teams to respond flexibly to changing demands.

3.3.3 Virtual teams

Virtual teams bring together individuals working in remote locations, reproducing the social, collaborative and information-sharing aspects of teamworking using Information and Communications Technology (ICT).

4   Team member roles

4.1 Who should belong in the team?

Team members should be selected for their potential to contribute to getting things done (**task performance**) and establishing good working relationships (**group maintenance**). This may include:

(a)   **Specialist skills**. A team might exist to combine expertise from different departments.

(b)   **Power** in the wider organisation. Team members may have influence.

(c)   **Access to resources**. Team members may contribute information, or be able to mobilise finance or staff for the task.

(d)   The **personalities and goals** of the individual members of the team. These will determine how the group functions.

The blend of the individual skills and abilities of its members will (ideally) **balance** the team.

4.2 Belbin: team roles

Ideally, team members should perform a **balanced mix of roles**. **Belbin** suggests: co-ordinator, shaper, plant, monitor-evaluator, resource-investigator, implementer, teamworker, completer-finisher and specialist.

Belbin (1981) researched business game teams at the Henley Management College and drew up a widely used framework for understanding roles within work groups.

Belbin insisted that a distinction needs to be made between:

(a)   **Team (process) role** ('a tendency to behave, contribute and interrelate with others at work in certain distinctive ways'), and

(b)   **Functional role** ('the job demands that a person has been engaged to meet by supplying the requisite technical skills and operational knowledge')

EXAM FOCUS POINT

Belbin's model of nine roles addresses the mix of team/process roles required for a fully functioning team.

4.2.1 Nine team roles

Belbin identifies nine team roles.

Role and description	Team-role contribution	Allowable weaknesses
Plant Creative, imaginative, unorthodox	Solves difficult problems	Ignores details, too preoccupied to communicate effectively
Resource investigator Extrovert, enthusiastic, communicative	Explores opportunities, develops contacts	Over-optimistic, loses interest once initial enthusiasm has passed
Co-ordinator (chairman) Mature, confident, a good chairperson	Clarifies goals, promotes decision-making, delegates well	Can be seen as manipulative, delegates personal work
Shaper Challenging, dynamic, thrives on pressure	Has the drive and courage to overcome obstacles	Can provoke others, hurts people's feelings
Monitor-evaluator Sober, strategic and discerning	Sees all options, judges accurately	Lacks drive and ability to inspire others, overly critical
Teamworker Co-operative, mild, perceptive and diplomatic	Listens, builds, averts friction, calms the waters	Indecisive in crunch situations, can be easily influenced
Implementer (company worker) Disciplined, reliable, conservative and efficient	Turns ideas into practical actions	Somewhat inflexible, slow to respond to new possibilities

BPP
LEARNING MEDIA

Role and description	Team-role contribution	Allowable weaknesses
Completer-finisher Painstaking, conscientious, anxious	Searches out errors and omissions, delivers on time	Inclined to worry unduly, reluctant to delegate, can be a nitpicker
Specialist Single-minded, self-starting, dedicated	Provides knowledge and skills in rare supply	Contributes only on a narrow front, dwells on technicalities, overlooks the 'big picture'

4.2.2 A balanced team

These team roles are not fixed within any given individual. Team members can occupy more than one role, or switch to 'backup' roles if required, hence there is no requirement for every team to have nine members. However, since role preferences are based on personality, it should be recognised that:

- Individuals will be naturally inclined towards some roles more than others.
- Individuals will tend to adopt one or two team roles more or less consistently.
- Individuals are likely to be more successful in some roles than in others.

The nine roles are complementary, and Belbin suggested that an 'ideal' team should represent a mix or balance of all of them. If managers know employees' team role preferences, they can strategically select, 'cast' and develop team members to fulfil the required roles.

Knowledge of these different roles may help you in leadership and management tasks under performance objective PO5, which requires you to demonstrate that you can 'show initiative within your team, working towards sustainable organisational goals, collaborating with and helping others.'

QUESTION

Belbin's team roles

The following phrases and slogans project certain team roles: identify which. (Examples are drawn from Belbin, 1993.)

(a) The small print is always worth reading.
(b) Let's get down to the task in hand.
(c) In this job you never stop learning.
(d) Without continuous innovation, there is no survival.
(e) Surely we can exploit that?
(f) When the going gets tough, the tough get going.
(g) I was very interested in your point of view.
(h) Has anyone else got anything to add to this?
(i) Decisions should not be based purely on enthusiasm.

ANSWER

(a) Completer-finisher
(b) Implementer/company worker
(c) Specialist
(d) Plant
(e) Resource investigator

(f) Shaper
(g) Teamworker
(h) Co-ordinator/chairman
(i) Monitor-evaluator

4.3 How do people contribute?

Team members make different types of **contribution** (eg proposing, supporting, blocking) in the areas of **task performance** and **team maintenance**.

In order to evaluate and manage team dynamics, it may be helpful for the team leader to:

(a)   Assess who (if anybody) is performing each of Belbin's **team roles**. Who is the team's plant? monitor-evaluator? and so on. There should be a mix of people performing task and team maintenance roles.

(b)   Analyse the **frequency and type of individual members' contributions** to group discussions and interactions.

   (i)   Identify which members of the team habitually make the most contributions, and which the least. (You could do this by taking a count of contributions from each member, during a sample 10-15 minutes of group discussion.)

   (ii)   If the same people tend to dominate discussion **whatever** is discussed (ie regardless of relevant expertise), the team has a problem in its communication process.

Rackham and Morgan have developed a helpful categorisation of the types of contribution people can make to team discussion and decision-making, including the following.

Category	Behaviour	Example
Proposing	Putting forward suggestions, new concepts or courses of action	'Why don't we look at a flexi-time system?'
Supporting	Supporting another person or their proposal	'Yes, I agree, flexi-time would be worth looking at.'
Seeking information	Asking for more facts, opinions or clarification	'What exactly do you mean by "flexi-time"?'
Giving information	Offering facts, opinions or clarification	'There's a helpful outline of flexi-time in this article.'
Blocking/difficulty stating	Putting obstacles in the way of a proposal, without offering any alternatives	'What if the other teams get jealous? It would only cause conflict.'
Shutting-out behaviour	Interrupting or overriding others; taking over	'Nonsense. Let's move onto something else – we've had enough of this discussion.
Bringing-in behaviour	Involving another member; encouraging contribution	'Actually, I'd like to hear what Fred has to say. Go on, Fred.'
Testing understanding	Checking whether points have been understood	'So flexi-time could work over a day or a week; have I got that right?'
Summarising	Drawing together or summing up previous discussion	'We've now heard two sides to the flexi-time issue: on the one hand, flexibility; on the other side possible risk. Now ...'

Each type of behaviour may be appropriate in the right situation at the right time. A team may be low on some types of contribution – and it may be up to the team leader to encourage, or deliberately adopt, desirable behaviours (such as bringing-in, supporting or seeking information) in order to provide balance.

5 Team development

You probably have had experience of being put into a group of people you do not know. Many teams are set up this way and it takes some time for the team to become effective.

A team **develops in stages**: forming, storming, norming, performing (**Tuckman**) and dorming or mourning/adjourning.

5.1 Tuckman's stages of group development

Four stages in group development were identified by Tuckman (1965).

Step 1	Forming
	The team is just coming together. Each member wishes to impress their personality on the group. The individuals will be trying to find out about each other, and about the aims and norms of the team. There will at this stage probably be a wariness about introducing new ideas. The objectives being pursued may as yet be unclear and a leader may not yet have emerged.

Step 2	Storming
	This frequently involves more or less open conflict between team members. There may be changes agreed in the original objectives, procedures and norms established for the group. If the team is developing successfully this may be a fruitful phase, as more realistic targets are set and trust between the group members increases.

Step 3	Norming
	A period of settling down: there will be agreements about work sharing, individual requirements and expectations of output. Norms and procedures may evolve which enable methodical working to be introduced and maintained.

Step 4	Performing
	The team sets to work to execute its task. The difficulties of growth and development no longer hinder the group's objectives.

Later writers added two stages to Tuckman's model.

(a) **Dorming**. Once a group has been performing well for some time, it may get complacent, and fall back into self-maintenance functions, at the expense of the task.

(b) **Mourning/adjourning**. The group sees itself as having fulfilled its purpose – or, if it is a temporary group, is due to physically disband. This is a stage of confusion, sadness and anxiety as the group breaks up. There is evaluation of its achievements, and gradual withdrawal of group members. If the group is to continue, going on to a new task, there will be a renegotiation of aims and roles: a return to the forming stage.

QUESTION

Team formation stages

Read the following descriptions of team behaviour and decide to which category they belong (forming, storming, norming, performing, dorming).

(a) Two of the group arguing as to whose idea is best
(b) Progress becomes static
(c) Desired outputs being achieved
(d) Shy member of group not participating
(e) Activities being allocated

ANSWER

Categorising the behaviour of group members in the situations described results in the following: (a) storming, (b) dorming, (c) performing, (d) forming, (e) norming.

6 Building a team

In Section 5, we suggested that teams have a natural evolutionary life cycle, and that four stages can be identified. Not all teams develop into mature teams and might be stuck, stagnating, in any one of the stages.

So, it often falls to the supervisor or manager to build the team. There are three main issues involved in team building.

Issues	Comments
Team identity	Get people to see themselves as part of this group
Team solidarity	Encourage loyalty so that members put in extra effort for the sake of the team
Shared objectives	Encourage the team to commit itself to shared work objectives and to co-operate willingly and effectively in achieving them

Team development can be facilitated by active **team-building** measures to support team identity, solidarity and commitment to shared objectives.

We can now discuss some of the techniques for building team identity, team solidarity and the commitment to shared objectives. But first try the question below.

QUESTION
Team-building exercises

Why might the following be effective as team-building exercises?

(a)   Sending a project team (involved in the design of electronic systems for racing cars) on a recreational day out karting.

(b)   Sending two sales teams on a day out playing 'War Games', each being an opposing combat team trying to capture the other's flag, armed with paint guns.

(c)   Sending a project team on a conference at a venue away from work, with a brief to review the past year and come up with a vision for the next year.

(These are actually commonly used techniques. If you are interested, you might locate an activity centre or company near you which offers outdoor pursuits, war games or corporate entertainment and ask them about team-building exercises and the effect they have on people.)

ANSWER

(a)   Recreation helps the team to build informal relationships: in this case, the chosen activity also reminds them of their tasks, and may make them feel special, as part of the motor racing industry, by giving them a taste of what the end user of their product does.

(b)   A team challenge forces the group to consider its strengths and weaknesses, to find its natural leader. This exercise creates an 'us' and 'them' challenge: perceiving the rival team as the enemy heightens the solidarity of the group.

(c)   This exercise encourages the group to raise problems and conflicts freely, away from the normal environment of work and also encourages brainstorming and the expression of team members' dreams for what the team can achieve in the future.

6.1 Team identity

A manager might seek to reinforce the sense of identity of the group. Arguably this is in part the creation of boundaries, identifying who is in the team and who is not.

(a) **Name**. Staff at McDonald's restaurants are known as the Crew. In other cases, the name would be more official, describing what the team actually does (eg Systems Implementation Task Force).

(b) **Badge or uniform**. This often applies to service industries, but it is unlikely that it would be applied within an organisation.

(c) Expressing the team's **self-image**. Teams often develop their own jargon, especially for new projects.

(d) Building a team **mythology**. Over time, groups and teams build up their own history and character. Stories from the past may take on an almost mythical nature (mistakes as well as successes).

(e) **A separate space**. It might help if team members work together in the same or adjacent offices, but this is not always possible. (A team intranet page may perform this function for a virtual team.)

6.2 Team solidarity

Team solidarity implies cohesion and loyalty inside the team. A team leader might be interested in:

(a) **Expressing** solidarity

(b) Encouraging **interpersonal relationships** – although the purpose of these is to ensure that work gets done

(c) **Dealing with conflict** by getting it out into the open; disagreements should be expressed and then resolved

(d) **Controlling competition** – the team leader needs to treat each member of the team fairly and to be seen to do so; favouritism undermines solidarity

(e) Encouraging some **competition with other groups**, if appropriate; for example, sales teams might be offered a prize for the highest monthly orders; London Underground runs best-kept station competitions

QUESTION

Group cohesion

Can you see any dangers in creating a very close-knit group? Think of the effect of strong team cohesion on:

(a) What the group spends its energies and attention on
(b) How the group regards outsiders, and any information or feedback they supply
(c) How the group makes decisions

What could be done about these dangerous effects?

ANSWER

Problems may arise in an ultra close-knit group because:

(a) The group's energies may be focused on its own maintenance and relationships, instead of on the task.

(b) The group may be suspicious or dismissive of outsiders, and may reject any contradictory information or criticism they supply; the group will be blinkered and stick to its own views, no matter what; cohesive groups thus often get the impression that they are infallible: they can't be wrong – and therefore can't learn from their mistakes.

(c)   The group may squash any dissent or opinions that might rock the boat. Close-knit groups tend to preserve a consensus – falsely, if required – and to take risky decisions, because they have suppressed alternative facts and viewpoints.

This phenomenon is called '**group think**' (Janis, 1982). In order to limit its effect, the team must be encouraged to:

(a)   Actively seek outside ideas and feedback
(b)   Welcome self-criticism within the group
(c)   Consciously evaluate conflicting evidence and opinions

6.3 Commitment to shared objectives

Getting commitment to the team's shared objectives may involve a range of leader activity.

- Clearly setting out the objectives of the team

- Allowing the team to participate in setting objectives

- Giving regular feedback on progress and results with constructive criticism

- Getting the team involved in providing performance feedback

- Offering positive reinforcement (praise etc) for co-operative working and task achievement by the team as a whole (rather than just 'star' individuals)

- Championing the success of the team within the organisation

7   Successful teams

A team can be evaluated on the basis of quantifiable and qualitative factors, covering its **operations** and its **output**, and team member **satisfaction**.

7.1 Evaluating team effectiveness

The task of the team leader is to build a 'successful' or 'effective' team. The criteria for team effectiveness include:

(a)   **Task performance**: fulfilment of task and organisational goals

(b)   **Team functioning**: constructive maintenance of team working, managing the demands of team dynamics, roles and processes

(c)   **Team member satisfaction**: fulfilment of individual development and relationship needs

There are a number of factors, both quantitative and qualitative, that may be assessed to decide whether or how far a team is operating effectively. Some factors cannot be taken as evidence on their own, but may suggest underlying problems – accident rates may be due to poor safety systems, for example – as well as poor morale and lack of focus due to team problems. Some of the characteristics of **effective** and **ineffective** teams may be summarised as follows.

Factor	Effective team	Ineffective team
Quantifiable		
Labour turnover	Low	High
Accident rate	Low	High
Absenteeism	Low	High
Output and productivity	High	Low

Factor	Effective team	Ineffective team
Quality of output	High	Low
Individual targets	Achieved	Not achieved
Stoppages and interruptions to the work flow	Low	High (eg because of misunderstandings, disagreements)
Qualitative		
Commitment to targets and organisational goals	High	Low
Understanding of team's work and why it exists	High	Low
Understanding of individual roles within the team	High	Low
Communication between team members	Free and open	Mistrust
Ideas	Shared for the team's benefit	'Owned' (and hidden) by individuals for their own benefit
Feedback	Constructive criticism	Point scoring, undermining
Problem-solving	Addresses causes	Only looks at symptoms
Interest in work decisions	Active	Passive acceptance
Opinions	Consensus	Imposed solutions
Job satisfaction	High	Low
Motivation in leader's absence	High	'When the cat's away ...'

7.2 Rewarding effective teams

Team-based rewards may be used to encourage co-operation and mutual accountability.

Organisations may try to encourage effective team performance by designing reward systems that recognise team, rather than individual, success. Indeed, **individual performance rewards** may act **against** team co-operation and performance.

(a) They emphasise individual rather than team performance.

(b) They encourage team leaders to think of team members only as individuals, rather than relating to them as a team.

For **team rewards** to be effective, the team must have certain characteristics.

- Distinct roles, targets and performance measures (so the team knows what it has to do to earn the reward)

- Significant autonomy and thus influence over performance (so the team perceives that extra effort will be rewarded)

- Maturity and stability

- Co-operation

- Interdependence of team members (so that the team manages member contribution, everyone 'pulls their weight', no one feels they could earn higher rewards on their own)

Reward schemes which focus on team (or organisation) performance include:

(a)   **Profit sharing** schemes, based on the distribution of a pool of cash related to profit

(b)   **Gain sharing** schemes, using a formula related to a suitable performance indicator, such as added value. Improvements in the performance indicator must be perceived to be within the employees' control, otherwise there will be no incentive to perform.

(c)   **Employee share option** schemes, giving staff the right to acquire shares in the employing company at an attractive price

CHAPTER ROUNDUP

↳ **Personality** is the total pattern of an individual's thoughts, feelings and behaviour. It is shaped by a variety of factors, both inherited and environmental.

↳ **Perception** is the process by which the brain selects and organises information in order to make sense of it. People behave according to what they perceive – not according to what really is.

↳ People develop **attitudes** about things, based on what they think, what they feel and what they want to do about it. Attitudes are formed by perception, experience and personality which in turn are shaped by wider social influences.

↳ **Role theory** suggests that people behave in any situation according to other people's expectations of how they should behave in that situation.

↳ A **group** is a collection of individuals who perceive themselves as a group. It thus has a sense of **identity**.

↳ People **contribute differently in groups** (due to group dynamics and synergy) than they do individually. This may have a positive or negative effect.

↳ A **team** is more than a group. It has joint **objectives** and **accountability** and may be set up by the organisation under the supervision or coaching of a team leader, although **self-managed teams** are growing in popularity.

↳ Teamworking may be used for: **organising** work; **controlling** activities; **generating** ideas; **decision-making**; pooling **knowledge.**

↳ Problems with teams include **conflict** on the one hand and **group think** (excessive cohesion) on the other.

↳ **Multi-disciplinary** teams contain people from different departments, pooling the skills of specialists.

Multi-skilled teams contain people who themselves have more than one skill.

↳ Ideally, team members should perform a **balanced mix of roles**. **Belbin** suggests: co-ordinator, shaper, plant, monitor-evaluator, resource-investigator, implementer, teamworker, completer-finisher and specialist.

↳ Team members make different types of **contribution** (eg proposing, supporting, blocking) in the areas of **task performance** and **team maintenance**.

↳ A team **develops in stages**: forming, storming, norming, performing (**Tuckman**) and dorming or mourning/adjourning.

↳ Team development can be facilitated by active **team-building** measures to support team identity, solidarity and commitment to shared objectives.

↳ A team can be evaluated on the basis of quantifiable and qualitative factors, covering its **operations** and its **output**, and team member **satisfaction**.

↳ **Team-based rewards** may be used to encourage co-operation and mutual accountability.

1   Stella used to be very unhappy in her job, complaining about the working conditions and the tasks, and so she left. She has been in a new job for four years and always takes on new challenges with enthusiasm. She regularly volunteers to take on extra work if other employees are busy and she rarely complains about the organisation or the management.

Which of the following options accounts for Stella's enthusiasm?

A   Her personality type   C   Her attitude
B   Her personality trait

2   'A small number of people with complementary skills who are committed to a common purpose, performance goals and approach for which they hold themselves basically accountable'. This is the definition of:

A   A group   C   A unit
B   A team

3   James is a team leader with a team of difficult employees. The work that the team does is critical and decisions made by James involve life or death situations. James has to follow correct procedures and sometimes shouts at members of the team in order to ensure the safety of everyone.

According to Belbin, what type of team member is James?

A   Shaper   C   Plant
B   Specialist   D   Complete-finisher

4   Chris is a quiet person who doesn't generally give his opinion unless he is asked for it but he is very creative and can solve difficult problems. Nicky is a loud person who gets very excited by Chris' ideas. Sonny sometimes upsets Nicky and Chris by challenging their ideas. Katja has to step in to avert friction between them.

According to Belbin's team roles, which of the team members is a teamworker?

A   Chris   C   Sonny
B   Nicky   D   Katja

5   Who described the stages of group development?

A   Woodcock   C   Tuckman
B   Belbin   D   Rackham and Morgan

6   High labour turnover is a characteristic of effective teams. True or false?

ANSWERS TO QUICK QUIZ

1   C   Her attitude. She is obviously in a positive mental state and this is influencing her responses.

2   B   This is the definition of a team. A group is a collection of individuals who perceive themselves as a group.

3   A   Shaper. James has the drive and courage to overcome obstacles but can hurt people's feelings.

4   D   Katja. Katja averts friction and calms the waters. (Chris is a plant, Nicky is a resource investigator and Sonny is a shaper.)

5   C   Tuckman. The four stages identified by Tuckman were forming, storming, norming and performing.

6   False.

Now try ...

Attempt the questions below from the **Practice Question Bank**

Q70

Q71

Q72

Q73

Q74

Human behaviour is a complex phenomenon. Managers need to understand something of what makes their team members 'tick' – particularly when it comes to the key question: how do you get them to perform well, or better?

That is what **motivation** is about.

Having explored motivation and its impact on performance in **Section 1**, we go on to look at a range of key **motivational theories** in **Sections 2 to 4.** There are some famous theoretical models here, and it is definitely worth learning them.

In **Sections 5 to 6**, we look at a range of **financial and non-financial rewards** that may be used to motivate people. Take note, as you proceed through the chapter, that money is by no means the only (or necessarily the most effective) incentive to higher levels of performance.

The ability to 'motivate' people is also a key skill of **leadership**, as we saw in Chapter 11.

Motivating individuals and groups

EXAM FOCUS POINT

Motivation is likely to appear regularly in the exam, since it is an essential aspect of managerial responsibility. Since there is a large body of academic work, you must understand the theories and authorities.

1 Overview of motivation

1.1 What is motivation?

Motivation is concerned with what causes people to act in a certain way, whether it be drinking a glass of water to reduce thirst or working hard to achieve a promotion at work.

Motivation is 'a decision-making process through which the individual chooses desired outcomes and sets in motion the behaviour appropriate to acquiring them'. (Huczynski and Buchanan, 2010).

In practice, the words **motives** and **motivation** are commonly used in different contexts to mean the following.

(a) **Goals or outcomes** that have become desirable for a particular individual. We say that money, power or friendship are motives for doing something.

(b) The **mental process of choosing desired outcomes**, deciding how to go about them (and whether the likelihood of success warrants the amount of effort that will be necessary) and setting in motion the required behaviour.

(c) The **social process** by which other people motivate us to behave in the ways they wish. Motivation in this sense usually applies to the attempts of organisations to get workers to put in more effort.

1.2 Needs and goals

People have certain **innate needs and goals**, through which they expect their needs to be satisfied. Both of these drive behaviour.

Individual behaviour is partly influenced by human biology, which requires certain basics for life. When the body is deprived of these essentials, biological forces called **needs** or **drives** are activated (eg hunger), and dictate the behaviour required to end the deprivation: eat, drink, flee, and so on. However, we retain freedom of choice about **how** we satisfy our drives: they do not dictate specific or highly predictable behaviour. (Say you are hungry: how many specific ways of satisfying your hunger can you think of?)

Each individual also has a set of **goals**. The relative importance of those goals to the individual may vary with time, circumstances and other factors.

Influence	Comment
Childhood environment and education	Aspiration levels, family and career models, and so on are formed at early stages of development.
Experience	This teaches us what to expect from life: we will either strive to repeat positive experiences, or to avoid or make up for negative ones.
Age and position	There is usually a gradual process of goal shift with age. Relationships and exploration may preoccupy young employees. Career and family goals tend to compete in the 20-40 age group: career launch and take-off may have to yield to the priorities associated with forming permanent relationships and having children.
Culture	Collectivist cultures (see Chapter 3) show a greater concern for relationships at work, while individualist cultures emphasise power and autonomy.
Self-concept	All the above factors are bound up with the individual's own self-image. The individual's assessments of their own abilities and place in society will affect the relative strength and nature of their needs and goals.

The **basic assumptions of motivation** are that:

(a)   People behave in such a way as to **satisfy their needs** and fulfil their goals.

(b)   An organisation is in a position to **offer some of the satisfactions** people might seek: relationships and belonging, challenge and achievement, progress on the way to self-actualisation, security and structure, and so on.

(c)   The organisation can therefore **influence** people to behave in ways it desires (to secure work performance) by offering them the means to satisfy their needs and fulfil their goals in return for that behaviour. (This process of influence is called motivation.)

(d)   If people's needs are being met, and goals being fulfilled, at work, they are more likely to have a **positive attitude** to their work and to the organisation, and to experience **job satisfaction**.

1.3 How useful is 'motivation' as a concept?

Motivation is a useful concept, despite the fact that the **impact** of motivation, job satisfaction and morale on performance are difficult to measure.

The impact of motivation and job satisfaction on **performance** is difficult to measure accurately.

(a)   Motivation is about getting **extra** levels of commitment and performance from employees, over and above mere compliance with rules and procedures. If individuals can be motivated, by one means or another, they might work more efficiently (and productivity will rise) or they will produce a better quality of work.

(b)   The case for job satisfaction as a factor in improved performance is not proven.

(c)   The key is to work 'smarter' – not necessarily 'harder'.

Morale is a term drawn primarily from a military context, to denote the state of mind or spirit of a group (esprit de corps), particularly regarding **discipline** and **confidence**. It can be related to satisfaction, since low morale implies a state of dissatisfaction.

The signs by which **low morale or dissatisfaction** are gauged are also ambiguous.

(a)   **Low productivity** is not invariably a sign of low morale. There may be more concrete problems (eg with work organisation or technology).

(b)   **High labour turnover** is not a reliable indicator of low morale: the age structure of the workforce and other factors in natural wastage will need to be taken into account. Low turnover, likewise, is no evidence of high morale: people may be staying because of a lack of other opportunities in the local job market, for example.

However, there is some evidence that satisfaction correlates with mental health, so symptoms of **stress** or psychological dysfunction may be a signal that all is not well. (Again, a range of non-work factors may be contributing.)

Attitude surveys may also be used to indicate workers' perception of their job satisfaction, by way of interview or questionnaire.

QUESTION

Personal motivation

What factors in yourself or your organisation motivate you to:

(a)   Turn up to work at all?
(b)   Do an average day's work?
(c)   'Bust a gut' on a task or for a boss?

Go on – be honest!

1.4 Theories of motivation

Many **theories** try to explain motivation and why and how people can be motivated.

One classification distinguishes between content and process theories.

(a)   **Content theories** ask the question: '**What** are the things that motivate people?'

They assume that human beings have a **set** of needs or desired outcomes. Maslow's hierarchy of needs and Herzberg's two-factor theory, both discussed shortly, are two of the most important approaches of this type.

(b)   **Process theories** ask the question: '**How** can people be motivated?'

They explore the process through which outcomes **become** desirable and are pursued by individuals. This approach assumes that people are able to select their goals and choose the paths towards them by a conscious or unconscious process of calculation. Expectancy theory and Handy's 'motivation calculus', discussed later, are theories of this type.

EXAM FOCUS POINT

There is an article on the ACCA website entitled "Let's get motivated" that is relevant to material in this chapter.

2   Content theories of motivation

Content theories of motivation suggest that the best way to motivate an employee is to find out what their needs are and offer them rewards that will satisfy those needs.

2.1 Maslow's hierarchy of needs

> **Maslow** identified a hierarchy of needs which an individual will be motivated to satisfy, progressing towards higher order satisfactions, such as self-actualisation.

Abraham Maslow (1943) described five innate human needs, and put forward certain propositions about the motivating power of each need.

- Self-actualisation — fulfilment of personal potential
- Esteem needs — for independence, recognition, status, respect from others
- Love/social needs — for relationships, affection, belonging
- Safety needs — for security, order, predictability, freedom from threat
- Physiological needs — food, shelter

(a) An individual's needs can be arranged in a '**hierarchy** of relative pre-potency' (as shown). Each level of need is **dominant until satisfied**; only then does the next level of need become a motivating factor. A need which has been satisfied no longer motivates an individual's behaviour.

(b) The need for self-actualisation can rarely be satisfied.

(c) In addition, Maslow described:

   (i) Freedom of enquiry and expression needs (for social conditions permitting free speech, and encouraging justice, fairness and honesty)

   (ii) Knowledge and understanding needs (to gain knowledge of the environment, to explore, to learn)

QUESTION
Maslow's hierarchy of needs

Decide which of Maslow's categories the following fit into.

(a) Receiving praise from your manager
(b) A family party
(c) An artist forgetting to eat
(d) A man washed up on a desert island

(e) A pay increase
(f) Joining a local drama group
(g) Being awarded the OBE
(h) Buying a house

ANSWER

Maslow's categories for the listed circumstances are as follows.

(a) Esteem needs
(b) Social needs
(c) Self-actualisation needs overriding lower-level needs!
(d) Physiological needs
(e) Safety needs initially; esteem needs above in a certain income level
(f) Social needs or self-actualisation needs
(g) Esteem needs
(h) Safety needs or esteem needs

2.1.1 Evaluating Maslow's theory

Maslow's hierarchy is simple and intuitively attractive: you are unlikely to worry about respect if you are starving! However, it is only a theory and has been shown to have several major limitations.

(a) An individual's behaviour may be in response to **several needs**, and the same need may cause **different behaviour** in different individuals, so it is difficult to use the model to explain or predict an individual's behaviour in response to rewards.

(b) The hierarchy ignores the concept of **deferred gratification** (by which people are prepared to ignore current suffering for the promise of future benefits) and **altruistic behaviour** (by which people sacrifice their own needs for others).

(c) **Empirical verification** of the hierarchy is hard to come by.

(d) Research has revealed that the hierarchy reflects UK and US **cultural values**, which may not transfer to other contexts.

2.2 Herzberg's two-factor theory

> **Herzberg** identified two basic need systems: the need to avoid unpleasantness and the need for personal growth. He suggested factors which could be offered by organisations to satisfy both types of need: hygiene and motivator factors respectively.

Herzberg's two-factor theory (Herzberg et al, 1959) is based on two needs: the need to avoid unpleasantness, and the need for personal growth.

(a) The need to avoid unpleasantness is satisfied through **hygiene factors**. Hygiene factors are to do with the environment and conditions of work, including:

- Company policy and administration
- Salary
- The quality of supervision
- Interpersonal relations
- Working conditions
- Job security

If inadequate, hygiene factors cause **dissatisfaction** with work (which is why they are also called 'dissatisfiers'). They work like sanitation, which minimises threats to health rather than actively promoting 'good health'.

(b) The need for personal growth is satisfied by **motivator factors**.

These actively create job satisfaction (they are also called 'satisfiers') and are effective in motivating an individual to superior performance and effort. These factors are connected to the work itself, including:

- Status (although this may be a hygiene factor too)
- Advancement (or opportunities for it)
- Recognition by colleagues and management
- Responsibility
- Challenging work
- A sense of achievement
- Growth in the job

A lack of motivator factors will encourage employees to concentrate on the hygiene factors. These, although they can be regarded as motivators in the very short term, will eventually dissatisfy.

Herzberg suggested that where there is evidence of poor motivation, such as low productivity, poor quality and strikes, management should not pay too much attention to hygiene factors, such as pay and conditions. Despite the fact that these are the traditional targets for the aspirations of organised labour, their potential for bringing improvements to work attitudes is limited. Instead, Herzberg suggested three types of **job design** which would offer job satisfaction through enhanced motivator factors.

- Job enlargement
- Job rotation   } discussed in Section 5 below.
- Job enrichment

2.3 Evaluating Herzberg's theory

Herzberg's original study was concerned with 203 Pittsburgh engineers and accountants. His theory has therefore been criticised as being based on:

(a)   An inadequately small sample size
(b)   A limited cultural context (Western professionals)

The impact of job satisfaction (from motivator factors) on work performance has proved difficult to verify and measure.

EXAM FOCUS POINT

There is an article on the ACCA website entitled "Understanding Herzberg's motivational theory" that is relevant to material in this section.

3 ▌ Process theories of motivation

Process theories of motivation help managers to understand the dynamics of employees' decisions about what rewards are worth going for.

3.1 Vroom's expectancy theory

Expectancy theory basically states that the strength of an individual's motivation to do something will depend on the extent to which they expect the results of their efforts to contribute to their personal needs or goals.

Victor Vroom (1964) stated a formula by which human motivation could be assessed and measured. He suggested that the strength of an individual's motivation is the product of two factors.

(a)   The strength of their **preference** for a certain outcome. Vroom called this **valence**: it can be represented as a positive or negative number, or zero – since outcomes may be desired, avoided or regarded with indifference.

(b)   His **expectation** that the outcome will in fact result from a certain behaviour. Vroom called this 'subjective probability' or **expectancy**. As a probability, it may be represented by any number between 0 (no chance) and 1 (certainty).

In its simplest form, the expectancy equation may be stated as:

$F = V \times E$

where: F   =   the force or strength of the individual's motivation to behave in a particular way

             V   =   valence: the strength of the individual preference for a given outcome or reward

             E   =   expectancy: the individual's perception that the behaviour will result in the outcome/ reward

In this equation, the lower the values of valence or expectancy, the less the motivation. An employee may have a high expectation that increased productivity will result in promotion (because of managerial promises, say), but if they are indifferent or negative towards the idea of promotion (because they dislike responsibility), they will not be motivated to increase their productivity. Likewise, if promotion is very important to them – but they do not believe higher productivity will get them promoted (because they have been passed over before, perhaps), their motivation will be low.

EXAM FOCUS POINT

This equation could form the subject of a one-mark question.

3.2 Managerial implications of process theories

Process theory suggests the following.

(a) **Intended results should be made clear**, so that the individual can complete the motivation calculation by knowing what is expected, the reward, and how much effort it will take.

(b) Individuals are more committed to **specific goals** which they **have helped to set themselves**, taking their needs and expectations into account.

(c) Immediate and ongoing **feedback** should be given. Without knowledge of actual results, there is no check that 'E' expenditure was justified (or will be justified in future).

(d) If an individual is **rewarded** according to performance tied to standards (management by objectives), however, they may well set lower standards: the expectancy part of the calculation (likelihood of success and reward) is greater if the standard is lower, so less expense of 'E' is indicated.

4 Choosing a motivational approach

Two influential writers of the neo-human relations school argue that a manager's approach to motivating people depends on the **assumptions** they make about 'what makes them tick'.

4.1 McGregor: Theory X and Theory Y

McGregor suggested that a manager's approach is based on attitudes somewhere on a scale between two extreme sets of assumptions: Theory X (workers have to be coerced) and Theory Y (workers want to be empowered).

McGregor (1987) suggested that managers (in the US) tended to behave as though they subscribed to one of two sets of assumptions about people at work: Theory X and Theory Y.

(a) **Theory X** suggests that most people dislike work and responsibility and will avoid both if possible. Because of this, most people must be coerced, controlled, directed and/or threatened with punishment to get them to make an adequate effort. Managers who operate according to these assumptions will tend to supervise closely, apply detailed rules and controls, and use 'carrot and stick' motivators.

(b) **Theory Y** suggests that physical and mental effort in work is as natural as play or rest. The ordinary person does not inherently dislike work: according to the conditions, it may be a source of satisfaction or dissatisfaction. The potentialities of the average person are rarely fully used at work. People can be motivated to seek challenge and responsibility in the job, if their goals can be integrated with those of the organisation. A manager with this sort of attitude to their staff is likely to be a consultative, facilitating leader, using positive feedback, challenge and responsibility as motivators.

Both are intended to be extreme sets of assumptions – not actual types of people. However, they also tend to be self-fulfilling prophecies. Employees treated as if 'Theory X' were true will begin to behave accordingly. Employees treated as if 'Theory Y' were true – being challenged to take on more responsibility – will rise to the challenge and behave accordingly.

Theory X and Theory Y can be used to heighten managers' awareness of the assumptions underlying their motivational style.

5 Rewards and incentives

Not all the **incentives** that an organisation can offer its employees are directly related to **monetary** rewards. The satisfaction of **any** of the employee's wants or needs may be seen as a reward for past performance, or an incentive for future performance.

- A **reward** is a token (monetary or otherwise) given to an individual or team in recognition of some contribution or success.
- An **incentive** is the offer or promise of a reward for contribution or success, designed to motivate the individual or team to behave in such a way as to earn it. (In other words, the 'carrot' dangled in front of the donkey!)

Different individuals have different goals, and get different things out of their working life: in other words, they have different **orientations** to work. Why might a person work, or be motivated to work well?

(a) The **human relations** school of management theorists regarded **work relationships** as the main source of satisfaction and reward offered to the worker.

(b) Later writers suggested a range of 'higher-order' motivations, notably:

- **Job satisfaction**, interest and challenge in the job itself – rewarding work
- **Participation** in decision-making – responsibility and involvement

(c) **Pay** has always occupied a rather ambiguous position, but since people need money to live, it will certainly be part of the reward package.

5.1 Intrinsic and extrinsic factors

Rewards may be **extrinsic** (external to the work and individual) or **intrinsic** (arising from performance of the work itself).

Rewards offered to the individual at work may be of two basic types.

(a) **Extrinsic rewards** are separate from (or external to) the job itself, and dependent on the decisions of others (that is, also external to the control of the workers themselves). Pay, benefits, non-cash incentives and working conditions (Herzberg's hygiene factors) are examples.

(b) **Intrinsic rewards** are those which arise from the performance of the work itself (Herzberg's motivator factors). They are therefore psychological rather than material and relate to the concept of job satisfaction. Intrinsic rewards include the satisfaction that comes from completing a piece of work, the status that certain jobs convey, and the feeling of achievement that comes from doing a difficult job well.

EXAM FOCUS POINT

The examining team has noted that candidates have performed poorly in the past on questions relating to the distinction between intrinsic and extrinsic rewards. A recent question tested the point that 'enjoyment of the job' is clearly an intrinsic reward, while securing a bonus or achieving promotion are driven by factors external to the job itself.

5.2 A reward system

It is suggested that a reward system should do six things.

(a)   Encourage people to **fill job vacancies** and not leave

(b)   Increase the **predictability of employees' behaviour**, so that employees can be depended on to carry out their duties consistently and to a reasonable standard

(c)   Increase **willingness to accept change** and flexibility (changes in work practices are often 'bought' from trade unions with higher pay)

(d)   Foster and **encourage innovative behaviour**

(e)   **Reflect the nature of jobs** in the organisation and the skills or experience required. The reward system should therefore be consistent with seniority of position in the organisation structure, and should be thought fair by all employees

(f)   **Motivate**: that is, increase commitment and effort

5.3 Job design as a motivator

The **job** itself can be used as a motivator, or it can be a cause of dissatisfaction. **Job design** refers to how tasks are organised to create 'jobs' for individuals.

5.3.1 Micro-design

One of the consequences of mass production and scientific management was what might be called a **micro-division** of labour, or **job simplification**. Micro-designed jobs have the following **advantages**.

(a)   **Little training**. A job is divided up into the smallest number of sequential tasks possible. Each task is so simple and straightforward that it can be learned with very little training.

(b)   **Replacement**. If labour turnover is high, this does not matter because unskilled replacements can be found and trained to do the work in a very short time.

(c)   **Flexibility**. Since the skill required is low, workers can be shifted from one task to another very easily.

(d)   **Control**. If tasks are closely defined and standard times set for their completion, production is easier to predict and control.

(e)   **Quality**. Standardisation of work into simple tasks means that quality is easier to predict.

Disadvantages of micro-designed jobs, however, include the following.

(a)   The work is **monotonous** and makes employees tired, bored and dissatisfied. The consequences will be high labour turnover, absenteeism, spoilage and unrest. People work better when their work is variable, unlike machines.

(b)   An individual doing a simple task feels like a small cog in a large machine, and has no **sense of contributing** to the organisation's end product or service.

(c)   Excessive specialisation **isolates** the individual in their work and inhibits not only social contacts with workmates, but knowledge generation.

(d)   In practice, excessive job simplification leads to **lower quality**, through inattention and loss of morale.

5.3.2 Job enrichment

Three ways of **improving job design** to make jobs more interesting to the employee, and hopefully to improve performance are job enrichment, job enlargement and job rotation.

Job enrichment is planned, deliberate action to build greater responsibility, breadth and challenge of work into a job. Job enrichment is similar to **empowerment**.

Job enrichment represents a 'vertical' extension of the job into greater levels of responsibility, challenge and autonomy. A job may be enriched by:

* Giving the job holder **decision-making tasks** of a higher order
* Giving the employee greater **freedom** to decide how the job should be done
* Encouraging employees to **participate** in the planning decisions of their superiors
* Giving the employee regular **feedback**

5.3.3 Job enlargement

Job enlargement is the attempt to widen jobs by increasing the number of operations in which a job holder is involved.

Job enlargement is a 'horizontal' extension of the job by increasing task variety and reducing task repetition.

(a) Tasks which span a larger part of the total production work should reduce boredom and add to task meaning, significance and variety.

(b) Enlarged jobs might be regarded as having higher status within the department, perhaps as stepping stones towards promotion.

Job enlargement is, however, limited in its intrinsic rewards, as asking workers to complete three separate tedious, unchallenging tasks is unlikely to be more motivating than asking them to perform just one tedious, unchallenging task!

5.3.4 Job rotation

Job rotation is the planned transfer of staff from one job to another to increase task variety.

Job rotation is a 'sequential' extension of the job. For example, in a factory where the worst job is seen as packing the products in to boxes, and the best job as being the fork lift truck driver: job rotation would ensure that individuals spent equal time on all jobs. Job rotation is also sometimes seen as a form of training, where individuals gain wider experience by rotating as trainees in different positions.

It is generally admitted that the developmental value of job rotation is limited – but it can reduce the monotony of repetitive work.

5.3.5 Job optimisation

A well-designed job should provide the individual with five **core dimensions** which contribute to job satisfaction.

(a) **Skill variety**: the opportunity to exercise different skills and perform different operations

(b) **Task identity**: the integration of operations into a 'whole' tasks (or meaningful segments of the task)

(c) **Task significance**: the task is perceived to have a role, purpose, meaning and value

(d) **Autonomy**: the opportunity to exercise discretion or self-management (eg in areas such as target-setting and work methods)

(e) **Feedback**: the availability of performance feedback, enabling the individual to assess their progress and the opportunity to **give** feedback, be heard and influence results

5.4 Feedback as a motivator

Constructive performance **feedback** is important in job satisfaction and motivation.

There are two main types of feedback, both of which are valuable in enhancing performance and development.

(a) **Motivational feedback** is used to reward and reinforce positive behaviour and performance by praising and encouraging the individual.

(b) **Developmental feedback** is given when a particular area of performance needs to be improved, helping the individual to identify what needs to be changed and how this might be done.

Constructive feedback is designed to widen options and encourage development. This does not mean giving only positive, motivational or 'encouraging' feedback about what a person has done: feedback about areas for improvement, given skilfully and sensitively, is in many ways more useful. It needs to be:

- Balanced with positives
- Specific
- Focused on behaviour/results – **not** personalities
- Objective (felt to be fair)
- Supportive/co-operative, emphasising the resources available to help the person improve
- Selective (not tackling all shortcomings at once)
- Encouraging

5.5 Participation as a motivator

Participation in decision-making (if genuine) can make people more committed to the task.

People generally want more interesting work and to have a say in decision-making. These expectations are a basic part of the movement towards greater **participation** at work.

Participation can involve employees and make them feel committed to their task, given the following conditions (5 Cs).

- **Certainty**. Participation should be genuine.
- **Consistency**. Efforts to establish participation should be made consistently over a long period.
- **Clarity**. The purpose of participation is made quite clear.
- **Capacity**. The individual has the ability and information to participate effectively.
- **Commitment**. The manager believes in and genuinely supports participation.

5.6 Inappropriate reward systems

Inappropriate reward systems may occur in practice. For example:

- Bonuses awarded regardless of performance
- Pay rises built into a contract regardless of performance

In these examples, the employee has no incentive to increase their performance or contribute to the organisation's prosperity. An employee could be rewarded with a bonus when they have completely failed to meet all their objectives. Another employee may have a contract with built-in pay rises, so spends time on the golf course instead of working. Both these examples will cause corporate governance problems, as the regime is effectively rewarding failure in the first case and paying for the pursuit of personal interests in the second case.

6 Pay as a motivator

Pay is the most important of the hygiene factors, but it is ambiguous in its effect on motivation.

Pay is important because:

- It is a major cost for the organisation.
- People feel strongly about it: it 'stands in' for a number of human needs and goals.
- It is a legal issue (minimum wage, equal pay legislation).
- It enables the organisation to attract and retain individuals with the knowledge, skills and experience required.

6.1 How is pay determined?

There are a number of ways in which organisations determine pay.

(a) **Job evaluation**. This is a systematic process for establishing the relative worth of jobs within an organisation. Its main purpose is to provide a rational basis for the design and maintenance of an equitable (and legally defensible) pay structure.

The salary structure is based on **job content**, and not on the personal merit of the job holder. (The individual job holder can be paid extra personal bonuses in reward for performance.)

(b) **Fairness**. Pay must be **perceived** and felt to match the level of work, and the capacity of the individual to do it.

(c) **Negotiated pay scales**. Pay scales, differentials and minimum rates may have been negotiated at plant, local or national level, according to such factors as legislation, government policy, the economy, the power of trade unions, the state of the labour market for relevant skills, productivity agreements, and so on.

(d) **Market rates**. Market rates of pay will have most influence on pay structures where there is a standard pattern of supply and demand in the open labour market. If an organisation's rates fall below the benchmark rates in the local or national labour market from which it recruits, it will have trouble attracting and holding employees.

(e) **Individual performance in the job**. This can result in merit pay awards, or performance-related bonuses.

6.2 Types of reward

An organisation may offer a range of rewards to employees, perhaps combined in a reward package. The range offered may include some or all of the following.

- Basic wages or salary
- Overtime payments (perhaps for employees paid a wage based on hours worked)
- Performance-related bonus
- Shares
- Share options (the opportunity to buy shares at a favourable price)
- Benefits in kind (for example personal use of a company vehicle)
- Pension contributions
- Service contracts and termination payments

Packages for employees at different levels are likely to differ.

6.3 What do people want from pay?

Pay has a central – but ambiguous – role in motivation theory. It is not mentioned explicitly in any need list, but it offers the satisfaction of many of the various needs.

Individuals may also have needs unrelated to money, however, which money cannot satisfy, or which the pay system of the organisation actively denies (eg the need for leisure/family time – not overtime!) So to what extent is pay an inducement to better performance? Can pay be an effective motivator or incentive?

Although the size of their income will affect their standard of living, most people tend not to be concerned about **maximising** their earnings. They may like to earn more but are probably more concerned about **earning enough** and knowing that their pay is fair in comparison with the pay of others both inside and outside the organisation.

Pay is a 'hygiene' factor: it gets taken for granted, and so is more often a source of dissatisfaction than satisfaction. However, pay is the most important of the hygiene factors, according to Herzberg. It is valuable not only in its power to be **converted** into a wide range of other satisfactions but also as a consistent **measure of worth** or value, allowing employees to compare themselves and be compared with other individuals or occupational groups inside and outside the organisation.

Research has also illustrated that workers may have an **instrumental orientation** to work: the attitude that work is not an end in itself but a means to other ends, through earning money.

Pay is only one of several intrinsic and extrinsic rewards offered by work. If pay is used to motivate, it can only do so in a wider context of the job and the other rewards. Thanks, praise and recognition, for example, are alternative forms of positive reinforcement.

QUESTION
Pay as a motivator

Herzberg says that money is a **hygiene** factor in the motivation process. If this is true, it means that lack of money can demotivate, but the presence of money will not in itself be a motivator.

How far do you agree with this proposition? Can individuals be motivated by a pay rise?

6.4 Performance-related pay (PRP)

Performance-related pay (PRP) is a form of incentive system, awarding extra pay for extra output or performance.

Performance-related pay (PRP) is related to output (in terms of the number of items produced or time taken to produce a unit of work), or results achieved (performance to defined standards in key tasks, according to plan).

The most common individual PRP scheme for wage earners is straight **piecework**: payment of a fixed amount per unit produced, or operation completed.

For managerial and other salaried jobs, however, a form of **management by objectives** will probably be applied. PRP is often awarded at the discretion of the line manager, although guidelines may suggest, for example, that those rated exceptional get a bonus of 10% whereas those who have performed less well only get, say, 3%.

(a)   Key results can be identified and specified, for which merit awards will be paid.

(b)   There will be a clear model for evaluating performance and knowing when, or if, targets have been reached and payments earned.

(c)   The exact conditions and amounts of awards can be made clear to the employee, to avoid uncertainty and later resentment.

For service and other departments, a PRP scheme may involve **bonuses** for achievement of key results, or **points schemes**, where points are awarded for performance of various criteria (efficiency, cost savings, quality of service, and so on). Certain points totals (or the highest points total in the unit, if a competitive system is used) then win cash or other awards.

6.4.1 Evaluating PRP

Benefits of PRP

- Improves commitment and capability
- Complements other HR initiatives

- Improves focus on the business's performance objectives
- Encourages two-way communication
- Allows greater supervisory responsibility
- Recognises achievement when other means are not available

Potential problems

- Subjectivity of awards for less measurable criteria (eg 'teamwork')
- Encouraging short-term focus and target-hitting (rather than improvements)
- Divisive/against teamworking (if awards are individual)
- Difficulties gaining union acceptance (if perceived to erode basic pay)

QUESTION

PRP

Why might PRP fail to motivate?

ANSWER

(a)   The rewards from PRP are often too small to motivate effectively. Anyhow, some employees may not expect to receive the rewards and hence will not put in the extra effort.

(b)   It is often unfair, especially in jobs where success is determined by uncontrollable factors.

(c)   If people are rewarded individually, they may be less willing to work as a team.

(d)   People may concentrate on short-term performance indicators rather than on longer-term goals such as innovation or quality. In other words, people put all their energy into hitting the target rather than doing their job better.

(e)   PRP schemes have to be well designed to ensure performance is measured properly, people consider them to be fair and there is consent to the scheme.

6.5 Rewarding the team

Various forms of **group rewards** can be used as an incentive to co-operative performance and mutual accountability.

6.5.1 Group bonus schemes

Group incentive schemes typically offer a bonus for a team which achieves or exceeds specified targets. Offering bonuses to a whole team may be appropriate for tasks where individual contributions cannot be isolated, workers have little control over their individual output because tasks depend on each other, or where team-building is particularly required. It may enhance team spirit and co-operation as well as provide performance incentives, but it may also create pressures within the group if some individuals are seen not to be pulling their weight.

6.5.2 Profit-sharing schemes

Profit-sharing schemes offer employees (or selected groups) bonuses, directly related to profits or value added. Profit sharing is based on the belief that all employees can contribute to profitability, and that that contribution should be recognised. The effects may include profit-consciousness and motivation in employees, commitment to the future prosperity of the organisation, and so on.

The actual incentive value and effect on productivity may be wasted, however, if the scheme is badly designed.

(a)   The sum should be **significant**.

(b)   There should be a **clear and timely link** between effort or performance and reward. Profit shares should be distributed as frequently as possible, consistent with the need for reliable information on profit forecasts, targets, etc and the need to amass significant amounts for distribution.

(c)   The scheme should only be introduced if profit forecasts indicate a **reasonable chance of achieving** the above: profit sharing is welcome when profits are high, but the potential for disappointment is great.

(d)   The greatest effect on productivity arising from the scheme may in fact arise from its use as a focal point for **discussion** with employees, about the relationship between their performance and results, areas and targets for improvement, etc. Management must be seen to be committed to the principle.

6.6 Other issues

It is important that **senior executive pay packages** provide incentives for them to improve business performance – that the package encourages behaviour that is consistent with achieving the organisation's strategic goals. Rewards should focus on the medium and long term, not just the short term.

Pensions are becoming an important part of the remuneration package. With individuals living longer and interest rates (and therefore investment income) being very low, pensions are the main source of income for a growing proportion of the population. Pension schemes in which the company pays significant contributions (rather than only the employee contributing) are very attractive to employees – pensions are an increasingly important element of the pay package.

In order to retain a key employee, particularly in a business where the workforce is traditionally highly mobile, the organisation may be prepared to offer long-term rewards, such as share option schemes to retain the employee longer. This approach, using a future reward to encourage staff retention, is referred to as **golden handcuffs**.

When a long-serving senior executive leaves, an organisation may make an additional payment called a **golden handshake** as part of the termination payment. The payment may be a reward for exceptional service, or in some circumstances the payment may be offered as an incentive to leave.

Sometimes an organisation may find that it has too many staff, perhaps because of reduced demand or more efficient working methods. In these circumstances, an organisation may ask for volunteers to give up their jobs – by offering **voluntary redundancy**. These volunteers are usually offered a relatively generous redundancy payment – and helps the organisation retain the goodwill of the remaining employees.

Pay can be a powerful **short-term** motivator (even according to Herzberg!); for example, a bonus payment for completing a piece of work in a specified period of time.

CHAPTER ROUNDUP

↪ **Motivation** is concerned with what causes people to act in a certain way, whether it be drinking a glass of water to reduce thirst or working hard to achieve a promotion at work.

↪ People have certain **innate needs and goals**, through which they expect their needs to be satisfied. Both of these drive behaviour.

↪ **Motivation** is a **useful concept**, despite the fact that the impact of motivation, job satisfaction and morale on performance are difficult to measure.

↪ Many **theories** try to explain motivation and why and how people can be motivated.

↪ **Content theories** of motivation suggest that the best way to motivate an employee is to find out what their needs are and offer them rewards that will satisfy those needs.

↪ **Maslow** identified a hierarchy of needs which an individual will be motivated to satisfy, progressing towards higher order satisfactions, such as self-actualisation.

↪ **Herzberg** identified two basic need systems: the need to avoid unpleasantness and the need for personal growth. He suggested factors which could be offered by organisations to satisfy both types of need: hygiene and motivator factors respectively.

↪ **Process theories** of motivation help managers to understand the dynamics of employees' decisions about what rewards are worth going for.

↪ **Expectancy theory** basically states that the strength of an individual's motivation to do something will depend on the extent to which they expect the results of their efforts to contribute to their personal needs or goals.

↪ **McGregor** suggested that a manager's approach is based on attitudes somewhere on a scale between two extreme sets of assumptions: Theory X (workers have to be coerced) and Theory Y (workers want to be empowered).

↪ Not all the **incentives** that an organisation can offer its employees are directly related to **monetary** rewards. The satisfaction of **any** of the employee's wants or needs may be seen as a reward for past performance, or an incentive for future performance.

↪ **Rewards** may be **extrinsic** (external to the work and individual) or **intrinsic** (arising from performance of the work itself).

↪ The **job** itself can be used as a motivator, or it can be a cause of dissatisfaction. **Job design** refers to how tasks are organised to create 'jobs' for individuals.

↪ Three ways of **improving job design** to make jobs more interesting to the employee, and hopefully to improve performance are job enrichment, job enlargement and job rotation.

↪ Constructive performance **feedback** is important in job satisfaction and motivation.

↪ **Participation** in decision-making (if genuine) can make people more committed to the task.

↪ **Pay** is the most important of the hygiene factors, but it is ambiguous in its effect on motivation.

↪ **Performance-related pay (PRP)** is a form of incentive system, awarding extra pay for extra output or performance.

↪ Various forms of **group rewards** can be used as an incentive to co-operative performance and mutual accountability.

QUICK QUIZ

1   Tick the correct box

                                                             Positive   *Self*

                                           reinforcement   *actualisation*

    Encouraging a certain type of behaviour by rewarding it   ☐   ☐

    Personal growth and fulfilment of potential   ☐   ☐

2   Which one of the following is not one of Maslow's hierarchy of needs?

    A   Esteem needs   C   Social needs

    B   Safety needs   D   Cultural needs

3   A reward is the offer or promise of a benefit for contribution or success, designed to motivate the individual of team. True or false?

4   In Vroom's expectancy theory, the lower the values of valence and expectancy, the higher the motivation. True or false?

5   According to Herzberg, leadership style is a motivator factor. True or false?

6   A 'horizontal' extension of the job to increase task variety is called:

    A   Job evaluation   C   Job enlargement

    B   Job enrichment   D   Job rotation

ANSWERS TO QUICK QUIZ

1
	Positive reinforcement	Self actualisation
Encouraging a certain type of behaviour by rewarding it	✓	☐
Personal growth and fulfilment of potential	☐	✓

2   D   Cultural needs. Maslow's hierarchy of needs includes physiological needs, safety needs, love/social needs, esteem needs and self actualisation.

3   False. This is an incentive.

4   False. Motivation would be lower. F= V × E so the lower that V and E are, the lower F (motivation) is.

5   False. It is a hygiene factor.

6   C   Make sure you can define all the other terms as well.

Now try ...

Attempt the questions below from the **Practice Question Bank**

Q75

Q76

Q77

Q78

Q79

16

Training and development

The development of people to meet current – and changing – job demands is a key leadership task.

In **Section 1**, we describe how people learn, and in **Sections 2 to 6**, we look at key aspects of a systematic approach to training: identifying training needs, selecting training **methods** and designing training that suits how people learn. **Evaluating** the effectiveness of training is also very important.

There are detailed procedures and models to learn, but at the core of this topic is the need to ensure that trainee learning is **applied** in the work context. Bear this in mind as you explore training methods, in particular.

In **Section 7**, we look at the wider topic of **development**, which is about more than just improving job performance.

This topic looks forward to performance appraisal (Chapter 17) because it is one of the formal ways of identifying training needs and development potential.

EXAM FOCUS POINT

'Training and development' contains a wide range of examinable topics. It could be linked with appraisal and performance management, where training needs are identified.

1 The learning process

There are different schools of thought as to **how people learn**.

1.1 Approaches to learning theory

There are different schools of learning theory which explain and describe how people learn.

(a) **Behaviourist psychology** concentrates on the relationship between stimuli (input through the senses) and responses to those stimuli. 'Learning' is the formation of new connections between stimulus and response, on the basis of conditioning. We modify our responses in future according to whether the results of our behaviour in the past have been good or bad.

(b) The **cognitive approach** argues that the human mind takes sensory information and imposes organisation and meaning on it: we interpret and rationalise. We use feedback information on the results of past behaviour to make rational decisions about whether to maintain successful behaviour or modify unsuccessful behaviour in future, according to our goals and our plans for reaching them.

1.2 Lessons from learning theory

Whichever approach it is based on, learning theory offers certain useful propositions for the design of **effective training programmes** and the role of the human resources department in developing such program.

Proposition	Comment
The individual should be **motivated** to learn.	The advantages of training should be made clear, according to the individual's motives – money, opportunity, valued skills or whatever.

Proposition	Comment
There should be clear **objectives and standards** set, so that each task has some meaning.	Each stage of learning should present a challenge, without overloading trainees or making them lose confidence. Specific objectives and performance standards will help trainees in the planning and control process that leads to learning, and provide targets against which performance will constantly be measured.
There should be timely, relevant **feedback** on performance and progress.	This will usually be provided by the trainer, and should be concurrent – or certainly not long delayed. If progress reports or performance appraisals are given only at the year end, for example, there will be no opportunity for behaviour adjustment or learning in the meantime.
Positive and negative **reinforcement** should be judiciously used.	Recognition and encouragement enhance individuals' confidence in their competence and progress: punishment for poor performance – especially without explanation and correction – discourages the learner and creates feelings of guilt, failure and hostility.
Active **participation** is more telling than passive reception (because of its effect on the motivation to learn, concentration and recollection).	If a high degree of participation is impossible, practice and repetition can be used to reinforce receptivity. However, participation has the effect of encouraging 'ownership' of the process of learning and changing – committing individuals to it as their own goal, not just an imposed process.

1.3 Learning styles: Honey and Mumford (1992)

Different people have different **learning styles** or preferences.

The way in which people learn best will differ according to their psychological preferences. That is to say, there are **learning styles** which suit different individuals. Peter **Honey** and Alan **Mumford** have drawn up a popular classification of four learning styles.

(a) **Theorists** seek to understand basic principles and to take an intellectual, 'hands-off' approach based on logical argument. They prefer training to be:

- Programmed and structured
- Designed to allow time for analysis
- Provided by teachers who share their preference for concepts and analysis

(b) **Reflectors**

- Observe phenomena, think about them and then choose how to act
- Need to work at their own pace
- Find learning difficult if forced into a hurried programme
- Produce carefully thought-out conclusions after research and reflection
- Tend to be fairly slow, non-participative (unless to ask questions) and cautious

(c) **Activists**

- Deal with practical, active problems and do not have patience with theory
- Require training based on hands-on experience
- Are excited by participation and pressure, such as new projects
- Are flexible and optimistic, but tend to rush at something without due preparation

(d) **Pragmatists**

- Only like to study if they can see a direct link to real, practical problems
- Are good at learning new techniques through on the job training
- Aim to implement action plans and/or do the task better
- May discard good ideas which only require some development

Training programmes should ideally be designed to accommodate the preferences of all four styles, or to suit individual trainees (where feasible).

QUESTION

Learning styles

With reference to the four learning styles drawn up by Honey and Mumford, which of these styles do you think most closely resembles your own? What implications has this got for the way you learn?

ANSWER

Depending on your answer you will learn most effectively in particular given situations. For example, the theorist will learn best from lectures and books, whereas the activist will get most from practical activities.

EXAM FOCUS POINT

Learning styles are the basic theories underpinning training. Bear in mind, though, that more practical aspects (such as training needs analysis and programme planning or the benefits of training), would be equally well suited to exam questions.

1.4 The learning cycle: Kolb

People can learn from everyday work experience, using the **learning cycle** of reflection, generalisation and application.

Another useful model is the **experiential learning cycle** devised by David **Kolb** (1984). Experiential learning involves doing and puts the learner in an active problem-solving role: a form of self-learning which encourages learners to formulate and commit themselves to their own learning objectives.

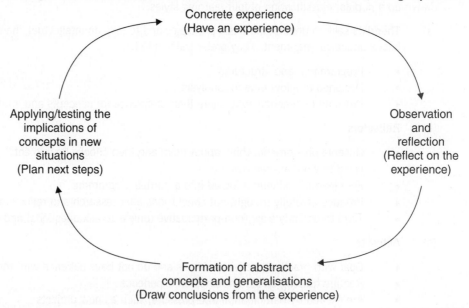

Suppose that an employee interviews a customer for the first time (concrete experience). They observe their own performance and the dynamics of the situation (observation) and afterwards, having failed to convince the customer to buy the product, the employee thinks about what they did right and wrong (reflection). They come to the conclusion that they failed to listen to what the customer really wanted and feared, underneath their general reluctance: they realise that the key to communication is active listening (abstraction/generalisation). They decide to apply active listening techniques in their next

interview (application/testing). This provides them with a new experience with which to start the cycle over again.

Simplified, this **learning by doing** approach involves:

Act ⟶ Analyse action ⟶ Suggest principles ⟶ Apply principles ⟶ Act ...

EXAM FOCUS POINT

Honey and Mumford and Kolb are specifically mentioned in the Study Guide for this syllabus.

1.5 Organisational learning

The **learning organisation** is an organisation that facilitates the learning of all its members (Pedler et al, 1991), by gathering and sharing knowledge, tolerating experience and solving problems analytically.

The learning organisation is an organisation that facilitates the acquisition and sharing of knowledge, and the learning of all its members, in order to continuously and strategically transform itself in response to a rapidly changing and uncertain environment.

The key dimensions of a learning organisation are:

- The generation and transfer of knowledge
- A tolerance for risk and failure as learning opportunities
- A systematic, ongoing, collective and scientific approach to problem-solving

1.5.1 Strengths of learning organisations

Learning organisations are good at certain key processes.

(a) **Experimentation**. Learning organisations systematically search for and test new knowledge. Decision-making is based on 'hypothesis-generating, hypothesis-testing' techniques: the plan-do-check-act cycle. Application of information and learning is key. Innovation is encouraged, with a tolerance for risk.

(b) **Learning from past experience**. Learning organisations freely seek and provide feedback on performance and processes: they review their successes and failures, assess them systematically and communicate lessons to all employees. Mistakes and failures are regarded as learning opportunities.

(c) **Learning from others**. Learning organisations recognise that the most powerful insights and opportunities come from looking 'outside the box' of the immediate environment. They encourage employees to seek information and learning opportunities outside the organisation as well as inside.

(d) **Transferring knowledge quickly and efficiently throughout the organisation**. Information is made available at all levels and across functional boundaries. Education, training and networking opportunities are constantly available.

2 Development and training

In order to achieve its goals, an organisation requires a **skilled workforce**. This is partly achieved by training.

2.1 Factors affecting job performance

There are many factors affecting a person's performance at work. Training and development is one method by which an organisation may seek to improve the performance of its staff.

2.2 What is training and development?

The main **purpose** of training and development is to raise competence and therefore performance standards. It is also concerned with personal development, helping and motivating employees to fulfil their potential.

- **Development** is 'the growth or realisation of a person's ability and potential through the provision of learning and educational experiences'.

- **Training** is 'the planned and systematic modification of behaviour through learning events, programmes and instruction which enable individuals to achieve the level of knowledge, skills and competence to carry out their work effectively'.

- **Education** is defined as that knowledge acquired gradually through learning and instruction. Someone who is 'educated' is regarded as being in possession of particular knowledge or skills, and having gone through a particular process in order to acquire them. Education is crucial for a person's professional development, but it is only one part of the development process.

The overall purpose of employee development is:

- To ensure the firm meets current and future performance objectives by ...
- Continuous improvement of the performance of individuals and teams, and ...
- Maximising people's potential for growth (and promotion)

We will discuss development separately in Section 7 of this chapter.

QUESTION

Self-appraisal

Note down key experiences which have developed your capacity and confidence at work, and the skills you are able to bring to your employer (or indeed a new employer!).

ANSWER

Few employers throw you in at the deep end – it is far too risky for them! Instead, you might have been given induction training to get acclimatised to the organisation, and you might have been introduced slowly to the job. Ideally, your employer would have planned a programme of tasks of steadily greater complexity and responsibility to allow you to grow into your role(s).

2.3 Training and development strategy

Organisations often have a **training and development strategy**, based on the overall strategy for the business. Development planning includes the following broad steps.

Step 1	Identify the **skills and competences** needed by the business plan or HR plan.
Step 2	Draw up the **development strategy** to show how training and development activities will assist in meeting the targets of the corporate plan.

Step 3   **Implement** the training and development strategy.

The advantage of such an approach is that the training is:

- Relevant
- Problem based (ie corrects a real lack of skills)
- Action oriented
- Performance related
- Forward looking

2.4 Benefits of training

Training offers significant **benefits** for both employers and employees – although it is **not** the solution to every work problem!

2.4.1 Benefits for the organisation

Training offers some significant benefits for the organisation.

Benefit	Comment
Minimised the costs of obtaining the skills the organisation needs	Training supports the business strategy.
Increased productivity, improving performance	Some people suggest that higher levels of training explain the higher productivity of German as opposed to many British manufacturers.
Fewer accidents, and better health and safety	EU health and safety directives require a certain level of training.
Less need for detailed supervision; reduced supervisory costs	If people are trained they can get on with the job, and managers can concentrate on other things. Training is an aspect of empowerment.
Flexibility	Training ensures that people have the variety of skills needed: multi-skilling is only possible if people are properly trained.
Recruitment and succession planning	Opportunities for training and development attract new recruits and ensure that the organisation has a supply of suitable managerial and technical staff for the future.
Retention	Training and development supports an internal job market (through transfer and promotion). It also helps to satisfy employees' self-development needs internally, without the need to change employers for task variety and challenge.
Change management	Training helps organisations manage change by letting people know why the change is happening and giving them the skills to cope with it.
Corporate culture	(1) Training programmes can be used to build the corporate culture or to direct it in certain ways. (2) Training programmes can build relationships between staff and managers in different areas of the business.
Motivation	Training programmes can increase commitment to the organisation's goals, by satisfying employees' self-actualisation needs (discussed in Chapter 13).

Note, however, that training cannot do everything! (Look at the wheel in Section 2.1 again.) Training cannot by itself improve performance problems arising out of:

- Bad management
- Poor job design
- Poor equipment, workplace layout or work organisation
- Lack of aptitude or intelligence
- Poor motivation (training gives a person the ability, but not necessarily willingness)

QUESTION

Limitations of training

Despite all the benefits to the organisation, many are still reluctant to train. Suggest reasons for this.

ANSWER

Cost: training can be costly. Ideally, it should be seen as an investment in the future or as something the firm has to do to maintain its position. In practice, many firms are reluctant to train because of poaching by other employers – trained staff are more marketable elsewhere. While some organisations encourage this 'employability' training, recognising their inability to offer employees long-term job security, others may experience it as a resource drain. In addition, it must be recognised that training by itself is not the solution to performance problems: it must be effectively planned and managed, as we will see later in this chapter.

2.4.2 Benefits for the employee

For the **individual employee**, the benefits of training and development are more clear-cut, and few refuse it if it is offered.

Benefit	Comment
Enhances portfolio of **skills**	Even if not specifically related to the current job, training can be useful in other contexts. The employee becomes more attractive in the labour market ('employability') and more profitable within the firm.
Psychological benefits	The trainee might feel reassured that they are of continuing value to the organisation. A perception of competence also enhances self-esteem and confidence.
Social benefit	People's social needs can be met by training courses, which can also develop networks of contacts.
The job	Training can help people do their job better, thereby increasing job satisfaction and possibly promotion and earning prospects.

2.5 A systematic approach to training

A **systematic approach** to training includes: need definition; objective setting; planning training programmes; delivering training; and evaluating results.

In order to ensure that training meets the real needs of the organisation, larger firms adopt a systematic approach.

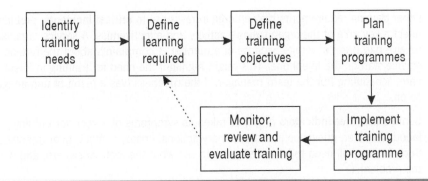

| Step 1 | **Identify and define** the **organisation's training needs** (from the human resource plan). (It may be that recruitment is a better solution to skill shortfalls.) |

| Step 2 | **Define the learning required** – in other words, specify the knowledge, skills or competences that have to be acquired. (For technical training, this is not difficult: for example, all finance department staff will have to become conversant with a new accounting system.) |

| Step 3 | **Define training objectives** – what must be learnt and what trainees must be able to do after the training exercise. |

| Step 4 | **Plan training programmes**. Training and development can be structured and implemented in a number of ways, as we shall discuss in Section 3. This covers:

• Who provides the training
• Where the training takes place
• Division of responsibilities between trainers, managers and the individual
• What training approaches, techniques, styles and technologies are used |

| Step 5 | **Implement the training programme** |

| Step 6 | **Monitor, review and evaluate** training. Has it been successful in achieving the learning objectives? |

| Step 7 | **Go back to Step 2** if more training is needed. |

We will now look at the stages of this process in more detail.

3 Training needs and objectives

A thorough analysis of **training needs** should be carried out to ensure that training programmes meet organisational and individual requirements.

3.1 Indicators of the need for training

Some training requirements will be obvious and 'automatic'.

(a) If a piece of legislation is enacted which affects the organisation's operations, training in its provisions will automatically be indicated. Thus, for example, HR staff have needed training as various EU Directives have been enacted in UK law.

(b) The introduction of new technology similarly implies a training need: for relevant employees to learn how to use it.

Other training requirements may emerge in response to **critical incidents**: problems or events which affect a key area of the organisation's activity and effectiveness. A service organisation may, for example, receive bad press coverage because of a number of complaints about the rudeness of its customer service staff on the telephone. This might highlight the need for training in telephone skills, customer care, scheduling (for the team manager, if the rudeness was a result of unmanageable workloads), and so on.

Some **qualitative indicators** might be taken as symptoms of a need for training: absenteeism, high labour turnover, grievance and disciplinary actions, crises, conflict, poor motivation and performance. Such factors will need to be investigated to see what the root causes are, and whether training will solve the problem.

3.2 Assessment for training

Another alternative is **self-assessment** by the employee. This may be highly informal (a list of in-house or sponsored courses is posted on the noticeboard or intranet and interested employees are invited to apply) or more systematic (employees complete surveys on training needs). The advantage of self-assessment, or self-nomination for training, is that it pre-supposes motivation on the part of the trainee and harnesses employees' knowledge of their own job requirements and skill weaknesses. The drawback, however, is that employees may be reluctant to admit to performance deficiencies.

A further alternative, therefore, is the use of **attitude surveys** and **360° feedback appraisal reports**, since the employee's superiors, subordinates, colleagues and customer contacts will be in a good position to identify performance deficiencies in areas that affect them: this will be particularly important in the case of customers.

3.3 Formal training need analysis

Other training requirements may only emerge from a formal **learning gap (or training need) analysis**.

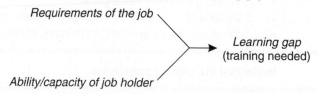

Requirements of the job

Learning gap (training needed)

Ability/capacity of job holder

Training needs may be defined as the gap between what people should be achieving and what they actually are achieving. In other words:

Required level of competence **minus** present level of competence = training need

The **required level of competence for the job** can be determined by:

(a) **Job analysis**, identifying the elements of the task

(b) **Skills analysis**, identifying the skill elements of the task, such as:

    (i) What senses (vision, touch, hearing, etc) are involved?
    (ii) What left-hand/right-hand/foot operations are required?
    (iii) What interactions with other operatives are required?

(c) **Role analysis**, for managerial and administrative jobs requiring a high degree of co-ordination and interaction with others

(d) **Existing records**, such as job specifications and descriptions, person specifications, the organisation chart (depicting roles and relationships), and so on

(e) **Competence analysis** or existing competence frameworks, such as NVQs relevant to the job

The **present level of employees' competence** (which includes not only skill and knowledge, but the employee's inclination or willingness to work competently as well) can be measured by an appropriate **pre-training test** of skills, knowledge, performance, attitude, and so on.

The ongoing system of **performance appraisal** (discussed in Chapter 17) will furnish some of this information. A **human resources audit** or **skills audit** may also be conducted for a more comprehensive account of the current level of competence, skill, knowledge (and so on) in the workforce.

3.4 Setting training objectives

Once training needs have been identified, they should be translated into **training objectives**.

If it is considered that training would improve work performance, training **objectives** can be defined. They should be clear, specific and related to observable, measurable targets, ideally detailing:

- **Behaviour** – what should the trainee be able to do?
- **Standard** – to what level of performance?
- **Environment** – under what conditions (so that the performance level is realistic)?

For example:

'At the end of the course the trainee should be able to describe ... or identify ... or distinguish x from y ... or calculate ... or assemble ...' and so on. It is insufficient to define the objectives of training as 'to give trainees a grounding in ...' or 'to encourage trainees in a better appreciation of ...': this offers no target achievement which can be measured.

Training objectives link the identification of training needs with the content, methods and technology of training.

Training needs	Learning objectives
To know more about the Data Protection Act	The employee will be able to answer four out of every five queries about the Data Protection Act without having to search for details.
To establish a better rapport with customers	The employee will immediately attend to a customer unless already engaged with another customers. The employee will greet each customer using the customer's name where known. The employee will apologise to every customer who has had to wait to be attended to.
To assemble clocks more quickly	The employee will be able to assemble each clock correctly within 30 minutes.

Having identified training needs and objectives, the manager will have to decide on the best way to approach training: there are a number of approaches and techniques, which we will discuss below.

3.5 Incorporating training needs into an individual development programme

Individuals can incorporate training and development objectives into a **personal development plan**.

A personal development plan is a clear developmental action plan for an individual which incorporates a wide set of developmental opportunities, including formal training.

The purposes of a personal development plan include:

- Improving performance in the existing job
- Developing skills for future career moves within and outside the organisation

3.5.1 Steps in personal development planning

Personal development planning includes the following basic steps.

Step 1	**Analyse the current position**. You could do a personal SWOT (strengths, weaknesses, opportunities, threats) analysis, or a **skills analysis** (as depicted in the following diagram).

Performance

	High	Low
High	Like and do well	Like but don't do well
Low	Dislike but do well	Dislike and don't do well

Liking of skills

The aim is to try to incorporate more of the employees' interests into their actual roles.

Step 2	**Set goals** to cover performance in the existing job, future changes in the current role, moving elsewhere in the organisation, developing specialist expertise. Such goals should have the characteristic of SMART objectives (specific, measurable, achievable, relevant and time-bounded).

Step 3	**Draw up an action plan** to achieve the goals, including:

- The objective
- Methods you will use to develop the identified skills (including learning experiences, opportunities to try and practise new behaviour, and so on)
- Timescales for review of progress
- Methods of monitoring and reviewing progress and achievement of the objective

4 Training methods

There are a variety of **training methods**. These include:

- Off the job education and training
- On the job training

4.1 Off the job training

Off the job training minimises risk but does not always support transfer of learning to the job.

Off the job training is formal training conducted outside the context of the job itself in special training rooms or off-site facilities.

(a) **Courses** may be run by the organisation's training department or may be provided by external suppliers. These may be:

  (i) **Day release**: the employee works in the organisation and on one day per week attends a local college or training centre for theoretical learning

(ii) **Distance learning, evening classes and correspondence courses**, which make demands on the individual's time outside work

(iii) **Revision courses** for examinations of professional bodies

(iv) **Block release** courses which may involve four weeks at a college or training centre followed by a period back at work

(v) **Sandwich courses**, which usually involve six months at college then six months at work, in rotation, for two or three years

(vi) A **sponsored full-time course** at a university for one or two years

(b) **Computer-based training** involves interactive training via PC. The typing program Mavis Beacon is a good example.

(c) **E-learning**

E-learning is computer-based learning through a network of computers or the internet (rather than standalone CD-Rom or software). Learning support is available from online tutors, moderators and discussion groups.

(d) **Techniques** used on the course might include lectures and seminars (theory and information) or role plays, case studies and in-tray exercises (to simulate work activities).

4.1.1 Evaluation of off the job training

The advantages and disadvantages of off the job training may be summarised as follows.

Advantages	Disadvantages
Allows exploration/experimentation without the risk of consequences for actual performance	May not be directly relevant or transferable to the job and/or job content
Allows focus on learning, away from distractions and pressures of work	May be perceived as a waste of working time
Allows standardisation of training Suits a variety of learning styles (depending on the method used)	Immediate and relevant feedback may not be available (eg if performance is assessed by exam)
May confer status, implying promotability	Tends to be more theoretical: does not suit 'hands-on' learning styles
	May represent a threat, implying inadequacy

4.2 On the job training

 On the job training maximises transfer of learning by incorporating it into 'real' work.

On the job training utilises real work tasks as learning experiences. Methods of on the job training include the following.

(a) **Demonstration/instruction:** show the trainee how to do the job and let them get on with it. It should combine telling a person what to do and showing them how, using appropriate media. The trainee imitates the instructor, and asks questions.

(b) **Job rotation:** the trainee is given several jobs in succession, to gain experience of a wide range of activities. (Even experienced managers may rotate their jobs to gain wider experience; this philosophy of job education is commonly applied in the Civil Service, where an employee may expect to move on to another job after a few years.)

(c) **Temporary promotion:** an individual is promoted into their superior's position while the superior is absent. This gives the individual a chance to experience the demands of a more senior position.

(d)   **'Assistant to' positions (or work shadowing):** an employee may be appointed as assistant to a more senior or experienced person, to gain experience of a new or more demanding role.

(e)   **Action learning:** managers are brought together as a problem-solving group to discuss a real work issue. An 'advisor' facilitates, and helps members of the group to identify how their interpersonal and problem-solving skills are affecting the process.

(f)   **Committees:** trainees might be included in the membership of committees, in order to obtain an understanding of interdepartmental relationships.

(g)   **Project work:** work on a project with other people can expose the trainee to other parts of the organisation.

4.2.1 Evaluation of on the job training

The advantages and disadvantages of on the job training may be summarised as follows.

Advantages	Disadvantages
Takes account of job context: high relevance and transfer of learning	Undesirable aspects of job context (group norms, corner-cutting) also learned
Suits 'hands-on' learning styles: offers 'learning by doing'	Doesn't suit 'hands-off' learning styles
No adjustment barriers (eg anti-climax after training) to application of learning on the job	Trial and error may be threatening (if the organisation has low tolerance of error!)
Develops working relationships as well as skills	Risks of throwing people in at the deep end with real consequences of mistakes
	Distractions and pressures of the workplace may hamper learning focus

QUESTION

Training methods

Suggest a suitable training method for each of the following situations.

(a)   A worker is transferred onto a new machine and needs to learn its operation.

(b)   An accounts clerk wishes to work towards becoming qualified with the relevant professional body.

(c)   An organisation decides that its supervisors would benefit from ideas on participative management and democratic leadership.

(d)   A new member of staff is about to join the organisation.

ANSWER

Training methods for the various workers indicated are as follows.

(a)   Worker on a new machine: on the job training, coaching

(b)   Accounts clerk working for professional qualification: external course – evening class or day-release

(c)   Supervisors wishing to benefit from participative management and democratic leadership: internal or external course. However, it is important that monitoring and evaluation takes place to ensure that the results of the course are subsequently applied in practice.

(d)   New staff: induction training

4.3 Induction training

Induction is the process whereby a person is formally introduced and integrated into an organisation or system.

4.3.1 The purposes of induction

The purposes of induction are:

(a)   To help new recruits to get their bearings

(b)   To begin to socialise new recruits into the culture and norms of the team/organisation

(c)   To support recruits in beginning performance

(d)   To identify ongoing training and development needs

(e)   To avoid initial problems at the 'induction crisis' stage of the employment life cycle, when frustration, disorientation and disappointment may otherwise cause new recruits to leave the organisation prematurely

4.3.2 The process of induction

The immediate superior should commence the **ongoing process of induction**.

Step 1	Pinpoint the areas that the recruit will have to learn about in order to start the job. Some things (such as detailed technical knowledge) may be identified as areas for later study or training.
Step 2	Introduce the recruit to the work premises and facilities, so they can get their bearings.
Step 3	Briefing by the HR Manager on relevant policies and procedures: conditions of employment, sickness and holiday absences, health and safety, and so on.
Step 4	Introduce the recruit to key people in the office: co-workers, health and safety officers, etc. One particular colleague may be assigned to recruits as a **mentor**, to keep an eye on them, answer routine queries, 'show them the ropes'.
Step 5	Introduce work procedures. (a) Explain the nature of the job, and the goals of each task. (b) Explain hours of work. (c) Explain the structure of the department: to whom the recruit will report, to whom they can go with complaints or queries and so on.
Step 6	Plan and implement an appropriate training programme for whatever technical or practical knowledge is required. Again, the programme should have a clear schedule and set of goals so that the recruit has a sense of purpose, and so that the programme can be efficiently organised to fit in with the activities of the department.
Step 7	Monitor initial progress, as demonstrated by performance, as reported by the recruit's mentor, and as perceived by the recruit themselves. This is the beginning of an ongoing cycle of feedback, review, problem-solving and development planning.

Note that induction is an **ongoing process**, embracing mentoring, coaching, training, monitoring, and so on. It is not just a first day affair! After three months, six months or one year the performance of a new recruit should be formally appraised and discussed. Indeed, when the process of induction has been finished, a recruit should continue to receive periodic appraisals, just like every other employee in the organisation.

5 Responsibility for training and development

> Increasingly, **responsibility for training and development** is being devolved to the individual learner, in collaboration with line managers and training providers.

5.1 The trainee

Many people now believe that the ultimate responsibility for training and development lies not with the employer but with the **individual**. People should seek to develop their own skills and improve their own careers, rather than wait for the organisation to impose training upon them. Why?

(a)   Delayering means there are fewer automatic promotion pathways: individuals need to seek non-'vertical' paths to greater interest and challenge in the job.

(b)   Technological change means that new skills are always needed, and people who can learn new skills will be more employable.

5.2 The human resources (HR) department or training department

The human resources department is centrally concerned with developing people. Larger organisations often have extensive learning and career planning programmes, managing the progression of individuals through the organisation, in accordance with the performance and potential of the individual and the needs of the organisation.

5.3 Line managers

Line managers bear some of the responsibility for training and development within the organisation by:

*   Identifying the training needs of the department or section
*   Assessing the current competences of the individuals within the department
*   Identifying opportunities for learning and development on the job
*   Coaching staff
*   Offering performance feedback for on the job learning
*   Organising training programmes where required

5.4 The training manager

The training manager is a member of staff appointed to arrange and sometimes run training. The training manager generally reports to the **human resources** or **personnel director**, but also needs a good relationship with line managers in the departments where the training takes place.

Responsibilities of the training manager include:

Responsibility	Comment
Liaison	With HR department and operating departments
Scheduling	Arranging training programmes at convenient times
Needs identification	Discerning existing and future skills shortages
Programme design	Developing tailored training programmes
Feedback	To the trainee, the department and the HR department
Evaluation	Measuring the effectiveness of training programmes

6 Evaluating training programmes

- **Validation of training** means observing the results of the course and measuring whether the training objectives have been achieved.

- **Evaluation of training** means comparing the costs of the scheme against the assessed benefits which are being obtained.

6.1 The five-level evaluation model

The effectiveness of a training scheme may be measured at different levels (Hamblin).

Level 1	**Trainees' reactions to the experience**. These are usually measured by post-training feedback forms.
Level 2	**Trainee learning** (new skills and knowledge): measuring what the trainees have learned on the course, usually by means of a test at the end of it.
Level 3	**Changes in job behaviour following training**: observing work practices and outputs (products, services, documents) to identify post-training differences.
Level 4	**Impact of training on organisational goals/results**: seeing whether the training scheme has contributed to the overall objectives of the organisation in terms of quality, productivity, profitability, employee retention, and so on.
Level 5	**Ultimate value**: the impact of training on the wider 'good' of the organisation in terms of stakeholder benefits, greater social responsibility, corporate growth/survival.

QUESTION
Evaluating and validating training

Outline why it is important to evaluate and validate a training programme.

ANSWER

Validation of a new course is important to ensure that objectives have been achieved. Evaluation of it is more difficult, but at least as important because it identifies the value of the training programme to the organisation. Both are required to improve effectiveness or cost effectiveness next time.

7 Development

Development includes a range of learning activities and experiences (not just training) to enhance employees' or managers' portfolio of competence, experience and capability, with a view to personal, professional or career progression.

7.1 What is development?

As we noted at the beginning of this chapter, development is a 'wider' approach to fulfilling an individual's potential than training and education. Development may include training, but may also include a range of learning experiences whereby employees are:

(a)   Given **work experience** of increasing challenge and responsibility, which will enable them to take on other more senior jobs in due course

(b)   Given **guidance, support and counselling** to help them formulate personal and career development goals

(c)   Given suitable **education and training** to develop their skills and knowledge

(d)   Helped to **plan their future** and identify opportunities open to them in the organisation

7.2 Approaches to development

Approaches to development include the following.

Approach	Comment
Management development	Improving managerial effectiveness through a planned process. This may include the development of management/leadership skills (or competences), management education (such as MBA programmes) and planned experience of different functions, positions and work settings, in preparation for increasing managerial responsibility.
Career development	Individuals plan career paths. The trend for delayered organisations has reduced opportunities for upward progression: opportunities may be planned for sideways/lateral transfers, secondments to project groups, short external secondments, and so on, to offer new opportunities.
Professional development	Professional bodies offer structured programmes of continuing professional development (CPD). The aim is to ensure that professional standards are maintained and enhanced through education, development and training self-managed by the individual. A CPD approach is based on the belief that a professional qualification should be the basis for a career lifetime of development **and** adherence to a professional code of ethics and standards.
Personal development	Businesses are increasingly offering employees wider-ranging development opportunities, rather than focusing on skills required in their current job. Personal development creates more rounded, competent employees who may contribute more innovatively and flexibly to the organisation's future needs. It may also help to foster employee job satisfaction, commitment and loyalty.

CHAPTER ROUNDUP

- There are different schools of thought as to **how people learn**.

- Different people have different **learning styles** or preferences.

- People can learn from everyday work experience, using the **learning cycle** of reflection, generalisation and application.

- The **learning organisation** is an organisation that facilitates the learning of all its members (Pedler et al, 1991), by gathering and sharing knowledge, tolerating experience and solving problems analytically.

- In order to achieve its goals, an organisation requires a **skilled workforce**. This is partly achieved by training.

- The main **purpose** of training and development is to raise competence and therefore performance standards. It is also concerned with personal development, helping and motivating employees to fulfil their potential.

- **Training** offers significant **benefits** for both employers and employees – although it is **not** the solution to every work problem!

- A **systematic approach** to training includes: need definition; objective setting; planning training programmes; delivering training; and evaluating results.

- A thorough analysis of **training needs** should be carried out to ensure that training programmes meet organisational and individual requirements.

- Once training needs have been identified, they should be translated into **training objectives**.

- Individuals can incorporate training and development objectives into a **personal development plan**.

- There are a variety of **training methods**. These include:
  - Off the job education and training
  - On the job training

- **Off the job training** minimises risk but does not always support transfer of learning to the job.

- **On the job training** maximises transfer of learning by incorporating it into 'real' work.

- **Induction** is the process whereby a person is formally introduced and integrated into an organisation or system.

- Increasingly, **responsibility for training and development** is being devolved to the individual learner, in collaboration with line managers and training providers.

- **Development** includes a range of learning activities and experiences (not just training) to enhance employees' or managers' portfolio of competence, experience and capability, with a view to personal, professional or career progression.

QUICK QUIZ

1   Which of the following are necessary for a training programme to be effective?

The trainee should be motivated to learn ☐

There should be clear objectives ☐

There should be timely feedback ☐

It should not be costly ☐

2   Which of the following is not one of the learning styles defined by Honey and Mumford?

A   Pragmatist   C   Abstractor
B   Theorist   D   Reflector

3   The 'learning by doing' approach based on Kolb's learning cycle begins with 'act'. Put the following stages of the cycle into the correct order.

A   Suggest principles
B   Apply principles
C   Analyse action

4   Tick the correct box to show what is being described by these phases.

	Development	Training	Education
The growth or realisation of a person's ability and potential through the provision of learning and educational experiences	☐	☐	☐
Knowledge that is acquired gradually, by learning and instruction	☐	☐	☐

5   Which type of training minimises risk but does not always support transfer of learning to the job?

A   On the job training
B   Off the job training

6   The formula 'required level of competence **minus** present level of competence describes
.... '.

7   Validation of training means comparing the costs of the scheme against the assessed benefits which are being obtained. True or false?

ANSWERS TO QUICK QUIZ

1 The trainee should be motivated to learn ☑

There should be clear objectives ☑

There should be timely feedback ☑

It should not be costly ☐

Training may be costly but if it is cost effective then it is worth it!

2 C The correct 'A' word (you may like to use the acronym PART or TRAP to remember the model) is 'Activist'.

3 C Analyse action

A Suggest principles

B Apply principles

4

	Development	Training	Education
The growth or realisation of a person's ability and potential through the provision of learning and educational experiences	☑	☐	☐
Knowledge that is acquired gradually, by learning and instruction	☐	☐	☑

5 B Off the job training.

6 Training needs.

7 False. This is evaluation of training. Validation of training means observing the results of the course and measuring whether the training objectives have been achieved.

Now try ...

Attempt the questions below from the **Practice Question Bank**

Q80

Q81

Q82

Q83

Q84

17

The **Accountant in Business** syllabus contains key management and people issues within its overall framework of 'business structure and purpose'. The general purpose of performance appraisal is to improve the efficiency of the organisation by ensuring that individuals within it are performing to the best of their ability, by developing their own potential (**Sections 1** and **2**). This links to training and development in Chapter 16.

This chapter also discusses the process of **appraisal** or **competence assessment** (**Section 3**): the measurement and evaluation of the individual's performance in relation to given plans and criteria. Barriers to effective appraisal often need to be overcome (**Section 4**).

You should be aware that this is part of a broader process of:

* Goal setting
* Performance monitoring
* Feedback giving
* Performance adjustment

This process occurs firmly within an organisational context, so that the performance of human resources supports the objectives of the organisation. It is therefore important that the effectiveness of the appraisal scheme is evaluated (**Section 5**).

Performance appraisal

EXAM FOCUS POINT

There is an article on the ACCA website entitled "Understanding the importance of appraisals" that is relevant to material in this chapter.

1 Performance management and assessment

Performance management aims to get better results for the organisation via the measurement and evaluation of individual performance.

Appraisal is part of the system of performance management, including goal setting, performance monitoring, feedback and improvement planning.

Performance management is a means of getting better results by managing performance within an agreed framework of goals, standards and competence requirements. It is a process to establish a shared understanding about what is to be achieved, and an approach to managing and developing people in order to achieve it.

This definition highlights key features of performance management.

Aspect	Comment
Agreed framework of goals, standards and competence requirements	The manager and the employee agree about a standard of performance, goals and the skills needed.
Performance management is a **process**	Managing people's performance is an ongoing activity involving continual monitoring and assessment, discussion and adjustment.
Shared understanding	The goals of the individual, unit and organisation as a whole need to be integrated: everyone needs to be 'on the same page' of the business plan.
Approach to **managing and developing people**	Managing performance is not just about plans, systems or resources: it is an **interpersonal** process of influencing, empowering, giving feedback and problem-solving.
Achievement	The aim is to enable people to realise their potential and maximise their contribution to the organisation's success.

1.1 The process of performance management

A systematic approach to performance management might include the following steps.

Step 1	From the **business plan**, identify the requirements and competences required to carry it out.

Step 2	Draw up a **performance agreement**, defining the expectations of the individual or team, covering standards of performance, performance indicators and the skills and competences people need.

Step 3	Draw up a **performance and development plan** with the individual. These record the actions needed to improve performance, normally covering development in the current job. They are discussed with job holders and will typically cover: <ul><li>The areas of performance the individual feels in need of development</li><li>What the individual and manager agree is needed to enhance performance</li><li>Development and training initiatives</li></ul>

Step 4	**Manage performance continually throughout the year**, not just at appraisal interviews done to satisfy the personnel department. Managers can review actual performance, with more informal interim reviews at various times of the year. (a) High performance is reinforced by praise, recognition and increasing responsibility. Low performance results in coaching or counselling. (b) Work plans are updated as necessary. (c) Deal with performance problems, by identifying what they are, establish the reasons for the shortfall, take control action (with adequate resources) and provide feedback.

Step 5	**Performance review**. At a defined period each year, success against the plan is reviewed, but the whole point is to assess what is going to happen in future.

In order for learning and motivation to be effective, it is essential that **people know exactly what their objectives are**. This enables them to do the following.

(a) Plan and direct their effort towards the objectives

(b) Monitor their performance against objectives and adjust (or learn) if required

(c) Experience the reward of achievement once the objectives have been reached

(d) Feel that their tasks have meaning and purpose, which is an important element in job satisfaction

(e) Experience the motivation of a challenge: the need to expend energy and effort in a particular direction in order to achieve something

(f) Avoid the demotivation of impossible or inadequately rewarded tasks. As we have discussed in the chapter on motivation, there is a calculation involved in motivated performance. If objectives are vague, unrealistic or unattainable, there may be little incentive to pursue them: hence the importance of SMART objectives.

Principles for devising performance measures include:

Principle	Comment
Job related	They should be related to the actual job, and the key tasks outlined in the job description.
Controllable	People should not be assessed in relation to factors which they cannot control.
Objective and observable	This is contentious. Certain aspects of performance can be measured, such as volume sales, but matters such as courtesy or friendliness which are important to some businesses are harder to measure.
Data must be available	There is no use identifying performance measures if the data cannot actually be collected.

2 The purpose of performance appraisal

2.1 Main components of appraisal

Appraisal can be used to **reward** but also to identify **potential**. It is part of performance management and can be used to establish areas for improvement and **training and development** needs.

The general purpose of any appraisal system is to improve the efficiency of the organisation by ensuring that the individuals within it are performing to the best of their ability and developing their potential for improvement. This has three main components.

(a) **Reward review**, measuring the extent to which an employee is deserving of performance-related bonuses or pay increases

(b) **Performance review**, for planning and following up training and development programmes: identifying training needs, validating training methods, and so on

(c) **Potential review**, as an aid to planning career development and succession, by attempting to predict the level and type of work the individual will be capable of in the future

2.2 Specific objectives of appraisal

More specific objectives of appraisal may be summarised as follows.

(a) Establishing **what the individual has to do** in a job in order that the objectives for the section or department are realised

(b) Establishing the **key or main results** which the individual will be expected to achieve in the course of their work over a period of time

(c) Comparing the individual's level of performance against a standard, to provide a basis for **remuneration** above the basic pay rate

(d) Identifying the individual's **training and development needs** in the light of actual performance

(e) Identifying potential candidates **for promotion**

(f) Identifying **areas for improvement**

(g) Establishing an **inventory** of actual and potential performance within the undertaking, as a basis for human resource planning

(h) Monitoring the undertaking's **selection procedures** against the subsequent performance of recruits

(i) **Improving communication** about work tasks between different levels in the hierarchy

2.3 Why have formal appraisal?

Formal appraisal systems support objective, positive, relevant, consistent feedback by managers.

You may argue that managers gather performance evaluations, and give feedback, on an ongoing basis, in the course of supervision. Why is a formal appraisal system required? What are the benefits?

(a) Managers and supervisors may obtain random impressions of subordinates' performance (perhaps from their more noticeable successes and failures), but rarely form a **coherent, complete and objective** picture.

(b) They may have a fair idea of their subordinates' shortcomings – but may not have devoted time and attention to the matter of **improvement and development**.

(c) Judgements are easy to make, but less easy to **justify** in detail, in writing, or to the subject's face.

(d) Different assessors may be applying a **different set of criteria**, and varying standards of **objectivity** and judgement. This undermines the value of appraisal for comparison, as well as its credibility in the eyes of the appraisees.

(e) Unless stimulated to do so, managers rarely give their subordinates adequate **feedback** on their performance.

An article in *Student Accountant* (April 2004) sets out the advantages and benefits for the individual and the organisation.

	Benefits
Individual	• Objectives are established in relation to the whole organisation • Key results and timescales are established • Compares past performance and future activities against standards • Basis for performance-related pay schemes
Organisation	• Suitable promotion candidates are identified • Areas of improvement can be seen • Communication is improved • Basis for medium- to long-term HR planning

QUESTION

Formal appraisal

List four disadvantages to the individual of not having a formal appraisal system.

ANSWER

Disadvantages to the individual of not having an appraisal system include: the individual is not aware of progress or shortcomings, is unable to judge whether they would be considered for promotion, is unable to identify or correct weaknesses by training and there is a lack of communication with the manager.

3 The process of performance appraisal

3.1 Overview of the appraisal process

Three basic requirements of a **formal appraisal system** are: defining what is to be appraised, recording assessments, and getting the appraiser and appraisee together for feedback and planning.

There are three basic requirements for a formal appraisal system.

(a) The **formulation of desired traits and standards** against which individuals can be consistently and objectively assessed

(b)   **Recording assessments**; managers should be encouraged to utilise a standard framework, but still be allowed to express what they consider important, and without too much form-filling

(c)   **Getting the appraiser and appraisee together,** so that both contribute to the assessment and plans for improvement and/or development

A systematic appraisal system can be depicted as follows.

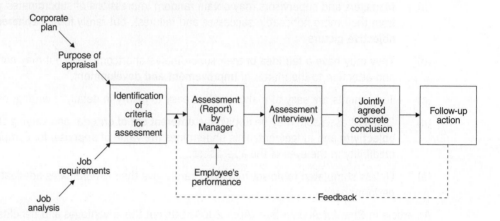

3.2 What is appraisal?

Assessments must be related to a common standard in order for comparisons to be made between individuals: on the other hand, they should be related to meaningful **performance criteria**, which take account of the critical variables in each job.

Some basic criteria might appear in a simple appraisal report form as follows.

APPRAISAL REPORT						
Name: Time in position:						
Position: Period of review:						
Company:						
Overall assessment	A	B	C	D	E	Comment
Job knowledge						
Effective output						
Co-operation						
Initiative						
Timekeeping						
Other relevant facts (specify)						
A = Outstanding B = Above standard C = To required standard D = Short of standard in some respects E = Not up to required standard						
Potential	A	B	C	D	E	Comment

A = Overdue for promotion	B = Ready for promotion	C = Potential for promotion
D = No evidence of promotion potential at present		
E = Has not worked long enough with me for judgement		
Training, if any, required:		
Assessment discussed with employee?	Yes	No
Signed	Date	
Confirmed	Date	

3.3 Appraisal techniques

There are a number of ways to judge or appraise performance. The most appropriate method will depend upon the circumstances and people involved.

A variety of appraisal techniques may be used, measuring different criteria in different ways.

(a) **Overall assessment**. The manager writes in narrative form his judgements about the appraisee. There will be no guaranteed consistency of the criteria and areas of assessment, however, and managers may not be able to convey clear, effective judgements in writing.

(b) **Guided assessment**. Assessors are required to comment on a number of specified characteristics and performance elements, with guidelines as to how terms such as 'application', 'integrity' and 'adaptability' are to be interpreted in the work context. This is more precise, but still rather vague.

(c) **Grading**. Grading adds a comparative frame of reference to the general guidelines, whereby managers are asked to select one of a number of levels or degrees to which the individual in question displays the given characteristic. These are also known as **rating scales**.

Numerical values may be added to ratings to give rating scores. Alternatively a less precise **graphic scale** may be used to indicate general position on a plus/minus scale.

Factor: job knowledge

High_____   Average _____   Low _____

(d) **Behavioural incident methods**. These concentrate on employee behaviour, which is measured against typical behaviour in each job, as defined by common critical incidents of successful and unsuccessful job behaviour reported by managers.

(e) **Results-orientated schemes**. These review performance against specific targets and standards of performance agreed in advance by manager and subordinate together. There are significant advantages to such an approach.

   (i) The subordinate is more involved in appraisal because they are able to evaluate their progress in achieving jointly agreed targets.

   (ii) The manager is relieved of a critic's role, and becomes a coach.

   (iii) Clear and known targets help modify behaviour.

The effectiveness of the scheme will depend on the **targets set** (are they clearly defined? realistic?) and the **commitment** of both parties to make it work.

QUESTION

Appraisal techniques

What sort of appraisal systems are suggested by the following examples?

(a) Teachers at a school send a brief report at the end of each term to the parents of the school's pupils. Typical phrases include 'a satisfactory term's work', and 'could do better'.

(b) A firm of auditors assess the performance of their staff in four categories: technical ability, relationships with clients, relationships with other members of the audit team, and professional attitude. On each of these criteria staff are marked from A (= excellent) to E (= poor).

(c) A firm of insurance brokers assesses the performance of its staff by the number of clients they have visited and the number of policies sold.

ANSWER

(a) Overall assessment
(b) A grading system, based on a guided assessment
(c) Results-orientated scheme

3.4 Self-appraisals

Self-appraisals occur when individuals carry out their own self-evaluation as a major input into the appraisal process.

Advantages include the following.

(a) It **saves the manager time**, as the employee identifies the areas of competence which are relevant to the job and their relative strengths.

(b) It offers **increased responsibility** to the individual, which may improve motivation.

(c) This **reconciles the goals** of the individual and the organisation.

(d) In giving the responsibility to an individual, the scheme may offer more **flexibility** in terms of the timing and relevance of the appraisal.

Disadvantages the following.

(a) People are often not the best judges of their own performance.

(b) People may deliberately over- (or under-) estimate their performance in order to gain approval or reward – or to conform to group norms.

Many schemes combine managerial and self appraisal.

3.5 The appraisal interview

The appraisal **interview** is an important stage in the process, as it can be used to encourage collaborative problem-solving and improvement planning. A 'problem-solving' style is preferable to a 'tell and sell' or 'tell and listen' style (Maier, 1975)).

The process of an appraisal interview may be as follows.

Step 1	Prepare
	• Plan interview time and environment: the aim is to facilitate collaborative problem-solving and communication. Privacy is essential.
	• Prepare relevant documentation: job description, employee records, and statement of performance (or appraisal form)
	• Review employee's history and self-appraisals/peer appraisals (if used)

	• Prepare for the interview.
	• Prepare report. Review employee's self-appraisal

Step 2	Interview
	• Select an appropriate style (see below): directional, persuasive or collaborative
	• Encourage employee to talk, identify problems and solutions
	• Be fair

Step 3	Agree
	• Summarise to check understanding
	• Gain employee commitment
	• Agree plan of action

Step 4	Report
	• Complete appraisal report, if not already prepared

Step 5	Follow up
	• Take action as agreed
	• Monitor progress
	• Keep employee informed

3.5.1 Three approaches: Maier (1975)

Maier identifies three types of approach to appraisal interviews. Most appraisees prefer the third of the alternatives suggested.

(a)   The **tell and sell style**. The manager tells the subordinate how they have been assessed, and then tries to 'sell' (gain acceptance of) the evaluation and the improvement plan. This requires unusual human relations skills in order to convey constructive criticism in an acceptable manner, and to motivate the appraisee to alter their behaviour.

(b)   The **tell and listen style**. The manager tells the subordinate how they have been assessed, and then invites the appraisee to respond. The manager therefore no longer dominates the interview throughout, and there is greater opportunity for coaching or counselling as opposed to pure direction.

    (i)   The employee is encouraged to participate in the assessment and the working out of improvement targets and methods: it is an accepted tenet of behavioural theory that participation in problem definition and goal setting increases the individual's commitment to behaviour and attitude modification.

    (ii)   This method does not assume that a change in the employee will be the sole key to improvement: the manager may receive helpful feedback about how job design, methods, environment or supervision might be improved.

(c)   The **problem-solving style**. The manager abandons the role of critic altogether, and becomes a coach and helper. The discussion is centred not on the assessment, but on the employee's work problems. The employee is encouraged to think solutions through, and to commit to the recognised need for personal improvement. This approach encourages intrinsic motivation through the element of self-direction, and the perception of the job itself as a problem-solving activity. It may also stimulate creative thinking on the part of employee and manager alike, to the benefit of the organisation's adaptability and methods.

EXAM FOCUS POINT

This is the accepted framework for discussing appraisal interviews and so is worth learning.

3.6 Follow-up

After the appraisal interview, the manager may complete the report, with an overall assessment, assessment of potential and/or the jointly reached conclusion of the interview, with **recommendations for follow-up action**. The manager should then discuss the report with the counter-signing manager (usually their own superior), resolving any problems that have arisen in making the appraisal or report, and agreeing on action to be taken. The report form may then go to the development adviser, training officer or other relevant people as appropriate for follow-up.

Follow-up procedures may include the following.

(a)   **Informing appraisees of the results** of the appraisal, if this has not been central to the review interview

(b)   **Carrying out agreed actions** on training, promotion, and so on

(c)   **Monitoring the appraisee's progress** and checking that they have carried out agreed actions or improvements

(d)   Taking necessary steps to **help the appraisee to attain improvement objectives**, by guidance, providing feedback, upgrading equipment, altering work methods, and so on

QUESTION

Follow-up

What would happen without follow-up?

ANSWER

The appraisal would merely be seen as a pleasant chat with little effect on future performance, as circumstances change. Moreover, the individual might feel cheated.

The appraisal can also be used as an input to the employee's personal **development plan** (see Chapter 16).

---

4   Barriers to effective appraisal

Problems with appraisal are its implementation in practice and a range of misperceptions about it (Lockett, 1992). New techniques of appraisal aim to monitor effectiveness from a number of perspectives.

4.1 Problems in practice

Lockett (1992) suggests that barriers to effective appraisal can be identified as follows.

Appraisal barriers	Comment
Appraisal as confrontation	Many people dread appraisals, or use them 'as a sort of show down, a good sorting out or a clearing of the air.' In this kind of climate: • There is likely to be a lack of agreement on performance levels and improvement needs. • The feedback may be subjective or exaggerated.

	• The feedback may be negatively delivered. • The appraisal may focus on negative aspects, rather than looking forward to potential for improvement and development.
Appraisal as judgement	The appraisal 'is seen as a one-sided process in which the manager acts as judge, jury and counsel for the prosecution'. This puts the subordinate on the defensive. Instead, the process of performance management 'needs to be jointly operated in order to retain the commitment and develop the self-awareness of the individual.'
Appraisal as chat	The appraisal is conducted as if it were a friendly chat 'without ... purpose or outcome ... Many managers, embarrassed by the need to give feedback and set stretching targets, reduce the appraisal to a few mumbled "well done!"s and leave the interview with a briefcase of unresolved issues.'
Appraisal as bureaucracy	Appraisal is a form-filling exercise, to satisfy the personnel department. Its underlying purpose, improving individual and organisational performance, is forgotten.
Appraisal as unfinished business	Appraisal should be part of a continuing future-focused process of performance management, not a way of 'wrapping up' the past year's performance issues.
Appraisal as annual event	Many targets set at annual appraisal meetings become irrelevant or out of date. Feedback, goal adjustment and improvement planning should be a continuous process.

4.2 Appraisal and pay

Another problem is the extent to which the appraisal system is related to the **pay and reward system**. Many employees consider that positive appraisals should be rewarded, but there are major drawbacks to this approach.

(a) **Funds available** for pay rises rarely depend on one individual's performance alone – the whole company has to do well.

(b) **Continuous improvement** should perhaps be expected of employees as part of their work and development, not rewarded as extra.

(c) Performance management is about a lot more than pay for **past** performance – it is often **forward looking** with regard to future performance.

4.3 Upward appraisal

New techniques of appraisal aim to monitor the appraisee's effectiveness from a number of perspectives. These techniques include upward, customer and 360 degree feedback.

A notable modern trend, adopted by some companies is **upward appraisal**, whereby employees are not rated by their superiors but by their subordinates. The followers appraise the leader.

Advantages of upward appraisal include the following.

(a) Subordinates tend to know their superior better than superiors know their subordinates.

(b) As all subordinates rate their managers statistically, these ratings tend to be more reliable – the more subordinates the better. Instead of the biases of individual managers' ratings, the various ratings of the employees can be converted into a representative view.

(c) Subordinates' ratings have more impact because it is more unusual to receive ratings from subordinates. It is also surprising to bosses because, despite protestations to the contrary,

information often flows down organisations more smoothly and comfortably than it flows up. When it flows up it is qualitatively and quantitatively different. It is this difference that makes it valuable.

Problems with the method include fear of reprisals, vindictiveness, and extra form processing. Some bosses in strong positions might refuse to act, even if a consensus of staff suggested that they should change their ways.

4.4 Customer appraisal

In some companies part of the employee's appraisal process includes taking into account **feedback** from 'customers' (whether internal or external). Some organisations go further and make customer feedback a key element of employee remuneration. This reflects the view that customers are the best judges of customer service.

4.5 360 degree appraisal

Taking downwards, upwards and customer appraisals together, some firms have instituted **360 degree appraisal** (or multi-source appraisal) by collecting feedback on an individual's performance from the following sources.

(a)   The person's immediate manager

(b)   People who report to the appraisee, perhaps divided into groups

(c)   Peers and co-workers: most people interact with others within an organisation, either as members of a team or as the receivers or providers of services, and can offer useful feedback

(d)   Customers: if salespeople know what customers thought of them, they might be able to improve their technique

(e)   The manager personally: all forms of 360 degree appraisal require people to rate themselves, and those 'who see themselves as others see them will get fewer surprises'

Sometimes the appraisal results in a counselling session, especially when the result of the appraisals are conflicting. For example, an appraisee's manager may have quite a different view of the appraisee's skills than subordinates.

Performance objective PO2, relating to stakeholder relationship management, includes the maintenance of 'productive business relationships'. Planning for and engaging positively with the appraisal process provides an example of a practical step you could take in this area.

CHAPTER ROUNDUP

↳ Performance management aims to get better results for the organisation and evaluation of individual performance.

↳ Appraisal is part of the system of performance management, including goal setting, performance monitoring, feedback and improvement planning.

↳ Appraisal can be used to **reward** but also to identify **potential**. It is part of performance management and can be used to establish areas for improvement and **training and development** needs.

↳ **Formal appraisal systems** support objective, positive, relevant, consistent feedback by managers.

↳ Three basic requirements of a **formal appraisal system** are: defining what is to be appraised, recording assessments, and getting the appraiser and appraisee together for feedback and planning.

↳ There are a number of ways to judge or appraise performance. The most appropriate method will depend upon the circumstances and people involved.

↳ The appraisal **interview** is an important stage in the process, as it can be used to encourage collaborative problem-solving and improvement planning. A 'problem-solving' style is preferable to a 'tell and sell' or 'tell and listen' style (Maier, 1975).

↳ **Problems** with appraisal are its implementation in practice and a range of misperceptions about it (Lockett, 1992). New techniques of appraisal aim to monitor effectiveness from a number of perspectives.

↳ New techniques of appraisal aim to monitor the appraisee's effectiveness from a number of perspectives. These techniques include upward, customer and 360 degree feedback.

QUICK QUIZ

1   Which one of the following is NOT a purpose of appraisal?

   A   To identify performance levels   C   To encourage communication between manager and employee
   B   To assess development needs   D   To highlight employees' weaknesses

2   The advantages of self-appraisals are: (tick all that apply)

   They save the manager time.   ☐

   They reconcile the goals of the individual and the organisation.   ☐

   They offer increased responsibility to the individual.   ☐

   They are more accurate as people are often the best judges of their own performance.   ☐

3   A 360 degree appraisal involves doing a downwards, upwards and customer appraisal together. True or false?

4   According to Maier, which style of appraisal interview is usually preferred by the appraisee?

   A   Tell and sell
   B   Tell and listen
   C   Problem-solving

5   When a subordinate rates their manager's leadership skills, this is an example of:

   A   Job evaluation   C   Performance management
   B   Job analysis   D   Upward appraisal

ANSWERS TO QUICK QUIZ

1   D   The appraisal must not be seen as a chance for the manager to act as judge, jury and counsel for the prosecution!

2   The advantages of self-appraisals are:

They save the manager time ☑

They reconcile the goals of the individual and the organisation ☑

They offer increased responsibility to the individual ☑

They are not more accurate, as people are often not the best judges of their own performance

3   True.   This is also called a multi-source appraisal.

4   C   Problem-solving.

5   D   Make sure you can define all these terms clearly.

Now try ...

Attempt the questions below from the **Practice Question Bank**

Q85

Q86

Q87

Q88

Q89

part

E

Personal effectiveness and communication in business

This chapter draws together a number of topics that relate to the way that people do their jobs.

Section 1 covers time management, a very necessary skill for all busy people. Good time management depends to some extent on ruthless prioritisation and this requires a good understanding by staff of just what their roles are. The role of information technology in improving personal effectiveness is discussed in **Section 2**.

In **Section 3, we look at the consequences of ineffectiveness at work.**

Section 4 covers competence frameworks, and coaching, mentoring and counselling as tools in personal development. We also focus on personal development plans, which are valuable for setting out the activities to ensure development and improved job performance.

Section 5 looks at conflict and the techniques for resolving it.

The rest of this chapter (**Sections 6 to 10**) is principally concerned with **communication**. Communication is fundamental to the success of any organisation of any size, since it is only **via** communication that we know what is to be done, by whom and how. Communication is also fundamental to **motivation**, as you discovered in Chapter 15.

Personal effectiveness and communication

TOPIC LIST	SYLLABUS REFERENCE
1 Time management	E1 (a)
2 The role of information technology	E1 (a), (b), (c)
3 Ineffectiveness at work	E2 (a),(b)
4 Competence frameworks and personal development	E3 (a)-(e)
5 Conflict	E4 (a)-(c)
6 Communication in the workplace	E5 (a)-(c), (i)
7 Formal communication processes	E5 (d)-(h)
8 Informal communication channels	E5 (f)
9 Barriers to communication	E5 (g),(h)
10 Communication methods	E5 (a)

Study Guide	Intellectual level
E1 Personal effectiveness techniques	
(a) Explain the importance of effective time management.	K
(b) Describe the barriers to effective time management and how they may be overcome.	K
(c) Describe the role of information technology in improving personal effectiveness.	S
E2 Consequences of ineffectiveness at work	
(a) Identify the main ways in which people and teams can be ineffective at work.	S
(b) Explain how individual or team ineffectiveness can affect organisational performance.	K
E3 Competence frameworks and personal development	
(a) Describe the features of a 'competence framework'.	S
(b) Explain how a competence framework underpins professional development needs.	S
(c) Explain how personal and continuous professional development can increase personal effectiveness at work.	S
(d) Explain the purpose and benefits of coaching, mentoring and counselling in promoting employee effectiveness.	K
(e) Describe how a personal development plan should be formulated, implemented, monitored and reviewed by the individual.	S
E4 Sources of conflict and techniques for conflict resolution and referral	
(a) Identify situations where conflict at work can arise.	S
(b) Describe how conflict can affect personal and organisational performance.	S
(c) Identify ways in which conflict can be managed.	S
E5 Communicating in business	
(a) Describe methods of communication used in the organisation and how they are used.	K
(b) Explain how the type of information differs and the purposes for which it is applied at different levels of the organisation: strategic, tactical and operational.	K
(c) List the attributes of good quality information.	K
(d) Explain a simple communication model: sender, message, receiver, feedback, noise.	K
(e) Explain formal and informal communication and their importance in the workplace.	K
(f) Identify the consequences of ineffective communication.	K
(g) Describe the attributes of effective communication.	K
(h) Describe the barriers to effective communication and identify practical steps that may be taken to overcome them.	K
(i) Identify the main patterns of communication.	K

EXAM FOCUS POINT

Many of these topics – such as barriers to communication, qualities of effective communication, counselling – may be set as questions. An article in *Student Accountant* has pointed out that 'if there is one prerequisite that sets accountancy apart from other professions, it is the need to communicate clearly and concisely both internally and externally. Communication is the core of the accountancy profession, transmitting information from one person to another, from one organisation to another – or a combination of both – and to the shareholders and other stakeholders of the organisation.' The article goes on to discuss various barriers to communication and how they can be overcome. The nature and direction of organisational communication, the need for good communication, the qualities of good communication, barriers to communication and ways to improve it are all key examinable topics, because of their importance to the accountant's role.

1 Time management

Time is a scarce resource and managers' time must be used to best effect. **Urgency** and **importance** must be recognised and distinguished. Tasks must be prioritised and scheduled. In-trays can be managed using the ABCD method. Other important matters are correct use of the telephone, availability to callers and seeing tasks through to completion.

The scarcest resource any of us has is time. No amount of investment can add more hours to the day or weeks to the year. All we can do is take steps to make more effective use of the time which is available to us. Planning how we spend our time is as normal to us as planning how we will spend our income, and you should already have considerable experience of both.

To be worth their pay, every employee needs to add more value than they cost per hour. If you do the same exercise for the whole team, you can see how expensive the time of your section actually is, and why keeping colleagues waiting to start a meeting or training course is more serious than just a breach of manners. It is important, therefore, that managers work as efficiently as possible.

Time management is the process of allocating time to tasks in the most effective manner.

Effective time management involves attention to:

- Goal or target setting
- Action planning
- Prioritising
- Focus
- Urgency
- Organisation

Time management tasks

(a) **Identifying objectives**: and the key tasks which are most relevant to achieving them – sorting out what the supervisor **must** do, from what he **could** do, and from what he would **like** to do. **Urgent** is not always the same as **important**.

(b) **Prioritising and scheduling**: assessing key tasks for relative importance and amount of time required. Routine non-essential tasks should be delegated – or done away with if possible. Routine key tasks should be organised as standard procedures and systems. Non-routine key tasks will have to be carefully scheduled as they arise, according to their urgency and importance; an up-to-date diary with a **carry forward system** to follow-up action will be helpful.

(c) **Planning and control**: Schedules should be regularly checked for disruption by the unexpected; priorities will indicate which areas may have to be set aside for more urgent items. Information and control systems in the organisation should be utilised so that problems can be anticipated, and sudden decisions can be made on the basis of readily available information.

1.1 Principles of time management

The key principles of time management can be depicted as follows.

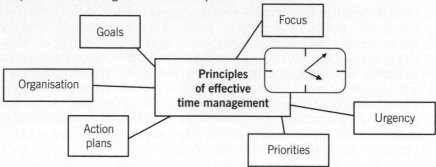

1.1.1 Goals

If you have no idea what it is you are supposed to accomplish, all the time in the world will not be long enough to get it done. Nor is there any way of telling whether you have done it or not. To be useful, goals need to be SMART:

Specific

Measureable

Attainable

Realistic

Time-bounded

1.1.2 Action plans

Now you must make **written action plans that set out how you intend to achieve your goals**.

1.1.3 Priorities

Now you can set priorities from your plan. You do this by deciding which tasks are the most important: what is the most valuable use of your time at that very moment?

Focus: one thing at a time

Work on **one thing at a time** until it is finished, where possible.

1.1.4 Urgency: do it now!

Do not put off large, difficult or unpleasant tasks simply because they are large, difficult or unpleasant.

1.1.5 Organisation

Apart from working to plans, checklists and schedules, your work organisation might be improved by the following.

(a) **An ABCD method of in-tray management**. Resolve to take one of the following approaches.

Act on the item immediately

Bin it, if you are sure it is worthless, irrelevant and unnecessary

Create a definite plan for coming back to the item: get it on your schedule, timetable or 'to do list'

Delegate it to someone else to handle

(b)   **Organise your work in batches**. Batches should contain jobs requiring the same activities, files, equipment, and so on.

(c)   **Take advantage of your natural work patterns**. Self-discipline is aided by developing regular hours or days for certain tasks, like dealing with correspondence first thing, or filing at the end of the day.

1.2 Improving time management

Plan each day. The daily list should include the most important tasks as well as urgent but less important tasks.

Produce a longer-term plan. This can highlight the important tasks so that sufficient time is spent on them on a daily basis.

Do not be available to everyone at all times. Constant interruptions can be prevented by, for example, setting 'surgery hours' during which your door is open to visitors.

Stay in control of the telephone. For example, only take calls during certain times and divert calls to your secretary during the rest of the day.

EXAM FOCUS POINT

In the examination you are likely to be faced with questions involving helping others with their time management. The list of ideas above may be useful examples, or suggestions for such questions, but add more of your own.

1.3 Prioritisation

Prioritising tasks involves ordering tasks in order of preference or priority, based on:

*   The relative consequences of timely or untimely performance
*   Importance
*   Dependency of other people on completion of the task(s)
*   Urgency
*   Defined deadlines, timescales and commitments

Prioritisation involves identifying key results (objectives which **must** be achieved if the section is to fulfil its aims) and key tasks (those things that **must** be done on time and to the required standard if the key results are to be achieved).

A job will be **important** compared with other tasks if it satisfies at least one of three conditions.

*   It adds value to the organisation's output.
*   It comes from a source deserving high priority, such as a customer or senior manager.
*   The potential consequences of failure are long term, difficult to reverse, far reaching and costly.

One of the problems managers have in allocating their time comes from determining which tasks are **important** as defined above and distinguishing these from **urgent** tasks, which may have a deadline but less importance.

*   Tasks both urgent and important should be dealt with now, and given a fair amount of time.

*   Tasks **not** urgent but still important will become urgent as the deadline looms closer. Some of these tasks can be delegated.

*   Tasks urgent but not important should be delegated, or designed out of your job. The task might be urgent to someone else, but not to you.

*   Tasks neither urgent nor important should be delegated or binned.

Performance objective PO5 of your Practical Experience Requirements requires you to be able to manage yourself effectively. You can apply the knowledge that you learn from this section on time management to help you demonstrate this competence.

1.4 Work planning

Work planning includes the following basic steps.

- Establishing priorities

- Loading, allocation of tasks

- Sequencing of tasks

- Scheduling: estimating the time taken to complete a task and working forwards or backwards to determine start or finish times

Work planning, as the term implies, means planning how, when and by whom work should be done, so that objectives can be efficiently met. At an individual level, this may involve the following.

Planning activity	Example
Scheduling **routine tasks** so that they will be completed at pre-determined times	You plan to complete bank reconciliations every month.
Handling **high-priority tasks and deadlines**: working into the routine any urgent tasks which interrupt the usual level of working	You adjust your plans so that you can prepare an urgent costing requested by the sales manager.
Adapting to **changes and unexpected demands**	A colleague may go off sick: there should be a contingency plan to enable to you to provide cover for them.
Setting **standards** against which performance will be measured	You set a target to complete a certain number of costings to a certain level of accuracy.
Co-ordinating your own plans and efforts with those of others	You plan to get your costings to the sales meeting in time for sales staff to prepare a quote for a client.

Work planning consists of a number of basic steps.

(a) **Allocating work** to people and machines (sometimes called **loading**)

(b) Determining the **order** in which activities are performed (prioritising: sometimes called **activity scheduling** or **task sequencing**)

(c) Determining exactly **when** each activity will be performed (timetabling: sometimes called **time scheduling**)

(d) Establishing **checks and controls** to ensure that deadlines are being met and that routine tasks are still achieving their objectives

EXAM FOCUS POINT

This topic may seem like common sense, but do not be tempted to ignore it. The specifics of time management, and time management principles, lend themselves very nicely to exam questions.

2 The role of information technology

In this section we discuss some of the most significant developments in communication technology, and the impact these developments have had on the way people do their work.

- Digital means 'of digits or numbers'. Digital information is information in a coded (binary) form.

- Information in analogue form uses continuously variable signals.

2.1 Modems and digital transmission

New technologies require **transmission systems** capable of delivering substantial quantities of data at great speed.

2.2 Mobile communications

Networks for portable telephone communications, also known as '**cellular**' or '**mobile phones**', have boomed in developed countries since the 1990s.

Digital networks have been developed which are better able to support data transmission than the older analogue networks, with **higher transmission speeds** and **less likelihood of data corruption**.

2.3 Voice messaging systems

Voice messaging systems answer and route telephone calls. Typically, when a call is answered a **recorded message** tells the caller to dial the extension required, or to hold if they want to speak to the operator.

2.4 Computer bulletin boards

A computer bulletin board consists of a central mailbox or area on a computer server where people can **deposit messages** for everyone to see and, in turn, **read what other people have left** in the system.

Bulletin boards can be appropriate for a team of individuals at different locations to compare notes. It becomes a way of keeping track of progress on a **project** between routine team meetings.

2.5 Videoconferencing

Videoconferencing is the use of computer and communications technology to **conduct meetings**.

Videoconferencing has become increasingly common as the internet and webcams have brought the service to desktop PCs at reasonable cost. More expensive systems feature a **separate room with several video screens**, which show the images of those participating in a meeting.

2.6 Electronic Data Interchange (EDI)

EDI is a form of computer-to-computer **data** interchange. Instead of sending each other reams of paper in the form of invoices, statements, and so on, details of inter-company transactions are sent via telecoms links, **avoiding the need for output** and paper at the sending end, and **for re-keying of data** at the receiving end.

2.7 Deciding on a communication tool

The **channel of communication** will impact on the effectiveness of the communication process. The characteristics of the message will determine what communication tool is best for a given situation.

Technological advances have increased the number of communication tools available. The features and limitations of ten common tools are outlined in the following table.

Tool	Features/Advantages	Limitations
Conversation	Requires little or no planning	May be easily forgotten
Meeting	Allows multiple opinions to be expressed	Can highlight differences and become time-wasting confrontations
Presentation	Visual aids such as slides can help the communication process	Requires planning and skill
Telephone	Good for communications that do not require (or you would prefer not to have) a permanent written record	No written record gives greater opportunity for misunderstandings
Facsimile	Enables reports and messages to reach remote locations quickly	Complex images do not transmit well
Memorandum	Provides a permanent record	Can come across as impersonal
Letter	Provides a permanent record of an external message Adds formality to external communications	If inaccurate or poorly presented provides a permanent record of incompetence May be slow to arrive depending on distance and the postal service
Report	Provides a permanent, often comprehensive written record	Complex messages may be misunderstood in the absence of immediate feedback
Email	Provides a written record Attachments (eg reports or other documents) can be included Quick – regardless of location Can be sent to multiple recipients easily, can be forwarded on to others	Long messages (more than one 'screen') may best be dealt with via other means, or as attached documents
Videoconference	This is in effect a meeting conducted using a computer and video system Some non-verbal messages (eg gestures) will be received	Image quality is often poor – resulting in not much more than an expensive telephone conference call!

2.8 The effect of office automation on business

Office automation has an enormous effect on business. We discuss some of the most significant effects in this section.

2.8.1 Routine processing

The processing of routine data can be done in **bigger volumes**, at **greater speed** and with **greater accuracy** than with non-automated, manual systems.

2.8.2 The paperless office

There might be **less paper** in the office (but not necessarily so) with more data processing done using computers. Many organisations print information held in computer files resulting in more paper in the office than with manual systems!

2.8.3 Management information

The nature and **quality of management information** has changed.

(a)   Managers are likely to have **access to more information** – for example from a database. Information is also likely to be **more accurate, reliable and up to date**. The range of **management reports** is likely to be wider and their content more comprehensive.

(b)   **Planning activities** should be more thorough, with the use of **models** (eg spreadsheets for budgeting) and **sensitivity analysis**.

(c)   Information for **control** should be more readily available. For example, a computerised sales ledger system should provide prompt reminder letters for late payers, and might incorporate other credit control routines. Stock systems, especially for companies with stocks distributed around several different warehouses, should provide better stock control.

(d)   Decision-making by managers can be helped by decision support systems.

2.8.4 Organisation structure

The **organisation structure** might change. PC networks give local office managers a means of setting up a good **local management information system**, and **localised data processing** while retaining access to **centrally held databases** and programs. Office automation can therefore encourage a tendency towards **decentralisation** of authority within an organisation.

On the other hand, such systems help **head office** to **keep in touch** with what is going on in local offices. Head office can therefore readily monitor and control the activities of individual departments, and retain a co-ordinating influence.

2.8.5 Customer service

Office automation, in some organisations, results in **better customer service**. When an organisation receives large numbers of telephone enquiries from customers, the staff who take the calls should be able to provide a prompt and helpful service if they have **online access** to the organisation's data files.

2.8.6 Homeworking or remote working

Advances in communications technology have, for some tasks, **reduced the need for the actual presence of an individual in the office**.

The **advantages to the organisation** of homeworking are as follows.

(a)   **Cost savings on space**. Office rental costs and other charges can be very expensive. If firms can move some of their employees on to a homeworking basis, money can be saved.

(b)   A **larger pool of labour**. The possibility of working at home might attract more applicants for clerical positions, especially from people who have other demands on their time (eg going to and from school) which cannot be fitted round standard office hours.

(c)   If the homeworkers are **freelance**, then the organisation **avoids the need to pay them** when there is insufficient work, when they are sick, on holiday, etc.

Performance objective PO5 of your Practical Experience Requirements requires you to be able to 'work with others to recognise, assess or improve business performance, using appropriate techniques and IT applications'. You can apply the knowledge that you learn from this section on the role of information technology to help you demonstrate this competence.

2.9 How technology can enhance personal effectiveness

2.9.1 Intranet

Many organisations use their intranets to deliver training modules eg ethics, work and safety procedures. Studying and assessment is carried out online, enabling employees to get immediate results as part of their ongoing learning and development.

2.9.2 Proprietary systems

Examples include:

- Skype – using your PC to telephone with video link, also useful for video conferencing
- Webex – web conferencing, online meetings and events

3 Ineffectiveness at work

3.1 The main ways in which employees can be ineffective

- Failing to communicate (eg problems, delays)
- Failing to meet deadlines
- Failing to comply with job specifications
- Failing to deliver the exact product needed

3.2 Effects on the organisation

- Potential problems are not identified and so no countermeasures can be taken in time to prevent the problem arising

- Problems are not dealt with as they arise

- Deadlines are not met

- Customers are angry and go elsewhere

4 Competence frameworks and personal development

4.1 Competence frameworks

A competence framework sets out what an employee **should be able to do** and what the employee **ought to know**.

An employee's job description should include a competence framework and the employee should be encouraged to keep up to date with developments in their field. This may involve regular attendance at conferences and update courses as part of the employee's professional development. Having a defined set of competences that are necessary for a job should help an organisation in the following ways.

- Assisting effective recruitment
- As a tool for performance evaluation
- Identifying skills gaps and planning training accordingly

4.1.1 Advantages of competence frameworks

Evaluating an individual's performance on the basis of what they can actually do is fairer than judging them on their personal qualities, qualifications or the amount of time spent on activities, providing a foundation for more objective performance reviews.

The framework also provides a basis for employees to plan their personal development.

4.1.2 Disadvantages of competence frameworks

Competency frameworks are hard to develop. They require a clear understanding of the job and a focus to think in terms of what employees need to be able to do rather than what they need to be.

Competences can be expressed at such a generic level ('innovativeness', 'leadership') that they become meaningless and difficult to measure.

4.2 Coaching

Coaching is an approach whereby a trainee is put under the guidance of an experienced employee who shows the trainee how to perform tasks. It is also a fashionable aspect of leadership style and a feature of superior/subordinate relationships, where the aim is to **develop** people by providing challenging opportunities and guidance in tackling them.

Step 1	**Establish learning targets**. The areas to be learnt should be identified, and specific, realistic goals (eg completion dates, performance standards) stated by agreement with the trainee.
Step 2	**Plan a systematic learning and development programme**. This will ensure regular progress, appropriate stages for consolidation and practice.
Step 3	**Identify opportunities for broadening the trainee's knowledge and experience**, eg by involvement in new projects, placement on interdepartmental committees, suggesting new contacts, or simply extending the job, adding more tasks, greater responsibility, etc.
Step 4	**Take into account the strengths and limitations of the trainee** in learning, and take advantage of learning opportunities that suit the trainee's ability, preferred style and goals.
Step 5	**Exchange feedback**. The coach will want to know how the trainee sees their progress and future. They will also need performance information in order to monitor the trainee's progress, adjust the learning programme if necessary, identify further needs which may emerge and plan future development for the trainee.

Note that coaching focuses on achieving specific objectives.

4.3 Mentoring

Mentoring is a long-term relationship in which a more experienced person acts as a teacher, counsellor, role model, supporter and encourager to another person with the aim of fostering the individual's personal and career development.

Mentoring differs from coaching in two main ways.

(a) The mentor is not usually the protégé's immediate superior.

(b) Mentoring covers a wide range of functions, not always related to current job performance.

Career functions include:

- Sponsoring within the organisation and providing exposure at higher levels
- Coaching and influencing progress through appointments
- Protection
- Drawing up personal development plans
- Advice with administrative problems that people face in their new jobs
- Help in tackling projects by pointing people in the right direction

Psychosocial functions include:

- Creating a sense of acceptance and belonging
- Counselling and friendship
- Providing a role model

Organisational arrangements for coaching and mentoring will vary, but in general a coach needs to be an expert in the trainee's professional field. Mentors are often drawn from other areas of the organisation but can open up lines of communication to those with power and influence across it. For this reason, a mentor is usually in a senior position.

4.4 Counselling

Counselling is an interpersonal interview, the aim of which is to facilitate another person in identifying and working through a problem.

The need for workplace counselling can arise in many different situations.

- During appraisal, to solve work or performance problems

- In grievance or disciplinary situations

- Following change, such as promotion or relocation

- On redundancy or dismissal

- As a result of domestic or personal difficulties

- In cases of sexual, racial or religious harassment or bullying at work (to support the victim and educate the perpetrator)

Note that counselling is non-directive. The individual decides what is to be achieved and how. Counselling helps people to help themselves.

4.5 Benefits of counselling

Effective counselling is not merely a matter of pastoral care for individuals, but is very much in the organisation's interests. Counselling can:

(a) **Prevent underperformance**, reduce labour turnover and absenteeism and increase commitment from employees

(b) Demonstrate an organisation's **commitment** to and concern for its employees

(c) Give employees the **confidence and encouragement** necessary to take responsibility for self and career development

(d) Recognise that the organisation may be contributing to the **employees' problems** and provide an opportunity to reassess organisational policy and practice

(e) Support the organisation in **complying with its obligations** (eg in regard to managing harassment in the workplace).

4.6 The counselling process

> Counselling is facilitating others through the process of **defining and exploring their own problems**: it is primarily a non-directive role.

Managers may be called on to use their expertise to help others make informed decisions or solve problems by:

(a)   **Advising:** offering information and recommendations on the best course of action. This is a relatively **directive** role, and may be called for in areas where you can make a key contribution to the **quality** of the decision: advising an employee about the best available training methods, say, or about behaviour which is considered inappropriate in the workplace.

(b)   **Counselling:** facilitating others through the process of defining and exploring their own problems and coming up with their own solutions. This is a relatively **non-directive** role, and may be called for in areas where you can make a key contribution to the **ownership** of the decision: helping employees to formulate learning goals, for example, or to cope with work (and sometimes non-work) problems.

The counselling process has three broad stages (Egan, 2014).

Step 1	**Reviewing the current scenario:** helping people to identify, explore and clarify their problem situations and unused opportunities. This is done mostly by listening, encouraging them to tell their 'story', and questioning/probing to help them to see things more clearly.

Step 2	**Developing a preferred scenario:** helping people to identify what they want, in terms of clear goals and objectives. This is done mostly by encouraging them to envisage their desired outcome, and what it will mean for them (in order to motivate them to make the necessary changes).

Step 3	**Determining how to get there:** helping people to develop action strategies for accomplishing goals, for getting what they want. This is done mostly by encouraging them to explore options and available resources, select the best option and plan their next steps.

4.7 Confidentiality

There will be situations when an employee cannot be completely open unless they are sure that any comments will be treated confidentially. However, certain information, once obtained by the organisation (for example about fraud or sexual harassment) calls for action. In spite of the drawbacks, employees must be made aware when their comments will be passed on to the relevant authority, and when they will be treated completely confidentially.

4.8 Personal development plans and objectives

- A **personal development plan** is a clear developmental action plan for an individual which incorporates a wide set of developmental opportunities, including formal training.

- **Self development** may be defined as: 'personal development, with the person taking primary responsibility for his or her own learning and for choosing the means to achieve this.' (Pedler, et al, 1991)

Personal development implies a wide range of activities with the objectives of:

- Improving **performance** in an existing job

- Improving **skills and competences**, perhaps in readiness for career development or organisational change

- Planning experience and pathways for **career development** and/or advancement within the organisation

- Acquiring **transferable skills** and competences for general 'employability' or change of direction

- Pursuing **personal growth** towards the fulfilment of one's personal interests and potential

4.9 A systematic approach to personal development planning

A systematic approach to planning your own development will include the following steps.

Step 1	Select an **area for development**: a limitation to overcome or a strength to build on. Your goals might be based on your need to **improve performance** in your current job and/or on your **career goals**, taking into account possible changes in your current role and opportunities within and outside the organisation. You might carry out a personal SWOT (strengths, weaknesses, opportunities, threats) analysis. One helpful tool is an interest/aptitude and performance matrix, on which you can identify skills which you require (don't do well) but for which you can build on your aptitudes and interests (like).

Performance

	High	*Low*
High	Like and do well	Like but don't do well
Low	Dislike but do well	Dislike and don't do well

Aptitude/interest

Step 2	Set a SMART (specific, measurable, agreed, realistic and time-bounded) **learning objective**: what you want to be able to do or do better, and in what timescale.

Step 3	Determine how you will move towards your objective:

- **Research** relevant learning resources and opportunities
- **Evaluate** relevant learning resources and opportunities for suitability, attainability and cost effectiveness
- Secure any **support or authorisation** required from your manager or training development

Step 4	Formulate a comprehensive and specific action plan, including:

- The SMART objective
- The learning approaches you will use, described as **specific actions** to take. (Ask a colleague to provide feedback; watch a training video; enrol in a course.) Each action should have a **realistic timescale** or schedule for completion.
- A **monitoring and review plan**. Precisely how and when (or how often) will you assess your progress and performance against your objectives? (Seek feedback? review results? pass an end of course test?)

Step 5	Secure agreement to your action plan (if required to mobilise organisational support or resources).

Step 6	**Implement** your action plan.

Make sure you don't neglect your study and revision in what may appear to be 'soft' syllabus topics, such as the preparation of a PDP.

Part of performance objective PO3 of your Practical Experience Requirement on strategy and innovation indicates that you should 'plan, identify and monitor appropriate personal targets and standards of delivery that meet the wider departmental and strategic objectives of your organisation'. You can apply the knowledge that you have learnt from this section to help fulfil this requirement.

5 Conflict

Key approaches to **managing disagreements and conflicts** include understanding the problem and the personalities involved; encouraging those involved to discuss the problem; exploring possibilities for mutual satisfaction (win-win); negotiating compromise where required; using formal grievance procedures where necessary.

5.1 How does conflict arise?

Conflict is the clash of opposing 'forces', including the personalities, interests, opinions or beliefs of individuals and groups. Conflict often arises within and between teams because of a number of factors.

(a) **Power and resources** are limited (and sometimes scarce) in the organisation. Individuals and groups **compete** for them, fearing that the more someone else has, the less there is to go around.

(b) Individuals and teams have their own **goals, interests and priorities** – which may be incompatible.

(c) There may be differences and incompatibilities of **personality** between individuals, resulting in 'clashes'.

(d) There may be differences and incompatibilities of **work methods, timescales and working style**, so that individuals or teams frustrate each other with apparent lack of co-ordination (especially if one person's task depends on the other's).

Difference and **competition** by themselves do not lead directly to conflict: they can even be positive forces, helping people to solve problems or to lift their performance.

However, they can **escalate** or **deteriorate** into destructive conflict if:

(a) There is **poor or limited communication**: assumptions go unchallenged, misunderstandings go unclarified, and feelings are left undealt with.

(b) There is **poor co-ordination**: working relationships are not managed or structured, and so are subject to interpersonal problems or unchecked competition.

(c) There are **status barriers**: problems in the relationship are glossed over by the superior asserting authority ('do it because I said so'), or hidden by the subordinate feeling powerless or threatened ('it's more than my job's worth to say anything').

(d) Work demands put pressure on individuals and teams: competition may escalate, feelings may become less manageable under stress, and there may be little time allowed for interpersonal problem-solving.

QUESTION
Conflict

Suggest how conflict may be (a) positive or constructive and (b) negative or destructive.

ANSWER

Conflict is constructive, when its effect is to:

(a) Introduce different **solutions** to problems
(b) **Define power relationships** more clearly
(c) Encourage **creativity**, the testing of ideas
(d) **Focus attention** on individual contributions
(e) **Bring emotions** out into the open
(f) **Release of hostile feelings** that have been, or may be, repressed otherwise

Conflict is destructive when its effect is to:

(a)   Distract attention from the task
(b)   Polarise views and 'dislocate' the group
(c)   Subvert objectives in favour of secondary goals
(d)   Encourage defensive or 'spoiling' behaviour
(e)   Force the group to disintegrate
(f)   Stimulate emotional, win-lose conflicts, ie hostility

5.2 Managing your own interpersonal conflicts

Performance objective PO2, covering stakeholder relationship management, mentions as an example demonstrating how you are able to discuss work problems or issues with colleagues or clients to improve or maintain relationships. If you have experienced any problems or conflicts while working with someone, you might attempt some of the methods discussed here..

Conflicts and sources of dissatisfaction can be managed informally in several ways.

(a)   **Communicate**

The first step in any conflict or difficulty should be **direct, informal discussion** with the person concerned.

(i)   Where there is a **personality or style clash**, this gets the problem out in the open and gives an opportunity to clear up any misunderstandings and misperceptions.

(ii)   Problems of **incompatible working styles** or **excessive work demands** are matters which can be taken, informally, to your supervisor: they will best be able to help you develop solutions to the problem.

(iii)   If your dissatisfaction is with someone in authority over you, or about your own **status**, you may have to discuss the matter with someone higher up in the organisation: this is probably best handled using more formal channels.

(b)   **Negotiate**

Where interests or styles are genuinely incompatible, or work demands are unmanageable, you may need to work together to explore a range of options that will at least partially satisfy both parties. You may have to make a concession in order to gain a concession: this is called **compromise**. However, the best approach is to attempt to find a mutually satisfying solution: a **win-win**.

(c)   **Separate**

If personality clash is the main source of conflict, you may have to arrange (or request) a way of dealing with the other person as little as possible. It may be within your power to simply walk away from potential conflicts, rather than allow yourself to participate. If the problems persist, you may need to initiate formal conflict resolution proceedings: to have a third party mediate – or to physically separate you in different areas, duties or departments.

5.2.1 Managing conflict in the team

Management responses to the handling of conflict (not all of which are effective).

Response	Comment
Denial/withdrawal	'Sweeping it under the carpet'. If the conflict is very trivial, it may indeed blow over without an issue being made of it, but if the causes are not identified, the conflict may grow to unmanageable proportions.
Suppression	'Smoothing over', to preserve working relationships despite minor conflicts.
Dominance	The application of power or influence to settle the conflict. The disadvantage of this is that it creates all the lingering resentment and hostility of 'win-lose' situations.
Compromise	Bargaining, negotiating, conciliating. To some extent, this will be inevitable in any organisation made up of different individuals. However, individuals tend to exaggerate their positions to allow for compromise, and compromise itself is seen to weaken the value of the decision, perhaps reducing commitment.
Integration/collaboration	Emphasis must be put on the task, individuals must accept the need to modify their views for its sake, and group effort must be seen to be superior to individual effort.
Encourage co-operative behaviour	Common goals may be set for all teams/departments. This would encourage co-operation and joint problem-solving.

QUESTION

Conflict resolution

In the light of the above consider how conflict could arise, what form it would take and how it might be resolved in the following situations.

(a) Two managers who share a secretary have documents to be typed.

(b) One worker finds out that another worker who does the same job as he does is paid a higher wage.

(c) A company's electricians find out that a group of engineers have been receiving training in electrical work.

(d) Department A stops for lunch at 12:30pm while Department B stops at 1pm. Occasionally the canteen runs out of puddings for Department B workers.

(e) The Northern Region and Southern Region sales teams are continually trying to better each other's results, and the capacity of production to cope with the increase in sales is becoming overstretched.

ANSWER

(a) Both might need work done at the same time. Compromise and co-ordinated planning can help them manage their secretary's time.

(b) Differential pay might result in conflict with management – even an accusation of discrimination. There may be good reasons for the difference (eg length of service). To prevent conflict such information should be kept confidential. Where it is public, it should be seen to be **not arbitrary**.

(c) The electricians are worried about their jobs, and may take industrial action. Yet if the engineer's training is unrelated to the electricians' work, management can allay fears by giving information. The electricians cannot be given a veto over management decisions: a 'win-lose' situation is inevitable, but both sides can negotiate.

(d) The kitchen should plan its meals better – or people from both departments can be asked in advance whether they want puddings.

(e) Competition **between** sales regions is healthy, as it increases sales. The conflict lies between sales regions and the production department. In the long term, an increase in production capacity is the only solution. Where this is not possible, proper co-ordination methods should be instituted.

5.3 A win-win approach

One useful model of conflict resolution is the **win-win model**. This states that there are three basic ways in which a conflict or problem can be worked out.

Method	Frequency	Explanation
Win-lose	This is quite common.	**One party gets what they want at the expense of the other party**: for example, Department A gets the new photocopier, while Department B keeps the old one (since there were insufficient resources to buy two new ones). However well justified such a solution is (Department A needed the facilities on the new photocopier more than Department B), there is often lingering resentment on the part of the 'losing' party, which may begin to damage work relations.
Lose-lose	This sounds like a senseless outcome, but actually **compromise** comes into this category. It is thus very common.	**Neither party gets what they really wanted**: for example, since Department A and B cannot both have a new photocopier, it is decided that neither department should have one. However 'logical' such a solution is, there is often resentment and dissatisfaction on **both** sides. (Personal arguments where neither party gives ground and both end up storming off or not talking are also lose-lose: the parties may not have lost the argument, but they lose the relationship ...) Even positive compromises only result in half-satisfied needs.
Win-win	This may not be common, but working towards it often brings out the best solution.	**Both parties get as close as possible to what they really want.** How can this be achieved?

It is critical to the **win-win approach** to discover **why both parties really want** something.

(a) They want something because they have not considered any other options.

(b) They can **get away with having something.**

(c) They need something in order to **avoid an outcome they fear**.

Department B may want the new photocopier because they have never found out how to use all the features (which do the same things) on the old photocopier; because they just want to have the same equipment as Department A; or because they fear that if they do not have the new photocopier, their work will be slower and less professionally presented.

To get to the heart of what people really need and want, the important questions in working towards win-win are:

(a) What do you want this for?

(b) What do you think will happen if you don't get it?

In our photocopier example, Department A says it needs the new photocopier to make colour copies (which the old copier does not do), while Department B says it needs the new copier to make clearer copies (because the copies on the old machine are a bit blurred). Now there are options to explore. It may be that the old copier just needs fixing in order for Department B to get what it really wants. Department A will still end up getting the new copier – but Department B has in the process been consulted and had its needs met.

Win-win is not always possible: it is **working towards it** that counts. The result can be mutual respect and co-operation, enhanced communication, more creative problem-solving and – at best – **satisfied needs all round**.

QUESTION

You win again

Suggest a (i) win-lose, (ii) compromise and (iii) win-win solution in the following scenarios.

(a)   Two of your team members are arguing over who gets the desk by the window: they both want it.

(b)   You and a colleague both need access to the same file at the same time. You both need it to compile reports for your managers, for the following morning. It is now 3pm, and each of you will need it for two hours to do the work.

(c)   Manager A is insisting on buying new computers for her department before the budgetary period ends. Manager B cannot understand why, since the old computers are quite adequate. She will moreover be severely inconvenienced by such a move, since her own systems will have to be upgraded as well in order to remain compatible with department A (the two departments constantly share data files). Manager B protests, and conflict erupts.

ANSWER

(a)   (i)   **Win-lose**: one team member gets the window desk, and the other does not. (Result: broken relationships within the team.)

        (ii)   **Compromise**: the team members get the window desk on alternate days or weeks. (Result: half satisfied needs.)

        (iii)   **Win-win**: what do they want the window desk for? One may want the view, the other better lighting conditions. This offers options to be explored: how else could the lighting be improved, so that both team members get what they really want? (Result: at least, the positive intention to respect everyone's wishes equally, with benefits for team communication and creative problem-solving.)

(b)   (i)   **Win-lose**: one of you gets the file and the other doesn't.

        (ii)   **Compromise**: one of you gets the file now, and the other gets it later (although this has an element of win-lose, since the other has to work late or take it home).

        (iii)   **Win-win**: you photocopy the file and **both** take it, or one of you consults your boss and gets an extension of the deadline (since getting the job done in time is the real aim – not just getting the file). These kind of solutions are more likely to emerge if the parties believe they **can** both get what they want.

(c)   (i)   **Win-lose**: Manager A gets the computers, and Manager B has to upgrade her systems.

        (ii)   **Compromise**: Manager A will get some new computers, but keep the same old ones for continued data sharing with Department B. Department B will also need to get some new computers, as a back-up measure.

        (iii)   **Win-win**: what does Manager A want the computers for, or to avoid? Quite possibly, she needs to use up her budget allocation for buying equipment before the end of the budgetary period: if not, she fears she will lose that budget allocation. However, that may not be the case, or there may be other equipment that could be more usefully purchased – in which case, there is no losing party.

5.4 The limits of your ability and authority to resolve relationship issues

Resolving difficulties in working relationships may be:

(a) **Beyond your authority**
Difficulties arising from work demands, work methods and status, for example, may require the intervention of someone who has the authority to change work schedules, reorganise work – and discipline unco-operative subordinates and colleagues (or even superiors) if necessary.

(b) **Beyond your ability**
You may have done your best to resolve personality clashes or to solve other problems, but the situation or relationship may just not be improving. It may require a wider perspective, more developed interpersonal skills, or special expertise in conflict resolution.

In these cases, you may need to mobilise organisational procedures for **formal grievance handling**.

5.5 Formal grievance procedures

A grievance occurs when an individual thinks that they are being wrongly treated by their colleagues or supervisors; that is, when working relationships break down.

The individual may consider that they are being picked on, being given an unfair workload, unfairly appraised in the annual report or unfairly blocked for promotion, or discriminated against.

When an individual has a grievance they should be able to pursue it and ask to have the problem resolved.

If one to one discussion has not worked, a more formal approach will be needed. A typical **grievance procedure** provides for the following steps.

Step 1	The grievance should be carefully explained to the aggrieved **individual's immediate boss** (unless they are the subject of the complaint, in which case it will be the next level up). Employees have the right to be accompanied by a colleague or representative to such an interview, if they feel they need support or a witness.
Step 2	If the immediate boss or other person cannot resolve the matter, or an employee is otherwise dissatisfied with the first interview, the case should be referred to the **next level of management** (and if necessary, in some cases, to an even higher authority).
Step 3	Cases referred to a higher manager should also be reported to the **personnel department**, for the assistance/advice of a personnel manager in resolving the problem.

All complaints should be thoroughly investigated, so if you do find that you have to go through a formal grievance procedure it is important that **you are honest and fair**. Records should be kept of all interviews and actions taken – and these should be confidential.

QUESTION
Grievance procedures

Check what the grievance procedures are in your organisation! If there is nothing set out in your job description or procedures manual, ask the personnel department.

ANSWER

Your own observations.

6 Communication in the workplace

6.1 Communication in the organisation

> **Communication** is a two-way process involving the transmission or exchange of information and the provision of feedback. It is necessary to direct and co-ordinate activities.

Communication is required for planning, co-ordination and control.

(a) **Management decision-making requires data**. Managers are at the hub of a communications system.

(b) Interdepartmental co-ordination depends on information flows. All the interdependent systems for purchasing, production, marketing and administration can be synchronised to perform the right actions at the right times to co-operate in accomplishing the organisation's aims.

(c) Individual motivation and effectiveness depends on communication, so that people know what they have to do and why.

Communication in the organisation may take the following forms.

- Giving **instructions**
- Giving or receiving **information**
- Exchanging **ideas**
- **Announcing** plans or strategies
- **Comparing** actual results against a plan
- **Rules or procedures**
- Communication about the **organisation structure** and job descriptions

6.2 Direction of communication

> Communication in an organisation **flows** downwards, upwards, sideways and diagonally.

Communication links different parts of the organisation.

(a) **Vertical communication** flows up and down the scalar chain from superior to subordinate and back.

(b) **Horizontal or lateral communication** flows between people of the same rank, in the same section or department, or in different sections or departments. Horizontal communication between peer groups is usually easier and more direct then vertical communication, being less inhibited by considerations of rank. It may be part of a **formal** work relationship, to co-ordinate the work of several people, and perhaps departments, who have to co-operate to carry out a certain operation. Alternatively, **informal** communication may furnish emotional and social support to an individual.

(c) Interdepartmental communication by people of different ranks may be described as **diagonal communication**. Departments in the technostructure which serve the organisation in general, such as Human Resources or Information Systems, have no clear line authority linking them to managers in other departments who need their involvement.

6.3 Communication patterns (or networks)

A **communication pattern** channels communication between people. One of the purposes of a **formal organisation structure** is the design of a communications pattern for the organisation.

Leavitt (1951), in a series of experiments, examined the effectiveness of four communication networks for **written** communication between members of a small group.

(a) The **circle**. Each member of the group could communicate with only two others in the group, as shown.

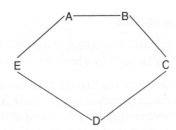

(b)   The **chain**

A — B — C — D — E

Similar to the circle, except that A and E cannot communicate with each other and are therefore at both ends of a communication chain.

(c)   The **'Y'**

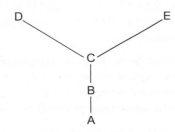

(d)   The **wheel**

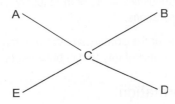

In both the 'Y' and the 'wheel' patterns, C occupies a more central position in the network.

In Leavitt's experiment, each member of a group of five people had to solve a problem and each had an essential piece of information. Only **written** communication, channelled according to one of the four patterns described above, was allowed. The findings of the experiment are tabulated below. A direct trade off between speed and job satisfaction is evident.

	Wheel	Y	Chain	Circle
Speed of problem-solving	Fastest	2nd fastest	3rd fastest	Slowest
Leader	C	C	C (less so than wheel and Y)	None emerged
Job satisfaction	Lowest	3rd highest	2nd highest	Highest(?)

6.4 Internal information

Data and **information** come from **sources** both **inside** and **outside** an organisation. An organisation's information systems should be designed so as to obtain – or **capture** – all the relevant data and information required.

Capturing data and information from inside the organisation involves designing a system for collecting or measuring data and information which sets out procedures for:

- What data and information is collected
- How frequently
- By whom
- By what methods
- How data and information is processed, filed and communicated

6.4.1 The accounting records

The accounting ledgers provide an excellent source of information regarding what has happened in the past. This information may be used as a basis for predicting future events eg budgeting.

Accounting records can provide more than purely financial information. For example, an inventory control system includes purchase orders, goods-received notes and goods-returned notes that can be analysed to provide information regarding the speed of delivery or the quality of supplies. Receivables ledgers can provide sales information for the marketing function.

6.4.2 Other internal sources

Much information that is not strictly part of the accounting records nevertheless is closely tied in to the accounting system.

(a) Information about **personnel** will be linked to the **payroll** system. Additional information may be obtained from this source if, say, a project is being costed and it is necessary to ascertain the availability and rate of pay of different levels of staff, or the need for and cost of recruiting staff from outside the organisation.

(b) Much information will be produced by a **production** department about machine capacity, fuel consumption, movement of people, materials, and work in progress, set up times, maintenance requirements, and so on. A large part of the traditional work of cost accounting involves ascribing costs to the **physical information** produced by this source.

(c) Many **service** businesses, notably accountants and solicitors, need to keep detailed records of the **time spent** on various activities, both to justify fees to clients and to assess the efficiency and profitability of operations.

Staff themselves are one of the primary sources of internal information. Information may be obtained either informally in the course of day-to-day business or through meetings, interviews or questionnaires.

6.5 External information

Formal collection of data from outside sources includes the following.

(a) A company's **tax specialists** will be expected to gather information about changes in tax law and how this will affect the company.

(b) Obtaining information about any new legislation on health and safety at work, or employment regulations, must be the responsibility of a particular person – for example the company's **legal expert** or **company secretary** – who must then pass on the information to other managers affected by it.

(c) Research and development (R&D) work often relies on information about other R&D work being done by another company or by government institutions. An **R&D official** might be made responsible for finding out about R&D work in the company.

(d) **Marketing managers** need to know about the opinions and buying attitudes of potential customers. To obtain this information, they might carry out market research exercises.

Informal gathering of information from the environment occurs naturally, consciously or unconsciously, as people learn what is going on in the world around them – perhaps from newspapers, television reports, meetings with business associates or the trade press.

Organisations hold external information, such as invoices, letters and advertisements, **received from customers and suppliers**. But there are many occasions when an active search outside the organisation is necessary.

The phrase **environmental scanning** is often used to describe the process of gathering external information, which is available from a wide range of sources.

(a)   The Government

(b)   Advice or information bureaux eg Reuters

(c)   Consultants

(d)   Newspaper and magazine publishers

(e)   There may be specific reference works which are used in a particular line of work

(f)   Libraries and information services

(g)   Increasingly businesses can use each other's systems as sources of information, for instance via extranets or electronic data interchange (EDI)

(h)   Electronic sources of information are becoming increasingly important

   (i)   For some time there have been 'viewdata' services, such as Prestel, offering a very large bank of information gathered from organisations including the Office for National Statistics, newspapers and the British Library. Topic offers information on the stock market. Companies like Reuters operate primarily in the field of provision of information – often in electronic form.

   (ii)   The **internet** is a vast source of information.

6.6 Efficient data collection

To produce meaningful information it is first necessary to capture the underlying data. The method of **data collection** chosen will depend on the nature of the **organisation**, **cost** and **efficiency**. Some common data collection methods are listed below.

- Document reading methods
- Magnetic ink character recognition (MICR)
- Optical mark reading (OMR)
- Scanners and optical character recognition (OCR)
- Bar coding and Electronic Point of Sale (EPOS)
- Electronic Funds Transfer at the Point of Sale (EFTPOS)
- Magnetic stripe cards
- Smart cards
- Touch screens
- Voice recognition

6.7 Why do organisations need information?

- **Data** is the raw material for data processing. Data consists of numbers, letters and symbols and relates to facts, events and transactions.

- **Information** is data that has been processed in such a way as to be meaningful to the person who receives it.

Organisations require **information** for a range of **purposes**.

- Planning   • Decision-making
- Controlling

6.7.1 Planning

Once any decision has been made, it is necessary to plan **how to implement** the steps necessary to make it effective. Planning requires a knowledge of, among other things, available **resources**, possible **timescales** for implementation and the likely **outcome under alternative scenarios**.

6.7.2 Controlling

Once a plan is implemented, its actual performance must be controlled. Information is required to assess **whether it is proceeding as planned** or whether there is some unexpected deviation from the plan. It may consequently be necessary to take some form of corrective action.

6.7.3 Decision-making

Information is also required to make informed decisions. This completes the full circle of organisational activity.

6.8 The qualities of good information

Good information has a number of specific qualities: the mnemonic **ACCURATE** is a useful way of remembering them.

The **qualities of good information** are outlined below – in mnemonic form. If you think you have seen this before, note that the second A here stands for '**Authoritative**', an increasingly important concern given the huge **proliferation of information sources** available today.

Quality	Example
Accurate	Figures should **add up**, the degree of **rounding** should be appropriate, there should be **no typos**, items should be allocated to the **correct category** and **assumptions should be stated** for uncertain information (no spurious accuracy).
Complete	Information should include everything that it **needs** to include, for example external data if relevant, or comparative information.
Cost-beneficial	It should not **cost more** to obtain the information than the **benefit** derived from having it. Providers of information should be given efficient means of collecting and analysing it. Presentation should be such that users do not waste time working out what it means.
User targeted	The **needs of the user** should be borne in mind, for instance senior managers may require summaries, junior ones may require detail.
Relevant	Information that is **not needed** for a decision should be omitted, no matter how 'interesting' it may be.
Authoritative	The **source** of the information should be a reliable one (**not**, for instance, 'Joe Bloggs Predictions Page' on the internet unless Joe Bloggs is known to be a reliable source for that type of information.
Timely	The information should be available **when it is needed**.
Easy to use	Information should be **clearly presented**, **not excessively long**, and sent using the **right medium** and **communication channel** (email, telephone, hard-copy report, etc).

EXAM FOCUS POINT

The attributes of good quality information are specifically mentioned in the Study Guide.

6.9 Information in the organisation

A modern organisation requires a **wide range of systems** to hold, process and analyse information. We will now examine the various information systems used to serve organisational information requirements.

Organisations require different types of information system to provide different **levels of information** in a range of functional areas.

System level	System purpose
Strategic	To help senior managers with long-term planning. Their main function is to ensure changes in the external environment are matched by the organisation's capabilities.
Management/ tactical	To help middle managers monitor and control. These systems check if things are working well or not. Some management-level systems support non-routine decision-making, such as 'what if?' analyses.
Operational	To help operational managers track the organisation's day-to-day operational activities. These systems enable routine queries to be answered, and transactions to be processed and tracked.

6.9.1 Example

Finance subsystem

- The **operational level** would deal with cash receipts and payments, bank reconciliations and so forth.

- The **tactical level** would deal with cash flow forecasts and working capital management.

- **Strategic level** financial issues are likely to be integrated with the organisation's commercial strategy, but may relate to the most appropriate source of finance (eg long-term debt, or equity).

The type of information at each level can be seen in the table below.

	Inputs	Process	Outputs
Strategic	Plans, competitor information, overall market information	Summarise Investigate Compare Forecast	Key ratios, ad hoc market analysis, strategic plans
Management/tactical	Historical and budget data	Compare Classify Summarise	Variance analyses Exception reports
Operational	Customer orders, programmed inventory control levels, cash receipts/payments	Update files Output reports	Updated file listings, invoices

7 Formal communication processes

7.1 The communication process

> Communication can be depicted as the **radio signal** model. The sender encodes the message and transmits it through a medium to the receiver who decodes it into information.

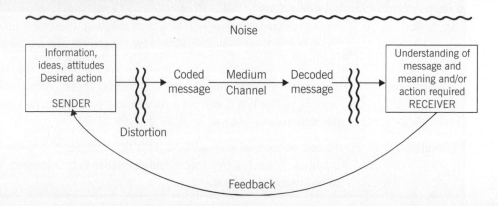

Process	Comment
Encoding of a message	The code or 'language' of a message may be verbal (spoken or written) or it may be non-verbal, in pictures, diagrams, numbers or body language.
Medium for the message	There are a number of channels for communication, such as a conversation, a letter, a noticeboard or via computer. The choice of medium used in communication depends on a number of factors, such as urgency, permanency, complexity, sensitivity and cost.
Feedback	The sender of a message needs feedback on the receiver's reaction. This is partly to test the receiver's understanding of it and partly to gauge the receiver's reaction.
Distortion	The meaning of a message can be lost at the coding and decoding stages. Usually the problem is one of language and the medium used; it is very easy to give the wrong impression in a brief email message.
Noise	Distractions and interference in the environment in which communication is taking place may be physical noise (passing traffic), technical noise (a bad telephone line), social noise (differences in the personalities of the parties) or psychological noise (anger, frustration, tiredness).

7.2 Desirable qualities of a communication system in an organisation

Clarity. The coder of a message must bear in mind the potential recipient. **Jargon can be used** – and will even be most appropriate – **where the recipient shares the same expertise**. It should be avoided for those who do not.

Recipient. The recipient should be clearly identified, and the right medium should be chosen, to minimise distortion and noise.

Medium. The channel or medium should be chosen to ensure it reaches the target audience. Messages of general application (eg health and safety signs) should be displayed prominently.

Timing. Information has to be timely to be useful.

7.3 Effective communication

Effective communication: the right person receives the right information in the right way at the right time.

What does 'good communication' look like? It is perhaps easiest to identify **poor** or ineffective communication, where information is not given; is given too late to be used; is too much to take in; is inaccurate or incomplete; is hard to understand. **Effective communication** is:

(a)   **Directed to appropriate people**. This may be defined by the reporting structure of the organisation, but it may also be a matter of discretion, trust, and so on.

(b)   **Relevant to their needs**. Information should be non-excessive in volume (causing overload); focused on relevant topics; communicated in a format, style and language that they can understand.

(c)   **Accurate and complete** (within the recipient's needs). Information should be 'accurate' in the sense of 'factually correct', but need not be minutely detailed: in business contexts, summaries and approximations are often used.

(d)   **Timely**. Information must be made available within the time period when it will be relevant (as input to a decision, say).

(e)   **Flexible**. Information should be suited in style and structure to the needs of the parties and situation. Assertive, persuasive, supportive and informative communication styles have different applications.

(f)   **Effective in conveying meaning**. Style, format, language and media all contribute to the other person's understanding or lack of understanding. If the other person doesn't understand the message, or misinterprets it, communication has not been effective.

(g)   **Cost effective**. In business organisations, all the above must be achieved, as far as possible, at reasonable cost.

8 Informal communication channels

Informal communication supplements the formal system.

The formal pattern of communication in an organisation is **always** supplemented by an informal one, which is sometimes referred to as the **grapevine**. People like to gossip about rumours and events.

8.1 The grapevine

The grapevine has a number of characteristics.

(a)   The grapevine acts **quickly**.

(b)   The working of the grapevine is **selective**: information is not divulged randomly.

(c)   The grapevine usually operates **at the place of work** and not outside it.

(d)   Oddly, the grapevine is most active when the formal communication network is active: the **grapevine does not fill a gap** created by an ineffective formal communication system.

(e)   **Higher-level executives were better communicators** and better informed than their subordinates.

(f)   More technostructure executives were in the know about events than line managers (because the staff executives are more mobile and get involved with more different functions in their work).

8.2 The importance of informal communications

Managers, rather than staff, might rely on the grapevine, as opposed to formal communication channels, because of the qualities informal communication possesses.

(a) It is more current than the formal system.

(b) It is relevant to the **informal** organisation (where many decisions are actually determined).

(c) It relates to **internal politics**, which may not be reflected in formal communications anyway.

(d) It can **bypass excessively secretive management**.

8.3 Interpersonal skills

Interpersonal skills are needed in order to understand and manage roles, relationships, attitudes and perceptions. They enable us to communicate effectively and to achieve our aims when dealing with other people.

Interpersonal skills

(a) The ability to interpret **body language** and to use it to reinforce messages

(b) The ability to **listen attentively and actively**

(c) The ability to put others at their ease, to persuade and to smooth over difficult situations

(d) The ability to **identify when false or dishonest arguments** are being used, and to construct logical ones

(e) The ability to recognise how much information, and of what kind, another person will **need and be able to take in**

(f) The ability to **use communication media effectively**: to speak well, write legibly, use appropriate vocabulary and use visual aids where required

(g) The ability to **sum up** or conclude an argument clearly and persuasively

(h) The ability to communicate and show enthusiasm, ie **leadership** or inspiration

The above list is by no means exhaustive.

Here are some more important things to consider in interpersonal relations.

Factor	Comment
Goal	What does the other person want from the process? What do you want from the process? What will both parties need and be trying to do to achieve their aims? Can both parties emerge satisfied?
Perceptions	What, if any, are likely to be the factors causing distortion of the way both parties see the issues and each other? (Attitudes, personal feelings, expectations?)
Roles	What roles are the parties playing? (Superior/subordinate, customer/server, complainer/soother?) What expectations does this create of the way they will behave?
Resistances	What may the other person be afraid of? What may they be trying to protect? (Their ego/self-image, attitudes?) Sensitivity will be needed in this area.
Attitudes	What sources of difference, conflict or lack of understanding might there be, arising from attitudes and other factors which shape them (sex, race, specialism, hierarchy)?
Relationships	What are the relative positions of the parties and the nature of the relationship between them? (Superior/subordinate? Formal/informal? Work/non-work)? What style is appropriate to it?
Environment	What factors in the immediate and situational environment might affect the issues and the people? (Eg competitive environment; customer care; pressures of disciplinary situation; nervousness; physical surroundings formality/informality)

8.3.1 Listening

Listening in the communications model is about decoding and receiving information. Effective listening has three consequences.

- It encourages the sender to listen effectively in return to what you have to say.
- It reduces the effect of noise.
- It helps resolve problems by encouraging understanding from someone else's viewpoint.

Advice for good listening

(a) **Be prepared to listen**. Put yourself in the right frame of mind and be prepared to grasp the main concepts.

(b) **Be interested**. Make an effort to analyse the message for its relevance.

(c) **Keep an open mind**. Your own beliefs and prejudices can get in the way of what the other person is actually saying.

(d) **Keep an ear open for the main ideas**. An awareness of how people generally structure their speech can help the process of understanding. Be able to distinguish between the thrust of the argument and the supporting evidence.

(e) **Listen critically**. This means trying to assess what the person is saying by identifying any **assumptions, omissions and biases**.

(f) **Avoid distraction**. People have a natural attention curve, high at the beginning and end of an oral message, but sloping off in the middle.

(g) **Take notes**. However, note taking can be distracting.

8.3.2 Non-verbal communication: body language

The hidden messages in face-to-face communication can be a common cause for communication breakdown, as they cause decoding problems. Observe others in meetings, presentations, interviews or just talking in the bar. Notice the signs of boredom or disagreement, support and interest. Picking up these signals will help you improve your own communication skills.

While watching others, also become more aware of yourself. Be aware of the signals you are sending and transmit only those you intend to.

Non-verbal communication can be controlled and used for several purposes.

(a) It can **provide appropriate feedback** to the sender of a message (a yawn, applause, clenched fists, fidgeting).

(b) It can **create a desired impression** (smart dress, a smile, punctuality, a firm handshake).

(c) It can **establish a desired atmosphere** or conditions (a friendly smile, informal dress, attentive posture, a respectful distance).

(d) It can **reinforce spoken messages** with appropriate indications of how interest and feelings are engaged (an emphatic gesture, sparkling eyes, a disapproving frown).

If we can learn to **recognise** non-verbal messages, our ability to listen is improved.

(a) When we are speaking, non-verbal **feedback** helps us to modify our message.

(b) We may recognise people's **real feelings** when their words are constrained by formal courtesies (an excited look, a nervous tic, close affectionate proximity).

(c) We can **recognise existing or potential personal problems** (the angry silence, the indifferent shrug, absenteeism or lateness at work, refusal to look someone in the eye).

Non-verbal cues

- Facial expression
- Gesture
- Posture and orientation
- Proximity and contact

- Movement and stillness
- Silence and sounds
- Appearance and grooming
- Response to norms and expectations

8.4 Observation

While not really a form of communication, **observation** as a management skill is linked to topics in communication such as interviewing, so it is convenient to deal with it here.

Observation is an important data-gathering technique. It can be used to measure the effectiveness of procedures, or, indeed, to establish just what procedures and processes are in use. It is perhaps most useful in establishing the nature of less formal aspects of the organisation, such as how the informal organisation works; how individuals perform their tasks; who interacts with whom; and how specified procedures are informally modified.

9 Barriers to communication

Barriers to communication include 'noise' from the environment, poorly constructed or coded/decoded messages (distortion) and failures in understanding caused by the relative position of the senders and receivers.

9.1 General faults in the communication process

Distortion or omission of information by the sender

Misunderstanding due to lack of clarity or technical jargon

Non-verbal signs (gesture, posture, facial expression) contradicting the verbal message, so that its meaning is in doubt

'Overload' – a person being given too much information to digest in the time available

People hearing **only what they want** to hear in a message

Differences in social, racial or educational **background**, compounded by age and personality differences, creating barriers to understanding and co-operation

(Mnemonic using words in bold above: Distorted Messages Never Overcome Personal Differences.)

9.2 Communication difficulties at work

Status (of the sender and receiver of information)

- A senior manager's words are listened to closely and a colleague's perhaps discounted.

- A subordinate might mistrust their superior believing that they might look for hidden meanings in a message.

Jargon. People from different job or specialist backgrounds (eg accountants, personnel managers, IT experts) can have difficulty in talking on a non-specialist's wavelength.

Suspicion. People discount information from those not recognised as having expert power.

Priorities. People or departments have different priorities or perspectives so that one person places more or less emphasis on a situation than another.

Selective reporting. Subordinates may give superiors incorrect or incomplete information (eg to protect a colleague, to avoid bothering the superior); also a senior manager may only be able to handle edited information because they do not have time to sift through details.

Use. Managers may be prepared to make decisions on a hunch without proper regard to the communications they may or may not have received.

Timing. Information which has **no immediate** use may be forgotten.

Opportunity. Opportunity, formal or informal, for people to say what they think may be lacking.

Conflict. Where there is conflict between individuals or departments, communications will be withdrawn and information withheld.

Personal differences. Differences such as age, educational/social background or personality mean that people have different views as to what is important or different ways of expressing those views. Sometimes individuals' views may be discounted because of who they are, not what they say.

9.2.1 Culture

Secrecy. Information might be given on a need-to-know basis, rather than be considered as a potential resource for everyone to use.

Can't handle bad news. The culture of some organisations may prevent the communication of certain messages. Organisations with a 'can-do' philosophy may not want to hear that certain tasks are impossible.

9.2.2 Categories of communication problems

(a)   **System.** There may be a bad formal communication system.

(b)   **Misunderstanding.** There may be misunderstanding about the actual content of a message.

(c)   **Personality.** Interpersonal difficulties may hamper communication.

9.3 Improving the communications system

Establish better communication links

- **Standing instructions** should be recorded in easily accessible manuals which are kept fully up to date.

- Management **decisions** should be sent to all people affected by them, preferably in writing.

- Regular **staff meetings** or formal consultations with trade union representatives should be held.

- **A house journal** should be issued regularly.

- **Appraisal interviews** should be held between a manager and their subordinates to discuss the job performance and career prospects of the subordinates.

- **Technology** should be utilised, for example ensuring organisational knowledge and information is captured and stored, and is easily searchable.

Use the **informal organisation** to supplement this increased freedom of communication.

9.4 Clearing up misunderstandings

Confirmation: issuing a message in more than one form (eg by word of mouth at a meeting, confirmed later in minutes) can help.

Reporting by exception should operate to prevent **information overload** on managers.

Train managers who do not express themselves clearly and concisely. Necessary jargon should be taught in some degree to people new to the organisation or unfamiliar with the terminology of the specialists.

Communication between managers and direct reports will be improved when **interpersonal trust** exists. Exactly how this is achieved will depend on the management style of the manager, the attitudes and personality of the individuals involved, and other environmental variables. Peters and Waterman advocate 'management by walking around' (MBWA), and informality in superior/subordinate relationships as a means of establishing closer links.

QUESTION

Communication

Is the statement below true or false?

'A clearly expressed verbal message will always be understood.'

ANSWER

False. 'Clear expression' is a matter of opinion and perception, or in terms of the communications model, of coding and decoding. We must also consider the effect of noise, such as cultural differences.

10 Communication methods

10.1 Communication methods

There are a wide range of communication methods available. In all situations, the method used should help the communication process.

Communication objective	Method	Reason for method
Generate new ideas On the spot feedback Spread information quickly	Face to face/meetings	People can 'bounce ideas' off one another.
Increase commitment and understanding of workforce	Teambriefing	A team briefing is more personal than a noticeboard.
Reach large membership spread over a wide area	Conference	A conference gives members a chance to discuss and understand what the organisation is doing.
Formal and confidential communication	Interview	Interviews are costly in terms of managerial time but are necessary for confidential communication.
Face to face communication without travel time	Telephone	The telephone is more impersonal than an interview but should save time.
Transmit information cheaply to a large number of people	Noticeboard	A noticeboard can provide a variety of information to any or all employees.
External communication/confidential written record	Letter	A letter is a flexible method of providing a written record.
Reach large number of people in several sites/countries	Email	Email messages need not interrupt the recipient's flow of work.
Explain complex facts and arguments	Report	A report allows people to study the material in their own time.

A key element of Practical Experience Requirement PO2 requires you to communicate effectively with stakeholder groups. You can apply the knowledge that you learn from this chapter to help you demonstrate this competence.

CHAPTER ROUNDUP

↳ **Time** is a scarce resource and managers' time must be used to best effect. **Urgency** and **importance** must be recognised and distinguished. Tasks must be prioritised and scheduled. In-trays can be managed using the ABCD method. Other important matters are correct use of the telephone, availability to callers and seeing tasks through to completion.

↳ **Effective time management** involves attention to:
  - Goal or target setting   – Focus
  - Action planning   – Urgency
  - Prioritising   – Organisation

↳ **Prioritising tasks** involves ordering tasks in order of preference or priority, based on
  - The relative consequences of timely or untimely performance
  - Importance
  - Dependency of other people of tasks
  - Urgency
  - Defined deadlines, timescales and commitments

↳ **Work planning** includes the following basic steps:
  - Establishing priorities
  - Loading, allocation of tasks
  - Sequencing of tasks
  - Scheduling estimating the time taken to complete a task and working forwards or backwards to determine start or finish times

↳ The **channel of communication** will impact on the effectiveness of the communication process. The characteristics of the message will determine what communication tool is best for a given situation.

↳ **Counselling** is an interpersonal interview, the aim of which is to facilitate another person in identifying and working through a problem.

↳ Counselling is facilitating others through the process of **defining and exploring their own problems**: it is primarily a non-directive role.

↳ Key approaches to **managing disagreements and conflicts** include understanding the problem and the personalities involved; encouraging those involved to discuss the problem; exploring possibilities for mutual satisfaction (win-win); negotiating compromise where required; using formal grievance procedures where necessary.

↳ **Communication** is a two-way process involving the transmission or exchange of information and the provision of feedback. It is necessary to direct and co-ordinate activities.

↳ Communication in an organisation **flows** downwards, upwards, sideways and diagonally.

↳ Data and **information** come from **sources** both **inside** and **outside** an organisation. An organisation's information systems should be designed so as to obtain – or **capture** – all the relevant data and information required.

↳ Organisations require **information** for a range of **purposes**.
  - Planning   – Decision-making
  - Controlling

↳ **Good information** has a number of specific qualities: the mnemonic **ACCURATE** is a useful way of remembering them.

↳ Communication can be depicted as the **radio signal** model. The sender codes the message and transmits it through a medium to the receiver who decodes it into information.

↳ **Effective communication**: the right person receives the right information in the right way at the right time.

↳ Informal communication supplements the formal system.

↳ **Barriers** to communication include 'noise' from the environments, poorly constructed or coded/decoded messages (distortion) and failures in understanding caused by the relative position of the senders and receivers.

1   List six elements of effective time management.

2   Which of the following necessarily makes a piece of work high priority?

A   Importance
B   Urgency
C   Importance and urgency
D   Other people want you to do the work by a given deadline

3   A list of activities in the order in which they must be completed is the product of task loading.
True or false?

4   When scheduling routine accounting tasks, you are more likely to use forward scheduling rather than
reverse scheduling. True or false?

5   Communication between two members of a project team from different functions, but with the same
level of authority, is:

A   Upward   C   Lateral
B   Downward   D   Diagonal

6   What are the stages of the counselling process?

7   Is the statement below true or false?

'Informal communication does not fill a gap created by an ineffective formal communication system, but
co-exists with it.'

8   Is the statement below true or false?

'Coaching encompasses a much wider range of functions than mentoring.'

ANSWERS TO QUICK QUIZ

1   Goals; action plans; priorities; focus; urgency; organisation

2   C   An important point: work may be urgent but not important or important but not urgent. You may have paused over D – but this is an assertiveness issue: if someone else 'wants' you to do something, you still have a right to consult your own priorities and commitments, assess their right to ask, and so on.

3   False: it is a product of task sequencing. Task loading is allocating tasks to people or machines.

4   True.   Reverse scheduling is more suitable for scheduling tasks for which you already have a completion date or deadline.

5   C

6   Reviewing the current scenario; developing a preferred scenario; determining how to get there

7   True.

8   False. Mentoring encompasses a wider range of functions than coaching.

Now try ...

Attempt the questions below from the **Practice Question Bank**

Q90

Q91

Q92

Q93

Q94

Q95

Q96

Q97

Q98

Q99

Q100

part

F

Professional ethics in accounting and business

467

part

F

Professional ethics in accounting
and business

19

Ethical conduct is a matter of continuing debate. This chapter begins by considering why society developed a framework of rules in **Section 1**. There have been many examples of misbehaviour at all levels of large organisations in recent years. All professional bodies are alarmed by these events and what they say about ethical standards in everyday life. They are determined to do everything they can to promote and ensure high standards of behaviour among their members. Ethics has an increased focus in this syllabus.

In **Section 2**, we look at the idea of managers' **accountability** and **fiduciary responsibility**. The vital theme here is that, even at the highest level, managers are not autonomous: they are always responsible to someone for their actions.

Section 3 looks at the wider background to ethical behaviour. Organisations are embedded in society and must respond not only to established ideas about ethical conduct but also to current public concerns, including some current notions about social responsibility.

Section 4 is about the way organisations manage ethical problems and, in particular, about the desirability of building and maintaining an ethical culture.

Sections 5 and 6 consider in particular why ethics are relevant to accountants, and the qualities that accountants should demonstrate. In particular, you are encouraged to make yourself familiar with **ACCA's own ethical code**.

Section 7 looks at ethical codes for businesses, while **Sections 8 and 9** deal with ethical dilemmas arising in business and their resolution.

Ethical considerations

TOPIC LIST	SYLLABUS REFERENCE
1 Framework of rules	F1 (a)
2 Management accountability	F1 (a)
3 The ethical environment	F1 (a),(d)
4 Ethics in organisations	F1 (a),(c),(d)
5 Accountants and ethics	F2 (a)-(d)
6 A code of ethics for accountants	F1(b); F2 (a)–(e)
7 Ethics in business	F3 (a)-(c)
8 Ethical dilemmas	F4 (a)-(c)
9 Resolution of ethical conflicts	F4 (d)

Study Guide	Intellectual level

F1 Fundamental principles of ethical behaviour

(a) Define business ethics and explain the importance of ethics to the organisation and to the individual. — K

(b) Describe and demonstrate the following principles from the IFAC (IESBA) code of ethics, using examples. — K
  (i) Integrity
  (ii) Objectivity
  (iii) Professional competence
  (iv) Confidentiality
  (v) Professional behaviour

(c) Describe organisational values which promote ethical behaviour using examples. — K
  (i) Openness
  (ii) Trust
  (iii) Honesty
  (iv) Respect
  (v) Empowerment
  (vi) Accountability

(d) Explain the concept of acting in the public interest. — K

F2 The role of regulatory and professional bodies in promoting ethical and professional standards in the accountancy profession

(a) Recognise the purpose of international and organisational codes of ethics and codes of conduct, IFAC (IESBA), ACCA etc. — K

(b) Describe how professional bodies and regulators promote ethical awareness and prevent or punish illegal or unethical behaviour. — K

(c) Identify the factors that distinguish a profession from other types of occupation. — K

(d) Explain the role of the accountant in promoting ethical behaviour. — K

(e) Recognise when and to whom illegal or unethical conduct by anyone within or connected to the organisation should be reported. — K

F3 Corporate codes of ethics

(a) Define corporate codes of ethics. — K

(b) Describe the typical contents of a corporate code of ethics. — K

(c) Explain the benefits of a corporate code of ethics to the organisation and its employees. — K

F4 Ethical conflicts and dilemmas

(a) Describe situations where ethical conflicts can arise. — K

(b) Identify the main threats to ethical behaviour. — K

(c) Outline situations at work where ethical dilemmas may be faced. — K

(d) List the main safeguards against ethical threats and dilemmas. — K

EXAM FOCUS POINT

There is an article on the ACCA website entitled "A question of ethics" that is relevant to material in this chapter.

1 Framework of rules

The society we live in could not exist without **rules and standards**. Think about it: what would life be like if everyone went about doing exactly what they felt like?

People may decide not to turn up for work. This would mean shops not opening, and that you could not buy food. What we consider **crime would spiral out of control** as members of the public decide to take what they want and the police would only tackle criminals if they felt like it. **Businesses would not function** and the financial markets could not operate.

As society developed from prehistoric tribes to the complex interrelationships we have today, rules regulating behaviour also had to evolve. This is because humans recognised the need for everyone to work together for the good of the group.

1.1 Development of society

Imagine a prehistoric tribe. They would have started as individuals, roaming for food and shelter to keep themselves alive. By working as a group, some could **find shelter**, while others **hunted** for things to eat. It would be no good if the hunters ate all the food they found, and those who found shelter refused to let the hunters into the shelter. The shelter finders would **starve** to death while the hunters would **freeze**.

Humans have evolved from these tribes and have built a strong society that has revolutionised our planet. This has only been possible because **individuals have worked together**, guided by rules.

1.2 A need for rules

Back in prehistoric times, there were no laws, no courts and no police. Rules would have **developed through need**. The tribe would have a collective idea of what was **right** and **wrong** for the good of the group and would have **punished** a group member who stepped out of line, for example by taking food from others.

Further rules developed as society grew and eventually the first **laws** were laid down to control the larger populations. **Religion** played a major role in developing the rules for the individual, and many of these rules are still in place today.

Business law is relatively new, and has only developed over the last couple of hundred years with **industrialisation** and the needs that grew from it.

1.3 How do the rules fit together?

There are three main sources of rules that regulate behaviour of individuals and businesses. These are:

- The law
- Non-legal rules and regulations
- Ethics

The diagram below shows how the three sources of regulation fit together.

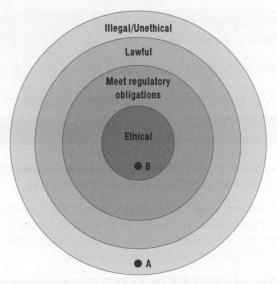

Point A shows a company's current behaviour. It indicates that it is currently breaking the law. It could be treating its employees in an illegal way, such as breaking health and safety laws.

The company wants to move to point B. This means taking the maximum care of employees that is expected by society. To get to this point, the company needs to meet its legal and non-legal obligations first.

The law is the minimum level of behaviour required. Any standard of behaviour below it is considered illegal and warrants punishment by society.

By meeting non-legal regulations (such as the rules of your workplace), you meet a higher level of behaviour than just the legal requirements.

Ethical behaviour is seen as the highest level of behaviour that society expects. Your behaviour goes further than just meeting your legal and non-legal obligations.

1.4 Corporate governance concepts

One view of governance is that it is based on a series of underlying concepts.

1.4.1 Fairness

The directors' deliberations and also the systems and values that underlie the company must be **balanced** by taking into account everyone who has a legitimate interest in the company, and respecting their rights and views. In many jurisdictions, corporate governance guidelines reinforce legal protection for certain groups; for example, minority shareholders.

1.4.2 Openness/transparency

Transparency means **open and clear disclosure** of relevant information to shareholders and other stakeholders, also not concealing information when it may affect decisions. It means open discussions and a default position of information provision, rather than concealment.

Disclosure in this context obviously includes information in the financial statements, not just the numbers and notes to the accounts but also narrative statements, such as the directors' report and the operating and financial review. It also includes all **voluntary disclosure**; that is, disclosure above the minimum required by law or regulation. Voluntary corporate communications include management forecasts, analysts' presentations, press releases, information placed on websites and other reports such as standalone environmental or social reports.

The main reason why transparency is so important relates to the agency problem, the potential conflict between owners and managers. Without effective disclosure the position could be unfairly weighted towards managers, since they have far more knowledge of the company's activities and financial situation than owner/investors. Avoidance of this **information asymmetry** requires not only effective disclosure rules but also strong internal controls that ensure that the information that is disclosed is **reliable**.

Linked with the agency issue, publication of relevant and reliable information **underpins stock market confidence** in how companies are being governed and thus **significantly influences market prices**. **International accounting standards** and **stock market regulations** based on corporate governance codes require information published to be **true and fair**. Information can only fulfil this requirement if adequate disclosure is made of uncertainties and adverse events.

Circumstances where concealment may be justified include discussions about **future strategy** (knowledge of which would benefit competitors), **confidential** issues relating to **individuals** and discussions leading to an agreed position that is then made public.

Independence is an important concept in relation to directors. Corporate governance reports have increasingly stressed the importance of **independent non-executive directors**, directors who are not primarily employed by the company and who have very strictly controlled other links with it. They should be free from conflicts of interest and in a better position to **promote the interests of shareholders and other stakeholders**. Freed from pressures that could influence their activities, independent non-executive directors should be able to carry out **effective monitoring** of the company in conjunction with equally independent external auditors on behalf of shareholders.

Non-executive directors' lack of links and limits on the time that they serve as non-executive directors should promote **avoidance of managerial capture** – accepting executive managers' views on trust without analysing and questioning them.

1.4.3 Probity/honesty

Hopefully this should be the most self-evident of the principles. It relates not only to telling the truth but also not misleading shareholders and other stakeholders. Lack of probity includes not only obvious examples of dishonesty such as taking bribes but also presenting information in a slanted way that is designed to give an unfair impression.

1.4.4 Responsibility

Responsibility means management accepting the credit or blame for governance decisions.

1.4.5 Accountability

Corporate accountability refers to whether an organisation (and its directors) are answerable in some way for the consequences of their actions.

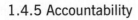

Accountability of directors to shareholders has always been an important part of company law, well before the development of the corporate governance codes. For example, companies in many regimes have been required to provide **financial information** to shareholders on an **annual basis** and hold **annual general meetings**. However, particularly because of the corporate governance scandals of the last 30 years, investors have demanded greater assurance that directors are acting in their interests. This has led to the development of corporate governance codes.

Making the accountability work is the responsibility of **both** parties. Directors, as we have seen, do so through the quality of information that they provide, whereas shareholders do so through their willingness to **exercise their responsibility as owners**, which means using the available mechanisms to query and assess the actions of the board.

The accountability relationship will be different for bodies owned or run by national or central government. The nature of the relationship may be clear – that government determines objectives. How accountability is demonstrated and enforced may depend though on how coherent the objectives are. The main problem will often be where the body's main objectives are non-economic, but the government also wishes to limit the amount it spends on the body.

As with responsibility, one of the biggest debates in corporate governance is the extent of management's **accountability** towards **other stakeholders**, such as the community within which the organisation operates. This has led on to a debate about the contents of accounts themselves.

In the context of public service, **holders of public office** are deemed **accountable** for their decisions and actions to **the public**, and must submit themselves to whatever scrutiny is appropriate for their office.

1.4.6 Reputation

Risks to an organisation's reputation depend on how likely other risks are to crystallise. In the same way, directors' concern for an organisation's reputation will be demonstrated by the extent to which they fulfil the other principles of corporate governance. There are **commercial reasons** for promoting and protecting an organisation's reputation. A key commercial reason relates to the company value, as reflected in the share price. Share price is often closely linked to reputation.

1.4.7 Judgement

Judgement means the board **making decisions that enhance the prosperity** of the organisation. This means that board members must acquire a broad enough knowledge of the **business and its environment** to be able to provide meaningful direction to it. This has implications not only for the attention directors have to give to the organisation's affairs but also to the way the directors are recruited and trained.

The complexities of senior management mean that the directors have to bring **multiple conceptual skills** to management that aim to maximise long-term returns. This means that corporate governance can involve balancing many competing people and resource claims against each other. Although risk management is an integral part of corporate governance, corporate governance isn't just about risk management.

1.4.8 Integrity

Integrity can be taken as meaning someone of **high moral character**, who sticks to principles no matter the pressure to do otherwise. In working life this means adhering to principles of professionalism and probity. **Straightforward dealing in relationships** with the different people and constituencies whom you meet is particularly important. Trust is vital in relationships and belief in the integrity of those with whom you are dealing underpins this.

Integrity is an essential principle of the **corporate governance relationship**, particularly in relationship to representing shareholder interests and exercising agency. Monitoring and hence agency costs can be reduced if there is trust in the integrity of the agents. In addition, we have seen that a key aim of corporate governance is to inspire confidence in participants in the market and this significantly depends upon a **public perception** of **competence and integrity**.

Integrity is also one of the fundamental principles discussed in the IFAC code of ethics. It provides assurance to those with whom the accountant deals of good intentions and truthfulness.

2 Management accountability

Organisations are not autonomous; they exist to serve some external purpose, usually manifested in a group such as shareholders in a company or trustees of a charity. In particular, the **strategic apex must not lose sight of this accountability**. All managers have a **duty of faithful service** to the external purpose of the organisation and this lies most heavily on the shoulders of those at the strategic apex.

2.1 Fiduciary responsibility

Organisations are not autonomous; that is to say, they do not exist to serve their own purposes or those of their senior managers. They exist to serve some external purpose and their managers have a duty to run them in a way that serves that purpose, whether it be to relieve distress (a charity), to keep the peace and manage the economy (a government), to promote the interests of its members (a trade union) or to make a profit (a business). Managers have a **fiduciary responsibility** (or duty of faithful service) in this respect and their behaviour must always reflect it.

2.2 Example

Managers need not be actually corrupt in order to fail in their fiduciary duty. The CEO who sets in motion a takeover bid that will enhance their prestige; the head of department who 'empire builds'; and the IT manager who buys an unnecessarily sophisticated enterprise resource management system are all failing in their fiduciary duty even though they receive no material benefit themselves.

2.3 Business objectives and management discretion

There are differing views about the extent to which external pressures modify business objectives and form boundaries to the exercise of management discretion.

(a)   **The stakeholder view of company objectives** is that many groups of people have a stake or legitimate interest in what the company does. Shareholders own the business, but there are also suppliers, managers, workers and customers. A business depends on appropriate relationships with these groups, otherwise it will find it hard to function. Each of these groups has its own objectives, so that a compromise or balance is required.

(b)   **The consensus theory of company objectives** was developed by Cyert and March (1992). They argued that managers run a business, but do not own it, and they do not necessarily set objectives for the company, but rather they look for objectives which suit their own inclinations. Objectives emerge as a consensus of the differing views of shareholders, managers, employees, suppliers, customers and society at large, but (in contrast to the stakeholder view) **they are not all selected or controlled by management**.

3 The ethical environment

Ethics and morality are about right and wrong behaviour. Western thinking about ethics tends to be based on ideas about **duty** and **consequences**. Unfortunately, such thinking often fails to indicate a single clear course of action. Ethical thinking is also influenced by the concepts of **virtue** and **rights**.

Ethics: a set of moral principles to guide behaviour

Whereas the political environment in which an organisation operates consists of laws, regulations and government agencies, the social environment consists of the customs, attitudes, beliefs and education of society as a whole, or of different groups in society; and the ethical environment consists of a set (or sets) of well-established rules of personal and organisational behaviour.

3.1 Ethical principles

Much of the practical difficulty with ethics lies in the absence of an **agreed basis** for decision-making. Effective **legal systems** are certain in their effects on the individual. While the complexity of such matters as tax law can make it difficult to determine just what the law says in any given case, it is still possible to determine the issue in court. Once the law is decided it is definite and there is little scope for argument.

The **certainty of legal rules** does not exist in ethical theory. Different ideas apply in different cultures. The two main important ideas in the Western ethical tradition are **duty** and **consequences**.

3.2 Ethics based on consequences

This approach judges actions by reference to their outcomes or consequences. **Utilitarianism,** propounded by Jeremy Bentham, is the best-known version of this approach and can be summed up as choosing the action that is likely to result in the **greatest good for the greatest number of people**.

3.2.1 Egoism

Egoism states that an act is ethically justified if decision makers freely decide to pursue their own short-term desires or their long-term interests. The subject to all ethical decisions is the self.

It has been argued that an egoistic pursuit of individual self-interest produces a desired outcome for society through **free competition and perfect information** operating in the marketplace. Producers of goods, for example, have to offer value for money, since competition means that customers will buy from competitors if they don't. Egoism can also link in with enlightened self-interest, such as a business investing in good facilities for its workforce to keep them content and hence maintain their loyalty.

3.2.2 Criticisms of egoism

One criticism of pure egoism is that it makes short-term selfish desires equivalent to longer-term, more beneficial, interests. A modified view would give most validity to exercising those short-term desires that were in long-term interests. A more serious criticism has been that the markets do not function perfectly, and that some participants can benefit themselves at the expense of others and also the wider environment – that it is unsustainable. Most fundamentally egoism is argued to be the **ethics of the thief** as well as the short-termist.

3.2.3 Pluralism

Pluralism accepts that different views may exist on morality, but suggests a consensus may be able to be reached in certain situations. A pluralist viewpoint is helpful in business situations where a range of perspectives have to be understood in order to establish a **course of action**. It emphasises the importance of morality as a **social phenomenon**. Some rules and arrangements need to be established for us to live together and we therefore need a good understanding of the different moralities that we will encounter.

However, a consensus may not always be possible, and this is a key message of this section of the text. Irreconcilable ethical disputes tend to arise when absolutists argue with relativists, or if you have a deontological viewpoint opposed to a teleological viewpoint. For example, during the recent debate in the UK about embryology, deontological arguments on the sanctity of life were opposed to teleological arguments about the scientific benefits of experimentation on embryos.

3.3 Ethics based on duty

We use **duty** as a label for the ethical approach technically called **deontology** (which means much the same thing as 'duty' in Greek). This set of ideas is associated with the German thinker Immanuel Kant and is based on the idea that behaviour should be governed by **absolute moral rules** that apply in all circumstances.

3.3.1 Ethical relativism

Relativism is the view that a **wide variety of acceptable ethical beliefs and practices** exist. The ethics that are most appropriate in a given situation will depend on the conditions at that time.

The relativist approach suggests that all moral statements are essentially subjective and arise from the culture, belief or emotion of the speaker.

3.3.2 Strengths of relativism

(a) Relativism highlights our **cognitive bias** in observing with our senses (we see only what we know and understand) and our **notational bias** (what we measure without using our senses is subject to the bias of the measurement methods used).

(b) Relativism also highlights differences in **cultural beliefs**. For example, all cultures may say that it is wrong to kill innocents, but different cultures may have different beliefs about who innocents actually are.

(c)   The philosopher Bernard Crick argued that differing absolutist beliefs result in **moral conflict** between people. (Relativist) ethics should act to resolve such conflicts.

(d)   In the global economy, where companies conduct businesses in many different countries and cultures, adopting a relativist approach presumes **more flexibility** and therefore greater success.

3.3.3 Criticisms of relativism

(a)   Put simply, strong relativism is a based on a **fundamental contradiction**. The statement that 'All statements are relative' is itself an absolute, non-relative statement. However, it is possible to argue that some universal truths (certain laws of physics) exist, but deny other supposedly objective truths.

(b)   A common criticism of relativism, particularly by religious leaders, is that it leads to a **philosophy of 'anything goes'**, denying the existence of morality and permitting activities that are harmful to others.

(c)   Alternatively some critics have argued for the existence of **natural moral laws** (discussed below). These are not necessarily religious laws. The atheist scientist Richard Dawkins has argued in favour of natural laws.

(d)   Ideas such as **objectivity and final truth** do have value – consider for example the ethical principle that we shall discuss later for accountants to be objective.

(e)   If it's valid to say that everyone's differing opinions are **right**, then it's equally valid to say that **everyone's differing opinions are wrong**.

3.3.4 Ethical absolutism

Absolutism is the view that there is an unchanging set of ethical principles that will apply in all situations, at all times and in all societies.

Absolutist approaches to ethics are built on the principle that **objective, universally applicable moral truths** exist and can be known. There is a set of moral rules that are always true.

Many absolutists would accept that some ethical truths may differ between different cultures. However, they would also believe in certain basic truths that should be common to all cultures (for example 'thou shall not kill').

3.3.5 Strengths of absolutism

(a)   Fundamentally the statement that **absolute truth does not exist** is **flawed**. If it does not exist, then the statement that it does not exist cannot be true.

(b)   Absolutism lays down certain unambiguous rules that people are able to follow, knowing that their **actions are right**.

3.3.6 Criticisms of absolutism

(a)   Absolutist ethics takes **no account of evolving norms** within society and the development of 'advances' in morality; for example, development of the belief that slavery is wrong.

(b)   From **what source** should absolutist ethics be derived? Should it be religion, universal laws, human nature? Whatever source is used, it is then possibly subject to human interpretation with the result that different views may exist on the same issue and there will never be universal agreement.

(c)   What happens when **two absolutist positions** appear **incompatible**? For example, is it permissible to tell a lie in order to save an innocent life?

(d)   A theory can be **true according to a relative framework** as well as true according to an absolute framework. What differs is the nature of the framework and not the truth of the statement.

3.4 Rights and virtues

The idea that individuals have natural **inherent rights** that should not be abused is a further, long-established influence on Western ethical thinking and one that has led to the development of law to protect certain 'human rights'.

Virtue ethics continues to exert a subtle influence. The idea is that, if people cultivate **virtue**, their behaviour is likely to be inherently ethical. Today it is suggested that managers should attempt to incorporate such virtues as firmness, fairness, objectivity, charity, forethought, loyalty, and so on into their daily behaviour and decision-making.

QUESTION   Categorical imperative

Is the statement below correct or incorrect?

'In Kant's approach to ethics, it is important to consider the consequences of an action in order to determine whether it is right or wrong.'

ANSWER

This statement is incorrect. Kant believes that certain rules must be obeyed no matter what the consequences may be.

3.5 Social attitudes

Social attitudes, such as a belief in the merits of education, progress through science and technology, and fair competition, are significant for the management of a business organisation. Other beliefs have either gained strength or been eroded in recent years.

(a)   There is a growing belief in preserving and improving the quality of life by reducing working hours, reversing the spread of pollution, developing leisure activities, and so on. Pressures on organisations to consider the environment are particularly strong because most environmental damage is irreversible and some is fatal to humans and wildlife.

(b)   Many pressure groups have been organised in recent years to protect social minorities and under-privileged groups. Legislation has been passed in an attempt to prevent racial discrimination and discrimination against women and disabled people.

(c)   Issues relating to the environmental consequences of corporate activities are currently debated, and respect for the environment has come to be regarded as an unquestionable good.

The ethical environment refers to justice, respect for the law and a moral code. The conduct of an organisation, its management and employees will be measured against ethical standards by the customers, suppliers and other members of the public with whom they deal.

3.6 Ethical problems facing managers

Managers have a duty (in most enterprises) to aim for profit. At the same time, modern ethical standards impose a duty to guard, preserve and enhance the value of the enterprise for the good of all touched by it, including the general public. Large organisations tend to be more often held to account over this than small ones.

In the area of **products and production**, managers have responsibility to ensure that the public and their own employees are protected from danger. Attempts to increase profitability by cutting costs may lead to dangerous working conditions or to inadequate safety standards in products. In the United States, **product liability litigation** is so common that this legal threat may be a more effective deterrent than general ethical standards.

Another ethical problem concerns **payments by companies to government or municipal officials** who have power to help or hinder the payers' operations. Walton (1978) refers to the fine distinctions which exist in this area.

(a)   **Extortion**. Foreign officials have been known to threaten companies with the complete closure of their local operations unless suitable payments are made.

(b)   **Bribery**. This refers to payments for services to which a company is not legally entitled. There are some fine distinctions to be drawn; for example, some managers regard political contributions as bribery.

(c)   **Grease money**. Multinational companies are sometimes unable to obtain services to which they are legally entitled because of deliberate stalling by local officials. Cash payments to the right people may then be enough to oil the machinery of bureaucracy.

(d)   **Gifts**. In some cultures (such as Japan) gifts are regarded as an essential part of civilised negotiation, even in circumstances where to Western eyes they might appear ethically dubious. Managers operating in such a culture may feel at liberty to adopt the local customs.

Business ethics are also relevant to competitive behaviour. This is because a market can only be free if competition is, in some basic respects, fair. There is a distinction between competing aggressively and competing unethically.

3.7 Social responsibility and businesses

Arguably, institutions like hospitals, schools and so forth exist because health care and education are seen to be desirable social objectives by government at large, if they can be afforded.

However, where does this leave businesses? How far is it reasonable, or even appropriate, for businesses to exercise 'social responsibility' by giving to charities, voluntarily imposing strict environmental objectives on themselves and so forth?

Social responsibility action is likely to have an adverse effect on shareholders' interests.

(a)   **Additional costs** such as those of environmental monitoring
(b)   **Reduced revenues** as a result of refusing to supply certain customers
(c)   **Diversion of employee effort** away from profitable activities
(d)   **Diversion of funds** into social projects

However, it is possible to argue that being socially responsible is in shareholders' interests, possibly over the longer term.

Corporate social responsibility is examined in more detail in Chapter 7.

3.8 Specific environmental responsibilities

Businesses are widely regarded as having a duty to safeguard the **natural environment**. There are six areas for action.

(a)   **Environmental auditing** to monitor such things as legal compliance, waste treatment, and emissions

(b)   **Economic action**: charges for environmental damage should be made internally to give managers an incentive to avoid it

(c)   **Accounting action**: a separate set of accounts incorporating **shadow prices** to represent environmental costs is prepared

(d)   **Ecological approach**: aspects of the business such as a product or a location are selected for examination to ascertain their environmental impact

(e)   **Production** is managed to minimise inputs of materials and energy

(f)   **Quality** management is applied using the principle of continuous improvement in environmental performance

3.9 Examples of social and ethical objectives

Companies are not passive in the social and ethical environment. Many organisations pursue a variety of social and ethical objectives.

(a)   **Employees**

    (i)   A minimum wage, perhaps with adequate differentials for skilled labour
    (ii)   Job security (over and above the protection afforded by legislation)
    (iii)   Good conditions of work (above the legal minima)
    (iv)   Job satisfaction
    (v)   Promotion of diversity and equal opportunities
    (vi)   A healthy and safe workplace

(b)   **Customers** may be regarded as entitled to receive a safe product of good quality at a reasonable price.

(c)   **Suppliers** may be offered regular orders and timely payment in return for reliable delivery and good service.

(d)   **Society as a whole**

    (i)   Control of pollution and use of sustainable resources
    (ii)   Provision of financial assistance to charities, sports and community activities
    (iii)   Not producing undesirable goods

4   Ethics in organisations

> Ethical conduct by all members should be a major concern for management. Inside the organisation, a **compliance-based** approach highlights **conformity with the law**. An **integrity-based** approach suggests a **wider remit**, incorporating ethics in the organisation's **values and culture**. Organisations sometimes issue codes of conduct to employees. Many employees are bound by professional codes of conduct.

Companies have to follow legal standards, or else they will be subject to fines and their officers might face similar charges. Ethics in organisations relates to **social responsibility** and **business practice**.

People that work for organisations bring their own values into work with them. Organisations contain a variety of ethical systems.

(a)   **Personal ethics**. These derive from a person's upbringing, religious or non-religious beliefs, political opinions, personality, and so on.

(b)   **Professional ethics**. These include ACCA's code of ethics and medical ethics.

(c)   **Organisation cultures** (eg 'customer first'). We discussed culture in an earlier chapter; culture, in denoting what is normal behaviour, also denotes what is the right behaviour in many cases.

(d)   **Organisation systems**. Ethics might be contained in a formal code, reinforced by the overall statement of values. A problem might be that ethics does not always save money, and there is a real cost to ethical decisions. Besides, the organisation has different ethical duties to different stakeholders. Who sets priorities?

Ethical problems can be approached from several directions, as we have attempted to show. Unfortunately, this means that difficult problems rarely have clear solutions and it is usually possible for the opportunist manager to find authority to support any decision. The Chartered Certified Accountant must make an effort to do the right thing bearing in mind the variety of ethical assumptions that other people may make; the varying expectations of legitimate stakeholders; and the attitudes of legislators and pressure groups.

4.1 Leadership practices and ethics

The role of culture in determining the ethical climate of an organisation can be further explored by a brief reflection on the role of leaders in setting the ethical standard. A culture is partly a collection of symbols and attitudes, embodying certain truths about the organisation. Senior managers are also symbolic managers; inevitably they decide priorities. They set an example, whether they like it or not.

Organisations of any kind must adopt values that will promote adherence to ethical principles, thereby maintaining the confidence of stakeholders. Senior leadership must endorse **organisational values** that promote ethical conduct, such as the following:

- Openness - being full and complete in the provision and disclosure of information
- Trust - relying on the judgments and information provided by others, and being trustworthy in turn
- Honesty - telling the truth, and being prepared to give information on which others can depend
- Respect - treating others with dignity and adopting a professional manner
- Empowerment - ensuring that those who are entrusted with responsibilities have the authority to carry out their tasks
- Accountability - taking full responsibility for outcomes

4.2 A corporate code of ethics

Corporate codes of ethics are published by organisations in order to communicate values to stakeholders. As well as stating the core principles governing how their commercial objectives are to be pursued, such codes might include statements specifically in relation to:

- Customers, whose purchases may be influenced by ethical considerations

- Shareholders, whose investment decisions may be influenced by ethical factors

- Employees, who need to know what is expected of them

- Suppliers, who need to understand the expectations of their customers, and who also should be treated ethically

- Lobby groups, who may have an interest in organisational practices

- Local communities, which may need reassurance that the organisation will act as a 'good citizen'

EXAM FOCUS POINT

The examining team has commented that candidates performed poorly in questions about corporate codes of ethics. Make sure that you are clear on what a typical corporate code of ethics might include.

4.3 The Seven Principles of Public Life

The UK Government's **Committee of Standards in Public Life** (1995) set out seven principles that individuals employed in the public sector must follow.

(a) **Selflessness**

Individuals should act solely in the public interest and not for personal gain or that of friends and family.

(b) **Integrity**

Individuals should avoid actions which would place them under financial or other obligations whereby the person holding their obligation could influence their public duties.

(c) **Objectivity**

All choices, especially those regarding awarding contracts, rewarding or providing benefits to others and making public appointments must be made purely on merit.

(d) **Accountability**

Individuals are responsible for their own actions and are accountable to others. They must subject themselves to whatever scrutiny comes with their office.

(e) **Openness**

Individuals must be open about their decisions and actions. Information regarding the reasons for their decisions must be freely available. Restrictions on information are only permitted when it is in the wider public interest.

(f) **Honesty**

Where individuals have private interests which relate to their public ones, they should declare them and seek to resolve any conflict to protect the public interest.

(g) **Leadership**

Individuals must promote and respect the other six principles through leadership and example.

Accountants must also follow these principles. Where they appear to be in a situation which **conflicts** with their legal, regulatory or other ethical frameworks they must ensure their concerns are heard.

4.4 Two approaches to managing ethics

There are two suggested approaches to the management of ethics in organisations.

- Compliance based
- Integrity based

4.4.1 Compliance-based approach

A compliance-based approach is primarily designed to ensure that the company **acts within the letter of the law**, and that violations are prevented, detected and punished. Some organisations, faced with the legal consequences of unethical behaviour, take legal precautions such as those below.

- Compliance procedures to detect misconduct
- Audits of contracts
- Systems for employees to report criminal misconduct without fear of retribution
- Disciplinary procedures to deal with transgressions

4.4.2 Integrity-based programmes

An integrity-based approach combines a concern for the law with an **emphasis on managerial responsibility** for ethical behaviour. Integrity strategies strive to define companies' guiding values, aspirations and patterns of thought and conduct. When integrated into the day-to-day operations of an organisation, such strategies can help prevent damaging ethical lapses, while tapping into powerful human impulses for moral thought and action.

Whistleblowing is the disclosure by an employee of illegal, immoral or illegitimate practices on the part of the organisation. This may appear to be in the public interest, but confidentiality is very important in the accountants' code of ethics. Whistleblowing frequently involves **financial loss** for the whistleblower.

(a) Whistleblowers may lose their jobs.

(b) A whistleblower who is a member of a professional body cannot, sadly, rely on that body to take a significant interest, or even offer a sympathetic ear. Some professional bodies have narrow interpretations of what is meant by ethical conduct. For many, the duties of **commercial confidentiality** are felt to be more important.

EXAM FOCUS POINT

The ethics codes described above can be related to mission, culture and control strategies. A compliance-based approach suggests that bureaucratic control is necessary; an integrity-based approach relies on cultural control.

5 Accountants and ethics

> As an accountant, your values and attitudes **flow through** everything you do professionally. They contribute to the **trust** the wider community puts in the profession and the **perception** it has of it.

Key reasons for accountants to behave ethically

(a) Ethical issues may be a matter of law and regulation and accountants are expected to apply them.

(b) The profession requires members to conduct themselves and provide services to the public according to certain standards. By upholding these standards, the profession's reputation and standing is protected.

(c) An accountant's ethical behaviour serves to protect the public interest.

5.1 Approaches to accountancy ethics

Professionals will have their own idea of what behaviour is ethical and what is not. Although there will be differences, collectively there are common views and values that shine through.

To help individuals judge whether or not they are acting ethically in particular circumstances, guidance should be given (usually by a governing body) that clarifies the matter. Such guidance is usually known as a '**Code of ethics**' or '**Code of conduct**'.

6 A code of ethics for accountants

> The **International Federation of Accountants** (IFAC) is an international body representing all the major accountancy bodies around the world. Its mission is to develop the **high standards** of professional accountants and enhance the quality of services they provide.

6.1 IFAC and the ACCA

To enable the development of high standards, IFAC's ethics committee established a **code of ethics**. The code indicates a minimum level of conduct that all accountants must adhere to. As a member of IFAC, ACCA released its own code of ethics, designed to align to the IFAC code. The IFAC code is now administered by the International Ethics Standards Board for Accountants (IESBA). The material contained in this section is from the ACCA's Code of Conduct and Ethics (ACCA, 2016).

6.1.1 Fundamental principles of the ACCA Code of Ethics and Conduct

When you become a member of the ACCA, you agree to be bound by the ACCA's Code of Ethics and Conduct (ACCA, 2016). Members are required to comply with the following fundamental principles.

- Integrity
- Objectivity
- Professional competence and due care
- Confidentiality
- Professional behaviour

The Code can be found in Section 3 of the ACCA rulebook (http://rulebook.accaglobal.com). It is quite long but you should try to read it (or at least skim read it). It will give you an insight into issues that may arise in questions in your exam.

For example, there is a section on receiving gifts from clients which states that a gift 'gives rise to threats to compliance with the fundamental principles'. It goes on to suggest that objectivity may be threatened and that gifts and hospitality should only be accepted if the value of the benefit is modest. Hopefully it is clear to you that this could easily be the subject of a question in your exam.

QUESTION

Gifts

Jayne, Will and Lesley work as auditors for a client called TV Co and Jayne is the senior auditor. TV Co manufactures large expensive televisions. The director of TV Co offers Jayne one of the newest, most expensive televisions as a thank you gift for doing the audit. If Jayne accepts the television, which one of the fundamental principles may be threatened?

A   Professional competence   C   Objectivity
B   Confidentiality   D   Reliability

ANSWER

C   Objectivity. This should have been easy for you because you have just read Section 6.1.1. Look at the question and the options again. Did you notice that the question asked for a **fundamental principle** and that only options A, B and C were fundamental principles? Option D is a personal quality. This means that option D could be ruled out straight away. You need to develop this skill at reading questions and options by practising lots of questions.

6.2 Personal qualities expected of an accountant

In meeting the fundamental principles, certain qualities are expected you. As a student of ACCA (and a future member) you need to develop the following qualities to ensure you meet the fundamental principles.

- Personal qualities
- Professional qualities

The personal qualities that an accountant should demonstrate are:

- Reliability
- Responsibility
- Timeliness
- Courtesy
- Respect

Personal quality	Detail
Reliability	When taking on work, you must ensure that it **gets done** and **meets professional standards**.
Responsibility	In the workplace you should take '**ownership**' of your work.
Timeliness	Clients and work colleagues rely on you to be **on time** and produce work within a **specified time frame**.
Courtesy	You should conduct yourself with **courtesy** and **consideration** towards clients and colleagues.
Respect	As an accountant, you should respect others by developing **constructive relationships** and recognising the **values** and **rights** of others.

6.3 Professional qualities expected of an accountant

The professional qualities an accountant should demonstrate are:

- Independence
- Scepticism
- Accountability
- Social responsibility

Professional quality	Detail
Independence	You must be able to complete your work **without bias** or **prejudice** and you must also **be seen** to be independent.
Scepticism	You should **question** information given to you so that you form your own opinion regarding its **quality** and **reliability**.
Accountability	You should recognise that you are **accountable** for your own judgements and decisions.
Social responsibility	Accountants have a **public duty** as well as a duty to their employer or client. Audit work, accountancy work and investment decisions may all affect the public in some way.

6.4 Conflicts of interest

There is a section in the ACCA's Code of Ethics and Conduct (ACCA, 2016) dedicated to the subject of conflicts of interest. ACCA members need to be aware that a **conflict** between **members'** and **clients' interests** might arise if members **compete directly** with a client, or have a **joint venture** with a company that is in competition with the client.

The rules state that members and firms should **not accept** or continue **engagements in which there are**, or are likely to be, **significant conflicts of interest** between members, firms and clients.

Members should **evaluate the threats** arising from a conflict of interest and, unless they are insignificant, they should apply **safeguards**. The test of whether a threat is significant is whether a **reasonable** and informed **third party**, having knowledge of all relevant information, would consider the conflict of interest **as likely to affect the judgement** of members and firms.

Disclosure (ie informing all known relevant parties of the possible conflict of interest) is the most important safeguard. There are other solutions depending on the situation, such as using a separate team of people or signing confidentiality agreements.

6.5 Self-interest threat

The ACCA Code of Ethics and Conduct (ACCA, 2016) highlights a great number of areas in which a self-interest threat to independence might arise.

6.5.1 Financial interests

Financial interests exist where an audit firm has a financial interest in a client's affairs; for example, the audit firm owns shares in the client, or is a trustee of a trust that holds shares in the client.

A financial interest in a client constitutes a substantial self-interest threat. According to the ACCA, **the parties listed below are not allowed to own a direct financial interest or an indirect material financial interest in a client**.

- The **assurance firm**
- **Partners in the same office** as the engagement partner (and their immediate families)
- A **member of the assurance team**
- An **immediate family member of a member of the assurance team**

The following safeguards will therefore be relevant.

- Disposing of the interest
- Removing the individual from the team if required
- Keeping the client's audit committee informed of the situation
- Using an independent partner to review work carried out if necessary

6.5.2 Close business relationships

Examples of when a firm and client have an inappropriately close business relationship include:

- Having a **material financial interest** in a joint venture with the assurance client

- **Arrangements to combine one or more services or products** of the firm with one or more services or products of the assurance client and to market the package with reference to both parties

- **Distribution or marketing arrangements** under which the firm acts as distributor or marketer of the assurance client's products or services or vice versa

Again, it will be necessary to judge the materiality of the interest and therefore its significance. However, unless the interest is clearly insignificant, an **assurance provider should not participate** in such a venture with a client. Appropriate safeguards are therefore to end the assurance provision or to terminate the (other) business relationship.

6.5.3 Employment with client

It is possible that staff might transfer between a firm and a client, or that negotiations or interviews to facilitate such movement might take place. Both situations are a threat to independence.

- An audit staff member might be **motivated by a desire to impress a future possible employer** (objectivity is therefore affected).
- A former partner turned finance director has **too much knowledge of the audit firm's systems** and procedures.

The extent of the threat to independence depends on various factors, such as the **role** the individual has taken up at the client, the **extent of their influence** on the audit previously, the length of time that has passed between the individual's connection with the audit and the new role at the client.

Various safeguards might be considered.

- Considering **modifying the assurance plan**

- Ensuring the audit is assigned to someone of **sufficient experience** compared with the individual who has left

- Involving an **additional professional accountant** not involved with the engagement to review the work done

- Carrying out a **quality control review** of the engagement

In respect of audit clients, ethical guidance states that a partner should not **accept a key management position** at an audit client until **at least two years** have elapsed since the conclusion of the audit they were involved with. An individual who has moved from the firm to a client should **not be entitled to any benefits or payments** from the firm unless these are made in accordance with predetermined arrangements. A firm should have procedures setting out that an individual involved in serious employment negotiations with an audit client should **notify the firm** and that this person would then be removed from the engagement.

6.5.4 Partner on client board

A partner or employee of an audit/assurance firm should **not serve on the board** of an assurance client. It may be acceptable for a partner or an employee of an assurance firm to perform the role of company secretary for an assurance client, if the role is essentially administrative (however don't forget the increased emphasis on the role of the company secretary in governance reports, aiming to enhance the secretary's role to go beyond routine administrative tasks).

6.5.5 Family and personal relationships

Family or close personal relationships between assurance firm and client staff could seriously threaten independence. Each situation has to be evaluated individually. Factors to consider are:

- The individual's responsibilities on the assurance engagement
- The closeness of the relationship
- The role of the other party at the assurance client

When an immediate family member of a member of the assurance team is a **director, an officer or an employee of the assurance client** in a position to exert direct and significant influence over the assurance engagement, the individual should be removed from the assurance team.

The audit firm should also consider whether there is any threat to independence if an employee who is not a member of the assurance team has a **close family or personal relationship** with a director, an officer or an employee of an assurance client.

A firm should have **quality control policies and procedures** under which staff should disclose if a close family member employed by the client is promoted within the client.

6.5.6 Gifts and hospitality

Unless the value of the gift/hospitality is clearly insignificant, a firm or a member of an assurance team should not accept it.

6.5.7 Loans and guarantees

The advice on loans and guarantees falls into two categories.

- The client is a bank or other similar institution
- Other situations

If a **lending institution client** lends an **immaterial amount to** an audit firm or member of assurance team on normal commercial terms, there is no threat to independence. If the loan were material it would be necessary to apply safeguards to bring the risk to an acceptable level. A suitable safeguard is likely to be an **independent review** (by a partner from another office in the firm).

Loans to members of the assurance team from a bank or other lending institution client are likely to be **material to the individual** but, provided that they are on normal commercial terms, these do not constitute a threat to independence.

However, an audit firm or individual on the assurance engagement should not enter into any loan or guarantee arrangement with a client that is not a bank or similar institution.

6.5.8 Overdue fees

In a situation where there are overdue fees, the auditor runs the risk of, in effect, making a loan to a client, whereupon the guidance above becomes relevant.

Audit firms should guard against fees building up and being significant by **discussing the issues with the audit committee or others involved in governance** and, if necessary, the possibility of resigning if overdue fees are not paid.

6.5.9 Percentage or contingent fees

Contingent fees are fees calculated on a predetermined basis relating to the outcome or result of a transaction or the result of the work performed.

Ethical guidelines state that a firm should not enter into any fee arrangement for an assurance engagement under which the amount of the fee is contingent on the result of the assurance work or on items that are the subject matter of the assurance engagement. It would also usually be inappropriate to accept a contingent fee for non-assurance work from an assurance client.

6.5.10 High percentage of fees

A firm should be alert to the situation arising where when the **total fees generated by an assurance client** represent a **large proportion of a firm's total fees**. Factors such as the **structure of the firm** and the length of time it has been trading will be relevant in determining whether there is a threat to independence. It is also necessary to beware of situations where the fees generated by an assurance client are a large proportion of the revenue of an individual partner.

Safeguards in these situations might include:

- Discussing the issues with the audit committee
- Taking steps to reduce the dependency on the client
- Obtaining external/internal quality control reviews
- Consulting a third party such as ACCA

Ethical guidance states that the public may perceive that a member's objectivity is likely to be in jeopardy where the fees for audit and recurring work paid by one client or group of connected clients **exceed 15%** of the firm's total fees. Where the entity is listed or public interest, this figure should be 10%.

It will be difficult for new firms establishing themselves to keep within these limits and firms in this situation should make use of the safeguards outlined.

6.5.11 Lowballing

When a firm quotes a significantly lower fee level for an assurance service than would have been charged by the predecessor firm, there is a significant self-interest threat. If the firm's tender is successful, the firm must apply safeguards such as:

- **Maintaining records** such that the firm is able to demonstrate that appropriate staff and time are spent on the engagement

- **Complying with all applicable assurance standards**, guidelines and quality control procedures

6.5.12 Recruitment

Recruiting senior management for an assurance client, particularly those able to affect the subject matter of an assurance engagement creates a self-interest threat for the assurance firm.

Assurance providers must not make management decisions for the client. Their involvement could be limited to reviewing a shortlist of candidates, providing that the client has drawn up the criteria by which they are to be selected.

6.6 Self-review threat

The key area in which there is likely to be a self-review threat is where an assurance firm provides services other than assurance services to an assurance client (providing multiple services). There is a great deal of guidance in the ACCA rules about various other services accountancy firms might provide to their clients, and these are dealt with below.

The distinction between listed companies, or public limited companies, and private companies, is perceived to be an important issue in the question of providing other services to clients.

Public interest companies are those that for some reason (size, nature, product) are in the 'public eye'. Auditors should treat these as if they are listed companies.

6.6.1 Recent service with an assurance client

Ethical guidance focuses on individuals who have been a **director or officer of the client**, or an employee in a position to exert **direct and significant influence** over the subject matter information of the assurance engagement in the period under review or the previous two years to the assurance team.

If an individual had been closely involved with the client prior to the time limits set out above, the assurance firm should consider the threat to independence arising and apply appropriate safeguards, such as:

- Obtaining a quality control review of the individual's work on the assignment
- Discussing the issue with the audit committee

6.6.2 General services

For assurance clients, accountants are not allowed to:

- Authorise, execute or consummate a transaction
- Determine which recommendations should be implemented
- Report in a management capacity to those charged with governance

Having custody of an assurance client's assets, supervising client employees in the performance of their normal duties, and preparing source documents on behalf of the client also pose significant self-review threats which should be addressed by safeguards. These could be:

- Ensuring non-assurance team staff are used for these roles
- Involving an independent professional accountant to advise
- Quality control policies on what staff are and are not allowed to do for clients
- Making appropriate disclosures to those charged with governance
- Resigning from the assurance engagement

6.6.3 Preparing accounting records and financial statements

There is clearly a significant risk of a self-review threat if a firm prepares **accounting records and financial statements** and then audits them. On the other hand auditors routinely assist management with the preparation of financial statements and give advice about accounting treatments and journal entries.

Therefore, assurance firms must analyse the risks arising and put safeguards in place to ensure that the risk is at an acceptable level. Safeguards include:

* **Using staff members other than assurance team members** to carry out work
* **Obtaining client approval for work** undertaken

The rules are more stringent when the client is listed or public interest. Firms should not prepare accounts or financial statements for listed or public interest clients, unless an emergency arises.

For any client, assurance firms are also not allowed to:

* Determine or change journal entries without client approval
* Authorise or approve transactions
* Prepare source documents

6.6.4 Valuation services

A **valuation** comprises the making of assumptions with regard to future developments, the application of certain methodologies and techniques, and the combination of both in order to compute a certain value, or range of values, for an asset, a liability or for a business as a whole.

If an audit firm performs a valuation which will be included in financial statements audited by the firm, a self-review threat arises.

Audit firms should not carry out valuations on matters that will be material to the financial statements.

If the valuation is for an immaterial matter, the audit firm should **apply safeguards** to ensure that the risk is reduced to an acceptable level. Matters to consider when applying safeguards are the extent of the audit client's knowledge of the relevant matters in making the valuation and the degree of judgement involved, how much use is made of established methodologies and the degree of uncertainty in the valuation. Safeguards include:

* Second partner review
* Confirming that the client understands the valuation and the assumptions used
* Ensuring the client acknowledges responsibility for the valuation
* Using separate personnel for the valuation and the audit

6.6.5 Taxation services

The **provision of taxation services** is generally not seen to impair independence.

6.6.6 Internal audit services

A firm may provide internal audit services to an audit client in most jurisdictions. However, it should ensure that the client **acknowledges its responsibility** for **establishing, maintaining and monitoring the system** of internal controls. It may be appropriate to use safeguards, such as ensuring that an employee of the client is designated as responsible for internal audit activities and that the board or audit committee approve all the work that internal audit does.

6.6.7 Corporate finance

Certain aspects of corporate finance will create self-review threats that cannot be reduced to an acceptable level by safeguards. Therefore, assurance firms are **not allowed to promote, deal in or underwrite** an assurance client's shares. They are also not allowed to commit an assurance client to the terms of a transaction or consummate a transaction on the client's behalf.

Other corporate finance services, such as assisting a client in defining corporate strategies, assisting in identifying possible sources of capital and providing structuring advice, may be acceptable in jurisdictions other than the US, providing that safeguards are in place, such as using different teams of staff, and ensuring no management decisions are taken on behalf of the client.

6.6.8 Other services

The audit firm might sell a variety of other services to audit clients, such as:

*   IT services
*   Temporary staff cover
*   Litigation support
*   Legal services

The assurance firm should consider whether there are any barriers to independence. Examples include the firm being asked to design internal control IT systems, which it would then review as part of its audit, or the firm being asked to provide an accountant to cover the chief accountant's maternity leave. The firm should consider whether the threat to independence could be reduced by appropriate safeguards. Again, the rules in America are stricter than elsewhere.

6.7 Advocacy threat

An advocacy threat arises in certain situations where the assurance firm is in a position of **taking the client's part** in a dispute or somehow **acting as their advocate**. The most obvious instances of this would be when a firm offered legal services to a client and, say, defended them in a legal case or provided evidence on their behalf as an expert witness. An advocacy threat might also arise if the firm carried out corporate finance work for the client; for example, if the audit firm was involved in advice on debt reconstruction and negotiated with the bank on the client's behalf.

As with the other threats above, the firm has to appraise the risk and apply safeguards as necessary. Relevant safeguards might be using **different departments** in the firm to carry out the work and making disclosures to the audit committee. Remember, the ultimate option is always to withdraw from an engagement if the risk to independence is too high.

6.8 Familiarity threat

A familiarity or association threat is where independence is jeopardised by the audit firm and its staff becoming overfamiliar with the client and its staff. There is a substantial risk of loss of professional scepticism in such circumstances.

We have already discussed some examples of when this risk arises, because very often a familiarity threat arises in conjunction with a self-interest threat.

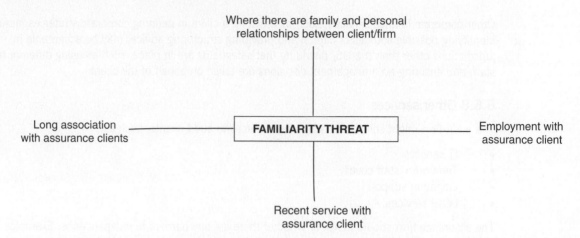

6.8.1 Long association of senior personnel with assurance clients

Senior members of staff at an audit firm having a long association with a client is a significant threat to independence. All firms should therefore monitor the relationship between staff and established clients and use safeguards to independence, such as **rotating senior staff off the assurance team**, involving **second partners** to carry out reviews and obtaining independent (but internal) quality control reviews.

6.9 Intimidation threat

An intimidation threat arises when members of the assurance team have reason to be intimidated by client staff.

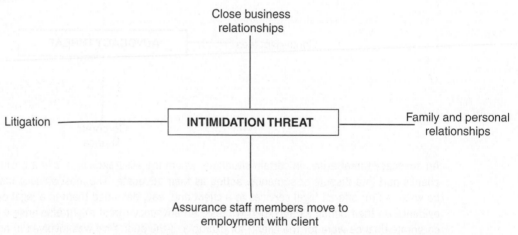

These are also examples of self-interest threats, largely because intimidation may only arise significantly when the assurance firm has something to lose.

6.9.1 Actual and threatened litigation

The most obvious example of an intimidation threat is when the client threatens to sue, or indeed sues, the assurance firm for work that has been done previously. The firm is then faced with the **risk of losing the client, bad publicity** and the **possibility that they will be found to have been negligent**, which will lead to further problems. This could lead to the firm being under pressure to produce an unqualified audit report when they have been qualified in the past, for example.

Generally, assurance firms should seek to avoid such situations arising. If they do arise, factors to consider are:

- The materiality of the litigation
- The nature of the assurance engagement
- Whether the litigation relates to a prior assurance engagement

The following safeguards could be considered.

- Disclosing to the audit committee the nature and extent of the litigation
- Removing specific affected individuals from the engagement team
- Involving an additional professional accountant on the team to review work

However, if the litigation is at all serious, it may be necessary to **resign from the engagement**, as the threat to independence is so great.

6.9.2 Second opinions

Another way that auditors can suffer an intimidation threat is when the audit client is unhappy with a proposed audit opinion, and seeks a **second opinion** from a different firm of auditors.

In such a circumstance, the second audit firm will not be able to give a formal audit opinion on the financial statements – only an appointed auditor can do that. However, the problem is that if a different firm of auditors indicates to someone else's client that a different opinion might be acceptable, the appointed auditors may feel under pressure to change their opinion. In effect, a self-interest threat arises, as the existing auditor may feel that they will lose next year's audit if they do not change this year's opinion.

There is nothing to stop a company director talking to a second firm of auditors about treatments of matters in the financial statements. However, the firm being asked for a second opinion should be very careful, because it is very possible that the opinion they form could be incorrect anyway if the director has not given them all the relevant information. For that reason, firms giving a second opinion should ensure that they **seek permission** to communicate with the existing auditor and they are appraised of all the facts. If permission is not given, the second auditors should decline to comment on the audit opinion.

Given that second opinions can cause independence issues for the existing auditors, audit firms should generally take great care if asked to provide one anyway.

7 Ethics in business

7.1 Businesses and ethics

Ethics in business: 'The application of ethical values to business behaviour'.

Businesses also have ethical values, based on the **norms** and **standards** of **behaviour** that their leaders believe will best help them express their identity and achieve their objectives. Some of these ethical values may be **explicit**; for example, expressed in a mission statement or in employee training programmes. Others may be **unwritten rules and customs** that form part of the organisation's culture: 'the way we do things around here'.

Business life is a fruitful source of **ethical dilemmas** because its whole purpose is material gain, the making of profit. Success in business requires a constant, avid search for potential advantage over others and business people are under pressure to do whatever yields such advantage.

The table below summarises **three elements** to ethics.

Element	Explanation
I	Ethics concern an **individual**'s professional responsibility to act.
DO	Ethics concern the 'real world' practical actions an individual can take. It is important to consider **how** an individual acts and not always **what** they do.
BEST	Ethics concern **choices** between different courses of action. These may involve taking a course of action which is less unpalatable than another.

7.1.1 An issue of trust

Whatever the situation, there is a public expectation (especially regarding professionals) that organisations will act ethically. This is known as the '**Trust me**' model and was the case for many years when most businesses were owned by families. Times have now changed and most companies are now run by directors and mangers rather than fathers and sons and the model changed to '**Involve me**' as more evidence was needed of their ethical credentials.

In recent times, trust in business has fallen and increasingly more evidence is required to demonstrate it. The '**Show me**' stage required some demonstration of trust, '**Prove to me**' required independent verification and assurance and the final stage of '**Obey me**' would exist when the law creates legislation to cure instances of unethical behaviour. We are some way off this point currently.

What caused this trust to disintegrate? Since the 1980s, the UK has seen a procession of corporate disasters including the names of **Barings Bank**, **Polly Peck** and **Maxwell**. The US has seen scandals concerning **Worldcom**, **Enron** and **Tyco**. Europe did not escape and has seen its share of problems with **Parmalat** while, in Asia, **Mitsubishi Motors** and **Daewoo** have had issues too. All these scandals have severely knocked public confidence and trust in major corporations.

In an attempt to counter this lack of trust, many corporations have developed **ethical strategies** and **policies** to provide **guidance** and **training** for their employees. The strategy is set by the leadership and this will feed into all areas of the business and become part of the cultural DNA of the organisation.

7.1.2 Corporate Responsibility Policies and Reports

An ethical strategy is not always visible to outsiders, and many companies now produce **Corporate Responsibility Policies (CRPs)** and **Corporate Responsibility Reports (CRRs)** for their stakeholders to demonstrate their commitment and to manage their relationships in the wider community. They reflect the view that an organisation has responsibilities beyond that of its shareholders.

(a)   **Corporate (Social) Responsibility policies**

Corporate Responsibility policies are also known as Corporate Social Responsibility policies. These are policies in which the organisation decides how to help the local community that it is part of and which charities to support. However, they also deal with the wider community, and policies often focus on reducing the environmental impact the organisation has and where to recruit new employs from. These policies must be consistent with the overall aims of the organisation to ensure support continues even when the organisation faces its own problems, such as a downturn in profit.

(b)   **Corporate Responsibility Reports**

Many new technological advances allow for the reporting of statistics as carbon footprints and a company's impact on the environment. These can be added to more conventional assessments such as staff turnover to provide quite a detailed report on the organisation.

Such **corporate values** also guide staff as to the expectations that employers have regarding their behaviour. The aim is to end up with consistent behaviour across the workforce in terms of personal conduct and professionalism. These policies are enforced on a voluntary basis and results are monitored through audits, surveys and interviews.

8   Ethical dilemmas

Ethical dilemmas are situations where two ethical values or requirements seem to be incompatible. They can also arise where two conflicting demands or obligations are placed on an individual.

A **conflict of interest** arises where an individual has a duty to two or more parties. While working, information or other matters may arise that mean they cannot continue work for one party without harming another.

We have discussed the **need** for accountants to be ethical, and the **consequences** of being unethical. It is therefore important that they can spot an **ethical problem** and be able to deal with it effectively and appropriately. Many dilemmas challenge both **personal integrity** and **business skills** and therefore a strong ethical understanding is important. We now consider potential situations where accountants have to make ethical decisions, and how they should resolve them.

8.1 Ethical dilemmas and conflicts of interest

Ethical dilemmas are situations where two ethical values or requirements seem to be incompatible. They can also arise where two conflicting demands or obligations are placed on an individual.

A **conflict of interest** arises where an individual has a duty to two or more parties. While working, information or other matters may arise that mean they cannot continue work for one party without harming another. Conflicts of interest are not wrong in themselves but they will become a problem if a professional continues with a course of action while being aware of, and not declaring, them.

8.2 Situations where ethical dilemmas and conflicts of interest occur

Ethical dilemmas occur as a result of **tensions** between four sets of values.

- **Societal values** – the law

- **Personal values** – values and principles held by the individual

- **Corporate values** – the values and principles of the organisation where the individual works, often laid down in ethical codes

- **Professional values** – the values and principles of the professional body that the individual is a member of, often laid down in ethical codes

Where society believes that businesses are not conducting themselves correctly, **laws may be introduced** to ensure a **minimum level** of **behaviour** is followed. Examples of this include laws created to deal with environmental issues, cartels and unfair competition, as well as fraud, insider dealing, bribery and corruption.

Ethical dilemmas involve **unclear choices** of what is right and wrong. In fact the choice could be what is the **least wrong** course of action to take. In such circumstances there is little an individual can do but to **seek advice** and trust their own **instincts** to make the correct choice.

Remember that **laws** do not necessarily help an individual to resolve an ethical issue – indeed many members of society feel torn when their **personal ethics** lead them to feel that following a particular **law** is **immoral**. That said, where a professional duty conflicts with statute, ACCA's advice is clear – the **law overrides** it every time.

8.2.1 Ethics and contractual obligations

Contractual obligations differ from statute in the sense that an individual enters into a contract **voluntarily**; there is no voluntary element to statutory obligations.

This means an individual may break contractual obligations without breaking the law. For this reason, professional **ethics should be followed even if this is at the expense of a contractual obligation**. Logically this means that, given the choice of breaking professional ethics or a term in your contract of employment, you must give the profession priority. The law and employment tribunals will support an employee whose employer required them to break their professional ethics – the problem is that many employees would not want to go to court over such matters.

8.2.2 Examples of ethical tensions

The following are examples of how tensions between sets of values can be created.

(a)   **Societal values and corporate values**

An individual may be asked by their employer to act in an illegal way, for example to discriminate against a disabled or ethnic employee.

(b)   **Personal values and corporate values**

An individual may not agree with certain activities of their organisation, such as the use of child labour in foreign factories. While not necessarily illegal, it goes against their own moral beliefs.

(c)   **Professional values and corporate values**

An individual is put into a position by their employer where they are required to amend a set of accounts to improve the profit figure. Such amendments go against the code of conduct of their accountancy body.

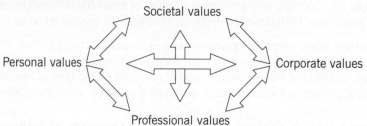

8.3 Spotting an ethical dilemma

Accountants will encounter situations throughout their professional life that present them with an **ethical dilemma** or **conflict of interest**. The following questions will help develop your ability to identify problems in the future. Use the information given to identify the ethical principles at stake.

EXAM FOCUS POINT

The key to answering exam questions in this area is to apply ACCA's fundamental principles. Also, you will probably get a feeling of whether a situation is unethical or not. Use the principles and your instinct to come to your own conclusion.

QUESTION
Time pressure

You are under time pressure to complete this month's management accounts. Important sales information is provided by the sales department, usually in good time for you to incorporate it into the final figures. The sales report is delayed this month due to staff sickness and you will not receive the information until a few hours before the accounts are due for presentation to the finance director.

ANSWER

There is an **integrity** issue here. While you may have time to include the information in the management accounts, it is unlikely that you will be able to check its accuracy as well. Therefore you risk misinforming the finance director of the month's sales.

QUESTION
Tax advice

During your lunch break, your company's human resources manager has asked you for some help. She has recently inherited a considerable sum of money and would like you to calculate her inheritance tax and capital gains tax liabilities. She has also asked you for advice on how she should invest the money.

ANSWER

The issues here are **professional competence and due care**. Unless you are a tax expert, it is unlikely that you would have sufficient competence to calculate the tax liabilities. Giving financial advice can be a minefield, and you may need to be qualified under the financial services regulations before you could do so.

Even if you did have the required competence, it is probable that you could not offer due care, as any advice you give would be on the spot, and you would not have been able to look into the matter in enough detail.

QUESTION

You have been asked to cover the duties of one of your colleagues while they are on holiday. One of their duties is to distribute the management accounts to the department managers a few days before they hold the monthly accounts meeting. Before they left, your colleague told you, 'Just print off the accounts and put them on each manager's desk'.

ANSWER

Confidentiality is the issue here. Management accounts are usually only for the eyes of top management, so you should reduce the risk of them getting into the hands of anyone else. Leaving unprotected copies on a desk makes them vulnerable. Ideally they should be handed directly to the manager concerned, or sealed in a confidential envelope if they must be left on their desk.

QUESTION

Your finance director has asked you to join a team planning a takeover of one of your company's suppliers. An old school friend works as an accountant for the company concerned, the finance director knows this, and has asked you to try and find out 'anything that might help the takeover succeed, but it must remain secret'.

ANSWER

There are three issues here. Firstly you have a **conflict of interest** as the finance director wants you to keep the takeover a secret, but you probably feel that you should tell your friend what is happening as it may affect their job.

Second, the finance director is asking you to deceive your friend. Deception is unprofessional behaviour and will break your ethical guidelines. Therefore the situation is presenting you with **two conflicting demands**. It is worth remembering that no employer can ask you to break your ethical rules.

Finally, the request to break your own ethical guidelines constitutes **unprofessional behaviour** by the finance director. You should consider reporting him to the relevant body.

QUESTION

Your company runs a cost-saving initiative whereby the department head that saves the most cost in the year receives a bonus. Your role is to collect the cost-saving data from each department and to present the results to the finance director.

After the initiative is over, the successful department head presents you with tickets to see your favourite music group in a sold-out concert.

ANSWER

The issue here is **objectivity**. The other department heads could see the gift as a reward for 'fixing' the result, or for 'special favours'. It may also bias your future work and therefore should be refused.

9 Resolution of ethical conflicts

Ethical conflicts may arise from:

- Pressure from an overbearing colleague or from family or friends
- Members asked to act contrary to technical and/or professional standards
- Divided loyalties between colleagues and professional standards
- Publication of misleading information
- Members having to do work beyond their degree of expertise or experience they possess
- Personal relationships with other employees or clients
- Gifts and hospitality being offered

We have seen there are many situations that could cause ethical conflicts, ranging from the trivial to the very serious (such as fraud or illegal acts). The method of resolving them that ACCA sets out for its members and students is laid down in its **ethical code** (ACCA, 2016); however, many organisations propose an alternative process to evaluate a decision.

Individuals should ask themselves:

(a) **Transparency**

Do I feel comfortable with others knowing about my decision, is my decision defensible?

(b) **Effect**

Have I considered all parties who may be affected by the decision and have all factors been taken into account such as mitigating circumstances?

(c) **Fairness**

Would a reasonable third party view the decision as fair?

QUESTION
Dealing with ethical dilemmas

Which of the following would **not** be a suitable question to ask yourself when resolving an ethical dilemma?

A   Would my colleagues think my solution is reasonable?
B   Have I thought about all the possible consequences of my solution?
C   Could I defend my solution under public scrutiny?
D   Does my solution benefit my career?

ANSWER

D   The best solution to an ethical dilemma should be taken whether or not it improves your career.

9.1 Raising and dealing with ethical dilemmas

A number of options are available for accountants wishing to raise ethical issues, for example:

- **Directly** with their accountancy body
- Within their organisation via a **help or whistleblower line**
- To **external organisations** such as customers, suppliers or agents
- **Anonymously**

However they choose to proceed, ACCA members and students should ensure it is **consistent** with ACCA's Ethical Code (ACCA, 2016).

The following diagram suggests an approach for **conflict resolution**.

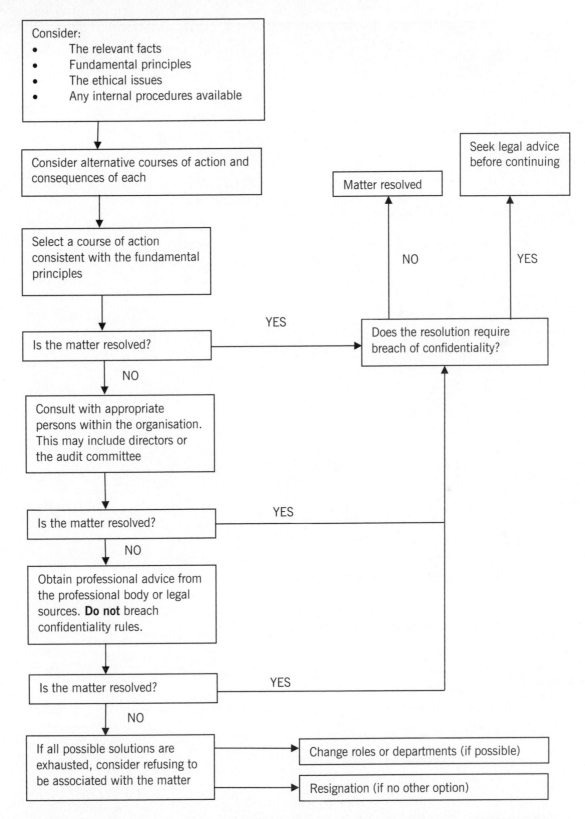

At all stages it is recommended that members document the substance of the issue and all discussions and decisions made.

PER performance objective PO1 requires you to apply professional ethics, values and judgement. The material covered in this chapter, and built on later in your studies in Paper P1 will help you achieve this.

CHAPTER ROUNDUP

↪ There are three main sources of rules that regulate behaviour of individuals and businesses. These are:

– The law
– Non-legal rules and regulations
– Ethics

↪ Organisations are not autonomous; they exist to serve some external purpose, usually manifested in a group such as shareholders in a company or trustees of a charity. In particular, the **strategic apex must not lose sight of this accountability**. All managers have a **duty of faithful service** to the external purpose of the organisation and this lies most heavily on the shoulders of those at the strategic apex.

↪ Ethics and morality are about right and wrong behaviour. Western thinking about ethics tends to be based on ideas about **duty** and **consequences**. Unfortunately, such thinking often fails to indicate a single clear course of action. Ethical thinking is also influenced by the concepts of **virtue** and **rights**.

↪ Ethical conduct by all members should be a major concern for management. Inside the organisation, a **compliance-based** approach highlights **conformity with the law**. An **integrity-based** approach suggests a **wider remit**, incorporating ethics in the organisation's **values and culture**. Organisations sometimes issue codes of conduct to employees. Many employees are bound by professional codes of conduct.

↪ As an accountant, your values and attitudes **flow through** everything you do professionally. They contribute to the **trust** the wider community puts in the profession and the **perception** it has of it.

↪ The **International Federation of Accountants** (IFAC) is an international body representing all the major accountancy bodies across the world. Its mission is to develop the **high standards** of professional accountants and enhance the quality of services they provide.

↪ The personal qualities that an accountant should demonstrate are:

– Reliability
– Responsibility
– Timeliness

– Courtesy
– Respect

↪ The professional qualities an accountant should demonstrate are:

– Independence
– Scepticism

– Accountability
– Social responsibility

↪ **Ethical dilemmas** are situations where two ethical values or requirements seem to be incompatible. They can also arise where two conflicting demands or obligations are placed on an individual.

↪ A **conflict of interest** arises where an individual has a duty to two or more parties. While working, information or other matters may arise that mean they cannot continue work for one party without harming another.

↪ **Ethical conflicts** may arise from:

- Pressure from an overbearing colleague or from family or friends
- Members asked to act contrary to technical and/or professional standards
- Divided loyalties between colleagues and professional standards
- Publication of misleading information
- Members having to do work beyond their degree of expertise or experience they possess
- Personal relationships with other employees or clients
- Gifts and hospitality being offered

QUICK QUIZ

1   Ethics are a set of .... that
     ....

2   What is the name given to guidance issued (usually by a governing body) to individuals to judge whether
     they are acting ethically in particular circumstances?

3   List five personal qualities expected of an accountant.

     (a)   R..   (d)   C..

     (b)   R..   (e)   R..

     (c)   T..

4   Fiduciary responsibility is a duty of faithful service. Is this true or false?

5   Why might social responsibility have an adverse effect on shareholders' interests?

6   One approach to managing ethics is to ensure primarily that the company acts within the letter of the
     law. What type of approach is this?

     A   Compliance-based approach   C   Commercial-based approach
     B   Integrity-based approach

7   Tick true or false for the following. The fundamental principles of the ACCA Code of Ethics and Conduct
     are

	True	False
Professional behaviour	☐	☐
Confidentiality	☐	☐
Social responsibility	☐	☐
Objectivity	☐	☐
Integrity	☐	☐
Professional competence and due care	☐	☐

1   Moral principles, guide behaviour

2   Code of Ethics or Code of Conduct

3   (a)   Reliability   (d)   Courtesy
    (b)   Responsibility   (e)   Respect
    (c)   Timeliness

4   True. Fiduciary responsibility is the duty of faithful service.

5   Social responsibility action may:

    • Incur additional costs (for example, environmental monitoring)
    • Decrease revenues (if, say, a company refused to supply to certain customers)
    • Divert employee effort away from profitable activities
    • Divert funds away from the business into social projects

6   A. The compliance-based approach is designed to ensure that the company acts within the letter of the law and that violations are prevented, detected and punished

7

	True	False
Professional behaviour	✓	
Confidentiality	✓	
Social responsibility		✓
Objectivity	✓	
Integrity	✓	
Professional competence and due care	✓	

Now try ...

Attempt the questions below from the **Practice Question Bank**

Q101

Q102

Q103

Q104

Practice question and answer bank

Practice question and answer bank

1   A .... company has a separate legal personality from its owners (shareholders).

Which word correctly completes this sentence?

A   Private   C   Limited
B   Public   **(1 mark)**

2   .... comprise all those individuals or groups who have a legitimate interest in an organisation's activities.

Which word or phrase correctly completes this sentence?

A   Key players   C   Stakeholders
B   Shareholders   **(1 mark)**

3   Complete the statement given below by using one of the words in the list below.

'Shareholders are .... stakeholders.'

A   External   C   Internal
B   Community   D   Connected   **(2 marks)**

4   ABC is a business controlled on the basis of one share, one vote; while DEF is controlled on the basis of one member, one vote.

(a)   **What sort of businesses are ABC and DEF?**

	ABC	DEF
A	Limited liability company	Partnership
B	Co-operative society	Limited liability company
C	Partnership	Limited liability company
D	Limited liability company	Co-operative society

(b)   Azif is a customer of both ABC and DEF. **What type of stakeholder is he?**

Select the correct answers from the list below.

ABC [▼]

DEF [▼]

Picklist

Internal
Connected
External
Not a stakeholder   **(4 marks)**

5   For which of the following reasons would dismissal automatically be considered unfair?

A   Redundancy   C   Pregnancy
B   Non-capability   D   Misconduct   **(2 marks)**

6   Under which component of PEST analysis would an organisation analyse the media through which segments of the youth market access new digital music products?

A   Political   C   Social
B   Economic   D   Technological   **(2 marks)**

7   The bargaining power of customers in an industry will be greater in which of the following circumstances?

    A   There are one or two dominant suppliers in the industry
    B   The product is highly important to the customer's business
    C   There are many customers in the industry
    D   Switching costs are low   **(2 marks)**

8   Health and safety regulations cover a range of workplace health and safety issues. Which of the following is not covered by regulation?

    A   Handling and storage of chemicals
    B   Lifting heavy objects
    C   Computers
    D   Pregnancy   **(2 marks)**

9   Workplace hazards cover a variety of situations including heavy lifting and VDU usage. What is the definition of a hazard?

    A   Heavy machinery
    B   Electrical equipment
    C   Something likely to cause injury, or a point of exposure to risk of accident, injury or illness
    D   Tippex   **(2 marks)**

10   Data security is crucially important to an organisation. Certain types of data may be particularly at risk.

To which of the following would this apply?

    A   Personal and private information
    B   Information relating to the security of the organisation
    C   Information integral to the outcome of dealings in the organisation
    D   Information integral to the organisation's standing and competitive advantage   **(2 marks)**

11   These are several possible risks to data in the workplace. These include **human error**, **technical malfunction** and which of the following:

    A   Catastrophic errors   C   Dishonesty
    B   Malicious damage   D   Political upheaval   **(2 marks)**

12   Constance is a sole trader operating in the UK. Her main business is in telecommunications: providing telephone, broadband and cable television services to the public. Demand for Constance's services is growing and she is considering outsourcing some of her operations. She is looking into using local contractors for a short period, until she can train her own operatives to cover the west of England and Wales.

    (a)   **How does the Government impact on Constance's business?**

	Yes	No
Company law		
Employment law		
Industry regulation		
Consumer protection		

    (b)   **What type of outsourcing is Constance considering?**

        A   Ad hoc   C   Partial
        B   Project management   D   Total   **(4 marks)**

13 Which type of government policy focuses on taxation, public borrowing and public spending?

A	Fiscal	C	Social
B	Monetary	D	Industry

(2 marks)

14 Which of the following is **not** likely to result from a fall in the exchange rate?

A A stimulus to exports
B An increase in the costs of imports
C Reducing demand for imports
D A reduction in the rate of domestic inflation

(2 marks)

15 .... inflation arises from an excess of aggregate need over the productive capacity of the economy.

Which word or words correctly complete this sentence?

A	Demand pull	C	Frictional
B	Cost push		

(1 mark)

16 XYZ Ltd operates an IT business. Recent developments in the IT industry mean that XYZ Ltd can use computers to replace some of its workers, who will be made redundant. At the same time, XYZ Ltd will be bringing in policies to limit environmental damage as a result of its actions.

(a) **What category of unemployment is the redundancy?**

A Frictional
B Seasonal
C Technological
D Structural

(b) **Which of the following actions would be of benefit to the environment?**

	Yes	No
Using renewable energy sources		
Burying non-biodegradable waste on site		
Minimising costs		
Buying recycled paper		
Encouraging staff not to print emails		

(4 marks)

17   In the diagram below, point 5 represents equilibrium. If the government starts to pay a cash
      subsidy to producers of the commodity, what will the new equilibrium be?

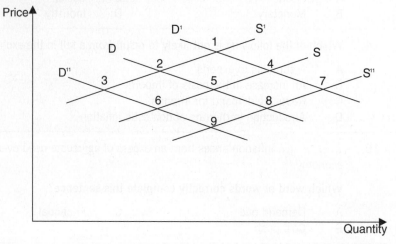

      A   Point 2
      B   Point 4
      C   Point 6
      D   Point 8   **(2 marks)**

18   Surpluses will be enjoyed by some suppliers and some consumers even when the market clears
      under perfect competition.

      Match the correct labels to the boxes on this diagram.

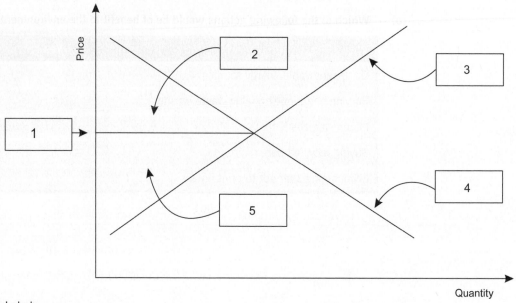

      Labels:

      A   Equilibrium price
      B   Consumer surplus
      C   Market supply
      D   Market demand
      E   Producer surplus   **(2 marks)**

19 If the cost of milk rises, and milk is a major ingredient in yoghurt, then the:

    A   Demand curve for yoghurt shifts to the left

    B   Supply for yoghurt curve shifts to the left

    C   Supply curve for yoghurt shifts to the right

    D   Demand and supply curves for yoghurt both shift to the right   **(2 marks)**

20 Which of the following is **not** one of the roles performed by prices in a market economy?

    A   A signal to consumers

    B   A signal to producers

    C   A way of allocating resources between competing uses

    D   A way of ensuring a fair distribution of incomes   **(2 marks)**

21 If all other factors remain unchanged, which one of the following would lead to a fall in share prices?

    A   A reduction in the rate of tax which companies have to pay

    B   Forecasts predicting a rise in company profits

    C   A rise in interest rates

    D   A reduction in the number of shares issued   **(2 marks)**

22 Indicate whether the following will cause a shift in the demand curve for a normal good, a shift in its supply curve, or neither:

	Shift in demand	Shift in supply	Neither
(i) An increase in household incomes			
(ii) A rise in wage costs			
(iii) A fall in the price of raw materials			
(iv) A fall in the price of the good			

(2 marks)

23 Which of the following statements is true?

    A   The grapevine springs up where there is inadequate formal communication in an organisation

    B   Cliques and other informal groups can be either helpful or dysfunctional in an organisation

    C   Not all organisations have an informal organisation

    D   The informal organisation promotes employee health and safety   **(2 marks)**

24 Henry Mintzberg's model analysed organisation structure into five basic components.

Which of the following components include analysts and designers of control systems?

    A   Strategic apex   C   Middle line

    B   Technostructure   D   Support staff   **(2 marks)**

25 Which of the following is not a component of Mintzberg's model of the organisation?

    A   Technostructure   C   Middle line

    B   Operating core   D   Administration staff   **(2 marks)**

26 Which feature of Mintzberg's organisational model is most heavily influential in a machine bureaucracy?

A   The operating core
B   The technostructure
C   The strategic apex
D   The middle line

(2 marks)

27 A business has the following features: narrow control spans, small groups with team members participating in decisions, and a large number of steps on the promotional ladder. It relies on the informal organisation to supply most of its internal communications.

(a) **What type of organisation is this business?**

Select the correct answer from the list below.

▼

Picklist

Flat organisation
Tall organisation

(b) **What are the advantages and disadvantages of an informal organisation?**

	Advantage	Disadvantage
Knowledge sharing		
Social groupings		
Informal work practices		
Responsiveness		
Speed		

(4 marks)

28 Which of the following is **not** one of the main objectives of Human Resource Management?

A   To obtain the right number and type of skilled employees for the organisation's current and future requirements

B   To develop and deploy the organisation's employees in such a way as to maximise flexibility and productivity

C   To ensure compliance with the organisation's social and legal responsibilities in relation to employees

D   To minimise labour turnover and maximise employee retention within the organisation

(2 marks)

29 Which of the following is most likely to be an example of an 'existential culture' in Harrison's model of cultural types?

A   An entrepreneurial start-up business
B   A partnership of graphic designers
C   A construction project
D   A large telecommunications company

(2 marks)

30 Committees are particularly effective for carrying out day–to-day work.

Is this statement true or false?

A   True   B   False   **(1 mark)**

31   Ralph founded a toy business, Raleigh's, many years ago. Although Ralph used to keep firm control in the early days, recently he has been happy to delegate authority to a vibrant new team of toy enthusiasts, although he remains Chairman of the Board. The team have brought out new toy ranges and are determined to make Raleigh's the leading toy manufacturer.

(a)   **Which of Handy's cultures is closest to the current situation at Raleigh's?**

A   Zeus
B   Apollo
C   Athena
D   Dionysus

(b)   **Which of the following roles are carried out by the Chair of a committee?**

Select the correct answers from the list below.

▼

▼

Picklist

Fixing the date and time of a meeting
Giving immediate rulings on points of dispute
Being seen to be impartial
Acting on decisions made   **(4 marks)**

32   Which of the following is **not** a major theme of corporate governance?

A   Ensuring the confidentiality of information
B   Accountability
C   Ethical treatment of stakeholders
D   The management and reduction of risk   **(2 marks)**

33   Under good corporate governance, who should set directors' remuneration?

A   An audit committee
B   Independent non-executive directors
C   The board of directors
D   The London Stock Exchange   **(2 marks)**

34   Corporate social responsibility (CSR) is incompatible with the interests of shareholders in a business organisation.

According to the stakeholder view, is this statement true or false?

A   True   B   False   **(1 mark)**

35 The following paragraphs describe corporate governance and social responsibility respectively. Some words have been omitted.

Corporate governance is the .... by which organisations are .... by senior officers. Most corporate governance .... are based around the principles of integrity, ..., independence and good management but there is disagreement on how much these principles need to be .... by detailed rules.

Businesses, particularly large ones, are subject to increasing .... that they will exercise social responsibility. This is an ill-defined concept, but appears to focus on the .... of specific benefits to society in general, such as charitable donations, the creation or preservation of ...., and spending on .... improvement or maintenance.

Complete the sentences using the following list of words/terms. Each word or term can only be used **once**.

Picklist

accountability
directed and controlled
employment
environmental
expectations
provision
reports
supplemented
system   **(4 marks)**

36 An organisation has to decide whether to buy or lease machinery for its new factory.

Which of the following members of the finance function would be responsible for this decision?

A The financial manager   C The financial accountant
B The management accountant   **(1 mark)**

37 Goods inwards checks are an example of a control in which business financial system?

A Payroll   C Sales
B Purchasing   D Cash management   **(2 marks)**

38 Which of the following is not an advantage of an accounting package compared with a manual system?

A A large amount of data can be processed very quickly
B The need for security checks for authorising access
C Accuracy of data
D Non-specialists can use packages   **(2 marks)**

39 Which of the following statements is true?

A Financial accountants provide historical information for internal use.
B Financial accountants provide historical information for external use.
C Financial accountants provide forward-looking information for internal use.
D Financial accountants provide forward-looking information for external use.   **(2 marks)**

40 Most management reports are made meaningful by the use of **comparison**. Which of the following comparisons is/are likely to be made by an organisation in reviewing financial data?

A With other organisations   C With forecast
B With budget   D With prior periods   **(2 marks)**

41 Management reports are often used to make comparisons within the organisation. Where comparisons are made between products, what measure would be used?

A Gross profit   C Contribution

B Net profit   D Return on capital   **(2 marks)**

42 GHI Ltd has a computerised accounting system. The system produces various reports and the draft financial statements.

(a) **What output would you expect to get from the sales ledger accounting system?**

A Bank statement

B Aged receivables listing

C Aged payables listing

D List of bankings

(b) **What information is included in the statement of financial position?**

	Yes	No
Income		
Assets		
Expenses		
Liabilities		
Sources of cash generated and spent		

(4 marks)

43 An organisation has a policy of checking all invoices from suppliers against goods-received notes before paying the invoices.

This is an example of what type of control procedure?

A Accounting controls   C Correct controls

B Detect controls   D Prevent controls   **(2 marks)**

44 Which of the following is **not** a feature of external audit?

A Its ultimate objective is to add value and improve operations.

B The auditors report to the shareholders or members of the organisation.

C It focuses on the financial statements and records of the organisation.

D The auditors are independent of the organisation and its management.   **(2 marks)**

45 The purpose of .... data is to ensure that the most recent usable copy of the data can be recovered and restored in the event of loss or corruption on the primary storage medium.

Which word correctly completes this sentence?

A Password-protecting   C Validating

B Backing up   D Verifying   **(2 marks)**

46 The mnemonic SPAMSOAP is often used to remember the range of financial control procedures. What does the 'O' stand for in this mnemonic?

A Operations   C Oversight

B Organisation   D Openness   **(2 marks)**

47 Which of the following is **not** an internal check?

A Separation of duties for authorising, custody and recording
B Pre-lists, post-lists and control totals
C Bank reconciliations
D Systems for authorising transactions within specified spending limits **(2 marks)**

48 JKL Ltd is a limited liability company incorporated in the UK. The company is listed on the UK Stock Exchange and applies International Financial Reporting Standards (IFRSs) when preparing its financial statements.

(a) **What are the features of internal and external audit?**

	Internal	External
Evaluating the adequacy and effectiveness of internal controls		
Carried out for the benefit of shareholders		
Part of the business's control system		
Examines the published financial statements		

(b) **Which body in the UK monitors the use of accounting standards in published financial statements?**

A Government
B HM Revenue and Customs
C International Accounting Standards Board
D Financial Reporting Review Panel **(4 marks)**

49 A warehouse manager instructs staff not to record returns of goods to suppliers if the goods have already been entered into inventory records, as this will be 'sorted out by the accounts department'.

Is this action potentially fraudulent?

A No
B Yes, as an example of removal of assets from a business
C Yes, as an example of intentional misrepresentation of the financial position of a business **(1 mark)**

50 Which of the following would be regarded as fraud prevention measures?

A Requiring all quantities to be written in words rather than numbers
B Requiring all staff to take full holiday entitlements
C Defining standard procedures for normal business operations
D All of the above **(2 marks)**

51 Only allowing purchasing staff to choose suppliers from an approved list is an example of what sort of fraud prevention measure?

A Segregation of duties   C Limitation controls
B Appropriate documentation   **(1 mark)**

52 Which of the following internal controls might be least effective in preventing fraud, if staff are in collusion with customers?

A Physical security
B Requiring signatures to confirm receipt of goods or services
C Sequential numbering of transaction documents
D Authorisation policies **(2 marks)**

53   Match the feature of the payables and creditors system to the control aims given:

A   Ordering   C   Accounting
B   Receipt and invoices

(i)   Cut-off is applied correctly to the purchase ledger
(ii)   All goods and services received are accurately recorded
(iii) Orders are only made to authorised suppliers   **(2 marks)**

---

54   Match the feature of the receivables and sales system to the control aims given:

A   Ordering and granting credit
B   Despatch and ordering
C   Recording, accounting and credit control

(i)   Credit notes are only given for valid reasons
(ii)   Orders are recorded correctly
(iii) All sales that have been invoiced are recorded on the nominal and sales ledgers
                                                                                      (2 marks)

---

55   Leticia runs a highly successful model agency. She relies on her bookkeeper to control the
      financial side of her business. However, the bookkeeper left recently and, due to business
      pressures, Leticia has employed a temp rather than spend time recruiting a permanent
      replacement. Leticia was looking at the business bank statements recently and became
      concerned by amounts of cash being paid into and out of the business account. She questioned
      the temp who said that one of the models had requested payment in cash and one of their new
      overseas customers was paying in cash 'to avoid tax problems at home'. This has never happened
      before. Leticia is extremely concerned that the temp and model may be colluding to commit fraud
      and that her bank account may be being used for money laundering.

      (a)   **Which of the following factors may indicate fraud?**

	Yes	No
New bookkeeper		
New overseas customer		
Lack of supervision		
Cash transactions		

      (b)   **If Leticia's bank account is being used for money laundering, what phase of the process
             may she be involved in?**

             Select the correct answer from the list below.

             [▼]

             Picklist

             Placement
             Integration
             Layering

      (c)   **What action should Leticia take?**

             Select the correct answer from the list below.

             [▼]

             Picklist

             Do nothing as it is only a suspicion
             Find more evidence of what is going on
             Report her suspicions to the authorities immediately   **(4 marks)**

---

56 Which type of power is associated with line authority?

A	Physical power	C	Legitimate power
B	Resource power	D	Expert power

(2 marks)

57 Which school of management thinking focused on a range of higher-order needs of workers for job satisfaction?

A	Scientific management	C	Neo-human relations
B	Human relations	D	Contingency

(2 marks)

58 What two factors in leadership style are plotted on Blake and Mouton's managerial grid?

A   Managerial discretion and subordinate discretion
B   Concern for production and concern for people
C   Psychological distance and favourability of the situation
D   Exercise of leadership and exercise of authority

(2 marks)

59 Which of the following is not one of Fayol's five functions of management?

A	Commanding	C	Communicating
B	Controlling	D	Co-ordinating

(2 marks)

60 Which of the following is not one of the interpersonal roles of managers identified by Henry Mintzberg?

A   Handling disturbances
B   Reconciling individual needs with the requirements of the organisation
C   Training staff
D   Liaising outside the scalar chain

(2 marks)

61 What managerial roles did Mintzberg describe and what categories did he group them into?

(2 marks)

62 Power arising from an individual's formal position in the organisation is called:

A	Referent power	C	Expert power
B	Legitimate power	D	Resource power

(2 marks)

63 What does a person specification describe?

A   The main tasks, responsibilities and conditions involved in a job
B   The attributes of the ideal person for a given job
C   The performance rating of a given job holder
D   The number of people required to fill job vacancies

(2 marks)

64 An organisation urgently needs to recruit an experienced cost accountant, but does not have a large budget for recruitment advertising.

Which of the following would be its most appropriate recruitment medium?

A   Recruitment consultancy
B   Advertisement in a national newspaper
C   Advertisement on local radio
D   Register with an online accountancy recruitment database

(2 marks)

65 Which selection method is the most reliable predictor of job performance?

A	Interviews	C	Work sampling
B	References	D	Personality tests

(2 marks)

66 Lin is the manager in charge of the financial accounts department for a large company. He is a very effective manager: making decisions, motivating his department and getting results. He is focused on the organisation's long-term goals and his department's part in them.

(a) **According to the Ashridge model, what is Lin's style of management?**

A Tells
B Sells
C Consults
D Joins

(b) **Where would Lin be in Blake and Mouton's managerial grid?**

(c) **According to Bennis, is Lin a manager or a leader?**

(4 marks)

67 Justine has offered to give evidence at an Employment Tribunal on behalf of a colleague who is claiming that he has been passed over for promotion because he is not married. Over the following weeks, her department head repeatedly denies her requests for work breaks, because she is already having 'time off in court'.

Justine may have a claim for what form of discrimination?

A Direct discrimination   C Victimisation
B Indirect discrimination   D Harassment   **(2 marks)**

68 Using age limits or phrases that imply restrictions (such as 'recent graduate') in job advertisements is age discrimination.

Is this statement true or false?

A True   B False   **(1 mark)**

69 SPQR uses individual interviews for its staff recruitment. Janine has been recruited as a goods outwards clerk. After two months, she complains that the other clerks are discriminating against her, using foul and abusive language and threatening her.

(a) **Which of the following are advantages and disadvantages of the interview method?**

	Advantage	Disadvantage
Interviewer may have knowledge gaps		
Direct face to face communication		
Flexibility in questioning		
Interviewer's perception may be selective		

(b) **Janine is the subject of what kind of behaviour?**

A Direct discrimination
B Harassment
C Indirect discrimination
D Victimisation   **(4 marks)**

70 Cohesive groups generally take more risky decisions than the same individuals working separately.

Is this statement true or false?

A True   B False   **(1 mark)**

71 In a project team, Jane is the person everyone turns to with their problems and interpersonal conflicts, knowing that she will listen and mediate.

Which of Belbin's team roles does Jane fulfil?

A Plant   C Co-ordinator
B Shaper   D Teamworker   **(2 marks)**

72 In which order does a team ordinarily progress through Tuckman's stages of development?

A Norming, storming, forming, performing
B Storming, forming, norming, performing
C Forming, storming, norming, performing
D Norming, forming, storming, performing   **(2 marks)**

73 The tendency of a group to follow what its members assume to be the group consensus, ending up following a course of action that no one in fact wants, is called:

A The risky-shift phenomenon   C The Abilene paradox
B Social facilitation   D Group think   **(2 marks)**

74 Which of the following would be an example of poor chairing of a meeting?

A Discussion is not limited to the items on the agenda
B Speakers are not allowed time to re-state their views
C Discussion of an item is cut short in order to move onto the next item
D People arrive and leave part-way through the meeting   **(2 marks)**

75 What type of motivation theory is expectancy theory?

A Process theory   B Content theory   **(1 mark)**

76 Bill believes that his team are innately lazy and will shirk work and responsibility unless he directs and supervises them closely, and applies strict discipline.

Which writer's motivational theory accounts for Bill's motivational approach?

A Herzberg   C Vroom
B Maslow   D McGregor   **(2 marks)**

77 Which of the following is **not** identified as a core dimension in job design for job satisfaction?

A Skill variety   C Performance-related pay
B Task identity   D Feedback   **(2 marks)**

78 The management of Guenguiss Cans Ltd runs a 'tight ship', with clocking-on timekeeping systems, close supervision and rules for everything. 'Well,' says the general manager, 'give people an inch and they'll take a mile.'

Which of Douglas McGregor's 'theories' does this management team subscribe to?

A Theory X   B Theory Y   **(1 mark)**

79 Meredith is a member of a team set up to complete a project. Meredith likes to review a project to see all the options and she is accurate in her judgements. However, she can be overly critical and lacks the ability to inspire others. The team leader feels that Meredith lacks drive and prefers to avoid responsibility.

(a) **Which is Meredith's team role according to the Belbin model?**

A   Plant
B   Shaper
C   Monitor-evaluator
D   Completer-finisher

(b) **If the team leader bases his approach on McGregor's theory, which one should he apply to Meredith?**

Select the correct answer from the list below.

[▼]

Picklist

Theory X
Theory Y   **(4 marks)**

80 What learning style would have a natural preference for (and learn best from) on-the-job training using such methods as project work or job instruction?

A   Theorist   C   Activist
B   Reflector   D   Pragmatist   **(2 marks)**

81 Which of the following is an advantage of on-the-job training?

A   Allows focus on learning
B   Supports transfer of learning
C   Allows standardisation of training
D   Minimises risk   **(2 marks)**

82 What is the lowest level at which the effectiveness of training can be evaluated?

A   Trainee learning
B   Changes in trainees' job behaviour
C   Trainee reaction
D   Changes in results   **(2 marks)**

83 .... is 'the planned and systematic modification of behaviour through learning events, programmes and instruction which enable individuals to achieve the level of knowledge, skills and competence to carry out their work effectively'.

Which word correctly completes this definition?

A   Conditioning   C   Education
B   Training   D   Development   **(2 marks)**

84 The learning cycle developed by David Kolb is a process for .... learning. Which of the following words correctly completes this sentence?

A   Programmed   C   Action
B   Experiential   **(1 mark)**

85 What is a key objective of a performance appraisal system?

A   To ensure that employees are developing their potential for improvement
B   To underpin the reward system of the organisation
C   To support promotion planning
D   To give employees feedback on the previous year's performance   **(2 marks)**

86   An organisation uses an appraisal form which enables managers to measure employees' behaviour in key situations against descriptions of key successful and unsuccessful job behaviour reported by managers.

What appraisal technique is being used by this organisation?

A   Overall assessment   C   A behavioural incident method
B   Guided assessment   D   A results-oriented scheme   **(2 marks)**

87   Which approach to appraisal interviewing gives the interviewer the least critical and dominant role in the process?

A   Tell and sell   C   Problem-solving
B   Tell and listen   **(1 mark)**

88   Appraisal is an example of what level of control?

A   Strategic   C   Operational
B   Tactical   D   Clan   **(2 marks)**

89   When a subordinate rates their superior's leadership skills, this is an example of:

A   360° feedback   C   Upward appraisal
B   Performance management   D   Results-oriented appraisal   **(2 marks)**

90   Fred is a team leader who keeps a detailed checklist of his daily tasks, and ranks them in order of importance and urgency. He only takes phone calls during particular times of day, to avoid interruptions. Even so, at the end of the day, he has to work late to complete a large number of urgent but low-level tasks for the following day.

Which of the following is Fred's weakness in the area of time management?

A   Planning   C   Focus
B   Delegation   D   Prioritisation   **(2 marks)**

91   Jihander, the payroll supervisor, has been asked to meet with Tom once a week for eight weeks, in order to help Tom to plan, implement and review a learning programme to improve his knowledge of the company's payroll system.

What term would be given to this type of relationship?

A   Coaching   C   Counselling
B   Mentoring   **(1 mark)**

92   Which of the following is **not** usually a barrier to effective communication?

A   Distortion   C   Connection between individuals
B   Noise   D   Technical vocabulary   **(2 marks)**

93   It has been suggested that work organisation might be improved by an ABCD method of in-tray management.

What does 'ABCD' stand for?

A   Act, Bin, Create, Delegate   C   Act, Blame, Create, Deliver
B   Apply, Bin, Collate, Delegate D   Apply, Bin, Collate, Deliver   **(2 marks)**

94   What makes a piece of work high priority?

A   It has to be completed by a deadline
B   Other tasks depend on it
C   The Chairman is involved in its outcome
D   Your promotion depends on it   **(2 marks)**

95 Compromise is an example of a:

A	Win-win result	C	Lose-win result
B	Win-lose result	D	Lose-lose result **(2 marks)**

96 Under the ACAS disciplinary code, an instance of gross misconduct should be dealt with after:

A	An oral warning	C	A final written warning
B	A disciplinary hearing	D	A full investigation **(2 marks)**

97 A grievance occurs when an employee infringes organisational rules or expectations. *True or false?* **(1 mark)**

98 An employer's treatment of an employee is so bad that eventually she resigns even though she liked her work. This would be an example of:

A	Wrongful dismissal	C	Automatically unfair dismissal
B	Potentially unfair dismissal	D	Constructive dismissal **(2 marks)**

99 Manesh is an accounts assistant who works from 9am to 5pm, with an hour for lunch. He has the following routine duties (duration of tasks are in brackets):

- Open the morning post (30 mins)

- Pass any cheques received to the cashier (30 mins)

- Enter sales invoices/credit notes daily in batches into the computer system by midday (2 hours)

- Match and check purchase invoices to goods received notes daily and pass them to the accountant for authorisation (6 mins per invoice)

- File sales invoices/credit notes (between 1 and 2 hours of filing)

Today is Friday 10am and Manesh has already opened the post and passed the cheques to the cashier, when he gets a telephone call from the accountant asking him to cover for a sick colleague. As a result, Manesh needs to enter the weekly purchase invoices into the computer today (which should only take an hour). Another colleague, who is back in the office this afternoon (2pm) needs to review a list of these invoices before the end of the day for forecasting purposes. The list is generated by the computer system.

Manesh has 20 purchase invoices that need to be matched to (and checked against) GRNs before the end of the day ready for authorisation first thing on Monday.

Decide on the order in which Manesh should carry out the tasks included in the picklist.

Order	Task	
1st task		▼
2nd task		▼
3rd task		▼
4th task		▼

Picklist

Filing
Match purchase invoices to goods received notes and pass to the accountant for authorisation
Enter weekly purchase invoices into the computer
Enter sales invoices/credit notes into computer system **(4 marks)**

100 Rajesh works in the accounts department of a large business. He receives communications from his two assistants, Lisa and Freda. He passes the information to the accountant, who in turn passes it to the chief accountant.

Lisa has only recently joined the firm and Rajesh is responsible for overseeing her training. He has delegated teaching the day-to-day workings to Freda, who has been with the firm for some years and is very capable. However, Freda is now complaining that Lisa is constantly interrupting her with queries, so that Freda cannot get her own work done. Freda is now seriously behind schedule and she asks Rajesh to relieve her of the 'burden' of teaching Lisa. Lisa in turn complains that Freda does not explain things properly, which is why she has to keep asking questions.

On further investigation, Rajesh discovers that Lisa is not as experienced as he had thought and decides to send her on a week's training course in the company's systems. He will then supervise her more closely when she returns from the course. Although Freda will still help with some queries, she is to let Rajesh know immediately if this starts to affect her own workload.

(a) **What type of communication pattern is being used?**

A   Chain
B   Circle
C   Y
D   Wheel

(b) **In resolving the conflict between Lisa and Freda, which model has Rajesh used?**

Select the correct answer from the list below.

▼

Picklist

Win-lose
Lose-lose
Win-win   (4 marks)

101 Which approach to ethics considers which actions are likely to result in 'the greatest good for the greatest number of people'?

A   Legalism   C   Categorical imperatives
B   Deontology   D   Utilitarianism   (2 marks)

102 What is the meaning of the ethical principal of 'independence in appearance'?

A   Accountants must complete their work free from bias or prejudice

B   Accountants must complete their work without excessive supervision

C   Accountants must complete their work in such a way as to give a reasonable person no cause to question their objectivity

D   Accountants must complete their work in such a way as to give a reasonable person confidence that they can work without supervision   (2 marks)

103 The Board of TUV Ltd are considering their organisational values in order to promote ethical behaviour. The Chair recounts a recent problem where they found that a waste disposal contractor was dumping their waste instead of recycling it according to their contract. The Board debates whether they are ethically liable for sorting out the problem, particularly as the contractor has ceased to trade.

Later in the meeting, a director reveals that his wife has been elected to the Board of a minor supplier. He says the supplier will offer substantial discounts if more goods are ordered from her firm.

(a) **Which ethical concept(s) is/are at issue in the case of the waste disposal situation?**

	Yes	No
Openness		
Honesty		
Accountability		
Integrity		
Objectivity		

(b) **What conflict of interest may arise in the case of the supplier?**

  A   Self-review threat
  B   Self-interest threat
  C   Familiarity threat
  D   Intimidation threat   **(4 marks)**

104 Which of the following would NOT be included in a corporate code of ethics for a company that buys products and raw materials from overseas?

  A   A statement detailing the behavioural standards expected of employees
  B   A summary of the company's quality promises to customers
  C   Details of environmental standards expected of suppliers
  D   A list of the laws and regulations that apply to the company   **(2 marks)**

1	C	A limited company is incorporated specifically to create a separate legal entity, allowing for the concept of limited liability. A limited company may be either public or private – but this is a separate distinction, based mainly on different sources of share capital. *(Chapter 1)*

2   C   Stakeholders are all individuals or groups with a 'stake' in the organisation's activities or results. Shareholders are merely one (connected) stakeholder group, while key players are one 'category' of stakeholders in Mendelow's power-interest matrix. *(Chapter 1)*

3   D   Connected *(Chapter 1)*

4   (a)   D   One share, one vote implies a limited liability company; one member, one vote is the basis of a co-operative or mutual society.

     (b)   ABC Connected, DEF Connected. *(Chapter 1)*

     As a customer, Azif is a connected stakeholder to both ABC and DEF. Note that any business has stakeholders, not just limited liability companies.

5   C   Redundancy, non-capability and misconduct are potentially fair grounds for dismissal, provided that the employee was fairly handled. Dismissal on the grounds of pregnancy is automatically unfair, partly as a form of sexual discrimination. *(Chapter 2)*

6   C   The developments in digital music products may be analysed under technological factors, but media consumption and buying patterns are sociocultural factors. *(Chapter 2)*

7   D   If the costs of switching to alternative suppliers is low, customers can demand more from their suppliers. The other circumstances tend to increase the power of suppliers, by reducing the customers' ability to take their business elsewhere (options A and B) or by decreasing the importance of individual customers' business (option C). *(Chapter 2)*

8   This was a trick question! All of the choices are covered by regulations which also encompass issues as diverse as noise regulations and the control of working hours and rest breaks. *(Chapter 2)*

9   C   This is the definition given in the chapter. The other alternatives are examples of things that may be hazards if misused. *(Chapter 2)*

10   All of these types of data are at risk. Remember that any data is at risk if it has a **monetary value**, could give a **competitive advantage** to whoever has it or has **nuisance value**. *(Chapter 2)*

11   The chapter suggests A, B and C would be the main risks to data. **D** is a remote possibility if the upheaval leads to unrest or control over data. *(Chapter 2)*

12   (a)

	Yes	No
Company law		✓
Employment law	✓	
Industry regulation	✓	
Consumer protection	✓	

As Constance is a sole trader, she will not be affected by company law. However, she could be affected by employment law, by industry regulation and by consumer protection.

     (b)   A   As Constance is considering using outsourcing for only a short period, this is ad-hoc outsourcing. *(Chapter 2)*

13   A   Monetary policy focuses on money supply, the monetary system, interest rates, exchange rates and the availability of credit. Social policy focuses on workplace regulation, labour supply, education and skills. Industry policy focuses on matters such as freedom of trade, entry barriers and capacity, and industry regulation. *(Chapter 3)*

14   D   A fall in the exchange rate makes a country's exports cheaper to overseas buyers, and imports more expensive: it therefore has the first three effects. The increase in the cost of imports, however, is likely to add to the rate of domestic inflation. *(Chapter 3)*

15   A   Demand pull inflation occurs when the economy is buoyant and there is a high aggregate demand, in excess of the economy's ability to supply. Cost push inflation occurs where the costs of factors of production rise. 'Frictional' is not a term applied to inflation, but to unemployment (referring to the lead time required to match workers with jobs). *(Chapter 3)*

16   (a)   C   Frictional and seasonal unemployment are short term, whereas XYZ's employees are being permanently laid off. Structural unemployment results from long-term changes in an industry. In XYZ's case, the workers are being made redundant because of new technology and so the correct answer is technological.

      (b)

	Yes	No
Using renewable energy sources	✓	
Burying non-biodegradable waste on site		✓
Minimising costs		✓
Buying recycled paper	✓	
Encouraging staff not to print emails	✓	

Burying non-biodegradable waste on site is causing an environmental problem for the future and could well be illegal. Minimising costs will not produce an environmental benefit. *(Chapters 2 and 3)*

17   D   The effect of a cash subsidy is to shift the supply curve to the right. Producers are willing to supply bigger quantities at the same market price, because they will get a cash subsidy from the government in addition to the market price. The new supply curve goes through points 7, 8 and 9, and so the new equilibrium, given no shift in the demand curve, is at point 8. *(Chapter 4)*

18   1   A   The market clears at the equilibrium price – there is neither surplus nor shortage.
      2   B   Some consumers would have paid a higher price.
      3   C   The higher the price, the more attractive it is to suppliers.
      4   D   The demand curve usually slopes downwards.
      5   E   Some suppliers would have sold at lower price. *(Chapter 4)*

19   B   Demand conditions, and therefore the demand curve, are unchanged. However, less will be supplied at any given price and so the supply curve will move to the left. *(Chapter 4)*

20   D   A government may intervene, for example through progressive taxation, to make the distribution of income fairer. *(Chapter 4)*

21   C   A reduction in corporation tax, and expectations of increased profits, will both increase the **demand** for shares. A reduction in the number of shares issued reduces the **supply** of shares. As the price of shares is determined by demand and supply (for shares) these options will cause the price of shares to rise.

      However, a rise in interest rates will lead to other investments becoming relatively more attractive instead of shares, so demand (and therefore price) for shares will fall. *(Chapter 4)*

22

	Shift in demand	Shift in supply	Neither
(i) An increase in household incomes	X		
(ii) A rise in wage costs		X	
(iii) A fall in the price of raw materials		X	
(iv) A fall in the price of the good			X

An increase in household incomes will lead to an increase in the quantity demanded at all prices, and so will lead to an outward shift in the demand curve.

A rise in wage costs will lead to an inward shift (contraction) of the supply curve, while a fall in the price of raw materials will lead to an outward shift (expansion) of the supply curve.

A fall in the price of the good will lead to a movement along both the demand and supply curves, but will not lead to a shift in either of them. *(Chapter 4)*

23 B Cliques can be helpful in encouraging cross-functional communication, but they can also 'freeze out' individuals and focus on their own agendas. The other statements are untrue: a grapevine flourishes even where formal communication is good; all organisations also have informal social systems; and informal organisation can undermine health and safety (eg by creating informal 'short-cuts' or a culture of recklessness). *(Chapter 5)*

24 B The technostructure is concerned with standardisation of work processes and outputs. The strategic apex and middle line are layers of management (controlling the operating core). Support staff fulfil ancillary functions.

25 D Mintzberg uses the term 'support staff'.

26 B Machine bureaucracies are characterised by multiple layers of management, formal (often rigid) procedures and standardised production processes, so the technostructure is very important *(Chapter 5)*

27 (a) Tall organisation   These are the perceived advantages of a tall organisation.

(b)

	Advantage	Disadvantage
Knowledge sharing	✓	
Social groupings		✓
Informal work practices		✓
Responsiveness	✓	
Speed	✓	

Knowledge sharing can give a wider perspective on an employee's role. Speed and responsiveness are another two advantages of the informal organisation. Social groupings, however, may act collectively against the organisation and informal work practices may violate safety or quality assurance measures. *(Chapter 5)*

28 D An organisation may not wish to minimise labour turnover and maximise retention, if the HR plan requires downsizing by natural wastage. The other three options are key objectives of HRM. *(Chapter 6)*

29 B An existential culture is shaped by the interests of contributing members, such as a professional partnership. An entrepreneurial start-up is likely to be a power culture; a construction project a task culture; and a large telecom firm a bureaucracy or role culture. *(Chapter 6)*

30 B Committees are useful for generating new ideas, but inefficient for ongoing work. *(Chapter 6)*

31   (a)   C   Athena represents a task culture where management is seen as completing a series of projects.

      (b)   Giving immediate rulings on points of dispute; Being seen to be impartial

            Fixing the date and time of a meeting, and acting on decisions made are the duties of the committee secretary. *(Chapter 6)*

32   A   Confidentiality may legitimately be breached in the public interest: corporate governance depends on the free flow of information to stakeholders. The other options are key themes in corporate governance. *(Chapter 7)*

33   B   Non-executive directors (sitting on a remuneration committee) have the independence required for this task – while the board of directors (including executive directors) does not. An audit committee has responsibilities for review of financial statements, internal controls and internal audits, and liaison with external auditors. *(Chapter 7)*

34   B   According to the stakeholder view, CSR is in the long-term interests of shareholders because it helps to secure stakeholder support, access to resources, sustainable business relationships, and so on. *(Chapter 7)*

35   Corporate governance is the **system** by which organisations are **directed and controlled** by senior officers. Most corporate governance **reports** are based around the principles of integrity, **accountability**, independence and good management but there is disagreement on how much these principles need to be **supplemented** by detailed rules.

            Businesses, particularly large ones, are subject to increasing **expectations** that they will exercise social responsibility. This is an ill-defined concept, but appears to focus on the **provision** of specific benefits to society in general, such as charitable donations, the creation or preservation of **employment**, and spending on **environmental** improvement or maintenance. *(Chapter 7)*

36   A   The financial manager is responsible for raising finance and controlling financial resources. The management accountant presents accounting information to support the management of the business. The financial accountant reports the results and financial position of a business. *(Chapter 8)*

37   B   Purchasing system tests are based around buying and goods inwards. The equivalent for sales would be selling and goods outwards. Payroll concerns the payment of wages and salaries. Cash management focuses on the authorisation, verification and recording of payments and receipts. *(Chapter 8)*

38   B   The need for security checks to ensure unauthorised personnel do not gain access to data files is a disadvantage rather than an advantage. *(Chapter 8)*

39   B   *(Chapter 8)*

40   All the options are valid comparisons that can be made. Note the difference between a **budget** which is an organisation's **plan** or **target** for a forthcoming period and a **forecast** which is a **prediction**. *(Chapter 8)*

41   C   Contribution. This refers to how much each product contributes to fixed costs and profit. *(Chapter 8)*

42   (a)   B   Supplier statements would be sent from the supplier, the aged payables listing is an output from the purchases ledger system, and the list of bankings is an output from the cash system.

(b)

	Yes	No
Income		✓
Assets	✓	
Expenses		✓
Liabilities	✓	
Sources of cash generated and spent		✓

The statement of financial position gives details of assets owned and liabilities owed by the business. Details of income and expenditure would be included in the statement of profit or loss and the sources of cash generated and spent appear in the statement of cash flows. *(Chapter 8)*

43   D   Prevent controls are designed to prevent errors (in this case, wrong payments) from happening. Detect controls are designed to detect errors once they have happened; correct controls to minimise or negate the effect of errors; and accounting controls to provide accurate accounting records. *(Chapter 9)*

44   A   This is the objective of internal audit. The (narrower) objective of external audit is to enable auditors to express an opinion on the financial statements of the organisation. *(Chapter 9)*

45   B   Backing up is making separately stored duplicate copies of data for this purpose. The other three options are other forms of integrity control: verification involves ensuring data entered matches source documents, while validation involves ensuring that it is not incomplete or unreasonable. *(Chapter 9)*

46   B   **Rationale**: **Organisation** in this context means identifying reporting lines, levels of authority and responsibility to ensure that everyone is aware of their control responsibilities. The full mnemonic stands for: Segregation of duties; Physical; Authorisation and approval; Management; Supervision; Organisation; Arithmetical and accounting; and Personnel. *(Chapter 9)*

47   D   **Rationale**: This is an **internal control**, rather than an **internal check**. Internal checks are more about dividing work (so that the work of one person can be independently proved by that of another) and using 'proof measures' to ensure the accuracy of records and calculations: options A, B and C are examples. *(Chapter 9)*

48   (a)

	Internal	External
Evaluating the adequacy and effectiveness of internal controls	✓	
Carried out for the benefit of shareholders		✓
Part of the business's control system	✓	
Examines the published financial statements		✓

Internal audit is part of the internal controls within an organisation, checking that the existing controls work and how to improve them. External audit is carried out by an external accounting firm on behalf of the shareholders to check that the published accounts give a true and fair view.

(b)   D   In the UK, the Financial Reporting Review Panel is responsible for examining and questioning the departure from accounting standards by large companies. *(Chapters 8 and 9)*

49   C   There is potential for inventory to be fraudulently overvalued for accounts purposes. *(Chapter 10)*

50   D   Trivial and unrelated as some of the options may seem, they are all fraud-prevention controls: making it difficult to alter quantities; creating time for frauds to come to light; and highlighting deviations from norms. *(Chapter 10)*

51   C   **Rationale: Limit controls** limit opportunity for fraud: another example is limiting access to the computer network by means of passwords. Segregation of duties means ensuring that functions which **together** facilitate fraud are performed by **different** individuals: eg separating the cheque signing function from the authorisation of payments. Appropriate documentation involves recording, authorising and tracking transactions through purchase requisitions, orders, invoices, and so on. *(Chapter 10)*

52   B   **Rationale:** This should be clear from the context, because of the collusion with customers (if you remembered what **collusion** was). Physical security refers to keeping assets under lock and key: not to be dismissed as a fraud prevention measure! Sequential numbering works because it is easy to spot if documents are missing. Authorisation policies increase checks and accountabilities. *(Chapter 10)*

53   A(iii), B(ii), C(i)   Refer back to the chapter if you didn't get this right. *(Chapter 10)*

54   A(ii), B(i), C(iii)   Make sure you know the features of the control system, as these relate to the main accounting systems in the organisation. *(Chapter 10)*

55   (a)

	Yes	No
New bookkeeper	✓	
New overseas customer	✓	
Lack of supervision	✓	
Cash transactions		✓

Cash transactions of themselves do not indicate fraud, as it seems that amounts are being paid in as well as out. This seems more likely to indicate money laundering.

(b)   Layering   Placement usually involves small sums of money. The business to business transactions with the overseas customer are more indicative of layering.

(c)   Report her suspicions to the authorities immediately

Once Leticia's suspicions are aroused, she should report the transactions to the authorities. Otherwise she may be committing the offence of failure to report. If found guilty she could go to prison for five years and/or suffer a fine. *(Chapter 10)*

56   C   Also known as 'position' power, as it derives from a given role in the chain of command. Physical power is based on superior force; resource power on control over valued resources or rewards; and expert power on possession of valued knowledge or expertise. *(Chapter 11)*

57   C   The neo-human relations school argued that a wide range of employee motivations impact on performance: the human relations school pioneered this insight, but focused on social or belonging needs. Scientific management focused instead on technical efficiency. The contingency school argued that a wide range of factors – human and non-human – impact on performance. *(Chapter 11)*

58   B   The grid plots concern for production and concern for people. A balance between managerial and subordinate discretion can be seen in other style theories, such as 'Tells-sells-consults-joins'. Psychological distance and situation are factors in Fiedler's contingency theory. The distinction between leadership and authority is used by Heifetz to distinguish between leaders (potentially informal or emergent) and managers (in positions of formal authority). *(Chapter 11)*

59   C   **Communicating** (*Chapter 11*)

60   A   This is a decisional role. The 'disturbances' referred to are unpredictable situations that require managerial input to resolve. (*Chapter 11*)

61   *Category*   *Roles*
      Interpersonal: Figurehead; Leader; Liaison
      Informational: Monitor; Spokesperson; Disseminator
      Decisional: Entrepreneur; Disturbance handler; Resource allocator; Negotiator
                       (*Chapter 11*)

62   B   (or 'position' power) (*Chapter 11*)

63   B   Option A is a job description: often confused with a person specification. One describes the job, while the other describes the ideal candidate for the job. A performance rating would be contained in a performance appraisal, and the number of people required in a job requisition or recruitment plan. (*Chapter 12*)

64   D   This e-recruitment option is suitably targeted (compared with a national newspaper or local radio), and low cost and low lead time (compared with retaining a consultancy). (*Chapter 12*)

65   C   Work sampling allows candidates to demonstrate actual capability in job-relevant tasks. Various forms of testing are less accurate. Interviews are very low on predictive validity, due to their limited scope, artificiality and subjectivity. References are even less accurate, due to bias and caution. (*Chapter 12*)

66   (a)   B   Lin makes the decisions but motivates his subordinates to accept them.

      (b)   9.9 team   High work accomplishment through leading committed people who identify themselves with the organisational aims.

      (c)   Leader   Lin focuses on people and inspires trust, holding a long-term view.
                                                                                (*Chapter 12*)

67   C   Victimisation occurs when a person is penalised for giving information or taking action in pursuit of a claim of discrimination. Direct discrimination occurs when one interested group is treated less favourably than another, and indirect discrimination when a policy or practice appears fair but is discriminatory in practice. Harassment is the use of threatening, intimidatory, offensive or abusive language or behaviour. (*Chapter 13*)

68   A   Age regulations make this practice unlawful in some countries. (*Chapter 13*)

69   (a)

	Advantage	Disadvantage
Interviewer may have knowledge gaps		✓
Direct face to face communication	✓	
Flexibility in questioning	✓	
Interviewer's perception may be selective		✓

The interviewer's perception being selective may weaken the interviewer's objectivity. An interviewer having knowledge gaps is a disadvantage if the candidate is able to disguise a lack of specialist knowledge required for the post.

      (b)   B   Janine is not being discriminated against; she is being subjected to harassment.
                                                                        (*Chapters 12 and 13*)

70   A   This is known as the 'risky-shift' phenomena: it is also a symptom of 'group think'. It is one of the ways in which people contribute differently in groups than they do individually – and not always in positive ways. (*Chapter 14*)

71   D   The Plant solves more conceptual, strategic problems for the team. The Shaper is a leader, but uses dynamism and challenge. The Co-ordinator pulls the team together, but

more as organiser or chairperson. It is the Teamworker who fulfils the relationship-maintenance function. *(Chapter 14)*

72   C   Forming is the 'coming together' stage, followed by conflict (storming) as roles and goals are tested, settling down (norming) as ways of working together are developed, and finally focus on the task (performing). *(Chapter 14)*

73   C   You should be able to describe the other group processes as well. *(Chapter 14)*

74   A   This is the best answer. A chairperson will be justified in cutting short a speaker who has nothing new to say and says it at great length. Brisk progress through the agenda is one mark of good meeting conduct. Some people may only need to be present for part of the meeting and it is a waste of their time to insist on their presence throughout. *(Chapter 14)*

75   A   Expectancy theory is a process theory, because it explores the process or 'calculation' by which outcomes become desirable and are pursued by individuals. Content theory focuses on the 'package' of needs or desired outcomes that motivate people (eg Herzberg's and Maslow's models). *(Chapter 15)*

76   D   McGregor's Theory X/Y accounts for the motivational approach of managers, based on their assumptions about their subordinates. You should be able to identify the other theories as two-factor theory, hierarchy of needs and expectancy theory respectively. *(Chapter 15)*

77   C   PRP is not an element of job design: nor is it directly related to job satisfaction. The five core dimensions are skill variety, task identity, task significance, autonomy and feedback: any or all of these can be increased in a job to increase employee satisfaction and commitment. *(Chapter 15)*

78   A   **Rationale**: Theory X is the managerial assumption that most people dislike work and responsibility and avoid them if possible. Managers use coercion and control to manage staff. Theory Y is the managerial assumption that people can be motivated to accept challenge and responsibility and contribute willingly to the firm. This results in quite a different management style. *(Chapter 15)*

79   (a)   C   Meredith fulfils the criteria of a monitor-evaluator.

       (b)   Theory X   Theory X suggests that people dislike work and want to avoid responsibility. They need to be closely supervised and motivated by 'carrot and stick' techniques. *(Chapters 14 and 15)*

80   D   Methods of learning by doing suit both Activists and Pragmatists, but Pragmatists have the additional preference for practical, job-related problem-solving. Theorists and Reflectors prefer to conceptualise or observe before applying learning. *(Chapter 16)*

81   B   On the job learning supports application of learning to the job (transfer of learning) far better than off the job learning. However, it is subject to the distractions and pressures of work, is not easy to standardise for large numbers of trainees, and creates the risk of poor initial performance and experimentation in real-work situations. *(Chapter 16)*

82   C   Trainee reaction or satisfaction is level 1; trainee learning is level 2; changes in job behaviour (ie application of learning) is level 3; and impact on goals/results is level 4. *(Chapter 16)*

83   B   **Rationale**: Conditioning may have sounded familiar if you only read as far as 'modification of behaviour', but it involves specific repetition and reward techniques. Education is the gradual acquisition of knowledge through learning and instruction, often leading to qualifications. Development is a wider experience of the growth or realisation of a person's ability and potential through a wide range of learning experiences.

            Pitfalls: This kind of related terminology lends itself to exam questions. Training, education and development all involve 'learning', but the learning experiences are of different types, and with different overall aims. *(Chapter 16)*

84   B   **Rationale**: The learning cycle is experiential learning or 'learning by doing'. 'Action learning' sounds similar, but is actually a specific learning method by which managers are brought together as a problem-solving group to discuss real work issues. Programmed learning is highly structured learning, which doesn't apply here. *(Chapter 16)*

85   A   The key objective of performance appraisal is performance improvement, through feedback, problem-solving and development planning. This is often not directly related to reward and/or promotion planning. While retrospective feedback is one tool of appraisal, it is not regarded as an end in itself. *(Chapter 17)*

86   C   Overall assessment is an unguided narrative evaluation; guided assessment a comment on specified characteristics and performance elements; and a results-oriented scheme a review of performance against specific targets and standards agreed in advance by the assessor and assessee. *(Chapter 17)*

87   C   The three options are listed in decreasing order of interviewer dominance and critical role, using Maier's popular classification. *(Chapter 17)*

88   B   **Tactical**. (Note that 'clan control' is a type of control strategy: not a level of control). *(Chapter 17)*

89   C   **Upward appraisal**. *(Chapter 17)*

90   B   Fred is not delegating tasks to his team: this is an important aspect of time management. The mini-scenario indicates that Fred plans, focuses and prioritises well. *(Chapter 18)*

91   A   This can be identified as coaching because it is short term, job specific and carried out by the immediate supervisor: unlike mentoring, which is long term, broad in focus and often carried out by an offline mentor. Counselling is a specific intervention in the case of personal or disciplinary problems, rather than directly addressing skill improvement. *(Chapter 18)*

92   C   Rapport is the term for establishing a 'connection' between yourself and another person, which generally facilitates communication: it involves a range of verbal and non-verbal communication techniques. Distortion refers to a fault in the 'coding' or 'decoding' of a message; noise to interference in the transmission or receipt of a message; and jargon to the use of technical vocabulary which non-users cannot understand. *(Chapter 18)*

93   A   Act, Bin, Create, Delegate. This is a useful shorthand for remembering good advice on managing what can be mountains of paper! *(Chapter 18)*

94   A, B   Answer C could also be correct in the sense that, if a piece of work is important, that makes it high priority. The Chairman's involvement **may** make it high priority. Answer D does make the work high priority for you but not necessarily for the organisation. *(Chapter 18)*

95   D   Neither party gets what they want. *(Chapter 18)*

96   D   The point of this question is to emphasise that all disciplinary issues should be properly investigated. After proper investigation and a disciplinary hearing, any of the usual sanctions may be appropriate. *(Chapter 18)*

97   False: this is a disciplinary action. (Try and define 'grievance' yourself.) *(Chapter 18)*

98   D   Little is certain in employment law but, on the face of it, this would seem to be a case of constructive dismissal. It may also turn out to be unfair dismissal. Wrongful dismissal is unlikely, as the employer may not have actually breached the contract of employment. It may emerge on investigation that the bad treatment of the employee was the result of one of the automatically unfair reasons for dismissal, such as membership of a trade union. However, on the facts we are given, option D is the best answer. *(Chapter 18)*

99   The correct answer is:

Order	Task
1st task (10am to 12 noon)	Enter sales invoices/credit notes into computer system
2nd task (12 noon to 1pm)	Enter weekly purchase invoices into the computer
3rd task (2pm to 4pm) (20 × 6 mins = 120 mins)	Match purchase invoices to goods-received notes and pass to the accountant for authorisation
4th task (4pm to 5pm)	Filing

The sales invoices and credit notes need to be entered into the computer system by midday and so take priority.

Next enter the purchase invoices into the computer, so that the report is available for Manesh's colleague by 2pm.

The third priority is to match the purchase invoices to the GRNs before the end of today, Friday, so that they are ready for the accountant first thing on Monday morning.

Any time left can then be spent on filing. *(Chapter 18)*

100   (a)   C   This is the classic Y pattern.

(b)   Win-win   Freda has won because she will be able to limit the disruption to her work. Lisa has also won because she will receive proper training. *(Chapter 18)*

101   D   Utilitarianism is based on the outcomes or consequences of actions. Deontology is based on duty: categorical imperatives are the 'rules' by which duty (or moral responsibility) can be judged. Legalism is based on the agreed rules or laws laid down by a group or society. *(Chapter 19)*

102   C   Independence in appearance is being **seen** to be independent or objective: it is an additional requirement to being objective in fact (independence of mind) – and nothing to do with freedom from supervision (or autonomy). *(Chapter 19)*

103   (a)

	Yes	No
Openness		✓
Honesty		✓
Accountability	✓	
Integrity	✓	
Objectivity		✓

Accountability refers to whether an organisation is responsible for the consequences of their actions and this is very much to the point in this case.

Openness means disclosing relevant information which may affect decisions to stakeholders. If TUV decide to incur the costs of a clean up, then this concept may come into play later.

Honesty means not only telling the truth but also not misleading stakeholders. Again this concept may come into play at a later stage.

Integrity means straightforward dealing and completeness, so this is an issue here.

Objectivity means that all choices are made purely on merit.

(b)   B   The self-interest threat may arise because the director's wife is on the Board of the supplier. This may lead to contracts being made with her firm regardless of which supplier would actually be better for the business. *(Chapter 19)*

104   D   Although a corporate code of ethics may refer to applicable laws and regulations, it would not necessarily list all those that the company has to comply with. Corporate codes of ethics usually represent statements of standards relating to a range of stakeholders – customers, shareholders, employees, suppliers, local communities etc *(Chapter 19)*

Bibliography

BPP
LEARNING MEDIA

ACCA. (2016). Code of Ethics and Conduct. [Online]. Available from: http://www.accaglobal.com/uk/en/member/standards/ethics/acca-code-of-ethics-and-conduct.html [Accessed 20 December 2016]

Adair, J. (1973) Action-Centred Leadership. New York, McGraw-Hill.

Anthony, R N. (1965) Planning and Control: a Framework for Analysis. Cambridge MA: Harvard University Press

Belbin, M. (1993) *Team Roles at Work.* Oxford, Butterworth-Heinemann.

Belbin, R.M. (1981) *Management Teams: Why They Succeed or Fail.* Butterworth-Heinemann.

Belbin, R.M. (1997) Changing the Way We Work. Oxford, Butterworth-Heinemann.

Bennis, W. (1985) Leaders: Strategies for Taking Charge. New York, HarperBusiness Essentials.

Blake, R. and Mouton, J. (1964) *The Management Grid.* Houston, Texas, Gulf Publishing.

Buchanan, D.A. and Huczynski, A.A. (2010) *Organisational Behaviour.* 7th edition. Harlow, Pearson Education Limited.

Chartered Institute of Marketing (2015) *7 Ps: A brief summary of marketing and how it works.* [Online]. Available from: https://www.cim.co.uk/files/7ps.pdf [Accessed 1 December 2016].

Committee for Standards in Public Life. (1995) The Seven Principles of Public LIfe. [Online]. Available from: https://www.gov.uk/government/publications/the-7-principles-of-public-life/the-7-principles-of-public-life--2 [Accessed 20 December 2016]

Companies Act 2006. (2006). London, TSO.

Consumer Rights Act 2015. (2015). London, TSO.

Criminal Justice Act 1993. (1993). London, HMSO.

Cyert, M., and March, J. (1992) *A Behavioral Theory of The Firm.* 2nd edition. New Jersey, Prentice-Hall Inc.

Data Protection Act 1998. (1998). London, TSO.

Drucker, P. (1989) *The Practice of Management.* Oxford, Butterworth-Heinemann.

Drucker, P. (1993) *Management: Tasks, Responsibilities, Practices.* New York, HarperBusiness.

Egan, G. (2014) The Skilled Helper. Belmont CA, Brooks/Cole.

Employment Rights Act 1996. (1996). London, TSO.

Equality Act 2010. (2010). London, TSO.

Fayol, H. (1967) *General and Industrial Management.* London, Pitman.

Fiedler, F.E. (1967) A Theory of Leadership Effectiveness. McGraw-Hill.

Fombrun, C.J., Tichy, N.M. and Devanna, M.A. (1984) Strategic Human Resource Management. New York: Wiley.

FRC. (2016) Senior management arrangements, systems and controls. [Online] Available from: https://www.handbook.fca.org.uk/handbook/SYSC.pdf [Accessed 19 December 2016]

FRC. (2016) The UK Corporate Governance Code. [Online]. Available from: https://www.frc.org.uk/Our-Work/Publications/Corporate-Governance/UK-Corporate-Governance-Code-April-2016.pdf [Accessed 19 December 2016]

Friedman, M. (1970) The Social Responsibility of Business is to Increase its Profits. [Online] Available from: http://umich.edu/~thecore/doc/Friedman.pdf [Accessed 19 December 2016]

Goold, M. and Campbell, A. (1988) Strategic Management Styles, in Competitiveness and the Management Process, (ed) A M Pettigrew. Oxford, Blackwell.

Handy, C B (2007) Gods of Management. The Changing Work of Organisations. United Kingdom, Arrow Books.

Haynes, M. (1997) *Project Management.* Fifty-Minute Series Book. Crisp Publications.

Health and Safety at Work Act 1974. (1974). London, HMSO.

Heifetz, R. (1994) Leadership Without Easy Answers. Cambridge MA, Havard University Press.

Herzberg, F. et al (1959) *The Motivation to Work.* New York, John Wiley & Sons Inc.

Hofstede, G. (2011). Dimensionalizing Cultures: The Hofstede Model in Context. [Online]. Available from: http://dx.doi.org/10.9707/2307-0919.1014 [Accessed 19 December 2016]

Honey, P. and Mumford, A. (1992) *The Manual of Learning Styles.* Maidenhead, Peter Honey.

http://www.nationalarchives.gov.uk/doc/open-government-licence/version/3/
Contains public sector information licensed under the Open Government Licence v3.

Ingham, J. (2003) How to Implement a Diversity Policy. People Management. 24th July.

Janis, J.L. (1982) *Groupthink.* 2nd edition. United States of America, Wadsworth Cengage Learning..

Johnson, G., Scholes, K., and Whittington, R. (2005) *Exploring Corporate Strategy.* 7th edition. Harlow, Pearson Education Limited.

Kolb, D. (1984) *Experiential Learning.* New York, Prentice Hall.

Leavitt, H. J. (1951). Some effects of certain communication patterns on group performance. Journal of Abnormal and Social Psychology, 46, 38-50.

Lockett, J. (1992) *Effective Performance Management.* London, Kogan Page.

Maier, N. (1975). The Appraisal Interview: Three Basic Approaches. New York, Wiley.

Maslow, A.H. (1943). A theory of human motivation. Psychological Review. 50 (4): 370–96.

Mayo, E. (1933) The Human Problems of an Industrial Civilisation, Macmillan.

McCarthy, Jerome E. (1964) Basic Marketing. A Managerial Approach. Homewood, IL: Irwin

McGregor, D. (1987) *The Human Side of Enterprise.* Penguin Books Ltd.

Mendelow, A. (1991) *Proceedings of the 2nd International Conference on Information Systems.* Cambridge, MA.

Mintzberg, H. (1979) *The Structuring of Organizations.* Prentice Hall.

Mintzberg, H. (1989) Mintzberg on Management: Inside our Strange World of Organisations. New York, The Free Press.

Mullins, L. (2002) *Management and Organisational Behaviour.* Harlow, Prentice Hall.

OECD. (2004) OECD Principles of Corporate Governance. [Online]. Available from: https://www.oecd.org/daf/ca/corporategovernanceprinciples/31557724.pdf [Accessed 19 December 2016]

Pedler, M., Burgoyne, J. and Boydell, T. (1991) *The Learning Company.* London, McGraw-Hill.

Porter, M. (1980) *Competitive Strategy.* New York, Free Press.

Porter, M. (1985) *Competitive Advantage: Creating and Sustaining Superior Performance.* New York, Free Press.

Rodger, A. (1952) *The Seven Point Plan.* London, National Institute of Industrial Psychology.

Schein, E. (1985) *Organisational Culture and Leadership.* San Francisco, Jossey-Bass.

Taylor, F. (1911) *The Principles of Scientific Management* (reprinted 1947). New York, Harper and Row.

The Myers & Briggs Foundation. (2014). My MBTI® Personality Type. Retrieved December 20, 2016, from http://www.myersbriggs.org/my-mbti-personality-type/mbti-basics/

Tuckman, B.W. (1965) Sequence in Small Groups. Psychological Bulletin, 63, 384-399.

Vroom, V. (1964) *Work and Motivation.* New York, Wiley.

Walton, C. (1978) *Ethics of Corporate Conduct.* Prentice Hall

Index

Note: **Key Terms** and their page references are given in **bold**

Review form

Name: _____   Address: _____

_____

_____

How have you used this Interactive Text?
(Tick one box only)

☐ Home study (book only)

☐ On a BPP in-centre course _____

☐ On a BPP online course

☐ On a course with another college

☐ Other _____

Why did you decide to purchase this Interactive Text? *(Tick one box only)*

☐ Have used BPP Texts in the past

☐ Recommendation by friend/colleague

☐ Recommendation by a lecturer at college

☐ Saw advertising

☐ Other _____

Which BPP products have you used?

☑ Text   ☐ Kit   ☐ i-Pass   ☐ Passcards

During the past six months do you recall seeing/receiving any of the following?
(Tick as many boxes as are relevant)

☐ Our advertisement in *ACCA Student Accountant*

☐ Our advertisement in *Teach Accounting*

☐ Other advertisement _____

☐ Our brochure with a letter through the post

☐ ACCA E-Gain email

☐ BPP email

☐ Our website www.bpp.com

Which (if any) aspects of our advertising do you find useful?
(Tick as many boxes as are relevant)

☐ Prices and publication dates of new editions

☐ Information on Interactive Text content

☐ Facility to order books

☐ None of the above

Your ratings, comments and suggestions would be appreciated on the following areas

	Very useful	Useful	Not useful
Introductory section (How to use this Interactive Text)	☐	☐	☐
Key terms	☐	☐	☐
Examples	☐	☐	☐
Questions and answers	☐	☐	☐
Fast forwards	☐	☐	☐
Quick quizzes	☐	☐	☐
Exam alerts	☐	☐	☐
Practice Question Bank	☐	☐	☐
Practice Answer Bank	☐	☐	☐
Index	☐	☐	☐
Structure and presentation	☐	☐	☐
Icons	☐	☐	☐

	Excellent	Good	Adequate	Poor
Overall opinion of this Interactive Text	☐	☐	☐	☐

Do you intend to continue using BPP products?   ☐ Yes   ☐ No

Please note any further comments and suggestions/errors on the reverse of this page.

The author of this edition can be emailed at: accaqueries@bpp.com

Please return this form to: Head of ACCA & Foundations in Accountancy Programmes, BPP Learning Media Ltd, FREEPOST, London, W12 8AA

Review form (continued)

Please note any further comments and suggestions/errors below